A Reformation Reader

"Denis Janz has succeeded in selecting key documents that illustrate the religious vision of the Reformers. While including the late medieval perspective, the English Reformation, and developments that initiated Catholic reform and the Counter Reformation, this anthology will prove to be particularly useful for undergraduate courses dealing with Martin Luther and John Calvin."

—Heiko A. Oberman
Regents Professor of History
University of Arizona
author, *The Dawn of the Reformation*

A Reformation Reader

Primary Texts with Introductions

edited by
Denis R. Janz

Fortress Press
Minneapolis

A REFORMATION READER
Primary Texts with Introductions

Cover design: Michael Mihelich
Author photo: Harold Baquet
Interior design: Beth Wright

Library of Congress Cataloging-in-Publication Data

A Reformation reader : primary texts with introductions / edited by Denis R. Janz
   p.   cm.
   Includes bibliographical references and index.
   ISBN 0-8006-3180-3 (alk. paper)
   1. Reformation Sources. I. Janz, Denis.
BR301.R44 1999
270.6—dc21   99-36070
                                                    CIP

Manufactured in the U.S.A.
08   07   06   05   04   2   3   4   5   6   7   8   9   10

For Don, Rob, and Jon

Contents

✠

Chapter 3. Zwingli and the Radical Reformation

Preface

✠

Many people have had a hand, directly or indirectly, in shaping this anthology. Over my twenty years at Loyola University New Orleans, some two thousand students, undergraduate and graduate, have read these Reformation texts with me. The enormous variety of perspectives they have brought to our discussions has been a source of continual enlightenment for me. Even more important have been the influence and encouragement of my colleagues, past and present, in the Department of Religious Studies. Not only have they accepted me, a somewhat unrepentant Protestant, into their ranks; not only have they given me the freedom and support to pursue my own research interests; but they have constantly held before me an exalted and profoundly "Catholic" vision of the value and dignity of intellectual work—a vision based ultimately on Augustine's dictum, "Behold, there He is, wherever truth is known." Their names deserve to be recorded: James Gaffney, Stephen Duffy, Thomas Smith, Catherine Wessinger, Fara Impastato, Vernon Gregson, Robert Gnuse, Earl Richard, Gerald Fagin, Tiina Allik, Kenneth Keulman, Daniel Sheridan, Peter Bernardi, and Timothy Cahill. Provost David Danahar facilitated this project in more practical ways, as did Dean Frank Scully and the Faculty Research Grants Committee. Computer experts Bret Jacobs and Jan Long faithfully and without laughing answered my numerous and undoubtedly inane inquiries. My graduate assistant Deborah Halter prepared the index. Finally, though they had nothing to do with this work, the unspoken love of my brothers has sustained me far more than they realize. It is to them that this book is dedicated.

17 May 1999

Introduction

✠

The purpose of this book is to introduce students, both undergraduate and graduate, to the Reformation of the sixteenth century. My view is that this is best done through guided reading in the primary sources. The texts I have chosen vary greatly. Some are short and relatively transparent. Others are longer and place great demands on the reader. Some are well known to specialists while others are not. All, in my opinion, will reward patient and careful reading. Each one can be thought of as a window, with its own angle of vision, through which one can glimpse a significant aspect of this tumultuous period. Together, I hope, they will enable the student to form a reasonably comprehensive picture of the whole.

The choice of texts for this reader is heavily theological. This reflects my view that the Reformation was not, in the first instance, an economic or political or even social movement. Important as these dimensions were, it was rather precisely religion that was the bone of contention. And the leaders of this movement, despite all their differences, had this one thing in common: they understood themselves as theologians, and what they wrote was to a large extent theology. Reading this material is the only way I know of to enter into their self-understandings.

For the sake of convenience, this book adopts several conventions about which the reader should be forewarned. First, the very term "Reformation" already carries with it an implicit value judgment. For "to reform" means to improve; it means that what went before was deficient in some way. Not all would agree that the various "reforms" of the sixteenth century, or even that the movement as a whole, marked such advancement. Second, to use the term "Reformation" in the singular may be to attribute a kind of unity to these events that they did not in fact have. Some today see the various religious currents of the time as being so diverse as to require that we use the plural "Reformations." Third, the documents collected here are neatly organized under six rubrics: the late medieval background, Martin Luther, Ulrich Zwingli and the radical reformers, John Calvin, the Reformation in England, and the Counter/Catholic Reformation. Readers should realize that the reality was considerably messier. Especially in the early stages of the movement, it was not always clear who belonged to which group. And at times, all dissident voices were simply lumped together under the label "Lutheran."

In my zeal to let the reformers speak for themselves, I have kept the introductions in this book to a minimum. Professors will undoubtedly want to supplement and further contextualize the texts with lectures. Then too, the texts in this anthology can easily be aligned with readings in standard surveys such as Steven Ozment's *The Age of Reform, 1250–1550: An Intellectual and Religious History of Late Medieval and Reformation Europe* (New Haven: Yale University Press, 1980); Euan Cameron's *The European Reformation* (Oxford: Clarendon Press, 1991); Carter Lindberg's *The European Reformations* (Oxford: Blackwell Publishers, 1996); Alister McGrath's *Reformation Thought: An Introduction* (Oxford: Blackwell Publishers, 1988); Lewis Spitz's *The Protestant Reformation, 1517–1559* (New York: Harper and Row, 1985); and so forth. Or these documents may be keyed to the splendid articles in the *Oxford Encyclopedia of the Reformation,* ed. Hans Hillerbrand (New York: Oxford University Press, 1996).

1

On the issue of language, my first concern has been not to distort the thought of the writers of these texts. The fact is that, despite all necessary qualifications, the world of the Reformation was undeniably sexist from top to bottom. Thus I have not modified the gender-exclusive language of its writers. Nor have I modified the gender-exclusive language of the translations, even when a case could be made for translating a term such as "Mensch" or "homo" as "human" or "person," rather than as "man." The gender-exclusive language of these texts is a constant reminder to us of the difference between our consciousness and that of the reformers—a difference that should not be minimized.

For those of us who teach using primary texts, the search for the perfect anthology is eternal, until of course we assemble our own! This one is the result of twenty years of experimentation in teaching the Reformation. My hope is that others may find it, if not ideal, then at least an improvement over what is currently available.

Chapter 1
The Late Medieval Background

✠

Introduction

A grasp of the European religious scene on the eve of the Reformation is absolutely indispensable to understanding the multiple crises that befell Western Christendom in the sixteenth century. For it was this scene that reformers of all types protested against. Only against this background can we grasp the full impact of the new theologies and confessions that now sprang to life. And only against this foil can we make judgments about what was innovative and what was traditional. It is not an exaggeration to say, therefore, that the more one knows about the late Middle Ages, the better one will understand the Reformation.

Yet it is a notoriously difficult matter to accurately summarize the theology, piety, and practice of so extensive a period and so vast an area. Even if we restrict ourselves to Germanic lands in the fifteenth century, we find no consensus among scholars. Where some see an exuberant flourishing of religious forms, others see only decadence and decline. What some recognize as stagnation in sub-Christian superstition, others identify as a rich and highly developed religiosity. Such judgments depend of course to some extent on the point of view of the observer, and students of this period do well to acknowledge their own prejudices. What is undeniable to all, however, and this becomes increasingly evident the more one studies the material, is that we are dealing here with enormous variety and complexity.

On the level of popular piety one finds manifestations ranging from the exalted spirituality of the mystics to the crude, and to us strange, pious practices of the illiterate peasants. Thus while some rhapsodized over the union of the soul with God, others insisted that their parish priests lead processions through the fields, reading the Gospel of John to the wheat. While some went on pilgrimage to the shrine of St. Thomas à Becket in Canterbury to see some of the clay (left over) from which God had made Adam, others spent a lifetime meditating in all simplicity and sincerity on the Psalms. And still others paid scant attention at all to religious matters. Yet all were late medieval Christians. It may be necessary for us to generalize about piety on the eve of the Reformation, but we should understand that it is hazardous to do so.

The same confused picture appears when we turn our attention to the institutional church. Much has been written about its corruption and venality. True, Pope Alexander VI did bribe twenty-five out of twenty-six cardinals to get elected. And a good number of village priests lived in concubinage. But this should not cause us to lose sight of the utterly sincere and caring pastor who gave a lifetime of service to his people, ministering to their needs even during episodes of the plague when it would have been safer to flee. Just as the laity included both saints and sinners, so too the official representatives of this institution, from popes to parish priests, ran the entire gamut.

As for theology, it too exhibited remarkable variety, even though it functioned largely within the parameters of official church teaching. Relatively discreet schools of thought vied for supremacy in the late medieval intellectual world, many of them anchored in the thought of one revered master. If any of these dominated, it was the nominalist school, building on the thought of William of Occam. But others presented viable, lively theological alternatives: the Thomists, the Albertists, the Augustinians, humanists, mystics, etc. Thus university theological faculties were often divided by these various loyalties and rivalries. A dynamic pluralism characterized late medieval theology, just as it characterizes Roman Catholic theology today. While some in the hierarchy saw this as a degeneration into chaos and confusion, others welcomed it as a healthy sign of a creative, energetic intellectual quest.

It was into this religious world that the first generation of Protestant reformers was born. And all of them protested against some of its features, accepted others, and modified still others. This chapter provides only a glimpse into various facets of the whole. Each document should serve as a window through which one can catch sight of an important part of this world. Together they constitute not a systematic but an impressionistic account of religion in the Christian West on the eve of the Reformation. They are a starting point for constructing a context which will allow one to understand the cataclysmic events which followed.

Spirituality

1. Thomas à Kempis, *The Imitation of Christ* (ca. 1420–1427)

Thomas à Kempis (1380–1471) joined the Order of Hermits of St. Augustine in 1406 and was ordained to the priesthood in 1413. Living at the monastery of Mount St. Agnes near Zwolle (in the Low Countries), he wrote his *Imitation of Christ* between 1420 and 1427. Written in all probability for novice monks, it soon became one of the most famous devotional books of the age, for laity and religious alike. It is a good representation, therefore, not only of clerical piety, but more importantly, of the types of piety which the church was recommending to all Christians. Our excerpt forcefully illustrates the otherworldly nature of this spirituality.

On the Imitation of Christ

"He who follows me shall not walk in darkness," says our Lord.

In these words Christ counsels us to follow His life and way if we desire true enlightenment and freedom from all blindness of heart. Let the life of Jesus Christ, then, be our first consideration.

The teaching of Jesus far transcends all the teachings of the saints, and whosoever has his spirit will discover concealed in it heavenly manna. But many people, although they often hear the gospel, feel little desire to follow it, because they lack the spirit of Christ. Whoever desires to understand and take delight in the words of Christ must strive to conform his whole life to him.

Of what use is it to discourse learnedly on the Trinity, if you lack humility and therefore displease the Trinity? Lofty words do not make a man just or holy; but a good life makes him dear to God. I would far rather feel contrition than be able to define it. If you knew the whole Bible by heart, and all the teachings of the philosophers, how would this help you without the grace and love of God? "Vanity of vanities, and all is vanity," except to love God and serve him alone. And this is supreme wisdom—to despise the world, and draw daily nearer the kingdom of heaven.

It is vanity to solicit honors, or to raise oneself to high station. It is vanity to be a slave to bodily desires and to crave for things which bring certain retribution. It is vanity to wish for long life, if you care little for a good life. It is vanity to give thought only to this present life, and to care nothing for the life to come. It is vanity to love things that so swiftly pass away, and not to hasten onwards to that place where everlasting joy abides. Keep constantly in mind the saying, "The eye is not satisfied with seeing, nor the ear filled with hearing." Strive to withdraw your heart from the love of visible things, and direct your affections to things invisible. For those who follow only their natural inclinations defile their conscience, and lose the grace of God.

On the Love of Solitude and Silence

Choose a suitable time for recollection and frequently consider the loving-kindness of God. Do not read to satisfy curiosity or to pass the time, but study such things as move your heart to devotion. If you avoid unnecessary talk and aimless visits, listening to news and gossip, you will find plenty of suitable time to spend in meditation on holy things. The greatest saints used to avoid the company of men whenever they were able, and chose rather to serve God in solitude.

A wise man once said "As often as I have been among men, I have returned home a lesser man." We often share this experience, when we spend much time in conversation. It is easier to keep silence altogether than not to talk more than we should. It is easier to remain quietly at home than to keep due watch over ourselves in public. Therefore, whoever is resolved to live an inward and spiritual life must, with Jesus, withdraw from the crowd. No man can live in the public eye without risk to his soul, unless he who would prefer to remain obscure. No man can safely speak unless he who would gladly remain silent. No man can safely command, unless he who has learned to obey well. No man can safely rejoice, unless he possesses the testimony of a good conscience.

The security of the saints was grounded in the fear of God, nor were they less careful and humble because they were resplendent in great virtues and graces. But the security of the wicked springs from pride and presumption, and ends in self-deception. Never promise yourself security in this life, even though you seem to be a good monk or a devout hermit.

Those who stand highest in the esteem of men are most exposed to grievous peril, since they often have too great a confidence in themselves. It is therefore, more profitable to many that they should not altogether escape temptations, but be often assailed lest they become too secure and exalted in their pride, or turn too readily to worldly consolations. How good a conscience would he keep if a man never sought after passing pleasures nor became preoccupied with worldly affairs! If only a man could cast aside all useless anxiety and think only on divine and salutary things, how great would be his peace and tranquillity!

No one is worthy of heavenly comfort, unless they have diligently exercised themselves in holy contrition. If you desire heart-felt contrition, enter into your room, and shut out the clamor of the world, as it is written, "Commune with your own heart, and in your chamber, and be still." Within your cell you will discover what you will only too often lose abroad. The cell that is dwelt in continually becomes a delight, but ill kept it breeds weariness of spirit. If in the beginning of your religious life you have dwelt in it and kept it well, it will later become a dear friend and a welcome comfort.

In silence and quietness the devout soul makes progress and learns the hidden mysteries of the Scriptures. There she finds floods of tears in which she may nightly wash and be cleansed. For the further she withdraws from all the tumult of the world, the nearer she draws to her maker. For God with his holy angels will draw near to him who withdraws himself from his friends and acquaintances. It is better to live in obscurity and to seek the salvation of his soul, than to neglect this even to work miracles. It is commendable in a religious, therefore, to go abroad but seldom, to avoid being seen, and to have no desire to see men.

Why do you long to see that which is not lawful for you to possess? The world itself passes away, and all the desires of it. The desires of the senses call you to roam abroad, but when their hour is spent, what do you bring back but a burdened conscience and a distracted heart? A cheerful going out often brings a sad homecoming, and a merry evening brings a sorry morning. For every bodily pleasure brings joy at first, but at length it bites and destroys.

What can you see elsewhere that you cannot see here? Look at the sky, the earth, and all the elements, for of these all things are made. What can you see anywhere under the sun that can endure for long? You hope, perhaps to find complete satisfaction; but this you will never do. Were you to see all things at present in existence spread out before your eyes, what would it be but an unprofitable vision? Lift up your eyes to God on high, and beg forgiveness for your sin and neglectfulness. Leave empty matters to the empty-headed, and give your attention to those things that God commands you. Shut your door upon you, and call upon Jesus the beloved. Remain with him in your cell, for you will not find so great a peace anywhere else. Had you never gone out and listened to idle talk, you would the better have remained perfectly at peace. But if it pleases you to hear the news of the world, you must always suffer disquiet of heart as a result.

On Contrition of Heart

If you wish to grow in holiness, you must live in the fear of God. Do not seek too much freedom, but discipline all your senses, and do not engage in foolish occupations; give yourself rather to contrition of heart, and you will find true devotion. Contrition reveals to us many good things to which dissipation rapidly blinds us. It is a wonder that any man can ever feel perfectly contented with this present life, if he weighs and considers his state of banishment, and the many perils which beset his soul.

Levity of heart and neglect of our faults make us insensible to the proper sorrows of the soul, and we often engage in empty laughter when we should rightly weep. There is no real liberty and true joy, save in the fear of God with a quiet conscience. Happy is he who can set aside every hindering distraction, and recall himself to the single purpose of contrition. Happy is he who abjures whatever may stain or burden his conscience. Fight manfully, for one habit

overcomes another. If you are content to let others alone, they will gladly leave you to accomplish your purpose unhindered.

Do not busy yourself with the affairs of others, nor concern yourself with the policies of your superiors. Watch yourself at all times, and correct yourself before you correct your friends. Do not be grieved if you do not enjoy popular favor; grieve rather that you do not live as well and carefully as befits a servant of God, and a devout religious person. It is often better and safer not to have many comforts in this life, especially those of the body. Yet, if we seldom or never feel God's comfort, the fault is our own; for we neither seek contrition of heart, nor entirely forego all vain and outward consolations.

Consider yourself unworthy of God's comfort, but rather deserving of much suffering. When a man is perfectly contrite, this present world becomes grievous and bitter to him. A good man always finds cause for grief and tears; for whether he considers himself or his neighbors, he knows that no man lives without trouble in this life. And the more strictly he examines himself, the more cause he finds for sorrow. Our sins and vices are grounds for rightful sorrow and contrition of heart; for they have so strong a hold on us that we are seldom able to contemplate heavenly things.

If you had more concern for a holy death than a long life, you would certainly be zealous to live better. And were you to ponder in your mind on the pains of hell and purgatory, you would readily endure toil and sorrow, and would shrink from no kind of hardship. But because considerations of this kind do not move the heart, we remain cold and unresponsive, clinging to old delights.

It is often our lack of spiritual life that allows our wretched body to rebel so easily.

Humbly beg our Lord, therefore, to grant you the spirit of contrition, and say with the prophet, "Feed me, O Lord, with the bread of tears, and give me plenteousness of tears to drink."

On Human Misery

Wherever you are and wherever you turn, you will not find happiness until you turn to God. Why are you so distressed when events do not turn out as you wish and hope? Is there anyone who enjoys everything as he wishes? Neither you, nor I, nor anyone else on earth. There is no one in the world without trouble or anxiety, be he king or pope. Whose, then, is the happiest lot? Surely, he who is able to suffer for love of God.

Many weak and foolish people say, "See what a good life that man enjoys! He is so rich, so great, so powerful, so distinguished!" But raise your eyes to the riches of heaven, and you will see that all the riches of this world are as nothing. All are uncertain and even burdensome, for they are never enjoyed without some anxiety or fear. The happiness of man does not consist in abundance of this world's goods, for a modest share is sufficient for him. The more spiritual a man desires to become, the more bitter does this present life grow for him, for he sees and realizes more clearly the defects and corruptions of human nature. For to eat and drink, to wake and sleep, to rest and labor, and to be subject to all the necessities of nature is a great trouble and affliction to the devout man, who would rather be released and set free from all sin.

The inner life of man is greatly hindered in this life by the needs of the body. Thus, the prophet devoutly prays that he may be set free from them, saying, "Lord, deliver me from my necessities!" Woe to those who refuse to recognize their own wretchedness, and doubly woe to those who love this miserable and corruptible life! For some cling so closely to it, that although by working or begging they can hardly win the bare necessities, they would yet be willing to live here for ever if it were possible, caring nothing for the kingdom of God.

How crazy and lacking in faith are such people, who are so deeply engrossed in earthly affairs that they care for nothing but material things! These unhappy wretches will at length know to their sorrow how vile and worthless were the things that they loved. But the saints of God and all the devoted friends of Christ paid little heed to bodily pleasures, nor to prosperity in this life, for all their hopes and aims were directed towards those good things that are eternal. Their whole desire raised them upward to things eternal and invisible, so that the love of things visible could not drag them down. My brother, do not lose hope of progress in the spiritual life; you have still time and opportunity.

Why put off your good resolution? Rise and begin this very moment, and say, "Now is the time to be up and doing; now is the time to fight; now is the time to amend." When things go badly and you are in trouble, then is the time to win merit. You must pass through fire and water, before you can come into the place of rest. You will never overcome your vices, unless you discipline yourself severely. For so long as we wear this frail body, we cannot be without sin, nor can we live without weariness and sorrow. We would gladly be free from all troubles; but since we have lost our innocence through sin, we have also lost true happiness. We must therefore have patience, and wait for God's mercy, until this wickedness pass away, and death be swallowed up in life.

How great is the frailty of man, ever prone to evil! Today you confess your sins; tomorrow you again commit the very sins you have confessed! Now you resolve to guard against them, and within the hour you act as though you had never made any resolution! Remembering, then, our weakness and instability, it is proper to humble ourselves, and never to have a high opinion of ourselves. For we can easily lose by carelessness that which by God's grace and our own efforts we had hardly won.

What will become of us in the end if our zeal so quickly grows cold? Unhappy our fate, if we rest on our oars as though we had already reached a haven of peace and security, when in fact no sign of holiness is apparent in our lives. It would be good for us to be instructed once more, like good novices, in the ways of the good life; there would then be some hope of our future improvement and greater spiritual progress.

A Meditation on Death

Very soon the end of your life will be at hand: consider, therefore, the state of your soul. Today a man is here; tomorrow he is gone. And when he is out of sight, he is soon out of mind. Oh, how dull and hard is the heart of man, which thinks only of the present, and does not provide against the future! You should order your every deed and thought as though today were the day of your death. Had you a good conscience, death would hold no terrors for you; even so, it were better to avoid sin than to escape death. If you are not ready to die today, will tomorrow find you better prepared? Tomorrow is uncertain; and how can you be sure of tomorrow?

Of what use is a long life, if we amend so little? Alas, a long life often adds to our sins rather than to our virtue!

Would to God that we might spend a single day really well! Many recount the years since their conversion, but their lives show little sign of improvement. If it is dreadful to die, it is perhaps more dangerous to live long. Blessed is the man who keeps the hour of his death always in mind, and daily prepares himself to die. If you have ever seen anyone die, remember that you, too, must travel the same road.

Each morning remember that you may not live until evening; and in the evening, do not presume to promise yourself another day. Be ready at all times, and so live that death may never find you unprepared. Many die suddenly and unexpectedly; for at an hour that we do not know the Son of man will come. When your last hour strikes, you will begin to think very differently of your past life, and grieve deeply that you have been so careless and remiss.

Happy and wise is he who endeavors to be during his life as he wishes to be found at his death. For these things will afford us sure hope of a happy death; perfect contempt of the world; fervent desire to grow in holiness; love of discipline; the practice of penance; ready obedience; self-denial; the bearing of every trial for the love of Christ. While you enjoy health, you can do much good; but when sickness comes, little can be done. Few are made better by sickness, and those who make frequent pilgrimages seldom acquire holiness by so doing.

Do not rely on friends and neighbors, and do not delay the salvation of your soul to some future date, for men will forget you sooner than you think. It is better to make timely provision and to acquire merit in this life, than to depend on the help of others. And if you have no care for your own soul, who will have care for you in time to come?

The present time is most precious; now is the accepted time, now is the day of salvation. It is sad that you do not employ your time better, when you may win eternal life hereafter. The time will come when you will long for one day or one hour in which to amend; and who knows whether it will be granted?

Dear soul, from what peril and fear you could free yourself, if you lived in holy fear, mindful of your death. Apply yourself so to live now, that at the hour of death, you may be glad and unafraid. Learn now to die to the world, that you may begin to live with Christ. Learn now to despise all earthly things, that you may go freely to Christ. Discipline your body now by penance, that you may enjoy a sure hope of salvation.

Foolish man, how can you promise yourself a long life, when you are not certain of a single day? How many have deceived themselves in this way, and been snatched unexpectedly from life! You have often heard how this man was slain by the sword; another drowned; how another fell from a high place and broke his neck; how another died at table; how another met his end in play. One perishes by fire, another by the sword, another from disease, another at the hands of robbers. Death is the end of all men; and the life of man passes away suddenly as a shadow.

Who will remember you when you are dead? Who will pray for you? Act now, dear soul; do all you can; for you know neither the hour of your death, nor your state after death. While you have time, gather the riches of everlasting life. Think only of your salvation, and care only for the things of God. Make friends now, by honoring the saints of God and by following their example, that when this life is over, they may welcome you to your eternal home.

Keep yourself a stranger and pilgrim upon earth, to whom the affairs of this world are of no concern. Keep your heart free and lifted up to God, for here you have no abiding city. Daily direct your prayers and longings to heaven, that at your death your soul may merit to pass joyfully into the presence of God.

On Judgment, and the Punishment of Sinners

Always keep in mind your last end, and how you will stand before the just judge from whom nothing is hid, who cannot be influenced by bribes and excuses, and who judges with justice. O wretched and foolish sinner, who trembles before the anger of man, how will you answer to God, who knows all your wickedness? Why do you not prepare yourself against the Day of Judgment, when no advocate can defend or excuse you, but each man will be hard put to answer for himself? While you live, your labor is profitable and your tears acceptable, for sorrow both cleanses the soul and makes peace with God.

The patient man undergoes a great and wholesome purgation; while suffering injuries, he grieves yet more for the malice of others than for his own wrongs; he gladly prays for his enemies, and from his heart forgives their offenses; he does not hesitate to ask pardon of others; he is more easily moved to compassion than to anger; he rules himself with strictness, and endeavors to make the body subject to the spirit in all things. It is better to expiate our sins and overcome our vices now, than to reserve them for purgation hereafter; but we deceive ourselves by our inordinate love of the body.

What will the flames feed upon, but your sins? The more you spare yourself now, and indulge the desires of the body, the more severe will be your punishment hereafter, and the more fuel you gather for the flames. In whatever things a man sins, in those will he be the more severely punished. Then will the slothful be spurred by fiery goads, and the gluttonous tormented by dire hunger and thirst. Then will the luxurious and pleasure-loving be plunged into burning pitch and stinking sulfur, while the envious will howl their grief like wild dogs.

There is no vice that will not receive its proper retribution. The proud will be subjected to the deepest humiliation, and the greedy experience misery and want. One hour's punishment then will be more bitter than a century of penance on earth. There will be neither rest nor comfort for the damned; but here we sometimes enjoy rest from our toil, and enjoy the comfort of our friends. Therefore, live rightly now, and grieve for your sins, that in the day of judgment you may stand secure in the company of the blessed. For then shall the righteous stand with great boldness before those who have afflicted and oppressed them. Then will he who now submits humbly to the judgment of man stand to judge others. Then will the poor and humble have great confidence, while the proud are encompassed by fears on every side.

It will then be seen that he who learned to be counted a fool and despised for Christ's sake in this world was indeed wise. Then will he be glad for every trial patiently borne, and the mouth of the wicked will be sealed. Then will every devout man be glad and the ungodly grieve. Then will he who kept his body in subjection have greater joy than he who lavished every pleasure upon it. Then will the rags of the poor shine with splendor, and the gorgeous raiment become tarnished. Then will the humble cottage of the poor be preferred to the gilded palace. Then will steadfast patience be of more avail than all worldly power. Then will humble obedience be exalted above all worldly cunning. Then will a good and clean conscience bring more

joy than learned philosophy. Then will contempt for riches far outweigh all the treasures of the world. Then will devout prayer yield greater pleasure than fine fare. Then will you rejoice more in having kept silence than in much talking. Then will holy deeds count for more than fine words. Then will a disciplined life and hard penance prove of more worth than all worldly delights.

Learn to endure a little now, that you may spare yourself more grievous troubles. Prove here what you can endure hereafter. If you can endure so little now, how could you endure the pains of hell? Be assured that a man cannot enjoy both kinds of happiness; he cannot enjoy all the pleasures of this life, and also reign with Christ in heaven. Moreover, if up to this very day you had lived in enjoyment of all honors and pleasures, how would all these profit you if you were to die at this moment? All, therefore, is vanity, save to love God and serve him alone. For he who loves God with all his heart fears neither death, punishment, judgment, nor hell; for perfect love enjoys sure access to God. But he who continues to delight in wickedness, what wonder is it if he fears death and judgment? Nevertheless, it is good that, if the love of God does not restrain you from sin, the fear of hell at least should restrain you. For he who sets aside the fear of God cannot long continue in a good life, but will rapidly fall into the snares of the devil.

Be watchful and diligent in the service of God, and frequently consider why you are come here, and why you have renounced the world. Was it not that you might live to God, and become a spiritual man? Endeavor, then, to make progress, and you will soon receive the reward of your labors; then neither fear nor sorrow will be able to trouble you. Labor for a short while now, and you will find great peace of soul, and everlasting joy. If you remain faithful in all your doings, be sure that God will be faithful and generous in rewarding you. Keep a firm hope that you will win the victor's crown; but do not be overconfident, lest you become indolent and self-satisfied.

There was once a man who was very anxious, and wavered between fear and hope. One day, overcome with sadness, he lay prostrate in prayer before the altar in church, and pondering these matters in his mind, said, "Oh, if only I knew that I should always persevere!" Then he heard within his heart an answer from God: "If you knew this, what would you do? Do now what you would then, and all will be well." So, comforted and strengthened, he committed himself to the will of God, and his anxious uncertainty vanished. Nor did he wish any longer to inquire into what would happen to him, but strove the more earnestly to learn the perfect and acceptable will of God, whenever he began or undertook any good work.

"Hope in the Lord, and do good," says the prophet: "dwell in the land, and you shall be fed with its riches." There is one thing that deters many in their spiritual progress and zeal for amendment, namely, fear of the difficulties and the cost of victory. But rest assured that those who grow in virtue beyond their fellows are they who fight most manfully to overcome whatever is most difficult and distasteful to them. For the more completely a man overcomes and cleanses himself in spirit, the more he profits and deserves abundant grace.

All men do not have the same things to overcome and mortify. But whoever is diligent and zealous—even though he has stronger passions to subdue—will certainly make greater progress than another, who is naturally self-controlled, but less zealous for

holiness. Two things in particular are a great help to amendment of life—a forcible withdrawal from any vice to which our nature inclines, and a fervent pursuit of any grace of which we stand in particular need. Especially study to avoid and overcome those things that most displease you in other people.

Strive to progress in all things, and let any examples that you see or hear inspire you to imitate them. But if you observe anything blameworthy, take care not to do the same yourself. And should you ever have done so, amend your conduct without delay. As you observe others, so do others observe you. How glad and pleasant it is to see fervent and devout brethren observing good manners and good discipline. And how sad and painful to see any who are disorderly and fail to live up to their calling. How harmful it is, if they neglect the true purpose of their vocation, and turn to matters that are not their proper concern.

Remember your avowed purpose, and keep ever before you the likeness of Christ crucified. As you meditate on the life of Jesus Christ, you should grieve that you have not tried more earnestly to conform yourself to him, although you have been a long while in the way of God. A religious who earnestly and devoutly contemplates the most holy life and passion of our Lord will find in it an abundance of all things profitable and needful to him, nor need he seek any other model than Jesus. Oh, if Jesus crucified would come into our hearts, how quickly and fully we should be instructed!

A zealous religious readily accepts and obeys all commands. But a careless and lukewarm religious has trouble after trouble, and finds sorrow on every side because he lacks true inward consolation, and is forbidden to seek it outside. Therefore a religious who disregards his Rule exposes himself to dreadful ruin. And he who desires an easier and undisciplined life will always be unstable, for one thing or another will always displease him.

Observe how many behave, who live strictly under the monastic discipline. They seldom go out, they live retired, they eat the poorest food; they work hard, they talk little, they keep long watches; they rise early, they spend much time in prayer, they study much, and always guard themselves with discipline. Consider the Carthusians, the Cistercians, and the monks and nuns of the various orders, how they rise each night to sing praises to our Lord. Were you slothful, this should shame you, when so great a company of religious are beginning the praises of God.

Would that our sole occupation were the perpetual praise of the Lord with heart and voice! Had you no need of food, drink, or rest, you could praise God without ceasing, and give yourself wholly to spiritual things. You would be far happier than now, when you are compelled to serve the needs of the body. Would that these needs did not exist, so that we might enjoy the spiritual feasts of the soul, which, alas, we taste so seldom.

When a man no longer seeks his comfort from any creature, then he first begins to enjoy God perfectly, and he will be well content with whatever befalls him. Then he will neither rejoice over having much, nor grieve over having little, but will commit himself fully and trustfully to God, who is all in all to him: in him nothing perishes or dies, for all things live for him, and serve his will continually.

Always remember your end, and that lost time never returns. Without care and diligence, you will never acquire virtue. If you begin to grow careless, all will begin to go amiss with you. But if you give yourself to prayer, you will find great peace, and your toil will grow lighter by the help of God's grace and your love of virtue. The fervent and sincere man is prepared for anything. The war against our vices and passions is harder than any physical toil; and whoever fails to overcome his lesser faults will gradually fall into greater. Your evenings will always be tranquil if you have spent the day well. Watch yourself, bestir yourself, admonish yourself; and whatever others may do, never neglect your own soul. The stricter you are with yourself, the greater is your spiritual progress.

From L. Sherley-Price, trans., Thomas à Kempis: The Imitation of Christ *(Baltimore: Penguin, 1972), 27–28, 50–66.*

The Papacy

2. Boniface VIII, *Unam Sanctam* (1302)

Boniface VIII, on the papal throne from 1294–1303, wrote the bull *Unam Sanctam* as a response to resistance by the king of France. It represents the high-water mark in papal claims to supreme authority, and it became for the late Middle Ages the foundation of the ecclesiastical hierarchy's self-understanding. In practice it was rudely belied by events such as the Avignon papacy (1309–1377), the Great Schism (1378–1415), the Council of Constance (1414–1418), etc. Yet the theory of papal absolutism laid down here persisted as the cornerstone of the way in which popes wished to be understood well into the modern era.

⊬

We are obliged by faith to believe and hold—and we do firmly believe and sincerely confess—that there is one holy, catholic and apostolic church, and that outside this church there is neither salvation nor remission of sins. . . . In which church there is one Lord, one faith, one baptism. At the time of the flood there was one ark of Noah, symbolizing the one church; this was completed in one cubit and had one, namely Noah, as helmsman and captain; outside which all things on earth, we read, were destroyed. . . . Of this one and only church there is one body and one head—not two heads, like a monster—namely Christ, and Christ's vicar is Peter, and Peter's successor, for the Lord said to Peter himself, "feed my sheep." "My sheep" he said in general, not these or those sheep; wherefore he is understood to have committed them all to him. Therefore, if the Greeks or others say that they were not committed to Peter and his successors, they necessarily confess that they are not of Christ's sheep, for the Lord says in John, "There is one fold and one shepherd."

And we learn from the words of the gospel that in this church and in her power are two swords, the spiritual and the temporal. For when the apostles said, "Behold here" (that is, in the church, since it was the apostles who spoke) "are two swords"—the Lord did not reply, "It is too much," but "It is enough." Truly he who denies that the temporal sword is in the power of Peter, misunderstands the words of the Lord, "Put up thy sword into the sheath." Both are in the power of the church, the spiritual sword and the material. But the latter is to be used for the church, the former by her; the former by the priest, the latter by kings and captains but at the will and by the permission of the priest. The one sword, then, should be under the other, and temporal authority subject to spiritual. For when the apostle says "There is no

power but of God, and the powers that be ordained of God," they would not be so ordained were not one sword made subject to the other. . . .

Thus, concerning the church and her power, is the prophecy of Jeremiah fulfilled, "See, I have this day set thee over the nations and over the kingdoms," etc. If, therefore, the earthly power err, it shall be judged by the spiritual power; and if a lesser power err, it shall be judged by a greater. But if the supreme power err, it can be judged only by God, not by man; for the testimony of the apostle is "The spiritual man judgeth all things, yet he himself is judged of no man." For this authority, although given to a man and exercised by a man, is not human, but rather divine, given at God's mouth to Peter and established on a rock for him and his successors in him whom he confessed, the Lord saying to Peter himself, "Whatsoever thou shalt bind," etc. Whoever therefore resists this power thus ordained of God, resists the ordinance of God. . . . Furthermore we declare, state, define and pronounce that it is altogether necessary to salvation for every human creature to be subject to the Roman pontiff.

✠

From G. H. Tavard, "The Bull Unam Sanctam of Boniface VIII," in P. Empie and T. Murphy, eds., Papal Primacy and the Universal Church *(Minneapolis: Augsburg, 1974), 106–7.*

The Status of Women

3. **Heinrich Kraemer, O.P., and Jacob Sprenger, O.P.,** *Malleficarum* **(1486)**

Heinrich Kraemer (d. 1505) and Jacob Sprenger (d. 1495), two Dominican inquisitors, wrote their *Hammer Against Witches* in 1486, two years after Pope Innocent VIII had affirmed the reality of witchcraft and encouraged its vigorous prosecution. The book was a training manual for neophyte inquisitors intent on protecting the faithful from the bane of witchcraft. Our excerpt reveals something of the current theory of what a witch is, but more importantly it betrays a view of women which can scarcely be surpassed in its misogyny. How large a segment of the population subscribed to this view is an open question.

Concerning Witches who Copulate with Devils
Why It Is That Women Are Chiefly Addicted to Evil Superstitions

There is also, concerning witches who copulate with devils, much difficulty in considering the methods by which such abominations are consummated. On the part of the devil: first, of what element the body is made that he assumes; secondly, whether the act is always accompanied by the injection of semen received from another; thirdly, as to time and place, whether he commits this act more frequently at one time than at another; fourthly, whether the act is invisible to any who may be standing by. And on the part of the women, it has to be inquired whether only they who were themselves conceived in this filthy manner are often visited by devils; or secondly, whether it is those who were offered to devils by midwives at the time of their birth; and thirdly, whether the actual venereal delectation of such is of a weaker sort. But we cannot here reply to all these questions, both because we are only engaged in a general study, and because in the second part of this work they are all singly explained by their operations, as will appear in the fourth chapter, where mention is made of

each separate method. Therefore let us now chiefly consider women; and first, why this kind of perfidy is found more in so fragile a sex than in men. And our inquiry will first be general, as to the general conditions of women; secondly, particular, as to which sort of women are found to be given to superstition and witchcraft; and thirdly, specifically with regard to midwives, who surpass all others in wickedness.

Why Superstition Is Chiefly Found in Women

As for the first question, why a greater number of witches is found in the fragile feminine sex than among men; it is indeed a fact that it were idle to contradict, since it is accredited by actual experience, apart from the verbal testimony of credible witnesses. And without in any way detracting from a sex in which God has always taken great glory that his might should be spread abroad, let us say that various men have assigned various reasons for this fact, which nevertheless agree in principle. Wherefore it is good, for the admonition of women, to speak of this matter; and it has often been proved by experience that they are eager to hear of it, so long as it is set forth with discretion.

For some learned men propound this reason; that there are three things in nature, the tongue, an ecclesiastic, and a woman, which know no moderation in goodness or vice; and when they exceed the bounds of their condition they reach the greatest heights and the lowest depths of goodness and vice. When they are governed by a good spirit, they are most excellent in virtue, but when they are governed by an evil spirit, they indulge the worst possible vices.

This is clear in the case of the tongue, since by its ministry most of the kingdoms have been brought into the faith of Christ;

and the Holy Spirit appeared over the apostles of Christ in tongues of fire. Other learned preachers also have had as it were the tongues of dogs, licking the wounds and sores of the dying Lazarus. As it is said: With the tongues of dogs ye save your souls from the enemy.

For this reason Saint Dominic, the leader and father of the Order of Preachers, is represented in the figure of a barking dog with a lighted torch in his mouth, that even to this day he may by his barking keep off the heretic wolves from the flock of Christ's sheep.

It is also a matter of common experience that the tongue of one prudent man can subdue the wrangling of a multitude; wherefore not unjustly Solomon sings much in their praise, in Proverbs 10: In the lips of him that hath understanding wisdom is found. And again, The tongue of the just is as choice silver: the heart of the wicked is little worth. And again, The lips of the righteous feed many; but fools die for want of wisdom. For this cause he adds in chapter 16, The preparations of the heart belong to man; but the answer of the tongue is from the Lord.

But concerning an evil tongue you will find in Ecclesiasticus 28: A backbiting tongue hath disquieted many, and driven them from nation to nation: strong cities hath it pulled down, and overthrown the houses of great men. And by a backbiting tongue it means a third party who rashly or spitefully interferes between two contending parties.

Secondly, concerning ecclesiastics, that is to say, clerics and religious of either sex, Saint John Chrysostom speaks on the text, He cast out them that bought and sold from the temple. From the priesthood arises everything good, and everything evil. Saint

Jerome in his epistle to Nepotian says: Avoid as you would the plague a trading priest, who has arisen from poverty to riches, from a low to a high estate. And blessed Bernard in his Twenty-third Homily *On the Psalms* says of clerics: If one should arise as an open heretic, let him be cast out and put to silence; if he is a violent enemy, let all good men flee from him. But how are we to know which ones to cast out or to flee from? For they are confusedly friendly and hostile, peaceable and quarrelsome, neighborly and utterly selfish.

And in another place: Our bishops are become spearmen, and our pastors shearers. And by bishops here is meant those proud abbots who impose heavy labors on their inferiors, which they would not themselves touch with their little finger. And Saint Gregory says concerning pastors: No one does more harm in the church than he who, having the name or order of sanctity, lives in sin; for no one dares to accuse him of sin, and therefore the sin is widely spread, since the sinner is honored for the sanctity of his order. Blessed Augustine also speaks of monks to Vincent the Donatist: I freely confess to your charity before the Lord our God, which is the witness of my soul from the time I began to serve God, what great difficulty I have experienced in the fact that it is impossible to find either worse or better men than those who grace or disgrace the monasteries.

Now the wickedness of women is spoken of in Ecclesiasticus 25: There is no head above the head of a serpent: and there is no wrath above the wrath of a woman. I had rather dwell with a lion and a dragon than to keep house with a wicked woman. And among much which in that place precedes and follows about a wicked woman, he concludes: All wickedness is but little to the wickedness of a woman. Wherefore Saint John Chrysostom says on the text, It is not good to marry (Matthew 19): What else is woman but a foe to friendship, an unescapable punishment, a necessary evil, a natural temptation, a desirable calamity, a domestic danger, a delectable detriment, an evil of nature, painted with fair colors! Therefore if it be a sin to divorce her when she ought to be kept, it is indeed a necessary torture; for either we commit adultery by divorcing her, or we must endure daily strife. Cicero in his second book of *The Rhetorics* says: The many lusts of men lead them into one sin, but the one lust of women leads them into all sins; for the root of all woman's vices is avarice. And Seneca says in his *Tragedies*: A woman either loves or hates; there is no third grade. And the tears of a woman are a deception, for they may spring from true grief, or they may be a snare. When a woman thinks alone, she thinks evil.

But for good women there is so much praise, that we read that they have brought beatitude to men, and have saved nations, lands, and cities; as is clear in the case of Judith, Debbora, and Esther. See also 1 Corinthians 7: If a woman hath a husband that believeth not, and he be pleased to dwell with her, let her not leave him. For the unbelieving husband is sanctified by the believing wife. And Ecclesiasticus 26: Blessed is the man who has a virtuous wife, for the number of his days shall be doubled. And throughout that chapter much high praise is spoken of the excellence of good women; as also in the last chapter of Proverbs concerning a virtuous woman.

And all this is made clear also in the New Testament concerning women and virgins and other holy women who have by faith led nations and kingdoms away from the worship of idols to the Christian religion. Anyone who looks at Vincent of Beauvais will find marvelous things of the conversion of Hungary by the most Christian Gilia, and of the Franks by Clotilda, the wife of Clovis. Wherefore in many vituperations that we read against women, the word *woman* is used to mean the lust of the flesh. As it is said: I have found a woman more bitter than death, and a good woman subject to carnal lust.

Others again have propounded other reasons why there are more superstitious women found than men. And the first is, that they are more credulous; and since the chief aim of the devil is to corrupt faith, therefore he rather attacks them. See Ecclesiasticus 19: He that is quick to believe is light-minded, and shall be diminished. The second reason is, that women are naturally more impressionable, and more ready to receive the influence of a disembodied spirit; and that when they use this quality well they are very good, but when they use it ill they are very evil.

The third reason is that they have slippery tongues, and are unable to conceal from their fellow-women those things which by evil arts they know; and, since they are weak, they find an easy and secret manner of vindicating themselves by witchcraft. See Ecclesiasticus as quoted above: I had rather dwell with a lion and a dragon than to keep house with a wicked woman. All wickedness is but little to the wickedness of a woman. And to this may be added that, as they are very impressionable, they act accordingly.

There are also others who bring forward yet other reasons, of which preachers should be very careful how they make use. For it is true that in the Old Testament the Scriptures have much that is evil to say about women, and this because of the first temptress, Eve, and her imitators; yet afterwards in the New

Testament we find a change of name, as from Eva to Ave (as Saint Jerome says), and the whole sin of Eve taken away by the benediction of Mary. Therefore preachers should always say as much praise of them as possible.

But because in these times this perfidy is more often found in women than in men, as we learn by actual experience, if anyone is curious as to the reason, we may add to what has already been said the following: that since they are feebler both in mind and body, it is not surprising that they should come more under the spell of witchcraft.

For as regards intellect, or the understanding of spiritual things, they seem to be of a different nature from men; a fact which is vouched for by the logic of the authorities, backed by various examples from the Scriptures. Terence says: Women are intellectually like children. And Lactantius: No woman understood philosophy except Temeste. And Proverbs 11, as it were describing a woman, says: As a jewel of gold in a swine's snout, so is a fair woman which is without discretion.

But the natural reason is that she is more carnal than a man, as is clear from her many carnal abominations. And it should be noted that there was a defect in the formation of the first woman, since she was formed from a bent rib, that is, a rib of the breast, which is bent as it were in a contrary direction to a man. And since through this defect she is an imperfect animal, she always deceives. For Cato says: when a woman weeps she weaves snares. And again: when a woman weeps, she labors to deceive a man. And this is shown by Samson's wife, who coaxed him to tell her the riddle he had propounded to the Philistines, and told them the answer, and so deceived him. And it is clear in the case of the first woman that she had little faith; for when the serpent asked why they did not eat of every tree in Paradise, she answered: Of every tree, etc.—lest perchance we die. Thereby she showed that she doubted, and had little faith in the word of God. And all this is indicated by the etymology of the word; for *Femina* comes from *Fe* and *Minus*, since she is ever weaker to hold and preserve the faith. And this as regards faith is of her very nature; although both by grace and nature faith never failed in the Blessed Virgin, even at the time of Christ's passion, when it failed in all men.

Therefore a wicked woman is by her nature quicker to waver in her faith, and consequently quicker to abjure the faith, which is the root of witchcraft.

And as to her other mental quality, that is, her natural will; when she hates someone whom she formerly loved, then she seethes with anger and impatience in her whole soul, just as the tides of the sea are always heaving and boiling. Many authorities allude to this cause. Ecclesiasticus 25: There is no wrath above the wrath of a woman. And Seneca: No might of the flames or of the swollen winds, no deadly weapon, is so much to be feared as the lust and hatred of a woman who has been divorced from the marriage bed.

This is shown too in the woman who falsely accused Joseph, and caused him to be imprisoned because he would not consent to the crime of adultery with her (Genesis 30). And truly the most powerful cause which contributes to the increase of witches is the woeful rivalry between married folk and unmarried women and men. This is so even among holy women, so what must it be among the others? For you see in Genesis 21 how impatient and envious Sarah was of Hagar when she conceived; how jealous Rachel was of Leah because she had no children (Genesis 30); and Hannah, who was barren, of the fruitful Peninnah (1 Kings 1);

and how Miriam (Numbers 12) murmured and spoke ill of Moses, and was therefore stricken with leprosy; and how Martha was jealous of Mary Magdalene, because she was busy and Mary was sitting down (Luke 10). To this point is Ecclesiasticus 37: Neither consult with a woman touching her of whom she is jealous. Meaning that it is useless to consult with her, since there is always jealousy, that is, envy, in a wicked woman. And if women behave thus to each other, how much more will they do so to men.

Valerius Maximus tells us how, when Phoroneus, the king of the Greeks, was dying, he said to his brother Leontius that there would have been nothing lacking to him of complete happiness if a wife had always been lacking to him. And when Leontius asked how a wife could stand in the way of happiness, he answered that all married men well knew. And when the philosopher Socrates was asked if one should marry a wife, he answered: If you do not, you are lonely, your family dies out, and a stranger inherits; if you do, you suffer perpetual anxiety, querulous complaints, reproaches concerning the marriage portion, the heavy displeasure of your relations, the garrulousness of a mother-in-law, cuckoldom, and no certain arrival of an heir. This he said as one who knew. For Saint Jerome in his *Contra Iouinianum* says: This Socrates had two wives, whom he endured with much patience, but could not be rid of their contumelies and clamorous vituperations. So one day when they were complaining against him, he went out of the house to escape their plaguing, and sat down before the house; and the women then threw filthy water over him. But the philosopher was not disturbed by this, saying, "I knew that the rain would come after the thunder."

There is also a story of a man whose wife was drowned in a river, who, when he was searching for the body to take it out of the water, walked up the stream. And when he was asked why, since heavy bodies do not rise but fall, he was searching against the current of the river, he answered: "When that woman was alive she always, both in word and in deed, went contrary to my commands; therefore I am searching in the contrary direction in case even now she is dead she may preserve her contrary disposition."

And indeed, just as through the first defect in their intelligence they are more prone to abjure the faith; so through their second defect of inordinate affections and passions they search for, brood over, and inflict various vengeances, either by witchcraft, or by some other means. Wherefore it is no wonder that so great a number of witches exist in this sex.

Women also have weak memories; and it is a natural vice in them not to be disciplined, but to follow their own impulses without any sense of what is due; this is her whole study, and all that she keeps in her memory. So Theophrastus says: If you hand over the whole management of the house to her, but reserve some minute detail to your own judgment, she will think that you are displaying a great want of faith in her, and will stir up strife; and unless you quickly take counsel, she will prepare poison for you, and consult seers and soothsayers; and will become a witch.

But as to domination by women, hear what Cicero says in the *Paradoxes*. Can he be called a free man whose wife governs him, imposes laws on him, orders him, and forbids him to do what he wishes, so that he cannot and dare not deny her anything that she asks? I should call him not only a slave, but the vilest of slaves, even if he comes of the noblest family. And Seneca, in the character of the raging Medea, says: Why do you cease to follow your happy impulse; how great is that part of vengeance in which you rejoice? Where he adduces many proofs that a woman will not be governed, but will follow her own impulse even to her destruction. In the same way we read of many women who have killed themselves either for love or sorrow because they were unable to work their vengeance.

Saint Jerome, writing of Daniel, tells a story of Laodice, wife of Antiochus king of Syria; how, being jealous lest he should love his other wife, Berenice, more than her, she first caused Berenice and her daughter by Antiochus to be slain, and then poisoned herself. And why? Because she would not be governed, but would follow her own impulse. Therefore Saint John Chrysostom says not without reason: O evil worse than all evil, a wicked woman, whether she be poor or rich. For if she be the wife of a rich man, she does not cease night and day to excite her husband with hot words, to use evil blandishments and violent importunations. And if she have a poor husband she does not cease to stir him also to anger and strife. And if she be a widow, she takes it upon herself everywhere to look down on everybody, and is inflamed to all boldness by the spirit of pride.

If we inquire, we find that nearly all the kingdoms of the world have been overthrown by women. Troy, which was a prosperous kingdom, was, for the rape of one woman, Helen, destroyed, and many thousands of Greeks slain. The kingdom of the Jews suffered much misfortune and destruction through the accursed Jezebel, and her daughter Athaliah, queen of Judah, who caused her son's sons to be killed, that on their death she might reign herself; yet each of them was slain. The kingdom of the Romans endured much evil through Cleopatra, queen of Egypt, that worst of women. And so with others. Therefore it is no wonder if the world now suffers through the malice of women.

And now let us examine the carnal desires of the body itself, whence has arisen unconscionable harm to human life. Justly may we say with Cato of Utica: If the world could be rid of women, we should not be without God in our intercourse. For truly, without the wickedness of women, to say nothing of witchcraft, the world would still remain proof against innumerable dangers. Hear what Valerius said to Rufinus: You do not know that woman is the Chimera, but it is good that you should know it; for that monster was of three forms; its face was that of a radiant and noble lion, it had the filthy belly of a goat, and it was armed with the virulent tail of a viper. And he means that a woman is beautiful to look upon, contaminating to the touch, and deadly to keep.

Let us consider another property of hers, the voice. For as she is a liar by nature, so in her speech she stings while she delights us. Wherefore her voice is like the song of the Sirens, who with their sweet melody entice the passersby and kill them. For they kill them by emptying their purses, consuming their strength, and causing them to forsake God. Again Valerius says to Rufinus: When she speaks it is a delight which flavors the sin; the flower of love is a rose, because under its blossom there are hidden many thorns. See Proverbs 5:3-4: Her mouth is smoother than oil; that is, her speech is afterwards as bitter as absinthe.

Let us consider also her gait, posture, and habit, in which is vanity of vanities. There is no man in the world who studies so hard to please God as even an ordinary woman studies by her vanities to please men. An example of this is to be found in the life of Pelagia, a worldly woman who was wont to go about Antioch tired and adorned most extravagantly. A holy father, named Nonnus, saw her and began to weep, saying to his companions, that never in all his life had he used such diligence to please God; and much more he added to this effect, which is preserved in his orations.

It is this which is lamented in Ecclesiastes 7, and which the Church even now laments on account of the great multitude of witches. And I have found a woman more bitter than death, who is the hunter's snare, and her heart is a net, and her hands are bands. He that pleaseth God shall escape from her; but he that is a sinner shall be caught by her. More bitter than death, that is, than the devil: Revelations 6:8, His name was Death. For though the devil tempted Eve to sin, yet Eve seduced Adam. And as the sin of Eve would not have brought death to our soul and body unless the sin had afterwards passed on to Adam, to which he was tempted by Eve, not by the devil, therefore she is more bitter than death.

More bitter than death, again, because that is natural and destroys only the body; but the sin which arose from woman destroys the soul by depriving it of grace, and delivers the body up to the punishment for sin.

More bitter than death, again, because bodily death is an open and terrible enemy, but woman is a wheedling and secret enemy.

And that she is more perilous than a snare does not speak of the snare of hunters, but of devils. For men are caught not only through their carnal desires, when they see and hear women: for Saint Bernard says: Their face is a burning wind, and their voice the hissing of serpents: but they also cast wicked spells on countless men and animals. And when it is said that her heart is a net, it speaks of the inscrutable malice which reigns in their hearts. And her hands are as bands for binding; for when they place their hands on a creature to bewitch it, then with the help of the devil they perform their design.

To conclude. All witchcraft comes from carnal lust, which is in women insatiable. See Proverbs 30. There are three things that are never satisfied, yea, a fourth thing which says not, It is enough; that is, the mouth of the womb. Wherefore for the sake of fulfilling their lusts they consort even with devils. More such reasons could be brought forward, but to the understanding it is sufficiently clear that it is no matter for wonder that there are more women than men found infected with the heresy of witchcraft. And in consequence of this, it is better called the heresy of witches than of wizards, since the name is taken from the more powerful party. And blessed be the highest who has so far preserved the male sex from so great a crime: for since he was willing to be born and to suffer for us, therefore he has granted to men this privilege.

What Sort of Women Are Found to Be above All Others Superstitious and Witches

As to our second inquiry, what sort of women more than others are found to be superstitious and infected with witchcraft; it must be said, as was shown in the preceding inquiry, that three general vices appear to have special dominion over wicked women, namely infidelity, ambition, and lust. Therefore they are more than others inclined towards witchcraft, who more than others are given to these vices. Again, since of these three vices the last chiefly predominates, women being insatiable, etc., it follows that those among ambitious women are more deeply infected who are more hot to satisfy their filthy lusts; and such are adulteresses, fornicatresses, and the concubines of the great.

Now there are, as it is said in the papal bull, seven methods by which they infect with witchcraft the venereal act and the conception of the womb: First, by inclining the minds of men to inordinate passion; second, by obstructing their generative force; third, by removing the members accommodated to that act; fourth, by changing men into beasts by their magic art; fifth, by destroying the generative force in women; sixth, by procuring abortion; seventh, by offering children to devils, besides other animals and fruits of the earth with which they work much harm. And all these will be considered later; but for the present let us give our minds to the injuries towards men.

And first concerning those who are bewitched into an inordinate love or hatred, this is a matter of a sort that it is difficult to discuss before the general intelligence. Yet it must be granted that it is a fact. For Saint Thomas, treating of obstructions caused by witches, shows that God allows the devil greater power against men's venereal acts than against their other actions; and gives this reason, that this is likely to be so, since those women are chiefly apt to be witches who are most disposed to such acts.

For he says that, since the first corruption of sin by which man became the slave of the devil came to us through the act of generation, therefore greater power is allowed by God to the devil in this act than in all others. Also the power of witches is more apparent in serpents, as it is said, than in other animals, because through the means of a serpent the devil tempted woman. For this reason also, as is shown afterwards, although matrimony is a work of God, as being instituted by him, yet it is sometimes wrecked by the work of the devil: not indeed through main force, since then he might be thought stronger than God, but with the permission of God, by causing some temporary or permanent impediment in the conjugal act.

And touching this we may say what is known by experience; that these women satisfy their filthy lusts not only in themselves, but even in the mighty ones of the age, of whatever state and condition; causing by all sorts of witchcraft the death of their souls through the excessive infatuation of carnal love, in such a way that for no shame or persuasion can they desist from such acts. And through such men, since the witches will not permit any harm to come to them either from themselves or from others once they have them in their power, there arises the great danger of the time, namely, the extermination of the faith. And in this way do witches every day increase.

And would that this were not true according to experience. But indeed such hatred is aroused by witchcraft between those joined in the sacrament of matrimony, and such freezing up of the generative forces, that men are unable to perform the necessary action for begetting offspring. But since love and hate exist in the soul, which even the devil cannot enter, lest these things should seem incredible to anyone, they must be inquired into; and by meeting argument with argument the matter will be made clear.

✠

From M. Summers, trans., The Malleus Maleficarum of Heinrich Kraemer and Jacob Sprenger *(New York: Dover Publications, 1971), 41–48.*

4. Henricus Cornelius Agrippa, *Declamation on the Nobility and Preeminence of the Female Sex* (1509)

At an opposite extreme to Kraemer and Sprenger in late medieval views of women, we find Henricus Agrippa's *Declamation on the Nobility and Preeminence of the Female Sex* (1509). Given Agrippa's maverick tendency to try to prove the opposite of popular opinion, historians are not sure how seriously to take his argument. Was this work designed to amuse rather than persuade? Nevertheless, here we have an individual of considerable humanist learning trying to turn more conventional wisdom on the status of women on its head.

✠

*Cease, inane babbler, to praise the male sex
more than is just, lest you build a worthless heap of
encomia.
Cease, if you are wise, to condemn the female sex
with malicious words that lack reason.
If you weigh each sex carefully in your balance,
whoever is male will yield to the female sex.
But if you hesitate to believe this, and the issue
seems still unsettled to you,
I have here a witness who has not appeared elsewhere,
a short work which studious Agrippa has recently
compiled,
Praising the female sex as superior to the male.*

Equality of Soul in Men and Women

God most beneficent, Father and creator of all good things, who alone possesses the fecundity of the two sexes, created humans in his image, male and female created he them. Sexual distinction consists only in the different location of the parts of the body for which procreation required diversity. But he has attributed to both man and woman an identical soul, which sexual difference does not at all affect. Woman has been allotted the same intelligence, reason, and power of speech as man and tends to the same end he does, that is, [eternal] happiness, where there will be no restriction by sex. For according to the truth of the gospel, although all will return to life in their own sex, they will no longer carry out the functions of their sex, but it has been promised to them that they will be similar to angels. Thus, there is no preeminence of nobility of one sex over the other by reason of the nature of the soul; rather, inwardly free, each is equal in dignity.

But, setting aside the divine essence of the soul in humans, in everything else that constitutes human being the illustrious feminine stock is almost infinitely superior to the ill-bred masculine race. This will appear indisputable when I have demonstrated it (and this is my purpose), not by forged or counterfeit speech or by the snares of logic in which many sophists love to entrap us, but by taking for authorities the best authors and by appealing to authentic historical accounts, clear explanations, the evidence of Holy Scripture, and prescriptions drawn from the two laws.

The Superior Beauty of Women

Since beauty itself is nothing other than the refulgence of the divine countenance and light which is found in things and shines through a beautiful body, women—who reflect the divine—were much more lavishly endowed and furnished with beauty than man. Whence follows the wonderful softness of the female body to sight and touch, her tender flesh, her fair and clear complexion, her shiny skin, the beauty of her head decked with long silky hair shining and supple, the great majesty of her face with its cheerful demeanor, her face the most fair of all creatures, her neck of a milky whiteness, her forehead large, high, noble. She has penetrating and sparkling eyes, which unite with grace and an amiable gaiety; the slender arch of her eyebrows rises above them, between them a beautiful open space, descending from which is a nose straight and properly proportioned. Under her nose is a red mouth, which owes its beauty to the symmetrical disposition of her tender lips; when she smiles we see her dainty teeth, well placed, as white as ivory, less numerous however than those of men, for woman is neither a glutton nor as aggressive as man. The cheeks and jaws impart to her a tender softness, a tinted rosy glow and modest demeanor; she has a delightful chin, round and with a charming dimple. Under this she has a slender neck, long enough, elevated above round shoulders. Her throat is delicate and white, of medium size. Her voice and her words are agreeable; her chest, large and prominent, makes for a harmonious unity of flesh and of breasts, with the same plumpness on each side both in the firmness of the breasts and in the roundness of both them and the belly. Her sides are supple, her back rises straight up; she has long arms, her hands are well made, her fingers slender with fine joints, her hips and thighs full, her calves plump, the ends of her hands and feet rounded off; all her members are full of vitality. In addition, she has a modest bearing, propriety in her movement, dignified gestures, and is, besides, in her whole body of a universally attractive proportion and symmetry, figure, and carriage.

There is no other creature who offers a sight so admirable, a similar marvel to behold, to the point that one would have to be blind not to see that God himself has put together in woman all that is beautiful in the whole world. All are dazzled by her beauty and love and venerate her on many accounts, to such an extent that we regularly see incorporeal spirits and demons perish with passionate love for women (and this is not an erroneous belief but a truth confirmed by many experiences).

The Superior Role of Women in Salvation

So then the blessing has been given because of woman, but the law because of man, and this was a law of wrath and curse; for it was to the man that the fruit of the tree had been prohibited, and not to the woman who had not yet been created. God wished her to be free from the beginning; it was therefore the man who committed the sin in eating, not the woman, the man who brought death, not the woman. And all of us have sinned in Adam, not in Eve, and we are infected with original sin not from our mother, who is a woman, but from our father, a man. Moreover, the ancient law ordained the circumcision of all males but left women uncircumcised, deciding without doubt to punish original sin in the sex that had sinned. And besides, God did not punish the woman for having eaten, but for having given to the man the occasion of evil, which she did through ignorance, tempted as she was by the devil. The man sinned in all knowledge, the woman fell into error through ignorance and because she was deceived. For she was also the first whom the devil tempted, knowing that she was the most excellent of creatures, and, as Bernard says: "The devil, seeing her admirable beauty and knowing that this beauty was the same that he had known in the divine light when he possessed it, that he enjoyed beyond all the other angels in conversation with God, directed his envy against the woman alone, by reason of her excellence."

Christ, born into our world in the greatest humility, took the more humble male sex and not the more elevated and noble female sex, in order to expiate by this humility the arrogant sin of the first father. In addition, because we have been condemned on account of the sin of the man and not of the woman, God wished that this sin be expiated by the sex that had sinned and that atonement come through the same sex that had been deceived in ignorance. This is why God said to the serpent that the woman, or rather, according to a better reading, the seed of the woman, would crush his head, and not the man or the seed of the man. Perhaps also this explains why the priesthood was conferred by the church on man rather than on woman, because every priest represents Christ, and Christ represents the first person who sinned, that is, Adam himself. One can thus understand the canon that begins with the words "this image" to assert that the woman has not been made in the image of God, that is to say, in corporeal resemblance to Christ.

Moreover, God—I speak of Christ—has not chosen to be the son of a man, but of a woman, whom he has honored to the point that he became incarnate from a woman alone. For Christ is called son of man because of a woman, not because of a husband. This is an extraordinary miracle, which causes the prophet to be astounded, that a woman has encircled a man as a protection, since the male sex has been engulfed by a virgin who carried Christ in her body.

Moreover, when Christ rose from the dead, he appeared first to women, not to men. And it is well known that after the death of Christ some men abjured their faith, although no text attests that women abandoned the faith and the Christian religion. Still further, no persecution, no heresy, no aberration in faith ever occurred because of the deeds of women; one knows that it was otherwise with men. Christ was betrayed, sold, bought, accused, condemned, suffered

the passion, was put on a cross, and finally delivered to death only by men. Even more, he was denied by Peter who loved him and abandoned by all the other disciples; only some women accompanied him to the cross and the tomb. Even a pagan, the wife of Pilate, made greater efforts to save Jesus than any of the men who had believed in him. Add to this the fact that theologians almost unanimously agree that the church at that time dwelled only in a single woman, the Virgin Mary, which makes it fitting to call the female sex religious and holy.

If one says with Aristotle that, among all living beings, the males are more courageous, wise, and noble, the apostle Paul, who was a more excellent teacher than he, responds in these words: "God has chosen foolish things of the world to confound the wise, God has chosen the weak of the world to confound the strong; and God has chosen vile things and those that are despised, things which are not, in order to reduce to nothing things which are."

Concluding Summary

Now, to sum up as briefly as possible, I have shown the preeminence of the female sex according to her name, order, place, and material of her creation, and the status superior to man she has received from God. Moreover, I have demonstrated this with respect to religion, nature, and human laws, and [in each case] through diverse authorities, reasons, and examples. However, as numerous as have been my arguments, I have left still more numerous points untreated, because neither personal ambition nor the desire to make the most of myself but duty and truth moved me to write. I did not want to appear, if I kept silent, to steal from so devoted a sex—by an impious silence—the praises owed to it (as it were burying the talent entrusted to me). But if anyone more diligent than I finds some argument I have overlooked that he thinks should be added to this work of mine, I shall believe that I have not been discredited but rather supported by him in the measure to which he will make better this good work of mine through his talent and his learning.

And now, lest this work turn into a huge book, let this be the end of it.

✠

From Albert Rabil, Jr., ed. and trans., Henricus Cornelius Agrippa: Declamation on the Nobility and Preeminence of the Female Sex *(Chicago: University of Chicago Press, 1996), 43–44, 50–51, 62–65, 96–97.*

Exegesis

5. Jacobus Faber Stapulensis, Introduction to the *Commentary on the Psalms* (1508)

As in every age, so too in the late Middle Ages, biblical exegesis was Christian theology's foundational discipline. The numerous biblical commentaries of the period contradict the later Protestant claim that pre-Reformation Catholicism ignored the Bible. The most advanced exegetical work of the period was done by humanists, among them Jacobus Faber Stapulensis (or Jacques Lefèvre d'Etaples, d. 1536). The introduction to his *Commentary on the Psalms* from 1508 illustrates his love of the Scriptures; his grappling with the traditional fourfold "senses" of the text (literal, allegorical, tropological, and anagogical); his sophistication in recognizing the complexity of the "literal" sense; and his altogether conventional anti-Jewish bias.

Whereas almost all studies are apt to yield nothing but pleasure and gain, only study of divine matters serves not merely pleasure and gain but promises the highest felicity. "Blessed are those," the psalmist said, "who study your testimonies." What is better for us to pursue? To what should we dedicate ourselves more completely? Indeed for a long time I pursued human concerns and paid only "lip service," as the expression goes, to theological studies (which are exalted and ought not to be approached casually). But even after a haphazard sampling of divine things I saw so much light shine forth that, by comparison, the human disciplines seemed like darkness. They breathed a fragrance of such sweetness that nothing like it can be found on earth, nor could I believe that there is any other earthly paradise whose odor could lead souls toward immortality.

I have frequently visited monasteries, but I have become convinced that those who do not love this sweetness certainly have not the slightest notion of the true food of the soul. For our spirits live "by every word that proceeds from the mouth of God," and what are these words but Holy Scripture itself? Those who do not love this sweetness are dead in spirit. And from the moment that these pious studies are no longer pursued, monasteries decay, devotion dies out, the flame of religion is extinguished, spiritual things are traded for earthly goods, heaven is given up and earth is accepted—the most disastrous transaction conceivable.

I often asked the few monks who tried to find nourishment in Sacred Scriptures what sweetness they experienced and savored. Most of them answered that as often as they fell into—I do not know what—literal sense, especially when they tried to understand the divine psalms, they became utterly sad and downcast from their reading.

Then I began to consider seriously that perhaps this had not been the true literal sense but rather, as quacks like to do with herbs, one thing is substituted for the other, a pseudo sense for the true literal sense. Therefore I went immediately for advice to our first leaders, I mean the apostles, the Gospel writers, and the prophets, who first entrusted the seed to the furrows of our souls and opened the door of understanding of the letter of Sacred Scripture, and I seemed to see another sense of Scripture: the intention of the prophet and of the Holy Spirit speaking in him. This I call "literal" sense but a literal sense which coincides with the Spirit. No other letter has the Spirit conveyed to the prophets or to those who have open eyes (not that I should want to deny the other sense, the allegorical, tropological, and anagogical, especially where the content of the text demands it).

To those who do not have open eyes but nevertheless *think* they have, another letter takes its place, which, as the apostle says, kills and opposes the Spirit. This letter is pursued today by the Jews, in whom even now this prophecy is being fulfilled. Their eyes are darkened so that they cannot see and their whole perspective is completely warped. This kind of sense they call literal, not the literal sense of their prophets, to be sure, but rather of certain of their rabbis. These interpret the divine hymns of David for the most part as applying to David himself, to his anxieties during the persecution by Saul and the other wars he fought. They do not regard him in these psalms as a prophet but rather as a chronicler of what he has seen and done, as if he were writing his own history. But David himself says regarding himself, "The Spirit of the Lord spoke through me, his word is upon my tongue." And divine Scripture calls him the man in all of Israel to whom it was given to sing about the Christ of the God of Jacob and the true Messiah. And where else is this granted to him than in the psalms?

And so I came to believe that there is a twofold literal sense. The one is the distorted sense of those who have no open eyes and interpret divine things according to the flesh and in human categories. The proper sense is grasped by those who can see and receive insight. The one is the invention of human understanding, the other is a gift of God's Spirit—the false sense depresses, the other bears it up on high. Hence there seems to be good reason for the complaint of those monks that as often as they fell for "literal" exposition they came away from it somber and upset. All their religious devotion had suddenly collapsed and had completely disappeared, as if ice water had been thrown on a burning fire. For just as the healthy body is aware of what is harmful to it, so also the spirit is aware of what threatens it. Therefore it is not without good reason that I feel this kind of letter should be avoided and that one should aspire to that sense which is animated by the Spirit, as colors are by light.

With this goal in mind, I have tried to write a short exposition of the psalms with the assistance of Christ, who is the key to the understanding of David and about whom David spoke, commissioned by the Holy Spirit, in the book of Psalms. In order that it might be more obvious how great the difference is between the proper and improper sense, I offer a few examples which demonstrate this. Let us first take Psalm 2: "Why do the nations conspire and the peoples plot in vain? The kings of the earth set themselves up and the rulers take counsel together against the Lord and his anointed." For the rabbinic interpreters, the literal meaning of the text is that the inhabitants of Palestine revolted against David, the anointed one of the Lord. But Paul and the other apostles take the literal sense to refer to the Anointed of the Lord, the true Messiah and the true Son of God (which is both true and appropriate).

For the rabbinic interpreters, the literal meaning of Psalm 18 is that David expresses thanks to God for being liberated from the hands of Saul and his other enemies. Paul has taken the literal sense to mean the Anointed One of the Lord. The rabbis understand Psalm 19 to deal with the first giving of the law. Paul takes it to be not the first but the second giving of the law when through the blessed apostles and their successors it was promulgated to all nations. Furthermore, the rabbis, in a literal interpretation of Psalms 1 and 21, refer them to the persecution of the Israelites in the time of Artaxerxes. Matthew, John, and Paul, full of God, took the psalms to refer, in a literal sense, to those things which happened to the Anointed of the Lord, the King of Glory, in his passion.

But it would be tedious to go through each psalm to show that what the rabbis contrive to be the literal sense is not the literal sense at all, but rather a fiction and a lie. Isaiah appropriately prophesied these things when he said: "For they are a rebellious people, lying sons, sons who will not hear the instruction of the Lord; who say to the seers, 'See not,' and to the prophets, 'Prophesy not to us what is right, speak to us smooth things, prophesy illusions, level the way, turn away from the path, let us hear no more of the Holy One of Israel.'"

Certainly those who see such "smooth things" see errors and stray from the true way, which is the Anointed One, and "turn away from the path" so that they cannot see "the Holy One of Israel," which is Christ Jesus, the most highly blessed forever.

How, therefore, can we rely on the interpretation of those whom God has stricken with blindness and terror, and not fear that when a blind man offers us guidance we will fall into a ditch together? It is impossible for

us to believe this one to be the literal sense which they call the literal sense, that which makes David a historian rather than a prophet. Instead, let us call that the literal sense which is in accord with the Spirit and is pointed out by the Spirit. "We know," says Paul, the spokesman of God, "that the law is spiritual," and if it *is* spiritual, how could the literal sense, if it is really to be the sense of the law, not be spiritual? Therefore the literal sense and the spiritual sense coincide. This true sense is not what is called the allegorical or tropological sense, but rather the sense the Holy Spirit intends as he speaks through the prophet. It has been our total purpose to draw out of this sense all the Holy Spirit has put into it.

Now, if anyone would hold against me that I have not done this as worthily as I should, I would be most ready to grant it. For who can interpret in a fitting manner a prophet who is not himself a prophet nor has received the spirit of a prophet? I cannot say that of myself nor do I claim what is described by Homer: "We are not led by man's divinations, but with my own eyes I have seen, and with my own ears I have heard, that God revealed all those things by bringing them to light."

But those by whose "divinations" I am led and whom I follow were able to say this [that they saw with their own eyes and heard with their own ears], and above all the joint witness of their Scriptures has been our abiding guide.

But perhaps there will be others who will stamp this enterprise of ours as redundant, since I am writing after Didymus, Origen, Arnobius, and Cassiodorus commented on the psalms. We shall answer that these Fathers treated everything most clearly, but that what they have done elaborately we shall treat succinctly. They worked with several senses; we have been intent on one primarily, namely, that sense which is the intention of both the Holy Spirit and the prophet. They had only one text of the psalms available, so that Augustine, for example, worked with the Old Psalter which is less reliable than the others. Therefore he was often forced to make excurses without relation to the text. Cassiodorus followed the Roman Psalter, and others have worked with the text that was available to them. We have consulted various text traditions, so that from these we could truly establish the original sense.

From H. A. Oberman, ed., Forerunners of the Reformation: The Shape of Late Medieval Thought *(New York: Holt, Rinehart and Winston, 1966), 297–301.*

Moral Instruction

6. The *Fasciculus Morum* (fourteenth century)

Moral instruction in the late medieval church took place in the contexts of catechesis, the sacrament of penance, and preaching. Given the often abysmal educational level of the ordinary parish priest, we can well imagine that many were at a loss as to what to say to their parishioners on Sunday morning. Hence the need for manuals to assist them. The one represented here by an anonymous fourteenth-century writer deals with the traditional seven deadly sins: pride, wrath, envy, avarice, sloth, gluttony, and lechery. It gives us a glimpse into how the church expected parish pastors to preach; it shows us the kind of illustrations, jokes, and anecdotes which ought to enliven the ideal sermon; and it illustrates the kind of moral instruction the faithful were subjected to. It

is noteworthy that in this particular handbook, far more space is devoted to the sin of sloth than any other sin. In other handbooks and especially in manuals for confessors, it is often sexual sins which receive the most attention.

What Sloth Is

After completing Part IV on the vice which especially serves the world, namely avarice and covetousness, together with the opposite virtues, we now come in the fifth place to treat those vices that spring from the stinking and corrupt flesh as its evil and damnable offspring, namely sloth, gluttony, and lechery, together with their opposite virtues, that is, holy activity, abstinence, and continence.

About sloth I shall proceed as follows: first I shall deal with what it is and how it is defined; second, with its characteristics and to what things it can be compared; and third, why it is harmful and rightly cursed. First, then, I say that sloth is boredom with respect to the good, or fearfulness. Now, to the devil, everything good is boring; therefore, this sin may rightly be said to serve not only the flesh but also the devil. Its characteristic is to want always to be at ease, even to reign with God if possible, and yet never to be busy but at all times to lie idle.

It can therefore be compared to a servant of whom Petrus Alphonsi speaks in his book *On Clerical Knowledge.* When his master ordered him at night to lock the doors after he had gone to bed, the servant replied, lying: "They are already shut." And when his master woke him in the morning to open the doors, he said: "I knew that you wanted them open; therefore I would not shut them last night." And when his master told him again: "It is day. Get up and do your work!" he replied: "If it is day, give me my dinner."

Then his master said to him: "It would be a shame for you to eat at night [i.e., since you get hungry again in the morning]." And the servant came back with: "If it is night, let me go to sleep." Thus, indeed, it goes with lazy, slothful people. You cannot ask them for anything to cast off their torpor and laziness without their having excuses freely ready, especially if they ought to endure any hardship for God's sake, such as in fasting, vigils, prayers, and the like. The first of these a slothful man cannot undertake because it would weaken his body; neither can he undertake the second because he gets a headache or eye-ache; nor the third either because he does not know the Our Father and other prayers, and if he does, he gets a swollen tongue and lips.

And yet they are perfectly capable of sitting and waking by the cup all day long and all the night, as it frequently happens, and of uttering useless things. Bernard challenges such people in a devout meditation, saying: "O ungrateful lazybones, why can you not endure anything for me, who have endured so much for you? Perhaps you say your head hurts and you have heartburn, which probably come from eating too much. Do I not have my head crowned for you and my heart pierced with a sharp spear? Your hands and feet are being eaten by worms that come from your corrupt humors, and I have both hands and both feet pierced for your sake with sharp nails and have them stuck on the cross. Is your body naked and worn thin by fasting? Look at me, I pray, how I am even more naked, worn, and despoiled on the gibbet. Do people rise against you with words? But nearly everybody shouts against me: 'Crucify, crucify him!' On you, some people have pity, but of me all people make fun. You are lying low, so that your shame may be somewhat hidden; but I am tormented high up in the air, that I may appear openly contemptible to everyone."

Such slothful people may therefore be compared to bums who sit all day long in the sun and do no work but refuse the burden of any good activity. Therefore they do not belong to the number of those whom Christ called to rest from their earthly labor when he said, in Matthew 11: "Come to me, all you that labor, and I will refresh you," that is, with eternal happiness.

They are also like the cuckoo, who does not hatch its own eggs but puts them into the nest of another bird and eats the other bird's eggs. In this way the slothful person lives off other people's labor, and what others have gained by hard and painful work, he eats up in idleness; the psalmist says: "They devour the poor man in secret," that is, the sustenance on which the poor should live. But that is food which perishes and does not last into eternal life, as the *Gloss* on John says: "The food that perishes is the bread which idle people eat who do no work in either the active or the contemplative life." Whence Chrysostom says in homily 14 of his *Imperfect Work on Matthew,* commenting on the words "Our daily bread": "He adds the word 'daily' to forbid luxurious food, so that we should eat only as much as our nature reasonably requires, not as much as our appetite craves. For if one spends as much on one dinner as might be enough for a hundred people who live modestly, one does not eat 'daily' food but food for many days." For this reason such people may well be called wasps or degenerate bees, which do not produce honey but consume it; as the psalmist says: "Strangers will plunder his labors."

Third, I say that such people may be likened to certain noblemen who hold on to their vineyards so tightly that they share them with no one but preserve it all for their heirs; but when the latter get these possessions into their hands, they waste and consume them without measure and reason. Thus, spiritually, many people today give their bodies over to idleness without doing any useful work, so that when their bodies come to their heirs, which are worms and snakes, the latter will eat them without measure and reason, according to the words of Ecclesiasticus 10: "When a man dies, he shall inherit serpents, beasts, and worms." And then he will, against his desire, give to the worms what he now refuses to give to divine worship or good deeds.

As a warning to such people there is a good story about a rich man who had three sons. As he wanted to know which of them was the worthiest to possess his heritage, he promised it to the laziest. When the oldest son heard this, he said: "Father, the heritage belongs to me, for I am so lazy that, if I were lying next to a fire and saw it spread all around me, I would rather let my feet and legs burn than draw them back from the fire." To whom the second brother replied: "Not so, but the heritage belongs to me. For if I were lying in a rainstorm and water were continuously dripping into my eyes, I would rather drown than move my head or close my eyelids." But when the third brother had heard this, he said: "Then the heritage is rightly mine, for I am so lazy that, if I were being led to the gallows with a rope around my neck and had a sharp sword in my hand, I would rather hang than cut the rope." By the first brother we can morally understand a lecher, who would rather be consumed in his burning lust than draw the feet of his evil affection from it. By the second we can understand the covetous person, who would

rather go blind than close the eye of his mind to covetousness, because just as drops that fall constantly blind the eyes of our body, so do riches blind the eyes of our mind. And by the third we can understand a proud man, or anyone that is caught and bound in any other sin, who would rather be drawn to hell by the rope of evil habit and be hanged there than free himself in confession with the sword of his tongue.

Therefore it is well said in Proverbs 26: "As the door turns upon its hinges, so does the slothful upon his bed," that is, in the bed of his perverse desire, from which he cannot escape any more easily than a fish from the net or a bird from the lime, because he is completely wrapped up and bound by the net and lime of the devil. Hence a lazy person can well be called "a door upon its hinges," because many such people lie indolent in the bed of somnolence that they would much rather snuggle in its warmth beyond a reasonable time than go to church and attend mass and God's service. And when at last they have got up, they hurry rather to the table than to church. If they should finally get there, it seems to them that they are standing on glowing coals, and so they can hardly stay there at all, whereas they really ought to remain until they are given leave to return home from church. This happens when mass is over and the priest says, "Go, the mass is ended," as if he were saying: this mass has been sent to the Father; therefore, go, that is, in the Lord's name return to your homes.

There are also some people of this kind who do not care about the mass except to get the blessed bread and holy water, and that, they think, is enough. They do not consider the fact that when the priest receives the body of Christ, he does so not only for himself but for all the faithful who are present or who would want to be if they somehow could; further, that the priest explicitly mentions "all here present" in the canon of the mass. It is therefore manifest that all who can be present and do not want to, lose the benefit of the mass, as far as this lies in their power. And many do not even care about the blessed bread and water. Perhaps that is so because they do not understand their value. . . .

The Nature of Lechery

Now, in the last place, we pass on to deal with lechery, the third and worst daughter of the flesh, and its members. Like a public whore, this vice is not ashamed to lie with anybody; whence it is rightly deemed to be accursed. Following it, we will deal with its opposite virtue, namely continence and purity, and its members. Concerning lechery I plan to proceed as follows: first, I will discuss what it is and how it is defined; second, its occasions and from where it originates; third, the species that follow it; and fourth, why those who fear God curse it.

On the first point we should know that lechery is variously defined by various authors. Some say: "Lechery is the failure to observe moderation in a soul that perversely loves bodily pleasures." Another author says: "Lechery is bodily incontinence which is born of or has its origin in the itching of our flesh." Yet another definition is this: "Lechery is the desire to have sex which rises beyond measure and against reason." And a fourth definition, according to Bernard, declares: "Lechery is drunken thirst, a momentary outburst, eternal bitterness; it shuns the light, seeks darkness, and entirely plunders man's mind." . . .

The Sex Act

The fifth occasion of lechery clearly lies in the sex act itself, of which it is said in Galatians 4: "The works of the flesh are manifest, which are uncleanness," etc. Against them is given the commandment of Deuteronomy 3: "Go well prepared, without your wives, children, and cattle." Notice that "wife" here means the flesh, to which one is married when one pampers and loves it immoderately. Her "children" are harmful delights and forbidden desires. And the "cattle" are the deeds of the flesh and animal-like acts. Therefore these three—wife, children, and cattle—are to be locked up in a fortified city, meaning they are to be reined in by the well-taught soul so that they do not go forth with us into battle. For whoever has these three with him is not well prepared but rather burdened down. Solinus in *The Marvels of the World* says that when the hyena has looked at an animal three times, the latter cannot move. This hyena is our flesh; it looks three times at those whom it binds to the aforementioned three. And therefore it is said in Joshua 1: "Your wives and children and cattle shall remain; but you pass over armed," as if to say: leave your fleshly desires and pleasures and works behind through the deeds of penance, and go forward against the vices armed with good virtues. If you do that, surely the words of Deuteronomy 7 will come true of you: "No one shall be barren among you of either sex." For when the spirit rules over the flesh, both sexes are fertile and bring forth the good fruit of virtues. Conversely, when the flesh rules over the spirit, both become sterile with respect to good habits. For Pliny says that when a goat licks an olive-tree, it renders it barren. The goat, which according to the philosopher is a bad-smelling and unclean animal, and smells worse behind than in front, symbolizes the flesh whose lusts and deeds are found to be ever more ugly and evil the more often they occur. But the olive-tree is man's mind; it is licked when the flesh with its fondling draws off its strength. Thus it is no wonder if the flesh does not allow it to yield fruit. Hence it is said in Jeremiah 22: "Write this man barren."

Concerning the flesh and its works it is written in Revelation 13: "I saw another beast coming up out of the earth, and he had two horns and spoke like a dragon." In spiritual terms, this beast is fleshly concupiscence, which rises from the earth of our flesh and has two horns, namely gluttony and lust, which do not look very terrifying and yet are quite deceptive. They are like the horns of a wanton lamb, because they invite to wantonness and yet in the end lead to insolence. This beast "spoke like a dragon." The dragon sends from his mouth poisonous breath; in the same way, the flesh stirs us to talk in this fashion. Hence there is hardly anyone who does not follow or hunt after wantonness in some manner, as can be seen in the variety of vanities, be it in food or clothing or gestures or speech or song or one's way of walking and similar wretched customs of the flesh that lead to damnation. Develop this point as you see fit.

And notice that in addition to these five occasions of lechery there are further the solicitations of old women called go-betweens, who cause many men and women to retreat from their good intention to live in continence and cleanness. They do the devil's work. For the devil's work is, above all, to strive with all diligence to cast people into sin and drown them. Now, when the devil himself cannot achieve this in people of great moral strength by his own ruses, he sends these go-betweens, full of wretched tricks, as his messengers to lure the minds of men and women into the sins of the flesh. Thus we can see that they are more powerful in evil than the devil himself and may be called the devil's coaches. Of them it is well said in Proverbs 16 that "the wrath of a king is the messenger of death." If David ordered to kill the man who seemingly brought good news, namely Saul's death, in 1 Kings 1, what do you think the heavenly David, that is, Christ, will do to those who, as it were, bring news of the fires of hell? Surely: King David could only inflict temporal death, but Christ can give eternal death; therefore, etc. Hence those cursed old women may be called sisters of the serpent that deceived Eve. According to Bede, the serpent has the face of a maiden, and this stands for those go-betweens that have been chosen by the devil to deceive our souls. Of them is said in Joel 1: "The girl they have sold for wine." But after the psalm, "their wine is the gall of dragons, and the venom of asps, which is incurable."

Observe the following: If a preacher of God's word were to win a single soul in all his life, he would do a great thing, because that soul, redeemed with the blood of Christ, is worth more than all the goods of the world. Therefore, if one of those go-betweens were to do no other evil in all her days than ruin a single soul, she would do a lot. But since no sacrifice pleases the devil as much as the ruin of souls, therefore—since this is what these go-betweens do—no sin is greater than theirs, as is plain to see. It lies in the nature of a noble falcon to fly up high, and yet he is often lured by the fowler's trick to come down, namely by means of some pigeon craftily set on the ground to lure him. In the same fashion, young women who climb up high on the way of chastity are tricked by the fowler of hell by means of such go-betweens that are assigned to this job.

For this we have a story about a young woman who loved her chastity but was loved unchastely and against her will by a cleric. As the cleric could make no headway in having her to his will, he thought of a ruse and secretly consulted such a go-between. When the latter had been hired by him, she took a bitch and starved it for two or three days. Then, on the fourth day, she fed it black bread and very sharp pepper, which made water and tears burst from its eyes. Then she took the bitch and went to the maiden's house. When the girl asked about the cause of the bitch's tears, the old dame answered, as if sad and grieving: "Alas, my daughter, woe to me. For God's sake, don't ask any further about this matter!" But when, like a woman, the girl was tempted even more to know the cause, the wretched dame at last answered with pretended tears: "This bitch you see thus crying once was my beloved daughter and was deeply loved by a cursed cleric. When he could not lure her with words or gifts to love him, he died of grief. But God in his anger took vengeance and changed my daughter into the shape of this bitch who is constantly weeping and mourning for her folly." When the girl heard this, she got frightened and said: "Alas, dear mother, what shall I do? For I am in the same case and condition. I implore you to give me your advice." Then she answered: "If you want to live, call the young man quickly and do his will in everything." That is what happened, and thus she tricked the girl. Wherefore it is well said: "I have found a woman more bitter than death," as if to say: in the course of nature, death can only catch one person at a time, but that wretched dame ruined three at once—herself and two others.

The Branches of Lechery
Fornication

As to the branches of this vice, there are several. The first may be said to be fornication, which is said to be more detestable than homicide or violent theft because the latter are not as evil in their substance as fornication is. For example, it is possible that someone wants to kill someone else by right, as does a judge out of love for justice; and likewise someone may steal someone else's goods out of great need. But no one can knowingly fornicate in any other way than by committing a mortal sin; therefore, etc. And thus, as can be seen in Numbers 25, when Israel had fornicated with the daughters of Moab, the Lord commanded their princes to be hanged. Therefore, we must understand that while fornication is any forbidden sexual intercourse, it particularly refers to intercourse with widows, prostitutes, or concubines. But the term "prostitute" must be applied only to those women who give themselves to anyone and will refuse none, and that for monetary gain.

People who claim that simple fornication is not a mortal sin because it is a natural act have to be shown the following three arguments in order: first, that it is absolutely forbidden; second, that it must be completely rejected; and third, that it has been called "diabolical" by the Lord. First, then, that simple fornication is absolutely forbidden is manifest from the commandments as in Deuteronomy 23: "There shall be no whore among the daughters of Israel"; and Exodus 24: "Thou shalt not commit fornication"; and Corinthians 6: "Flee fornication"; and Galatians 5: "The works of the flesh are manifest, which are fornication," etc.; and the text continues: "They who do such things shall not obtain the kingdom of God." Thus the first argument is manifest. . . .

Violating a Virgin

The second branch of lechery is violating, that is, unlawfully deflowering, a virgin. This is much to be detested. For as can be seen in Genesis 34, when Shechem, the son of Hamor, deflowered Dinah, he and his father and the entire population of the town were killed for this sin. Likewise, once the good of virginity has thus been lost, it is irrecoverable, just as a glass vessel cannot be made whole again once it has been broken; whence the psalmist says: "My heart is become like a vessel that is destroyed." Orosius tells in book 4 that Hannibal, the leader of the Carthaginians, though he was such a great champion that, as a sign of his victory, he had sent to Carthage three measures of gold rings taken from the fingers of rich Romans that had been killed, yet after being undefeated in battle he was, as Valerius reports in book 4, captured and overcome by the fire of lechery. And the Chartrian concludes from this reasonably that a prince's reign cannot stand for long or remain if it is corrupted by lechery.

Adultery

The third branch of lechery is adultery, which is the unlawful approaching of another man's marriage bed. It can be divided into two species, namely adultery between a married and a single person, and adultery between two married persons. That adultery is a crime is obvious from the fact that, first, it goes against the common sacrament of marriage which God instituted in paradise in the state of innocence. Moreover, Christ himself in his sinlessness deigned to be born in wedlock—not only in the purity of virginity but also in the honorable state of matrimony—that he might show how eminently worthy this sacrament is. And that one should more earnestly refrain from violating

this sacrament, he laid the offense under a grave penalty, for in Leviticus 20 it is said: "If a man has defiled another man's wife and committed adultery, let them be put to death, both the adulterer and the adulteress." And in Numbers 5 it is similarly written: "Since you have gone away from your husband and have been defiled and have lain with another man, these curses shall light upon you: May the Lord make you a curse and an example to all among his people; may he make your thigh rot, and may your womb burst asunder."

In his book *On the Nature of Things* Alexander reports that once there were two storks; the female sat on her eggs in the nest to hatch them, and the male flew about the country to seek food for himself and his mate. It so happened that while she was left behind in her nest she committed adultery with other storks. Out of her natural instinct then, lest her husband on his return should notice the smell of adultery, she washed herself in a spring that was in front of the gate of a knight. After she had done so twice or three times, the knight, who had noticed this, had the spring closed off. When she came as usual to wash herself but could not, she returned to her nest unclean. Upon his return at night, her mate perceived her smell and tore her completely to pieces in revenge for her adultery. This applies spiritually to God and man's soul, which God has taken to himself as his spouse, according to the words of Hosea: "I will espouse you to myself in faith." God leaves her here, as if in the nest of this world, so that she may bring forth good works. She does not need to worry about her livelihood, only about living a good life, because God himself will supply all her needs, after the words of Isaiah: "Learn to do well," etc., because "if you are willing and listen to me, you shall eat the good things of the land." But the wretched soul commits adultery with other wretches, and when she becomes afraid of the judgment, washes herself in the fountain of penance. This penance is in front of the door of the confessor, of which the psalmist speaks as follows: "This is the gate of the Lord; the just shall enter into it." In front of this door must be the wellspring of penance and the water of contrition. After she washes herself, the stench of sin disappears totally. Hence God, too, covers up our sins; Wisdom 2: "You have mercy upon all because you can do all things, and you overlook the sins of men because of their repentance." Now it frequently happens that since God offers such mercy, the wretched soul relapses into sin. And when she wants to wash herself through penance as usual, she is often prevented from doing so by sudden vengeance, because the wellspring of contrition is closed off by the knight of death. Therefore, as Ecclesiasticus 15 fittingly speaks to sinful man: "Do not delay to turn to the Lord," etc., "for his wrath shall come of a sudden, and in the time of vengeance he will destroy you." . . .

Incest

The fourth branch of lechery is connected with the previous ones; it is called incest, which means sexual intercourse with a person related by blood or spiritual kinship. How grave this sin is can be seen in three ways. First, by the punishment established for it in the Law; for in Leviticus 18 it is said: "Every soul that commits any of these abominations shall perish from the midst of the people." In this passage Scripture speaks specifically of incest and the sin against nature. Second, according to 1 Corinthians 5, the apostle has given people who sin in this fashion over to Satan for punishment. Third,

its gravity is further seen in its evil consequences. For it leads to manslaughter, as we find in Amnon, in 1 Kings 12, who corrupted his sister, for which he was killed by his brother Absalom. Tell the entire story. Similarly, this vice makes a man like a dog, who pays no attention to his blood relationship when it comes to sex.

Notice that this branch comprises lechery among clerics and religious. Their sin is more grievous than that of other people; therefore Bernard says: "Where there is a greater gift of grace, the transgressor is liable to greater punishment"; and the same is true of his guilt. Notice also that the sin of people in this state is made more grievous by three reasons. The first is that they break their vow. Two circumstances can aggravate the sin of theft, namely the value of what is stolen and its size—for one's neighbor suffers greater harm in this case—and also its sanctity, for in the latter case a thief does not merely commit theft but also sacrilege. Now when a cleric commits a sexual sin, he loses that chastity which he had promised to maintain when he received holy orders, and it is thus irrecoverable; Ecclesiasticus 26: "No price is worthy of a continent soul." The second reason is that a cleric belongs to God's household and lives on its budget. If he then commits lechery with the goods of God, he is to be expelled from his service like a traitor. Whence Bernard says: "Woe to those who walk in the flesh, for they cannot please God." Therefore, when they break their vow, they bring greater harm upon themselves and consequently incur a greater penalty, because it is better not to make a vow than to make it and then break it voluntarily. The third reason is that they deceive the people on whose alms they live and for whom they promise to pray; but they hardly fulfill their promises at all or do so in a state of sin and uncleanness. Therefore Gregory says: "We live off the church's patrimony and receive from it our food and drink. If we do not pray in return, indeed we eat and drink the people's sins."

With regard to sexual sins of the religious, which fall under incest, we should know that this sin is made more grievous for five reasons in particular. The first can be found in the fact that, as we read in Genesis 7, this was the cause of the flood. If, as is written there, it displeased God so much that the sons of God took the daughters of men as their wives, how much must those fear to displease him who commit fornication with them! The second reason derives from the notion of apostasy. A person is called an "apostate" when he audaciously abandons his religious habit. But the virtue of chastity belongs more intimately to the religious life than the habit; therefore it is plain that abandoning chastity is much more grievous than abandoning one's habit. Hence it is said in Proverbs 6: "An apostate is an unprofitable man." The third aggravating factor is that, obviously, the devil tries very hard to bring a religious person to a fall, since he rejoices more over the fall of one religious than over that of many other people. . . .

Sodomy

The fifth and last branch of lechery is the diabolical sin against nature called sodomy. I pass it over in horror and leave it to others to describe it.

The commentator on Virgil reports that when the Greeks were devastating Ilion, that is, Troy, they found there the daughter of Priam, by the name of Cassandra, in the temple of Minerva. The good knight Ajax was so overcome by her beauty that he raped the maiden. For that deed Minerva, the goddess of chastity, took the following revenge on him: when he was sailing back to his homeland, she stirred up the elements on the sea and the sea itself violently and sent lightning bolts and flashes from above, whereby she tossed the ship on a rock so that he and all his companions perished in the tempest. This Cassandra raped by Ajax symbolizes any woman who engages in sex with any fornicator against the will of God and his church. Minerva, the goddess of chastity, stands for Christ. What wonder, then, if Christ takes vengeance on those who scorn his commandment by getting involved, not just in simple fornication but in that vile and abominable sin against nature that is not to be named? To be sure, it is no wonder at all.

An explicit type of this occurs in Genesis 19, in Sodom and Gomorrah, which are five cities of that region. Not only did fire and sulfur falling from above kill people and animals, but the earth opened its mouth and swallowed all the living. Thus it is certain that on account of the said sin they perished forever in hell. As an open sign the sea there remains dead even in our days; no living being can submerge or remain in it; and it is all for just revenge in horror of such a sin. As it is said in the book *On the Nature of Things,* if a burning light is thrown into this sea, it floats on the surface and cannot drown until it is put out, as a sign that nothing alive that is done in the light of grace for those for whose sake such vengeance was taken is of any use. And a further testimony, according to writers on natural history and several moderns who have observed this with their own eyes, is that while the apples that grow on the shore of that sea are most beautiful to look at, when they are ripe and are cut open they give forth a sulfurous smoke and dusty ashes. The same applies to those evil lechers who are devoted to the aforementioned abhorrent sins: though they show great external beauty in their body, like green apples, the riper they grow, the more they give forth a sickening ash in their lust that burns and smells like sulfur. Therefore, according to Augustine, "God hated this vice so much that, seeing it being committed by men before his incarnation, he almost refrained from becoming a man." And thus God did not want to entrust any angel or man with the execution of this punishment but kept its vengeance for himself, after the words: "Revenge is mine, and I will repay." . . .

From S. Wenzel, ed. and trans., Fasciculus Morum: A Fourteenth Century Preacher's Handbook *(University Park, Pa.: Pennsylvania State University Press, 1989), 399–405, 649, 663–69, 677–79, 683–89.*

Theology

7. Thomas Bradwardine, *The Cause of God against the Pelagians* (ca. 1344)

One important item on the busy theological agenda of the late Middle Ages was the subject of justification, the Christian understanding of how human beings become righteous before God. Thomas Bradwardine (d. 1349), English archbishop and theologian, staked out his position on this issue in his book *The Cause of God against the Pelagians* (ca. 1344). Labeling his contemporary theological opponents as "Pelagians," Bradwardine defended the Augustinian teaching. In this excerpt from his book, Bradwardine argues that the logic of this position leads inexorably to a strong doctrine of predestination.

The Pelagians now oppose our whole presentation of predestination and reprobation, attempting either to eliminate them completely or, at least, to show that they are dependent on personal merits.

[The "Pelagian" Arguments]

1. They use the following arguments: God does nothing unreasonable and there is no reason why he should predestine or reprobate one man rather than another. Therefore, he either predestines and reprobates everyone or no one. And since there is a consensus that not everyone is predestined or rejected, they conclude that no one is. Or, if they grant that there be such a thing as a reason for predestination or reprobation, this reason can then only be based on several different kinds of merit.

2. Thus Abbot Joachim of Flora (d.1202) in his dialogues with Benedict assigns two reasons or causes for the election, predestination, and mercy of God, of which the first is man's own capacity for mercy, salvation, and goodness, and the second is the good act itself. He assigns opposite causes and reasons for reprobation.

3. The Gospel of John states: "He gave them power to become sons of God." Since, therefore, in accordance with predestination and grace men become sons of God, this lies within their own free power and occurs in no other way than by merits acceptable to God.

4. The psalmist agrees with this when, after reciting certain sins, he says, "Let them [the sinners] be blotted out of the book of the living; let them not be enrolled among the righteous."

5. Again the Apocalypse says, "Hold fast what you have, lest anyone should seize your crown," which is the crown God has promised to his elect.

6. Likewise, if Adam had not sinned no one would have been reprobated. Therefore,

predestination or reprobation corresponds to individual merit.

7. Likewise, since it would be unfair and cruel for either man or an angel to harm someone without provocation, and such an action would be necessarily unjust, how much less befitting would such action be for a God who is the most right and the most righteous? Nor would it befit God that anyone should be reprobated and predestined to eternal fire unless it were done on account of preceding guilt.

[The "Augustinian" Responses]

1. The first of these arguments is unreasonable and can be answered with complete clarity by referring to the argumentation of previous chapters [that is, the sovereign God, creator and redeemer, cannot be dependent on anything outside of him].

2. Now turning to the support drawn from Joachim, it should be pointed out that although Joachim was a great doctor, he did not have great authority. He was an Arian in his Trinitarian doctrine, as is clear from the book he wrote against Peter Lombard, *On the Trinity,* and from his condemnation by Innocent III at the Fourth Lateran Council. And just as he was an Arian in Trinitarian doctrine he was a Pelagian in attributing the original cause of predestination and reprobation, not to the God who predestines and reprobates but to man's own capacity and to the actions of the men predestined or reprobated, as indicated above.

Nevertheless he tried to avoid the most extreme Pelagian position by asserting that the cause of divine election and reprobation was man's own capacity for mercy or wrath, not his capacity for works or acts themselves. When Benedict asks what the capacity for good and evil might be if not for good and evil works, as the apostle says about Isaac and Jacob, Joachim answers that this capacity is not an act but "a repository of grace or wrath from which the good and evil works have their origin." And farther on he says that when God elects certain men he does not look for righteousness in them, for he himself will give them that. The only factors necessary are humility and wretchedness, that is to say, "a propensity for mercy." Thus in approaching too close to the banks of the Pelagian flood he slips over and is sucked completely into the whirlpool, when he says that one's merits are the cause of predestination and reprobation.

As I briefly reconstruct the diffuse course of his argument, he means to say that humility is the cause of predestination, and pride the cause of reprobation, for he claims that the state of despair and misery is the underlying cause of divine election—as the apostle says, "Brother, look to your calling because not many are wise according to the flesh but those whom the world thinks foolish, God chooses."

As one reads farther it becomes clear that man is claimed by God, not for his righteousness but for his wretchedness, not for his works but for his need, not for his strength but for his weakness, not for his wisdom but for his foolishness, not for his high station but for his obscurity. "Just as the Pharisee of the biblical account is rejected for his righteousness, so the publican is chosen for his sin. This does not mean that God loves unrighteousness or hates the purity of innocence, but rather that he rejects self-righteousness and has mercy on the humble penitence of the sinner."

And later Joachim says the causes of election are despair and affliction, "not because these things in themselves please God but because they give birth to humility, the sole virtue required by God of men and angels." And again he says that because "the Lord had foreknowledge of the pride of the people of Israel he hated and rejected them."

All of this makes it quite obvious that Joachim contradicts himself. How can it be possible for man's own capacity to be the cause of predestination or reprobation when sometimes, between two of equal capacity, one is chosen and one is abandoned or, at other times, the one of lesser capacity is chosen while the one of greater is abandoned? How can despair and misery be the cause of divine predestination when, as I suspect, many men who in this world live in despair, misery, and poverty are ultimately rejected, while others who have always enjoyed high station, prosperity, and wealth are predestined unto life? Among the holy angels who have been predestined and ultimately confirmed there was never any despair or misery, for they were never guilty or subject to punishment. And above all what is the misery and despair which, according to Joachim's theory, caused Christ's predestination, he whom St. Paul calls the "Son of God in power"?

Joachim's whole position could be "reprobated" by other arguments, but since so few of his arguments hold, these few of my rebuttals will suffice.

3. Now when they bring forward the quotation from the Gospel of John, "He gave them power to become sons of God," they seem to wish to conclude from this that some become or can become the elect sons of God in the course of their life. That is, that from the number of those who are not predestined or who are reprobate, some at the present time can become predestined and at the same time cease to belong to the reprobate. This conflicts with what has been established in Chapters 23 and 45 and, furthermore, contains evident contradictions in itself as can plainly be shown from these chapters.

The quotation from the Gospel of John seems rather to prove the opposite. For he did not say, "He gave them power to make themselves sons of God," but "to be made sons of God." But by whom? Not by themselves. Not out of their own will. Whoever has produced himself? Whoever was born out of himself? What son of the devil can give birth to himself and appear to be the son of God? Hear what follows: "who are born not from human flesh or will but from God." Therefore they do not make themselves sons of God. God does this.

Furthermore Aristotle shows that power, or capability, is of two kinds, active and passive. Now that which is meant by the quotation, "He gave them power to become sons of God," is also asserted in Romans, "Whoever are led by the Spirit of God are sons of God." God gives men power, that is to say, a rational soul and free will with which man can freely and voluntarily receive grace in the present and glory in the future so that, in both the present and the future, they might become sons of God. Thus in the present, as they are being made sons of God by faith and prevenient grace, which makes them into adopted sons of God, they freely accomplish the pleasing work of sons and so freely persevere in this to such an extent that no one could take away their sonship unless they would permit it.

Chrysostom supports this argument in his exegesis of the text which indicates that there is need of much zeal to preserve unspoiled the image with which man is endowed in the baptism of adoption. At the same time, however, he indicates that no one can take this power away from us but ourselves and that this grace comes to those who zealously desire it. Indeed it is in the power of free will and grace to become sons of God by their joint operation.

And Augustine, commenting on John, asks, "'Why were all born in sin?' That we are children of Adam implies damnation by necessity. But to be children of Christ is man's act through his will and through grace, since men are not forced to become children of Christ. Even though they did not choose to be born children of Adam, all of them are sinners in the true sense of the word. All those who are children of Christ are justified and are just, not because of themselves but because of Christ." He does not say, "He gave them power to become sons of God," as if only man were included and God excluded in this process. Nor did he give man the priority while making God a subordinate factor. Therefore John says, "He gave them power to become sons of God," not "to make themselves sons of God." And again, "They are born not out of the will of flesh nor out of the will of men but out of God who is the origin and author of this divine birth."

Furthermore, Bede is quoted as saying, "The carnal begetting of each individual is due to the conjugal embrace, but his spiritual begetting is due to the grace of the Holy Spirit." And Chrysostom said, "St. John the evangelist tells us this so that learning the weakness and humility of the first birth, which takes place through blood and the will of flesh, and knowing the sublimity of the second, which is through grace and excellence, we might receive from this text a profound understanding appropriate to the gift of him who begets us, and show the appropriate zeal."

And Augustine said, preaching on this passage from John, "To as many as received him he gave power to become sons of God." If they became children, they were born. If they were born, whatever may have caused it, it was not flesh or blood or the will of flesh or the will of men but God. Let them rejoice, therefore, that they are born of God. Let them anticipate their return to God. Let them receive the proof because they are born of God.

And, "The Word was made flesh and dwelt among us." If the Word was not ashamed to be born of men, should man be ashamed to be born of God? Saying "He gave them power to become sons of God" does not at all mean, as Pelagius dreamed, that he gave them power to become sons of God by preceding works of merit. It is inconceivable that St. John could contradict his Lord, who said, as John himself reports, "No one is able to come unto me unless the Father who sent me draws him." And "No one is able to come unto me unless it has been given to him by my father." It is equally inconceivable that he could in such short compass make contradictory assertions. Since following hard on the above he says that the Word was full of grace and truth and then adds, "From this fullness we have all received grace for grace." We have received first of all, as I say, grace freely given and truth because we receive grace promised of old and thus grace for grace, that is to say, grace given freely to fulfill the grace promised earlier through the prophets. Secondly, we have received according to our certain hope the grace of beatitude in the future for grace now operative during this dispensation.

Therefore Augustine commenting on John says, "He did not say, 'And from his fullness we all have received grace for grace,' but he said, 'And from his fullness we all have received, and, beyond that, grace for grace.'" Now I do not know what he wants us to understand with the words "have received from the fullness of his grace and, beyond that, grace for grace." Have we not received from his fullness first grace and then again grace for the grace we have received initially?

Does Augustine mean we receive faith before we receive grace? But we cannot walk in faith without being in grace. How would we ever have received this grace? By our preceding merits? Grace is *given* to you, it is not a payment. For this reason it is called grace, because it is freely given. With preceding merits you cannot buy what you have already received as a gift. Therefore the sinner has received first grace in order that his sins might be forgiven. What has he merited? When he demands justice he will receive punishment and when he asks for mercy he will receive grace. But this is exactly what had been promised by God through the prophets. Therefore when he comes to give what he has promised he gives not only grace but also truth. How is this truth manifested? When that which has been promised is fulfilled. What, in fact, does "grace for grace" mean? By faith we merit God. That you received the immortal reward, that is, eternal life, is grace. On account of what merit do you receive eternal life? On account of grace. "God crowns His gifts, not your merits." But this text can also very appropriately be exegeted literally by saying that those who are actually now children of God through faith and grace in this dispensation are granted the power, that is to say, grace helping free will, so that they might become children of God in the future, in the kingdom of heaven.

For this very reason he introduces the statement with "Whoever received him," that is, by believing in him through faith active in love, "He gave them power to become sons of God." Therefore Theophilus is quoted in the gloss, "Because we shall attain the most perfect sonship in the resurrection—as the apostle says, we are awaiting the adoption of the sons of God, the redemption of our bodies—he grants us the power to

become sons of God, that is, this grace will be consummated in future grace."

4. Let us turn now to the objection from Psalm 68 [69], "Let them be erased from the book of the living." If this is understood with superficial literalness, we must concede that predestination and reprobation are subject to change; it would imply that someone who was previously elected and not reprobated is now reprobated and not elected. If someone can at any time be erased from the book of the living, this contradicts everything which previously has been shown.

It is necessary, therefore, to interpret the quotation in a different way. It can be understood as a deletion in accordance with present justice. Or "let them be erased" could be taken to mean "let them be regarded as erased," that is, "as never entered in the book," since the following statement actually says, "Let them not be written with the just." Or "let them be erased" could be taken to mean that their hope of being entered in the book is shown to be vain, just as God is said to feel regrets.

Therefore when Augustine interprets this psalm he says, "Brethren, let us not take this to mean that God would have enrolled someone in the book of life and then erased him out of the book. If Pilate, a mere human, insisted that the inscription 'King of the Jews' should stay on Christ's cross once he said, 'What I have written, I have written,' is it not more certain that God would not change his mind?"

God knows in advance, before the foundation of the world he has predestined all who will reign with his Son in eternal life. Those whom he has enrolled are contained in the book of life. How can they be erased from a book where they were never written? This quotation expresses their hope, that is, they thought themselves to have been entered in the book of life. What does this mean, "Let them be erased from the book of life"? It is obvious they were never there to begin with.

Thus, therefore, those who had hoped, by reason of their righteousness, that they were written in the book of God, when confronted by their damnation, are made aware that they are "erased from the book of life," and they realize that they were never there. The second part of the statement ["Let them not be enrolled with the righteous"] explains the first part. As I have said, "Let them be erased" is to be understood to refer to their vain hopes. And this can correctly be summarized by saying, "Let them not be enrolled."

5. Likewise, to those who understand the Apocalypse literally, "Hold what you have" seems to say that it is possible for someone's crown to be taken away at any time and given to another man, and that, therefore, such a one can cease to be predestined and begin to be reprobated, while for the man who takes his place it is the other way around. But all that has been said does not allow of this. Neither John nor indeed the Spirit in John said or suggested that man through his own strength, without the help of God, holds or can hold his crown, that is, can persevere in a good life and good works until death. Nor did John say that anyone by himself and his own strength, alone without the special help of God, can receive the crown of predestination or grace in the present, or the crown of glory in the future. The following trustworthy words confirm this conclusion: "Thus says the holy and true one who has the key of David, who opens and no one closes, who closes and no one opens: Behold, I have set before you an open door which no one is able to shut. Although you

have little power, still you have preserved my word. Therefore I shall preserve you from the hour of temptation. Behold I come quickly. Hold fast to what you have, etc." Here it is clearly taught that perseverance depends first of all on divine preservation and secondly on human cooperation. How much the less does the beginning and attainment of an upright life depend on man alone! Therefore the quotation "Hold fast to what you have, etc." means that the good act is preceded and elicited by God's grace in order that man might persevere to the very end. Thus he who heard this exhortation was perhaps predestined [to life eternal] by means of this exhortation, be it from God or man, so that he might persevere to the end and hold fast to his crown.

Augustine said that we should pray that those who have not yet been called might be called; perhaps they have been thus predestined to be won over by our prayers and to accept the grace by which they desire election and actually receive it. For God who has predestined all things will fulfill all. It is possible to exegete the passage from Revelations just like the earlier one of the Psalms; it is possible for man to gain or lose the crown of life in terms of present justice, that is, in terms of certain hope.

Accordingly, Augustine proves that the gift of final perseverance cannot be lost and he suggests the following clarification for what we mean by its being lost. Because final perseverance actually means persevering until the end, it is possible for many to have it but, by definition, impossible for them to lose it. Let us beware, however, of saying that the gift of final perseverance can never be lost once it has been granted, that is, once one had the ability to persevere until the end. Let us rather say that it is lost in that moment when man rejects the gift so that he cannot reach the goal—just as we say that the man who does not persevere until the end has lost eternal life or the kingdom of God. It is not that he ever actually had it but he would have had it if he had been able to persevere. And let us not quarrel about words, but let us simply say that there are things we can refer to as losing which, in reality, we do not possess but only hope to acquire.

6. The argument that if Adam had not sinned, no one would have been reprobated but all would have been predestined does not prove at all that predestination and reprobation depend on merit. The opposite of this thesis follows obviously. As was shown above, God does not predestine a certain end for man or man for a certain end; that is to say, God does not grant man eternal life on account of his future good works, but, on the contrary, he grants the good works that may bring him to eternal life. But it does not follow the other way around that if man had acted differently God would have drawn up a different eternal plan. The contrary is true.

Take Christ as an example. If Christ had not done good works he would not have been predestined Son of God—this is obviously untenable! If Paul had not preached he would not have been elected—or was he elected in order that he might preach? No, the contrary is true. If the sun had never shone or the fire given heat, would they not have been predestined to do so? Have they now been predestined to do so because they actually do it? No, that the sun actually shines and the fire actually heats is because they have been predestined or preordained to do this. Moreover, it is by no means clear that if Adam had not sinned no one would have been reprobated. It seems possible that even if Adam had not sinned, all his descendants would not necessarily have been made sinless

and confirmed until the end. Rather they would have had the freedom to choose or accept good or evil.

But even when we grant Anselm's point that if Adam had not fallen, all his descendants would have remained sinless to the end, still we say with Gregory that none of the reprobate would have been born, but only the predestined. Therefore, the sin of Adam is not the primary cause of reprobation, but rather, as said above, if Adam had not sinned, God would have ordained differently. And when you object to this argument on the grounds that a predestined son may sometimes have a reprobate father, and that such a son would not have had a father at all if Adam had not sinned, and, in that case, not only the *now* predestined but *all* who have been predestined would not have been born, you argue against St. Gregory, not against me. At the same time several things can be said in defense of St. Gregory's position. One answer would be that if Adam had not sinned, only those who are now elect would have been born, that is to say, only that number of those now elect would have been born. If Adam had not sinned, God would have created only those souls as are now given to the elect, although some he might perhaps have joined to other bodies than they have now. Or, if we wish to keep body and soul together as an elect unit, only those would have been born who are now elect. In that case an elect who has actually been born of a reprobate parent would have instead been born of another father who belongs to the elect.

7. Now we turn to the argument which accuses God of injustice and cruelty. It should be noted that not every punishment appropriately given to one man by another is imposed because of preceding guilt. Sometimes the punishment is given as a warning

or for other reasons, as many passages in divine as well as human writings show. As a certain law said, "No one who has not committed a crime ought to be punished unless there be a cause." Both civil and canon law agree on this.

Furthermore, Peter Lombard shows that there are five reasons for man's punishment in this dispensation, which are: (1) the correction of sin, (2) the beginning of punishment for sin, (3) the growth in merits, as it was in the cases of Job and Tobith, (4) the avoidance of sin, as Paul says about the thorn in his flesh, (5) the glory of God, as John makes clear in his passage about the man blind from birth. One can also be publicly punished, to frighten others, to deter them from evil and strengthen them in goodness, in accordance with the laws, be they divine, canonical, or civil. If a man may undergo temporal punishment for the temporal benefit of others, why should he not be punished temporally and eternally for the temporal and eternal benefit of the elect, in order that they might all the more flee from evil and choose the good in the present, that in the future they might have greater joy, deeper love, and higher praise for God?

Thus great profit, both in the present and in the future, accrues to the elect from the reprobate, indeed the whole purpose of being for the reprobate is that they have been created for the sake of the elect. What injustice and cruelty can be charged to God because he chooses to predestine and create one of his creatures for the service of another creature and both of them for his own service, praise, glory, and honor? This is particularly true, since he punishes no man with eternal damnation unless such a man deserves it, that is to say, unless through his sins he deservedly and justly requires eternal punishment. And God always punishes most

mercifully and appropriately because innumerable times he finds a way to punish less than is deserved.

If indeed, as Augustine seems to say, it is more desirable to be wretched than not to exist at all, what injustice or cruelty can be ascribed to God if he gives to some creature many and great goods, even though he may punish him with other of his creaturely goods, such as physical pain? When all is taken into account, this creature's position is more attractive than repulsive, and, therefore, even for this state he owes God thanks as for a great gift.

Why do they not accuse God because he punishes innocent beasts and baptized infants with no small physical pain? Indeed he gave up his own most innocent Son, our Lord Jesus Christ, to a most painful, cruel, and tormenting punishment. But since God is omnipotent, completely free Lord of his whole creation, whose will alone is the most righteous law for all creation—if he should eternally punish the innocent, particularly since he does it for the perfection of the universe, for the profit of others, and for the honor of God himself, who would presume to dispute with him, to contradict him, or ask, "Why do you do this?" I firmly believe, no one! "Has the potter no right over the clay to make of the same lump one vessel for honor and another for menial use?"

✠

From Oberman, **Forerunners of the Reformation,** *151–62.*

8. Gabriel Biel, *The Circumcision of the Lord* (ca. 1460)

Gabriel Biel (d. 1495), a representative of the nominalist theological school, lectured and wrote at the University of Tübingen.

Like Bradwardine, he took up the question of justification but defended a position undoubtedly at odds with Augustinianism. In fact, his views have frequently been described as at least "semi-Pelagian." In this sermon, intended for a university audience, Biel summarizes his theology of justification—one which the young Luther studied assiduously.

✝

"His name shall be called Jesus."

(Luke 2:21)

A few days ago we celebrated that glorious day which the birth of our Savior has made so wonderful and lovely for us and which he gave us as an example for our imitation. To this rejoicing is now added a new exultation when today in the circumcision of the newborn king "that name" is given "which is above every name," which was chosen by the Father from eternity before all worlds, which was enunciated by angels, by the mother and by Joseph, the legal father, which was according to Origen announced to them by the new man.

On this day of his circumcision we have no less reason for wonder, praise, and imitation than on the day of his birth. On that day we marveled that the highest majesty appeared in the form of a servant. Today we marvel that this God who is born sinlessly, true God from God the Father and true man from the Virgin Mary, was circumcised just like a sinner.

On Christmas Day we, in our small way, gave thanks, expressing our love and praise for the redeemer who came into the prison of this world to lead the captives out of this prison. Today we magnify him with all our hearts because he put on our fetters and bonds and because he put his own innocent hands into our chains in order that we criminals might be set free.

At his birth we saw with the shepherds the Word which was abbreviated to fit the dimensions of the world; we saw lying in the manger the holy and tender child whose humility we are urged to imitate. Today we see that he who gave the law made himself subject to the law by his circumcision and thus we are instructed even more clearly in obedience of the law to which we are subject. And just as on that day at the moment of his birth, or beginning, he joined together the human with the divine, now at his circumcision he shows that he is truly man, while simultaneously "that name which is above every name" bespeaks the glory of majesty. In order that his divine nature by which he saves his people from their sins might be better known, he has, by his circumcision, destroyed sin in the children of wrath and infused his grace in them. Therefore, it is most appropriate that the text, "His name shall be called Jesus," is selected at the beginning as our theme. Pray now for the needed assistance of grace with a "Hail Mary"!

"Unto us a Child is born, unto us a Son is given": that is Jesus.

He is called Savior. Not just through human preaching but through the message of the angels it is already well enough known to Christians that the Child who has been born and the Son who has been given to us is called Jesus, that is, Savior. Savior, not because of some limited and temporal salvation, as some men have sometimes been called "savior," but Savior because of that universal, spiritual, and eternal salvation which no one else has bestowed or has ever been able to bestow.

To resume, Gabriel said to Joseph, "You will call his name Jesus for he will save his people from their sins." In truth he *has already saved* his people by preparing medicine. *He continues to save* them daily by driving out disease. *He will save* them ultimately by giving them perfect health and preserving them from every ill. The preparation of the medicine is the task of the human nature of Christ, the driving out of disease the task of the divine nature, and the perfect health the task of both natures.

He prepared the medicine when he instituted and commanded the medicinal sacraments. To heal the wounds inflicted by our sins, he, through the effusion of his blood, earned efficacy for the sacraments. Since I remember having preached about this at length a year ago on this very day, I comment no further on this point and turn to another. In the present sermon three issues are to be raised.

First, in what does this driving out of disease consist? How does this accord with Christ's divine nature? *Second,* what is actually accomplished by grace? We ought to see what grace is and what its effects are. *Third*, some truths should be deduced regarding the significance of grace by which we can be exhorted to come to know and to praise the power of God.

I said that our Savior saves us daily by driv-ing out disease, which is the task of his divine nature. Now it is obvious that this disease is sin, which he drives out when he forgives and ceases to impute to the sinner eternal punishment. As the prophet says, "Blessed is the man to whom the Lord does not impute sin, whose sin is covered." And Jerome, commenting on that said, "When the Lord forgives sins he covers the sinner lest in the judgment it be revealed to his damnation." For, as Augustine said, when God sees sins he charges them unto punishment. But when he forgives sins he also always restores the lost grace which is the health and life of the soul. Since, now, "all the works of God are perfect," he does not

imperfectly heal the disease by merely driving it out, but he also gives health by the infusion of grace. For a man does not enjoy perfect health when, although without pain in his body, he is unable to use it for the tasks of life. But this capacity is a gift of grace. This is what Augustine meant when he said, "The Lamb takes away the sins both by forgiving what has been done and by helping the sinner not to sin again." This help is extended through grace.

Both operations are ascribed primarily to the divine nature. No one removes sins except God alone, who is the lamb taking away the sins of the world, as Augustine said. For this reason, namely, that he forgives sins, the Jews accused Christ of blasphemy, since they did not believe him to be God. Now no one confers grace except God. It is clear that grace comes into being only through God's creative action, since grace cannot be acquired through our works like other moral habits which, as Aristotle said, are naturally engendered in us by repetition of our own moral actions. The apostle Paul said, "But if it is by grace, it is no longer on the basis of works, otherwise grace would no longer be grace." Because nature cannot make something out of nothing, that which is created comes from God alone. If grace could come from the creature, a grace which would suffice unto salvation, then any creature would be able to save himself by his own natural powers, that is, do what only grace can do. That is the error of Pelagius. Therefore the prophet said, "The Lord will give grace and glory."

In order that we understand with what great kindness God saves us by his justification of sinners or the forgiveness of sins (and thus understand the mercy of the Lord), let us be found even more acceptable to him and let us in gratitude prepare for the reception of even greater gifts.

Now we must see just what this grace is by which the sinner is justified and what is actually accomplished in us. The grace of which we speak is a gift of God supernaturally infused into the soul. It makes the soul acceptable to God and sets it on the path to deeds of meritorious love.

There are many other supernatural gifts which are also infused into the soul. The apostle Paul says, "There are varieties of gifts but the same Spirit," and goes on to enumerate gifts of the Spirit—wisdom, knowledge, faith, healing, miracles, etc. "To one is given through the Spirit the utterance of wisdom and to another the utterance of knowledge, etc." But none of them make the man who receives them acceptable to God, nor does it make his work worthy of merit.

Now the many praiseworthy effects of grace can be summarized under three headings: (a) making acceptable, (b) justifying, and (c) making the works which result meritorious and worthy of eternal life, of grace and glory.

(a) Grace makes acceptable for this reason alone, that it is present in and is part of that nature which can be beatified, that is, man. According to Scotus, grace is an enrichment of nature that is pleasing to God's will. Grace makes human nature acceptable to God by adorning it not with an ordinary acceptation but with that special acceptation by which man is according to God's decision ordained toward life eternal. For to be acceptable, to be beloved by God and to be his friend, means to be in such a state that one will attain eternal life unless one loses this state through sin. For example, in just this way, grace makes acceptable to God children who neither desire nor are able to desire the good. This is what the apostle Paul said to Timothy, "So that we might be justified by his grace and become heirs to a firm hope of eternal life." And Peter said, "Through the grace of our Lord Jesus Christ we believe unto salvation."

(b) And because grace makes the sinner acceptable to God it follows that it also justifies him. Justification has two aspects: remission of guilt, and acceptance to eternal life, since it is impossible for one who is going to be accepted to eternal life to be at the same time condemned to eternal punishment. If it were otherwise, the same person would be both worthy and unworthy of eternal life. Therefore, it is necessary that he who has been accepted unto life have his guilt forgiven (if he has any).

But if grace is infused into someone who is already justified, that which it accomplishes is not justification. An example would be the grace once given to the holy angels and now daily given to those who are upright of heart, who through their good works earn an additional gift of grace above and beyond the grace already in them. About this justification by grace Paul writes, "They are justified by his grace as a gift through the redemption which is in Christ Jesus."

(c) Thus God makes these our works meritorious and acceptable for eternal reward, not actually all our works but only those which have been brought forth by the prompting of grace. It is assumed of a meritorious work that the person who performs it is accepted, since the acts of a person who has not been accepted or of an enemy cannot please God. As Genesis says, "The Lord had regard for Abel and his offering," that is, God's acceptance went first to the person of Abel and only secondly to his gifts. And this acceptance is due to the mere presence of grace in a person, as we saw above.

But an act is not meritorious just because it is performed by one who has been accepted, since such a person can commit venial sins or perform morally indifferent [neutral] acts. Therefore, a meritorious act must be brought forth by the prompting of grace. This grace prompts us to love God above all things and in all things, that is, to seek after the glory of God as the goal of every action, and to prefer the ultimate good, God, ahead of one's self and everything else. Therefore, all those things which are not directed consciously or unconsciously toward God do not come from the prompting of grace and therefore are surely not worthy of eternal life.

And although, according to some doctors, man can love God above everything else with his natural powers alone [without grace], this applied particularly to man before the fall; but man can never love God as perfectly and easily as with grace. Moreover, without grace it is absolutely impossible for him to love God meritoriously. Such is the rule established by God that no act should be accepted as meritorious unless it be prompted by grace. Therefore, the apostle said, "We are not sufficient of ourselves to claim anything as coming from us, our sufficiency is from God." And again after having said that he had worked hard for others, the apostle quickly added, "Though it was not I, but the grace of God which is within me."

Thus, as Lombard said, meritorious acts depend on two factors, our free will and grace. There is no human merit that does not depend partly on free will. The principal cause of meritorious moral action, however, is attributed to grace. But grace does not determine the will. The will can ignore the prompting of grace and lose it by its own default. The prompting of grace is toward meritorious acts for the sake of God. Therefore, the act as such stems primarily from grace. This is the case because it is performed by someone who has grace in accordance with the prompting of grace. Augustine

speaks in this way when he says that the will is related to grace like a footservant to her lady—it accompanies but does not precede grace. And in his book on free will he says that grace is related to free will as a rider to the horse. The rider guides the horse and chooses the direction in which to go. Indeed it is in this way that grace steers and prompts the will to direct itself toward God.

Thus it is clear that grace is nothing other than infused love [charity], because the same effects are attributed to both. For love [charity] is that which prompts us to love God above everything else, which makes us beloved to God, without which no one is beatified. Now this is exactly what grace does, therefore both Holy Scripture and the Fathers identify love with grace. What love accomplishes they attribute to grace alone and vice versa. So the apostle says that no gifts are of benefit without love. And again the apostle reported that the Lord had spoken to him, "My grace is sufficient for you." Now these two assertions are consistent only if love and grace are exactly the same.

Augustine, too, says, "The whole difference between salvation and perdition is grace alone," and elsewhere: "It is love alone that makes the difference between salvation and perdition." This thesis rests not only on authorities but also on reason based on Scripture, for if grace and love were different they could be separated by God. Then it would be possible for a man to have grace but not be a friend of God, or man could even be an enemy of God, if he had grace and not love, or, again, man could be a friend of God but not accepted by God, if he had love but not grace. Therefore, we conclude that it is one and the same to be accepted, beloved, and a friend of God.

Scotus, however, argues for a rational distinction between the two. Grace, he says, refers to God as the loving subject, on the grounds that the word "grace" is used when God loves someone. Love [charity] on the other hand refers to God as the object of love, because this word has the connotation of love for God.

Likewise it is clear why the doctors call grace a habit, although it is not acquired but infused. Grace accomplishes in the soul something similar to the effects of a naturally acquired habit, although in a far more perfect fashion than an acquired habit. The naturally acquired habit is a permanent quality in the power of the soul which stems from frequently repeated acts. This habit prompts and urges the man to repeat the same act. As Aristotle says, "Experience teaches us with certainty that all these acts leave behind a capacity which allows us to do these acts with greater care, readiness, pleasure, and correctness."

But grace elevates human power beyond itself, so that acts which had been turned by sin toward evil or inward toward one's self now can be meritoriously redirected against the law of the flesh and toward God. Grace leads, assists, and directs in order that man may be prompted in a way which corresponds with divine charity. And thus grace weakens the remaining power of sin, not—as many doctors say—because it forgives or wipes out sins, but because it strengthens human power.

We could use the illustration of a bird that has a stone tied to it so that it could scarcely fly away. Now if this bird's wings were strengthened, then we would say that the impediment to flight had been lessened, although the weight of the stone had not been lessened. Thus the apostle knew that he was assisted by grace when he cried out against the law of the flesh by which he was

tortured, "Wretched man that I am! Who will deliver me from the body of death? The grace of God through Jesus Christ our Lord."

The preceding has made clear how much the grace given to us by Christ excels the original righteousness we lost in Adam. Because, although original righteousness completely subdued the tincture of sin and ordered the lower powers of man in perfect obedience to the higher powers, it did not give to human power the capacity to perform meritorious works. Nor could Adam have been saved by original righteousness alone without grace. From this we can understand how great a gift that grace is by which Christ saves in the present dispensation. Grace is a gift above every created thing, as the apostle makes clear. Referring to this the Lord said to the disciples, "No longer shall I call you servants but friends." Augustine says, "Behold the gifts given to the church, and know that from among them all, the most excellent is the gift of love." Grace is "the gift by which alone we are made good, as by no other created gifts." Whatever you want, have this. This is the only gift which is indispensable, without which all the others are useless. "Even if you do not have the others, knowledge or prophecy, having this you have fulfilled the law." Not only is this gift more glorious than all others, it is so great that it is never given unless the Holy Trinity gives itself with it. The Trinity never gives itself without this gift nor the gift without itself. As the apostle has said, "God's love has been poured into our hearts through the Holy Spirit which has been given to us." And the Gospel of John asserts that the Holy Spirit is not given without the Father and the Son.

In all these things, my beloved, magnify and praise the loving mercy and goodness of our Lord Jesus Christ which is shown in the justification of the sinner. He could very well have forgiven sins by abstaining from punishment for them, without going so far as embracing the sinner as a friend—for this is all that man usually does. But God thought it too little to forgive the sins of him who had lost God's friendship through sinning, without also restoring (*reformaret*) him to his personal friendship.

But even this does not exhaust the infinite mercy of the Savior; he also gives a special aid of grace. By this grace we are able to remain without difficulty in his friendship, and to grow continually through good works. On such a foundation we can easily overcome the onslaughts of the devil, the world, and flesh, and gain a great reward in store for us.

No doubt he could have simultaneously made us his friends and accepted our work as meritorious without this gift of grace. But how could we have remained in friendship with God without the assistance of grace? Thus God has established the rule [covenant] that whoever turns to him and does what he can will receive forgiveness of sins from God. God infuses assisting grace into such a man, who is thus taken back into friendship. As is written in John: "Grace and truth came through Christ."

So that this might be more easily understood I shall tell a parable: Let us say that there is a most lenient king who shows so much mercy to his people that he publishes a decree saying that he will embrace with his favor any of his enemies who desire his friendship, provided they mend their ways for the present and the future. Furthermore, the king orders that all who have been received in this fashion into his friendship will receive a golden ring to honor all who are dedicated to his regime, so that such a

friend of the king may be known to all. The king gives to such a man by way of delegation of his royal authority such a position that every work done to the honor of the king, regardless of where performed or how large or small it is, shall be rewarded by the king above and beyond its value. And to give him extra strength to perform this kind of meritorious work, precious and powerful stones are inserted in the ring to encourage him who wears it, so that his body does not fail him when he needs it but increases in ability to gain further rewards the more the body is exercised and accustomed to resist every adverse force.

How could one ever praise highly enough the clemency and the preciousness of the gifts of such a king? Behold, such is our King and Savior! The gift is grace, which is bestowed abundantly on us, which is to the soul what the ring is to the body in the parable.

Therefore, it is indeed fitting that the name of such a great Savior be Jesus, because he alone can save his people by his gift of grace. We pray that he deign to give us this grace in the present and glory in the future. Amen.

✠

From Oberman, Forerunners of the Reformation, *165–74.*

Indulgences

Indulgences were an integral part of the religious landscape on the eve of the Reformation. The theory behind them was given official status in Pope Clement VI's bull *Unigenitus* in 1343. In 1476 Pope Sixtus IV, in his bull *Salvator noster*, first applied indulgences to the souls in purgatory. Thus, by the sixteenth century, the machinery of indulgences was well-established and their sale was commonplace. We can see just how the system functioned from Archbishop Albert of Mainz's instructions to his indulgence sales staff in 1515.

9. Clement VI, *Unigenitus* (1343)

The only-begotten Son of God deigned to come down from his father's bosom into the womb of his mother, in whom and from whom he joined, by an ineffable union, the substance of our mortality to his divinity, in unity of person. . . . His purpose was in this way to redeem fallen humanity and make satisfaction for him to God the Father. . . . Nor did he redeem us with corruptible things—with silver and gold but with his own precious blood, which he is known to have poured out as an innocent victim on the altar of the cross: not a mere measured drop of blood (which however because of its union with the Word would have sufficed for the redemption of all humanity) but as it were an unmeasured flood. . . .What a great treasure, then, did the holy Father acquire therefrom for the church militant, lest the mercy of so great an outpouring be made empty, useless or superfluous! . . . those who avail themselves of this infinite treasure are given a share in God's friendship [*Wisdom*, 8:14].

Now this treasure he entrusted to be dispensed for the weal of the faithful . . . through blessed Peter, who bore the keys of heaven, and Peter's successors as God's own representatives on earth. The purposes served should be proper and reasonable: sometimes total, sometimes partial remission of punishment due for temporal sins, as well generally as specially (according as they learn it to be expedient with God); and for these ends the treasure should be applied in mercy to those who are truly penitent and have made their confession.

The mass of this treasure is known to have been increased by the merits of the blessed mother of God and of all the elect, from the first righteous man to the last. Nor is there any fear of its being used up or diminished, as well because of the infinite merits of Christ . . . as because the greater the number who are drawn to righteousness by its application, the greater grows the mass of merits themselves.

10. Sixtus IV, *Salvator noster* (1476)

Our aim is that the salvation of souls may be secured above all at that time when they most need the intercessions of others and are least able to help themselves. We wish by our apostolic authority to draw on the treasury of the church and to succor the souls in purgatory who died united with Christ through love and whose lives have merited that such intercessions should now be offered through an indulgence of this kind.

With the longings of such great paternal affection as with God's help we can achieve, in reliance on the divine mercy and the plenitude of our power, we grant by concession an indulgence as follows: If any parents, friends or other Christians are moved by obligations of piety towards these very souls who are exposed to the fire of purgatory for the expiation of punishments which by divine justice are their due: let them during the stated period of ten years give a fixed amount or value of money, as laid down by its dean and chapter or by our own collector, for the repair of the church of saints, paying either in person at the Church or by duly accredited messengers: it is then our will that plenary remission should avail by intercession for the said souls in purgatory, to win them relief from their punishments—the souls, that is, for whose sakes the stated quantity or value of money has been paid in the manner declared.

✠

11. Albert of Mainz, *Instructio summaria* (1515)

The following are the four principal gifts of grace that have been granted by the apostolic bull: any one of them can be had separately. It is on these four indulgences that the preachers must concentrate their utmost diligence, infiltrating them one by one into the ears of the faithful in the most effective way, and explaining them with all the ability they have.

The first principal grace is the plenary remission of all sins—the greatest of all graces, for the reason that man, a sinner who is deprived of divine grace, obtains through it perfect remission and God's grace anew. In addition, through this remission of sins, punishments to be undergone in purgatory because of offense done to the divine majesty, are remitted in full, and the punishments of the said purgatory are totally wiped out. Now it is true that no possible repayment could be sufficient to earn so great a grace, for the reason that God's gift and his grace are beyond valuation; nevertheless, that the invitation of Christians to secure it may be made easier, we lay down the following procedure:

First, let every penitent who has made oral confession visit as least seven of the churches appointed for this purpose—that is, those in which the papal arms are installed—and in each church let him say with devotion five Paternosters and five Ave Marias to render honor to the five wounds of our Lord Jesus Christ, through whom has been enacted our redemption. . . .

For those who are confined to their beds there may be deputed a dedicated image before which or to which they may say certain prayers according to the ruling of the penitentiary. . . .

If anyone for any reason seeks to be excused the visit to the said churches or altars, the penitentiaries, having heard the reason, may allow it: such a visit may be compounded by a larger financial contribution.

This money must be placed in a box. But the contributions for the repository in aid of the construction of the building of the chief of the apostles will be sought as follows: first the penitentiaries and confessors, after expounding the magnitude of such plenary remission and indulgences to those who confess, will ask them how much in money or other temporal possessions their consciences tell them it is worth to make good the lack of such plenary remission and indulgences; they will ask this to facilitate their subsequent inducements to contribute. And since human conditions vary far too much for us to take separate account of them all and lay an appropriate assessment on each, we classify them in general terms and assess the classes as follows. . . . [Albert then assesses at fixed amounts all classes from kings and archbishops down through abbots and barons to priests and merchants and the lesser orders of society concluding with] the penniless, who may make good their contribution by prayers and fasting: for the kingdom of heaven should not stand open for the rich more than for the poor. . . .

The second principal grace is the confessional, carrying with it the greatest, most relevant and previously unknown indulgences.

. . . Its contents and their significance the preachers and confessors must explain and extol with all their power. In the confessional the following concessions are made for those who pay for it:

The right to choose as a suitable confessor even a regular of a mendicant order who can in the first place absolve them from having to seek a settlement of complaints that other men can bring against them.

He can absolve them once in the course of their lives and also in *articulo mortis* from certain of the gravest sins, even those which are reserved for the apostolic see. He can absolve them from cases not reserved for the apostolic see as often as is necessary.

He can apply plenary indulgence of all sins once in the course of the confessing person's life and in *articulo mortis* as often as death threatens, even if the threat does not materialize.

He can commute any kind of vows for other works of piety, except solemn vows undertaken overseas or of a pilgrimage to the thresholds of the apostles (and of St. James in Compostela) or of the religious life and of chastity.

He can administer the sacrament of the Eucharist at any time of the year except Easter day and *in articulo mortis*.

We order that one of these confessionals must be made generally available to ensure that the poor are not excluded from the graces it contains, . . . the reckoning being a quarter of a golden Rhenish florin which (quite apart from the usual assessment) must be placed in the indulgence-repository. . . .

The third principal grace is participation in all the blessings of the universal church. . . .

The fourth principal grace is the plenary remission of all sins for the souls that exist in purgatory, which the pope grants and con-cedes by means of intercessions, so that a contribution placed by the living in the repository on their behalf counts as one which a man might make or give for himself. . . . There is no need for the contributors to be of contrite heart or to make oral confession, since this grace depends (as the bull makes clear) on the love in which the departed died and the contributions which the living pay.

✠

From E. G. Rupp and B. Drewery, eds., Martin Luther (London: Edward Arnold; and New York: St. Martin's Press, 1970), 13–17.

Eating, Sleeping, and Dying

12. Dietrich Kolde, *Mirror for Christians* (1470)

Dietrich Kolde (d. 1515) was first an Augustinian and then a Franciscan priest who served various constituencies in German-speaking lands and the Low Countries. His catechism was written in German for the instruction of uneducated lay people, and after its first printing in 1470 it went on to become one of the most popular of these pedagogical tools. In it he rehearses and explains the traditional matter of catechesis—the creed, the Lord's Prayer, and the Ten Commandments. And along the way he inserts practical advice about how Christians should conduct themselves in the most mundane events of ordinary life. He also adds a section on how to die, a major theme in late medieval devotional literature.

✠

A Lesson About How a Person Should Conduct Himself at Meals

When you are about to sit down to eat and drink at the table, you should bless God first with an Our Father or two, and make the sign of the cross over the meal and say: Bless us and these gifts that we will receive by your generosity through Jesus Christ your dear Son. Amen. May God allow us to partake at the heavenly table. God is love. Whoever remains in love, remains in God, and God remains in him. May his love bless us and lead us to eternal life. Amen.

You should speak of God during the meal, because God's angels are standing at your table and at your door. Further, you should eat and drink in moderation. Further, you should not eat your fill, even though you would like more, since otherwise you would be acting like the beasts that stuff themselves until they can eat no more. You should think thus during the meal: O dear Lord, how many holy people there are who scarcely have bread to eat, and they thank you much more than I! O dear Lord, our ancestors in the wilderness did not live so luxuriously with food and drink as we do now. But nevertheless we would like to be in heaven. O dear Lord, please console and nourish all the souls in purgatory. Amen.

After the meal you should get up and say an Our Father and thank him for his gifts, and then say this as well: O dear Lord, give favor and grace to the living. Give eternal rest to the dead. To holy Christendom give peace, and give us poor sinners eternal life after this life. Amen.

How A Person Should Conduct Himself When He Goes to Bed

In the evening, when you go to bed, you should kneel down in front of your bed, and if you wish you can stretch out your arms like a cross, as Christ did on the cross, and raise your eyes to heaven and say: O dear Lord, almighty God, I am a poor sinful person. I am guilty of not serving you fervently today; and of not saying my prayers with fervor; and of passing many hours, nearly all the time, idly; and of neglecting to do many good works. Further, here you should say what sins you committed that day, and cry out and ask God the Lord for compassion and grace and forgiveness for your sins, and resolve firmly to go to confession and to commit the sins no more. And if you were to die that night with such a resolution, you would never be damned. Further, you should thank our dear Lord and Mary his dear mother for the bitter suffering and the pain that Mary endured at the time of vespers when she saw her dear child taken from the cross and laid on her virgin bosom; further, for how he was buried at the time of Compline and Mary, the blessed mother of our dear Lord, had to go away so bitterly grieving and weeping; and for how she came again to Jerusalem with bloody clothes; and how the women of Jerusalem stood before the entrance and said: Oh Lord God, how can the dear mother be so sadly troubled; oh what state the holy maternal heart must be in; oh the poor woman, what pain she has endured as she lost such a sweet dear child; and they said to her: O Mary, why are your clothes so bloody? You should weep when you think of this, and ask Mary on your behalf to ask her dear child for forgiveness of your sins, and for solace and rest for the poor souls in purgatory. And in this state of great fervor you should go to bed and think how the great lords of this world and many rich people who have lived and died in sins are now burning in hell, where they will never again rest or sleep. And because you know this, you should sleep sweetly and think about resting with Saint John the Evangelist at the breast of Jesus. Oh how sweetly you will sleep, and how happily you will awake in the morning, and how happy you will be all day. If you awake in the night, you should say: O dear Lord Jesus Christ, have mercy on me and give rest to the souls in purgatory, because they are in great pain.

How One Should Die, and This Is the Most Fruitful Lesson in the World

First of all, a person should say his creed repeatedly in German and with devotion; and if he cannot say the creed himself, he should have it spoken before him by another person. And he should always say: O dear Lord, I believe all that a good Christian is obliged to believe, and I desire to live and die in the faith. And if anything else occurs to me that is contrary to this creed I renounce it now for then and then for now. O dear Lord Jesus Christ, strengthen me in this holy faith. O dear Lord, even though I have sinned much and confessed badly and improved badly, I still do not want to despair of you, because you are so very compassionate; I have become so bitterly sour toward you and you have suffered so much for me. And you also said: Anyone who comes to your vineyard at the time of vespers should receive payment equal to those who worked the whole day. O dear Lord, I come to my conversion late. Have mercy on me. You can speak a word and forgive me all my sins. O dear Lord, what would you gain if I should lie a long time in purgatory, a fate which I surely deserve? O dear Lord, you said: Ask and it will be given to you. I ask you, Lord, just say a word and make my soul healthy. O dear Lord, please be mindful that the dead will not praise you nor all those who are in hell. O dear Lord, I will gladly endure everything that you send to me for my sins. O dear Lord, please let this small suffering, and your great and manifold suffering, stand for all my sins.

Further, one should say the following prayers repeatedly to sick people:

O dear Lord Jesus Christ, you untied the bonds of all my sins with your holy suffering. Therefore, dear Lord, I want to offer you an offering of praise, namely my poor soul, which I offer into your hands. Now I will die patiently and willingly if that is your dearest will. O dear Lord Jesus Christ, I am sorry from the bottom of my heart that I have angered you. O dear Lord God, I wish I were a thousand times more sorry. I wish I could cry tears of blood for my sins. Oh, dear Lord, accept my good intentions in place of works. O dear Lord, I give you my body and my soul. Do with me as your holy will dictates, and not as my earthly nature wills. The spirit is prepared but the flesh is weak: O dear Lord Jesus Christ, please do not reject me, a poor sinner.

Further, when it gets to the point of separation, or when bitter death is coming, then you should say the following repeatedly:

O dear Lord Jesus Christ, father and mother have left me. I ask you, dear Lord, to receive me now into your kingdom.

O holy God! O powerful God! O compassionate God! O strict and righteous judge, have mercy on me, a poor sinner, when I must answer at your terrifyingly strict court, and when I am to give testimony as a poor human being about all my words and all my deeds. O dear Lord Jesus, then may your holy bitter death, your precious blood and your unspeakable manifold suffering stand between you and all my sins.

O dear Lord Jesus, I am the poor human being that you yourself created in your own image with your divine strength and power. O dear Lord, I am the poor human being that you yourself redeemed and delivered from all strength and power of the devil with your innocent bitter death.

O dearest Lord Jesus Christ, I am the poor human being that you can preserve with your unfathomable compassion. Stand by me in my hour of death, when all the world departs from me.

O Father, into your hands I commit my spirit, because you have redeemed me, O my God of truth.

O Mary, mother of grace and mother of compassion, shelter and protect me from the devils and receive my poor soul in my hour of death. O gentle advocate and guiding star, please do not depart from me. O esteemed sweet Virgin Mary, let me see your chosen pure child rejoicing now. O dear Mary, let me hear the voices of the angels. Go out, O beautiful bride of Christ, you noble soul! Jesus, your bridegroom, is coming! O Mary, let me never hear the voice of Jesus the strict judge. O gentle, compassionate and sweet Mary, stand by me now, because today I must fight a battle on which my poor soul's eternal bliss or eternal damnation depends. O Mary, mother of God, and all God's dear saints, stand by me and help me fight, for if you do not help me my battle is lost. O dear, most sweet, gentle, compassionate maid Mary, have mercy on me, a poor, sorrowful, sinful human, because you are my mother and my only comfort, my hope and my confidence. Further, it is very useful and good to read with fervor the passion of our Lord for the sick person, and the Our Father in German and the creed in German.

✠

From D. Janz, ed., Three Reformation Catechisms: Catholic, Anabaptist, Lutheran. *(Toronto: Edwin Mellen Press, 1982), 101–2, 104–5, 121–24.*

Criticism

13. Desiderius Erasmus, *In Praise of Folly* (1509)

Late medieval religion was not without its critics, ranging from harmless cranks and troublemakers, to fire and brimstone preachers of the impending apocalypse, to sophisticated and subtle thinkers gently prodding the church in the direction of reform. At one extreme we have the illiterate peasant in the remote village of Montaillu who opined that Mary was certainly not a virgin. And on the other, we have a figure like Desiderius Erasmus (d. 1536), standing at the pinnacle of culture and learning. In his 1509 book *In Praise of Folly,* Erasmus launched a scathing attack on the manifold stupidities and blatant immoralities of the religious establishment. The fact that he remained to the end of his life a loyal son of the Roman Catholic Church shows that critical thought did not necessarily have to move in the Protestant direction.

✠

As for the theologians, perhaps it would be better to pass them over in silence, "not stirring up the hornets' nest" and "not laying a finger on the stinkweed," since this race of men is incredibly arrogant and touchy. For they might rise up en masse and march in ranks against me with six hundred conclusions and force me to recant. And if I should refuse, they would immediately shout "heretic." For this is the thunderbolt they always keep ready at a moment's notice to terrify anyone to whom they are not very favorably inclined.

Certainly, though no one is less willing than they are to recognize my good will toward them, still these men are also obliged to me for benefits of no little importance. They are so blessed by their self-love as to be fully persuaded that they themselves dwell in the third heaven, looking down from high above on all other mortals as if they were earth-creeping vermin almost worthy of their pity. They are so closely hedged in by rows of magistral definitions, conclusions, corollaries, explicit and implicit propositions, they have so many "holes they can run to," that Vulcan himself couldn't net them tightly enough to keep them from escaping by means of distinctions, with which they cut all knots as cleanly as the fine-honed edge of "the headsman's axe"—so many new terms have they thought up and such monstrous jargon have they coined. Moreover, they explicate sacred mysteries just as arbitrarily as they please, explaining by what method the world was established and arranged, by what channels original sin is transmitted to Adam's posterity, by what means, by what proportion, in how short a period of time Christ was fully formed in the virgin's womb, how accidents subsist in the Eucharist without any domicile. But such questions are run-of-the-mill. There are others which they think worthy of great and "illuminated" theologians, as they say. If they ever encounter these, then they really perk up. Whether there is any instant in the generation of the divine persons? Whether there is more than one filial relationship in Christ? Whether the following proposition is possible: God the Father hates the Son. Whether God could have taken on the nature of a woman, of the devil, of an ass, of a cucumber, of a piece of flint? And then how the cucumber would have preached, performed miracles, and been nailed to the cross? And what Peter would have consecrated (if he had consecrated) during the time Christ was hanging on the cross? And whether during that same time Christ could be called a man? And

whether it will be permissible to eat and drink after the resurrection?—taking precautions even now against hunger and thirst.

There are numberless petty quibbles even more fine-spun than these, concerning notions, relations, instants, formalities, quiddities, ecceities—things to which no eyesight could ever penetrate, unless it were an "x-ray vision" so powerful it could perceive through the deepest darkness things that are nowhere. Also throw in those *sententiae* of theirs, so paradoxical that those oracular sayings which the Stoics called paradoxes seem downright crude and commonplace by comparison—such as this, for example: it is a less serious crime to murder a thousand men than to fix just one shoe for a poor man on the Lord's day; or it would be better to let the whole world be destroyed—"lock, stock, and barrel," as they say—than to tell just one, tiny, little white lie. And then these most subtle subtleties are rendered even more subtle by the various "ways" or types of scholastic theology, so that you could work your way out of a labyrinth sooner than out of the intricacies of the Realists, Nominalists, Thomists, Albertists, Occamists, Scotists—and I still haven't mentioned all the sects, but only the main ones.

In all of these there is so much erudition, so much difficulty, that I think the apostles themselves would need to be inspired by a different spirit if they were forced to match wits on such points with this new breed of theologians. Paul could provide a living example of faith, but when he said "Faith is the substance of things to be hoped for and the evidence of things not seen," his definition was not sufficiently magisterial. So too, he lived a life of perfect charity, but he neither distinguished it nor defined it with sufficient dialectical precision in the first epistle to the Corinthians, chapter 13.

Certainly the apostles consecrated the Eucharist very piously, but still if they had been asked about the "terminus a quo" and the "terminus ad quem," about transubstantiation, about how the same body can be in different places, about the difference between the body of Christ as it is in heaven, as it was on the cross, and as it is in the Eucharist, about the exact point at which transubstantiation takes place (since the speech through which it is accomplished is a divisible quantity which takes place in a flowing period of time), I don't think they would have responded with a subtlety equal to that of the Scotists when they discuss and define these points. They knew Jesus' mother, but which of them has shown how she was preserved from the stain of Adam's sin as philosophically as our theologians have done it? Peter received the keys, and received them from one who would not have committed them to someone unworthy of them, but still I don't know whether he understood—certainly he never attained sufficient subtlety to understand—how even a person who does not have knowledge can still have the keys of knowledge. They baptized everywhere, but nowhere did they teach what are the formal, material, efficient, and final causes of baptism, nor do they even so much as mention the delible and indelible marks of the sacraments. Certainly they worshiped God, but they did so in the spirit, following no other directive than the one given in the gospel: "God is a spirit and those who worship him should worship him in the spirit and in truth." But it is hardly clear that it was also revealed to them that a charcoal sketch drawn on a wall should be worshiped with the same worship as Christ himself, provided

that the picture has two fingers extended, long hair, and three rays in the halo stuck on the back of the skull. For who could perceive these things unless he had spent thirty-six whole years in studying the physics and metaphysics of Aristotle and the Scotists? So too, the apostles preach grace very forcefully, but nowhere do they distinguish between grace "*gratis data*" and grace "*gratificans*." They exhort us to good works, without distinguishing "*opus operans*" from "*opus operatum*." Everywhere they inculcate charity, without separating infused from acquired charity or explaining whether charity is an accident or a substance, a created or an uncreated thing. They detest sin, but I would stake my life they couldn't define scientifically what it is that we call sin, unless perchance they had been instructed by the spirit of the Scotists. Nor can I bring myself to believe that Paul, from whose learning we may judge that of the others, would so often have condemned questions, disputes, genealogies, and (as he calls them) quarrels about words, if he had been so expert in subtle argumentation, especially since all the quarrels and disputes of that time were coarse and crude by comparison with the supersubtleties of our doctors of theology.

But they are men of the greatest modesty: if the apostles have perhaps written something a bit loosely, without magisterial precision, far be it from them to condemn it; rather, they make the proper allowances in their interpretation, paying at least that much respect to the antiquity of Scripture on the one hand and to the title of apostle on the other. And Lord knows it would be a little unfair to demand from them things about which they never heard a single word from their teacher. But if the same thing happens in Chrysostom, Basil, or Jerome, then they consider it sufficient to write next to it "non tenetur" (untenable). These Fathers certainly did confute pagan philosophers and Jews, who are by temperament extraordinarily stubborn, but they did it by the lives they led and the miracles they performed rather than by manufacturing syllogisms. They also convinced people whose minds were completely incapable of following even a single quodlibet of Scotus. But nowadays what pagan, what heretic would not immediately yield to so many fine-spun subtleties, unless he should be too crude to follow them, or so impudent as to make fun of them, or provided with the same snares so that the two sides would be evenly matched, just as if you should match one magician against another or as if one man with a charmed sword should fight against another whose sword was also charmed. For then it would be like the loom of Penelope: weaving and unweaving the same piece of cloth over and over again. So far as I can judge, Christians would be wise if, instead of sending out those regiments of thick-skulled soldiers who have been fighting for so long now without winning a decisive victory, they should send against the Turks and Saracens these most clamorous Scotists and most stubborn Occamists and invincible Albertists, together with the whole band of dialecticians: they would behold, I think, the finest battle imaginable and such a victory as was never seen before. For who could be so cold as not to be inflamed by their acumen? Who could be so dull as not to be stimulated by the sharpness of their wit? Who so sharp-sighted that they could not pull the wool over his eyes?

But I may seem to be saying all this merely as a joke. No wonder, indeed, since among the theologians themselves there are some better educated men who are disgusted by these theological quibbles, which they consider utterly pointless. There are those who denounce it as a form of sacrilege and consider it the worst sort of impiety to talk in such a tawdry fashion, to dispute with the worldly subtleties of the pagans, to lay down such arrogant definitions, about sacred mysteries which should be reverently contemplated rather than explicated, and to besmirch the majesty of divine theology with words and ideas so bloodless and even squalid.

But meanwhile they themselves are so completely contented and self-satisfied, they even applaud themselves so enthusiastically, that they spend their days and nights in these most delightful trifles and have not a moment to spare to read through the gospel or Paul's epistles even once. At the same time, while they are talking nonsense in the schools, they think they are supporting the universal church, which otherwise would collapse, with their syllogistic props in much the same way that Atlas, in the mythology of the poets, holds up the world on his shoulders. You can imagine how happy a life they lead while they distort and reshape Holy Scripture however they like (just as if it were a lump of wax), while they demand that their conclusions (to which some schoolmen have subscribed) should be more revered than the laws of Solon and more binding than the papal decretals, while—like moral guardians of the whole world—they demand a recantation of whatever doesn't square "to a 'T'" with their explicit and implicit conclusions, while they deliver their oracular pronouncements: "This proposition is scandalical," "This one is not sufficiently reverential," "This one gives off a whiff of heresy," "This one does not tinkle true," so that not even baptism, not the gospel, not Paul or Peter, not St. Jerome or St. Augustine, in fact not even Thomas himself *Aristotelicissimus,* can make someone a Christian unless he has the vote of these bachelors of divinity, so fine-honed is the edge of their judgment. Who would ever have thought that someone who said that the two parts of such paired expressions as *"matula putes"* and *"matula putet"* or *"ollae feruere"* and *"ollam feruere"* are equally congruent is no true Christian if these wise men had not taught us about it? Who would ever have delivered the church from the darkness of such grave errors—which, in fact, no one would ever have heard of if they had not read them in pronouncements issued with the great seals of the universities? But aren't they as happy as can be while they do such things? And also while they depict every detail of the infernal regions so exactly that you would think they had spent several years in that commonwealth. And also while they manufacture at their pleasure new heavenly spheres, finally adding the largest and most beautiful of all just to make sure that the blessed souls would have plenty of room to take walks, to stage their dinner-parties, or even to play ball. With these trifles and thousands more like them their heads are so swollen and stuffed that I don't think Jupiter's brain was any more burdened when he called for Vulcan's axe to give birth to Pallas. Therefore don't be surprised when you see them at public disputations with their heads so carefully wrapped up in swaths of cloth, for otherwise they would clearly explode.

Sometimes I myself have to laugh at them: they think they have finally reached the very acme of theology if they plumb the depths of barbarous and foul language; and when they mumble so badly that only another mumbler could understand them, they call it ingenuity beyond the reach of the ordinary listener. For they assert that it is not consonant with the dignity of sacred writing for them to be compelled to obey the rules of grammar. Wonderful indeed is the majesty of theologians if they alone have the right to speak faultily, though they have that in common with many lowly cobblers. Finally, they think they are most godlike whenever they are scrupulously addressed with the title "Magister noster," for they seem to find in that name something of the same mysterious profundity that the Jews reverenced in the ineffable four letters of Yahweh. Hence they say it is quite improper to write MAGISTER NOSTER in anything but capital letters. But if anyone should say it backwards—"Noster magister"—at one stroke he has corrupted the entire majesty of the theological title.

Almost as happy as the theologians are those men who are commonly called "religious" and "monks"—though both names are quite incorrect, since a good part of them are very far removed from religion and no one is encountered more frequently everywhere you go. I cannot imagine how anything could be more wretched than these men, if it were not for the many sorts of assistance I give them. For even though everyone despises this breed of men so thoroughly that even a chance meeting with one of them is considered unlucky, still they maintain a splendid opinion of themselves. First of all, they consider it the very height of piety to have so little to do with literature as not even to be able to read. Moreover, when they roar out their psalms in church like braying asses (counting their prayers indeed, but understanding them not at all), then (of all things!) they imagine that the listening saints are soothed and caressed with manifold delight.

Among them are some who make a great thing out of their squalor and beggary, who stand at the door bawling out their demands for bread—indeed there is no inn or coach or ship where they do not make a disturbance, depriving other beggars of no small share of their income. And in this manner these most agreeable fellows, with their filth, ignorance, coarseness, impudence, re-create for us, as they say, an image of the apostles.

But what could be more charming than to observe how they do everything by rules, as if they were entering figures in a ledger where it would be a terrible sin to overlook the smallest detail: how many knots to the shoe, what colors and different styles for each garment, of what material and how many straws wide the cincture may be, the cut of the hood and how many pecks it should hold, how many inches long the hair may be, how many hours are allowed for sleep. Who cannot see, considering the variety in physical and mental constitutions, how unequal this equality really is? Nevertheless, because of such trifles, not only do they consider outsiders beneath their contempt but one order scorns another, and men who profess apostolic charity raise a catastrophic uproar about a garment that is belted somewhat differently or a color that is a little darker. You can see some of them who are so strictly religious that their outer garments are of coarse goat's hair, but their undergarments are of fine silk; and then again you will see others who wear linen outside, but lamb's wool underneath. Or others who shrink from contact with money as if it were a deadly poison, but at the same time do not refrain from contact with wine and women. In short, they are all amazingly eager to avoid any agreement in their manner of life. Nor do they strive to be like Christ, but to be unlike each other. Then too, a great part of their happiness consists in their titles: one order likes to be called Cordeliers, and among them some are Coletans, others Friars Minor, some Minims, others Bullists. Then some are Benedictines, others Bernardines; some are Brigetines, others Augustinians; some Williamites, others Jacobites—as if it weren't enough to be called Christians. The majority of them rely so much on their ceremonies and petty human traditions that they think one heaven is hardly a fitting reward for such merits, never quite realizing that Christ will scorn all such things and will require the fulfillment of his own precept, namely charity. One will display his barrel-belly, bloated with all kinds of fish. Another will pour out a hundred pecks of psalms. One will reckon up thousands of fasts and will claim that his belly has almost burst because he had only one lunch so often. Another will bring forth such a pile of ceremonies that seven freighters could hardly transport it. One will boast that for sixty years he never once touched money unless his fingers were protected by two pairs of gloves. Another will bring in a hood so filthy and greasy that no common seaman would consider it fit to put on. One will tell how for more than five and fifty years he led the life of a sponge, always fixed to one spot. Another will assert that his voice grew hoarse from continually singing, another that he became almost catatonic from solitude, another that his tongue atrophied from constant silence. But Christ, interrupting their boasts (which would otherwise never come to an end), will say, "Where did this new race of Jews come from? The only law I recognize as truly mine is the only one I hear nothing about. Long ago, not speaking obliquely in parables but quite openly, I promised my Father's inheritance not to hoods, or trifling prayers, or fasts, but rather deeds of faith and charity. Nor do I acknowledge those who too readily acknowledge their own deeds: those who want to appear even holier than I am can go dwell in the heavens of the Abraxasians if they like, or they can order that a new heaven be built for them by the men whose petty traditions they have placed before my precepts." When they hear this and see sailors and teamsters chosen in preference to them, how do you suppose their faces will look as they stare at each other?

But meanwhile they are happy in their hopes, not without a helping hand from me. Then too, though these men are cut off from political office, still no one dares to scorn them, especially the mendicants, because they have complete knowledge of everyone's secrets from what they call confession. Of course, they hold that it is wrong to reveal them, except every now and then when they are in their cups and want to amuse themselves with some funny stories, but then they make their point obliquely and hypothetically, without mentioning any names. But if anyone stirs up these hornets, they get their full measure of revenge in their sermons to the people, pointing out their enemy indirectly, so covertly that no one who understands anything at all can fail to understand who is meant. Nor will they ever make an end of barking until you throw "a sop to Cerberus."

Tell me now, is there any comedian or pitchman you would rather see than these men when they orate in their sermons, imitating quite absurdly but still very amusingly what the rhetoricians have handed down about the way to make a speech? Good lord! How they gesticulate, how fittingly they vary their tone of voice, how they croon, how they strut, continually changing their facial expressions, drowning out everything with their shouts! And the mysterious secret of this oratorical artistry is passed down personally from one little friar to another. Though it is not lawful for me to know it, I will guess at it anyway and come as close as I can.

First of all, they make an invocation, a device they have borrowed from the poets. Then, if they are going to talk about charity, their exordium has to do with the Nile River in Egypt. Or if they are going to discourse on the mystery of the cross, they open their sermon very auspiciously with Bel, the dragon of Babylon. Or if they are going to discuss fasting, they open with the twelve signs of the zodiac. Or if they are going to speak about faith, they go through a long prologue about squaring the circle. I myself once heard an eminent fool—I beg your pardon, I mean scholar—who was going to explain the Holy Trinity in a sermon before a large audience. To show that his learning was far above the ordinary and to meet the expectations of the theologians among the hearers, he invented a completely new approach—namely, to start with the letters, syllables, and the whole word, then to take up the agreement of noun and verb, adjective and substantive, to the amazement of many listeners, some of whom muttered to themselves that question in Horace "What is he driving at with all this damned nonsense?" He finally came to the conclusion that the rudiments of grammar give such a clear picture of the whole Trinity that no mathematician could make it any plainer by drawing in the dust. And this *theologicissimus* had sweated over this oration for eight whole months, so much so that to this day he is blind as a bat, since all the acumen of his sight was diverted to the sharpness of his wit. But the man hardly regrets his blindness and considers it a small price to pay for such glory.

We once heard another preacher, an old man of eighty, so thoroughly theological that you would have thought he was Scotus come back to life. Undertaking to explain the mystery of the name *Jesus,* he showed with amazing subtlety that whatever could be said on this subject was hidden in the very letters of the name. That it has only three inflectional endings is a clear sign of the Trinity. Then, that the first inflection (Jesus) ends in "s," the second (Jesum) in "m" and the third (Jesu) in "u" conceals an *unspeakable* mystery: namely, the three letters show that he is first (summum), middle (medium), and last (ultimum). He had in store for us an even more recondite mystery: dividing "Jesus" into two equal parts leaves a penthemimer in the middle. Then he explained that in Hebrew this letter is sh, pronounced "sin." Now in the language of the Scots, I think, "sin" means "peccatum." Thus we have a very clear indication that it was Jesus who took away the sins of the world. Everyone was struck with open-mouthed wonder at this novel *exordium,* especially the theologians, so that they almost shared the fate of Niobe. But my fate was nearly that of Priapus, that good-for-nothing figwood statue, who, much to his dismay, watched the nocturnal ceremonies of Canidia and Sagana. And certainly with good reason. For when did Demosthenes among the Greeks or Cicero among the Romans ever think up such an *exordium* as this? They considered an introduction faulty if it strayed too far from the subject at hand. As if any swineherd, taught by nature alone, wouldn't have enough common sense to begin with something relevant. But these learned friars think their preamble (for that's their word for it) will be most exquisitely rhetorical only if it has absolutely nothing to do with the subject matter, so that the bewildered listener mutters under his breath "What is he up to now?"

In the third part, which serves as a narration, they interpret something from the gospel, but fleetingly and as if in passing, though that is the only thing they ought to be doing in the whole sermon. In the fourth section, assuming an entirely new character, they raise some theological question, often enough one that is neither here nor there, and they think that this too belongs to the art of preaching. Here they really ruffle their theological feathers, quoting solemn doctors, subtle doctors, most subtle doctors, seraphic doctors, cherubic doctors, holy doctors, irrefragable doctors, dinning these grandiose titles into our ears. Then, preaching to uneducated lay people, they put on display their syllogisms, majors, minors, conclusions, corollaries, most jejune hypotheses and utterly pedantic quibbles. There remains now the fifth act, in which it behooves them to perform with the greatest artistry. Here they haul out some foolish folktale, something from the *Speculum Historiale,* say, or the *Gesta Romanorum,* and interpret it allegorically, tropologically, and anagogically. In this fashion they put together their chimera, one far beyond what Horace imagined when he wrote "If to a human head, etc."

But they have heard from somebody or other that the beginning of a speech should be quite restrained, not at all loud. And so in the opening they start out so softly that they can't even hear their own voices, as if it did any good to say something that no one can understand. They have heard that exclamations should sometimes be employed to stir up the emotions. Thus, in the middle of a passage delivered in a low voice, every now and then they suddenly raise their voices and shout like crazy men, even when there is no need for it at all. You would think they needed a dose of hellebore, as if it made no difference at what point you raise your voice! Moreover, because they have heard that a sermon should gradually become more and more fiery, they begin the individual parts in a more or less reasonable tone of voice; but then they suddenly burst out in an incredible vocal barrage, even if the subject is quite dry and abstract, breaking off at last in such a way that you would think they had run out of breath.

Finally, they have learned that the rhetoricians have something to say about laughter and hence they also take pains to sprinkle in a few jokes. But those jokes (by all that's refined!) are so elegant and so appropriate that they would remind you of an ass playing a harp. Sometimes they are also satirical, but in such a way as to titillate rather than wound. And they never serve up more genuine flattery than when they try hardest to give the impression of speaking sharply. In short, their whole performance is such that you would imagine they had taken lessons from some street peddler, except that the friars lag far behind them. Still, they resemble each other so closely that no one can doubt that the friars learned their rhetoric from the peddlers or the peddlers from the friars.

And even so, these preachers, with my help, find people who listen to them with as much admiration as if they were Demosthenes himself or Cicero. This group consists mostly of merchants and fine ladies. The friars devote all their energies to pleasing the ears of these people because the merchants, if they are rubbed the right way, will usually give them some of their booty, a little slice of their ill-gotten gains. The women have many reasons for granting their favors to the friars, but the chief one is that they are accustomed to

pour into the sympathetic ear of the friars the grievances they hold against their husbands.

You can see, I think, how much this class of men owes me: though in fact they browbeat mankind with their petty observances and ridiculous nonsense and screaming and shouting, they think they are veritable Pauls or Anthonys. But I am glad to be done with these playactors, whose ungrateful disavowal of my benefits is matched by their disgraceful pretense to piety. . . .

Then too, the lifestyle of princes has long since been diligently imitated, and almost surpassed, by popes, cardinals, and bishops. In fact, if anyone should consider the moral meaning of the linen rochet, so striking because of its snowy whiteness, namely a life innocent in all respects; or the significance of the miter, with its two horns joined by one knot at the top, namely a thorough knowledge of both the Old Testament and the New; or the meaning of hands protected by gloves, namely, administering the sacraments with purity undefiled by merely human considerations; or of the crosier, the most watchful care of the flock entrusted to him; or of the cross carried before him, that is, victory over all human passions; if, I say, anyone should consider these things and others like them, would he not lead a life full of grief and anxiety? But now they do a fine job if they feed themselves. The care of the sheep they either commend to Christ himself or pass on to their brothers, as they call them, and vicars. They don't so much as remember their own name—what the word "bishop" means—namely, painstaking labor and concern. But in casting their nets for money, there they play the bishop, and keep a sharp enough lookout.

In the same way, if cardinals realized that they have succeeded in the place of the apostles and are required to perform the same functions; then, if they thought that they are not lords but ministers of spiritual gifts, for every one of which they will soon have to give a most exact account; indeed, if they even gave a little serious consideration to their apparel and thought to themselves: "What does the whiteness of this garment mean? Isn't it the most eminent and flawless innocence of life? What does the scarlet underneath mean? Isn't it the most burning love of God? And then what is meant by the scarlet outside, flowing down in such wide undulations and completely covering the Most Reverend Father's mule?—though, for that matter, it would be enough by itself to cover a camel. Isn't it charity reaching out far and wide to help everyone, that is, to teach, exhort, console, reproach, advise, settle wars, resist wicked princes, and freely give not merely riches but even life-blood for Christ's flock—though why should any riches at all belong to those who act in the place of the poor apostles?"—if they considered these things, I say, they would not strive to get that office and would gladly relinquish it, or at least they would lead very laborious and anxious lives, such as those ancient apostles lived.

Now, as for the popes, who act in Christ's place, if they tried to imitate his way of life—namely poverty, labor, teaching, the cross, *contemptus mundi*—if they thought of the name "pope" (that is, "father") or of the title "most holy," who on earth could be more miserable? Or who would spend everything he has to buy that office? Or defend it, once it was bought, with sword, poison, and all manner of violence? How many advantages would these men be deprived of if they were ever assailed by wisdom? Wisdom, did I say? No, even by a single grain of that salt

mentioned by Christ. So much wealth, honor, power, so many victories, offices, dispensations, taxes, indulgences, so many horses, mules, retainers, so many pleasures! You see what a warehouse, what a harvest, what a sea of good things I have gathered together. These would be replaced by vigils, fasts, tears, prayers, sermons, studies, sighs, and thousands of such wretched labors. Nor should we neglect another point: so many scribes, copyists, notaries, advocates, ecclesiastical prosecutors, so many secretaries, mule-curriers, stableboys, official bankers, pimps (I had almost added something more delicate, but I am afraid it might sound indelicate to some ears), in short, the huge mass of humanity which weighs down—pardon me, I meant "waits on"—the see of Rome would be turned out to starve. Certainly an inhuman and monstrous crime! And, what is even more abominable, the very highest princes of the church, the true lights of the world, would be reduced to a scrip and a staff.

But as it is now, they leave whatever work there is to Peter and Paul, who have plenty of free time. But the splendor and the pleasures, those they take for themselves. And thus, through my efforts, I have brought things to such a pass that almost no sort of person leads a softer, more carefree life, since they think they have done quite well by Christ if they play a bishop's role with mystical and almost theatrical pomp, with ceremonies, with titles like "your Beatitude," "your Reverence," "your Holiness," with blessings and anathemas. For them, to perform miracles is old-fashioned, outworn, completely out of step with the times; to teach the people is burdensome; to interpret Holy Scripture, academic; to pray, otiose; to pour forth tears, base and womanish; to be in want, degrading; to be conquered, disgraceful and quite unsuitable for one who hardly allows even the greatest kings to kiss his blessed foot; and finally, to die seems disagreeable; to be lifted up on the cross, disreputable.

All that is left are the weapons and sweet benedictions mentioned by Paul, and with such things they are sufficiently liberal: with interdicts, suspensions, formal warnings—denounced and reiterated—solemn excommunications, pictures of vengeance meted out to heretics, and that horrific lightning bolt which they employ with a mere nod to send the souls of mortals to the bottomless pit of perdition. That bolt, however, these most holy fathers in Christ and Christ's vicars on earth hurl at no one more fiercely than at those who, at the instigation of the devil, seek to diminish and gnaw away the patrimony of Peter. Though Peter says in the gospel, "We have left all and followed you," they interpret his patrimony as fields, towns, taxes, imposts, dominions. While they fight for such things with burning Christian zeal and defend them with fire and sword, not without the loss of much Christian blood, they believe this is the very way to defend apostolically the church, the bride of Christ, manfully putting her enemies to flight, as they say. As if the church had any more deadly enemies than impious popes, who allow Christ to fade away in silence, who bind him with mercenary laws, who defile him with forced interpretations, who murder him with the pestilent wickedness of their lives.

Thus, although the Christian church was founded with blood, confirmed with blood, expanded with blood, nowadays they settle everything with the sword, just as if Christ had perished completely and would no longer protect his own in his own way. And although war is so inhuman that it befits beasts, not men, so insane that even the poets imagine that it is unleashed by the Furies, so noxious that it spreads moral corruption far and wide, so unjust that it is normally carried on best by robbers, so impious that it is utterly foreign to Christ, still they neglect everything else and do nothing but wage war. Here you can see rickety old men demonstrate the hardiness of a youthful spirit, not upset by any expense, not wearied by any labors, not the least bit disturbed by the thought of reducing all human affairs, laws, religion, peace, to utter chaos. Nor is there any lack of learned flatterers who call this patent madness by the names zeal, piety, fortitude, having devised a way to allow someone to unsheathe cold steel and thrust it into his brother's guts without any offense against that highest duty of charity which, according to Christ's precept, he owes to his fellow Christian. Indeed, I am still not sure whether the popes have set or followed the example of some German bishops who pay no attention to vestments or benedictions or any such ceremonies but carry on as secular lords, plain and simple, so much so that they consider it cowardly and hardly worthy of a bishop to render up their courageous souls to God anywhere but on the front lines of the battle.

Now the general run of priests, thinking it would be a crime for them to fall behind the holy dedication of their superiors—good lord! how stoutly they fight for their right to tithes, with sword, spear, stones, with every imaginable sort of armed force. In this point how sharp-sighted they are in ferreting out of the writings of the Fathers anything they can use to intimidate the simple people and make them think they owe even more than a tenth. But at the same time, it never occurs to them how often those writings explain the duties which priests in turn are supposed to perform for the people. They do not even consider what their tonsure means: that a priest is supposed to be free from all worldly desires and ought to meditate on nothing but heavenly matters. But these agreeable fellows say they have fulfilled their duty perfectly once they have mumbled through their office in some fashion or other—as for me, by heaven, I would be amazed if any god either heard or understood such prayers, since they themselves can hardly be said to hear or understand them at the very time their mouths are bawling them out.

But priests have this in common with laymen: they all keep a sharp lookout to harvest their profits, and in that point no one is ignorant of the laws. But if there is some responsibility, they prudently shift that onto someone else's shoulders and pass the buck down the line from one to another. In fact, even lay princes, just as they parcel out the duties of ruling to deputies, and the deputies pass them on to subdeputies, so too they leave all the practice of piety, in their modesty, to the common people. The people foist it off on those whom they call ecclesiastics, for all the world as if they themselves had nothing to do with the church, as if their baptismal vows had had no effect whatever. Then the priests who call themselves secular—as if they were united to the world rather than to Christ—pass on the burden to the canons regular, the canons to the monks, the laxer monks to the stricter ones, both groups to the mendicant orders, the mendicants to the Carthusians, and with them alone piety lies buried, hidden away in such a manner that it hardly ever appears. In the same way popes, however diligent in harvesting money, delegate their excessively apostolic labors to the bishops, the bishops to the pastors, the pastors to their vicars, the vicars

to the mendicant friars, and they too foist off their charge on those who shear the fleece of the flock.

But it is no part of my present plan to rummage through the lives of popes and priests, lest I should seem to be composing a satire rather than delivering an encomium, or lest anyone should imagine I am reproaching good princes when I praise bad ones. Rather, I have touched briefly on these matters to make it perfectly clear that no mortal can live happily unless he is initiated into my mysteries and has gained my favor.

From C. H. Miller, trans., Desiderius Erasmus: The Praise of Folly *(New Haven: Yale University Press, 1979), 87–106, 110–15.*

Chapter 2
Martin Luther

✠

Introduction

"The Reformation" could well be defined as that whirlwind of personalities, ideas, and events in the sixteenth century that led to the disintegration of Western Christendom. While the various currents in this whirlwind are notoriously difficult to disentangle, one thing remains clear. At its vortex stands the figure of Martin Luther (1483–1546), who, despite all necessary qualifications, retains the title of "Father of the Protestant Reformation." But like many great historical figures who tower over their age, he resists easy classifications and facile description.

The question of precisely who this man was stirred controversy from the very outset. Some of his contemporaries saw him as no less than a prophet and saint who was now restoring "true Christianity" after a thousand years of darkness. And others saw in him a veritable child of the devil, destroying Christendom out of sheer perversity. By today the more strident voices in this controversy have been muted, thanks largely to the coming to maturity of an ecumenical consciousness. Yet new studies continue to appear at an amazing rate, all trying in some way to sharpen our picture of who this man was. This chapter aims to give readers a first glimpse at the person and his ideas.

In Luther's case, these two things—person and idea—cannot easily be separated. Dispassionate scholarly discussion, purposely fostered by the medieval scholastic method, was foreign to Luther's temperament. His personal likes and dislikes shine through almost every page that he wrote, and his personal experience is the anvil on which his theology was forged. The person, therefore, cannot be ignored if we want to understand the ideas. Accordingly, we begin here with a diverse sampling of the texts, each of which allows us to glimpse an aspect of his character. And this obviously sheds light on his ideas. Yet we must be careful not to reduce the ideas solely to products of psychological conflict of some sort. Luther's ideas are clearly related to his personal experience. Yet they are also, and above all, products of a thinking mind. And it is on this level that they must be grappled with.

Luther wore many hats during his turbulent lifetime: first monk, then husband and father, university professor, pastor, church organizer, political advisor, translator, publicist, counselor, and so on. But he was first and foremost a professional theologian. His preparation for this career was a thorough one. He was trained for many years, at both the Universities of Erfurt and Wittenberg, in the nominalist current of scholastic theology. And the doctorate that he received in 1512 remained for him the confirmation and legitimization of his calling to the end of his life. God, he believed, had called him to be a theologian, and this meant a lifelong struggle to understand and explain what Christianity was all about. To this task he gave himself unreservedly.

What kind of theologian was he? Prolific, by any standard. He had an enormous intellectual curiosity and studied incessantly. And out of this came a prodigious number of writings:

commentaries, disputations, treatises, tracts, meditations, sermons, letters, translations, etc. They fill well over a hundred volumes in the modern critical edition. Only a small handful of experts today have read it all. Even Luther himself, towards the end of his life, was somewhat appalled at the sheer volume of his writings. "What a blabbermouth I am," he said.

Luther's academic post at Wittenberg was as professor of biblical interpretation. In this capacity he lectured on the Bible continually to the end of his life. His knowledge of the biblical languages enabled him not only to translate the Bible into German, but to give detailed exegetical analyses. And from those he invariably drew theological conclusions for his time. In this sense he was a "biblical theologian." His favorite books—the Psalms, the Gospel of John, and the letters of St. Paul—occupied him endlessly, and he thought their riches were inexhaustible.

He was also a "controversial theologian" in the sense that his theology at almost every point was developed and worked out in the heat of controversy. From the very beginning, already in 1518 his views were viciously attacked by a multitude of opponents. To begin with these foes were Roman Catholic of course, but in the 1520s they were joined by others of various opinions and persuasions. Though he was now attacked from all sides, Luther remained undaunted, replying with a vehemence, wit, and polemical skill rarely matched in the history of Christian theology. The urgency of the situation often demanded that calm reflection and careful formulation of positions be set aside. And this Luther was more than willing to do. His opponents, in other words, frequently determined his theological agenda.

Because most of Luther's theological authorship came about in this way, some have concluded that his theology is not "systematic." If one means by this that he did not write a single, unified, and all-embracing theological tome as did Thomas Aquinas or John Calvin or Karl Barth, then this is correct. But if by "systematic theology" we mean a coherent and internally consistent set of theological ideas that are all related to and governed by a single central theme, then Luther the theologian was supremely "systematic." This unitary, controlling concept is often summed up in the slogan "justification through faith alone." Luther never tired of explaining this, for he believed it to be the heart of Christianity, the "gospel" as he called it. This, he said, was the "hinge on which all else turns," the "issue on which the church stands or falls." And Luther saw with an astonishing clarity its implications for every other Christian teaching or belief. He also came to see, in the end, how this doctrine ultimately relativized the value of his own life's work—a point his followers have often failed to grasp.

The Person

14. Autobiographical Fragment: Preface to the Complete Edition of Luther's Latin Writings (1545)

At the incessant urging of his followers, and with considerable reluctance, Luther agreed in 1545 to allow his Latin writings to be republished in one collection. For this he wrote a preface, orienting the prospective reader and giving his version of the crucial events up to 1521. Experts still debate the exact date of his Reformation "discovery," with some placing it as early as 1513 and others as late as 1519.

✠

Martin Luther wishes the sincere reader salvation!

For a long time I strenuously resisted those who wanted my books, or more correctly my confused lucubrations, published. I did not want the labors of the ancients to be buried by my new works and the reader kept from reading them. Then, too, by God's grace a great many systematic books now exist, among which the *Loci communes* of Philip excel, with which a theologian and a bishop can be beautifully and abundantly prepared to be mighty in preaching the doctrine of piety, especially since the Holy Bible itself can now be had in nearly every language. But my books, as it happened, yes, as the lack of order in which the events transpired made it necessary, are accordingly crude and disordered chaos, which is now not easy to arrange even for me.

Persuaded by these reasons, I wished that all my books were buried in perpetual oblivion, so that there might be room for better ones. But the boldness and bothersome perseverance of others daily filled my ears with complaints that it would come to pass, that if I did not permit their publication in my lifetime, men wholly ignorant of the causes and the time of the events would nevertheless most certainly publish them, and so out of one confusion many would arise. Their boldness, I say, prevailed and so I permitted them to be published. At the same time the wish and command of our most illustrious Prince, Elector, etc., John Frederick was added. He commanded, yes, compelled the printers not only to print, but to speed up the publication.

But above all else, I beg the sincere reader, and I beg for the sake of our Lord Jesus Christ himself, to read those things judiciously, yes, with great commiseration. May he be mindful of the fact that I was once a monk and a most enthusiastic papist when I began that cause. I was so drunk, yes, submerged in the pope's dogmas, that I would have been ready to murder all, if I could have, or to cooperate willingly with the murderers of all who would take but a syllable from obedience to the pope. So great a Saul was I, as are many to this day. I was not such a lump of frigid ice in defending the papacy as Eck and his like were, who appeared to me actually to defend the pope more for their own bellies' sake than to pursue the matter seriously. To me, indeed, they seem to laugh at the pope to this day, like Epicureans! I pursued the matter with all seriousness, as one, who in dread of the last day, nevertheless from the depth of my heart wanted to be saved.

So you will find how much and what important matters I humbly conceded to the pope in my earlier writings, which I later and now hold and execrate as the worst blasphemies and abomination. You will, therefore, sincere reader, ascribe to this error, or, as they slander, contradiction, to the time and my inexperience. At first I was all alone and certainly very inept and unskilled in conducting such great affairs. For I got into these turmoils by accident and not by will or intention. I call upon God himself as witness.

Hence, when in the year 1517 indulgences were sold (I wanted to say promoted) in these regions for most shameful gain—I was then a preacher, a young doctor of theology, so to speak—and I began to dissuade the people and to urge them not to listen to the clamors of the indulgence-hawkers; they had better things to do. I certainly thought that in this case I should have a protector in the pope, on whose trustworthiness I then leaned strongly, for in his decrees he most clearly damned the immoderation of the quaestors, as he called the indulgence-preachers.

Soon afterward I wrote two letters, one to Albrecht, the archbishop of Mainz, who got half of the money from the indulgences, the pope the other half—something I did not know at the time—the other to the ordinary (as they call them) Jerome, the bishop of Brandenburg. I begged them to stop the shameless blasphemy of the quaestors. But the poor little brother was despised. Despised, I published the *Theses* and at the same time a German *Sermon on Indulgences,* shortly thereafter also the *Explanations,* in which, to the pope's honor, I developed the idea that indulgences should indeed not be condemned, but that good works of love should be preferred to them.

This was demolishing heaven and consuming the earth with fire. I am accused by the pope, am cited to Rome, and the whole papacy rises up against me alone. All this happened in the year 1518, when Maximilian held the diet at Augsburg. In it, the Cardinal Cajetan served as the pope's Lateran legate. The most illustrious Duke Frederick of Saxony, elector prince, approached him on

my behalf and brought it about that I was not compelled to go to Rome, but that he himself should summon me to examine and compose the matter. Soon the diet adjourned.

The Germans in the meantime, all tired of suffering the pillagings, traffickings, and endless impostures of Roman rascals, awaited with bated breath the outcome of so great a matter, which no one before, neither bishop nor theologian, had dared to touch. In any case that popular breeze favored me, because those practices and "Romanations," with which they had filled and tired the whole earth, were already hateful to all.

So I came to Augsburg, afoot and poor, supplied with food and letters of commendation from Prince Frederick to the senate and to certain good men. I was there three days before I went to the cardinal, though he cited me day by day through a certain orator, for those excellent men forbade and dissuaded me most strenuously, not to go to the cardinal without a safe conduct from the emperor. The orator was rather troublesome to me, urging that if I should only revoke, everything would be all right! But as great as the wrong, so long is the detour to its correction.

Finally, on the third day he came demanding to know why I did not come to the cardinal, who expected me most benignly. I replied that I had to respect the advice of those very fine men to whom I had been commended by Prince Frederick, but it was their advice by no means to go to the cardinal without the emperor's protection or safe conduct. Having obtained this (but they took action on the part of the imperial senate to obtain it), I would come at once. At this point he blew up. "What?" he said, "Do you suppose Prince Frederick will take up arms for your sake?" I said, "This I do not at all desire." "And where will you stay?" I replied,

"Under heaven." Then he, "If you had the pope and the cardinals in your power, what would you do?" "I would," said I, "show them all respect and honor." Thereupon he, wagging his finger with an Italian gesture, said, "Hem!" And so he left, nor did he return.

On that day the imperial senate informed the cardinal that the emperor's protection or a safe conduct had been granted me and admonished him that he should not design anything too severe against me. He is said to have replied, "It is well. I shall nevertheless do whatever my duty demands." These things were the start of that tumult. The rest can be learned from the accounts included later.

Master Philip Melanchthon had already been called here that same year by Prince Frederick to teach Greek literature, doubtless so that I should have an associate in the work of theology. His works attest sufficiently what the Lord has performed through this instrument, not only in literature but also in theology, though Satan is mad and all his adherents.

Maximilian died, in the following year, 1519, in February, and according to the law of the empire Duke Frederick was made deputy. Thereupon the storm ceased to rage a bit, and gradually contempt of excommunication or papal thunderbolts arose. For when Eck and Caraccioli brought a bull from Rome condemning Luther and revealed it, the former here, the latter there to Duke Frederick, who was at Cologne at the time together with the other princes in order to meet Charles who had been recently elected, Frederick was most indignant. He reproved that papal rascal with great courage and constancy, because in his absence he and Eck had disturbed his and his brother John's dominion. He jarred them so magnificently that they left him in shame and disgrace. The prince, endowed with incredible insight, caught on to the devices of the Roman Curia and knew how to deal with them in a becoming manner, for he had a keen nose and smelled more and farther than the Romanists could hope or fear.

Hence they refrained from putting him to a test. For he did not dignify with the least respect the Rose, which they call "Golden," sent him that same year by Leo X, indeed ridiculed it. So the Romanists were forced to despair of their attempts to deceive so great a prince. The gospel advanced happily under the shadow of that prince and was widely propagated. His authority influenced very many, for since he was a very wise and most keen-sighted prince, he could incur the suspicion only among the hateful that he wanted to nourish and protect heresy and heretics. This did the papacy great harm.

That same year the Leipzig debate was held, to which Eck had challenged us two, Karlstadt and me. But I could not, in spite of all my letters, get a safe conduct from Duke George. Accordingly, I came to Leipzig not as a prospective debater, but as a spectator under the safe conduct granted to Karlstadt. Who stood in my way I do not know, for till then Duke George was not against me. This I know for certain.

Here Eck came to me in my lodging and said he had heard that I refused to debate. I replied, "How can I debate, since I cannot get a safe conduct from Duke George?" "If I cannot with you," he said, "neither do I want to with Karlstadt, for I have come here on your account. What if I obtain a safe conduct for you? Would you then debate with me?" "Obtain," said I, "and it shall be." He left and soon a safe conduct was given me too and the opportunity to debate.

Eck did this because he discerned the certain glory that was set before him on account of my proposition in which I denied that the pope is the head of the church by divine right. Here a wide field was open to him and a supreme occasion to flatter in praiseworthy manner the pope and to merit his favor, also to ruin me with hate and envy. He did this vigorously throughout the entire debate. But he neither proved his own position nor refuted mine, so that even Duke George said to Eck and me at the morning meal, "Whether he be pope by human right or divine right, yet he is pope." He would in no case have said this had he not been influenced by the arguments, but would have approved of Eck only.

Here, in my case, you may also see how hard it is to struggle out of and emerge from errors which have been confirmed by the example of the whole world and have by long habit become a part of nature, as it were. How true is the proverb, "It is hard to give up the accustomed," and, " Custom is second nature." How truly Augustine says, "If one does not resist custom, it becomes a necessity." I had then already read and taught the sacred Scriptures most diligently privately and publicly for seven years, so that I knew them nearly all by memory. I had also acquired the beginning of the knowledge of Christ and faith in him, i.e., not by works but by faith in Christ are we made righteous and saved. Finally, regarding that of which I speak, I had already defended the proposition publicly that the pope is not the head of the church by divine right. Nevertheless, I did not draw the conclusion, namely, that the pope must be of the devil. For what is not of God must of necessity be of the devil.

So absorbed was I, as I have said, by the example and the title of the holy church as well as by my own habit, that I conceded human right to the pope which nevertheless, unless it is founded on divine authority, is a diabolical lie. For we obey parents and magistrates not because they themselves command it, but because it is God's will, 1 Peter 3 [2:13]. For that reason I can bear with a less hateful spirit those who cling too pertinaciously to the papacy, particularly those who have not read the sacred Scriptures, or also the profane, since I, who read the sacred Scriptures most diligently so many years, still clung to it so tenaciously.

In the year 1519, Leo X, as I have said, sent the Rose with Karl von Miltitz, who urged me profusely to be reconciled with the pope. He had seventy apostolic briefs that if Prince Frederick would turn me over to him, as the pope requested by means of the Rose, he should tack one up in each city and so transfer me safely to Rome. But he betrayed the counsel of his heart toward me when he said, "O Martin, I believed you were some aged theologian who, sitting behind the stove, disputed thus with himself; now I see you are still young and strong. If I had twenty-five thousand armed men, I do not believe I could take you to Rome, for I have sounded out the people's mind all along the way to learn what they thought of you. Behold, where I found one standing for the pope, three stood for you against the pope." But that was ridiculous! He had also asked simple little women and girls in the hostelries, what they thought of the Roman chair. Ignorant of this term and thinking of the domestic chair, they replied, "How can we know what kind of chairs you have in Rome, wood or stone?"

Therefore he begged me to seek the things which made for peace. He would put forth every effort to have the pope do the same. I also promised everything abundantly. Whatever I could do with a good conscience with respect to the truth, I would do most promptly. I, too, desired and was eager for peace. Having been drawn into these disturbances by force and driven by necessity, I had done all I did: the guilt was not mine.

But he had summoned Johann Tetzel of the preaching order, and the primary author of this tragedy, and had with verbose threats from the pope so broken the man, till then so terrible to all, a fearless crier, that from that time on he wasted away and was finally consumed by illness of mind. When I found this out before his death, I comforted him with a letter, written benignly, asking him to be of good cheer and not to fear my memory. But perhaps he succumbed a victim of his conscience and of the pope's indignation.

Karl von Miltitz was regarded as vain and his advice as vain. But, in my opinion, if the man at Mainz had from the start, when I admonished him, and, finally, if the pope, before he condemned me unheard and raged with his bulls, had taken this advice, which Karl took although too late, and had at once quenched Tetzel's fury, the matter would not have come to so great a tumult. The entire guilt belongs to the one at Mainz, whose smartness and cleverness fooled him, with which he wanted to suppress my doctrine and have his money, acquired by the indulgences, saved. Now counsels are sought in vain; in vain efforts are made. The Lord has awakened and stands to judge the people. Though they could kill us, they still do not have what they want, yes, have less than they have, while we live in safety. This some of them who are not entirely of a dull nose smell quite enough.

Meanwhile, I had already during that year returned to interpret the Psalter anew. I had

confidence in the fact that I was more skillful, after I had lectured in the university on St. Paul's epistles to the Romans, to the Galatians, and the one to the Hebrews. I had indeed been captivated with an extraordinary ardor for understanding Paul in the Epistle to the Romans. But up till then it was not the cold blood about the heart, but a single word in Chapter 1 [:17], "In it the righteousness of God is revealed," that had stood in my way. For I hated that word "righteousness of God," which, according to the use and custom of all the teachers, I had been taught to understand philosophically regarding the formal or active righteousness, as they called it, with which God is righteous and punishes the unrighteous sinner.

Though I lived as a monk without reproach, I felt that I was a sinner before God with an extremely disturbed conscience. I could not believe that he was placated by my satisfaction. I did not love, yes, I hated the righteous God who punishes sinners, and secretly, if not blasphemously, certainly murmuring greatly, I was angry with God, and said, "As if, indeed, it is not enough, that miserable sinners, eternally lost through original sin, are crushed by every kind of calamity by the law of the Decalogue, without having God add pain to pain by the gospel and also by the gospel threatening us with his righteousness and wrath!" Thus I raged with a fierce and troubled conscience. Nevertheless, I beat importunately upon Paul at that place, most ardently desiring to know what St. Paul wanted.

At last, by the mercy of God, meditating day and night, I gave heed to the context of the words, namely, "In it the righteousness of God is revealed, as it is written, 'He who through faith is righteous shall live.'" There I began to understand that the righteousness of God is that by which the righteous lives by a gift of God, namely by faith. And this is the meaning: the righteousness of God is revealed by the gospel, namely, the passive righteousness with which merciful God justifies us by faith, as it is written, "He who through faith is righteous shall live." Here I felt that I was altogether born again and had entered paradise itself through open gates. There a totally other face of the entire Scripture showed itself to me. Thereupon I ran through the Scriptures from memory. I also found in other terms an analogy, as, the work of God, that is, what God does in us, the power of God, with which he makes us strong, the wisdom of God, with which he makes us wise, the strength of God, the salvation of God, the glory of God.

And I extolled my sweetest word with a love as great as the hatred with which I had before hated the word "righteousness of God." Thus that place in Paul was for me truly the gate to paradise. Later I read Augustine's *The Spirit and the Letter,* where contrary to hope I found that he, too, interpreted God's righteousness in a similar way, as the righteousness with which God clothes us when he justifies us. Although this was heretofore said imperfectly and he did not explain all things concerning imputation clearly, it nevertheless was pleasing that God's righteousness with which we are justified was taught. Armed more fully with these thoughts, I began a second time to interpret the Psalter. And the work would have grown into a large commentary, if I had not again been compelled to leave the work begun, because Emperor Charles V in the following year convened the diet at Worms.

I relate these things, good reader, so that, if you are a reader of my puny works, you may keep in mind, that, as I said above, I was all alone and one of those who, as Augustine says of himself, have become proficient by writing and teaching. I was not one of those who from nothing suddenly become the topmost, though they are nothing, neither have labored, nor been tempted, nor become experienced, but have with one look at the Scriptures exhausted their entire spirit.

To this point, to the year 1520 and 1521, the indulgence matter proceeded. Upon that followed the sacramentarian and the Anabaptist affairs. Regarding these a preface shall be written to other tomes, if I live.

Farewell in the Lord, reader, and pray for the growth of the Word against Satan. Strong and evil, now also very furious and savage, he knows his time is short and the kingdom of his pope is in danger. But may God confirm in us what he has accomplished and perfect his work which he has begun in us, to his glory, Amen. March 5, in the year 1545.

From J. Pelikan and H. Lehman, eds., Luther's Works: American Edition, 55 vols. (St. Louis: Concordia; Philadelphia: Fortress; 1955–1987), vol. 34, 327–38. Note: Hereafter, this work will be abbreviated LW with volume number and page or citation numbers following.

15. Letter to His Father: Dedication of *On Monastic Vows* (21 November 1521)

In 1505, against the wishes of his father, Luther entered the Augustinian monastery at Erfurt. By 1521, when he wrote his book *On Monastic Vows*, he had come to see the error of his ways. His prefatory letter indicates regret and seeks to overcome the long years of alienation from his father.

To Hans Luther, his father, Martin Luther, his son, sends greetings in Christ.

In dedicating this book to you, dearest father, . . . I am taking the opportunity, which this interchange between us conveniently provides, of telling my pious readers the cause of the book, its argument, and the example it offers. . . .

It is now nearly sixteen years since I became a monk, against your wishes and without your knowledge. In your paternal affection you feared for my weakness, since I was then a youth, just entering my twenty-second year, "clothed in hot youth" (as Augustine says), and you had learned from many examples that this kind of life has turned out badly for many. Your own plan for my future was to tie me down with an honorable and wealthy marriage. Your fears for me got on your mind and your anger against me was for a time implacable. . . . At last you gave it up and submitted your will to God, although your fears for me remained. For I remember only too well that after you were reconciled and talking with me again, I told you that I had been called by terrors from heaven and become a monk against my own will and desire (to say nothing of the inclinations of the flesh!): I had been beleaguered by the terror and agony of sudden death, and I made my vows perforce and of necessity. Then you said—"May it not prove an illusion and a deception." That word penetrated and lodged in the depths of my soul, as if God had spoken through your mouth; but I hardened my heart against you and your word as much as I could. You said something else as well: when I presumed as your son to rebuke you for your anger, you suddenly lashed me with the retort—so fitting and so pointed that hardly any word spoken to me in my whole life has sounded more power-

fully in my ears or lingered so long—"Have you not also heard that parents are to be obeyed?" . . . For my vow was not worth a straw, because in taking it I was withdrawing myself from the will and authority of my parent.

From E. G. Rupp and B. Drewery, eds., Martin Luther *(London: Edward Arnold; New York: St. Martin's Press, 1970), 2–3.*

16. Luther on His Monastic Life

At various points in his later writings, Luther commented on his career in the monastery. These comments reveal an utterly sincere piety, a sense of spiritual failure, and an extreme if not pathological scrupulosity.

I was indeed a good monk and kept the rules of my order so strictly that I can say: if ever a monk got to heaven through monasticism, I should have been that man. All my brothers in the monastery who know me will testify to this. I would have become a martyr through fasting, prayer, reading and other good works had I remained a monk very much longer. . . .

When I was a monk I tried with all diligence to live according to the rule, and I used to be contrite, to confess and sedulously perform my allotted penance. And yet my conscience could never give me certainty: I always doubted and said "You did not do that correctly. You were not contrite enough. You left that out of your confession." The more I tried to remedy an uncertain, weak and afflicted conscience with the traditions of men, the more each day I found it more uncertain, weaker, more troubled. . . .

Then remorse comes and terrifies the sinner. Then all's right with the world and he alone is a sinner. God is gracious to the whole world, save to him alone. Nobody has to meet the wrath of God save he alone; he believes there is no wrath anywhere than that which he feels, and he finds himself the most miserable of men. That is how it was with Adam and Eve when they sinned. Had God not come in the cool of the day they would never have noticed their sin. But when he came, they crawled away. . . .

I knew a man who said that he had suffered [the pains of eternal torments] in the shortest possible time, so great and infernal that "nor tongue nor pen can show" nor those believe who have not experienced them, so that if they were to be completed, or lasted half an hour, or even the tenth part of an hour, he would utterly perish and his bones be reduced to ashes. Then God appears horrifyingly angry and with him the whole creation. There can be no flight, nor consolation either from within or from without, but all is accusation.

✝

From Rupp and Drewery, Martin Luther, 4–5.

17. From Luther's *Table Talk*

The Black Cloister in Wittenberg, previously home to Augustinian monks, became home in 1525 to Luther and his wife Katherine, six children of their own, Katherine's maiden aunt, several orphaned nephews and nieces, a few servants, and several impoverished students. After 1530 Luther's fame and hospitality meant that they were very frequently joined at mealtime by colleagues, government officials, escaped nuns, foreign visitors, etc. This "miscellaneous and promiscuous crowd" made for lively mealtime conversation, and Luther himself was not reluctant to hold forth

on almost every conceivable topic. Inevitably, some began to take notes, and these were compiled and published for the first time in 1566.

✝

On Writing against Opponents

"The papists and I write against each other in different ways. I enter the fray after careful reflection and in a sufficiently hostile frame of mind. For ten years I battled with the devil and established all my positions, and so I knew that they would stand up. But neither Erasmus nor any of the others took the matters seriously. Only Latomus has written excellently against me. Mark this well: Only Latomus wrote against Luther; all the rest, even Erasmus were croaking toads."

LW *vol. 54, no. 463.*

On Aging

"Young fellows are tempted by girls, men who are thirty years old are tempted by gold, when they are forty years old they are tempted by honor and glory, and those who are sixty years old say to themselves, 'What a pious man I have become!'"

LW *vol. 54, no. 1601.*

On Theologians

"God makes fools of both theologians and princes. . . . We want to set things straight and make everything right. To this God says, 'Well, then, go ahead! Be clever and do a good job! Be a preacher and make the people godly! Be a lord and mend the people's ways! Get to it at once!' . . . We are fools and bunglers in all we do and attempt."

LW *vol. 54, no. 547.*

On Human Sinfulness

The doctor took his son on his lap, and the child befouled him. Thereupon he [Martin

Luther} said, "How our Lord has to put up with many a murmur and stink from us, worse than a mother must endure from her child!"

LW *vol. 54, no. 1615.*

On Schoolboy Pranks

"Then they asked each pupil to parse precisely, according to *Donatus, legeris, legere, legitur,* and even *lecti mei ars.* These tests were nothing short of torture."

LW *vol. 54, no. 3566A.*

On His Own Writings

When he {Martin Luther} heard that his books were in the library of the prince he said, "My books ought by no means to be placed in that library, especially not the earliest books which I wrote at the beginning, for they are offensive not only to my adversaries but also to me."

LW *vol. 54, no. 3493.*

On March 29 [1538] the Strassburgers asked for permission to publish the collected works of Luther with a reliable index to the same. Luther replied, "I'd like all my books to be destroyed so that only the sacred writings in the Bible would be diligently read. For one is referred from one book to another, as it happened in the ancient church, when one turned from a reading of the Bible to a reading of Eusebius, then of Jerome, then of Gregory, and finally of the scholastics and philosophers. This will happen to us too. I'd like them {my books} to be preserved for the sake of history, in order that men may observe the course of events and the conflict with the pope, who once seemed formidable but is now regarded with disdain."

LW *vol. 54, no. 3797.*

On the Illness and Death of His Daughter

When the illness of his daughter became more grave he {Martin Luther} said, "I love her very much. But if it is thy will to take her, dear God, I shall be glad to know that she is with thee." . . .

Among other things he then said, "In the last thousand years God has given no bishop such great gifts as he has given to me. . . ."

LW *vol. 54, no. 5494.*

When his daughter was in the agony of death, he {Martin Luther} fell on his knees before the bed and, weeping bitterly, prayed that God might will to save her. Thus she gave up the ghost in the arms of her father.

LW *vol. 54, no. 5496.*

When his dead daughter was placed in the coffin, he {Martin Luther} said, "You dear little Lena! How well it has turned out for you!"

He looked at her and said, "Ah, dear child, to think that you must be raised up and will shine like the stars, yes, like the sun!"

LW *vol. 54, no. 5498.*

On Lawyers

"Every lawyer is either a good-for-nothing or a know-nothing. If a lawyer wants to dispute this, tell him, 'You hear? A lawyer shouldn't talk until a sow breaks wind!' Then he should say 'Thank you, dear grandmother, I haven't heard a sermon in a long time!' . . ."

LW *vol. 54, no. 5663.*

On German Drinking Habits

"Tomorrow I have to lecture on the drunkenness of Noah [Gen. 9:20-27], so I should drink enough this evening to be able to talk about that wickedness as one who knows by experience."

Dr. Cordatus [his guest] said, "By no means; you ought to do the opposite!"

To this Luther responded, "One must make the best of the vices that are peculiar to each land. The Bohemians gorge themselves, the Wends [Slavic settlers in Saxony] steal, the Germans swill without stopping. How would you outdo a German, dear Cordatus, except by making him drunk—especially a German who doesn't love music and women?"
LW *vol. 54, no. 3476.*

18. Letter to Katie (2 July 1540)

Luther's marriage to the former nun Katherine von Bora in 1525 was, by all accounts, a happy one. This letter, with its gently teasing tone, reveals not only deep affection but also concern for the mundane aspects of family life.

To my dearly beloved Katie, Mrs. Doctor Luther, etc., to the lady at the new pig market:
Personal.

Grace and peace! Dear Maid Katie, Gracious Lady of Zölsdorf (and whatever other names your Grace has)! I wish humbly to inform your Grace that I am doing well here. I eat like a Bohemian and drink like a German; thanks be to God for this. Amen. The reason for this is that Master Philip truly has been dead, and really, like Lazarus, has risen from death. God, the dear Father, listens to our prayers. This we [can] see and touch [with our hands], yet we still do not believe it. No one should say Amen to such disgraceful unbelief of ours.

I have written to Doctor Pomer, the pastor, that the Count of Schwarzburg is asking that a pastor be sent to Greussen. As a wise woman and doctor, you, with Master George Major and Master Ambrose, might also give counsel as to which of the three candidates I suggested to Pomer might be convinced [to go]. It is not a bad parish. Yet you people are wise and will find a better solution [than I suggested].

There at Arnstadt the pastor has driven a devil out of a young girl in a truly Christian way. Regarding this event we say: may the will of God, who is still alive, be done, even though the devil should be sorry about this.

I have received the letters from the children, also the one from the *baccalaureus* (who is no child)—(Marushe [is] also not [one])—but from your Grace I have received nothing. If it please God, then you might now, at least once, answer this, the fourth letter, with your gracious hand.

I am sending along with Master Paul the silver apple which my gracious lord presented to me. As I previously said, you may divide it among the children and ask them how many cherries and apples they would wish in exchange for it; give them these at once, and you retain the stalk, etc.

Give my hearty greetings and good will to our dear boarders, especially to Doctor Severus or Schiefer, and tell them to help in all the affairs of the church, school, house—wherever the need arises. Also [tell] Master George Major and Master Ambrose to help you around the house. By God's will we shall be here until Sunday, and then, with Philip, we shall travel from Weimar to Eisenach.

With this I commend you to God. Tell our Lycaon not to neglect the mulberries by oversleeping; of course, he won't oversleep unless he forgets about it. Also, he should tap the wine at the right time. All of you be happy and pray. Amen.
Martin Luther,
who loves you from his heart.

From LW vol. 50, 208–12.

Theological Writings

19. *Ninety-five Theses* or *Disputation on the Power and Efficacy of Indulgences* (1517)

While this is the most famous document of Luther's Reformation, it is not the most important. It is a series of theses for an academic disputation, written in Latin for a university audience. A close reading shows that in them Luther rejects neither indulgences as such, nor purgatory, nor the sacrament of penance. Their importance lies in the fact that they are a small initial step that stirred up an international furor and thereby set in motion the dramatic events that followed.

✠

Out of love and zeal for truth and the desire to bring it to light, the following theses will be publicly discussed at Wittenberg under the chairmanship of the reverend father Martin Luther, Master of Arts and Sacred Theology and regularly appointed Lecturer on these subjects at that place. He requests that those who cannot be present to debate orally with us will do so by letter.

In the Name of Our Lord Jesus Christ. Amen.

1. When our Lord and Master Jesus Christ said, "Repent" [Matt. 4:17], he willed the entire life of believers to be one of repentance.

2. This word cannot be understood as referring to the sacrament of penance, that is, confession and satisfaction, as administered by the clergy.

3. Yet it does not mean solely inner repentance; such inner repentance is worthless unless it produces various outward mortifications of the flesh.

4. The penalty of sin remains as long as the hatred of self, that is, true inner repentance, until our entrance into the kingdom of heaven.

5. The pope neither desires nor is able to remit any penalties except those imposed by his own authority or that of the canons.

6. The pope cannot remit any guilt, except by declaring and showing that it has been remitted by God; or, to be sure, by remitting guilt in cases reserved to his judgment. If his right to grant remission in these cases were disregarded, the guilt would certainly remain unforgiven.

7. God remits guilt to no one unless at the same time he humbles him in all things and makes him submissive to his vicar, the priest.

8. The penitential canons are imposed only on the living, and, according to the canons themselves, nothing should be imposed on the dying.

9. Therefore the Holy Spirit through the pope is kind to us insofar as the pope in his decrees always makes exception of the article of death and of necessity.

10. Those priests act ignorantly and wickedly who, in the case of the dying, reserve canonical penalties for purgatory.

11. Those tares of changing the canonical penalty to the penalty of purgatory were evidently sown while the bishops slept [Matt. 13:25].

12. In former times canonical penalties were imposed, not after, but before absolution, as tests of true contrition.

13. The dying are freed by death from all penalties, are already dead as far as the canon laws are concerned, and have a right to be released from them.

14. Imperfect piety or love on the part of the dying person necessarily brings with it great fear; and the smaller the love, the greater the fear.

15. This fear or horror is sufficient in itself, to say nothing of other things, to constitute the penalty of purgatory, since it is very near the horror of despair.

16. Hell, purgatory, and heaven seem to differ the same as despair, fear, and assurance of salvation.

17. It seems as though for the souls in purgatory fear should necessarily decrease and love increase.

18. Furthermore, it does not seem proved, either by reason or Scripture, that souls in purgatory are outside the state of merit, that is, unable to grow in love.

19. Nor does it seem proved that souls in purgatory, at least not all of them, are certain and assured of their own salvation, even if we ourselves may be entirely certain of it.

20. Therefore the pope, when he uses the words "plenary remission of all penalties," does not actually mean "all penalties," but only those imposed by himself.

21. Thus those indulgence-preachers are in error who say that a man is absolved from every penalty and saved by papal indulgences.

22. As a matter of fact, the pope remits to souls in purgatory no penalty which, according to canon law, they should have paid in this life.

23. If remission of all penalties whatsoever could be granted to anyone at all, certainly it would be granted only to the most perfect, that is, to very few.

24. For this reason most people are necessarily deceived by that indiscriminate and high-sounding promise of release from penalty.

25. That power which the pope has in general over purgatory corresponds to the power which any bishop or curate has in a particular way in his own diocese or parish.

26. The pope does very well when he grants remission to souls in purgatory, not by the power of the keys, which he does not have, but by way of intercession for them.

27. They preach only human doctrines who say that as soon as the money clinks into the money chest, the soul flies out of purgatory.

28. It is certain that when money clinks in the money chest, greed and avarice can be increased; but when the church intercedes, the result is in the hands of God alone.

29. Who knows whether all souls in purgatory wish to be redeemed, since we have exceptions in St. Severinus and St. Paschal, as related in a legend.

30. No one is sure of the integrity of his own contrition, much less of having received plenary remission.

31. The man who actually buys indulgences is as rare as he who is really penitent; indeed, he is exceedingly rare.

32. Those who believe that they can be certain of their salvation because they have indulgence letters will be eternally damned, together with their teachers.

33. Men must especially be on their guard against those who say that the pope's pardons are that inestimable gift of God by which man is reconciled to him.

34. For the graces of indulgences are concerned only with the penalties of sacramental satisfaction established by man.

35. They who teach that contrition is not necessary on the part of those who intend to buy souls out of purgatory or to buy confessional privileges preach unchristian doctrine.

36. Any truly repentant Christian has a right to full remission of penalty and guilt, even without indulgence letters.

37. Any true Christian, whether living or dead, participates in all the blessings of Christ and the church; and this is granted

him by God, even without indulgence letters.

38. Nevertheless, papal remission and blessing are by no means to be disregarded, for they are, as I have said [Thesis 6], the proclamation of the divine remission.

39. It is very difficult, even for the most learned theologians, at one and the same time to commend to the people the bounty of indulgences and the need of true contrition.

40. A Christian who is truly contrite seeks and loves to pay penalties for his sins; the bounty of indulgences, however, relaxes penalties and causes men to hate them— at least it furnishes occasion for hating them.

41. Papal indulgences must be preached with caution, lest people erroneously think that they are preferable to other good works of love.

42. Christians are to be taught that the pope does not intend that the buying of indulgences should in any way be compared with works of mercy.

43. Christians are to be taught that he who gives to the poor or lends to the needy does a better deed than he who buys indulgences.

44. Because love grows by works of love, man thereby becomes better. Man does not, however, become better by means of indulgences but is merely freed from penalties.

45. Christians are to be taught that he who sees a needy man and passes him by, yet gives his money for indulgences, does not buy papal indulgences but God's wrath.

46. Christians are to be taught that, unless they have more than they need, they must reserve enough for their family needs and by no means squander it on indulgences.

47. Christians are to be taught that the buying of indulgences is a matter of free choice, not commanded.

48. Christians are to be taught that the pope, in granting indulgences, needs and thus desires their devout prayer more than their money.

49. Christians are to be taught that papal indulgences are useful only if they do not put their trust in them, but very harmful if they lose their fear of God because of them.

50. Christians are to be taught that if the pope knew the exactions of the indulgence-preachers, he would rather that the basilica of St. Peter were burned to ashes than built up with the skin, flesh, and bones of his sheep.

51. Christians are to be taught that the pope would and should wish to give of his own money, even though he had to sell the basilica of St. Peter, to many of those from whom certain hawkers of indulgences cajole money.

52. It is vain to trust in salvation by indulgence letters, even though the indulgence commissary, or even the pope, were to offer his soul as security.

53. They are enemies of Christ and the pope who forbid altogether the preaching of the Word of God in some churches in order that indulgences may be preached in others.

54. Injury is done the Word of God when, in the same sermon, an equal or larger amount of time is devoted to indulgences than to the Word.

55. It is certainly the pope's sentiment that if indulgences, which are a very insignificant thing, are celebrated with one bell, one procession, and one ceremony, then the gospel, which is the very greatest thing, should be preached with a hundred

bells, a hundred processions, a hundred ceremonies.

56. The treasures of the church, out of which the pope distributes indulgences, are not sufficiently discussed or known among the people of Christ.

57. That indulgences are not temporal treasures is certainly clear, for many [indulgence-]preachers do not distribute them freely but only gather them.

58. Nor are they the merits of Christ and the saints, for, even without the pope, the latter always work grace for the inner man, and the cross, death, and hell for the outer man.

59. St. Laurence said that the poor of the church were the treasures of the church, but he spoke according to the usage of the word in his own time.

60. Without want of consideration we say that the keys of the church, given by the merits of Christ, are that treasure;

61. For it is clear that the pope's power is of itself sufficient for the remission of penalties and cases reserved by himself.

62. The true treasure of the church is the most holy gospel of the glory and grace of God.

63. But this treasure is naturally most odious, for it makes the first to be last [Matt. 20:16].

64. On the other hand, the treasure of indulgences is naturally most acceptable, for it makes the last to be first.

65. Therefore the treasures of the gospel are nets with which one formerly fished for men of wealth.

66. The treasures of indulgences are nets with which one now fishes for the wealth of men.

67. The indulgences which the demagogues acclaim as the greatest graces are actually understood to be such only insofar as they promote gain.

68. They are nevertheless in truth the most insignificant graces when compared with the grace of God and the piety of the cross.

69. Bishops and curates are bound to admit the commissaries of papal indulgences with all reverence.

70. But they are much more bound to strain their eyes and ears lest these men preach their own dreams instead of what the pope has commissioned.

71. Let him who speaks against the truth concerning papal indulgences be anathema and accursed;

72. But let him who guards against the lust and license of the indulgence-preachers be blessed;

73. Just as the pope justly thunders against those who by any means whatsoever contrive harm to the sale of indulgences.

74. But much more does he intend to thunder against those who use indulgences as a pretext to contrive harm to holy love and truth.

75. To consider papal indulgences so great that they could absolve a man even if he had done the impossible and had violated the mother of God is madness.

76. We say on the contrary that papal indulgences cannot remove the very least of venial sins as far as guilt is concerned.

77. To say that even St. Peter, if he were now pope, could not grant greater graces is blasphemy against St. Peter and the pope.

78. We say on the contrary that even the present pope, or any pope whatsoever, has greater graces at his disposal, that is, the gospel, spiritual powers, gifts of healing, etc., as it is written in 1 Cor. 12 [:28].

79. To say that the cross emblazoned with the papal coat of arms, and set up by the

indulgence-preachers, is equal in worth to the cross of Christ is blasphemy.

80. The bishops, curates, and theologians who permit such talk to be spread among the people will have to answer for this.

81. This unbridled preaching of indulgences makes it difficult even for learned men to rescue the reverence which is due the pope from slander or from the shrewd questions of the laity,

82. Such as: "Why does not the pope empty purgatory for the sake of holy love and the dire need of the souls that are there if he redeems an infinite number of souls for the sake of miserable money with which to build a church? The former reasons would be most just; the latter is most trivial."

83. Again, "Why are funeral and anniversary masses for the dead continued and why does he not return or permit the withdrawal of the endowments founded for them, since it is wrong to pray for the redeemed?"

84. Again, "What is this new piety of God and the pope that for a consideration of money they permit a man who is impious and their enemy to buy out of purgatory the pious soul of a friend of God and do not rather, because of the need of that pious and beloved soul, free it for pure love's sake?"

85. Again, "Why are the penitential canons, long since abrogated and dead in actual fact and through disuse, now satisfied by the granting of indulgences as though they were still alive and in force?"

86. Again, "Why does not the pope, whose wealth is today greater than the wealth of the richest Crassus, build this one basilica of St. Peter with his own money rather than with the money of poor believers?"

87. Again, "What does the pope remit or grant to those who by perfect contrition already have a right to full remission and blessings?"

88. Again, "What greater blessing could come to the church than if the pope were to bestow these remissions and blessings on every believer a hundred times a day, as he now does but once?"

89. "Since the pope seeks the salvation of souls rather than money by his indulgences, why does he suspend the indulgences and pardons previously granted when they have equal efficacy?"

90. To repress these very sharp arguments of the laity by force alone, and not to resolve them by giving reasons, is to expose the church and the pope to the ridicule of their enemies and to make Christians unhappy.

91. If, therefore, indulgences were preached according to the spirit and intention of the pope, all these doubts would be readily resolved. Indeed, they would not exist.

92. Away then with all those prophets who say to the people of Christ, "Peace, peace," and there is no peace! [Jer. 6:14].

93. Blessed be all those prophets who say to the people of Christ, "Cross, cross," and there is no cross!

94. Christians should be exhorted to be diligent in following Christ, their head, through penalties, death, and hell;

95. And thus be confident of entering into heaven through many tribulations rather than through the false security of peace [Acts 14:22].

✠

From LW vol. 31, 25–33.

20. *A Meditation on Christ's Passion* (1519)

By 1519 Luther was deeply involved in the polemic for which he is best known. Yet his pastoral instincts and concern for the laity surfaced frequently, as in this Good Friday sermon. In it one can see a stage in the evolution of his theology as it grew to maturity in the following years.

✠

1. Some people meditate on Christ's passion by venting their anger on the Jews. This singing and ranting about wretched Judas satisfies them, for they are in the habit of complaining about other people, of condemning and reproaching their adversaries. That might well be a meditation on the wickedness of Judas and the Jews, but not on the sufferings of Christ.

2. Some point to the manifold benefits and fruits that grow from contemplating Christ's passion. There is a saying ascribed to Albertus about this, that it is more beneficial to ponder Christ's passion just once than to fast a whole year or to pray a psalm daily, etc. These people follow this saying blindly and therefore do not reap the fruit of Christ's passion, for in so doing they are seeking their own advantage. They carry pictures and booklets, letters and crosses on their person. Some who travel afar do this in the belief that they thus protect themselves against water and sword, fire, and all sorts of perils. Christ's suffering is thus used to effect in them a lack of suffering contrary to his being and nature.

3. Some feel pity for Christ, lamenting and bewailing his innocence. They are like the women who followed Christ from Jerusalem and were chided and told by Christ that it would be better to weep for themselves and their children [Luke 23:27-28]. They are the kind of people who go far afield in their meditation on the passion, making much of Christ's farewell from Bethany and of the Virgin Mary's anguish, but never progressing beyond that, which is why so many hours are devoted to the contemplation of Christ's passion. Only God knows whether that is invented for the purpose of sleeping or of waking.

Also to this group belong those who have learned what rich fruits the holy mass offers. In their simplemindedness they think it enough simply to hear mass. In support of this several teachers are cited to us who hold that the mass is *opere operati, non opere operantis,* that it is effective in itself without our merit and worthiness, and that this is all that is needed. Yet the mass was not instituted for its own worthiness, but to make us worthy and to remind us of the passion of Christ. Where that is not done, we make of the mass a physical and unfruitful act, though even this is of some good. Of what help is it to you that God is God, if he is not God to you? Of what benefit is it to you that food and drink are good and wholesome in themselves if they are not healthful for you? And it is to be feared that many masses will not improve matters as long as we do not seek the right fruit in them.

4. They contemplate Christ's passion aright who view it with a terror-stricken heart and a despairing conscience. This terror must be felt as you witness the stern wrath and the unchanging earnestness with which God looks upon sin and sinners, so much so that he was unwilling to release sinners even for his only and dearest Son without his payment of the severest penalty for them. Thus he says in Isaiah 53[:8], "I have chastised him for the transgressions of my people." If the dearest child is punished thus, what will

be the fate of sinners? It must be an inexpressible and unbearable earnestness that forces such a great and infinite person to suffer and die to appease it. And if you seriously consider that it is God's very own Son, the eternal wisdom of the Father, who suffers, you will be terrified indeed. The more you think about it, the more intensely will you be frightened.

5. You must get this thought through your head and not doubt that you are the one who is torturing Christ thus, for your sins have surely wrought this. In Acts 2 [:36-37] St. Peter frightened the Jews like a peal of thunder when he said to all of them, "You crucified him." Consequently three thousand alarmed and terrified Jews asked the apostles on that one day, "O dear brethren, what shall we do now?" Therefore, when you see the nails piercing Christ's hands, you can be certain that it is your work. When you behold his crown of thorns, you may rest assured that these are your evil thoughts, etc.

6. For every nail that pierces Christ, more than one hundred thousand should in justice pierce you, yes, they should prick you forever and ever more painfully! When Christ is tortured by nails penetrating his hands and feet, you should eternally suffer the pain they inflict and the pain of even more cruel nails, which will in truth be the lot of those who do not avail themselves of Christ's passion. This earnest mirror, Christ, will not lie or trifle, and whatever it points out will come to pass in full measure.

7. St. Bernard was so terrified by this that he declared, "I regarded myself secure; I was not aware of the eternal sentence that had been passed on me in heaven until I saw that God's only Son had compassion upon me and offered to bear this sentence for me. Alas, if the situation is that serious, I should not

make light of it or feel secure." We read that Christ commanded the women not to weep for him but for themselves and their children [Luke 23:28]. And he adds the reason for this, saying, "For if they do this to the green wood, what will happen when it is dry?" [Luke 23:31] He says as it were: From my martyrdom you can learn what it is that you really deserve and what your fate should be. Here the saying applies that the small dog is whipped to frighten the big dog. Thus the prophet said that all the generations on earth will bewail him, but that they will bewail themselves because of him. In like manner the people of whom we heard in Acts 2 [:36-37] were so frightened that they said to the apostles, "O brethren, what shall we do?" This is also the song of the church: "I will ponder this diligently and, as a result, my soul will languish within me."

8. We must give ourselves wholly to this matter, for the main benefit of Christ's passion is that man sees into his own true self and that he be terrified and crushed by this. Unless we seek that knowledge, we do not derive much benefit from Christ's passion. The real and true work of Christ's passion is to make man conformable to Christ, so that man's conscience is tormented by his sins in like measure as Christ was pitiably tormented in body and soul by our sins. This does not call for many words but for profound reflection and a great awe of sins. Take this as an illustration: a criminal is sentenced to death for the murder of the child of a prince or a king. In the meantime you go your carefree way, singing and playing, until you are cruelly arrested and convicted of having inspired the murderer. Now the whole world closes in upon you, especially since your conscience also deserts you. You should be terrified even more by the meditation on Christ's passion.

For the evildoers, the Jews, whom God has judged and driven out, were only the servants of your sin; you are actually the one who, as we said, by his sin killed and crucified God's Son.

9. He who is so hardhearted and callous as not to be terrified by Christ's passion and led to a knowledge of self, has reason to fear. For it is inevitable, whether in this life or in hell, that you will have to become conformable to Christ's image and suffering. At the very least, you will sink into this terror in the hour of death and in purgatory and will tremble and quake and feel all that Christ has suffered on the cross. Since it is horrible to lie waiting on your deathbed, you should pray God to soften your heart and let you ponder Christ's passion with profit to you. Unless God inspires our heart, it is impossible for us of ourselves to meditate thoroughly on Christ's passion. No meditation or any other doctrine is granted to you that you might be boldly inspired by your own will to accomplish this. You must first seek God's grace and ask that it be accomplished by his grace and not by your own power. That is why the people we referred to above fail to view Christ's passion aright. They do not seek God's help for this, but look to their own ability to devise their own means of accomplishing this. They deal with the matter in a completely human but also unfruitful way.

10. We say without hesitation that he who contemplates God's sufferings for a day, an hour, yes, only a quarter of an hour, does better than to fast a whole year, pray a psalm daily, yes, better than to hear a hundred masses. This meditation changes man's being and, almost like baptism, gives him a new birth. Here the passion of Christ performs its natural and noble work, strangling the old

Adam and banishing all joy, delight, and confidence which man could derive from other creatures, even as Christ was forsaken by all, even by God.

11. Since this [strangling of the old Adam] does not rest with us, it happens that we occasionally pray for it, and yet do not attain it at once. Nevertheless we should neither despair nor desist. At times this happens because we do not pray for it as God conceives of it and wishes it, for it must be left free and unfettered. Then man becomes sad in his conscience and grumbles to himself about the evil in his life. It may well be that he does not know that Christ's passion, to which he gives no thought, is effecting this in him, even as the others who do think of Christ's passion still do not gain this knowledge of self through it. For these the passion of Christ is hidden and genuine, while for those it is only unreal and misleading. For these the passion of Christ is hidden and genuine, while for those it is only unreal and misleading. In that way God often reverses matters, so that those who do not meditate on Christ's passion do meditate on it, and those who do not hear mass do hear it, and those who hear it do not hear it.

12. Until now we have sojourned in Passion Week and rightly celebrated Good Friday. Now we come to the resurrection of Christ, to the day of Easter. After man has thus become aware of his sin and is terrified in his heart, he must watch that sin does not remain in his conscience, for this would lead to sheer despair. Just as [our knowledge of] sin flowed from Christ and was acknowledged by us, so we must pour this sin back on him and free our conscience of it. Therefore beware, lest you do as those perverse people who torture their hearts with their sins and strive to do the impossible, namely,

get rid of their sins by running from one good work or penance to another, or by working their way out of this by means of indulgences. Unfortunately such false confidence in penance and pilgrimages is widespread.

13. You cast your sins from yourself and onto Christ when you firmly believe that his wounds and sufferings are your sins, to be borne and paid for by him, as we read in Isaiah 53 [:6], "The Lord has laid on him the iniquity of us all." St. Peter says, "in his body has he borne our sins on the wood of the cross" [1 Pet. 2:24]. St. Paul says, "God has made him a sinner for us, so that through him we would be made just" [2 Cor. 5:21]. You must stake everything on these and similar verses. The more your conscience torments you, the more tenaciously must you cling to them. If you do not do that, but presume to still your conscience with your contrition and penance, you will never obtain peace of mind, but will have to despair in the end. If we allow sin to remain in our conscience and try to deal with it there, or if we look at sin in our heart, it will be much too strong for us and will live on forever. But if we behold it resting on Christ and [see it] overcome by his resurrection, and then boldly believe this, even it is dead and nullified. Sin cannot remain on Christ, since it is swallowed up by his resurrection. Now you see no wounds, no pain in him, and no sign of sin. Thus St. Paul declares that "Christ died for our sin and rose for our justification" [Rom. 4:25]. That is to say, in his suffering Christ makes our sin known and thus destroys it, but through his resurrection he justifies us and delivers us from all sin, if we believe this.

14. If, as was said before, you cannot believe, you must entreat God for faith. This too rests entirely in the hands of God. What we said about suffering also applies here, namely, that sometimes faith is granted openly, sometimes in secret.

However, you can spur yourself on to believe. First of all, you must no longer contemplate the suffering of Christ (for this has already done its work and terrified you), but pass beyond that and see his friendly heart and how this heart beats with such love for you that it impels him to bear with pain your conscience and your sin. Then your heart will be filled with love for him, and the confidence of your faith will be strengthened. Now continue and rise beyond Christ's heart to God's heart and you will see that Christ would not have shown this love for you if God in his eternal love had not wanted this, for Christ's love for you is due to his obedience to God. Thus you will find the divine and kind paternal heart, and, as Christ says, you will be drawn to the Father through him. Then you will understand the words of Christ, "For God so loved the world that he gave his only Son, etc." [John 3:16]. We know God aright when we grasp him not in his might or wisdom (for then he proves terrifying), but in his kindness and love. Then faith and confidence are able to exist, and then man is truly born anew in God.

15. After your heart has thus become firm in Christ, and love, not fear of pain, has made you a foe of sin, then Christ's passion must from that day on become a pattern for your entire life. Henceforth you will have to see his passion differently. Until now we regarded it as a sacrament which is active in us while we are passive, but now we find that we too must be active, namely, in the following. If pain or sickness afflicts you, consider how paltry this is in comparison with the thorny crown and the nails of Christ. If you are obliged to do or to refrain from doing things

against your wishes, ponder how Christ was bound and captured and led hither and yon. If you are beset by pride, see how your Lord was mocked and ridiculed along with criminals. If unchastity and lust assail you, remember how ruthlessly Christ's tender flesh was scourged, pierced, and beaten. If hatred, envy, and vindictiveness beset you, recall that Christ, who indeed had more reason to avenge himself, interceded with tears and cries for you and for all his enemies. If sadness or any adversity, physical or spiritual, distresses you, strengthen your heart and say, "Well, why should I not be willing to bear a little grief, when agonies and fears caused my Lord to sweat blood in the Garden of Gethsemane? He who lies abed while his master struggles in the throes of death is indeed a slothful and disgraceful servant."

So then, this is how we can draw strength and encouragement from Christ against every vice and failing. That is a proper contemplation of Christ's passion, and such are its fruits. And he who exercises himself in that way does better than to listen to every story of Christ's passion or to read all the masses. This is not to say that masses are of no value, but they do not help us in such meditation and exercise.

Those who thus make Christ's life and name a part of their own lives are true Christians. St. Paul says, "Those who belong to Christ have crucified their flesh with all its desires" [Gal. 5:24]. Christ's passion must be met not with words or forms, but with life and truth. Thus St. Paul exhorts us, "Consider him who endured such hostility from evil people against himself, so that you may be strengthened and not be weary at heart" [Heb. 12:3]. And St. Peter, "Since therefore Christ suffered in the flesh, strengthen and arm yourselves by meditating on this" [1

Pet. 4:1]. However, such meditation has become rare, although the letters of St. Paul and St. Peter abound with it. We have transformed the essence into semblance and painted our meditations on Christ's passion on walls and made them into letters.

From LW *vol. 42, 7–14.*

21. *To the Christian Nobility of the German Nation Concerning the Reform of the Christian Estate* (1520)

The year 1520 was a watershed for Luther. On June 15, Pope Leo X had issued his bull *Exsurge Domine* condemning Luther's teaching. Luther's *To the Christian Nobility* appeared in August, and *The Babylonian Captivity of the Church*, an attack on the sacramental system, was published in October. Then in early November came the *pièce de résistance*, his "The Freedom of a Christian." Here, in *To the Christian Nobility*, Luther argues that the Roman Catholic Church had made itself impervious to reform, and that therefore the political authorities should take matters into their own hands.

The Romanists have very cleverly built three walls around themselves. Hitherto they have protected themselves by these walls in such a way that no one has been able to reform them. As a result, the whole of Christendom has fallen abominably.

In the first place, when pressed by the temporal power they have made decrees and declared that the temporal power had no jurisdiction over them, but that, on the contrary, the spiritual power is above the temporal. In the second place, when the attempt is made to reprove them with the Scriptures, they raise the objection that only the pope may interpret the Scriptures. In the third place, if threatened with a council, their story is that no one may summon a council but the pope.

In this way they have cunningly stolen our three rods from us, that they may go unpunished. They have ensconced themselves within the safe stronghold of these three walls so that they can practice all the knavery and wickedness which we see today. Even when they have been compelled to hold a council they have weakened its power in advance by putting the princes under oath to let them remain as they were. In addition, they have given the pope full authority over all decisions of a council, so that it is all the same whether there are many councils or no councils. They only deceive us with puppet shows and sham fights. They fear terribly for their skin in a really free council! They have so intimidated kings and princes with this technique that they believe it would be an offense against God not to be obedient to the Romanists in all their knavish and ghoulish deceits.

May God help us, and give us just one of those trumpets with which the walls of Jericho were overthrown to blast down these walls of straw and paper in the same way and set free the Christian rods for the punishment of sin, [and] bring to light the craft and deceit of the devil, to the end that through punishment we may reform ourselves and once more attain God's favor.

Let us begin by attacking the first wall. It is pure invention that pope, bishop, priests, and monks are called the spiritual estate while princes, lords, artisans, and farmers are called the temporal estate. This is indeed a piece of deceit and hypocrisy. Yet no one

need be intimidated by it, and for this reason: all Christians are truly of the spiritual estate, and there is no difference among them except that of office. Paul says in 1 Corinthians 12 [:12-13] that we are all one body, yet every member has its own work by which it serves the others. This is because we all have one baptism, one gospel, one faith, and are all Christians alike; for baptism, gospel, and faith alone make us spiritual and a Christian people.

The pope or bishop anoints, shaves heads, ordains, consecrates, and prescribes garb different from that of the laity, but he can never make a man into a Christian or into a spiritual man by so doing. He might well make a man into a hypocrite or a humbug and blockhead, but never a Christian or a spiritual man. As far as that goes, we are all consecrated priests through baptism, as St. Peter says in 1 Peter 2 [:9], "You are a royal priesthood and a priestly realm." The Apocalypse says, "Thou hast made us to be priests and kings by thy blood" [Rev. 5:9-10]. The consecration by pope or bishop would never make a priest, and if we had no higher consecration than that which pope or bishop gives, no one could say mass or preach a sermon or give absolution.

Therefore, when a bishop consecrates it is nothing else than that in the place and stead of the whole community, all of whom have like power, he takes a person and charges him to exercise this power on behalf of the others. It is like ten brothers, all king's sons and equal heirs, choosing one of themselves to rule the inheritance in the interests of all. In one sense they are all kings and of equal power, and yet one of them is charged with the responsibility of ruling. To put it still more clearly: suppose a group of earnest Christian laymen were taken prisoner and set down in a desert without an episcopally ordained priest among them. And suppose they were to come to a common mind there and then in the desert and elect one of their number, whether he were married or not, and charge him to baptize, say mass, pronounce absolution, and preach the gospel. Such a man would be as truly a priest as though he had been ordained by all the bishops and popes in the world. That is why in cases of necessity anyone can baptize and give absolution. This would be impossible if we were not all priests. Through canon law the Romanists have almost destroyed and made unknown the wondrous grace and authority of baptism and justification. In times gone by, Christians used to choose their bishops without all the fuss that goes on nowadays. St. Augustine, Ambrose, and Cyprian each became [a bishop in this way]. . . .

It follows from this argument that there is no true, basic difference between laymen and priests, princes and bishops, between religious and secular, except for the sake of office and work, but not for the sake of status. They are all of the spiritual estate, all are truly priests, bishops, and popes. But they do not all have the same work to do. Just as all priests and monks do not have the same work. This is the teaching of St. Paul in Romans 12 [:4-5] and 1 Corinthians 12 [:12] and in 1 Peter 2 [:9], as I have said above, namely, that we are all one body of Christ the Head, and all members one of another. Christ does not have two different bodies, one temporal, the other spiritual. There is but one Head and one body.

Therefore, just as those who are now called "spiritual," that is, priests, bishops, or popes, are neither different from other Christians nor superior to them, except that they are charged with the administration of the

Word of God and the sacraments, which is their work and office, so it is with the temporal authorities. They bear the sword and rod in their hand to punish the wicked and protect the good. A cobbler, a smith, a peasant—each has the work and office of his trade, and yet they are all alike consecrated priests and bishops. Further, everyone must benefit and serve every other by means of his own work or office so that in this way many kinds of work may be done for the bodily and spiritual welfare of the community, just as all members of the body serve one another [1 Cor. 12:14-26]. . . .

So, then, I think this first paper wall is overthrown. Inasmuch as the temporal power has become a member of the Christian body it is a spiritual estate, even though its work is physical. Therefore, its work should extend without hindrance to all the members of the whole body to punish and use force whenever guilt deserves or necessity demands, without regard to whether the culprit is pope, bishop, or priest. Let the Romanists hurl threats and bans about as they like. That is why guilty priests, when they are handed over to secular law, are first deprived of their priestly dignities. This would not be right unless the secular sword previously had had authority over these priests by divine right. Moreover, it is intolerable that in canon law so much importance is attached to the freedom, life, and property of the clergy, as though the laity were not also as spiritual and as good Christians as they, or did not also belong to the church. Why are your life and limb, your property and honor, so cheap and mine not, inasmuch as we are all Christians and have the same baptism, the same faith, the same Spirit, and all the rest? If a priest is murdered, the whole country is placed under interdict. Why not when a peasant is murdered? How does this great difference come between two men who are both Christians? It comes from the laws and fabrications of men. . . .

The second wall is still more loosely built and less substantial. The Romanists want to be the only masters of Holy Scripture, although they never learn a thing from the Bible all their life long. They assume the sole authority for themselves, and, quite unashamed, they play about with the words before our very eyes, trying to persuade us that the pope cannot err in matters of faith, regardless of whether he is righteous or wicked. Yet they cannot point to a single letter. This is why so many heretical and unchristian, even unnatural, ordinances stand in the canon law. But there is no need to talk about these ordinances at present. Since these Romanists think the Holy Spirit never leaves them, no matter how ignorant and wicked they are, they become bold and decree only what they want. And if what they claim were true, why have Holy Scripture at all? Of what use is Scripture? Let us burn the Scripture and be satisfied with the unlearned gentlemen at Rome who possess the Holy Spirit! And yet the Holy Spirit can be possessed only by pious hearts. If I had not read the words with my own eyes, I would not have believed it possible for the devil to have made such stupid claims at Rome, and to have won supporters for them.

But so as not to fight them with mere words, we will quote the Scriptures. St. Paul says in 1 Corinthians 14 [:30], "If something better is revealed to anyone, though he is already sitting and listening to another in God's word, then the one who is speaking shall hold his peace and give place." What would be the point of this commandment if we were compelled to believe only the man who is talking, or the man who is at the top? Even Christ said in John 6 [:45] that all Christians shall be taught by God. If it were to happen that the pope and his cohorts were wicked and not true Christians, were not taught by God and were without understanding, and at the same time some obscure person had a right understanding, why should the people not follow the obscure man? Has the pope not erred many times? Who would help Christendom when the pope erred if we did not have somebody we could trust more than him, somebody who had the Scriptures on his side?

Therefore, their claim that only the pope may interpret Scripture is an outrageous fancied fable. They cannot produce a single letter [of Scripture] to maintain that the interpretation of Scripture or the confirmation of its interpretation belongs to the pope alone. They themselves have usurped this power. And although they allege that this power was given to St. Peter when the keys were given to him, it is clear enough that the keys were not given to Peter alone but to the whole community. Further, the keys were not ordained for the doctrine or government, but only for the binding or loosing of sin. Whatever else or whatever more they arrogate to themselves on the basis of the keys is a mere fabrication. But Christ's words to Peter, "I have prayed for you that your faith fail not" [Luke 22:32], cannot be applied to the pope, since the majority of the popes have been without faith, as they must themselves confess. Besides, it is not only for Peter that Christ prayed, but also for all apostles and Christians, as he says in John 17 [:9, 20], "Father, I pray for those whom thou hast given me, and not for these only, but for all who believe on me through their word." Is that not clear enough? . . .

The third wall falls of itself when the first two are down. When the pope acts contrary to the Scriptures, it is our duty to stand by the Scriptures, to reprove him and to constrain him, according to the word of Christ, Matthew 18 [:15-17], "If your brother sins against you, go and tell it to him, between you and him alone; if he does not listen to you, then take one or two others with you; if he does not listen to them, tell it to the church; if he does not listen to the church, consider him a heathen." Here every member is commanded to care for every other. How much more should we do this when the member that does evil is responsible for the government of the church, and by his evil-doing is the cause of much harm and offense to the rest! But if I am to accuse him before the church, I must naturally call the church together.

The Romanists have no basis in Scripture for their claim that the pope alone has the right to call or confirm a council. This is just their own ruling, and it is only valid as long as it is not harmful to Christendom or contrary to the laws of God. Now when the pope deserves punishment, this ruling no longer obtains, for not to punish him by authority of a council is harmful to Christendom.

Thus we read in Acts 15 that it was not St. Peter who called the apostolic council but the apostles and the elders. If then that right had belonged to St. Peter alone, the council would not have been a Christian council, but a heretical *conciliabulum*. Even the Council of Nicaea, the most famous of all councils, was neither called nor confirmed by the bishop of Rome, but by the emperor Constantine. Many other emperors after him have done the same, and yet these councils were the most Christian of all. But if the pope alone has the right to convene councils, then these councils would have all been heretical. Further, when I examine the councils the pope did summon, I find that they did nothing of special importance.

Therefore, when necessity demands it, and the pope is an offense to Christendom, the first man who is able should, as a true member of the whole body, do what he can to bring about a truly free council. No one can do this so well as the temporal authorities, especially since they are also fellow-Christians, fellow-priests, fellow-members of the spiritual estate, fellow-lords over all things. Whenever it is necessary or profitable they ought to exercise the office and work which they have received from God over everyone. Would it not be unnatural if a fire broke out in a city and everybody were to stand by and let it burn on and on and consume everything that could burn because nobody had the authority of the mayor, or because, perhaps, the fire broke out in the mayor's house? In such a situation is it not the duty of every citizen to arouse and summon the rest? How much more should this be done in the spiritual city of Christ if a fire of offense breaks out, whether in the papal government, or anywhere else! The same argument holds if an enemy were to attack a city. The man who first roused the others deserves honor and gratitude. Why, then, should he not deserve honor who makes known the presence of the enemy from hell and rouses Christian people and calls them together?

But all their boasting about an authority which dare not be opposed amounts to nothing at all. Nobody in Christendom has authority to do injury or to forbid the resisting of injury. There is no authority in the church except to promote good. Therefore, if the pope were to use his authority to prevent the calling of a free council, thereby preventing the improvement of the church, we should have regard neither for him nor for his authority. And if he were to hurl his bans and thunderbolts, we should despise his conduct as that of a madman. On the contrary, we should excommunicate him and drive him out as best we could, relying completely upon God. This presumptuous authority of his is nothing. He does not even have such authority. He is quickly defeated by a single text of Scripture, where Paul says to the Corinthians, "God has given us authority not to ruin Christendom but to build it up" [2 Cor. 10:8]. Such power is not to be obeyed, but rather resisted with life, property, and with all our might and main. . . .

We shall now look at the matters which ought to be properly dealt with in councils, matters with which the popes, cardinals, bishops, and all scholars ought properly to be occupied day and night if they loved Christ and his church. But if this is not the case, let ordinary people and the temporal authorities do it without regard to papal bans and fulminations, for an unjust ban is better than ten just and proper absolutions, and one unjust, improper absolution is worse than ten just bans. Therefore, let us awake, dear Germans, and fear God more than man [Acts 5:29], lest we suffer the same fate of all the poor souls who are so lamentably lost through the shameless, devilish rule of the Romanists. The devil grows stronger every day, if such a thing were possible, if such a hellish regime could grow any worse—a thing I can neither conceive nor believe. . . .

It is horrible and shocking to see the head of Christendom, who boasts that he is the vicar of Christ and successor of St. Peter, going about in such a worldly and ostentatious style that neither king nor emperor can equal or approach him. He claims the title of "most holy" and "most spiritual," and yet he is more worldly than the world itself. He wears a triple crown, whereas the highest monarchs wear but one. If that is like the poverty of Christ and of St. Peter, then it is a new and strange kind of likeness! When anybody says anything against it, the Romanists bleat, "Heresy!" They refuse to hear how unchristian and ungodly all this is. In my opinion, if the pope were to pray to God with tears, he would have to lay aside his triple crown, for the God we worship cannot put up with pride. In fact, the pope's office should be nothing else but to weep and pray for Christendom and to set an example of utter humility. . . .

Now, although I am too insignificant a man to make propositions for the improvement of this dreadful state of affairs, nevertheless I shall sing my fool's song through to the end and say, so far as I am able, what could and should be done, either by the temporal authority or by a general council.

1. Every prince, every noble, every city should henceforth forbid their subjects to pay annates to Rome and should abolish them entirely. . . .

2. Since the pope with his Romanist practices—his commends, coadjutors, reservations, *gratiae expectativae,* papal months, incorporations, unions, pensions, pallia, chancery rules, and such knavery—usurps for himself all the German foundations without authority and right, and gives and sells them to foreigners at Rome who do nothing for Germany in return, and since he robs the local bishops of their rights and makes mere ciphers and dummies of them, and thereby acts contrary to his own canon law, common sense, and reason, it has finally reached the point where the livings and benefices are sold to coarse, unlettered asses and ignorant knaves at Rome

out of sheer greed. Pious and learned people do not benefit from the service or skill of these fellows. Consequently the poor German people must go without competent and learned prelates and go from bad to worse.

For this reason the Christian nobility should set itself against the pope as against a common enemy and destroyer of Christendom for the salvation of the poor souls who perish because of this tyranny.

3. An imperial law should be issued that no bishop's cloak and no confirmation of any dignity whatsoever shall henceforth be secured from Rome, but that the ordinance of the most holy and famous Council of Nicaea be restored. This ordinance decreed that a bishop shall be confirmed by the two nearest bishops or by the archbishop. . . .

4. It should be decreed that no temporal matter is to be referred to Rome, but that all such cases shall be left to the temporal authority, as the Romanists themselves prescribe in that canon law of theirs, which they do not observe. . . .

5. Reservations should no longer be valid, and no more benefices should be seized by Rome, even if the incumbent dies, or there is a dispute, or even if the incumbent is a member of the pope's household or on the staff of a cardinal. . . .

6. The *casus reservati,* reserved cases, should also be abolished. . . .

7. The Roman see should do away with the *officia,* and cut down the creeping, crawling swarm of vermin at Rome, so that the pope's household can be supported out of the pope's own pocket. . . .

8. The harsh and terrible oaths which the bishops are wrongfully compelled to swear to the pope should be abolished. . . .

9. The pope should have no authority over the emperor, except the right to anoint and crown him at the altar just as a bishop crowns a king. . . .

10. The pope should restrain himself, take his fingers out of the pie, and claim no title to the kingdom of Naples and Sicily. . . .

Further, the kissing of the pope's feet should cease. . . .

12. Pilgrimages to Rome should either be abolished or else no one should be allowed to make such a pilgrimage for reasons of curiosity or his own pious devotion, unless it is first acknowledged by his parish priest, his town authorities, or his overlord that he has a good and sufficient reason for doing so. . . .

13. Next we come to the masses who make many vows but keep few. Do not be angry, my noble lords! I really mean it for the best. It is the bittersweet truth that the further building of mendicant houses should not be permitted. God help us, there are already too many of them. . . .

14. We also see how the priesthood has fallen, and how many a poor priest is overburdened with wife and child, his conscience troubled. . . .

15. Nor must I forget the poor monasteries. The evil spirit, who has now confused all the estates of life and made them unbearable through man-made laws, has taken possession of some abbots, abbesses, and prelates. As a result they govern their brothers and sisters in such a way that they quickly go to hell and lead a wretched existence here and now, as do the devil's martyrs. . . .

16. It is also necessary to abolish all endowed masses for the dead, or at least to reduce their number, since we plainly see that they have become nothing but a mockery. . . .

17. Certain penalties or punishments of canon law should be abolished, too, especially the interdict, which without any doubt was invented by the evil spirit. . . .

18. All festivals should be abolished, and Sunday alone retained. . . .

19. The grades or degrees within which a marriage is forbidden, such as those affecting godparents or the third and fourth degree of kinship, should be changed. If the pope in Rome can grant dispensations and scandalously sell them for money, then every priest may give the same dispensations without price and for the salvation of souls. . . .

20. The chapels in forests and the churches in fields, such as Wilsnack, Sternberg, Trier, The Grimmenthal, and now Regensburg and a goodly number of others which recently have become the goal of pilgrimages, must be leveled. . . .

21. One of the greatest necessities is the abolition of all begging throughout Christendom. Nobody ought to go begging among Christians. It would even be a very simple matter to make a law to the effect that every city should look after its own poor, if only we had the courage and the intention to do so. . . .

22. It is also to be feared that the many masses which were endowed in ecclesiastical foundations and monasteries are not only of little use, but arouse the great wrath of God. It would therefore be profitable not to endow any more of these masses, but rather to abolish many that are already endowed. . . .

23. The brotherhoods, and for that matter, indulgences, letters of indulgence, butter letters, mass letters, dispensations, and everything of that kind, should be snuffed out and brought to an end. There is nothing good about them. . . .

24. It is high time we took up the Bohemian question and dealt seriously and honestly with it. We should come to an understanding with them so that the terrible slander, hatred, and envy on both sides comes to an end. . . .

25. The universities, too, need a good, thorough reformation. . . .

That is enough for the moment. (I think I have said enough in my little book *Treatise on Good Works* about what the secular authorities and the nobility ought to do. There is certainly room for improvement in their lives and in their rule, yet the abuses of the temporal power are not to be compared with those of the spiritual power, as I have shown in that book.)

I know full well that I have been very outspoken. I have made many suggestions that will be considered impractical. I have attacked many things too severely. But how else ought I to do it? I am duty-bound to speak. If I had the power, these are the things I would do. I would rather have the wrath of the world upon me than the wrath of God. The world can do no more to me than take my life. In the past I have made frequent overtures of peace to my enemies, but as I see it, God has compelled me through them to keep on opening my mouth wider and wider and to give them enough to say, bark, shout, and write because they have nothing else to do. Well, I know another little song about Rome and the Romanists. If their ears are itching to hear it, I will sing that one to them, too— and pitch it in the highest key! You understand what I mean, dear Rome.

Moreover, many times have I offered my writings for investigation and hearing, but to no avail. Nevertheless, I know full well that if my cause is just, it must be condemned on earth and be justified only by Christ in heaven, for all the Scriptures show that the cause of Christians and of Christendom must be judged by God alone. Moreover, no cause has ever yet been justified on earth by men because the opposition has always been too great and too strong. It is still my greatest concern and anxiety that my cause may not be condemned, by which I would know for certain that it is not yet pleasing to God.

Therefore, just let them go hard at it, pope, bishop, priest, monk, or scholar. They are just the ones to persecute the truth, as they have always done.

God give us all a Christian mind, and grant to the Christian nobility of the German nation in particular true spiritual courage to do the best they can for the poor church. Amen.

☩

From LW vol. 44, 126–40, 156–217.

22. *The Freedom of a Christian* (1520)

This treatise, published in early November, is an early and succinct statement of Luther's most fundamental theological idea. Two influential Augustinian friends had pressed him to write a conciliatory letter to the pope. This he now did, though it was laced with sly ambiguity. And to it he appended *The Freedom of a Christian.*

☩

To Leo X, Pope at Rome, Martin Luther wishes salvation in Christ Jesus our Lord. Amen.

Living among the monsters of this age with whom I am now for the third year waging war, I am compelled occasionally to look up to you, Leo, most blessed father, and to think of you. Indeed, since you are occasionally regarded as the sole cause of my warfare, I cannot help thinking of you. To be sure, the undeserved raging of your godless flatterers against me has compelled me to appeal from your see to a future council, despite the decrees of your predecessors Pius and Julius, who with a foolish tyranny forbade such an appeal. Nevertheless, I have never alienated myself from your Blessedness to such an extent that I should not with all my heart wish you and your see every blessing, for which I have besought God with earnest prayers to the best of my ability. It is true that I have been so bold as to despise and look down upon those who have tried to frighten me with the majesty of your name and authority. There is one thing, however, which I cannot ignore and which is the cause of my writing once more to your Blessedness. It has come to my attention that I am accused of great indiscretion, said to be my great fault, in which, it is said, I have not spared even your person.

I freely vow that I have, to my knowledge, spoken only good and honorable words concerning you whenever I have thought of you. If I had ever done otherwise, I myself could by no means condone it, but should agree entirely with the judgment which others have formed of me; and I should do nothing more gladly than recant such indiscretion and impiety. I have called you a Daniel in Babylon; and everyone who reads what I have written knows how zealously I defended your innocence against your defamer Sylvester. Indeed, your reputation and the fame of your blameless life, celebrated as they are throughout the world. . . .

I have truly despised your see, the Roman Curia, which, however, neither you nor anyone else can deny is more corrupt than any Babylon or Sodom ever was, and which, as far as I can see, is characterized by a completely depraved, hopeless, and notorious godlessness. I have been thoroughly incensed over the fact that good Christians are mocked in your name and under the cloak of the Roman church I have resisted and will continue to resist your see as long as the spirit of faith lives in me. Not that I shall strive for the impossible or hope that by my efforts alone anything will be accomplished in that most disordered Babylon, where the fury of so many flatterers is turned against me; but I acknowledge my indebtedness to my Christian brethren, whom I am duty-bound to warn so that fewer of them may be destroyed by the plagues of Rome, at least so that their destruction may be less cruel.

As you well know, there has been flowing from Rome these many years—like a flood covering the world—nothing but a devastation of men's bodies and souls and possessions, the worst examples of the worst of all things. All this is clearer than day to all, and the Roman church, once the holiest of all, has become the most licentious den of thieves [Matt. 21:13], the most shameless of all brothels, the kingdom of sin, death, and hell. It is so bad that even Antichrist himself, if he should come, could think of nothing to add to its wickedness.

Meanwhile you, Leo, sit as a lamb in the midst of wolves [Matt. 10:16] and like Daniel in the midst of lions [Dan. 6:16]. With Ezekiel you live among scorpions [Ezek. 2:6]. How can you alone oppose these monsters? Even if you would call to your aid three or four well-learned and thoroughly reliable cardinals, what are these among so many? You would all be poisoned before you could begin to issue a decree for the purpose of remedying the situation. The Roman Curia is already lost, for God's wrath has relentlessly fallen upon it. It detests church councils, it fears a reformation, it cannot allay its own corruption; and what was said of its mother Babylon also applies to it: "We would have cured Babylon, but she was not healed. Let us forsake her" [Jer. 51:9]. . . .

So I come, most blessed father, and, prostrate before you, pray that if possible you intervene and stop those flatterers, who are the enemies of peace while they pretend to keep peace. But let no person imagine that I will recant unless he prefer to involve the whole question in even greater turmoil. Furthermore, I acknowledge no fixed rules for the interpretation of the Word of God, since the Word of God, which teaches freedom in all other matters, must not be bound [2 Tim. 2:9]. If these two points are granted, there is nothing that I could not or would not most willingly do or endure. I detest contentions. I will challenge no one. On the other hand, I do not want others to challenge me. If they do, as Christ is my teacher, I will not be speechless. When once this controversy has been cited before you and settled, your Blessedness will be able with a brief and ready word to silence both parties and command them to keep the peace. That is what I have always wished to hear.

Therefore, my Father Leo, do not listen to those sirens who pretend that you are no mere man but a demigod so that you may command and require whatever you wish. It will not be done in that manner and you will not have such remarkable power. You are a servant of servants, and more than all other men you are in a most miserable and dangerous position. Be not deceived by those who pretend that you are lord of the world, allow no one to be considered a Christian unless he accepts your authority, and prate that you have power over heaven, hell, and purgatory. These men are your enemies who seek to destroy your soul [1 Kings 19:10], as Isaiah says: "O my people, they that call thee blessed, the same deceive thee" [Isa. 3:12]. They err who exalt you above a council and the church universal. They err who ascribe to you alone the right of interpreting Scripture. Under the protection of your name they seek to gain support for all their wicked deeds in the church. Alas! Through them Satan has already made much progress under your predecessors. In short, believe none who exalt you, believe those who humble you. This is the judgment of God, that ". . . he has put down the mighty from their thrones and exalted those of low degree" [Luke 1:52]. See how different Christ is from his successors, although they all would wish to be his vicars. I fear that most of them have been too literally his vicars. A man is a vicar only when his superior is absent. If the pope rules, while Christ is absent and does not dwell in his heart, what else is he but a vicar of Christ? What is the church under such a vicar but a mass of people without Christ? Indeed, what is such a vicar but an Antichrist and an idol? How much more properly did the apostles call themselves servants of the present Christ and not vicars of an absent Christ?

Perhaps I am presumptuous in trying to instruct so exalted a personage from whom we all should learn and from whom the thrones of judges receive their decisions, as those pestilential fellows of yours boast. But I am following the example of St. Bernard in his book, *On Consideration,* to Pope Eugenius, a book every pope should know from memory. I follow him, not because I am eager to instruct you, but out of pure and loyal concern which compels us to be interested in all the affairs of our neighbors, even when they are protected, and which does not permit us to take into consideration either their dignity or lack of dignity since it is only concerned with the dangers they face or the advantages they may gain. I know that your Blessedness is driven and buffeted about in Rome, that is, that far out at sea you are threatened on all sides by dangers and are working very hard in the miserable situation so that you are in need of even the slightest help of the least of

your brothers. Therefore I do not consider it absurd if I now forget your exalted office and do what brotherly love demands. I have no desire to flatter you in so serious and dangerous a matter. If men do not perceive that I am your friend and your most humble subject in this matter, there is One who understands and judges [John 8:50].

Finally, that I may not approach you empty-handed, blessed father, I am sending you this little treatise dedicated to you as a token of peace and good hope. From this book you may judge with what studies I should prefer to be more profitably occupied, as I could be, provided your godless flatterers would permit me and had permitted me in the past. It is a small book if you regard its size. Unless I am mistaken, however, it contains the whole of Christian life in a brief form, provided you grasp its meaning. I am a poor man and have no other gift to offer, and you do not need to be enriched by any but a spiritual gift. May the Lord Jesus preserve you forever. Amen.

A Christian is a perfectly free lord of all, subject to none.

A Christian is a perfectly dutiful servant of all, subject to all.

These two theses seem to contradict each other. If, however, they should be found to fit together they would serve our purpose beautifully. Both are Paul's own statements, who says in 1 Cor. 9 [:19], "For though I am free from all men, I have made myself a slave to all," and in Rom. 13 [:8], "Owe no one anything, except to love one another." Love by its very nature is ready to serve and be subject to him who is loved. So Christ, although he was Lord of all, was "born of woman, born under the law" [Gal. 4:4], and therefore was at the same time a free man and a servant, "in the form of God" and "of a servant" [Phil. 2:6-7].

Let us start, however, with something more remote from our subject, but more obvious. Man has a twofold nature, a spiritual and a bodily one. According to the spiritual nature, which men refer to as the soul, he is called a spiritual, inner, or new man. According to the bodily nature, which men refer to as flesh, he is called a carnal, outward, or old man, of whom the apostle writes in 2 Cor. 4 [:16], "Though our outer nature is wasting away, our inner nature is being renewed every day." Because of this diversity of nature the Scriptures assert contradictory things concerning the same man, since these two men in the same man contradict each other, "for the desires of the flesh are against the Spirit, and the desires of the Spirit are against the flesh," according to Gal. 5 [:17].

First, let us consider the inner man to see how a righteous, free, and pious Christian, that is, a spiritual, new, and inner man, becomes what he is. It is evident that no external thing has any influence in producing Christian righteousness or freedom, or in producing unrighteousness or servitude. A simple argument will furnish the proof of this statement. What can it profit the soul if the body is well, free, and active, and eats, drinks, and does as it pleases? For in these respects even the most godless slaves of vice may prosper. On the other hand, how will poor health or imprisonment or hunger or thirst or any other external misfortune harm the soul? Even the most godly men, and those who are free because of clear consciences, are afflicted with these things. None of these things touches either the freedom or the servitude of the soul. It does not help the soul if the body is adorned with the sacred robes of priests or dwells in sacred places or is occupied with sacred duties or prays, fasts, abstains from certain kinds of food, or does any work that can be done by the body and in the body. The righteousness and the freedom of the soul require something far different since the things which have been mentioned could be done by any wicked person. Such works produce nothing but hypocrites. On the other hand, it will not harm the soul if the body is clothed in secular dress, dwells in unconsecrated places, eats and drinks as others do, does not pray aloud, and neglects to do all the abovementioned things which hypocrites can do.

Furthermore, to put aside all kinds of works, even contemplation, meditation, and all that the soul can do, does not help. One thing, and only one thing, is necessary for Christian life, righteousness, and freedom. That one thing is the most holy Word of God, the gospel of Christ, as Christ says, John 11 [:25], "I am the resurrection and the life; he who believes in me, though he die, yet shall he live"; and John 8 [:36], "So if the Son makes you free, you will be free indeed"; and Matt. 4 [:4], "Man shall not live by bread alone, but by every word that proceeds from the mouth of God." Let us then consider it certain and firmly established that the soul can do without anything except the Word of God and that where the Word of God is missing there is no help at all for the soul. If it has the Word of God it is rich and lacks nothing since it is the Word of life, truth, light, peace, righteousness, salvation, joy, liberty, wisdom, power, grace, glory, and of every incalculable blessing. This is why the prophet in the entire psalm [119] and in many other places yearns and sighs for the Word of God and uses so many names to describe it.

On the other hand, there is no more terrible disaster with which the wrath of God can afflict men than a famine of the hearing of his Word, as he says in Amos [8:11]. Likewise there is no greater mercy than when he sends forth his Word, as we read in Psalm 107 [:20]: "He sent forth his word, and healed them, and delivered them from destruction." Nor was Christ sent into the world for any other ministry except that of the Word. Moreover, the entire spiritual estate—all the apostles, bishops, and priests—has been called and instituted only for the ministry of the Word.

You may ask, "What then is the Word of God, and how shall it be used, since there are so many words of God?" I answer: The apostle explains this in Romans 1. The Word is the gospel of God concerning his Son, who was made flesh, suffered, rose from the dead, and was glorified through the Spirit who sanctifies. To preach Christ means to feed the soul, make it righteous, set it free, and save it, provided it believes the preaching. Faith alone is the saving and efficacious use of the Word of God, according to Rom. 10 [:9]: "If you confess with your lips that Jesus is Lord and believe in your heart that God raised him from the dead, you will be saved." Furthermore, "Christ is the end of the law, that every one who has faith may be justified" [Rom. 10:4]. Again, in Rom. 1 [:17], "He who through faith is righteous shall live." The Word of God cannot be received and cherished by any works whatever but only by faith. Therefore it is clear that, as the soul needs only the Word of God for its life and righteousness, so it is justified by faith alone and not any works; for if it could be justified by anything else, it would not need the Word, and consequently it would not need faith. . . .

Should you ask how it happens that faith alone justifies and offers us such a treasure of great benefits without works in view of the fact that so many works, ceremonies, and laws are prescribed in the Scriptures, I answer: First of all, remember what has been said, namely, that faith alone, without works, justifies, frees, and saves; we shall make this clearer later on. Here we must point out that the entire Scripture of God is divided into two parts: commandments and promises. Although the commandments teach things that are good, the things taught are not done as soon as they are taught, for the commandments show us what we ought to do but do not give us the power to do it. They are intended to teach man to know himself, that through them he may recognize his inability to do good and may despair of his own ability. That is why they are called the Old Testament and constitute the Old Testament. For example, the commandment, "You shall not covet" [Exod. 20:17], is a command which proves us all to be sinners, for no one can avoid coveting no matter how much he may struggle against it. Therefore, in order not to covet and to fulfill the commandment, a man is compelled to despair of himself, to seek the help which he does not find in himself elsewhere and from someone else, as stated in Hosea [13:9]: "Destruction is your own, O Israel: your help is only in me." As we fare with respect to one commandment, so we fare with all, for it is equally impossible for us to keep any one of them. . . . From what has been said it is easy to see from what source faith derives such great power and why a good work or all good works together cannot equal it. No good work can rely upon the Word of God or live in the soul, for faith alone and the Word of God rule in the soul. Just as the heated iron glows like fire because of the union of fire with it, so the Word imparts its qualities to the soul. It is clear, then, that a Christian has all that he needs in faith and needs no works to justify him; and if he has no need of works, he has no need of the law; and if he has no need of the law, surely he is free from the law. It is true that "the law is not laid down for the just" [1 Tim. 1:9]. This is that Christian liberty, our faith, which does not induce us to live in idleness or wickedness but makes the law and works unnecessary for any man's righteousness and salvation.

This is the first power of faith. Let us now examine also the second. It is a further function of faith that it honors him whom it trusts with the most reverent and highest regard since it considers him truthful and trustworthy. There is no other honor equal to the estimate of truthfulness and righteousness with which we honor him whom we trust. Could we ascribe to a man anything greater than truthfulness and righteousness and perfect goodness? On the other hand, there is no way in which we can show greater contempt for a man than to regard him as false and wicked and to be suspicious of him, as we do when we do not trust him. So when the soul firmly trusts God's promises, it regards him as truthful and righteous. Nothing more excellent than this can be ascribed to God. The very highest worship of God is this: that we ascribe to him truthfulness, righteousness, and whatever else should be ascribed to one who is trusted. When this is done, the soul consents to his will. Then it hallows his name and allows itself to be treated according to God's good pleasure for, clinging to God's promises, it does not doubt that he who is true, just, and wise will do, dispose, and provide all things well. . . .

The third incomparable benefit of faith is that it unites the soul with Christ as a bride is united with her bridegroom. By this mystery, as the apostle teaches, Christ and the soul become one flesh [Eph. 5:31-32]. And if they are one flesh and there is between them a true marriage—indeed the most perfect of all marriages since human marriages are but poor examples of this one true marriage—it follows that everything they have they hold in common, the good as well as the evil. Accordingly the believing soul can boast of and glory in whatever Christ has as though it were its own, and whatever the soul has Christ claims as his own. Let us compare these and we shall see inestimable benefits. Christ is full of grace, life, and salvation. The soul is full of sins, death, and damnation. Now let faith come between them and sins, death and damnation will be Christ's, while grace, life, and salvation will be the soul's; for if Christ is a bridegroom, he must take upon himself the things which are his bride's and bestow upon her the things that are his. If he gives her his body and very self, how shall he not give her all that is his? And if he takes the body of the bride how shall he not take all that is hers?

Not only are we the freest of kings, we are also priests forever, which is far more excellent than being kings, for as priests we are worthy to appear before God to pray for others and to teach one another divine things. These are the functions of priests, and they cannot be granted to any unbeliever. Thus Christ has made it possible for us, provided we believe in him, to be not only his brethren, co-heirs, and fellow-kings, but also his fellow-priests. Therefore we may boldly come into the presence of God in the spirit of faith [Heb. 10:19, 22] and cry "Abba, Father!" pray for one another, and do all things which we see done and foreshadowed in the outer and visible works of priests.

He, however, who does not believe is not served by anything. On the contrary, nothing works for his good, but he himself is a servant of all, and all things turn out badly for him because he wickedly uses them to his own advantage and not to the glory of God. So he is no priest but a wicked man whose prayer becomes sin and who never comes into the presence of God because God does not hear sinners [John 9:31]. Who then can comprehend the lofty dignity of the Christian? By virtue of his royal power he rules over all things, death, life, and sin, and through his priestly glory is omnipotent with God because he does the things which God asks and desires, as it is written, "He will fulfill the desire of those who fear him; he also will hear their cry and save them" [cf. Phil. 4:13]. To this glory a man attains, certainly not by any works of his, but by faith alone.

From this anyone can clearly see how a Christian is free from all things and over all things so that he needs no works to make him righteous and save him, since faith alone abundantly confers all these things. Should he grow so foolish, however, as to presume to become righteous, free, saved, and a Christian by means of some good work, he would instantly lose faith and all its benefits, a foolishness aptly illustrated in the fable of the dog who runs along a stream with a piece of meat in his mouth and, deceived by the reflection of the meat in the water, opens his mouth to snap at it and so loses both the meat and the reflection. . . .

To return to our purpose, I believe that it has now become clear that it is not enough or in any sense Christian to preach the works, life, and words of Christ as historical facts, as if the knowledge of these would suffice for the conduct of life; yet this is the fashion among those who must today be regarded as our best preachers. Far less is it sufficient or

Christian to say nothing at all about Christ and to teach instead the laws of men and the decrees of the Fathers. Now there are not a few who preach Christ and read about him that they may move men's affections to sympathy with Christ, to anger against the Jews, and such childish and effeminate nonsense. Rather ought Christ to be preached to the end that faith in him may be established that he may not only be Christ, but be Christ for you and me, and that what is said of him and is denoted in his name may be effectual in us. Such faith is produced and preserved in us by preaching why Christ came, what he brought and bestowed, what benefit it is to us to accept him. This is done when that Christian liberty which he bestows is rightly taught and we are told in what way we Christians are all kings and priests and therefore lords of all and may firmly believe that whatever we have done is pleasing and acceptable in the sight of God, as I have already said.

What man is there whose heart, upon hearing these things, will not rejoice to its depth, and when receiving such comfort will not grow tender so that he will love Christ as he never could by means of any laws or works? Who would have the power to harm or frighten such a heart? If the knowledge of sin or the fear of death should break in upon it, it is ready to hope in the Lord. It does not grow afraid when it hears tidings of evil. It is not disturbed when it sees its enemies. This is so because it believes that the righteousness of Christ is its own and that its sin is not its own, but Christ's, and that all sin is swallowed up by the righteousness of Christ. This, as has been said above, is a necessary consequence on account of faith in Christ. So the heart learns to scoff at death and sin and to say with the apostle, "O death, where is thy victory? O death, where is thy sting? The sting of death is sin, and the power of sin is the law. But thanks be to God, who gives us the victory through our Lord Jesus Christ" [1 Cor. 15:55-57]. Death is swallowed up not only in the victory of Christ but also by our victory, because through faith his victory has become ours and in that faith we also are conquerors.

Let this suffice concerning the inner man, his liberty, and the source of his liberty, the righteousness of faith. He needs neither laws nor good works but, on the contrary, is injured by them if he believes that he is justified by them.

Now let us turn to the second part, the outer man. Here we shall answer all those who, offended by the word "faith" and by all that has been said, now ask, "If faith does all things and is alone sufficient unto righteousness, why then are good works commanded? We will take our ease and do no works and be content with faith." I answer: not so, you wicked men, not so. That would indeed be proper if we were wholly inner and perfectly spiritual men. But such we shall be only at the last day, the day of the resurrection of the dead. As long as we live in the flesh we only begin to make some progress in that which shall be perfected in the future life. For this reason the Apostle in Romans 8 [:23] calls all that we attain in this life "the first fruits of the Spirit" because we shall indeed receive the greater portion, even the fullness of the Spirit, in the future. This is the place to assert that which was said above, namely, that a Christian is the servant of all and made subject to all. Insofar as he is free he does no works, but insofar as he is a servant he does all kinds of works. How this is possible we shall see.

Although, as I have said, a man is abundantly and sufficiently justified by faith inwardly, in his spirit, and so has all that he needs, except insofar as this faith and these riches must grow from day to day even to the future life; yet he remains in this mortal life on earth. In this life he must control his own body and have dealings with men. Here the works begin; here a man cannot enjoy leisure; here he must indeed take care to discipline his body by fastings, watchings, labors, and other reasonable discipline and to subject it to the Spirit so that it will obey and conform to the inner man and faith and not revolt against faith and hinder the inner man, as it is the nature of the body to do if it is not held in check. The inner man, who by faith is created in the image of God, is both joyful and happy because of Christ in whom so many benefits are conferred upon him; and therefore it is his one occupation to serve God joyfully and without thought of gain, in love that is not constrained.

While he is doing this, behold, he meets a contrary will in his own flesh which strives to serve the world and seeks its own advantage. This the spirit of faith cannot tolerate, but with joyful zeal it attempts to put the body under control and hold it in check, as Paul says in Romans 7 [:22-23], "For I delight in the law of God, in my inmost self, but I see in my members another law at war with the law of my mind and making me captive to the law of sin," and in another place, "But I pommel my body and subdue it, lest after preaching to others I myself should be disqualified" [1 Cor. 9:27], and in Galatians [5:24], "And those who belong to Christ Jesus have crucified the flesh with its passions and desires."

In doing these works, however, we must not think that a man is justified before God by them, for faith, which alone is righteousness before God, cannot endure that erroneous opinion. We must, however, realize that these works reduce the body to subjection and purify it of its evil lusts, and our whole purpose is to be directed only toward the driving out of lusts. Since by faith the soul is cleansed and made to love God, it desires that all things, and especially its own body, shall be purified so that all things may join with it in loving and praising God. Hence a man cannot be idle, for the need of his body drives him and he is compelled to do many good works to reduce it to subjection. Nevertheless the works themselves do not justify him before God, but he does the works out of spontaneous love in obedience to God and considers nothing except the approval of God, whom he would most scrupulously obey in all things. . . .

From LW vol. 31, 334–59.

23. Preface to the New Testament (1546/1522)

In May of 1521, for reasons having to do with his personal safety, Luther was taken to the Wartburg castle where he remained for the next months. There, in less than eleven weeks, he produced what was to become a classic—his German translation of the entire New Testament. In 1522 he wrote a preface for it which he revised in 1546. Because his translation was an instant best-seller, the preface is one of Luther's most influential writings. In it he tells the reader "what to look for in this book," namely, the "gospel" as he understood it. Here already was a highly significant qualification of his *sola scriptura* principle.

It would be right and proper for this book to go forth without any prefaces or extrane-

ous names attached and simply have its own say under its own name. However many unfounded [*wilde*] interpretations and prefaces have scattered the thought of Christians to a point where no one any longer knows what is gospel or law, New Testament or Old. Necessity demands, therefore, that there should be a notice or preface, by which the ordinary man can be rescued from his former delusions, set on the right track, and taught what he is to look for in this book, so that he may not seek laws and commandments where he ought to be seeking the gospel and promises of God.

Therefore it should be known, in the first place, that the notion must be given up that there are four gospels and only four evangelists. The division of the New Testament books into legal, historical, prophetic, and wisdom books is also to be utterly rejected. Some make this division, thinking thereby (I know not how) to compare the New with the Old Testament. On the contrary it is to be held firmly that . . .

Just as the Old Testament is a book in which are written God's laws and commandments, together with the history of those who kept and of those who did not keep them, so the New Testament is a book in which are written the gospel and the promises of God, together with the history of those who believe and of those who do not believe them.

For "gospel" [*Euangelium*] is a Greek word and means in Greek a good message, good tidings, good news, a good report which one sings and tells with gladness. For example, when David overcame the great Goliath, there came among the Jewish people the good report and encouraging news that their terrible enemy had been struck down and that they had been rescued and given joy and peace; and they sang and danced and were glad for it [1 Sam. 18:6].

Thus this gospel of God or New Testament is a good story and report, sounded forth into all the world by the apostles, telling of a true David who strove with sin, death, and the devil, and overcame them, and thereby rescued all those who were captive in sin, afflicted with death, and overpowered by the devil. Without any merit of their own he made them righteous, gave them life, and saved them, so that they were given peace and brought back to God. For this they sing, and thank and praise God, and are glad forever, if only they believe firmly and remain steadfast in faith.

This report and encouraging tidings, or evangelical and divine news, is also called a New Testament. For it is a testament when a dying man bequeaths his property, after his death, to his legally defined heirs. And Christ, before his death, commanded and ordained that his gospel be preached after his death in all the world [Luke 24:44-47]. Thereby he gave to all who believe, as their possession, everything that he had. This included: his life, in which he swallowed up death; his righteousness, by which he blotted out sin; and his salvation, with which he overcame everlasting damnation. A poor man, dead in sin and consigned to hell, can hear nothing more comforting than this precious and tender message about Christ; from the bottom of his heart he must laugh and be glad over it, if he believes it true.

Now to strengthen this faith, God has promised this gospel and testament in many ways, by the prophets in the Old Testament, as St. Paul says in Romans 1 [:1], "I am set apart to preach the gospel of God which he promised beforehand through his prophets in the Holy Scriptures, concerning his Son, who was descended from David," etc.

To mention some of these places: God gave the first promise when he said to the serpent, in Genesis 3 [:15], "I will put enmity between you and the woman, and between your seed and her seed; he shall bruise your head, and you shall bruise his heel." Christ is this woman's seed, who has bruised the devil's head, that is, sin, death, hell, and all his power. For without this seed, no man can escape sin, death, or hell.

Again, in Genesis 22 [:18], God promised Abraham, "Through your descendant shall all the nations of the earth be blessed." Christ is that descendant of Abraham, says St. Paul in Galatians 3 [:16]; he has blessed all the world, through the gospel [Gal. 3:8]. For where Christ is not, there is still the curse that fell upon Adam and his children when he had sinned, so that they all are necessarily guilty and subject to sin, death, and hell. Over against this curse, the gospel now blesses all the world by publicly announcing, "Whoever believes in this descendant of Abraham shall be blessed." That is, he shall be rid of sin, death, and hell, and shall remain righteous, alive, and saved forever, as Christ himself says in John 11 [:26], "Whoever believes in me shall never die."

Again God made this promise to David in 2 Samuel 7 [:12-14] when he said, "I will raise up your son after you, who shall build a house for my name, and I will establish the throne of his kingdom forever. I will be his father, and he shall be my son," etc. This is the kingdom of Christ, of which the gospel speaks: an everlasting kingdom, a kingdom of life, salvation, and righteousness, where all those who believe enter in from out of the prison of sin and death.

There are many more such promises of the gospel in the other prophets as well, for example Micah 5[:2], "But you, O Bethlehem Ephrathah, who are little to be among the clans of Judah, from you shall come forth for me one who is to be ruler in Israel"; and again, Hosea 13 [:14], "I shall ransom them from the power of hell and redeem them from death. O death, I will be your plague; O hell, I will be your destruction."

The gospel, then, is nothing but the preaching about Christ, Son of God and of David, true God and man, who by his death and resurrection has overcome for us the sin, death, and hell of all men who believe in him. Thus the gospel can be either a brief or a lengthy message; one person can write of it briefly, another at length. He writes of it at length, who writes about many words and works of Christ, as do the four evangelists. He writes of it briefly, however, who does not tell of Christ's works, but indicates briefly how by his death and resurrection he has overcome sin, death, and hell for those who believe in him, as do St. Peter and St. Paul.

See to it, therefore, that you do not make a Moses out of Christ, or a book of laws and doctrines out of the gospel, as has been done heretofore and as certain prefaces put it, even those of St. Jerome. For the gospel does not expressly demand works of our own by which we become righteous and are saved; indeed it condemns such works. Rather the gospel demands faith in Christ: that he has overcome for us sin, death, and hell, and thus gives us righteousness, life, and salvation not through our works, but through his own works, death, and suffering, in order that we may avail ourselves of his death and victory as though we had done it ourselves.

To be sure, Christ in the gospel, and St. Peter and St. Paul besides, do give many commandments and doctrines, and expound the law. But these are to be counted like all Christ's other works and good deeds. To know his works and the things that happened to him is not yet to know the true gospel, for you do not yet thereby know that he has overcome sin, death, and the devil. So,

too, it is not yet knowledge of the gospel when you know these doctrines and commandments, but only when the voice comes that says, "Christ is your own, with his life, teaching, works, death, resurrection, and all that he is, has, does, and can do."

Thus we see also that he does not compel us but invites us kindly and says, "Blessed are the poor," etc. [Matt. 5:3]. And the apostles use the words, "I exhort," "I entreat," "I beg," so that one sees on every hand that the gospel is not a book of law, but really a preaching of the benefits of Christ, shown to us and given to us for our own possession, if we believe. But Moses, in his books, drives, compels, threatens, strikes, and rebukes terribly, for he is a lawgiver and driver.

Hence it comes that to a believer no law is given by which he becomes righteous before God, as St. Paul says in 1 Timothy 1 [:9], because he is alive and righteous and saved by faith, and he needs nothing further except to prove his faith by works. Truly, if faith is there, he cannot hold back; he proves himself, breaks out into good works, confesses and teaches this gospel before the people, and stakes his life on it. Everything that he lives and does is directed to his neighbor's profit, in order to help him—not only to the attainment of this grace, but also in body, property, and honor. Seeing that Christ has done this for him, he thus follows Christ's example.

That is what Christ meant when at the last he gave no other commandment than love, by which men were to know who were his disciples [John 13:34-35] and true believers. For where works and love do not break forth, there faith is not right, the gospel does not yet take hold, and Christ is not rightly known. See, then, that you so approach the books of the New Testament as to learn to read them in this way.

Which Are the True and Noblest Books of the New Testament?

From all this you can now judge all the books and decide among them which are the best. John's Gospel and St. Paul's epistles, especially that to the Romans, and St. Peter's first epistle are the true kernel and marrow of all the books. They ought properly to be the foremost books, and it would be advisable for every Christian to read them first and most, and by daily reading to make them as much his own as his daily bread. For in them you do not find many works and miracles of Christ described, but you do find depicted in masterly fashion how faith in Christ overcomes sin, death, and hell, and gives life, righteousness, and salvation. This is the real nature of the gospel, as you have heard.

If I had to do without one or the other—either the works or the preaching of Christ—I would rather do without the works than without his preaching. For the works do not help me, but his words give life, as he himself says [John 6:63]. Now John writes very little about the works of Christ, but very much about his preaching, while the other evangelists write much about his works and little about his preaching. Therefore John's Gospel is the one, fine, true, and chief gospel, and is far, far to be preferred over the other three and placed high above them. So, too, the epistles of St. Paul and St. Peter far surpass the other three gospels, Matthew, Mark, and Luke.

In a word St. John's Gospel and his first epistle, St. Paul's epistles, especially Romans, Galatians, and Ephesians, and St. Peter's first epistle are the books that show you Christ and teach you all that is necessary and salvatory for you to know, even if you were never to see or hear any other book or doctrine. Therefore St. James's epistle is

really an epistle of straw, compared to these others, for it has nothing of the nature of the gospel about it. But more of this in the other prefaces.

From LW vol. 35, 235–37.

24. Preface to the Old Testament (1545/1523)

Luther's translation work occupied him throughout his career, with continual revisions. His translation of the Pentateuch appeared in 1523 along with this preface (revised in 1545). In it he gives the reader his view of what, in essence, the Old Testament is about.

There are some who have little regard for the Old Testament. They think of it as a book that was given to the Jewish people only and is now out of date, containing only stories of past times. They think they have enough in the New Testament and assert that only a spiritual sense is to be sought in the Old Testament. Origen, Jerome, and many other distinguished people have held this view. But Christ says in John 5 [:35], "Search the Scriptures, for it is they that bear witness to me." St. Paul bids Timothy attend to the reading of the Scriptures [1 Tim. 4:13], and in Romans 1 [:2] he declares that the gospel was promised by God in the Scriptures, while in 1 Corinthians 15 he says that in accordance with the Scriptures Christ came of the seed of David, died, and was raised from the dead. St. Peter, too, points us back, more than once, to the Scriptures.

They do this in order to teach us that the Scriptures of the Old Testament are not to be despised, but diligently read. For they themselves base the New Testament upon them mightily, proving it by the Old Testament and appealing to it, as St. Luke also writes in Acts 17 [:11], saying that they at Thessalonica examined the Scriptures daily to see if these things were so that Paul was teaching. The ground and proof of the New Testament is surely not to be despised, and therefore the Old Testament is to be highly regarded. And what is the New Testament but a public preaching and proclamation of Christ, set forth through the sayings of the Old Testament and fulfilled through Christ?

In order that those who are not more familiar with it may have instruction and guidance for reading the Old Testament with profit, I have prepared this preface to the best of the ability God has given me. I beg and really caution every pious Christian not to be offended by the simplicity of the language and stories frequently encountered there, but fully realize that, however simple they may seem, these are the very words, works, judgments, and deeds of the majesty, power, and wisdom of the most high God. For these are the Scriptures which make fools of all the wise and understanding, and are open only to the small and simple, as Christ says in Matthew 11 [:25]. Therefore dismiss your own opinions and feelings, and think of the Scriptures as the loftiest and noblest of holy things, as the richest of mines which can never be sufficiently explored, in order that you may find that divine wisdom which God here lays before you in such simple guise as to quench all pride. Here you will find the swaddling clothes and the manger in which Christ lies, and to which the angel points the shepherds [Luke 2:12]. Simple and lowly are these swaddling clothes, but dear is the treasure, Christ, who lies in them.

Know, then, that the Old Testament is a book of laws, which teaches what men are to do and not to do—and in addition gives examples and stories of how these laws are kept or broken—just as the New Testament is gospel or book of grace, and teaches where one is to get the power to fulfill the law. Now in the New Testament there are also given, along with the teaching about grace, many other teachings that are laws and commandments for the control of the flesh—since in this life the Spirit is not perfected and grace alone cannot rule. Similarly in the Old Testament too there are, beside the laws, certain promises and words of grace, by which the holy fathers and prophets under the law were kept, like us, in the faith of Christ. Nevertheless just as the chief teaching of the New Testament is really the proclamation of grace and peace through the forgiveness of sins in Christ, so the chief teaching of the Old Testament is really the teaching of laws, the showing up of sin, and the demanding of good. You should expect this in the Old Testament.

From LW *vol. 35, 235–37.*

25. *The Small Catechism* (1529)

Dismayed over the ignorance of the laity, Luther in 1529 prepared this brief introduction to the fundamentals of the Christian faith. Its foundations were the elements of traditional catechesis—the Ten Commandments, the creed, and the Lord's Prayer, now explained in a distinctively "Lutheran" fashion. To this Luther added other things which he thought were indispensable for all Christians to know. This text, which Luther thought was one of his best, was taught by schoolmasters, parents, and pastors, and it

thereby became one of his most influential writings, truly a "consolidation tract of the Reformation."

✠

Preface

Grace, mercy, and peace in Jesus Christ, our Lord, from Martin Luther to all faithful, godly pastors and preachers. The deplorable conditions which I recently encountered when I was a visitor constrained me to prepare this brief and simple catechism or statement of Christian teaching. Good God, what wretchedness I beheld! The common people, especially those who live in the country, have no knowledge whatever of Christian teaching, and many pastors are quite incompetent and unfitted for teaching. Although the people are supposed to be Christian, are baptized, and receive the holy sacrament, they do not know the Lord's Prayer, the creed, or the Ten Commandments, they live as if they were pigs and irrational beasts, and now that the gospel has been restored they have mastered the fine art of abusing liberty.

How will you bishops answer for it before Christ that you have so shamefully neglected the people and paid no attention at all to the duties of your office? May you escape punishment for this! You withhold the cup in the Lord's supper and insist on the observance of human laws, yet you do not take the slightest interest in teaching the people the Lord's Prayer, the creed, the Ten Commandments, or a single part of the Word of God. Woe to you forever!

I therefore beg of you for God's sake, my beloved brethren who are pastors and preachers, that you take the duties of your office seriously, that you have pity on the people who are entrusted to your care, and that you help me to teach the catechism to the people, especially those who are young. Let those who lack the qualifications to do better at least take this booklet and these forms and read them to the people word for word in this manner:

In the first place, the preacher should take the utmost care to avoid changes or variations in the text and wording of the Ten Commandments, the creed, the Lord's Prayer, the sacraments, etc. On the contrary, he should adopt one form, adhere to it, and use it repeatedly year after year. Young and inexperienced people must be instructed on the basis of a uniform, fixed text and form. They are easily confused if a teacher employs one form now and another form—perhaps with the intention of making improvements—later on. In this way all the time and labor will be lost.

This was well understood by our good fathers, who were accustomed to use the same form in teaching the Lord's Prayer, the creed, and the Ten Commandments. We, too, should teach these things to the young and unlearned in such a way that we do not alter a single syllable or recite the catechism differently from year to year. Choose the form that pleases you, therefore, and adhere to it henceforth. When you preach to intelligent and educated people, you are at liberty to exhibit your learning and to discuss these topics from different angles and in such a variety of ways as you may be capable of. But when you are teaching the young, adhere to a fixed and unchanging form and method. Begin by teaching them the Ten Commandments, the creed, the Lord's Prayer, etc., following the text word for word so that the young may repeat these things after you and retain them in their memory.

If any refuse to receive your instructions, tell them that they deny Christ and are no

Christians. They should not be admitted to the sacrament, be accepted as sponsors in Baptism, or be allowed to participate in any Christian privileges. On the contrary, they should be turned over to the pope and his officials, and even to the devil himself. In addition, parents and employers should refuse to furnish them with food and drink and should notify them that the prince is disposed to banish such rude people from his land.

Although we cannot and should not compel anyone to believe, we should nevertheless insist that the people learn to know how to distinguish between right and wrong according to the standards of those among whom they live and make their living. For anyone who desires to reside in a city is bound to know and observe the laws under whose protection he lives, no matter whether he is a believer or, at heart, a scoundrel or knave.

In the second place, after the people have become familiar with the text, teach them what it means. For this purpose, take the explanations in this booklet, or choose any other brief and fixed explanations which you may prefer, and adhere to them without changing a single syllable, as stated above with reference to the text. Moreover, allow yourself ample time, for it is not necessary to take up all the parts at once. They can be presented one at a time. When the learners have a proper understanding of the First Commandment, proceed to the Second Commandment, and so on. Otherwise they will be so overwhelmed that they will hardly remember anything at all.

In the third place, after you have thus taught this brief catechism, take up a large catechism so that the people may have a richer and fuller understanding. Expound every commandment, petition, and part, pointing out their respective obligations, benefits, dangers, advantages, and disadvantages, as you will find all of this treated at length in the many books written for this purpose. Lay the greatest weight on those commandments or other parts which seem to require special attention among the people where you are. For example, the Seventh Commandment, which treats of stealing, must be emphasized when instructing laborers and shopkeepers, and even farmers and servants, for many of these are guilty of dishonesty and thievery. So, too, the Fourth Commandment must be stressed when instructing children and the common people in order that they may be encouraged to be orderly, faithful, obedient, and peaceful. Always, adduce many examples from the Scriptures to show how God punished and blessed.

You should also take pains to urge governing authorities and parents to rule wisely and educate their children. They must be shown that they are obliged to do so, and that they are guilty of damnable sin if they do not do so, for by such neglect they undermine and lay waste both the kingdom of God and the kingdom of the world and are the worst enemies of God and man. Make very plain to them the shocking evils they introduce when they refuse their aid in the training of children to become pastors, preachers, notaries, etc., and tell them that God will inflict awful punishments on them for these sins. It is necessary to preach about such things. The extent to which parents and governing authorities sin in this respect is beyond telling. The devil also has a horrible purpose in mind.

Finally, now that the people are freed from the tyranny of the pope, they are unwilling to receive the sacrament and they treat it with contempt. Here, too, there is need of exhortation, but with this understanding: No one is to be compelled to believe or to receive the sacrament, no law is to be made concerning it, and no time or place should be appointed for it. We should so preach that, of their own accord and without any law, the people will desire the sacrament and, as it were, compel us pastors to administer it to them. This can be done by telling them: It is to be feared that anyone who does not desire to receive the sacrament at least three or four times a year despises the sacrament and is no Christian, just as he is no Christian who does not hear and believe the gospel. Christ did not say, "Omit this," or "Despise this," but he said, "Do this, as often as you drink it," etc. Surely he wishes that this be done and not that it be omitted and despised. "*Do* this," he said.

He who does not highly esteem the sacrament suggests thereby that he has no sin, no flesh, no devil, no world, no death, no hell. That is to say, he believes in none of these, although he is deeply immersed in them and is held captive by the devil. On the other hand, he suggests that he needs no grace, no life, no paradise, no heaven, no Christ, no God, nothing good at all. For if he believed that he was involved in so much that is evil and was in need of so much that is good, he would not neglect the sacrament in which aid is afforded against such evil and in which such good is bestowed. It is not necessary to compel him by any law to receive the sacrament, for he will hasten to it of his own accord, he will feel constrained to receive it, he will insist that you administer it to him.

Accordingly you are not to make a law of this, as the pope has done. All you need to do is clearly set forth the advantage and disadvantage, the benefit and loss, the blessing and danger connected with this sacrament.

Then the people will come of their own accord and without compulsion on your part. But if they refuse to come, let them be, and tell them that those who do not feel and acknowledge their great need and God's gracious help belong to the devil. If you do not give such admonitions, or if you adopt odious laws on the subject, it is your own fault if the people treat the sacrament with contempt. How can they be other than negligent if you fail to do your duty and remain silent? So it is up to you, dear pastor and preacher! Our office has become something different from what it was under the pope. It is now a ministry of grace and salvation. It subjects us to greater burdens and labors, dangers and temptations with little reward or gratitude from the world. But Christ himself will be our reward if we labor faithfully. The Father of all grace grant it! To him be praise and thanks forever, through Christ, our Lord. Amen.

[I] The Ten Commandments
in the plain form in which the head of the family shall teach them to his household
The First
You shall have no other gods.

What does this mean?

Answer: We should fear, love, and trust in God above all things.
The Second
You shall not take the name of the Lord your God in vain.

What does this mean?

Answer: We should fear and love God, and so we should not use his name to curse, swear, practice magic, lie, or deceive, but in every time of need call upon him, pray to him, praise him, and give him thanks.
The Third
Remember the Sabbath day, to keep it holy.

What does this mean?

Answer: We should fear and love God, and so we should not despise his Word and the preaching of the same, but deem it holy and gladly hear and learn it.

The Fourth

Honor your father and your mother.

What does this mean?

Answer: We should fear and love God, and so we should not despise our parents and superiors, nor provoke them to anger, but honor, serve, obey, love, and esteem them.

The Fifth

You shall not kill.

What does this mean?

Answer: We should fear and love God, and so we should not endanger our neighbor's life, nor cause him any harm, but help and befriend him in every necessity of life.

The Sixth

You shall not commit adultery.

What does this mean?

Answer: We should fear and love God, and so we should lead a chaste and pure life in word and deed, each one loving and honoring his wife or her husband.

The Seventh

You shall not steal.

What does this mean?

Answer: We should fear and love God, and so we should not rob our neighbor of his money or property, nor bring them into our possession by dishonest trade or by dealing in shoddy wares, but help him to improve and protect his income and property.

The Eighth

You shall not bear false witness against your neighbor.

What does this mean?

Answer: We should fear and love God, and so we should not tell lies about our neighbor, nor betray, slander, or defame him, but should apologize for him, speak well of him, and interpret charitably all that he does.

The Ninth

You shall not covet your neighbor's house.

What does this mean?

Answer: We should fear and love God, and so we should not seek by craftiness to gain possession of our neighbor's inheritance or home, nor to obtain them under pretext of legal right, but be of service and help to him so that he may keep what is his.

The Tenth

You shall not covet your neighbor's wife, or his manservant, or his maidservant, or his ox, or his ass, or anything that is your neighbor's.

What does this mean?

Answer: We should fear and love God, and so we should not abduct, estrange, or entice away our neighbor's wife, servants, or cattle, but encourage them to remain and discharge their duty to him.

[Conclusion]

What does God declare concerning all these commandments?

Answer: He says, "I the Lord your God am a jealous God, visiting the iniquity of the fathers upon the children to the third and the fourth generation of those who hate me, but showing steadfast love to thousands of those who love me and keep my commandments."

What does this mean?

Answer: God threatens to punish all who transgress these commandments. We should therefore fear his wrath and not disobey these commandments. On the other hand, he promises grace and every blessing to all who keep them. We should therefore love him, trust in him, and cheerfully do what he has commanded.

[II] The Creed
in the plain form in which the head of the family shall teach it to his household

The First Article: Creation
I believe in God the Father almighty maker of heaven and earth.

What does this mean?

Answer: I believe that God has created me and all that exists; that he has given me and still sustains my body and soul, all my limbs and senses, my reason and all the faculties of my mind, together with food and clothing, house and home, family and property; that he provides me daily and abundantly with all the necessities of life, protects me from all danger, and preserves me from all evil. All this he does out of his pure, fatherly, and divine goodness and mercy, without any merit or worthiness on my part. For all of this I am bound to thank, praise, serve, and obey him. This is most certainly true.

The Second Article: Redemption
And in Jesus Christ, his only son our Lord: who was conceived by the Holy Spirit, born of the virgin Mary, suffered under Pontius Pilate, was crucified, dead, and buried: he descended into hell, the third day he rose from the dead, he ascended into heaven, and is seated on the right hand of God the Father almighty whence he shall come to judge the living and the dead.

What does this mean?

Answer: I believe that Jesus Christ, true God, begotten of the Father from eternity, and also true man, born of the Virgin Mary, is my Lord, who has redeemed me, a lost and condemned creature, delivered me and freed me from all sins, from death, and from the power of the devil, not with silver and gold but with his holy and precious blood and with his innocent sufferings and death, in order that I may be his, live under him in his kingdom, and serve him in everlasting right-eousness, innocence, and blessedness, even as he is risen from the dead and lives and reigns to all eternity. This is most certainly true.

The Third Article: Sanctification
I believe in the Holy Spirit, the holy Christian church, the communion of saints, the forgiveness of sins, the resurrection of the body, and the life everlasting. Amen.

What does this mean?

Answer: I believe that by my own reason or strength I cannot believe in Jesus Christ, my Lord, or come to him. But the Holy Spirit has called me through the gospel, enlightened me with his gifts, and sanctified and preserved me in true faith, just as he calls, gathers, enlightens, and sanctifies the whole Christian church on earth and preserves it in union with Jesus Christ in the one true faith. In this Christian church he daily and abundantly forgives all my sins, and the sins of all believers, and on the last day he will raise me and all the dead and will grant eternal life to me and to all who believe in Christ. This is most certainly true.

[III] The Lord's Prayer
in the plain form in which the head of the family shall teach it to his household

[Introduction]
Our Father who art in heaven.

What does this mean?

Answer: Here God would encourage us to believe that he is truly our Father and we are truly his children in order that we may approach him boldly and confidently in prayer, even as beloved children approach their dear father.

The First Petition
Hallowed be thy name.

What does this mean?

Answer: To be sure, God's name is holy in itself, but we pray in this petition that it may also be holy for us.

How is this done?

Answer: When the Word of God is taught clearly and purely and we, as children of God, lead holy lives in accordance with it. Help us to do this, dear Father in heaven! But whoever teaches and lives otherwise than as the Word of God teaches, profanes the name of God among us. From this preserve us, heavenly Father!

The Second Petition

Thy kingdom come.

What does this mean?

Answer: To be sure, the kingdom of God comes of itself, without our prayer, but we pray in this petition that it may also come to us.

How is this done?

Answer: When the heavenly Father gives us his Holy Spirit so that by his grace we may believe his holy Word and live a godly life, both here in time and hereafter forever.

The Third Petition

Thy will be done, on earth as it is in heaven.

What does this mean?

Answer: To be sure, the good and gracious will of God is done without our prayer, but we pray in this petition that it may also be done by us.

How is this done?

Answer: When God curbs and destroys every evil counsel and purpose of the devil, of the world, and of our flesh which would hinder us from hallowing his name and prevent the coming of his kingdom, and when he strengthens us and keeps us steadfast in his Word and in faith even to the end. This is his good and gracious will.

The Fourth Petition

Give us this day our daily bread.

What does this mean?

Answer: To be sure, God provides daily bread, even to the wicked, without our prayer, but we pray in this petition that God may make us aware of his gifts and enable us to receive our daily bread with thanksgiving.

What is meant by daily bread?

Answer: Everything required to satisfy our bodily needs, such as food and clothing, house and home, fields and flocks, money and property; a pious spouse and good children, trustworthy servants, godly and faithful rulers, good government; seasonable weather, peace and health, order and honor; true friends, faithful neighbors, and the like.

The Fifth Petition

And forgive us our debts, as we also have forgiven our debtors.

What does this mean?

Answer: We pray in this petition that our heavenly Father may not look upon our sins, and on their account deny our prayers, for we neither merit nor deserve those things for which we pray. Although we sin daily and deserve nothing but punishment, we nevertheless pray that God may grant us all things by his grace. And assuredly we on our part will heartily forgive and cheerfully do good to those who may sin against us.

The Sixth Petition

And lead us not into temptation.

What does this mean?

Answer: God tempts no one to sin, but we pray in this petition that God may so guard and preserve us that the devil, the world, and our flesh may not deceive us or mislead us into unbelief, despair, and other great and shameful sins, but that, although we may be so tempted, we may finally prevail and gain the victory.

The Seventh Petition

But deliver us from evil.

What does this mean?

Answer: We pray in this petition, as in a summary, that our Father in heaven may deliver us from all manner of evil, whether it affect body or soul, property or reputation, and that at last, when the hour of death comes, he may grant us a blessed end and graciously take us from this world of sorrow to himself in heaven.

[Conclusion]

Amen.

What does this mean?

Answer: It means that I should be assured that such petitions are acceptable to our heavenly Father and are heard by him, for he himself commanded us to pray like this and promised to hear us. "Amen, amen" means "Yes, yes, it shall be so."

[IV] The Sacrament of Holy Baptism

in the plain form in which the head of the family shall teach it to his household

First

What is baptism?

Answer: Baptism is not merely water, but it is water used according to God's command and connected with God's Word.

What is the word of God?

Answer: As recorded in Matthew 28:19, our Lord Christ said, "Go therefore and make disciples of all nations, baptizing them in the name of the Father and of the Son and of the Holy Spirit."

Second

What gifts or benefits does Baptism bestow?

Answer: It effects forgiveness of sins, delivers from death and the devil, and grants eternal salvation to all who believe, as the Word and promise of God declare.

What is this Word and promise of God?

Answer: As recorded in Mark 16:16, our Lord Christ said, "He who believes and is baptized will be saved; but he who does not believe will be condemned."

Third

How can water produce such great effects?

Answer: It is not the water that produces these effects, but the Word of God connected with the water, and our faith which relies on the Word of God connected with the water. For without the Word of God the water is merely water and no Baptism. But when connected with the Word of God it is a Baptism, that is, a gracious water of life and a washing of regeneration in the Holy Spirit, as St. Paul wrote to Titus (3:5-8), "He saved us by the washing of regeneration and renewal in the Holy Spirit, which he poured out upon us richly through Jesus Christ our Savior, so that we might be justified by his grace and become heirs in hope of eternal life. The saying is sure."

Fourth

What does such baptizing with water signify?

Answer: It signifies that the old Adam in us, together with all sins and evil lusts, should be drowned by daily sorrow and repentance and be put to death, and that the new man should come forth daily and rise up, cleansed and righteous, to live forever in God's presence.

Where is this written?

Answer: In Romans 6:4, St. Paul wrote, "We were buried therefore with him by baptism into death, so that as Christ was raised from the dead by the glory of the Father, we too might walk in newness of life."

[V] [Confession and Absolution]

How Plain People Are to Be Taught to Confess

What is confession?

Answer: Confession consists of two parts. One is that we confess our sins. The other is that we receive absolution or forgiveness from the confessor as from God himself, by no means doubting but firmly believing that our sins are thereby forgiven before God in heaven.

What sins should we confess?

Answer: Before God we should acknowledge that we are guilty of all manner of sins, even those of which we are not aware, as we do in the Lord's Prayer. Before the confessor, however, we should confess only those sins of which we have knowledge and which trouble us.

What are such sins?

Answer: Reflect on your condition in the light of the Ten Commandments: whether you are a father or mother, a son or daughter, a master or servant; whether you have been disobedient, unfaithful, lazy, ill-tempered, or quarrelsome; whether you have harmed anyone by word or deed; and whether you have stolen, neglected, or wasted anything, or done other evil.

Please give me a brief form of confession.
Answer: You should say to the confessor:
Dear Pastor, please hear my confession and declare that my sins are forgiven for God's sake.
Proceed.

I, a poor sinner, confess before God that I am guilty of all sins. In particular I confess in your presence that, as a manservant or maidservant, etc., I am unfaithful to my master, for here and there I have not done what I was told. I have made my master angry, caused him to curse, neglected to do my duty, and caused him to suffer loss. I have also been immodest in word and deed. I have quarreled with my equals. I have grumbled and sworn at my mistress, etc. For all this I am sorry and pray for grace. I mean to do better.

A master or mistress may say:
In particular I confess in your presence that I have not been faithful in training my children, servants, and wife to the glory of God. I have cursed. I have set a bad example by my immodest language and actions. I have injured my neighbor by speaking evil of him, overcharging him, giving him inferior goods and short measure.

Masters and mistresses should add whatever else they have done contrary to God's commandments and to their station in life, etc.

If, however, anyone does not feel that his conscience is burdened by such or by greater sins, he should not worry, nor should he search for and invent other sins, for this would turn confession into torture; he should simply mention one or two sins of which he is aware. For example, "In particular I confess that I once cursed. On one occasion I also spoke indecently. And I neglected this or that," etc. Let this suffice.

If you have knowledge of no sin at all (which is quite unlikely), you should mention none in particular, but receive forgiveness upon the general confession which you make to God in the presence of the confessor.

Then the confessor shall say:
God be merciful to you and strengthen your faith. Amen.

Again he shall say:
Do you believe that this forgiveness is the forgiveness of God?

Again he shall say:
Be it done for you as you have believed. According to the command of our Lord Jesus Christ, I forgive you your sins in the name of the Father and of the Son and of the Holy Spirit. Amen. Go in peace.

A confessor will know additional passages of the Scriptures with which to comfort and to strengthen the faith of those whose consciences are heavily burdened or who are distressed and sorely tried. This is intended simply as an ordinary form of confession for plain people.

[VI] The Sacrament of the Altar

in the plain form in which the head of the family shall teach it to his household

What is the Sacrament of the Altar?

Answer: Instituted by Christ himself, it is the true body and blood of our Lord Jesus Christ, under the bread and wine, given to us Christians to eat and to drink.

Where is this written?

Answer: The holy evangelists Matthew, Mark, and Luke, and also St. Paul, write thus:

> Our Lord Jesus Christ, on the night when he was betrayed, took bread, and when he had given thanks, he broke it, and gave it to his disciples and said, "Take, eat; this is my body which is given for you. Do this in remembrance of me." In the same way also he took the cup, after supper, and when he had given thanks he gave it to them, saying, "Drink of it, all of you. This cup is the new covenant in my blood, which is poured out for many for the forgiveness of sins. Do this, as often as you drink it, in remembrance of me."

What is the benefit of such eating and drinking?

Answer: We are told in the words "for you" and "for the forgiveness of sins." By these words the forgiveness of sins, life, and salvation are given to us in the sacrament, for where there is forgiveness of sins, there are also life and salvation.

How can bodily eating and drinking produce such great effects?

Answer: The eating and drinking do not in themselves produce them, but the words "for you" and "for the forgiveness of sins." These words, when accompanied by the bodily eating and drinking, are the chief thing in the sacrament, and he who believes these words has what they say and declare: the forgiveness of sins.

Who, then, receives this sacrament worthily?

Answer: Fasting and bodily preparation are a good external discipline, but he is truly worthy and well prepared who believes these words: "for you" and "for the forgiveness of sins." On the other hand, he who does not believe these words, or doubts them, is unworthy and unprepared, for the words "for you" require truly believing hearts.

[VII] Morning and Evening Prayers

How the head of the family shall teach his household to say morning and evening prayers

In the morning, when you rise, make the sign of the cross and say, "In the name of God, the Father, the Son, and the Holy Spirit. Amen."

Then, kneeling or standing, say the Apostles' Creed and the Lord's Prayer. Then you may say this prayer:

> I give Thee thanks, heavenly Father, through thy dear Son Jesus Christ, that Thou hast protected me through the night from all harm and danger. I beseech Thee to keep me this day, too, from all sin and evil, that in all my thoughts, words, and deeds I may please Thee. Into thy hands I commend my body and soul and all that is mine. Let thy holy angel have charge of me, that the wicked one may have no power over me. Amen.

After singing a hymn (possibly a hymn on the Ten Commandments) or whatever your devotion may suggest, you should go to your work joyfully.

In the evening, when you retire, make the sign of the cross and say, "In the name of God, the Father, the Son, and the Holy Spirit. Amen."

Then, kneeling or standing, say the Apostles' Creed and the Lord's Prayer. Then you may say this prayer:

I give Thee thanks, heavenly Father, through thy dear Son Jesus Christ, that Thou hast this day graciously protected me. I beseech Thee to forgive all my sin and the wrong which I have done. Graciously protect me during the coming night. Into thy hands I commend my body and soul and all that is mine. Let thy holy angels have charge of me, that the wicked one may have no power over me. Amen.

Then quickly lie down and sleep in peace.

[VIII] Grace at Table

How the head of the family shall teach his household to offer blessing and thanksgiving at table

[Blessing Before Eating]

When children and the whole household gather at the table, they should reverently fold their hands and say:

The eyes of all look to Thee, O Lord, and Thou givest them their food in due season. Thou openest thy hand; Thou satisfiest the desire of every living thing.

(It is to be observed that "satisfying the desire of every living thing" means that all creatures receive enough to eat to make them joyful and of good cheer. Greed and anxiety about food prevent such satisfaction.)

Then the Lord's Prayer should be said, and afterwards this prayer:

Lord God, heavenly Father, bless us, and these thy gifts which of thy bountiful goodness Thou hast bestowed on us, through Jesus Christ our Lord. Amen.

[Thanksgiving after Eating]

After eating, likewise, they should fold their hands reverently and say:

O give thanks to the Lord, for he is good; for his steadfast love endures forever. He gives to the beasts their food, and to the young ravens which cry. His delight is not in the strength of the horse, nor his pleasure in the legs of a man; but the Lord takes pleasure in those who fear him, in those who hope in his steadfast love.

Then the Lord's Prayer should be said, and afterwards this prayer:

We give Thee thanks, Lord God, our Father, for all thy benefits, through Jesus Christ our Lord, who lives and reigns forever. Amen.

[IX] Table of Duties

consisting of certain passages of the Scriptures, selected for various estates and conditions of men, by which they may be admonished to do their respective duties

Bishops, Pastors, and Preachers

"A bishop must be above reproach, married only once, temperate, sensible, dignified, hospitable, an apt teacher, no drunkard, not violent but gentle, not quarrelsome, and no lover of money. He must manage his own household well, keeping his children submissive and respectful in every way. He must not be a recent convert," etc. (1 Tim. 3:2-6).

Duties Christians Owe Their Teachers and Pastors

"Remain in the same house, eating and drinking what they provide, for the laborer deserves his wages" (Luke 10:7). "The Lord commanded that those who proclaim the gospel should get their living by the gospel" (1 Cor. 9:14). "Let him who is taught the word share all good things with him who teaches. Do not be deceived; God is not mocked" (Gal. 6:6, 7). "Let the elders who rule well be considered worthy of double honor, especially those who labor in preaching and teaching; for the scripture says, 'You shall not muzzle an ox when it is treading out the grain,' and 'The laborer deserves his wages'" (1 Tim. 5:17, 18). "We beseech you, brethren, to respect those who labor among you and are over you in the Lord and admonish you, and to esteem them very highly in love because of their work. Be at peace among yourselves" (1 Thess. 5:12, 13). "Obey your leaders and submit to them; for they are keeping watch over your souls, as men who will have to give account. Let them do this joyfully, and not sadly, for that would be of no advantage to you" (Heb. 13:17).

Governing Authorities

"Let every person be subject to the governing authorities. For there is no authority except from God, and those that exist have been instituted by God. Therefore he who resists the authorities resists what God has appointed, and those who resist will incur judgment. He who is in authority does not bear the sword in vain; he is the servant of God to execute his wrath on the wrongdoer" (Rom. 13:1-4).

Duties Subjects Owe to Governing Authorities

"Render therefore to Caesar the things that are Caesar's, and to God the things that are God's" (Matt. 22:21). "Let every person be subject to the governing authorities. Therefore one must be subject, not only to avoid God's wrath but also for the sake of conscience. For the same reason you also pay taxes, for the authorities are ministers of God, attending to this very thing. Pay all of them their dues, taxes to whom taxes are due, revenue to whom revenue is due, respect to whom respect is due, honor to whom honor is due" (Rom. 13:1, 5-7). "I urge that supplications, prayers, intercessions, and thanksgivings be made for all men, for kings and all who are in high positions, that we may lead a quiet and peaceable life, godly and respectful in every way" (1 Tim. 2:1, 2). "Remind them to be submissive to rulers and authorities, to be obedient, to be ready for any honest work" (Titus 3:1). "Be subject for the Lord's sake to every human institution, whether it be the emperor as supreme, or to governors as sent by him to punish those who do wrong and to praise those who do right" (1 Pet. 2:13, 14).

Husbands

"You husbands, live considerately with your wives, bestowing honor on the woman as the weaker sex, since you are joint heirs of the grace of life, in order that your prayers may not be hindered" (1 Pet. 3:7).

"Husbands, love your wives, and do not be harsh with them" (Col. 3:19).

Wives

"You wives, be submissive to your husbands, as Sarah obeyed Abraham, calling him Lord. And you are now her children if you do right and let nothing terrify you" (1 Pet. 3:1, 6).

Parents

"Fathers, do not provoke your children to anger, lest they become discouraged, but bring them up in the discipline and instruction of the Lord" (Eph. 6:4; Col. 3:21).

Children

"Children, obey your parents in the Lord, for this is right. 'Honor your father and mother' (this is the First Commandment with a promise) 'that it may be well with you and that you may live long on the earth'" (Eph. 6:1-3).

Laborers and Servants, Male and Female

"Be obedient to those who are your earthly masters, with fear and trembling, with singleness of heart, as to Christ; not in the way of eye-service, as men-pleasers, but as servants of Christ, doing the will of God from the heart, rendering service with a good will as to the Lord and not to men, knowing that whatever good anyone does, he will receive the same again from the Lord, whether he is a slave or free" (Eph. 6:5-8).

Masters and Mistresses

"Masters, do the same to them, and forbear threatening, knowing that he who is both their Master and yours is in heaven, and that there is no partiality with him" (Eph. 6:9).

Young Persons in General

"You that are younger, be subject to the elders. Clothe yourselves, all of you, with humility toward one another, for 'God opposes the proud, but gives grace to the humble.' Humble yourselves therefore under the mighty hand of God, that in due time he may exalt you" (1 Pet. 5:5, 6).

Widows

"She who is a real widow, and is left all alone, has set her hope on God and continues in supplications and prayers night and day; whereas she who is self-indulgent is dead even while she lives" (1 Tim. 5:5, 6).

Christians in General

"The commandments are summed up in this sentence, 'You shall love your neighbor as yourself'" (Rom. 13:9). "I urge that supplications, prayers, intercessions, and thanksgivings be made for all men" (1 Tim. 2:1).

Let each his lesson learn with care
And all the household well will fare.

From T. Tappert, ed., The Book of Concord *(Philadelphia: Fortress Press, 1959), 338–56.*

26. *The Smalcald Articles* (1537)

In 1536, Pope Paul III called a council for the following year to deal with the Protestant challenge. It did not in fact convene until 1545. The elector of Saxony asked Luther to prepare for this event by setting down a statement of faith, and indicating where there was room for negotiation and where there was not. The result appeared in 1537 and came to be known as the "Smalcald Articles." Their combative tone indicates the extent to which Luther, by this time, was unwilling to compromise with the Roman Catholic Church. Note, for instance, the stark contrast Luther now emphasizes between the Roman Catholic "mass" and his reformed "Lord's Supper."

[Part II]

The second part treats the articles which pertain to the office and work of Jesus Christ, or to our redemption.

Article I. [Christ and Faith]

The first and chief article is this, that Jesus Christ, our God and Lord, "was put to death for our trespasses and raised again for our justification" [Rom. 4:25]. He alone is "the Lamb of God, who takes away the sin of the world" [John 1:29]. "God has laid upon him the iniquities of us all" (Isa. 53:6). Moreover, "all have sinned," and "they are justified by his grace as a gift, through the redemption which is in Christ Jesus, by his blood" [Rom. 3:23-25].

Inasmuch as this must be believed and cannot be obtained or apprehended by any work, law, or merit, it is clear and certain that such faith alone justifies us, as St. Paul says in Romans 3, "For we hold that a man is justified by faith apart from the works of law" [Rom. 3:28], and again, "that he [God] himself is righteous and that he justifies him who has faith in Jesus" [Rom. 3:26].

Nothing in this article can be given up or compromised, even if heaven and earth and things temporal should be destroyed. For as St. Peter says, "there is no other name under heaven given among men by which we must be saved" [Acts 4:12]. "And with his stripes we are healed" [Isa. 53:5].

On this article rests all that we teach and practice against the pope, the devil, and the world. Therefore we must be quite certain and have no doubts about it. Otherwise all is lost, and the pope, the devil, and all our adversaries will gain the victory.

Article II. [The Mass]

The mass in the papacy must be regarded as the greatest and most horrible abomination because it runs into direct and violent conflict with this fundamental article. Yet, above and beyond all others, it has been the supreme and most precious of the papal idolatries, for it is held that this sacrifice or work of the mass (even when offered by an evil scoundrel) delivers men from their sins, both here in this life and yonder in purgatory, although in reality this can and must be done by the Lamb of God alone, as has been stated above. There is to be no concession or compromise in this article either, for the first article does not permit it.

If there were reasonable papists, one would speak to them in the following friendly fashion:

Why do you cling so tenaciously to your masses?

1. After all, they are a purely human invention. They are not commanded by God. And we can discard all human inventions, for Christ says, 'In vain do they worship me, teaching as doctrines the precepts of men' [Matt. 15:9].

2. The mass is unnecessary, and so it can be omitted without sin and danger.

3. The sacrament can be had in a far better and more blessed manner—indeed, the only blessed manner—according to the institution of Christ. Why, then, do you drive the world into wretchedness and woe on account of an unnecessary and fictitious matter when the sacrament can be had in another and more blessed way?

Let the people be told openly that the mass, as trumpery, can be omitted without sin, that no one will be damned for not observing it, and that one can be saved in a better way without the mass. Will the mass not then collapse of itself—not only for the rude rabble, but also for all godly, Christian, sensible, God-fearing people—especially if they hear that it is a dangerous thing which was fabricated and invented without God's Word and will?

4. Since such countless and unspeakable abuses have arisen, everywhere through the buying and selling of masses, it would be prudent to do without the mass for no other reason than to curb such abuses, even if it actually possessed some value in and of itself. How much the more should it be discontinued in order to guard forever against such abuses when it is so unnecessary, useless, and dangerous and when we can obtain what is more necessary, more

useful, and more certain without the mass.

5. The mass is and can be nothing else than a human work, even a work of evil scoundrels (as the canon and all books on the subject declare), for by means of the mass men try to reconcile themselves and others to God and obtain and merit grace and the forgiveness of sins. It is observed for this purpose when it is best observed. What other purpose could it have? Therefore, it should be condemned and must be abolished because it is a direct contradiction to the fundamental article, which asserts that it is not the celebrant of a mass and what he does but the Lamb of God and the Son of God who takes away our sin.

Somebody may seek to justify himself by saying that he wishes to communicate himself [take communion] for the sake of his own devotion. This is not honest, for if he really desires to commune, he can do so most fittingly and properly in the sacrament administered according to Christ's institution. To commune by himself is uncertain and unnecessary, and he does not know what he is doing because he follows a false human opinion and imagination without the sanction of God's Word. Nor is it right (even if everything else is in order) for anyone to use the sacrament, which is the common possession of the church, to meet his own private need and thus trifle with it according to his own pleasure apart from the fellowship of the church.

This article concerning the mass will be the decisive issue in the council. Even if it were possible for the papists to make concessions to us in all other articles, it would not be possible for them to yield on this article. It is as Campegio said in Augsburg: he would suffer himself to be torn to pieces before he would give up the mass. So by God's help I would suffer myself to be burned to ashes before I would allow a celebrant of the mass and what he does to be considered equal or superior to my Savior, Jesus Christ. Accordingly we are and remain eternally divided and opposed the one to the other. The papists are well aware that if the mass falls, the papacy will fall with it. Before they would permit this to happen, they would put us all to death.

Besides, this dragon's tail—that is, the mass—has brought forth a brood of vermin and the poison of manifold idolatries.

The first is purgatory. They were so occupied with requiem masses, with vigils, with the weekly, monthly, and yearly celebrations of requiems, with the common week, with All Souls' Day, and with soul-baths that the mass was used almost exclusively for the dead although Christ instituted the sacrament for the living alone. Consequently purgatory and all the pomp, services, and business transactions associated with it are to be regarded as nothing else than illusions of the devil, for purgatory, too, is contrary to the fundamental article that Christ alone, and not the work of man, can help souls. Besides, nothing has been commanded or enjoined upon us with reference to the dead. All this may consequently be discarded, apart entirely from the fact that it is error and idolatry.

The papists here adduce passages from Augustine and some of the Fathers who are said to have written about purgatory. They suppose that we do not understand for what purpose and to what end the authors wrote these passages. St. Augustine does not write that there is a purgatory, nor does he cite any passage of the Scriptures that would constrain him to adopt such an opinion. He leaves it undecided whether or not there is a purgatory and merely mentions that his mother asked that she be remembered at the altar or sacrament. Now, this is nothing but

a human opinion of certain individuals and cannot establish an article of faith. That is the prerogative of God alone. But our papists make use of such human opinions to make men believe their shameful, blasphemous, accursed traffic in masses which are offered for souls in purgatory, etc. They can never demonstrate these things from Augustine. Only when they have abolished their traffic in purgatorial masses (which St. Augustine never dreamed of) shall we be ready to discuss with them whether statements of St. Augustine are to be accepted when they are without the support of the Scriptures and whether the dead are to be commemorated in the sacrament. It will not do to make articles of faith out of the holy Fathers' words or works. Otherwise what they ate, how they dressed, and what kind of houses they lived in would have to become articles of faith—as has happened in the case of relics. This means that the Word of God shall establish articles of faith and no one else, not even an angel.

The second is a consequence of this: evil spirits have introduced the knavery of appearing as spirits of the departed and, with unspeakable lies and cunning, of demanding masses, vigils, pilgrimages, and other alms. We had to accept all these things as articles of faith and had to live according to them. Moreover, the pope gave his approval to these things as well as to the mass and all the other abominations. Here, too, there can be no concession or compromise.

The third are pilgrimages. Masses, forgiveness of sins, and God's grace were sought here, too, for masses dominated everything. It is certain that we have not been commanded to make pilgrimages, nor are they necessary, because we may obtain forgiveness and grace in a better way and may omit pilgrimages without sin and danger. Why do they neglect their own parishes, the Word of God, their wives and children, etc. and pursue these unnecessary, uncertain, harmful will-o'-the-wisps of the devil? They do so simply because the devil has possessed the pope to praise and approve of these practices in order that great multitudes of people may turn aside from Christ to their own merits and (what is worst of all) become idolaters. Besides, it is an unnecessary, uncommanded, abortive, uncertain, and even harmful thing. Therefore there may be no concession or compromise here either.

The fourth are fraternities. Here monasteries, chapters, and vicars have obligated themselves to transfer (by legal and open sale) all masses, good works, etc. for the benefit of the living and the dead. Not only is this mere human trumpery, utterly unnecessary and without command, but it is contrary to the first article, concerning redemption. Therefore, it is under no circumstances to be tolerated.

The fifth are relics. In this connection so many manifest lies and so much nonsense has been invented about the bones of dogs and horses that even the devil has laughed at such knavery. Even if there were some good in them, relics should long since have been condemned. They are neither commanded nor commended. They are utterly unnecessary and useless. Worst of all, however, is the claim that relics effect indulgences and the forgiveness of sin and that, like the mass, etc., their use is a good work and a service of God.

The sixth place belongs to the precious indulgences, which are granted to the living and the dead (for money) and by which the pope sells the merits of Christ together with the superabundant merits of all the saints and the entire church. These are not to be tolerated. Not only are they unnecessary and without commandment, but they are also contrary to the first article, for the merits of Christ are obtained by grace, through faith, without our work or pennies. They are offered to us without our money or merit, not by the power of the pope but by the preaching of God's Word.

The Invocation of Saints: The invocation of saints is also one of the abuses of the Antichrist. It is in conflict with the first, chief article and undermines knowledge of Christ. It is neither commanded nor recommended, nor does it have any precedent in the Scriptures. Even if the invocation of saints were a precious practice (which it is not), we have everything a thousandfold better in Christ.

Although angels in heaven pray for us (as Christ himself also does), and although saints on earth, and perhaps also in heaven, do likewise, it does not follow that we should invoke angels and saints, pray to them, keep fasts and festivals for them, say masses and offer sacrifices to them, establish churches, altars, and services for them, serve them in still other ways, regard them as helpers in time of need, and attribute all sorts of help to them, assigning to each of them a special function, as the papists teach and practice. This is idolatry. Such honor belongs to God alone. As a Christian and a saint on earth, you can pray for me, not in one particular necessity only, but in every kind of need. However, I should not on this account pray to you, invoke you, keep fasts and festivals and say masses and offer sacrifices in your honor, or trust in you for my salvation. There are other ways in which I can honor, love, and thank you in Christ. If such idolatrous honor is withdrawn from angels and dead saints, the honor that remains will do no harm and will quickly be forgotten. When spiritual and physical benefit and help are no longer expected, the saints will cease to be molested in their graves and in heaven, for no one will long remember, esteem, or honor them out of love when there is no expectation of return.

In short, we cannot allow but must condemn the mass, its implications, and its consequences in order that we may retain the holy sacrament in its purity and certainty according to the institution of Christ and may use and receive it in faith.

Article III. [Chapters and Monasteries]

The chapters and monasteries which in former times had been founded with good intentions for the education of learned men and decent women should be restored to such purposes in order that we may have pastors, preachers, and other ministers in the church, others who are necessary for secular government in cities and states, and also well-trained girls to become mothers, housekeepers, etc.

If they are unwilling to serve this purpose, it would be better to abandon them or tear them down rather than preserve them with their blasphemous services, invented by men, which claim to be superior to the ordinary Christian life and to the offices and callings established by God. All this, too, is in conflict with the first, fundamental article concerning redemption in Jesus Christ. Besides, like other human inventions, all this is without commandment, unnecessary, and useless. Moreover, it causes dangerous and needless effort, and accordingly the prophets call such service of God *aven*, that is, vanity.

Article IV. [The Papacy]

The pope is not the head of all Christendom by divine right or according to God's Word, for this position belongs only to one, namely, to Jesus Christ. The pope is only the bishop and pastor of the churches in Rome and of such other churches as have attached themselves to him voluntarily or through a human institution (that is, a secular government). These churches did not choose to be under him as under an overlord but chose to stand beside him as Christian brethren and companions, as the ancient councils and the time of Cyprian prove. But now no bishop dares to call the pope "brother," as was then customary, but must address him as "most gracious lord," as if he were a king or emperor. This we neither will nor should nor can take upon our consciences. Those who wish to do so had better not count on us!

Hence it follows that all the things that the pope has undertaken and done on the strength of such false, mischievous, blasphemous, usurped authority have been and still are purely diabolical transactions and deeds (except what pertains to secular government, where God sometimes permits much good to come to a people through a tyrant or scoundrel) which contribute to the destruction of the entire holy Christian church (insofar as this lies in his power) and come into conflict with the first, fundamental article which is concerned with redemption in Jesus Christ.

All the pope's bulls and books, in which he roars like a lion (as the angel in Rev. 10:3 suggests), are available. Here it is asserted that no Christian can be saved unless he is obedient to the pope and submits to him in all that he desires, says, and does. This is nothing less than to say, "Although you believe in Christ, and in him have everything that is needful for salvation, this is nothing and all in vain unless you consider me your god and are obedient and subject to me." Yet it is manifest that the holy church was without a pope for more than five hundred years at the least and that the churches of the Greeks and of many other nationalities have never been under the pope and are not at the present time. Manifestly (to repeat what has already been said often) the papacy is a human invention, and it is not commanded, it is unnecessary, and it is useless. The holy Christian church can exist very well without such a head, and it would have remained much better if such a head had not been raised up by the devil. The papacy is of no use to the church because it exercises no Christian office. Consequently the church must continue to exist without the pope.

Suppose that the pope would renounce the claim that he is the head of the church by divine right or by God's command; suppose that it were necessary to have a head, to whom all others should adhere in order that the unity of Christendom might better be preserved against the attacks of sects and heresies; and suppose that such a head would then be elected by men and it remained in their power and choice to change or depose this head. This is just the way in which the Council of Constance acted with reference to the popes when it deposed three and elected a fourth. If, I say, the pope and the see of Rome were to concede and accept this (which is impossible), he would have to suffer the overthrow and destruction of his whole rule and estate, together with all his rights and pretensions. In short, he cannot do it. Even if he could, Christendom would not be helped in any way. There would be even more sects than before because, inasmuch as subjection to such a head would depend on the good pleasure of men rather than on a divine command, he would very easily and quickly be despised and would ultimately be without any adherents at all. He would not always

have to have his residence in Rome or some other fixed place, but it could be anywhere and in whatever church God would raise up a man fitted for such an office. What a complicated and confused state of affairs that would be!

Consequently the church cannot be better governed and maintained than by having all of us live under one head, Christ, and by having all the bishops equal in office (however they may differ in gifts) and diligently joined together in unity of doctrine, faith, sacraments, prayer, works of love, etc. So St. Jerome writes that the priests of Alexandria governed the churches together and in common. The apostles did the same, and after them all the bishops throughout Christendom, until the pope raised his head over them all.

This is a powerful demonstration that the pope is the real Antichrist who has raised himself over and set himself against Christ, for the pope will not permit Christians to be saved except by his own power, which amounts to nothing since it is neither established nor commanded by God. This is actually what St. Paul calls exalting oneself over and against God. Neither the Turks nor the Tartars, great as is their enmity against Christians, do this; those who desire to do so they allow to believe in Christ, and they receive bodily tribute and obedience from Christians.

However, the pope will not permit such faith but asserts that one must be obedient to him in order to be saved. This we are unwilling to do even if we have to die for it in God's name. All this is a consequence of his wishing to be the head of the Christian church by divine right. He had to set himself up as equal to and above Christ and to proclaim himself the head, and then the lord of the church, and finally of the whole world. He went so far as to claim to be an earthly god and even presumed to issue orders to the angels in heaven.

When the teaching of the pope is distinguished from that of the Holy Scriptures, or is compared with them, it becomes apparent that, at its best, the teaching of the pope has been taken from the imperial, pagan law and is a teaching concerning secular transactions and judgments, as the papal decretals show. In keeping with such teaching, instructions are given concerning the ceremonies of churches, vestments, food, personnel, and countless other puerilities, fantasies, and follies without so much as a mention of Christ, faith, and God's commandments.

Finally, it is most diabolical for the pope to promote his lies about masses, purgatory, monastic life, and human works and services (which are the essence of the papacy) in contradiction to God, and to damn, slay, and plague all Christians who do not exalt and honor these abominations of his above all things. Accordingly, just as we cannot adore the devil himself as our lord or God, so we cannot suffer his apostle, the pope or Antichrist, to govern us as our head or lord, for deception, murder, and the eternal destruction of body and soul are characteristic of his papal government, as I have demonstrated in many books.

In these four articles they will have enough to condemn in the council, for they neither can nor will concede to us even the smallest fraction of these articles. Of this we may be certain, and we must rely on the hope that Christ, our Lord, has attacked his adversaries and will accomplish his purpose by his Spirit and his coming. Amen. In the council we shall not be standing before the emperor or the secular authority, as at Augsburg, where we responded to a gracious summons and were given a kindly hearing, but we shall stand before the pope and the devil himself, who does not intend to give us a hearing but only to damn, murder, and drive us to idolatry. Consequently we ought not here kiss his feet or say, "You are my gracious lord," but we ought rather speak as the angel spoke to the devil in Zechariah, "The Lord rebuke you, O Satan" (Zech. 3:2).

[Part III]

The following articles treat matters which we may discuss with learned and sensible men, or even among ourselves. The pope and his court do not care much about these things; they are not concerned about matters of conscience but only about money, honor, and power.

I. Sin

Here we must confess what St. Paul says in Rom. 5:12, namely, that sin had its origin in one man, Adam, through whose disobedience all men were made sinners and became subject to death and the devil. This is called original sin, or the root sin.

The fruits of this sin are all the subsequent evil deeds which are forbidden in the Ten Commandments, such as unbelief, false belief, idolatry, being without the fear of God, presumption, despair, blindness—in short, ignorance or disregard of God—and then also lying, swearing by God's name, failure to pray and call upon God, neglect of God's Word, disobedience to parents, murder, unchastity, theft, deceit, etc.

This hereditary sin is so deep a corruption of nature that reason cannot understand it. It must be believed because of the revelation in the Scriptures (Ps. 51:5, Rom. 5:12ff., Exod. 33:20, Gen. 3:6ff.). What the scholastic theologians taught concerning this article is therefore nothing but error and stupidity, namely,

1. That after the fall of Adam the natural powers of man have remained whole and uncorrupted, and that man by nature possesses right understanding and a good will, as the philosophers teach.

2. Again, that man has a free will, either to do good and refrain from evil or to refrain from good and do evil.

3. Again, that man is able by his natural powers to observe and keep all the commandments of God.

4. Again, that man is able by his natural powers to love God above all things and his neighbor as himself.

5. Again, if man does what he can, God is certain to grant him his grace.

6. Again, when a man goes to the sacrament there is no need of a good intention to do what he ought, but it is enough that he does not have an evil intention to commit sin, for such is the goodness of man's nature and such is the power of the sacrament.

7. That it cannot be proved from the Scriptures that the Holy Spirit and his gifts are necessary for the performance of a good work. Such and many similar notions have resulted from misunderstanding and ignorance concerning sin and concerning Christ, our Savior. They are thoroughly pagan doctrines, and we cannot tolerate them. If such teachings were true, Christ would have died in vain, for there would be no defect or sin in man for which he would have had to die, or else he would have died only for the body and not for the soul inasmuch as the soul would be sound and only the body would be subject to death.

II. The Law

Here we maintain that the law was given by God first of all to restrain sins by threats and fear of punishment and by the promise and offer of grace and favor. But this purpose failed because of the wickedness which sin has worked in man. Some, who hate the law because it forbids what they desire to do and commands what they are unwilling to do, are made worse thereby. Accordingly, insofar as they are not restrained by punishment, they act against the law even more than before. These are the rude and wicked people who do evil whenever they have opportunity. Others become blind and presumptuous, imagining that they can and do keep the law by their own powers, as was just said above concerning the scholastic theologians. Hypocrites and false saints are produced in this way.

However, the chief function or power of the law is to make original sin manifest and show man to what utter depths his nature has fallen and how corrupt it has become. So the law must tell him that he neither has nor cares for God or that he worships strange gods—something that he would not have believed before without a knowledge of the law. Thus he is terror-stricken and humbled, becomes despondent and despairing, anxiously desires help but does not know where to find it, and begins to be alienated from God, to murmur, etc. This is what is meant by Rom. 4:15, "The law brings wrath," and Rom. 5:20, "Law came in to increase the trespass."

III. Repentance

This function of the law is retained and taught by the New Testament. So Paul says in Rom. 1:18, "The wrath of God is revealed from heaven against all ungodliness and wickedness of men," and in Rom. 3:19, 20, "The whole world may be held accountable to God, for no human being will be justified in his sight." Christ also says in John 16:8, "The Holy Spirit will convince the world of sin."

This, then, is the thunderbolt by means of which God with one blow destroys both open sinners and false saints. He allows no one to justify himself. He drives all together into terror and despair. This is the hammer of which Jeremiah speaks, "Is not my word like a hammer which breaks the rock in pieces?" (Jer. 23:29). This is not *activa contritio* (artificial remorse), but *passiva contritio* (true sorrow of the heart, suffering, and pain of death).

This is what the beginning of true repentance is like. Here man must hear such a judgment as this: "You are all of no account. Whether you are manifest sinners or saints, you must all become other than you now are and do otherwise than you now do, no matter who you are and no matter how great, wise, mighty, and holy you may think yourselves. Here no one is godly," etc.

To this office of the law the New Testament immediately adds the consoling promise of grace in the gospel. This is to be believed, as Christ says in Mark 1:15. "Repent and believe in the gospel," which is to say, "Become different, do otherwise, and believe my promise." John, who preceded Christ, is called a preacher of repentance—but, for the remission of sins. That is, John was to accuse them all and convince them that they were sinners in order that they might know how they stood before God and recognize themselves as lost men. In this way they were to be prepared to receive grace from the Lord and to expect and accept from him the forgiveness of sins. Christ himself says this in Luke 24:47, "Repentance and the forgiveness of sins should be preached in his name to all nations."

But where the law exercises its office alone, without the addition of the gospel, there is only death and hell, and man must despair like Saul and Judas. As St. Paul says, the law slays through sin. Moreover, the gospel offers consolation and forgiveness in more ways than one, for with God there is plenteous redemption (as Ps. 130:7 puts it) from the dreadful captivity to sin, and this comes to us through the Word, the sacraments, and the like, as we shall hear.

Now we must compare the false repentance of the sophists with true repentance so that both may be better understood.

The False Repentance of the Papists: It was impossible for them to teach correctly about repentance because they did not know what sin really is. For, as stated above, they did not have the right teaching concerning original sin but asserted that the natural powers of man have remained whole and uncorrupted, that reason is capable of right understanding and the will is capable of acting accordingly, and that God will assuredly grant his grace to the man who does as much as he can according to his free will.

From this it follows that people did penance only for actual sins, such as wicked thoughts to which they consented (for evil impulses, lust, and inclinations they did not consider sin), wicked words, and wicked works which man with his free will might well have avoided. Such repentance the sophists divided into three parts—contrition, confession, and satisfaction—with the added consolation that a man who properly repents, confesses, and makes satisfaction has merited forgiveness and has paid for his sins before God. In their teaching of penance the sophists thus instructed the people to place their confidence in their own works. Hence the expression in the pulpit when the general confession was recited to the people: "Prolong my life, Lord God, until I make satisfaction for my sins and amend my life."

There was no mention here of Christ or of faith. Rather, men hoped by their own works to overcome and blot out their sins before God. With this intention we, too, became priests and monks, that we might set ourselves against sin.

As for contrition, this was the situation: Since nobody could recall all his sins (especially those committed during the course of a whole year), the following loophole was resorted to, namely, that when a hidden sin was afterwards remembered, it had also to be repented of, confessed, etc., but meanwhile the sinner was commended to the grace of God. Moreover, since nobody knew how much contrition he had to muster in order to avail before God, this consolation was offered: If anybody could not be contrite (that is, really repentant), he should at least be attrite (which I might call halfway or partially repentant). They understood neither of these terms, and, to this day they are as far from comprehending their meaning as I am. Nevertheless, such attrition was reckoned as a substitute for contrition when people went to confession. And when somebody said that he was unable to repent or be sorry for his sin (which might have been committed, let us say, in whoredom, revenge, or the like), such a person was asked if he did not wish or desire to be repentant. If he said yes (for who but the devil himself would want to say no?) it was counted as contrition and, on the basis of this good work of his, his sin was forgiven. Here the example of St. Bernard, etc. was cited.

Here we see how blind reason gropes about in matters which pertain to God, seeking consolation in its own works, according to its own inventions, without being able to consider Christ and faith. If we examine this in the light, we see that such contrition is an artificial and imaginary idea evolved by man's own powers without faith and without knowledge of Christ. A poor sinner who reflected on his lust or revenge in this fashion would sooner have laughed than wept, unless perchance he was really smitten by the law or vainly vexed with a sorrowful spirit by the devil. Apart from cases like this, such repentance surely was pure hypocrisy. It did not extinguish the lust for sin. The person involved was obliged to grieve, but he would rather have sinned if he had been free to do so.

As for confession, the situation was like this: Everybody had to give an account of all his sins—an impossibility and the source of great torture. The sins which had been forgotten were pardoned only when a man remembered them and thereupon confessed them. Accordingly he could never know when he had made a sufficiently complete or a sufficiently pure confession. At the same time his attention was directed to his own works, and he was told that the more completely he confessed, the more he was ashamed, and the more he abased himself before the priest, the sooner and the better he would make satisfaction for his sins, for such humiliation would surely earn grace before God. Here, again, there was neither faith nor Christ. A man did not become aware of the power of absolution, for his consolation was made to rest on his enumeration of sins and on his self-abasement. But this is not the place to recount the torture, rascality, and idolatry which such confession has produced.

Satisfaction was even more complicated, for nobody could know how much he was to do for one single sin, to say nothing of all his sins. Here the expedient was resorted to of imposing small satisfactions which were easy to render, like saying five Our Fathers, fasting for a day, etc. For the penance that was still lacking, man was referred to purgatory.

Here, too, there was nothing but anguish and misery. Some thought that they would never get out of purgatory because, according to the ancient canons, seven years of penance were required for a single mortal sin. Nevertheless, confidence was placed in man's own works of satisfaction. If the satisfaction could have been perfect, full confidence would have been placed in it, and neither faith nor Christ would have been of any value. But such confidence was impossible. Even if one had done penance in this way for a hundred years, one would still not have known whether this was enough. This is a case of always doing penance but never coming to repentance.

Here the holy see in Rome came to the aid of the poor church and invented indulgences. By these satisfaction was remitted and cancelled, first for seven years in a single case, then for a hundred, etc. The indulgences were distributed among the cardinals and bishops so that one could grant them for a hundred years, another for a hundred days, but the pope reserved for himself alone the right to remit the entire satisfaction.

When this began to yield money and the bull market became profitable, the pope invented the jubilee year and attached it to Rome. This was called remission of all penalty and guilt, and the people came running, for everyone was eager to be delivered from the heavy, unbearable burden. Here we have the discovery and digging up of the treasures of the earth. The popes went further and quickly multiplied the jubilee years. The more money they swallowed, the wider became their maws. So they sent their legates out into all lands until every church and house was reached by jubilee indulgences. Finally

the popes forced their way into purgatory, first by instituting masses and vigils for the dead and afterwards by offering indulgences for the dead through bulls and jubilee years. In time souls got to be so cheap that they were released at six pence a head.

Even this did not help, however, for although the pope taught the people to rely on and trust in such indulgences, he again introduced uncertainty when he declared in his bulls, "Whoever wishes to benefit from the indulgence or jubilee year must be contrite, make confession, and pay money." But the contrition and confession practiced by these people, as we have heard above, are uncertain and hypocritical. Moreover, nobody knew which soul was in purgatory, and nobody knew which of those in purgatory had truly repented and properly confessed. So the pope took the money, consoled the people with his power and indulgences, and once again directed attention to uncertain human works.

There were some who did not think they were guilty of actual sins—that is, of sinful thoughts, words, and deeds. I and others like myself who wished to be monks and priests in monasteries and chapters fought against evil thoughts by fasting, vigils, prayers, masses, coarse clothing, and hard beds and tried earnestly and mightily to be holy, and yet the hereditary evil which is born in us did what is its nature to do, sometimes while we slept (as St. Augustine, St. Jerome, and others confess). Each one, however, held that some of the others were, as we taught, without sin and full of good works, and so we shared our good works with others and sold them to others in the belief that they were more than we ourselves needed for heaven. This is certainly true, and there are seals, letters, and examples to show it. Such persons did not need to repent, for what were they to repent of when they did not consent to evil thoughts? What should they confess when they refrained from evil words? What satisfaction should they render when they were innocent of evil deeds and could even sell their superfluous righteousness to other poor sinners? The scribes and Pharisees in Christ's time were just such saints.

Here the fiery angel St. John, the preacher of true repentance, intervenes. With a single thunderbolt he strikes and destroys both. "Repent," he says. On the one hand there are some who think, "We have already done penance," and on the other hand there are others who suppose, "We need no repentance." But John says:

> Repent, both of you. Those of you in the former group are false penitents, and those of you in the latter are false saints. Both of you need the forgiveness of sins, for neither of you knows what sin really is, to say nothing of repenting and shunning sin. None of you is good. All of you are full of unbelief, blindness, and ignorance of God and God's will. For he is here present, and from his fullness have we all received, grace upon grace. No man can be just before God without him. Accordingly, if you would repent, repent rightly. Your repentance accomplishes nothing. And you hypocrites who think you do not need to repent, you brood of vipers, who has given you any assurance that you will escape the wrath to come?

St. Paul teaches the same thing in Rom. 3:10-12: "None is righteous, no, not one; no one understands, no one seeks for God. All have turned aside, together they have gone wrong." And in Acts 17:30, "Now he commands all men everywhere to repent." He says "all men," that is, excepting no one who is a man. Such repentance teaches us to acknowledge sin—that is, to acknowledge that we are all utterly lost, that from head to foot there is no good in us, that we must become altogether new and different men.

This repentance is not partial and fragmentary like repentance for actual sins, nor is it uncertain like that. It does not debate what is sin and what is not sin, but lumps everything together and says, "We are wholly and altogether sinful." We need not spend our time weighing, distinguishing, differentiating. On this account there is no uncertainty in such repentance, for nothing is left that we might imagine to be good enough to pay for our sin. One thing is sure: We cannot pin our hope on anything that we are, think, say, or do. And so our repentance cannot be false, uncertain, or partial, for a person who confesses that he is altogether sinful embraces all sins in his confession without omitting or forgetting a single one. Nor can our satisfaction be uncertain, for it consists not of the dubious, sinful works which we do but of the sufferings and blood of the innocent Lamb of God who takes away the sin of the world.

This is the repentance which John preaches, which Christ subsequently preaches in the gospel, and which we also preach. With this repentance we overthrow the pope and everything that is built on our good works, for all of this is constructed on an unreal and rotten foundation which is called good works or the law, although no good work but only wicked works are there and although no one keeps the law (as Christ says in John 7:19) but all transgress it. Accordingly the entire building, even when it is most holy and beautiful, is nothing but deceitful falsehood and hypocrisy.

In the case of a Christian such repentance continues until death, for all through life it contends with the sins that remain in the flesh. As St. Paul testifies in Rom. 7:23, he wars with the law in his members, and he does this not with his own powers but with the gift of the Holy Spirit which follows the forgiveness of sins. This gift daily cleanses and expels the sins that remain and enables man to become truly pure and holy. This is something about which the pope, the theologians, the jurists, and all men understand nothing. It is a teaching from heaven, revealed in the gospel, and yet it is called a heresy by godless saints.

Some fanatics may appear (and perhaps they are already present, such as I saw with my own eyes at the time of the uprising) who hold that once they have received the Spirit or the forgiveness of sins, or once they have become believers, they will persevere in faith even if they sin afterwards, and such sin will not harm them. They cry out, "Do what you will, it matters not as long as you believe, for faith blots out all sins," etc. They add that if anyone sins after he has received faith and the Spirit, he never really had the Spirit and faith. I have encountered many foolish people like this and I fear that such a devil still dwells in some of them.

It is therefore necessary to know and to teach that when holy people, aside from the fact that they still possess and feel original sin and daily repent and strive against it, fall into open sin (as David fell into adultery, murder, and blasphemy), faith and the Spirit have departed from them. This is so because the Holy Spirit does not permit sin to rule and gain the upper hand in such a way that sin is committed, but the Holy Spirit represses and restrains it so that it does not do what it wishes. If sin does what it wishes, the Holy Spirit and faith are not present, for St. John says, "No one born of God commits sin; he cannot sin." Yet it is also true, as the same St.

John writes, "If we say we have no sin, we deceive ourselves, and the truth is not in us."

IV. The Gospel

We shall now return to the gospel, which offers counsel and help against sin in more than one way, for God is surpassingly rich in his grace: First, through the spoken word, by which the forgiveness of sin (the peculiar function of the gospel) is preached to the whole world; second, through Baptism; third, through the holy sacrament of the altar; fourth, through the power of keys; and finally, through the mutual conversation and consolation of brethren. Matt. 18:20, "Where two or three are gathered," etc.

V. Baptism

Baptism is nothing else than the Word of God in water, commanded by the institution of Christ; or as Paul says, "the washing of water with the word"; or, again, as Augustine puts it, "The Word is added to the element and it becomes a sacrament." Therefore we do not agree with Thomas and the Dominicans who forget the Word (God's institution) and say that God has joined to the water a spiritual power which, through the water, washes away sin. Nor do we agree with Scotus and the Franciscans who teach that Baptism washes away sin through the assistance of the divine will, as if the washing takes place only through God's will and not at all through the Word and the water.

As for infant Baptism, we hold that children should be baptized, for they, too, are included in the promise of redemption which Christ made, and the church should administer Baptism to them.

VI. The Sacrament of the Altar

We hold that the bread and the wine in the supper are the true body and blood of Christ and that these are given and received not only by godly but also by wicked Christians.

We also hold that it is not to be administered in one form only. We need not resort to the specious learning of the sophists and the Council of Constance that as much is included under one form as under both. Even if it were true that as much is included under one form as under both, yet administration in one form is not the whole order and institution as it was established and commanded by Christ. Especially do we condemn and curse in God's name those who not only omit both forms but even go so far as autocratically to prohibit, condemn, and slander the use of both as heresy and thus set themselves against and over Christ, our Lord and God, etc.

As for transubstantiation, we have no regard for the subtle sophistry of those who teach that bread and wine surrender or lose their natural substance and retain only the appearance and shape of bread without any longer being real bread, for that bread is and remains there agrees better with the Scriptures, as St. Paul himself states, "The bread which we break" (1 Cor. 10:16), and again, "Let a man so eat of the bread" (1 Cor. 11:28).

VII. The Keys

The keys are a function and power given to the church by Christ to bind and loose sins, not only the gross and manifest sins but also those which are subtle and secret and which God alone perceives. So it is written, "Who can discern his errors?" (Ps. 19:12). And Paul himself complains (Rom. 7:23) that in his flesh he was a captive to "the law of sin." It is not in our power but in God's alone to judge which, how great, and how many our sins are. As it is written, "Enter not into judgment with thy servant, for no man living is righteous before thee" (Ps. 143:2), and Paul also says in 1 Cor. 4:4, "I am not

aware of anything against myself, but I am not thereby acquitted."

VIII. Confession

Since absolution or the power of the keys, which was instituted by Christ in the gospel, is a consolation and help against sin and a bad conscience, confession and absolution should by no means be allowed to fall into disuse in the church, especially for the sake of timid consciences and for the sake of untrained young people who need to be examined and instructed in Christian doctrine.

However, the enumeration of sins should be left free to everybody to do or not as he will. As long as we are in the flesh we shall not be untruthful if we say, "I am a poor man, full of sin. I see in my members another law," etc. (Rom. 7:23). Although private absolution is derived from the office of the keys, it should not be neglected; on the contrary, it should be highly esteemed and valued, like all other functions of the Christian church.

In these matters, which concern the external, spoken Word, we must hold firmly to the conviction that God gives no one his Spirit or grace except through or with the external Word which comes before. Thus we shall be protected from the enthusiasts—that is, from the spiritualists who boast that they possess the Spirit without and before the Word and who therefore judge, interpret, and twist the Scriptures or spoken Word according to their pleasure. Müntzer did this, and many still do it in our day who wish to distinguish sharply between the letter and the spirit without knowing what they say or teach. The papacy, too, is nothing but enthusiasm, for the pope boasts that "all laws are in the shrine of his heart," and he claims that whatever he decides and commands in his churches is spirit and law, even when it is above and contrary to the Scriptures or spoken

Word. All this is the old devil and the old serpent who made enthusiasts of Adam and Eve. He led them from the external Word of God to spiritualizing and to their own imaginations, and he did this through other external words. Even so, the enthusiasts of our day condemn the external Word, yet they do not remain silent but fill the world with their chattering and scribbling, as if the Spirit could not come through the Scriptures or the spoken word of the apostles but must come through their own writings and words. Why do they not stop preaching and writing until the Spirit himself comes to the people without and before their writings since they boast that the Spirit came upon them without the testimony of the Scriptures? There is no time to dispute further about these matters. After all, we have treated them sufficiently elsewhere.

Even those who have come to faith before they were baptized and those who came to faith in Baptism came to their faith through the external Word which preceded. Adults who have attained the age of reason must first have heard, "He who believes and is baptized will be saved" (Mark 16:16), even if they did not at once believe and did not receive the Spirit and Baptism until ten years later. Cornelius (Acts 10:1 ff.) had long since heard from the Jews about the coming Messiah through whom he was justified before God, and his prayers and alms were acceptable to God in this faith (Luke calls him "devout" and "God-fearing"), but he could not have believed and been justified if the Word and his hearing of it had not preceded. However, St. Peter had to reveal to him that the Messiah, in whose coming he had previously believed, had already come, and his faith concerning the coming Messiah did not hold him captive with the hardened, unbelieving Jews, but he knew that he now had to be saved by the present Messiah and not deny or persecute him as the Jews did.

In short, enthusiasm clings to Adam and his descendants from the beginning to the end of the world. It is a poison implanted and inoculated in man by the old dragon, and it is the source, strength, and power of all heresy, including that of the papacy and Mohammedanism [Islam]. Accordingly, we should and must constantly maintain that God will not deal with us except through his external Word and sacrament. Whatever is attributed to the Spirit apart from such Word and sacrament is of the devil. For even to Moses God wished to appear first through the burning bush and the spoken word, and no prophet, whether Elijah or Elisha, received the Spirit without the Ten Commandments. John the Baptist was not conceived without the preceding word of Gabriel, nor did he leap in his mother's womb until Mary spoke. St. Peter says that when the prophets spoke, they did not prophesy by the impulse of man but were moved by the Holy Spirit, yet as holy men of God. But without the external Word they were not holy, and the Holy Spirit would not have moved them to speak while they were still unholy. They were holy, St. Peter says, because the Holy Spirit spoke through them.

IX. Excommunication

We consider the greater excommunication, as the pope calls it, to be merely a civil penalty which does not concern us ministers of the church. However, the lesser (that is, the truly Christian) excommunication excludes those who are manifest and impenitent sinners from the sacrament and other fellowship of the church until they mend their ways and avoid sin. Preachers should not mingle civil punishments with this spiritual penalty or excommunication.

X. Ordination and Vocation

If the bishops were true bishops and were concerned about the church and the gospel, they might be permitted (for the sake of love and unity, but not of necessity) to ordain and confirm us and our preachers, provided this could be done without pretense, humbug, and unchristian ostentation. However, they neither are nor wish to be true bishops. They are temporal lords and princes who are unwilling to preach or teach or baptize or administer Communion or discharge any office or work in the church. More than that, they expel, persecute, and condemn those who have been called to do these things. Yet the church must not be deprived of ministers on their account.

Accordingly, as we are taught by the examples of the ancient churches and Fathers, we shall and ought ourselves ordain suitable persons to this office. The papists have no right to forbid or prevent us, not even according to their own laws, for their laws state that those who are ordained by heretics shall also be regarded as ordained and remain so. St. Jerome, too, wrote concerning the church in Alexandria that it was originally governed without bishops by priests and preachers in common.

XI. The Marriage of Priests

The papists had neither authority nor right to prohibit marriage and burden the divine estate of priests with perpetual celibacy. On the contrary, they acted like antichristian, tyrannical, and wicked scoundrels, and thereby they gave occasion for all sorts of horrible, abominable, and countless sins, in which they are still involved. As little as the power has been given to us or to them to make a woman out of a man or a man out of a woman or abolish distinctions of sex altogether, so little have they had the power to separate such creatures of God or forbid them to live together honestly in marriage. We are therefore unwilling to consent to their abominable celibacy, nor shall we suffer it. On the contrary, we desire marriage to be free, as God ordained and instituted it, and we shall not disrupt or hinder God's work, for St. Paul says that to do so is a doctrine of demons.

XII. The Church

We do not concede to the papists that they are the church, for they are not. Nor shall we pay any attention to what they command or forbid in the name of the church, for, thank God, a seven-year-old child knows what the church is, namely, holy believers and sheep who hear the voice of their Shepherd. So children pray, "I believe in one holy Christian church." Its holiness does not consist of surplices, tonsures, albs, or other ceremonies of theirs which they have invented over and above the Holy Scriptures, but it consists of the Word of God and true faith.

XIII. How Man Is Justified before God, and His Good Works

I do not know how I can change what I have heretofore constantly taught on this subject, namely, that by faith (as St. Peter says) we get a new and clean heart and that God will and does account us altogether righteous and holy for the sake of Christ, our mediator. Although the sin in our flesh has not been completely removed or eradicated, he will not count or consider it.

Good works follow such faith, renewal, and forgiveness. Whatever is still sinful or imperfect in these works will not be reckoned as sin or defect for the sake of the same Christ. The whole man, in respect both of his person and of his works, shall be accounted and shall be righteous and holy through the pure grace and mercy which have been poured out upon us so abundantly in Christ. Accordingly we cannot boast of the great merit in our works if they are considered apart from God's grace and mercy, but, as it is written, "Let him who boasts, boast of the Lord" (1 Cor. 1:31). That is to say, all is well if we boast that we have a gracious God. To this we must add that if good works do not follow, our faith is false and not true.

XIV. Monastic Vows

Since monastic vows are in direct conflict with the first chief article, they must be absolutely set aside. It is of these that Christ says in Matt. 24:5, "I am the Christ," etc. Whoever takes the vows of monastic life believes that he is entering upon a mode of life that is better than that of the ordinary Christian and proposes by means of his work to help not only himself but also others to get to heaven. This is to deny Christ, etc. And on the authority of their St. Thomas, such people boast that a monastic vow is equal to Baptism. This is blasphemy.

XV. Human Traditions

The assertion of the papists that human traditions effect forgiveness of sins or merit salvation is unchristian and to be condemned. As Christ says, "In vain do they worship me, teaching as doctrines the precepts of men" (Matt. 15:9), and it is written in Titus 1:14, "They are men who reject the truth." When the papists say that it is a mortal sin to break such precepts of men, this, too, is false.

These are the articles on which I must stand and on which I will stand, God willing, until my death. I do not know how I can change or concede anything in them. If anybody wishes to make some concessions, let him do so at the peril of his own conscience.

Finally, there remains the pope's bag of

magic tricks which contains silly and childish articles, such as the consecration of churches, the baptism of bells, the baptism of altar stones, the invitation to such ceremonies of sponsors who might make gifts, etc. Such baptizing is a ridicule and mockery of holy Baptism which should not be tolerated. In addition, there are blessings of candles, palms, spices, oats, cakes, etc. These cannot be called blessings, and they are not, but are mere mockery and fraud. Such frauds, which are without number, we commend for adoration to their god and to themselves until they tire of them. We do not wish to have anything to do with them.

✠

From Tappert, Book of Concord, *292–318.*

Lutheranism

27. The *Augsburg Confession* (1530)

In 1530 the emperor Charles V summoned an imperial diet to meet in Augsburg to restore religious unity to the empire. The Lutheran side was asked for a summary statement of its position, and this was prepared by Luther's most prominent follower, Philip Melanchthon (1497–1560). It received Luther's approval and was widely accepted as Lutheranism's public and official confessional statement. Only its central article on justification is printed here.

✠

Justification

It is also taught among us that we cannot obtain forgiveness of sin and righteousness before God by our own merits, works, or satisfactions, but that we receive forgiveness of sin and become righteous before God by grace, for Christ's sake, through faith, when we believe that Christ suffered for us and that for his sake our sin is forgiven and righteousness and eternal life are given to us. For God will regard and reckon this faith as righteousness, as Paul says in Rom. 3:21-26 and 4:5.

✠

From Tappert, Book of Concord, 30.

28. Philip Melanchthon, *Apology of the Augsburg Confession* (1531)

After the Augsburg negotiations broke down, Melanchthon prepared a lengthy explanation and defense of the *Augsburg Confession*. In its section on justification (printed here), we can see how the most prominent of Luther's followers now understood the heart of his Reformation protest.

✠

[Article IV. Justification]

In the fourth, fifth, and sixth articles, and later in the twentieth, they condemn us for teaching that men do not receive the forgiveness of sins because of their own merits, but freely for Christ's sake, by faith in him. They condemn us both for denying that men receive the forgiveness of sins because of their merits, and for affirming that men receive the forgiveness of sins by faith and by faith in Christ are justified.

In this controversy the main doctrine of Christianity is involved; when it is properly understood, it illumines and magnifies the honor of Christ and brings to pious consciences the abundant consolation that they need. We therefore ask his Imperial Majesty kindly to hear us out on this important issue. For since they understand neither the forgiveness of sins nor faith nor grace nor right-

eousness, our opponents confuse this doctrine miserably, they obscure the glory and the blessings of Christ, and they rob pious consciences of the consolation offered them in Christ. To substantiate our Confession and to refute the objections of our opponents, we shall have to say a few things by way of preface so that the sources of both kinds of doctrine, the opponents' and our own, might be recognized.

All Scripture should be divided into these two chief doctrines, the law and the promises. In some places it presents the law. In others it presents the promise of Christ; this it does either when it promises that the Messiah will come and promises forgiveness of sins, justification, and eternal life for his sake, or when, in the New Testament, the Christ who came promises forgiveness of sins, justification, and eternal life. By "law" in this discussion we mean the commandments of the Decalogue, wherever they appear in the Scriptures. For the present we are saying nothing about the ceremonial and civil laws of Moses. Of these two doctrines our opponents select the law and by it they seek forgiveness of sins and justification. For to some extent human reason naturally understands the law since it has the same judgment naturally written in the mind. But the Decalogue does not only require external works that reason can somehow perform. It also requires other works far beyond the reach of reason, like true fear of God, true love of God, true prayer to God, true conviction that God hears prayer, and the expectation of God's help in death and all afflictions. Finally, it requires obedience to God in death and all afflictions, lest we try to flee these things or turn away when God imposes them. Here the scholastics have followed the philosophers. Thus they teach only the righteousness of reason—that is, civil works—and maintain that without the Holy Spirit reason can love God above all things. As long as a man's mind is at rest and he does not feel God's wrath or judgment, he can imagine that he wants to love God and that he wants to do good for God's sake. In this way the scholastics teach men to merit the forgiveness of sins by doing what is within them, that is, if reason in its sorrow over sin elicits an act of love to God or does good for God's sake. Because this view naturally flatters men, it has produced and increased many types of worship in the church, like monastic vows and the abuses of the mass; someone has always been making up this or that form of worship or devotion with this view in mind. To support and increase trust in such works, the scholastics have declared that by necessity—the necessity of unchanging order, not of compulsion—God grants grace to those who do this.

In this point of view there are many vicious errors that would take a long time to enumerate. But let the intelligent reader just consider this. If this is Christian righteousness, what difference is there between philosophy and the teaching of Christ? If we merit the forgiveness of sins by these elicited acts of ours, of what use is Christ? If we can be justified by reason and its works, what need is there of Christ or of regeneration? On the basis of these opinions, things have come to such a pass that many people ridicule us for teaching that men ought to seek some righteousness beyond the philosophical. We have heard of some who, in their sermons, laid aside the gospel and expounded the ethics of Aristotle. If the opponents' ideas are correct, this was perfectly proper, for Aristotle wrote so well on natural ethics that nothing further needs to be added. We see that there are books in existence which compare certain teachings of Christ with the teachings of

Socrates, Zeno, and others, as though Christ had come to give some sort of laws by which we could merit the forgiveness of sins rather than receiving it freely for his merits. So if we accept this teaching of the opponents that we merit forgiveness of sins and justification by the works of reason, there will be no difference between philosophical or Pharisaic righteousness and Christian righteousness.

In order not to bypass Christ altogether, our opponents require a knowledge of the history about Christ and claim that he merited for us a certain disposition or, as they call it, "initial grace," which they understand as a disposition inclining us to love God more easily. It is clear, however, what they ascribe to this disposition, for they imagine that the acts of the will before the disposition and those after it are of the same type. They imagine that the will can love God, but that this disposition stimulates it to do so more freely. They bid us merit this first disposition by our preceding merits. Then they bid us merit an increase of this disposition and eternal life by the works of the law. Thus they bury Christ; men should not use him as mediator and believe that for his sake they freely receive the forgiveness of sins and reconciliation, but should dream that they merit the forgiveness of sins and are accounted righteous by their own keeping of the law before God. This in spite of the fact that the law is never satisfied, that reason performs only certain external works and meanwhile neither fears God nor truly believes that he cares. Though they talk about this disposition, yet without the righteousness of faith man can neither have nor understand the love of God.

When they make up a distinction between merit of congruity and merit of condignity, they are only playing in order to avoid the impression that they are outright Pelagians.

For if God necessarily gives grace for the merit of congruity, it is no longer merit of congruity but merit of condignity. They do not know what they are talking about. They imagine that after that disposition of love a man can earn the merit of condignity, but they would have him doubt whether the disposition is truly present. How is one to know whether one has the merit of congruity or the merit of condignity? But this whole business is the invention of idle men who do not know how the forgiveness of sins takes place, or how the judgment of God and the terrors of conscience drive out our trust in works. Smug hypocrites always believe that they have the merit of condignity, whether or not the disposition is there, because men naturally trust their own righteousness. But terrified consciences waver and doubt and then seek to pile up other works to find peace. They never suppose that they have the merit of condignity, and so they run headlong into despair, unless they hear, beyond the teaching of the law, the gospel of the free forgiveness of sins and the righteousness of faith.

Thus our opponents teach nothing but the righteousness of reason or of law, at which they look as the Jews did at the veiled face of Moses. In smug hypocrites, who think that they are keeping the law, they arouse presumption, a vain trust in works and a contempt for the grace of Christ. Timid consciences, on the other hand, they drive to despair because in their doubt they can never experience what faith is and how effective it is. And at last they despair utterly.

We for our part maintain that God requires the righteousness of reason. Because of God's command, honorable works commanded in the Decalogue should be performed, according to Gal. 3:24, "The law is a custodian," and 1 Tim. 1:9, "The law is laid down for the lawless." For God wants this civil discipline to restrain the unspiritual, and to preserve it he has given laws, learning, teaching, governments, and penalties. To some extent, reason can produce this righteousness by its own strength, though it is often overwhelmed by its natural weakness and by the devil, who drives it to open crimes. We freely give this righteousness of reason its due credit; for our corrupt nature has no greater good than this, as Aristotle correctly says, "Neither the evening star nor the morning star is more beautiful than righteousness." God even honors it with material rewards. Nevertheless, it ought not be praised at the expense of Christ.

For it is false that by our works we merit the forgiveness of sins.

It is false, too, that men are accounted righteous before God because of the righteousness of reason.

It is false, too, that by its own strength reason can love God above all things and keep his law, truly fear him, truly believe that he hears prayer, willingly obey him in death and in his other visitations, and not covet. But reason can produce civil works.

It is false, too, and a reproach to Christ, that men who keep the commandments of God outside a state of grace do not sin.

We have proof for this position of ours not only in the Scriptures, but also in the Fathers. Against the Pelagians, Augustine maintains at length that grace is not given because of our merits. In *Nature and Grace* he says:

> If natural capacity, with the help of free will, is in itself sufficient both for discovering how one ought to live, and also for leading a holy life, then "Christ died to no purpose" (Gal. 2:21), and therefore also "the stumbling-block of the cross has been removed" (Gal. 5:11). Why then may I not

myself exclaim, too—yes, I will exclaim and chide them with a Christian's sorrow—"You are severed from Christ, you who would be justified by the law; you have fallen away from grace" (Gal. 5:4); for "being ignorant of the righteousness that comes from God, and seeking to establish your own, you did not submit to God's righteousness" (Rom. 10:3). For even as Christ is "the end of the law," so likewise he is the Savior of man's corrupted nature, for righteousness to "every one who has faith" (Rom. 10:4).

John 8:36 says, "If the Son makes you free, you will be free indeed." Therefore reason cannot free us from our sins or merit for us the forgiveness of sins. And in John 3:5 it is written, "Unless one is born of water and the Spirit, one cannot enter the kingdom of God." But if we must be born again through the Holy Spirit, then the righteousness of reason does not justify us before God, it does not keep the law. And Rom. 3:23 says, "All fall short of the glory of God," that is, they lack the wisdom and righteousness of God which acknowledge and glorify him. And Rom. 8:7, 8, "The mind that is set on the flesh is hostile to God; it does not submit to God's law, indeed it cannot; and those who are in the flesh cannot please God." These words are so clear that they do not need an acute understanding but only attentive listening—to use the words that Augustine uses in discussing this matter.

If the mind that is set on the flesh is hostile to God, then the flesh sins even when it performs outward civil works. If it cannot submit to God's law, it is certainly sinning even when it produces deeds that are excellent and praiseworthy in human eyes. Our opponents concentrate on the commandments of the second table, which contain the civil righteousness that reason understands. Content with this, they think they satisfy the law of God. Meanwhile they do not see the first table, which commands us to love God, to be sure that God is wrathful at our sin, to fear him truly, and to be sure that he hears us. But without the Holy Spirit, the human heart either despises the judgment of God in its smugness, or in the midst of punishment it flees and hates his judgment. So it does not obey the first table. It is inherent in man to despise God and to doubt his Word with its threats and promises. Therefore men really sin even when they do virtuous things without the Holy Spirit; for they do them with a wicked heart, and (Rom. 14:23) "whatever does not proceed from faith is sin." Such people despise God when they do these things, as Epicurus did not believe that God cared for him or regarded or heard him. This contempt for God corrupts works that seem virtuous, for God judges the heart.

Finally, it was very foolish of our opponents to write that men who are under eternal wrath merit the forgiveness of sins by an elicited act of love, since it is impossible to love God unless faith has first accepted the forgiveness of sins. A heart that really feels God's wrath cannot love him unless it sees that he is reconciled. While he terrifies us and seems to be casting us into eternal death, human nature cannot bring itself to love a wrathful, judging, punishing God. It is easy enough for idle men to make up these dreams that a man guilty of mortal sin can love God above all things, since they themselves do not feel the wrath or judgment of God. But in the agony of conscience and in conflict, the conscience experiences how vain these philosophical speculations are. Paul says (Rom. 4:15), "The law brings wrath." He does not say that by the law men merit the forgiveness of sins. For the law always accuses and terrifies consciences. It does not justify, because a conscience terrified by the law flees before God's judgment. It is an error, therefore, for men to trust that by the law and by their works they merit the forgiveness of sins. We have said enough about the righteousness of law or of reason which our opponents teach. Later on, in the exposition of our doctrine of the righteousness of faith, the subject itself will compel us to cite further evidence; this will also help refute those errors of our opponents that we have been considering.

Therefore men cannot keep the law by their own strength, and they are all under sin and subject to eternal wrath and death. On this account the law cannot free us from sin or justify us, but the promise of the forgiveness of sins and justification was given because of Christ. He was given for us to make satisfaction for the sins of the world and has been appointed as the mediator and the propitiator. This promise is not conditional upon our merits but offers the forgiveness of sins and justification freely. As Paul says (Rom. 11:6), "If it is by works, it is no longer on the basis of grace." Elsewhere he says, "Now, the righteousness of God has been manifested apart from law" (Rom. 3:21), that is, the forgiveness of sins is offered freely. Reconciliation does not depend upon our merits. If the forgiveness of sins depended upon our merits and if reconciliation were by the law, it would be useless. For since we do not keep the law, it would follow that we would never obtain the promise of reconciliation. So Paul reasons in Rom. 4:14, "If it is the adherents of the law who are to be the heirs, faith is null and the promise is void." For if the promise were conditional upon our merits and the law, which we never keep, it would follow that the promise is useless.

Since we obtain justification through a free promise, however, it follows that we cannot justify ourselves. Otherwise, why would a promise be necessary? The gospel is, strictly speaking, the promise of forgiveness of sins and justification because of Christ. Since we can accept this promise only by faith, the gospel proclaims the righteousness of faith in Christ, which the law does not teach. And this is not the righteousness of the law. For the law requires our own works and our own perfection. But to us, oppressed by sin and death, the promise freely offers reconciliation for Christ's sake, which we do not accept by works but by faith alone. This faith brings to God a trust not in our own merits, but only in the promise of mercy in Christ. Therefore, when a man believes that his sins are forgiven because of Christ and that God is reconciled and favorably disposed to him because of Christ, this personal faith obtains the forgiveness of sins and justifies us. In penitence and the terrors of conscience it consoles and encourages our hearts. Thus it regenerates us and brings us the Holy Spirit, so that we can finally obey God's law, love him, truly fear him, be sure that he hears us, and obey him in all afflictions. It mortifies our lust. By freely accepting the forgiveness of sins, faith sets against God's wrath not our merits of love, but Christ the mediator and propitiator. This faith is the true knowledge of Christ, it uses his blessings, it regenerates our hearts, it precedes our keeping of the law. About this faith there is not a syllable in the teaching of our opponents. Therefore we condemn our opponents for teaching the righteousness of the law instead of the righteousness of the gospel, which proclaims the righteousness of faith in Christ.

What Is Justifying Faith?

Our opponents imagine that faith is only historical knowledge and teach that it can exist with mortal sin. And so they say nothing about faith by which, as Paul says so often, men are justified, because those who are accounted righteous before God do not live in mortal sin. The faith that justifies, however, is no mere historical knowledge, but the firm acceptance of God's offer promising forgiveness of sins and justification. To avoid the impression that it is merely knowledge, we add that to have faith means to want and to accept the promised offer of forgiveness of sins and justification.

It is easy to determine the difference between this faith and the righteousness of the law. Faith is that worship which receives God's offered blessings; the righteousness of the law is that worship which offers God our own merits. It is by faith that God wants to be worshipped, namely, that we receive from him what he promises and offers.

Paul clearly shows that faith does not simply mean historical knowledge but is a firm acceptance of the promise (Rom. 4:16): "That is why it depends on faith, in order that the promise may be guaranteed." For he says that only faith can accept the promise. He therefore correlates and connects promise and faith. It will be easy to determine what faith is if we pay attention to the article of the creed on the forgiveness of sins. So it is not enough to believe that Christ was born, suffered, and was raised unless we add this article, the purpose of the history, "the forgiveness of sins." The rest must be integrated with this article, namely, that for Christ's sake and not because of our own merits the forgiveness of sins is bestowed upon us. For why did Christ have to be offered for our sins if our merits make satisfaction for them?

In speaking of justifying faith, therefore, we must remember that these three elements always belong together: the promise itself, the fact that the promise is free, and the merits of Christ as the price and propitiation.

The promise is accepted by faith; the fact that it is free excludes our merits and shows that the blessing is offered only by mercy; the merits of Christ are the price because there must be a certain propitiation for our sins. Scripture contains many pleas for mercy, and the holy Fathers often say that we are saved by mercy. And so at every mention of mercy we must remember that this requires faith, which accepts the promise of mercy. Similarly, at every mention of faith we are also thinking of its object, the promised mercy. For faith does not justify or save because it is a good work in itself, but only because it accepts the promised mercy.

This service and worship is especially praised throughout the prophets and the psalms. Even though the law does not teach the free forgiveness of sins, the patriarchs knew the promise of the Christ, that for his sake God intended to forgive sins. As they understood that the Christ would be the price for our sins, they knew that our works could not pay so high a price. Therefore they received free mercy and the forgiveness of sins by faith, just as the saints in the New Testament. The frequent references to mercy and faith in the psalms and the prophets belong here; for example, "If thou, O Lord, shouldst mark iniquities, Lord, who shall stand?" (Ps. 130:3). Here the psalmist confesses his sins, but he does not lay claim to any merit of his own. He adds, "There is forgiveness with thee" (v. 4). Here he comforts himself with his trust in God's mercy. He quotes the promise: "My soul waits for his word, my soul hopes in the Lord," that is, because thou hast promised the forgiveness of sins I am sustained by thy promise. Therefore the patriarchs, too, were justified not by the law but by the promise and faith. It is strange that our opponents make so little of faith when they see it praised everywhere as the foremost kind of worship, as in Ps. 50:15: "Call upon me in the day of trouble; I will deliver you, and you shall glorify me." This is how God wants to be known and worshipped, that we accept his blessings and receive them because of his mercy rather than because of our own merits. This is the greatest consolation in all afflictions, and our opponents take it away when they despise and disparage faith and teach men to deal with God only by works and merits.

From Tappert, Book of Concord, *107–15.*

29. *Formula of Concord* (1580)

Luther's death in 1546 heralded energetic debate and even factionalism among his followers. What precisely had he meant, especially in his diverse writings about justification? "Lutheran" theologians, or as they called themselves "theologians of the Augsburg Confession," reached a measure of agreement in 1580, and the result was the *Formula of Concord.* In it the movement unified itself around a normative restatement of what Luther had intended.

IV. Good Works

The Chief Issue in the Controversy Concerning Good Works

Two controversies have arisen in some churches concerning the doctrine of good works:

1. The first division among some theologians was occasioned when one party asserted that good works are necessary to salvation; that it is impossible to be saved without good works; and that no one has ever been saved without good works. The other party asserted that good works are detrimental to salvation.

2. The second controversy arose among certain theologians concerning the use of the words "necessary" and "free." The one party contended that we should not use the word "necessary" when speaking of the new obedience, since it does not flow from necessity or coercion but from a spontaneous spirit. The other party held with reference to the word "necessary" that the new obedience is not a matter of our choice but that regenerated persons are bound to render such obedience. At first this was merely a semantic issue. Later on, a real controversy developed. The one party contended that the law should not be preached at all to Christians but that people should be admonished to do good works solely on the basis of the gospel. This the other party denied.

Affirmative Theses

The Pure Doctrine of the Christian Church in This Controversy: In order to explain this controversy from the ground up and to resolve it, this is our doctrine, faith, and confession:

1. That good works, like fruits of a good tree, certainly and indubitably follow genuine faith—if it is a living and not a dead faith.

2. We believe, teach, and confess that good works should be completely excluded from a discussion of the article of man's salvation as well as from the article of our justification before God. The apostle affirms in clear terms, "So also David declares that salvation pertains only to the man to whom God reckons righteousness apart from works, saying, 'Blessed are those whose iniquities are forgiven, and whose sins are covered'" (Rom. 4:6-8). And again, "For by grace you have been saved through faith; and this is not your own doing, it is the gift of God—not

because of works, lest any man should boast" (Eph. 2:8, 9).

3. We believe, teach, and confess further that all men, but especially those who are regenerated and renewed by the Holy Spirit, are obligated to do good works.

4. In this sense the words "necessary," "ought," and "must" are correctly and in a Christian way applied to the regenerated and are in no way contrary to the pattern of sound words and terminology.

5. However, when applied to the regenerated the words "necessity" and "necessary" are to be understood as involving not coercion but the due obedience which genuine believers, insofar as they are reborn, render not by coercion or compulsion of the law but from a spontaneous spirit because they are "no longer under the law but under grace."

6. Therefore we also believe, teach, and confess that the statement, "The regenerated do good works from a free spirit," should not be understood as though it were left to the regenerated person's option whether to do or not to do good and that he might keep his faith even if he deliberately were to persist in sin.

7. This, however, should be understood exactly as our Lord and the apostles themselves explain it, as applying only to the liberated spirit which does good works not from a fear of punishment, like a slave, but out of a love of righteousness, like a child (Rom. 8:15).

8. However, in the elect children of God this spontaneity is not perfect, but they are still encumbered with much weakness as St. Paul complains of himself in Rom. 7:14-25 and Gal. 5:17.

9. Nevertheless, for Christ's sake the Lord does not reckon this weakness against his elect, as it is written, "There is therefore now no condemnation for those who are in Christ Jesus" (Rom. 8:1).

10. We also believe, teach, and confess that not our works but only the Holy Spirit, working through faith, preserves faith and salvation in us. The good works are testimonies of the Holy Spirit's presence and indwelling.

False Antitheses

1. Accordingly we reject and condemn spoken and written formulations which teach that good works are necessary to salvation; likewise, that no one has ever been saved without good works; likewise, that it is impossible to be saved without good works.

2. We also reject and condemn as offensive and as subversive of Christian discipline that bald statement that good works are detrimental to salvation.

Especially in these last times, it is just as necessary to exhort people to Christian discipline and good works, and to remind them how necessary it is that they exercise themselves in good works as an evidence of their faith and their gratitude toward God, as it is to warn against mingling good works in the article of justification. Such an Epicurean dream concerning faith can damn people as much as a papistic and Pharisaic confidence in one's own works and merit.

3. We also reject and condemn the teaching that faith and the indwelling of the Holy Spirit are not lost through malicious sin, but that the holy ones and the elect retain the Holy Spirit even though they fall into adultery and other sins and persist in them.

V. Law and Gospel

The Chief Question at Issue in This Controversy

The question has been, Is the preaching of the holy gospel strictly speaking only a preaching of grace which proclaims the forgiveness of sins, or is it also a preaching of repentance and reproof that condemns unbelief, since unbelief is condemned not in the law but wholly through the gospel?

Affirmative Theses

The Pure Doctrine of God's Word:

1. We believe, teach, and confess that the distinction between law and gospel is an especially glorious light that is to be maintained with great diligence in the church so that, according to St. Paul's admonition, the Word of God may be divided rightly.

2. We believe, teach, and confess that, strictly speaking, the law is a divine doctrine which teaches what is right and God-pleasing and which condemns everything that is sinful and contrary to God's will.

3. Therefore everything which condemns sin is and belongs to the proclamation of the law.

4. But the gospel, strictly speaking, is the kind of doctrine that teaches what a man who has not kept the law and is condemned by it should believe, namely, that Christ has satisfied and paid for all guilt and without man's merit has obtained and won for him forgiveness of sins, the "righteousness that avails before God," and eternal life.

5. The word "gospel" is not used in a single sense in Holy Scripture, and this was the original occasion of the controversy. Therefore we believe, teach, and confess that when the word "gospel" means the entire doctrine of Christ which he proclaimed personally in his teaching ministry and which his apostles also set forth (examples of this meaning occur in Mark 1:15 and Acts 20:24), then it is correct to say or write that the gospel is a proclamation both of repentance and of forgiveness of sins.

6. But when law and gospel are opposed to each other, as when Moses is spoken of as a teacher of the law in contrast to Christ as a preacher of the gospel, then we believe, teach, and confess that the gospel is not a proclamation of contrition and reproof but is, strictly speaking, precisely a comforting and joyful message which does not reprove or terrify but comforts consciences that are frightened by the law, directs them solely to the merit of Christ, and raises them up again by the delightful proclamation of God's grace and favor acquired through the merits of Christ.

7. Now as to the disclosure of sin, as long as men hear only the law and hear nothing about Christ, the veil of Moses covers their eyes, as a result they fail to learn the true nature of sin from the law, and thus they become either conceited hypocrites, like the Pharisees, or they despair, as Judas did, etc. Therefore Christ takes the law into his own hands and explains it spiritually (Matt. 5:21-48; Rom 7:14). Then "God's wrath is revealed from heaven" over all sinners and men learn how fierce it is. Thus they are directed back to the law, and now they learn from it for the first time the real nature of their sin, an acknowledgment which Moses could never have wrung from them.

Therefore the proclamation of the suffering and death of Christ, the Son of God, is an earnest and terrifying preaching and advertisement of God's wrath which really directs people into the law, after the veil of Moses has been removed for them, so they now know for the first time what great things God demands of us in the law, none of which we could fulfill, and that we should now seek all our righteousness in Christ.

8. Nevertheless, as long as all this—namely, the passion and death of Christ—proclaims God's wrath and terrifies people, it is not, strictly speaking, the preaching of the gospel but the preaching of Moses and the

law, and therefore it is an "alien work" of Christ by which he comes to his proper office—namely, to preach grace, to comfort, to make alive. And this is the preaching of the gospel, strictly speaking.

Antithesis
Rejected Contrary Doctrine:

1. Hence we reject and deem it as false and detrimental when men teach that the gospel, strictly speaking, is a proclamation of conviction and reproof and not exclusively a proclamation of grace. Thereby the gospel is again changed into a teaching of the law, the merit of Christ and the Holy Scriptures are obscured, Christians are robbed of their true comfort, and the doors are again opened to the papacy.

VI. The Third Function of the Law
The Chief Question at Issue in This Controversy

The law has been given to men for three reasons: (1) to maintain external discipline against unruly and disobedient men, (2) to lead men to a knowledge of their sin, (3) after they are reborn, and although the flesh still inheres in them, to give them on that account a definite rule according to which they should pattern and regulate their entire life. It is concerning the third function of the law that a controversy has arisen among a few theologians. The question therefore is whether or not the law is to be urged upon reborn Christians. One party said yes, the other says no.

Affirmative Theses
The Correct Christian Teaching in This Controversy:

1. We believe, teach, and confess that although people who genuinely believe and whom God has truly converted are freed through Christ from the curse and the coercion of the law, they are not on that account without the law: on the contrary. they have been redeemed by the Son of God precisely that they should exercise themselves day and

night in the law (Ps. 119:1). In the same way our first parents even before the fall did not live without the law, for the law of God was written into their hearts when they were created in the image of God.

2. We believe, teach, and confess that the preaching of the law is to be diligently applied not only to unbelievers and the impenitent but also to people who are genuinely believing, truly converted, regenerated, and justified through faith.

3. For although they are indeed reborn and have been renewed in the spirit of their mind, such regeneration and renewal is incomplete in this world. In fact, it has only begun, and in the spirit of their mind the believers are in a constant war against their flesh (that is, their corrupt nature and kind), which clings to them until death. On account of this old Adam, who inheres in people's intellect, will, and all their powers, it is necessary for the law of God constantly to light their way lest in their merely human devotion they undertake self-decreed and self-chosen acts of serving God. This is further necessary lest the old Adam go his own self-willed way. He must be coerced against his own will not only by the admonitions and threats of the law, but also by its punishments and plagues, to follow the Spirit and surrender himself a captive. 1 Cor. 9:27; Rom. 6:12; Gal. 6:14; Ps. 119:1; Heb. 13:21.

4. Concerning the distinction between works of the law and fruits of the Spirit we believe, teach, and confess that works done according to the law are, and are called, works of the law as long as they are extorted from people only under the coercion of punishments and the threat of God's wrath.

5. Fruits of the Spirit, however, are those works which the Spirit of God, who dwells in the believers, works through the regenerated, and which the regenerated perform

insofar as they are reborn and do them as spontaneously as if they knew of no command, threat or reward. In this sense the children of God live in the law and walk according to the law of God. In his epistles St. Paul calls it the law of Christ and the law of the mind. Thus God's children are "not under the law, but under grace" (Rom. 7:23, 8:1, 14).

6. Therefore both for penitent and impenitent, for regenerated and unregenerated people the law is and remains one and the same law, namely, the unchangeable will of God. The difference, as far as obedience is concerned, rests exclusively with man, for the unregenerated man—just like the regenerated according to the flesh—does what is demanded of him by the law under coercion and unwillingly. But the believer without any coercion and with a willing spirit, insofar as he is reborn, does what no threat of the law could ever have wrung from him.

Antithesis

1. Accordingly we condemn as dangerous and subversive of Christian discipline and true piety the erroneous teaching that the law is not to be urged, in the manner and measure above described, upon Christians and genuine believers, but only upon unbelievers, non-Christians, and the impenitent.

From Tappert, Book of Concord, *475–81*.

Chapter 3
Zwingli and the Radical Reformation

✠

Introduction

Whereas the Reformation in Germany began with a theological critique of indulgences, the Reformation in Switzerland began with the eating of sausages. Ulrich Zwingli (1484–1531), born into a peasant family, had been fortunate enough to study at the Universities of Vienna, Basel and Bern, where he sampled lightly of scholastic theology and imbibed heavily at the fountain of Renaissance humanism. Ordained to the priesthood in 1506, Zwingli served as parish priest in the towns of Glarus and Einsiedeln until 1518 when he was promoted to the cathedral church in Zurich. Here, as he later explained, he discovered what was to become for him the "touchstone" of all Christian belief and action, reform and protest, namely the Bible. But although Zwingli now (in 1519) began to preach exclusively out of Scripture, it was not until 1522 that the reform group he had gathered about him made its protest public. And it did so by eating sausages during Lent. In doing this it defied both tradition and ecclesiastical authority in the name of Scripture, which of course says nothing about the Lenten fast.

As Zwingli's protest gathered public support in Zurich, his reform movement escalated. All preaching in the city's churches was now to be strictly out of the Bible. In 1524 pictures and statues were removed from the churches. In 1525 the mass was abolished in Zurich. Understandably, the Roman Catholic response was to accuse Zwingli of "Lutheranism." But from the beginning Zwingli emphasized his independence. His biblical preaching had begun before he began to read Luther seriously, probably in 1520. By 1529 it was clear to almost everyone that there were major differences between the two. In that year, they met at Marburg where seemingly irreconcilable differences on the Eucharist heralded the definitive parting of the ways. It was only after Zwingli's early demise in 1531 that his followers, in tandem with Calvinists, built the foundation of Reformed Protestantism.

Ulrich Zwingli

30. Letter to Utinger (5 December 1518)

Zwingli was often charged with a certain moral laxity, and there is little doubt that there was some substance to those charges. This revealing letter is Zwingli's response to accusations that arose while he was being considered for the pastoral posting in Zurich. He got the job, perhaps because his chief rival for the position had a permanent mistress and six children. There is little evidence that the laity in the sixteenth century took offense at such lapses from the ideal of celibacy.

✠

One of the most learned and amiable of our friends [Myconius] has written to me that a rumor has been spread in Zurich about me, alleging that I have seduced the daughter of a high official, and that this has given offense to a number of my friends. I must answer this calumny so that you, dear friend, and others, can clear my life from these false rumors. . . . First, you know that three years ago I made a firm resolution not to interfere with any female: St. Paul said it was good not to touch a woman. That did not turn out very well. . . .

As to the charge of seduction I needn't take long in dealing with that. They make it out to concern the daughter of an important citizen. I don't deny that she is the daughter of an important person: anyone who could touch the emperor's beard is important—a barber forsooth! No one doubts that the lady concerned is the barber's daughter except possibly the barber himself who has often accused his wife, the girl's mother, a supposedly true and faithful wife, of adultery, blatant but not true. At any rate he has turned the girl, about whom all this fuss is being

made, out from his house and for two years has given her neither board nor lodging. So what is the daughter of such a man to me? . . .

With intense zeal day and night even at the cost of harm to his body, [I] study the Greek and Latin philosophers and theologians, and this hard work takes the heat out of such sensual desires even if it does not entirely eliminate them.

Further, feelings of shame have so far restrained me that when I was still in Glarus and let myself fall into temptation in this regard a little, I did so so quietly that even my friends hardly knew about it.

And now we will come to the matter before us and I will cast off what they call the last anchor taking no account of public opinion which takes a poor view of open resort to loose women. In this instance it was a case of maiden by day, matron by night, and not so much of the maiden by day but everybody in Einsiedeln knew about her . . . no one in Einsiedeln thought I had corrupted a maiden. All the girl's relations knew that she had been caught long before I came to Einsiedeln, so that I was not in any way concerned. . . .

To close: I have written a good deal of facetious chatter, but these people don't understand anything else. You can say whatever you think suitable to anyone who is concerned.

✠

From G. R. Potter, ed., Huldrych Zwingli *(New York: St. Martin's Press, 1977), 11–12.*

31. *Of Freedom of Choice in the Selection of Food* (16 April 1522)

One result of Zwingli's biblical preaching was that early in Lent 1522, some of his followers ate meat, though Zwingli himself apparently did not. His 23 March sermon, later printed under this title, states his position on the issue.

✠

To sum up briefly: if you want to fast, do so; if you do not want to eat meat, don't eat it; but allow Christians a free choice. If you are a person of leisure, you should fast often and abstain from food that excites you; the worker moderates his desires by hoeing and plowing in the field. You say, 'but the idlers will eat meat without needing to.' The answer is that these very same people fill themselves with even richer foods, which enflame them even more than the highly-seasoned highly-spiced meats.

If you would be a Christian at heart, act in this way. If the spirit of your belief teaches you thus, then fast, but grant also your neighbor the privilege of Christian liberty, and fear God greatly, if you have transgressed his laws, nor make what man has invented greater before God than what God himself has commanded. . . . You should neither scorn nor approve anyone for any reason connected with food or with feast days whether observed or not (an exception is always to be made about Sunday until after hearing the Word of God and partaking of the Lord's Supper). Take no notice of feasting on the Sabbath or at new moon, for these are now only symbols of Christian celebrations, freeing men from their sins and keeping them so.

Further, we should not let ourselves be concerned about such "works" but be saved by the grace of God only. With the coming of Christ shadows and forebodings have assuredly passed away.

Here is another sign of the times. I think that there is danger of this age being evil and corrupt rather than reaching out towards everlasting righteousness. Further, simple people think everything is all right if they go to confession in Lent only, observe the fast, take Communion and thus account for the whole year. God should, however, be acknowledged at all times and our life should be one of piety, whereas we act to the contrary when we think that it is quite enough if we pay attention only to the times of fasting whereas Christ says, "Be vigilant: for you know not the day or the hour" [Matt. 25:13].

✠

From Potter, Huldrych Zwingli, *17–18.*

32. Petition to the Bishop of Constance (2 July 1522)

Zwingli's call for a married clergy, signed also by other Zurich priests, went unanswered. A year later, priests were publicly marrying, and Zwingli himself, in 1524, married Anna Reinhard, a woman who had been his mistress for two years.

✠

You cannot but know, very reverend Father, how inadequately and poorly the priests from time past to the present have commonly upheld the rule of celibacy. It was easy enough to give orders but it was not possible to ensure that the orders could be carried out. For God would not entrust this measure of authority to any human being since a gift which is from God and the angels should not come from the hand of man but from God himself. This is plainly shown by Christ's own words [Matt. 19:10-12] . . . . Chastity is a gift from God bestowed upon a few who clearly recognize it. . . . Christ left everyone free to remain single or not with the words "let those accept it who can." . . .

If in no circumstances can you agree to the principle of [clerical] marriage we beg of you at least not to oppose it. Another beside ourselves has called for it [i.e. Christ]. For we believe you to be strong enough not to be afraid of doing a good deed without regard to those who can slay the body. Indeed there is really no need for you to interfere. For there is a report that most of the clergy have already chosen wives, not only here in Switzerland but among all peoples everywhere. So to settle this affair peacefully is not only beyond your power but even beyond that of those with greater authority than you have.

✠

From Potter, Huldrych Zwingli, *18.*

33. *Of the Clarity and Certainty of the Word of God* (6 September 1522)

It was also in 1522 that Zwingli expanded on his "Scripture as touchstone" principle: tradition and even human interpretation were to be set aside in favor of the biblical text itself. This document is an elaboration of an earlier sermon preached to a convent of nuns.

✠

The Word of God is so vital, strong and powerful that all things must necessarily obey it, and that fully and at such time as God himself appoints. . . .

The whole evangelical doctrine is nothing but a sure guarantee that what God has promised will certainly be performed. For the gospel is now nothing other than a present fulfillment. For he who was promised to our forefathers and to the whole human race has been brought to us and with him all our hopes turned to certainty, as Simeon said in Luke, chapter 2. . . .

Those who defend the doctrines of men say: it is true that above all other teaching we ought to esteem the teaching of the gospel which is inspired and taught by God more highly than any other—but we understand the gospel differently. If there is a conflict between your and my understanding there must be someone to decide between us and to be able to silence the one who is wrong. This they all say so as to subordinate the understanding of God's word to men. Thus anyone who preaches the gospel can be taken and brought before Caiaphas and Annas. And in direct opposition to what Paul says, that all knowledge, thought and ability depend upon the will and service of God, they want to subject God's doctrine to the judgment of men. . . .

By the gospel we do not mean only the writings of Matthew, Mark, Luke, and John but . . . all that God has revealed to man in order that he may instruct him and give him a sure knowledge of his will. . . .

Even if you hear the gospel of Jesus Christ from an apostle you will not follow it unless the heavenly Father teaches and draws you by his Spirit. The words are clear: God's teaching clearly enlightens, teaches and gives certainty without any intervention on the part of human knowledge. If people are taught by God they are well taught with clarity and conviction. If they had first to be taught and assured by men, they would be more correctly described as men-taught rather than taught by God.

You must be *theodidacti,* that is, taught of God, not of men: that is what truth itself said [John 6:45] and it cannot lie. If you do not believe, and believe firmly, leaving the vanities of men and submitting yourselves solely to God's teaching, you have no true faith. . . .

I know for certain that God teaches me, for I know this by experience. In order that you may not misrepresent my meaning let me tell you how I know that God teaches me. In my youth I devoted myself as much to human learning as did others of my age. Then, some seven or eight years ago, I undertook to devoting myself entirely to the Scriptures, and the conflicting philosophy and theology of the schoolmen constantly presented difficulties. But eventually I came to a conclusion—led thereto by the Scriptures and the Word of God—and decided "You must drop all that and learn God's will directly from his own word." . . .

Finally here is the answer to any opposition. It is my conviction that the word of God must be held by us in the highest esteem (the Word of God being that alone which comes from God's Spirit) and no such credence is to be given to any other word. It is certain and cannot fail us; it is clear and does not let us wander in darkness. It teaches itself, it explains itself and it brings the light of full salvation and grace to the human soul. . . . In these it has its being, through these it strives, rejecting all human consolation, relying on God alone for comfort and confidence. Without God there is no rest, for repose is with him alone. Yes, salvation comes to us here and now, not in any material form but in the certainty of consolation and hope. May God increase this in us and may it never be lacking. Amen.

✝

From Potter, Huldrych Zwingli, *29–30.*

34. *Sixty-seven Theses* (27 January 1523)

In 1523 Zurich city officials called for a public debate to settle the contention which was by then causing unrest in the city. In preparation for this event, Zwingli wrote his *Sixty-*

seven Theses, which his reform party then successfully defended on 27 January. This victory was an important step towards consolidating the Reformation in Zurich. The theses clearly reveal Zwingli's reform agenda.

✝

I. All who say that the gospel is invalid without the confirmation of the church err and slander God.

II. The sum and substance of the gospel is that our Lord Jesus Christ, the true son of God, has made known to us the will of his heavenly Father, and has with his sinlessness released us from death and reconciled us to God.

III. Hence Christ is the only way to salvation for all who ever were, are and shall be.

IV. He who seeks or shows another way errs, and, indeed, he is a murderer of souls and a thief.

V. Hence all who consider other teachings equal to or higher than the gospel err, and do not know what the gospel is.

VI. For Christ Jesus is the guide and leader, promised by God to all mankind, which promise was fulfilled.

VII. He is eternal salvation and head of all who believe; these are his body, for his own human body is dead. Nothing is of avail without him.

VIII. From this follows first that all who dwell in the head [i.e., Christ] are members and children of God, forming the church or communion of the saints, which is the bride of Christ, *ecclesia catholica.*

IX. Furthermore, as the members of the body can not function without the control of the head, so no one in the body of Christ can do anything without its head, Christ.

X.   As that man is mad whose limbs [try to] do something without his head, tearing, wounding, injuring himself, so when the members of Christ undertake something without their head, Christ, they are stupid and injure and burden themselves with foolish laws.

XI.   Hence we see in the so-called spiritual laws, concerning their splendor, riches, orders, titles, decrees, a cause of all foolishness because they do not agree with the head.

XII. Thus they behave foolishly, not because of their head [i.e., Christ]— for every possible effort is made by the grace of God to bring them back to the light—but their foolish behavior is no longer to be tolerated and they must pay heed to the head alone.

XIII. If anyone wants to hear, he can learn clearly and plainly the will of God, and by his Spirit be drawn to him and become a changed man through him.

XIV. Therefore all Christian people shall use their best diligence that the gospel of Christ alone be preached everywhere.

XV.   For in faith rests our salvation, and in unbelief our damnation; for all truth is clear in him.

XVI. In the gospel one learns that human doctrines and decrees are useless for salvation.

XVII. Christ is the only eternal high priest, from which it follows that those who have called themselves high priests have opposed the honor and power of Christ—have, indeed, completely rejected him.

XVIII. Christ, having sacrificed himself once and for all, is for all eternity a perpetual and acceptable offering for the sins of all believers, from which it follows that the mass is not a sacrifice, but is a commemoration of the sacrifice and assurance of the salvation which Christ has given us.

XIX. Christ is the only mediator between God and ourselves.

XX.   God will give us everything in his [Christ's] name, whence it follows that for our part after this life we need no mediator except him.

XXI. When we pray for one another on earth, we do so in such a way that we believe that all things are to be given to us through Christ alone.

XXII. Christ is our justification, from which it follows that our works, if they are of Christ, are good; but if ours, they are neither right nor good.

XXIII. Christ utterly rejects the material goods and show of this world, from which it follows that those who amass wealth in his name grossly abuse him when they make him a cloak to hide their avarice and arrogance.

XXIV. No Christian is bound to do those things which God has not decreed; hence one may eat at all times all food, whence one learns that the dispensations about cheese and butter are a Roman imposture.

XXV. Time and place are controlled by Christian men and not men by them; hence we learn that those who make rules about time and place deprive Christians of their freedom.

XXVI. Nothing is more displeasing to God than hypocrisy; so we learn that all that is a show before men is gross hypocrisy and iniquity. Included in this are cowls, vestments, tonsures, etc.

XXVII. All Christian men are brethren of Christ and brothers to one another: and the title of Father should not be assumed by anyone on earth. This includes orders, sects and factions.

XXVIII. All that God has allowed or not forbidden is right, hence marriage is permitted to all human beings.

XXIX. All so-called clerics sin if, after they have an inward conviction that God has denied them the gift of chastity, they do not protect themselves by marriage.

XXX. Those who promise chastity take childishly or foolishly too much upon themselves, whence is learnt that those who make such vows do wrong to God-fearing people.

XXXI. Excommunication cannot be imposed by any single individual but only by the church, that is the congregation of those among whom the wrongdoer dwells, in conjunction with their overseer, that is, their minister.

XXXII. Only those who give public offense should be excommunicated.

XXXIII. Property unrighteously acquired should not be given to churches, monasteries, monks, priests or nuns, but to the needy, if it cannot be returned to the legal owner.

XXXIV. There is no ground in the teaching of Christ for the pretensions of the so-called spiritual authority,

XXXV. Whereas the jurisdiction and authority of the secular power is based on the teaching and actions of Christ.

XXXVI. All the rights and protection that the so-called spiritual authority claims belong to secular governments provided they are Christian.

XXXVII. To them, likewise, all Christians owe obedience without exception,

XXXVIII. Insofar as they do not order that which is contrary to God.

XXXIX. Therefore all their laws should be in harmony with the divine will, so that they protect the oppressed, even if these do not complain.

XL. They [i.e. governments] alone have the right to exact the death penalty without bringing the wrath of God upon themselves, and then only for those who have offended against public order.

XLI. If they give good advice and help to those for whom they must account to God, then these owe them material assistance.

XLII. But if they are unfaithful and transgress the laws of Christ they may be deposed in accordance with God's will.

XLIII. To sum up; that realm is best and most stable which is ruled in accordance with God's will alone, and the worst and weakest is that which is ruled arbitrarily.

XLIV. Those who call on God in spirit and in truth should do so without great publicity.

XLV. Those who act in order that they may be seen by men and secure praise during their lifetime are hypocrites. It must therefore follow that:

XLVI. Choral or spoken church services that are performed without true intent but only for reward are carried out either for the sake of reputation or for profit.

XLVII. A man should be willing to die rather than offend or disgrace a fellow Christian.

XLVIII. He who is offended without cause through weakness or ignorance should not be allowed to remain weak or ignorant but should be strengthened so that he does not regard what is really not sinful as sin.

XLIX. I know of no greater scandal than that priests are not allowed to take lawful wives but may keep mistresses if they pay a fine.

L. God alone remits sins through Jesus Christ, his son, our only Lord.

LI. He who gives this authority to an individual takes away the honor due to God to give to one who is not God. This is real idolatry.

LII. Hence the confession which is made to the priest or other person shall not be regarded as remission of sin, but only a seeking for advice.

LIII. Acts of penance imposed by human counsel (excommunication excepted) do not cancel sin but are imposed to deter others.

LIV. Christ has borne all our toil and sorrows. Hence whoever attributes to works of penance that which belongs to Christ alone, errs and dishonors God.

LV. Anyone who refuses absolution to one truly penitent is no agent of God or of St. Peter but of the devil.

LVI. Whoever remits any sin only for the sake of money is the companion of Simon [Magus] and Balaam, and the real messenger of the devil.

LVII. The true Holy Scriptures know nothing of purgatory after this life.

LVIII. The fate of the dead is known to God alone.

LIX. And the less God has let us know concerning it, the less we should endeavor to know about it.

LX. I do not reject human prayer to God to show grace to the departed; but to fix a time for this and to lie for the sake of gain is not human but demonic.

LXI. The divine Scriptures know nothing of the "indelible character" conferred in recent times on the priesthood.

LXII. Furthermore, they know no priests except those who proclaim the word of God.

LXIII. They command that honor, that is to say, material subsistence, shall be shown [to priests].

LXIV. Those who acknowledge their errors shall not be deprived of their endowments but shall be allowed to die in peace and after that their property shall be dealt with in Christian fashion.

LXV. God will deal with those who do not acknowledge their errors. Hence they should not receive corporal punishment unless they behave so violently that action is essential.

LXVI. All those in spiritual authority shall quickly humble themselves and serve solely the cross of Christ and not money-chests; otherwise perdition is upon them and the axe is laid to the root of the tree.

LXVII. If anyone wishes to discuss with me concerning interest, tithes, unbaptized children, or confirmation, I am ready to answer.

From Potter, Huldrych Zwingli, *21–25.*

35. *On True and False Religion* (1525)

Zwingli made his most systematic theological statement in his 1525 book, *On True and False Religion*. This work dealt with God, human nature, sin, grace, church, sacraments, ethics, etc. What follows is a short excerpt from the section on the Eucharist.

What, therefore, will their authority avail, however great and excellent they are? The truth is more excellent. To the others, who break out with, "You seem to me to hold that the bodily flesh and also the blood of Christ are not present in the Eucharist," I answer: Do you say this of yourself or have others said it to you? If you are a believer, you are aware how salvation comes; and then the Word of God has such power with you that you raise no question about bodily flesh. But if others have told you that this is my view, I say to them that in this matter I hold as the church of Christ holds. She will not even brook the question whether the body of Christ is in the Sacrament of the Eucharist in actual, physical, or essential form. For when you bring up these elements of the world, she will thrust this buckler in your face: "The flesh profiteth nothing" [John 6:63]; why, then, do you dispute about the flesh? Even if you now cry out, "O heaven! O earth!" nay, even "Stars and seas!" I shall simply say, "The flesh profiteth nothing"; why, then, is it better for you to be curious rather than anxious about it? Be this, then, a wall of bronze, "The flesh profiteth nothing." Go now, and bring up all your engines of war, catapults, battering rams, sheds, and every kind of weapon; far from shattering this wall, you will be able not even to shake it. We must, then, hold a different view of the flesh and blood of this sacrament from that which the theologians

have thus far laid down, whose opinion is opposed by all sense and reason and understanding and by faith itself. For I do not think we have to listen to those who are so bold as to say, "I have always firmly believed that in this sacrament I eat the essential body, or the bodily and sensible flesh, of Christ." As if in saying this they could persuade anyone to believe that his senses perceive what they do not perceive! When, therefore, they say that the whole thing is established by faith and therefore cannot be denied, for we must firmly believe that we have a sense perception of the bodily flesh, I reply: "I know what faith is and I know also what sense is; but you, either not having this knowledge or supposing that I have it not, are trying to cast darkness upon my light. Faith exists in our hearts through the Spirit of God, and we are sensible of it. In fact, that there is an inward change of heart is not an obscure matter, but we do not perceive it by means of the senses." But now these persons come and, because they fancy that faith is a violent and deliberate turning of our hearts towards some even quite incongruous thing, they therefore aver that here the belief that the bodily and sensible flesh is present is held with unwavering faith. Yet in this they make two mistakes: first, in thinking that faith has its origin in man's decision and election. They make a mistake here because, although faith is hope and trust in things quite remote from sense, nevertheless it does not rest upon our decision or election. The things upon which we set our hopes themselves cause us to put all our hopes upon them; for if we were made believers by our own election or determination, all men could become believers by their own strength, even the impious. Since, therefore, faith has not its origin in sense or reason and looks not to the things of sense, it is easy to discover how they err in the second place. They err in the second place, then, in applying faith to things of sense, and in saying that through these it brings us certainty. But of that there is no need, for what is perceived by sense owes nothing to faith. Why should anyone hope for that which he already sees? For things which are perceived when presented to the senses are things of sense. Let us see now how finely these things fit together: By faith we believe that the bodily and sensible flesh of Christ is here present. By faith things quite remote from sense are believed. But all bodily things are so entirely things of sense that unless they are perceived by sense they are not bodily. Therefore, to believe and to perceive by sense are essentially different. Observe, therefore, what a monstrosity of speech this is: I believe that I eat the sensible and bodily flesh. For if it is bodily, there is no need of faith, for it is perceived by the sense; and things perceived by sense have no need of faith, for by sense they are perceived to be perfectly sure. On the other hand, if your eating is a matter of belief, the thing you believe cannot be sensible or bodily. Therefore what you say is simply a monstrosity. Observe, too, that the theologians asserted here another thing, which even the senses know not, namely, that bread is flesh; for if this had been so, it would have been established by the verdict of sense, not by faith. For faith springs not from things accessible to the sense nor are they objects of faith. Nor do I think we have to listen to those who, seeing that the view mentioned is not only crude but even frivolous and impious, make this pronouncement: "We eat, to be sure, the true and bodily flesh of Christ, but spiritually"; for they do not yet see that the two statements cannot stand, "It is body" and "It

is eaten spiritually." For body and spirit are such essentially different things that whichever one you take, it cannot be the other. If spirit is the one that has come into question, it follows by the law of contraries that body is not; if body is the one, the hearer is sure that spirit is not. Hence, to eat bodily flesh spiritually is simply to assert that to be body which is spirit. I have adduced these things from the philosophers against those men who, in spite of Paul's warning to be on our guard against philosophy, Col. 2:8, have made it the mistress and instructress of the Word of God, that they may see clearly how nicely they sometimes weigh their decisions and pronouncements. In short, faith does not compel sense to confess that it perceives what it does not perceive, but it draws us to the invisible and fixes all our hopes on that [cf. Heb. 11:1]. For it dwelleth not amidst the sensible and bodily, and hath nothing in common therewith. Come now, understand what happiness is born in you if you believe that you eat the bodily and sensible flesh of Christ, or, as others say, eat his bodily flesh spiritually! You will undoubtedly admit that nothing arises therefrom but perplexity, dullness, and to speak freely, suspicion in regard to other things of faith which are most certain and most sacred. Yet these fine fellows were all the while saying that this monstrous eating of sensible and bodily flesh is a prop to faith, and sometimes they brought it forward as a miracle, which yet no man perceived. Who, pray, ever made up such nonsense, and that before the eyes of those who clung in their hearts to the true and most high God, and who, as soon as they examined their faith, saw that there was no need of paradoxes of this sort? For what did God ever promise of those who believed that bodily flesh is eaten here? Did not those who were truly faithful know for certain that salvation is found in relying upon the mercy of God, of which we have the sure sign or pledge in Jesus Christ the only begotten Son of God? What, then, do you imagine this invention—subtle, forsooth, since it consists of words only (for no mind can take it in, and neither does faith teach it, as we have seen)—effected with the pious? Nothing, by heaven. Hence it undoubtedly came about that those who were truly pious either believed nothing of the kind, or when pressed to believe took to flight in their hearts, even though with their lips they confessed that they believed it was as the impious declared. For who, when confronted with anything so monstrous, did not flee, saying: "Do not examine this thing; believe the Fathers." And whenever the goading voice of the truth said: "It is a strange thing. How can it be that you should be compelled to believe that which you cannot see to be possible? When the Jews did not comprehend it, Christ showed that it was to be understood spiritually, but now these persons say it is done in a bodily and material sense, which yet you do not perceive or experience," did not everyone say to himself: "It is not for you to take anxious thought about these things"? But these fellows had taught men thus to run away that the truth might not shine forth and be understood. And as to the impious, they did not trust even in Christ, so far were they from giving him thanks for the redemption given to us. What, then, did they do but tyrannically thrust upon us what it is impossible that they themselves believed, even though they said so a thousand times? For faith is the gift of God; and since God never taught this thing, he surely has not drawn men to believe it. That he did not teach it is clear, because the flesh profiteth absolutely nothing. . . .

From S. M. Jackson and C. N. Heller, eds., Zwingli: Commentary on True and False Religion *(Durham, NC: Labyrinth Press, 1981), 212–15.*

36. Letter to Vadian (20 October 1529)

In an attempt to unify the Protestant forces, in 1529 Philip of Hesse invited Zwingli and Luther to meet in the city of Marburg. There, from October 1 to 4, discussion turned into rancorous debate, as it quickly became evident that on the paramount issue of the Eucharist neither side was ready to make concessions. This letter is Zwingli's account of the exchange.

The landgrave decided that there should be separate preliminary conferences in private, Oecolampadius with Luther and Melanchthon with Zwingli, to seek between themselves for any possible measure of agreement that could lead to peace. Here Luther's reaction to Oecolampadius was such that he came to me and privately complained that once again he had come up against Eck! Don't tell this to anyone you can't trust. Melanchthon I found uncommonly slippery; he kept changing his shape like another Proteus, forced me—in lieu of salt!—to use my pen as a weapon and keep my hand dry, so that I could hold him fast for all his chafings and wrigglings and dodgings. I am sending you a copy of a few extracts from our very lengthy conversations on the understanding that you will only show it to those you can trust—I mean, to those who will not use it to stir up another crisis: remember that Philip [Melanchthon] has a copy too, for I drew it up in his presence and under his eye, and many of his own words he actually dictated. But the last thing we want is to bring on a new crisis. Philip and I spent six hours together, Luther and Oecolampadius three.

On the next day the four of us entered the arena in the presence of the landgrave and a few others—twenty-four at most; we fought it out in this and in three further sessions, thus making four in all in which, with witnesses, we fought our winning battle. Three times we threw at Luther the fact that he had at other times given a different exposition from the one he was now insisting on of those ridiculous ideas of his, that Christ suffered in his divine nature, that the body of Christ is everywhere, and that the flesh profits nothing; but the dear man had nothing to say in reply—except that on the matter of the flesh profiting nothing he said: "You know, Zwingli, that all the ancient writers have again and again changed their interpretations of passages of Scripture as time went on and their judgment matured." He said: "The body of Christ is eaten and received into our body in the bodily sense [*corporaliter*], but at the same time I reserve my judgment on whether the human spirit eats his body too"—when a little before he had said: "the body of Christ is eaten by the mouth in the bodily sense, but the human spirit does not eat him in the bodily sense." He said: "[the bread and wine] are made into the body of Christ by the utterance of these words—'This is my body'—however great a criminal one might be who pronounces them." He conceded that the body of Christ is finite. He conceded that the Eucharist may be called a "sign" of the body of Christ. These and others are examples of the countless inconsistencies, absurdities and follies which he babbles out like water lapping on the shore; but we refuted him so successfully that the land-

grave himself has now come down on our side, though he does not say so in the presence of some of the princes. The Hessian entourage, almost to a man, has withdrawn from Luther's position. The landgrave himself has given permission for our books to be read with impunity, and in future will not allow "bishops" who share our views to be ejected from their place. John, the Saxon prince, was not there, but [Ulrich of] Württemberg was.

We finally left [Marburg] with certain agreements which you will soon see in print. The truth prevailed so manifestly that if ever anyone was beaten it was the foolish and obstinate Luther. He was clearly defeated, as any wise and fair judge would agree, although he now makes out that he was not beaten. We have, however, achieved this much good, that our agreement on the rest of the doctrines of the Christian religion will prevent the papal party from hoping any longer that Luther will be on their side.

✠

From Potter, Huldrych Zwingli, 106–8.

37. Zwingli's Death: Two Accounts

The Swiss Confederacy, made up of relatively independent districts or cantons, functioned throughout most of the 1520s by allowing each canton to determine its own religious policy. This arrangement eventually fell apart, with battles breaking out between Protestant and Catholic cantons. On 11 October 1531, Zwingli himself enthusiastically took up the sword in a skirmish with a neighboring Catholic canton and was killed. The following very different accounts are revealing.

A Catholic Version (Salat)

Zwingli was found in the front line where the Zurich force had been drawn up. He was lying on his face which had not been scratched or wounded. A Catholic soldier, not knowing who he was, turned him over and shook him so that he might have air and be able to breathe. He opened his eyes and looked round. Then he was asked if he wished to confess his sins. He shook his head and indicated that he did not wish to do so. Thereupon another warrior standing by struck Zwingli a fatal blow on the neck under the chin with his broadsword. Then a number of men arrived who had known Zwingli when he was alive, looked at him and sought for identification marks on his body. They found that it really was Zwingli. Then they had much to say, rejoicing in his death and calling him a good many entirely suitable names. They added their repeated thanks to almighty God whose vengeance lay there in the blood of the miscreant who had been the true founder, originator, creator and initiator of all their evils, calamities and alarms. Even so God had graciously allowed him to die in the presence of, and surrounded by, good, honorable men, perhaps because he had once been a priest. It would not have been remarkable if there had been more devils by him at his end than there were soldiers in the field. For the whole evening more and more Catholics came up to look at the dead body of one who had been responsible for bringing more discontent, disorder, trouble, need and anxiety than had all the princes, lords, peoples and cities. He now lay there given by God's instrumentality into their hands and he had paid the price for his wickedness. There, at last, was the representative of all the Confederates and (by the grace of God) all his schemes perished with him.

A Protestant Version (Bullinger)

On the battlefield, not far from the line of attack, Mr. Ulrich Zwingli lay under the dead and wounded. While men were looting . . . he was still alive, lying on his back, with his hands together as if he was praying, and his eyes looking upwards to heaven. So some approached who did not know him and asked him, since he was so weak and close to death (for he had fallen in combat and was stricken with a mortal wound), whether a priest should be fetched to hear his confession. Thereat Zwingli shook his head, said nothing and looked up to heaven. Later they told him that if he was no longer able to speak or confess he should yet have the mother of God in his heart and call on the beloved saints to plead to God for grace on his behalf. Again Zwingli shook his head and continued gazing straight up to heaven. At this the Catholics grew impatient, cursed him and said that he was one of the obstinate cantankerous heretics and should get what he deserved. Then Captain Fuckinger of Unterwalden appeared and in exasperation drew his sword and gave Zwingli a thrust from which he at once died. So the renowned Mr. Ulrich Zwingli, true minister and servant of the churches of Zurich, was found wounded on the battlefield along with his flock (with whom he remained until his death). There, because of his confession of the true faith in Christ, our only savior, the mediator and advocate of all believers, he was killed by a captain who was a pensioner, one of those against whom he had always preached so eloquently. . . .

The crowd then [Oct. 12] spread it abroad throughout the camp that anyone who wanted to denounce Zwingli as a heretic and betrayer of a pious confederation should come onto the battlefield. There, with great contempt, they set up a court of injustice on Zwingli which decided that his body should be quartered and the portions burned. All this was carried into effect by the executioner from Lucerne with abundance of abuse; among other things he said that although some had asserted that Zwingli was a sick man he had in fact never seen a more healthy-looking body.

They threw into the fire the entrails of some pigs that had been slaughtered the previous night and then they turned over the embers so that the pigs' offal was mixed with Zwingli's ashes. This was done close to the high road to Scheuren.

Verdicts on Zwingli from scholars and ignorant alike were varied. All those who knew him were constant in their praises. Even so there were still more who were critical either because they really did not know him or, if they had known him a little, were determined to show their resentment and spoke ill of him.

From Potter, Huldrych Zwingli, *143–46.*

Thomas Müntzer

38. *A Sermon before the Princes* (1524)

The figure of Thomas Müntzer (ca. 1491–1525) remains almost as controversial today as he was in his own time. There is little doubt, however, that he was one of Luther's most bitter opponents, that his extreme apocalypticism entailed a call for radical social transformation, and that this was one of the catalysts for the German Peasants' War in 1525. In his *Sermon before the Princes* of 13 July 1524, Müntzer portrays himself as the

prophet who heralds a momentous upheaval which will then usher in a new age in which the righteous shall reign. He calls on the princes to be God's instruments in this revolution. Less than a year later, the Peasants' War was over and Müntzer, as one of its leaders, was beheaded outside the city walls of Mühlhausen.

Whoever wishes, by reason of his fleshly judgment, to be utterly hostile about visions [and dreams] without any experience of them, rejecting them all, or [again, whoever] wishes to take them all in without any distinction . . . will have a poor run of it and will hurl himself against the Holy Spirit. For God speaks clearly, like this text of Daniel [Ch.2], about the transformation of the world. He will prepare it in the last days in order that his name may be rightly praised. He will free it of its shame, and will pour out his Holy Spirit over all flesh, and our sons and daughters shall prophesy and shall have dreams and visions. For if Christendom is not to become apostolic (Acts 2:16) in the way anticipated in Joel, why should one preach at all? To what purpose then the Bible with its visions?

It is true, and I know it to be true, that the Spirit of God is revealing to many elect, pious persons a decisive, inevitable, imminent reformation [accompanied] by great anguish, and it must be carried out to completion. Defend oneself against it as one may, the prophecy of Daniel remains unweakened, even if no one believes it, as also Paul says to the Romans (3:3). This passage of Daniel is thus as clear as the sun, and the process of ending the fifth monarchy of the world is in full swing. . . .

O beloved lords, how handsomely the Lord will go smashing among the old pots with his rod of iron (Ps. 2:9). Therefore, you much beloved and esteemed princes, learn your judgments directly from the mouth of God and do not let yourselves be misled by your hypocritical parsons nor be restrained by false consideration and indulgence. For the stone [made] without hands, cut from the mountain [which will crush the fifth kingdom], has become great. The poor laity [of the towns] and the peasants see it much more clearly than you. Yea, God be praised, it has become so great [that] already, if other lords or neighbors should wish to persecute you for the gospel's sake, they would be driven back by their own people! . . .

The pitiable corruption of holy Christendom has become so great that at the present time no tongue can tell it all. Therefore a new Daniel must arise and interpret for you your vision and this [prophet], as Moses teaches (Deut. 20:2), must go in front of the army. He must reconcile the anger of the princes and the enraged people. . . .

Now if you want to be true governors, you must begin government at the roots, and, as Christ commanded, drive his enemies from the elect. For you are the means to this end. . . .Christ says it sufficiently (Matt. 7:19; John 15:2, 6): Every tree that bringeth not forth good fruit is rooted out and cast into the fire. . . . For the godless person has no right to live when he is in the way of the pious. In Exodus 22:18 God says: Thou shalt not suffer evildoers to live. Saint Paul also means this where he says of the sword of rulers that it is bestowed upon them for the retribution of the wicked as protection for the pious (Rom. 13:4). God is your protection and will teach you to fight against his foes (Ps. 18:34). He will make your hands skilled in fighting and will also sustain you. But you will have to suffer for that reason a great cross and temptation in order that the fear of God may be declared upon you. . . .

Look at Ps. 44:5 and 1 Chr. 14:11. There you will find the solution in this way. They did not conquer the land by the sword but rather through the power of God. But the sword was the means, as eating and drinking is for us a means of living. In just this way the sword is necessary to wipe out the godless (Rom. 13:4). That this might now take place, however, in an orderly and proper fashion, our cherished fathers, the princes, should do it, who with us confess Christ. If, however, they do not do it, the sword will be taken from them (Dan. 7:26-27). . . . Otherwise the Christian church cannot come back again to its origin. The weeds must be plucked out of the vineyard of God in the time of harvest. Then the beautiful red wheat will acquire substantial rootage and come up properly (Matt. 13:24-30). The angels, however, who sharpen their sickles for this purpose are the serious servants of God who execute the wrath of the divine wisdom (Mal. 3:1-6). . . .

✠

From L. H. Zuck, ed., Christianity and Revolution: Radical Christian Testimonies, 1520–1650 *(Philadelphia: Temple University Press, 1975), 36–37.*

The Peasant Revolt

39. The *Twelve Articles* of the Peasants (1525)

In 1525, longstanding peasant grievances and Reformation religious impulses coalesced in a widespread uprising of the "common man." The revolt was brutally crushed by both Catholic and Protestant authorities, with between seventy thousand and one hundred thousand peasants killed. The *Twelve Articles* are a representative and widely disseminated list of their demands, written by the furrier Sebastian Lotzer and the Lutheran pastor Christoph Schappeler in February of that same year.

To the Christian reader peace and the grace of God through Christ.

There are many Antichrists who on account of the assembling of the peasants, cast scorn upon the gospel, and say: Is this the fruit of the new teaching, that no one obeys but all everywhere rise in revolt, and band together to reform, extinguish, indeed kill the temporal and spiritual authorities? The following articles will answer these godless and blaspheming faultfinders. They will first of all remove the reproach from the Word of God and secondly give a Christian excuse for the disobedience or even the revolt of the entire peasantry. . . .Therefore, Christian reader, read the following articles with care, and then judge. Here follow the articles:

The First Article. First, it is our humble petition and desire, indeed our will and resolution, that in the future we shall have power and authority so that the entire community should choose and appoint a minister, and that we should have the right to depose him should he conduct himself improperly. The minister thus chosen should teach us the holy gospel pure and simple, without any human addition, doctrine or ordinance. For to teach us continually the true faith will lead us to pray God that through his grace his faith may increase within us and be confirmed in us. For if his grace is not within us, we always remain flesh and blood, which avails nothing; since the Scripture clearly teaches that only through true faith can we come to God. Only through his mercy can we become holy. . . .

The Second Article. Since the right tithe is established in the Old Testament and fulfilled in the New, we are ready and willing to pay the fair tithe of grain. Nonetheless it should be done properly. The Word of God plainly provides that it should be given to God and passed on to his own. If it is to be given to a minister, we will in the future collect the tithe through our church elders, appointed by the congregation, according to the judgment of the whole congregation. The remainder shall be given to the poor of the place, as the circumstances and the general opinion demand. . . .

The Third Article. It has been the custom hitherto for men to hold us as their own property, which is pitiable enough considering that Christ has redeemed and purchased us without exception, by the shedding of his precious blood, the lowly as well as the great. Accordingly, it is consistent with Scripture that we should be free and we wish to be so. Not that we want to be absolutely free and under no authority. God does not teach us that we should lead a disorderly life according to the lusts of the flesh, but that we should live by the commandments, love the Lord our God and our neighbor. . . .

The Fourth Article. In the fourth place it has been the custom heretofore that no poor man was allowed to catch venison or wild fowl, or fish in flowing water, which seems to us quite unseemly and unbrotherly, as well as selfish and not according to the word of God. . . . Accordingly, it is our desire if a man holds possession of waters that he should prove from satisfactory documents that his right has been wittingly acquired by purchase. We do not wish to take it from him by force, but his rights should be exercised in a Christian and brotherly fashion. . . .

The Fifth Article. In the fifth place we are aggrieved in the matter of woodcutting, for our noble folk have appropriated all the woods to themselves alone. . . . It should be free to every member of the community to help himself to such firewood as he needs in his home. Also, if a man requires wood for carpenter's purposes he should have it free, but with the approval of a person appointed by the community for that purpose. . . .

The Sixth Article. Our sixth complaint is in regard to the excessive services demanded of us, which increase from day to day. We ask that this matter be properly looked into, so that we shall not continue to be oppressed in this way, and that some gracious consideration be given to us, since our forefathers served only according to the Word of God.

The Seventh Article. Seventh, we will not hereafter allow ourselves to be further oppressed by our lords. What the lords possess is to be held according to the agreement between the lord and the peasant. . . .

The Eighth Article. In the eighth place, we are greatly burdened by holdings which cannot support the rent exacted from them. The peasants suffer loss in this way and are ruined. We ask that the lords may appoint persons of honor to inspect these holdings and fix a rent in accordance with justice, so that the peasant shall not work for nothing, since the laborer is worthy of his hire.

The Ninth Article. In the ninth place, we are burdened with the great evil in the constant making of new laws. We are not judged according to the offense but sometimes with great ill will, and sometimes much too leniently. In our opinion we should be judged according to the old written law, so that the case shall be decided according to its merits, and not with favors.

The Tenth Article. In the tenth place we are aggrieved that certain individuals have appropriated meadows and fields which at one time belonged to the community. These we will take again into our own hands unless they were rightfully purchased.

The Eleventh Article. In the eleventh place we will entirely abolish the custom called "Todfall" (heriot), and will no longer endure it, nor allow widows and orphans to be thus shamefully robbed against God's will. . . .

Conclusion. In the twelfth place it is our conclusion and final resolution, that if any one or more of these articles should not be in agreement with the Word of God, which we do not think, we will willingly recede from such article when it is proved to be against the Word of God by a clear explanation of the Scripture. For this we shall pray God, since he can grant all this and he alone. The peace of Christ abide with us all.

✠

From Zuck, Christianity and Revolution, *14–16.*

The Anabaptists

Among the various conflicting currents of reform in the turbulent decade of the 1520s, one came to be known almost immediately as "Anabaptists." The name is misleading. For one thing, it means "rebaptizers" and yet these people, who believed in adult baptism, held that infant baptism was no baptism at all. For another, it implies that baptism was for them the most important thing. This was not always the case, and in fact, from a theological point of view, baptism was far more important for Catholics and Luther's followers. Then, too, the name implies that we are dealing here with a unified movement with a consistent religious position. In fact, historians now agree, significantly different "Anabaptist" groups emerged almost contemporaneously and relatively independently in Switzerland, central and south Germany, north Germany, and the Netherlands. And no one person can be given the title of founder.

Yet, all necessary qualifications notwithstanding, it seems clear that a set of core beliefs united most of these people most of the time, differentiating them from others, and making it possible for us to speak of an Anabaptist movement. Besides adult baptism, they believed in a voluntary church, freedom of conscience, and pacifism. All of this was based on their conception of discipleship: to be a "Christian" meant simply and above all to be a follower of Christ. For these beliefs, many of which were politically subversive in the sixteenth-century context, the Anabaptists suffered enormously. Catholic and Protestant authorities alike hunted them mercilessly, and tortured, drowned or burned those who would not recant.

For centuries, most historians followed Luther in regarding this group as a fanatical sect of ignorant extremists. Today, however, such a judgment is no longer possible. While we may hesitate to go along with their descendants (the Mennonites, the Amish, the Hutterites, etc.) who sometimes depict them as holy martyrs for truth, we must at the very least see these sixteenth-century Anabaptists as heroic precursors of some of the values on which our own society is built.

40. *Reminiscences* of George Blaurock (1525)

Swiss Anabaptism had its origins in a major rift that developed between Zwingli and some of his younger and more radical followers. The first adult baptism took place late in

January 1525, in the home of Felix Mantz. The eyewitness description by George Blaurock (d. 1529) sets the context, captures the moment, and reflects the deep alienation from Zwingli.

✠

It came to pass that Ulrich Zwingli and Conrad Grebel, one of the aristocracy, and Felix Mantz—all three much experienced and men learned in the German, Latin, Greek, and also the Hebrew, languages—came together and began to talk through matters of belief among themselves and recognized that infant baptism is unnecessary and recognized further that it is in fact no baptism. Two, however, Conrad and Felix, recognized in the Lord and believed [further] that one must and should be correctly baptized according to the Christian ordinance and institution of the Lord, since Christ himself says that whoever *believes* and is baptized will be saved. Ulrich Zwingli, who shuddered before Christ's cross, shame, and persecution, did not wish this and asserted that an uprising would break out. The other two, however, Conrad and Felix, declared that God's clear commandment and institution could not for that reason be allowed to lapse.

At this point it came to pass that a person from Chur came to them, namely, a cleric named George of the House of Jacob, commonly called "Bluecoat" (*Blaurock*) because one time when they were having a discussion of matters of belief in a meeting this George Cajacob presented his view also. Then someone asked who it was who had just spoken. Thereupon someone answered: The person in the blue coat spoke. Thus thereafter he got the name of Blaurock. . . . This George came, moreover, with the unusual zeal which he had, a straightforward, simple parson. As such he was held by everyone. But in matters of faith and in divine zeal, which had been given him out of God's grace, he acted wonderfully and valiantly in the cause of truth. He first came to Zwingli and discussed matters of belief with him at length, but accomplished nothing. Then he was told that there were other men more zealous than Zwingli. These men he inquired for diligently and found them, namely, Conrad Grebel and Felix Mantz. With them he spoke and talked through matters of faith. They came to one mind in these things, and in the pure fear of God they recognized that a person must learn from the divine Word and preaching a true faith which manifests itself in love, and receive the true Christian baptism on the basis of the recognized and confessed faith, in the union with God of a good conscience, [prepared] henceforth to serve God in a holy Christian life with all godliness, also to be steadfast to the end in tribulation. And it came to pass that they were together until fear began to come over them, yea, they were pressed in their hearts. Thereupon, they began to bow their knees to the most high God in heaven and called upon him as the knower of hearts, implored him to enable them to do his divine will and to manifest his mercy toward them. For flesh and blood and human forwardness did not drive them, since they well knew what they would have to bear and suffer on account of it. After the prayer, George Cajacob arose and asked Conrad to baptize him, for the sake of God, with the true Christian baptism upon his faith and knowledge. And when he knelt down with that request and desire, Conrad baptized him, since at that time there was no ordained deacon to perform such work. After that was done the others similarly desired George to baptize them, which he also did upon their request. Thus they together gave themselves to the name of the Lord in the high fear of God. Each confirmed the other in the service of the gospel, and they began to teach and keep the faith. Therewith began the separation from the world and its evil works.

Soon thereafter several others made their way to them, for example, Balthasar Hubmaier of Friedberg, Louis Haetzer, and still others, men well instructed in the German, Latin, Greek, and Hebrew languages, very well versed in Scripture, some preachers and other persons, who were soon to have testified with their blood.

The aforementioned Felix Mantz they drowned at Zurich because of this true belief and true baptism, who thus witnessed steadfastly with his body and life to this truth. Afterward Wolfgang Ullmann, whom they burned with fire and put to death in Waltzra, also in Switzerland, himself the eleventh, his brethren and associates witnessing in a valorous and knightly manner with their bodies and their lives unto death that their faith and baptism were grounded in the divine truth. . . .

Thus did it [the movement] spread through persecution and much tribulation. The church increased daily, and the Lord's people grew in numbers. This the enemy of the divine truth could not endure. He used Zwingli as an instrument, who thereupon began to write diligently and to preach from the pulpit that the baptism of believers and adults was not right and should not be tolerated—contrary to his own confession which he had previously written and taught, namely, that infant baptism cannot be demonstrated or proved with a single clear word from God. But now, since he wished rather to please men than God, he contended against the true Christian baptism. He also stirred up the magistracy to act on imperial authorization and behead as Anabaptists those who had properly given themselves to God, and with a good understanding had made covenant of a good conscience with God.

Finally it reached the point that over twenty men, widows, pregnant wives, and maidens were cast miserably into dark towers, sentenced never again to see either sun or moon as long as they lived, to end their days on bread and water, and thus in the dark towers to remain together, the living and the dead, until none remained alive—there to die, to stink, and to rot. Some among them did not eat a mouthful of bread in three days, just so that others might have to eat.

Soon also there was issued a stern mandate at the instigation of Zwingli that if any more people in the canton of Zurich should be rebaptized, they should immediately, without further trial, hearing, or sentence, be cast into the water and drowned. Herein one sees which spirit's child Zwingli was, and those of his party still are.

However, since the work fostered by God cannot be changed and God's counsel lies in the power of no man, the aforementioned men went forth, through divine prompting, to proclaim and preach the evangelical word and the ground of truth. George Cajacob or Blaurock went into the county of Tyrol. In the meantime Balthasar Hubmaier came to Nicolsburg in Moravia, began to teach and preach. The people, however, accepted the teaching and many people were baptized in a short time.

✠

From G. H. Williams, ed., Spiritual and Anabaptist Writers *(Philadelphia: Westminster Press, 1957), 41–46.*

41. Balthasar Hubmaier, *Concerning Heretics and Those Who Burn Them* (1524)

Balthasar Hubmaier (1480–1528) was ordained to the priesthood in 1510 and earned a doctorate in theology shortly thereafter. By 1523 he was favoring Zwinglian ideas, and in 1525 he joined the Anabaptists, becoming one of their most able spokespersons. Thus it was in his pre-Anabaptist phase, in 1524, that he wrote the tract printed here. It is one of the earliest pleas for religious toleration in a profoundly intolerant age. Hubmaier was burned at the stake by Catholic authorities in Vienna on March 10, 1528.

✠

1. Heretics are those who wickedly oppose the Holy Scriptures, the first of whom was the devil, when he said to Eve, "Ye shall not surely die" (Gen. 3:4), together with his followers.

2. Those also are heretics who cast a veil over the Scriptures and interpret them otherwise than the Holy Spirit demands; as those who everywhere proclaim a concubine as a benefice, pastoring and ruling the church at Rome, and compelling us to believe this talk.

3. Those who are such one should overcome with holy knowledge, not angrily but softly, although the Holy Scriptures contain wrath.

4. But this wrath of the Scriptures is truly a spiritual fire and zeal of love, not burning without the Word of God.

5. If they will not be taught by strong proofs or evangelic reasons, then let them be, and leave them to rage and be mad (Titus 3:2, 3), that those who are filthy may become more filthy still (Rev. 22:11).

6. The law that condemns heretics to the fire builds up both Zion in blood and Jerusalem in wickedness.

7. Therefore will they be taken away in sighs, for the judgments of God (whose right it is to judge) either convert or harden them, that the blind lead the blind and both the seduced and the seducer go from bad to worse.

8. This is the will of Christ who said, "Let both grow together till the harvest, lest while ye gather up the tares ye root up also the wheat with them" (Matt. 13:29). "For there must also be heresies among you, that they that are approved may be made manifest among you" (1 Cor. 11:19).

9. Though they indeed experience this, yet they are not put away until Christ shall say to the reapers, "Gather first the tares and bind them in bundles to burn them" (Matt. 13:30).

10. This word does not teach us idleness but strife; for we should unceasingly contend, not with men but with their godless doctrine.

11. The unwatchful bishops are the cause of the heresies. "When men slept, the enemy came" (Matt. 13:25).

12. Again, "Blessed is the man who is a watcher at the door of the bridegroom's chamber" (Prov. 8:34), and neither sleeps nor "sits in the seat of the scornful" (Ps. 1:1).

13. Hence it follows that the inquisitors are the greatest heretics of all, since, against the doctrine and example of Christ, they condemn heretics to fire, and before the time of harvest root up the wheat with the tares.

14. For Christ did not come to butcher, destroy and burn, but that those that live might live more abundantly (John 10:10).

15. We should pray and hope for repentance, as long as man lives in this misery.

16. A Turk or a heretic is not convinced by our act, either with the sword or with fire, but only with patience and prayer; and so we should await with patience the judgment of God.

17. If we do otherwise, God will treat our sword as stubble, and burning fire as mockery (Job 41:29).

18. So unholy and far off from evangelical doctrine is the whole order of preaching friars (of which variegated birds our Antony is one), that hitherto out of them alone the inquisitors have come.

19. If these only knew of what spirit they ought to be, they would not so shamelessly pervert God's Word, nor so often cry, "To the fire, to the fire!" (Luke 9:54-56).

20. It is no excuse (as they chatter) that they give over the wicked to the secular power, for he who thus gives over sins more deeply (John 19:11).

21. For each Christian has a sword against the wicked, which is the word of God (Eph. 6:17), but not a sword against the malignant.

22. The secular power rightly and properly puts to death the criminals who injure the bodies of the defenseless (Rom. 13:3, 4). But he who is God's cannot injure anyone, unless he first deserts the gospel.

23. Christ has shown us this clearly, saying, "Fear not them that kill the body" (Matt. 10:28).

24. The [secular] power judges criminals, but not the godless who cannot injure either body or soul, but rather are a benefit; therefore God can in wisdom draw good from evil.

25. Faith which flows from the gospel fountain, lives only in contests, and the rougher they become so much the greater becomes faith.

26. That every one has not been taught the gospel truth, is due to the bishops no less than to the common people—these that they have not cared for a better shepherd, the

former that they have not performed their office properly.

27. If the blind lead the blind, according to the just judgment of God, they both fall together into the ditch (Matt. 15:14).

28. Hence to burn heretics is in appearance to profess Christ (Titus 1:10, 11), but in reality to deny him, and to be more monstrous than Jehoiakim, the King of Judah (Jer. 37:23).

29. If it is blasphemy to destroy a heretic, how much more is it to burn to ashes a faithful herald of the Word of God, unconvicted, not arraigned by the truth.

30. The greatest deception of the people is a zeal for God that is unscripturally expended, the salvation of the soul, honor of the church, love of truth, good intention, use or custom, episcopal decrees, the teaching of the reason that comes by the natural light. For they are deadly arrows where they are not led and directed by the Scriptures.

31. We should not presume, led away by the deception of our own purpose, to do better or more securely than God has spoken by his own mouth.

32. Those who rely on their good intention and think to do better, are like Uzziah and Peter. The latter was called Satan by Christ (Matt. 16:23), but the former came to a wretched end (1 Chr. 13:10).

33. Elnathan, Delaiah and Gemariah acted wisely in withstanding Jehoiakim, the King of Judah, when he cast the book of Jehovah into the fire (Jer. 36:25).

34. But in that, after one book was burnt, Baruch by the express direction of Jeremiah, wrote another much better (Jer. 36:27-32), we see the just punishment of God on the unrighteous burning. For so it shall be that on those who fear the frost, a cold snow falls (Job. 6:16).

35. But we do not hold that it was unchristian to burn their numerous books of incantations, as the fact in the Acts of the Apostles shows (Acts 19:19). It is a small thing to burn innocent paper, but to point out an error and to disprove it by Scripture, that is art.

36. Now it is clear to every one, even the blind, that a law to burn heretics is an invention of the devil. "Truth is immortal."

✠

From Henry C. Vedder, Balthasar Hubmaier: The Leader of the Anabaptists (New York: AMS Press, 1971), 84–88.

42. Balthasar Hubmaier, *A Christian Catechism* (1526)

While Hubmaier was one of the more theologically sophisticated of the early Anabaptist leaders, he sets this aside in his catechism in favor of clarity and simplicity. The work takes the form of a question and answer dialogue. It abandons the traditional catechetical structure of Ten Commandments, Lord's Prayer, and creed in favor of a structure based on the two "ordinances" of Christ, namely baptism and the Lord's Supper. Here we have an excerpt dealing with the closely related doctrines of baptism and the church.

✠

Leon: What do you desire after faith?
Hans: The baptism of water.
Leon: How many kinds of baptism are there?
Hans: Three kinds.
Leon: What are they?
Hans: Baptism of the Spirit, baptism of water, and baptism of blood.
Leon: What is the baptism of the Spirit?

Hans: It is an inner illumination of our heart which is brought about by the Holy Spirit through the living word of God.

Leon: What is the baptism of water?

Hans: It is an external and evident sign of the internal baptism of the Spirit which man gives with the reception of water, whereby he confesses his sins before all men. He shows also thereby that he believes that these are forgiven through the death and resurrection of our Lord Jesus Christ. By this he also lets himself be externally registered, enlisted, and thus, by the baptism of water, incorporated into the community of the church, according to the institution of Christ; before this church the person also openly and verbally makes a vow to God and promises in the power of God the Father, and the Son, and the Holy Spirit, that he will from now on believe and live according to his divine Word. And where he trespasses in this regard, he will submit to brotherly punishment according to the ordinance of Christ (Matt. 18:15ff.). And this then is the correct baptismal vow which we have lost for a thousand years; in the meantime Satan's monastic and priestly vows were introduced and placed on the saints in their stead.

Leon: What is the baptism of blood?

Hans: It is a daily mortifying of the flesh until death.

Leon: Where has Christ informed us of these baptisms?

Hans: On the baptism of the Spirit, John 3:5; on the baptism of water, Matt. 28:18ff. and Mark 16:15f.; on the baptism of blood, Luke 12:50.

Leon: Why were you not baptized in childhood?

Hans: Because as a child I did not yet believe, nor did I know what faith, Christ, or baptism were.

Leon: What is your opinion of the infant baptism which the water-priests use?

Hans: Simply this: that the old child bathes the young child, and through this the true water baptism of Christ is perverted.

Leon: Since Christ has instituted the baptism of water only for the faithful (Matt. 28, Mark 16), one should baptize only the faithful, i.e., those who openly and verbally confess their faith; should we then allow ourselves to be rebaptized? What is your opinion?

Hans: Our opinions should count for and mean nothing; we must ask advice from the mouth of the Lord and he has said: Go out teaching and baptizing all peoples; whoever believes and is baptized will be saved. Now, while Christ commands his disciples to preach and baptize, we are at the same time commanded to hear the preaching and to allow ourselves to be baptized. Because whoever breaks the least of Christ's commandments, the same will be called the least in the kingdom of heaven (Matt. 5:19, James 2). Now, however, the baptism of water is given as a very serious commandment to be done in the name of the Father and Son and of the Holy Spirit. Whatever baptism we receive, even if we are a hundred years old, it is still not a rebaptism, since infant baptism is no baptism, nor is it worthy of the name. Because the child knows neither good nor evil, nor can he promise or pledge anything to God or the church.

Leon: What is the baptismal vow?

Hans: It is a pledge, given to God by the person openly and verbally before the church, in which he renounces Satan and all his demons and works. He vows too that from now on he will place his faith, hope and trust in God alone, and will lead his life according to the divine word, by the power of Jesus Christ our Lord; and where he does not do this, he hereby promises the church that he will not separate himself from it and virtuously accept from it brotherly punishment, as was already said above.

Leon: Where is baptism treated in the articles of faith?

Hans: In the ninth and tenth articles where one expresses belief in a catholic Christian church, a community of saints, and the remission of sins; these articles also include the supper of Christ. Because with external baptism the church opens its gates to all the faithful who verbally confess their faith before it, and takes them into her bosom, into the community and fellowship of saints for the forgiveness of their sins. Therefore, as much as one values the forgiveness of sins and the community of saints outside of which there is no salvation, so much should he value the baptism of water, through which he enters and becomes part of the universal Christian church. This too is the understanding and resolution which emerged from the Council of Nicaea in these words: I confess a single baptism for the remission of sins. And Peter also agreed

when he said: And everyone was baptized in the name of our Lord Jesus Christ for the forgiveness of sins (Acts 2:38).

Leon: Since you have now assured the church of your faith by means of the baptism of water, tell me, what is the church?

Hans: The church is sometimes taken to be all people who are gathered and united in one God, in one Lord, in one faith, and in one baptism, and who confess this faith with the mouth, wherever these people may be on earth. Now, this is the universal bodily Christian church and community of the saints gathered in the Spirit of God alone, as we have confessed in the ninth article of the creed. Sometimes the church is taken to be each particular and outward gathering, church group, or parish, which belongs to a pastor or bishop, and which comes together bodily for teaching, baptism and the supper. This daughter church has just the same power to bind and to loose on earth as her mother, the universal church, who uses the keys according to the command of Christ, her spouse and marriage partner.

Leon: What is the difference between these two churches?

Hans: The particular church can indeed err, as the papal church has erred in many cases. But the universal church cannot err. She is without spot, without wrinkle, is governed by the Holy Spirit, and Christ is with her until the end of the world (Matt. 28:20). And God himself has always reserved seven thousand men who have not bowed the knee to the idol Baal (1 Kgs. 19:18, Rom. 11).

Leon: What is the Christian church built upon?

Hans: On the verbal confession of faith that Jesus is Christ, a Son of the living God. This external confession, and not faith alone, is what makes a church, because that which has power to bind and loose is external and bodily not abstract, while faith is internal. And although faith alone makes one righteous, yet faith alone does not save, since the open confession must also accompany it. We have beautiful testimony for this in Matt. 16:18. There Christ says: You are Peter, a rock, and on the rock (understand as "what you confess"), I will build my church. He also speaks thus: Anyone who confesses me before men, him will I confess before my Father who is in heaven, and whoever denies or is ashamed of my words before men, him will I deny and be ashamed of before my Father (Matt. 10:32, Luke 9:26; 12:5f.). And Paul says: With the heart man believes unto righteousness, but with the mouth confession is made unto salvation (Rom. 10:10).

Leon: What power do those in the church have over one another?

Hans: The power of brotherly correction.

Leon: What is brotherly correction?

Hans: When one, seeing his brother sinning, goes to him out of love and corrects him in private, so that he renounces such sins. He who does so has won his brother's soul. If the brother does not renounce his sins, the other takes two or three witnesses with him and corrects the brother once again before them. If the brother follows this correction, he is saved; if the brother does not, he reports it to the church. The church calls the brother up and corrects him for a third time. If he now renounces his sin, then they have won his soul (Matt. 18:15ff.).

Leon: From where does the church get this power?

Hans: From the commandment of Christ when he said to his disciples: Everything that you will bind on earth will also be bound in heaven, and everything that you will loose on earth will also be loosed in heaven (Matt. 18:18; John 20:23).

Leon: When may a brother use this power over another?

Hans: From the time of the baptismal vow in which the person has subjected himself to the church and all its members, according to the word of Christ.

Leon: What happens when the corrected sinner does not want to reform himself?

Hans: Then the church has the power and right to exclude him and put him under the ban as a person who is a perjurer and vowbreaker.

Leon: What is the ban?

Hans: It is an exclusion and cutting off, so that from now on Christians shall have no association with such men, neither in speaking, eating, drinking, milling, baking, nor in any other way. Rather he is regarded as a heathen and publican, that is, as an annoying, improper, contaminated man, who is bound and given over to the devil. He must be avoided and shunned not only because by his association the whole church hears and tastes evil and by his evil example it is worsened, but much more because the church, terrified by this correction, will fear and thus extinguish sin. For as surely as God lives, what the church thus admits or excludes on earth, that is admitted or excluded also in heaven.

Leon: What are the grounds for exclusion?

Hans: Unwillingness to be reconciled to one's brother or to renounce sin.

Leon: What does one exclude people for?

Hans: Not for "six schillings worth of hazelnuts" [insignificant trifles], as our papists used to do, but for a grievous sin; and it works to the good of the sinner who looks into himself, knows himself, and renounces the sin.

Leon: How does the church deal with him if he renounces sin, avoids the path which might lead him to fall again, and reforms himself?

Hans: It takes him up again with joy, as the father received his lost son and as Paul received the Corinthians (Luke 15:20; 2 Cor. 2:10); it opens up the doors of heaven for him, and allows him to come again to the communion of the supper of Christ. So, in sum: Where baptism of water according to the institution of Christ is not set up and used, there one does not know who his brother or sister is, there is no church, no brotherly discipline or correction, no ban, no supper, nor anything like a Christian existence and reality. God lives; it is therefore true. Or heaven and earth must break in pieces. . . .

✠

From D. Janz, ed., Three Reformation Catechisms: Catholic, Anabaptist, Lutheran *(Toronto: Edwin Mellen Press, 1982), 147–56.*

43. The *Schleitheim Confession* (1527)

This first major expression of consensus among Anabaptist leaders emerged from a conference held in the town of Schleitheim in February of 1527. The meeting was presided over by Michael Sattler (1490–1527), a former prior of a Benedictine monastery who had joined the movement in 1525.

✠

The articles we have dealt with, and in which we have been united, are these: baptism, ban, the breaking of bread, separation from abomination, shepherds in the congregation, the sword, the oath.

I. Notice concerning baptism. Baptism shall be given to all those who have been taught repentance and the amendment of life and [who] believe truly that their sins are taken away through Christ, and to all those who desire to walk in the resurrection of Jesus Christ and be buried with him in death, so that they might rise with him; to all those who with such an understanding themselves desire and request it from us; hereby is excluded all infant baptism, the greatest and first abomination of the pope. For this you have the reasons and the testimony of the writings and the practice of the apostles. We wish simply yet resolutely and with assurance to hold to the same.

II. We have been united as follows concerning the ban. The ban shall be employed with all these who have given themselves over to the Lord, to walk after [him] in his commandments; those who have been baptized into the one body of Christ, and let themselves be called brothers or sisters, and still somehow slip and fall into error and sin, being inadvertently overtaken. The same [shall] be warned twice privately and the third time be publicly admonished before the entire congregation according to the command of Christ (Matthew 18). But this shall be done according to the ordering of the Spirit of God before the breaking of bread, so that we may all in one spirit and in one love break and eat from one bread and drink from one cup.

III. Concerning the breaking of bread, we have become one and agree thus: all those who desire to break the one bread in remembrance of the broken body of Christ and all those who wish to drink of one drink in remembrance of the shed blood of Christ, they must beforehand be united in the one body of Christ, that is the congregation of God, whose head is Christ, and that by baptism. For as Paul indicates, we cannot be partakers at the same time of the table of the Lord and the table of devils. Nor can we at the same time partake and drink of the cup of the Lord and the cup of devils. That is: all those who have fellowship with the dead works of darkness have no part in the light. Thus all who follow the devil and the world, have no part with those who have been called out of the world unto God. All those who lie in evil have no part in the good.

So it shall and must be, that whoever does not share the calling of the one God to one faith, to one baptism, to one spirit, to one body together with all the children of God, may not be made one loaf together with them, as must be true if one wishes truly to break bread according to the command of Christ.

IV. We have been united concerning the separation that shall take place from the evil and the wickedness which the devil has planted in the world, simply in this: that we have no fellowship with them, and do not run with them in the confusion of their abomination. So it is; since all who have not entered into the obedience of faith and have not united themselves with God so that they will to do His will, are a great abomination before God, therefore nothing else can or really will grow or spring forth from them than abominable things. Now there is nothing else in the world and all creation than good or evil, believing and unbelieving, darkness and light, the world and those who are [come] out of the world, God's temple and idols, Christ and Belial, and none will have part with the other.

To us, then, the commandment of the Lord is also obvious, whereby he orders us to be and to become separated from the evil one, and thus he will be our God and we shall be his sons and daughters.

Further, he admonishes us therefore to go out from Babylon and from the earthly Egypt, that we may not be partakers in their torment and suffering, which the Lord will bring upon them.

From all this we should learn that everything which has not been united with our God in Christ is nothing but an abomination which we should shun. By this are meant all popish and repopish works and idolatry, gatherings, church attendance, winehouses, guarantees and commitments of unbelief, and other things of the kind, which the world regards highly, and yet which are carnal or flatly counter to the command of God, after the pattern of all the iniquity which is in the world. From all this we shall be separated and have no part with such, for they are nothing but abominations, which cause us to be hated before our Christ Jesus, who has freed us from the servitude of the flesh and fitted us for the service of God and the Spirit whom he has given us.

Thereby shall also fall away from us the diabolical weapons of violence—such as sword, armor, and the like, and all of their use to protect friends or against enemies—by virtue of the word of Christ: "you shall not resist evil."

v. We have been united as follows concerning shepherds in the church of God. The shepherd in the church shall be a person according to the rule of Paul, fully and completely, who has a good report of those who are outside the faith. The office of such a person shall be to read and exhort and teach, warn, admonish, or ban in the congregation, and properly to preside among the sisters and brothers in prayer, and in the breaking of the bread, and in all things to take care of the body of Christ, that it may be built up and developed, so that the name of God might be praised and honored through us, and the mouth of the mocker be stopped.

He shall be supported, wherein he has need, by the congregation which has chosen him, so that he who serves the gospel can also live therefrom, as the Lord has ordered. But should a shepherd do something worthy of reprimand, nothing shall be done with him without the voice of two or three witnesses. If they sin they shall be publicly reprimanded, so that others might fear.

But if the shepherd should be driven away or led to the Lord by the cross, at the same hour another shall be ordained to his place, so that the little folk and the little flock of God may not be destroyed, but be preserved by warning and be consoled.

vi. We have been united as follows concerning the sword. The sword is an ordering of God outside the perfection of Christ. It punishes and kills the wicked, and guards and protects the good. In the law the sword is established over the wicked for punishment and for death, and the secular rulers are established to wield the same.

But within the perfection of Christ only the ban is used for the admonition and exclusion of the one who has sinned, without the death of the flesh, simply the warning and the command to sin no more.

Now many, who do not understand Christ's will for us, will ask: whether a Christian may or should use the sword against the wicked for the protection and defense of the good, or for the sake of love.

The answer is unanimously revealed: Christ teaches and commands us to learn from him, for he is meek and lowly of heart and thus we shall find rest for our souls. Now Christ says to the woman who was taken in adultery, not that she should be stoned according to the law of his Father (and yet he says, "what the Father commanded me, that I do") but with mercy and forgiveness and the warning to sin no more, says: "Go, sin no more." Exactly thus should we also proceed, according to the rule of the ban.

Second, is asked concerning the sword: whether a Christian shall pass sentence in disputes and strife about worldly matters, such as the unbelievers have with one another. The answer: Christ did not wish to decide or pass judgment between brother and brother concerning inheritance, but refused to do so. So should we also do.

Third, is asked concerning the sword: whether the Christian should be a magistrate if he is chosen thereto. This is answered thus: Christ was to be made king, but he fled and did not discern the ordinance of his Father. Thus we should also do as he did and follow after him, and we shall not walk in darkness.

For he himself says: "Whoever would come after me, let him deny himself and take up his cross and follow me." He himself further forbids the violence of the sword when he says, "The princes of this world lord it over them etc., but among you it shall not be so." Further Paul says: "Whom God has fore-known, the same he has also predestined to be conformed to the image of his Son," etc. Peter also says: "Christ has suffered (not ruled) and has left us an example, that you should follow after in his steps."

Lastly one can see in the following points that it does not befit a Christian to be a magistrate: the rule of the government is according to the flesh, that of the Christians according to the spirit. Their houses and dwelling remain in this world, that of the Christians is in heaven. Their citizenship is in this world, that of the Christians is in heaven. The weapons of their battle and warfare are carnal and only against the flesh, but the weapons of Christians are spiritual, against the fortification of the devil. The worldly are armed with steel and iron, but Christians are armed with the armor of God, with truth, righteousness, peace, faith, salvation, and with the Word of God. In sum: as Christ our Head is minded, so also must be minded the members of the body of Christ through him, so that there be no division in the body, through which it would be destroyed. Since then Christ is as is written of him, so must his members also be the same, so that his body may remain whole and unified for its own advancement and upbuilding. For any kingdom which is divided within itself will be destroyed.

VII. We have been united as follows concerning the oath. The oath is a confirmation among those who are quarreling or making promises. In the law it is commanded that it should be done only in the name of God, truthfully and not falsely. Christ, who teaches the perfection of the law, forbids his [followers] all swearing, whether true nor false; neither by heaven nor by earth, neither by Jerusalem nor by our head; and that for the reason which he goes on to give: "For you cannot make one hair white or black." You see, thereby all swearing is forbidden. We cannot perform what is promised in swearing, for we are not able to change the smallest part of ourselves.

Now there are some who do not believe the simple commandment of God and who say, "But God swore by himself to Abraham, because he was God (as he promised him that he would do good to him and would be his God if he kept his commandments). Why then should I not swear if I promise something to someone?" The answer: hear what Scripture says. "God, since he wished to prove over-abundantly to the heirs of his promise that his will did not change, inserted an oath so that by two immutable things we might have a stronger consolation (for it is impossible that God should lie)." Notice the meaning of the passage: God has the power to do what he forbids you, for everything is possible to him. God swore an oath to Abraham, Scripture says, in order to prove that his counsel is immutable. That means: no one can withstand and thwart his will; thus he can keep his oath. But we cannot, as Christ said above, hold or perform our oath, therefore we should not swear.

Others say that swearing cannot be forbidden by God in the New Testament when it was commanded in the Old, but that it is forbidden only to swear by heaven, earth Jerusalem, and our head. Answer: hear the Scripture. He who swears by heaven, swears by God's throne and by him who sits thereon.

Observe: swearing by heaven is forbidden, which is only God's throne; how much more is it forbidden to swear by God himself. You blind fools, what is greater, the throne or he who sits upon it?

Others say, if it is then wrong to use God for truth, then the apostles Peter and Paul also swore. Answer: Peter and Paul only testify to that which God promised Abraham, whom we long after have received. But when one testifies, one testifies concerning that which is present, whether it be good or evil. Thus Simeon spoke of Christ to Mary and testified: "Behold: this one is ordained for the falling and rising of many in Israel and to be a sign which will be spoken against."

Christ taught us similarly when he says: Your speech shall be yea, yea; and nay, nay; for what is more than that comes of evil. He says, your speech or your word shall be yes and no, so that no one might understand that he had permitted it. Christ is simply yea and nay, and all those who seek him simply will understand his Word. Amen.

✠

From John H. Yoder, The Legacy of Michael Sattler *(Scottdale, Pa.: Herald Press, 1973), 36–42.*

44. The Trial and Martyrdom of Michael Sattler (1527)

Shortly after the Schleitheim conference, Sattler was arrested by Austrian Roman Catholic authorities. He was put on trial along with other Anabaptists, found guilty, and executed. The following is an account of the trial and execution.

✠

After many legal transactions on the day of his departure from this world, the articles against him being many, Michael Sattler . . . requested that they might once more be read to him and that he might again be heard upon them. This the bailiff, as the attorney [for the defense] of his lord [the emperor], opposed and would not consent to it. Michael Sattler then requested a ruling. After a consultation, the judges returned as their answer that, if his opponents would allow it, they, the judges, would consent. Thereupon the town clerk of Ensisheim, as the spokesman of the said attorney, spoke thus: "Prudent, honorable, and wise lords, he has boasted of the Holy Spirit. Now if his boast is true, it seems to me, it is unnecessary to grant him this; for, if he has the Holy Spirit, as he boasts, the same will tell him what has been done here." To this Michael Sattler replied: "You servants of God, I hope my request will not be denied, for the said articles are as yet unclear to me [because of their number]." The town clerk responded: "Prudent, honorable, and wise lords, though we are not bound to do this, yet in order to give satisfaction, we will grant him his request that it may not be thought that injustice is being done him in his heresy or that we desire to abridge him of his rights. Hence let the articles be read to him again." [The nine charges, seven against all fourteen defendants, two specifically against Sattler, are here omitted, as they are answered seriatim by Sattler.]

Thereupon Michael Sattler requested permission to confer with his brethren and sisters, which was granted him. Having conferred with them for a little while, he began and undauntedly answered as follows: "In regard to the articles relating to me and my brethren and sisters, hear this brief answer:

First, that we have acted contrary to the imperial mandate, we do not admit. For the same says that the Lutheran doctrine and delusion is not to be adhered to, but only the gospel and the Word of God. This we have kept. For I am not aware that we have acted contrary to the gospel and the Word of God. I appeal to the words of Christ.

Secondly, that the real body of Christ the Lord is not present in the sacrament, we admit. For the Scripture says: Christ ascended into heaven and sitteth on the right hand of his heavenly Father, whence he shall come to judge the quick and the dead, from which it follows that, if he is in heaven and not in the bread, he may not be eaten bodily.

Thirdly, as to baptism we say infant baptism is of no avail to salvation. For it is written [Rom. 1:17] that we live by faith alone. Again [Mark 16:16]: He that believeth and is baptized shall be saved. Peter says the same [1 Pet. 3:21]: Which doth also now save you in baptism (which is signified by that [Ark of Noah]), not the putting away of the filth of the flesh but rather the covenant of a good conscience with God by the resurrection of Jesus Christ.

Fourthly, we have not rejected the oil [of extreme unction]. For it is a creature of God, and what God has made is good and not to be refused, but that the pope, bishops, monks, and priests can make it better we do not believe; for the pope never made anything good. That of which the Epistle of James [5:14] speaks is not the pope's oil.

Fifthly, we have not insulted the mother of God and the saints. For the mother of Christ is to be blessed among all women because unto her was accorded the favor of giving birth to the Savior of the whole world. But that she is a mediatrix and advocatess—of this the Scriptures know nothing, for she must with us await the judgment. Paul said to Timothy [1 Tim. 2:5]: Christ is our mediator and advocate with God. As regards the saints, we say

that we who live and believe are the saints, which I prove by the epistles of Paul to the Romans [1:7], the Corinthians [1Cor. 1:2], the Ephesians [1:1], and other places where he always writes "to the beloved saints." Hence, we who believe are the saints, but those who have died in the faith we regard as the blessed.

Sixthly, we hold that we are not to swear before the authorities, for the Lord says [Matt. 5:34]: Swear not, but let your communication be, Yea, yea; nay, nay.

Seventhly, when God called me to testify of his Word and I had read Paul and also considered the unchristian and perilous state in which I was, beholding the pomp, pride, usury, and great whoredom of the monks and priests, I went and took unto me a wife, according to the command of God; for Paul well prophesies concerning this to Timothy [1 Tim. 4:3]: In the latter time it shall come to pass that men shall forbid to marry and command to abstain from meats which God hath created to be received with thanksgiving.

Eighthly, if the Turks should come, we ought not to resist them. For it is written [Matt. 5:21]: Thou shalt not kill. We must not defend ourselves against the Turks and others of our persecutors, but are to beseech God with earnest prayer to repel and resist them. But that I said that, if warring were right, I would rather take the field against so-called Christians who persecute, capture, and kill pious Christians than against the Turks was for the following reason. The Turk is a true Turk, knows nothing of the Christian faith, and is a Turk after the flesh. But you who would be Christians and who make your boast of Christ persecute the pious witnesses of Christ and are Turks after the spirit!

In conclusion, ministers of God, I admonish you to consider the end for which God has appointed you, to punish the evil and to defend and protect the pious. Whereas, then, we have not acted contrary to God and the gospel, you will find that neither I nor my brethren and sisters have offended in word or deed against any authority. Therefore, ministers of God, if you have neither heard nor read the word of God, send for the most learned men and for the sacred books of the Bible in whatsoever language they may be and let them confer with us in the Word of God. If they prove to us with the Holy Scriptures that we err and are in the wrong, we will gladly desist and recant and also willingly suffer the sentence and punishment for that of which we have been accused; but if no error is proven to us, I hope to God that you will be converted and receive instruction.

Upon this speech the judges laughed and put their heads together, and the town clerk of Ensisheim said: "Yes, you infamous, desperate rascal of a monk, should we dispute with you? The hangman will dispute with you, I assure you!"

Michael said: "God's will be done."

The town clerk said: "It were well if you had never been born."

Michael replied: "God knows what is good."

The town clerk: "You archheretic, you have seduced pious people. If they would only now forsake their error and commit themselves to grace!"

Michael: "Grace is with God alone."

One of the prisoners also said: "We must not depart from the truth."

The town clerk: "Yes, you desperate villain, you archheretic, I say, if there were no hangman here, I would hang you myself and be doing God a service thereby."

Michael: "God will judge aright." Thereupon the town clerk said a few words to him in Latin, what, we do not know. Michael Sattler answered him, *Judica*.

The town clerk then admonished the judges and said: "He will not cease from this chatter anyway. Therefore, my Lord Judge, you may proceed with the sentence. I call for a decision of the court."

The judge asked Michael Sattler whether he too committed it to the court. He replied: "Ministers of God, I am not sent to judge the Word of God. We are sent to testify and hence cannot consent to any adjudication, since we have no command from God concerning it. But we are not for that reason removed from being judged and we are ready to suffer and to await what God is planning to do with us. We will continue in our faith in Christ so long as we have breath in us, unless we be dissuaded from it by the Scriptures."

The town clerk said: "The hangman will instruct you, he will dispute with you, archheretic."

Michael: "I appeal to the Scriptures."

Then the judges arose and went into another room where they remained for an hour and a half and determined on the sentence. In the meantime some [of the soldiers] in the room treated Michael Sattler most unmercifully, heaping reproach upon him. One of them said: "What have you in prospect for yourself and the others that you have so seduced them?" With this he also drew a sword which lay upon the table, saying: "See, with this they will dispute with you." But Michael did not answer upon a single word concerning himself but willingly endured it all. One of the prisoners said: "We must not cast pearls before swine." Being also asked why he had not remained a lord in the convent, Michael answered: "According to the flesh I was a lord, but it is better as it is." He did not say more than what is recorded here, and this he spoke fearlessly.

The judges having returned to the room, the sentence was read. It was as follows: "In the case of the attorney of His Imperial Majesty vs. Michael Sattler, judgment is passed that Michael Sattler shall be delivered to the executioner, who shall lead him to the place of execution and cut out his tongue, then forge him fast to a wagon and thereon with red-hot tongs twice tear pieces from his body; and after he has been brought outside the gate, he shall be plied five times more in the same manner. . . ."

After this had been done in the manner prescribed, he was burned to ashes as a heretic. His fellow brethren were executed with the sword, and the sisters drowned. His wife, also after being subjected to many entreaties, admonitions, and threats, under which she remained steadfast, was drowned a few days afterward. Done the 21st day of May, A.D. 1527.

From Williams, Spiritual and Anabaptist Writers, *138–44.*

45. Hans Denck, *Concerning True Love* (1527)

Born in Bavaria around 1500, Hans Denck pursued humanistic studies in Ingolstadt and Basel before joining the Anabaptist movement in 1526. He died of the plague in the following year, but in that brief interim he produced a number of writings and became an important leader of South German Anabaptism. The work printed here, *Concerning True Love*, is remarkable for several reasons. On one level it can be read as an almost mystical meditation on the Christian understanding of love, with echoes of Bernard of Clairvaux and the *Devotio Moderna*. On another level it is a theologically sophisticated and systematically coherent summary of the major Anabaptist teachings, showing their relationship to what Denck understands as the central core of Christianity, namely love. The somewhat

naïve biblicism of some other early Anabaptist writers is absent here.

Love is a spiritual power. The lover desires to be united with the beloved. Where love is fulfilled, the lover does not objectify the beloved. The lover forgets himself, as if he were no more, and without shame he yearns for his beloved. The lover cannot be content until he has proven his love for the beloved in the most dangerous situations. The lover would gladly and willingly face death for the benefit of the beloved. Indeed, the lover might be so foolish as to die to please his beloved, even knowing that no other benefit could come from the act. And the less his beloved acknowledges his love, the more passion the lover feels. He will not cease in his love but strive the more to prove his love, even if it will never be acknowledged.

When love is true and plays no favorites, it reaches out in desire to unite with all people (that is, without causing division and instability). Love itself can never be satisfied by lovers. Even if all lovers were to desert their loving, even if the joy of loving were no more with them, love is such a richness in itself that it was, is, and will be satisfied into eternity. Love willingly denies all things, no matter how cherished. Yet love cannot deny itself.

If it were possible, love would even deny itself for the sake of love. Love would allow itself to cease and become as nothing so that love's object could become what love is. We might even say that love hates itself, for love selflessly desires only the good of others. If love were unwillingly to deny itself for the sake of the beloved, it would not be true loving but a form of selfishness in love's own eyes. Love knows and recognizes that total giving for the sake of the beloved is good.

That is why love cannot deny itself. Love must finally love itself, not selfishly, but as loving what is good.

The spark of love is found in many people to a certain degree, although it seems to have been extinguished in many more of our contemporaries. Yet we may be sure that because love is spiritual and human beings are but flesh, no matter how small this spark of love may be, it comes not from a human source but from the source of perfect love. God, himself uncreated but the maker of all things, is this love. God cannot destroy himself, but all things will be broken by God. For God is eternally immutable. This means that God must love himself because God is good. God is sufficient within himself, yet were it possible, God would gladly become as nothing for the sake of those in need.

Humanity could not comprehend such love if God did not show it to them in particular people. Such people are called holy and children of God, for they favor God, their spiritual Father. This love is more readily understood by human beings when it is most perfectly shown. The more perfectly this love is comprehended, the more attractive it becomes. Salvation is nearest to those most attracted by this love. Therefore, the person in whom it pleased eternal love to show itself most clearly is called the savior of his people. Not that it would be possible for one of humanity to save others. But God is so perfectly united in love with this one that all that God would do is done in him. The suffering of this one is the very suffering of himself.

This person is Jesus of Nazareth, promised in Scripture by the true God and fulfilled in his time. All the qualities proper to love were publicly demonstrated in Israel in the events of his life through the power of the Holy Spirit.

Even now, though our time seems without love, we may also know that this has been accomplished. We acknowledge this highest love and may be sure through the Spirit of God that the love of God toward humanity and humanity toward God cannot be shown more perfectly than has happened in Jesus. For in him God had such compassion for the world that he willingly renounced his righteous judgment against us for our sinfulness, asking only that we not despise that which is shown to us in the human aspect of Jesus— that is, as he was led by God and not his human nature. In doing so, a person who loves God most truly and as much as possible can help his neighbor to also know and love God.

Whoever wants to know true love can receive it no better than through Jesus Christ. Indeed, it cannot be known except through him. Salvation is not limited by flesh and blood or time and place. But it is not possible without these. For just as a person must be saved by God, so God also cannot save a person except through his humanity. All who are saved are one in spirit with God. But that one who is most perfect in love is a forerunner of those who are being saved. Jesus is not with us himself. But in all times God has been pleased by those who, in his name, follow and are obedient to those who teach his will. The more clearly it is taught, the more rightly it can be followed. But it has never been more perfectly taught than by that one in whom it was perfectly accomplished. That one is Jesus Christ, whom God sent to lead both Jews and Gentiles together out of spiritual bondage. But now in our time, he is denied not just by Jews and pagans, but by Christians themselves. All people who sought and found the way of God are one with God. But this one who never strayed from the way of God was always united with God. He was one with God's Spirit from eternity. Yet he was born as a human being and, other than in sin, was subject to all human failings.

That is why it is written that all who are saved must be saved through this Jesus to behold the perfection of the Spirit. This is the one aim toward which all who are being saved should seek. Only to the extent that one beholds the perfection of the Spirit is one saved. The closer one comes to it, the farther one is from condemnation.

What is taught and done by love is truly good and right. Without love, nothing is truly good and right. Whoever knows what is good and right, yet teaches something different, even if it seems good it is evil and useless. That is how it is with the teachings and works of Moses, David and the patriarchs. They were good. But where they displace love (that is, Jesus) they must be considered dross for the sake of that which is better. For indeed they are dross when you consider what they lack and how they could be improved. When Moses killed the Egyptian who was beating the Israelite, this was in a sense good, for his passion was for justice and against injustice. But if Moses had known and possessed perfect love, he would have given himself to be killed in place of his brother. But he would not have strangled the Egyptian, the enemy of his brother. Therefore the teachings and Law of Moses, which said an eye for an eye, to protect the innocent by force, to defeat evil with force, and concerning usury, divorce, oath swearing and so on, were good teachings and law for the people of Israel at that time (out of whom God would create and bring forth a new Israel). But if it had been possible that (before Jesus) one would have presented a more perfect

teaching and love, and the people had been disposed to accept it, then the previous love would have had to fade. Then, anyone who would have resisted or spoken against the new way would by this show the uselessness and evil of the old teaching.

We can see then why it is written that works of the law cannot justify anyone before God. The justification by faith which is worthy before God far surpasses the works of the law. For perfection forsakes the concessions contained in the law.

The righteousness of faith is prepared and yearns to restore to the Lord God all that belongs to him—that is, all our possession and capacities. Legal justification, on the other hand, consents to no more than what is expressly written in the law and takes advantage of every possible concession it can squeeze out of it. So those under law are slaves who do no more than is explicit in the law. But those under faith are called children of God, for they do all that they are able to do for God's sake, which is more than could be made literally explicit. They therefore have the benefit of God in that God has not given them an explicit or written law, but asks only that they love God. A slave under obligation to his master must get up at four or five in the morning and work late at night. But the master's son gets up and retires as he chooses, without obligation. But while the slave gives no thought to the fate of the master, the son remains by his side through all dangers, even unto death. Therefore, the slave cannot remain indefinitely in the master's house, be blessed or enjoy peace with his master, unless he first becomes a child or household member. Then he no longer thinks of obligations or rewards, but only of how and in what ways he can please his lord and best carry out the lord's will. Not that the obligations that the

Lord made with his people Israel in the Law of Moses were wrong. But it is wrong to oppose the Lord's purpose to lead his people to an even better way through Jesus, the firstborn in the Spirit. The way of Jesus was not against the law, though it sometimes seemed to be. For all slaves are obligated to be true and devoted to their lord. After all, it is also explicitly written in the law that one should love God with all one's heart, soul and abilities (that is, with all one has and is capable of). Jesus taught and did exactly that. All of his teachings and deeds stand in this aim and purpose. Therefore, all who follow him in his teachings and deeds are promised eternal life. But there is very little written in the law about eternal life, for as said above, the slave does not remain forever in his master's house. His time of service is limited.

Now one might object that nothing can be added to or taken away from the law. In other words, it is improper to elevate that law in love, thereby reducing and not observing its practices. Yet to this one must reply that love is the very essence of the law, which nobody can practice too perfectly or understand too profoundly.

Whoever daily grows in love does not add to the law but rather fulfills it more perfectly. Love means to know and love God, surrendering for his sake those things which are so valued by people after the flesh, and to accept and bear those things which run counter to the flesh. Therefore, one can understand that in the old and new law (as they are called) there is only one love. But in the new law it is more perfectly explained and shown to God's people through Jesus the helper. The old law had become a source of bondage because the people lacked understanding. At the same time, however, they were partially gathered in by God (like bondsmen) in that they were obligated to service. In the same way that the covenantal sign, circumcision, was given without regard to human desire for it; all descendants of Abraham were duty-bound to the law, whether they wanted to be or not. But the new law is a matter of becoming God's children. Therefore, all who are under the new law are not forced to be there by other people. Rather, they are drawn to it in the deepest part of their soul by the merciful God, the true Father. He makes known to them his most perfect will, which is love itself. This was exhibited in Christ Jesus and was and is proclaimed through the good news of his magnificent resurrection.

Baptism, the sign of the covenant, will only be given to those who by God's power through knowledge of true love are invited to it, who desire it and are willing to follow. They will be uncoerced by other members and relatives to remain in this love—only love itself may constrain them. As it is written in the Psalter, "Your people will be there of their own will!"

That ceremonies prescribed in the law are no longer practiced is not a result of a command, but is a freedom permitted by love. The holy patriarchs of old sometimes must have broken these ceremonies also. Yet they were without blame because they were excused through love. Out of true love, Jesus was silent about these things, neither commanding nor forbidding. It was as if he wanted them to understand that one can come to this love without such ceremonies. For one without love, these ceremonies are of themselves of no benefit. But whoever has this love and understanding should practice and observe them even as Jesus did. But when preaching the gospel of love to the Gentiles, it is unnecessary to teach them such things. For if they take on love, they will know how to act in terms of such rites when they need to. It is also unnecessary to throw this in the face of Jews when preaching love to them. For otherwise love may become the source of tearing down love. Love gives its friends freedom from such rites because they love the Father in truth, even if they once stood under the kind of obligation which a slave owes his master.

Now it might be asked why love forsakes the old ceremonies only to replace them with new ones such as baptism and the Lord's supper. It is because these are only a confession and remembrance. In these rites the children should confess and remember from where and to what they have been called. They have been called out of the world to God to serve God in holiness and righteousness, as Zacharias, father of John the Baptist said.

Holiness is once and for all to separate oneself from this evil world and the impurities of the flesh to serve only the Lord God. This is the meaning and witness of water baptism. In baptism one confesses the old way of living as useless and desires from then on to walk in a new way of living. Righteousness is, as was said, to give each person his due. Because we owe everything to the one Lord God, everything we have and do in body and soul, honor and worldly goods, we should give for his name's sake. We should risk everything in highest submission. It should be with all children as it was for the firstborn. He was transformed into our nature that we might become one bread, broken for one another. Since he became bread for us and was crushed and baked for our benefit, we should remember this in the breaking of bread.

That is why we break bread often but baptize only once. For initiation into the new covenant happens only once, even if it is sometimes transgressed and recommitment is needed. It is like a child born to his father. He may run off and then return, yet he remains his father's child. He need not go through the birthing process again. But the fruition of the covenant of righteousness must be strived for constantly and acted upon.

The ceremonies of baptism and breaking bread were not instituted that salvation would depend on keeping them. But where they are held, one should do so earnestly. Although they may appear to be rather foolish and simple to the world, the Lord does not want them to be scorned. The Lord practiced these things himself. He fulfilled all works of righteousness, from the smallest to the greatest, as an example for us. By doing these things he wanted to show us that nothing is too simple to be used as a remembrance of something of great value.

This then is a summation of the teaching of Jesus Christ. By this all contention which arises concerning the truth may be settled by those who have a heartfelt desire to understand. Whatever teaching is not built on the foundation of love should not be maintained in favor of love. Whoever knows this principle and yet teaches otherwise cannot be defended by love. Even if he tries to defend his teaching by love, saying in effect that it is done for love's sake, it can come to nothing. The children of love should not act contrary to love for the sake of love. In such things the wise need wisdom and all friends of God need love, so as not to replace God's love with human love. To love someone other than through God's truth and love is actually a form of hatred. It is more loving to hate someone for the sake of God's love! Of course you cannot hate someone for the sake of love.

But this means earnestly to censure him and, if he will not take heed, with deep sorrow to avoid him. This is the basis for separation between the children of God and the children of the world. Indeed, this is the basis for banning or exclusion of false brothers, which also clearly must occur for the sake of true love. Otherwise we would have to deny the foundation of the covenant of the children of God, which is holiness and separation from worldly company. This is what happens in baptism, as was said before.

From what has been said, then, it is easy to see what to make of things like infant baptism, vows and oaths and governing evildoers. God tolerated these things in the world to bring about improvement (though this does not apply to infant baptism, which God never willed). But among those who know the truth (or at least assume they know the truth) God does not cause these things to happen any more than God causes any sort of evil.

Truth strongly witnesses to the spuriousness of infant baptism. The most important task of disciples of Jesus Christ is to teach and make disciples of the Lord, seeking above all else the kingdom of God. When you baptize before a person has become a disciple you are by that act saying, in effect, that baptism is more important than teaching and knowledge. In the eyes of God this is a terrible error. So if teaching is more important than baptism, let baptism wait until teaching has taken place. To baptize before teaching is saying that baptism is more important, but this is contrary to Christian doctrine. Now some say they give priority to teaching for those willing to listen. But in his commission, Christ did not say to go to the Jews and preach but go to the Gentiles and baptize! One does not baptize Isaac

because his father Abraham is a disciple! The commission says clearly, "Go forth and teach, making disciples of all nations, baptizing them (those who have become disciples!) in the name of the Father (who draws them to him) and the Son (who now leads them) and the Holy Spirit (through whose power they are made firm in fulfillment of the Father's will)." In short, just as Christ is Christ before anyone believes in him, so teaching is done before baptism. Where there is no Christ there is no faith. So baptism without teaching is not true baptism.

Oaths and swearing should not be done because no human has power to keep them. What a friend of God knows to be right should simply be done, so far as he is able, without oaths and promises. He might ask the Lord to help him accomplish something. But he should not make presumptuous promises, as if the Lord were obligated to do what he wants the Lord to do. Humans do not have power over a single hair! Therefore, if someone swears that he is able to do something, he either acts brazenly without understanding, or if he does understand, then he acts as a hypocrite—that is, he says something which in his heart he knows is not true. As Scripture says, "You cannot make even one hair white or black," and "Do not fall into hypocrisy!"

Now some say that God himself swears oaths and that is not wrong. So we should swear as well, for it is written, "Be perfect, even as your Father in heaven!" Here is the answer to that. If we could be as sure as God that we have the power to keep our word, then we could swear as God did. We might say the same for killing and governing, if we could do them like God, totally without revenge or self-seeking. But we cannot. The only person who could have done this purposely did not do it, as an example to us. For his time had not yet come. So we should abstain gladly from such things and follow the one through whom we come to the Father, the Father we could not know without such a mediator.

You should not be too quick to say yes or no. For if you say yes as a guarantee or assurance, this is really a kind of oath, in that by doing this one expects what was promised to be fulfilled as God's will. Then you must break your word if you cannot keep it. If you do right this will not happen—as Paul did when he apologized before God to the Corinthians that despite his promise he was not able to visit them.

This is all that needs to be said concerning swearing about future events. As for testimony concerning things past, according to the Lord's teaching we should do it simply, using as few words as possible—yes or no. For we must answer to God for anything we say. One might call on God as a witness that what he says is true, as Paul did. But do not forget never to use God's name frivolously. This is forbidden in the law and also in the New Testament, where we are forbidden to swear at all. It is not wrong to use God's name in itself. In fact, love requires all her children to do so so that God might be known and alone be eternally loved and praised.

No Christian who wants to bring honor to his Lord can use force or be a ruler. For the governance of our King consists only in teaching and in the power of the Spirit. Whoever truly acknowledges Christ as Lord should not act contrary to his commandments. And Christ has commanded his disciples to deal with evildoers in no way other than to teach and admonish them for their own improvement. If they will not listen, one should leave them alone and avoid them.

Those who are outsiders (that is, unbelievers) do not concern the community of Christ, except that Christians hope to serve by teaching. Not that power is wrong in itself, in view of how wicked the world is. It can serve as God's wrath. But love teaches its children something better—that they should serve the grace of God.

It is the nature of love never to desire the worst for anyone. Rather, love seeks to serve for improvement wherever that is possible. The head of a household should treat the household members as he himself would want God to treat him, that is, not contrary to love. And if it would be possible for a governor to do the same, he might also be a Christian in that position. But because the world would not tolerate this, a friend of God should not be a ruler. He should leave that position if he wants Christ as Lord and Master. One may love the Lord in any station in life. But he must not forget what is proper for one who loves the Lord—to forsake all violence for the Lord's sake and to be subject to others as unto the Lord.

Now one might say that John the Baptist, when asked by the soldiers what they should do, did not tell them to give up their profession. Here is the answer to that. The Law and the Prophets lasted up to John. John did not come to overthrow the law. Only the Light himself and he alone could do this—that is, as far as it was to happen. John was not the Light, but a witness to the Light. The one who takes away sin may also take away the law—that is, Jesus Christ, the Lamb of God, to whom John pointed. John preached the wrath of God for repentance to those who would not keep that law. But Christ preached to them grace and free forgiveness that they might live without rebuke in God's good favor.

All that is written here flows from the perfect love of Christ, and from it one may perceive who has the Spirit of the Lord. Whoever understands and yet teaches otherwise is a true Antichrist. And whoever cannot understand it does not know the Lord. Although the whole world does not tolerate this teaching, it is a comfort to all of God's children. God is stronger and mightier than the whole world or the prince of this world, the devil himself. God is faithful and will not allow harm to come to those who trust him.

Woe to anyone who shrinks from the truth to avoid scandal and yet claims to be doing right. For this is love of the devil. He blinds his children and seeks to blind the children of God also, so that they fear men more than God. Whoever wishes to avoid offending the Lord should first see what the Lord commands and then not fail to do it for any reason. Stand on the solid rock, don't trip on it!

The person who teaches a command and then does not hold it himself and allows others to break it is the real offender! He will have the least place in the kingdom of heaven. What can be said of one who violates all or most of the very commandments he himself teaches? Never forget that one who teaches in the Lord's name must himself be a disciple of Christ. A disciple of Christ never acts without sanction or neglects the Master's commandments.

Oh, all of you who long for love, seek love and you will find it! For the Lord God offers it freely to all whose hearts desire it. Whoever longs for love prepares for the wedding. If he lacks the proper dress, the bridegroom will see to it that no shame is brought upon him. But woe to those who come to the wedding in worn-out garments, when atonement has already been accomplished.

✠

From D. Liechty, ed., Early Anabaptist Spirituality *(New York: Paulist Press, 1994), 112–21.*

46. Menno Simons, *A Meditation on the Twenty-fifth Psalm* (1537)

Born in 1496 in Holland, Menno Simons was ordained to the Roman Catholic priesthood in 1524. While he seems to have had Anabaptist sympathies for quite some time, it was only in 1536 that he joined the movement. The final catalyst for this move was undoubtedly the debacle at Münster in 1535: under the leadership of millenarian prophets, Anabaptists of an apocalyptic revolutionary persuasion had established the "New Jerusalem," with disastrous consequences. Menno in effect rescued Dutch Anabaptism from these radical tendencies, organizing and leading the movement until his death in 1561. Today the largest group of Anabaptist descendants, the Mennonites, take their name from him. The following sample from his spiritual writings bears within it the unmistakable influence of Augustine's *Confessions*.

✠

1. *To you, O Lord, I lift my soul; in you I trust, O my God. Do not let me be put to shame.* Lord and king, sovereign of heaven and earth! I call you my Lord, though I am not worthy to be called your servant. For I have not served only you from my youth, but your enemy, the devil. Even so, I do not doubt your grace, for I find in your word of truth that you are an abundant and good Lord to all who call on you. Therefore, Lord, I do call on you. Hear me, Lord, hear me! I lift up my soul to you with a sure heart and in full confidence—not my head or my hands, as the hypocrites do. I

lift up my soul to you alone, I say, not to Abraham, who never knew us, nor to Israel, who never knew us. But you are our Lord and Father. You are our redeemer. As the prophet said, this has been your name since ancient times. Loving Father, that is why I trust in you. For I know without a doubt that you are a faithful God for all those who put their trust in you. When I am in darkness, you are my light. When I am in prison, you are there with me. When I am deserted, you are my comfort. In death, you are my life. When people curse me, you bless me. When people cause me sorrow, you bring me joy. When people kill me, you bring resurrection. When I walk through the valley of darkness, you are always with me. Lord, it is right that I raise my troubled and miserable soul to you, trusting in your promises without shame.

2. Nor let my enemies triumph over me. No one whose hope is in you will ever be put to shame. Lord of hosts, Lord of lords! My flesh is weak, my affliction and need is great. Even so, I do not fear the physical mocking of my enemies. But this I do fear more and more, that I would deny your great and praiseworthy name and fall away from your truth. Then my enemies would revel in my weakness and disobedience, mocking me, saying, "Now where is your God? Now where is your Christ?" Your divine honor would be blasphemed because of me. Lord, protect me! Protect me, Lord! My enemies are powerful and numerous, more than the hairs on my head and the grass of the field. My corrupt flesh finds no peace. Satan stalks me like a bellowing lion, looking to devour me. The murderous world seeks to kill me, just as all those who seek your honor have been hated, persecuted, burned and murdered. Miserable human being that I am, I do not know where

to turn. There is oppression, tribulation, distress and fear everywhere. There is fighting within and persecution outside. Even so, I say with King Jehoshaphat that if I do not know where to go, I will lift my eyes to you and trust in your grace and goodness, just as Abraham did at Gerar, as Jacob did in Mesopotamia, as Joseph did in Egypt, as Moses did in Midian, as Israel did in the wilderness, as David did in the mountains, as Hezekiah did in Jerusalem, as the young men did in the fiery furnace and as Daniel did in the den of lions. These God-fearing ancestors all placed their hope in you, waited on you. And they were not put to shame.

3. But they will be put to shame who are treacherous without excuse. Sovereign Lord, just as all who fear you are covered by your merciful grace, so also does your solemn wrath go out toward all those who scorn you, who walk according to their own desires and who say, with foolishness in their hearts,

> There is no God. We have made an agreement with death and a covenant with hell. God knows nothing of our dealings. Thick clouds cover over the works of human beings. We eat and drink, and tomorrow we die. Life is short and full of troubles and hard work and there is no revival when it is all over. We will live as we want to for as long as it lasts, and use the creation as it pleases us. We will oppress the poor and deceive the righteous. We will condemn them to a most shameful death.

Beloved Lord, that is the error of the world. It is nothing other than the lusts of the flesh, lusts of the eyes and prideful living. There is nothing but idle falsehood, injustice and tyranny wherever you look. Very few are those who truly fear your name. Paul said, "The mind of sinful man is death" (Rom. 8:6). That judgment is true. He who lives according to the flesh will die, as the whole of Scripture teaches. If people do not repent, nothing is more sure than your stern wrath. Therefore, beloved Lord, threaten, punish, admonish and teach them. Then perhaps they will regret their ways, recognize the truth and be saved. They are, after all, the work of your hand, created in your image and purchased at a great price. Let them not, therefore, come to a shameful end, as did Cain, Sodom, Pharaoh and Antiochus and all others who unjustly scorned you.

4. *Show me your ways, O Lord, teach me your paths.* Lord of hosts, I know your grace through your word. There is but one way which leads to life. For the flesh, it is too small and narrow—but a foot wide, as Esdras says it. It is ringed on all sides by thorns and other dangers. Few find it, and even fewer walk along it. It is like a gem hidden in a field which nobody can find unless the Spirit shows it to him. Beloved Lord, there is no other way than you alone. All who walk in you will find the portals of life. But the other way seems attractive to the flesh. Its appearance is pleasing. It is wide and straight. But it leads to death. The whole world walks along this way without fear or even a second thought. Along this way, that which is corruptible is valued above that which is incorruptible, evil is valued above what is good, and darkness is valued above the light of the world. They walk along this reversed and twisted way. They weary themselves in the ways of injustice and do not acknowledge the way of the Lord. It is clearly true that the way of error seems right in the eyes of the fool. But I know through your Spirit and your word that it is the way which leads to certain hell. Therefore, I pray, beloved Lord, be gracious toward this miserable sinner. Show me your pathway and teach me your ways. For your way is the true path, the way of blessing and love, humility,

chastity, full of peace and goodness, and will lead my soul into eternal life.

5. *Guide me in your truth and teach me, for you are God my Savior, and my hope is in you all day long.* Lord, Lord! As David said, "My tears have been my food day and night" (Ps. 42:3). My heart moves within my body. My strength has left me. The light of my eyes is almost gone because of the many perils and entanglements set for my soul. I fear constantly that I might be lured from your truth by human fallacies or Satan's trickery.

Lord, the guile of the learned is sharp and cunning. Satan masterfully uses his subtlety. There are those who teach nothing but human doctrines and commandments, which are fruitless and foul trees. Others constantly speak of grace, Spirit and Christ. But at the same time they daily trample on your grace, betray your Holy Spirit and crucify your son with their idle and worldly lives, as is well known. There are those who at one time came out from Sodom, Egypt and Babylon and accepted the yoke of the cross of Christ. Yet now they are again devoured by the devil, led astray by false prophets, just as if they had never known your word and your will. They are possessed of seven spirits worse than before and their present errors are worse than that which they left behind. They bedeck themselves with your holy word and ordinances, imagining that what you never contemplated, much less commanded, is now your preference, word and will. This is why I am troubled and full of sadness and heartache. For I know that your true word is not the deceitful lies which they teach. It is the upright truth to which your perfect mouth witnesses here on earth and is taught in this troubled world. All who are in the truth hear your voice, the voice of the one true shepherd and bridegroom. They flee from the voice of strangers, fearing they will be deceived.

Lord! Consider your troubled and poor servants. You examine every heart. You know me. You know that I seek and desire nothing but your will. Loving Lord, direct and teach me in your truth. For you alone are my God and Lord, my salvation. Apart from you I know no other. You alone are my hope, my comfort, my shield, fortress and protection. I place my trust in you and in my fear, tribulation and suffering I daily wait on you.

6. *Remember, O Lord, your great mercy and love, for they are from of old.* Lord of Hosts! When I swim in the merciful waters of your grace I find that I can neither plumb nor measure the depths. Your compassion is the greatest of all your works. Lord, who ever came to you with a devout heart and was turned away? Who ever sought you and did not find you? Who ever desired aid from you and was not given help? Who ever prayed for your grace and did not receive it? Who ever called upon you and was not heard? Yes, beloved Lord, how many you have received in grace when according to your strict sense of justice they would have deserved something else. Adam departed from you and believed the counsel of the serpent. He transgressed your covenant and became for you a child of death. But your fatherly love would not allow him to be thrown aside. In grace you sought after him, you called and admonished him and covered his nakedness with pelts of fur. You mercifully comforted him with a promise concerning his seed. Paul, your chosen vessel, was at one time like a roaring lion and a ravaging wolf against your holy mountain. Yet you shone your grace upon him and enlightened his blindness. You called him from heaven and chose him to be an apostle and servant in your house.

Beloved Lord, I am the greatest of sinners and the least among the saints. I am unworthy to be called your child or servant, for I have sinned against heaven and before you. There was a time when I opposed your glorious word and your holy will with all my power. With open eyes and understanding heart I disputed against your clear truth. I taught and lived according to the flesh and sought my own selfish honor rather than your justice, honor, and word. Yet this miserable sinner was never abandoned by your fatherly grace. You accepted me in love and converted me to a new understanding. You led me with your right hand and taught me through your Holy Spirit. Then by my own free will I began also to strive against the world, the flesh and the devil. I renounced all my comforts, serenity, honor and easy living and willingly took upon myself the heavy cross of the Lord Jesus Christ. Now I also am an inheritor of that promised kingdom with all servants of God and disciples of Christ. So again I say, your mercy is the greatest of all your works. Therefore, beloved Lord, come to my aid. Stand by me and comfort me. Comfort this miserable sinner.

My soul is in mortal need and I am surrounded by the danger of hell. Lord, help me, protect me and do not scorn me. Consider your great goodness in which all take part who have placed their hope in your holy name and gracious mercy since the beginning of the world.

7. *Remember not the sins of my youth and my rebellious ways; according to your love remember me, for you are good, O Lord.* Sovereign Lord! I was born of sinful seed and was conceived in sin. I am born of sinful flesh. The evil seed of Adam is sown in my heart and much sorrow has flowed from it. Miserable sinner that I am, I did not recognize my transgressions

until your Spirit showed them to me. I thought I was a Christian. But when I saw myself truly, what I found was wholly earthly, of the flesh, and outside of your word. What was light to me is darkness. What was truth to me is falsehood. What was righteousness to me is sinful. My worship of God was idolatry and my life was surely death. Loving God, I did not recognize who I was until I saw myself mirrored in your holy word. Then I recognized my blindness, nakedness and inborn sinfulness. As Paul, I saw that nothing good was in my flesh. All was ulcerous and blistery from head to toe. My gold was filth, my wheat was chaff, my deeds were deceptions and lies. I walked before you according to the flesh. My thoughts were of the flesh and my words and works were without reverence to God. I was impure whether waking or sleeping, my praying was hypocrisy and nothing I did was without sin. Lord, think not on the sins of my youth which I committed in such great number, both knowingly and unknowingly, before you. Also, do not remember the transgressions I commit daily because of my extreme weakness. But consider me according to your great mercy. Where I am blind, enlighten me. Where I am naked, clothe me. Where I am injured, heal me. Where I am dead, raise me up. I know of no other light, life and healing balm apart from you. Accept me in grace and give me your mercy, blessing and confidence, Lord, for the sake of your own goodness. . . .

✠

From Liechty, Early Anabaptist Spirituality, *248–53.*

47. Peter Walpot, *True Yieldedness and the Christian Community of Goods* (1577)

In the emerging early capitalist economic system of the sixteenth century, Christians of all types paid increasing attention to their religion's economic implications. Among the most radical of these was the Hutterite branch of Anabaptism, named after Jacob Hutter, burned at the stake in 1538. In continuity with the medieval monastic tradition, this group advocated complete economic "communism," but now for all followers of Christ. In the following document, Peter Walpot (1521–1578), a second-generation Hutterite leader, developed a cogent defense of this option, all the more remarkable in that he lacked any formal education.

✠

"Just as gold is tried in the fire, so are humans tried in the ovens of humiliation."
(Ecclesiasticus 2)

God's word would not be so difficult if not for human selfishness.

1. The Lord commanded Israel: Above all, there should be no poor among you (Deuteronomy 15). How much more should this be fulfilled in the full community of goods among the New Testament people. For if the Old had been fulfilled and sufficient, no place would have been sought for another Testament (Hebrews 8). . . .

21. The Lord called as his disciple Simon Peter and his brother Andrew: also James, son of Zebedee and John his brother. And he said to them, "Follow me!" (Matthew 4; Mark 1; Luke 5). And they left their nets, their boats, and their father and followed him. See then how Christ places demands on one's possessions and how these men left their parents and friends and followed him in the way he led, the path of yieldedness and community.

22. Christ spoke saying, "Blessed are the poor in spirit" (Matthew 5; Luke 6). The poor in spirit are those who have relinquished their possessions and left them behind for the sake of Christ. They possess nothing anymore but stand and persevere in the community of the true Christian church. It follows that the opposite of these are not in a state of blessing.

Here is not meant by "poor" those who have nothing as a result of their own laziness or those who have nothing because they have gambled, whored or been drunkards, or those who have nothing and yet are as wicked as any other person. He means those whom the Spirit has made poor (2 Corinthians 6). In the same way that the Spirit led Christ into the wilderness to be tempted by the devil, so the Spirit leads these ones into poverty where, like Christ their master, they have nothing themselves. That is what is meant by "poor in spirit." Therefore, whoever dreads this poverty, you should dread them. And whoever shuns this community, you should shun them.

23. Christ said to his disciples, "You are the light of the world. But not a light under a basket which is useful and a light only unto itself. You are rather a light in a lamp which is useful to the whole house." You do this with your good works. He also called them salt, that they should be useful to the community and show to all what good things they have received from God. The light or salt or yeast is of no use to itself. Its usefulness is rather in its relation to others. In the same way, our usefulness should be directed toward others and not ourselves. Where the salt does not make salty, there is no salt, but something less. So when we do works of love and kindness we become an example of good works to others.

24. No one may serve two masters (Matthew 6; Luke 16). For you will hate the one and love the other or obey the one and despise the other. You cannot serve God and Mammon—that is, earthly possessions and riches. For like a lock, the love of and concern for money occupies the heart. Therefore, you should not strive for surplus and then seek to justify it. For Christ said that it is impossible to serve and nurture both of these two masters. So don't say that it is possible! For one master commands you to deny yourself. The other master says to take for yourself what is not yours and keep it for yourself. One master says you should be in community; the other says you should be selfish and possessive. So how is it possible to bring these two stubborn things into agreement? Whoever is a servant of Mammon is certainly no servant of Christ. You must be finished with the one master in order to serve the other.

No one can go two directions at once; no one can put his foot in two places at once; a bird can only sit on one perch at a time; no one can cook two stews in the same pot; a sick person cannot become well by both water and fire. One of these must be gone. *To have one, let the other one go.* No one has more than one heart. And no one can love and serve God and at the same time love and serve earthly possessions and riches, money and wealth. For then they have their god, which is, as Paul said, their own bellies (Philippians 3). They trust and serve wealth as God himself. If day and night they care for house and field, land and water with the highest diligence and greatest care and most earnestness, they cannot give even the tenth part of that diligence, care and earnestness to God and his service. We are redeemed by Christ. Therefore we should not now serve money and wealth and cling to them but rather give them to God's poor. In this way we will not end up in the place where the rich man was thrown and punished (Luke 16).

25. "Do not store up for yourselves treasure on earth, where moth and rust destroy, and where thieves break in and steal. But store up for yourselves treasures in heaven, where moth and rust do not destroy, and where thieves do not break in and steal. For where your treasure is, there your heart will be also" (Matt. 6:19-21). The temporal is fleeting, here today and gone tomorrow. Today there is a beautiful flower, tomorrow a dry piece of dust. Today there is a burning fire, tomorrow cold ashes, useless soot, smoke, which is soon forgotten and swept out of the fireplace. Nothing remains, all is consumed and makes no more difference. We may achieve nothing by the temporal. This is why Christ said, "Where your treasure is, there is your heart also." For it is surely true that where one places his treasure, there he also places his soul. The selfish person can hardly maintain that he can both possess his treasures and riches and at the same time have his heart and mind set on God. For that is impossible. They may say with their mouth that they are ardent, but their heart follows after its own good and greed. For that is their treasure. One sees this in many who serve and honor temporal, earthly things. They would give up their faith before they would leave their riches behind. They are really worse than the heathen, for they have Christ in their mouth but their heart is on the money purse. They are idol-worshippers of the worst sort.

26. Someone might ask, so what happens then if I renounce all my possessions? Christ said, "Look at the birds of the air; they do not sow or reap or store away in barns, and yet your heavenly Father feeds them. Are you not much more valuable than they?" (Matt. 6:26). In the same way Elijah was fed by ravens and the five thousand were fed with five loaves of barley bread (Matt. 14:13ff.; John 16). So therefore, don't worry. For these are the things which the heathen do, each providing for himself regardless of the others. You should seek first the kingdom of God and his righteousness and these other things will be given you, even if you don't have provisions stored up for days and years like the rich. He will care for us as he did for Adam before the time Adam had to worry about food and clothing. Caring belongs to God; work belongs to us. It is through community that God cares for our daily needs and relieves us of greed. For we belong only to him and our concern is only for the divine.

27. Community is also taught in the Lord's Prayer. Christ taught us not to ask for our own bread. Not "give me my bread," but "give us our bread," that is, the communal bread. It is a false supplicator who prays, give us our bread, but then treats the bread received as his own! Whoever has his own shouldn't ask of God. Paul the apostle wrote (2 Thessalonians 3) that whoever lives in disorderly fashion and will not work, but goes around as a busybody, should eat his own bread, as a punishment to his shame.

28. Whoever lives in wealth is false in his confession of faith. For the Christian faith sets up a holy Christian church and a community of saints. Where there is no community of saints there is no true and worthy Christian church. Therefore all lie who say that community is unnecessary and has no foundation in doctrine (Acts 2 and 4). For it is indeed an article of the faith and instituted by Christ and the Holy Spirit and his teaching. Therefore, just as it is necessary to hold to the Apostles' Creed, the Lord's Prayer and

Holy Communion, it is also necessary to hold community of goods. Community is no simple oddity, which the apostles tried out for novelty. Rather, it is divinely earnest and just as right and proper now as it was in Jerusalem and elsewhere.

29. "Enter through the narrow gate" (Matthew 7), Christ said. "For narrow is the gate and small is the way which leads to life, and few find it." A life of Christian community is the narrow gate. For the carnal man it is a small needle's eye. Indeed, it is an oven of yieldedness in which the person is tried like gold in the fire. That is why there are few who enter this narrow port or find this small way. They always think it is too difficult for a person to be so unencumbered, giving up everything. They simply cannot believe this and therefore will never enter into the narrow door or gate, before which one must give up all things. But the broad way with the wide gate is that of the society of the possessive life of the world, full of selfishness and greed. There are many who go that way, indeed, the whole world. As the saying goes—merchants are drawn to where the money is. In other words, people are drawn to greed and possessions and therefore mock the humble Christ who said you cannot serve both God and Mammon. . . .

139. We are all called to one hope and common inheritance. For when a father has many children—excepting those who are bastards and disobedient, disinheriting themselves—they are equally heirs to his goods and inheritance. Therefore, if we say that we have communion in spiritual things such as faith, God, gospel, Christ, gifts of the Holy Spirit, and want to inherit the goods of heaven equally with each other, then we should show this here in temporal things all the more. Therefore we are children and not

slaves, as it would be if each had only his own. We will be called the children of God.

140. We are also brothers because we have and show brotherhood. As Christ said, you shall not be called master, for you have only one Master, Christ. But you are all brothers. Now, to be like brothers, all things are shared with each other—the more evenly, the more brotherly it is. Those who do not divide things evenly, but rather each one seeks his own advantage and fate, and who cheat one another, do not treat each other as brothers. Even if they call themselves brothers, they are false brothers. Therefore, act according to the truth in the brotherhood of Christ, which alone proves that one is a fellow heir to the kingdom of heaven. So should we also be fellow inheritors here.

141. God does not want his children to live here on earth like cattle, like cows, like donkeys, like buffalo, where each one only seeks to fill his own belly. To do so is to be less than dogs, who never know when they have had enough. Or like a sow, who wants the feeding trough all to herself and will give to the others only what is left over. Rather, God wants his own to live here on earth as a new humanity and as members of one body.

142. Community means nothing else than to have all things in common out of love for one's neighbor, to have everything equal and for no one to have private property. There is nothing higher, better or more perfect than someone presenting himself and his wealth for the common good and from that point on sharing with each other both sickness and health, love and suffering, each one wanting to be the other's neighbor, debtor, fellow member and loyal comrade. That is the Christian church and the community of the saints, which is neither forced nor unnatural, nor impossible to do, so long as love is there.

Earthly fathers will live sparingly and do without food themselves in order to help their children. Likewise, a mother will take something from her own hungry belly to give to her child. So should believers not be able to hold their temporal goods in common with each other? It would be unchristian not to do so, because we are to love our neighbors and fellows members as ourselves, to have together, to want together, to suffer together, to experience ups and downs together. No matter what you say, it is no community, no unity, no common use, when each has his own house, his own field and goods, his own kitchen, his own cellar and his own table.

143. Private property does not belong in the Christian church. Private property is a thing of the world, of the heathen, of those without divine love, of those who will have their own way. For there would be no property if it were not for selfish will. But the true community of goods belongs among believers. For by divine law all things should be held in common and nobody should take for himself what is God's any more than the air, rain, snow or water, the sun or other elements. Just as these cannot be divided up, so it is with temporal goods, which God has given in the same portion and measure for the common good. These should not be made private, and surely this cannot be done according to divine or Christian law. For owning private property is contrary to the nature and conditions of his creation. Whoever encloses and holds privately that which is and should be free, sins and goes against the one who created it free and made it free. The writer of the *German Theology* says this as well. But because of the wickedness humanity has taken on, out of envy and greed, each one stashes away in his own sack. One says, "this is mine," while another says, "that is mine." And so there is in any case a dividing of goods among humans, but it has become in this life one of great inequality. It has unfortunately gone so far that if they could reach the sun and moon and contain the elements, they would call them their private possession and then sell them for money.

144. Some desires are necessary. For example, an animal must eat, drink and sleep. Other desires are natural, even if they cannot be said to be necessary—for example physical love. But the desire for and love of money is neither natural nor necessary. It is simply excessive. For gold and silver were for a long time hidden. Therefore, it is an acquired corruption, a result of the advice of the snake. The devil once led Eve astray with the apple. Now the whole world is led astray with gold and money. Concerning being a eunuch for the kingdom, Christ said that whoever can accept it should accept it. But of money he said that whoever does not renounce all that he has cannot be his disciple. For one single soul is not able to handle too many desires. One will subdue the others. Whoever has only one child loves that child without measure. But whoever has many children has his affections divided. That is why it is impossible for a person to give full enthusiasm and exertion to both things at once. For the same reason it is very dangerous for a child to have a knife in his hand or for a lunatic to have a sword. That is just how harmful property and wealth are to humans. In fact, it is more dangerous, for if the lunatic sticks himself with the sword, his lunacy leaves him and he has peace. But as for the greedy and selfish person it is not so. He receives his wounds a thousand times a day, for the desire for money and wealth is a thing which includes countless wounds. Therefore we must rid our hearts of these desires.

145. Greed is a serious and evil sickness which blinds a person's eyes and stops up his ears. Nothing is more wretched and vexing to such a one than to hear about community and yieldedness. The disease of greed withers the hand so that it is useless in helping others. The greedy lose their reason and do not know what or why they are here on this earth. Greed allows neither the self, the conscience, nor the soul to know salvation. For the most corrupt kind of metal commands them and rules them. All the while they think they are commanding and ruling over others. Therefore, there is nothing more senseless and more adverse than to serve and cling to money and greed. Their joy is to be tangled up in bondage, and they are happy and jubilant to see themselves be pressed under by a greedy dog. They give that dog all the more to gorge on so that it becomes even stronger and in this way make for themselves countless roads into hell. For greed is like putting more wood on the fire to make it greater. The more a person brings to it, the more it rises up. The greedy do not care what they already have. They put it behind them and snap after more in front of them. And finally they come to the same fate as Aesop's dog.

That is why we should ponder this and flee from it with highest diligence. We should search out the antidote for this disease with which we may kill this terrible beast and pull all greed out by the roots. This pestilent disease has spoiled the earth. This sin has mixed things all up so that while one dies of hunger, another bursts from being too full. One must go around naked while another piles clothes upon clothes, only to be eaten by moths. That is why there are so many vagrants and beggars on all the streets, knocking on doors and crying for alms. This affliction of Belial has filled the streets with blood and the towns with weeping and wailing. It has taken us away from the most holy service of Christ and eats away our hearts from the word and seed of God. Even when we do something good, greed comes along and spoils it, the longer the more wicked. Greed is such a hateful affliction before God that if "anyone calls himself a brother, but is greedy, have nothing to do with him and do not even eat with him," said Paul (1 Corinthians 5). Greed is counted as one of the cursed, deadly afflictions that separates a person from the kingdom of God. It has spoiled the glorious image of God in humans, who made us of honorable standing, so that we could look up toward the heavens. Greed strikes human beings down to the earth so that they cannot get up, but rather like a sow are drawn toward the mud by the devil, choosing to live like worms. This craving made Judas into a betrayer, ruined Ananias and his wife and covered Gehazi, who could have been a disciple and prophet, with leprosy. Indeed, it is a general plague in the world, which allows no one to be satisfied with what he has. All eyes and hearts are set on nothing other than greed, caring for nothing else than how much money they can get. And they never even think about how they may justly invest it. They dress their mules and horses with gold and let Christ and his own go unclothed.

146. God so loved the world that he gave (did not spare) his only begotten son for our sakes (John 3). It is to our shame that we are unworthy of such a great love. And it is our pain that we wanted to spare our money for ourselves and did not want to give even a little to his own. How can we repay this, when we see that another person suffered for our sake? We can entrust all we have to him and

still not think we have done enough for him. Well, how much more then do we owe to Christ and his own!

147. The old church histories, such as Eusebius show and witness to the fact that the believers held to community, not only in Jerusalem but in many other places. He quotes from Philo's little book, titled *The Contemplative Life* or *The Life of Prayer,* which reports that the believers among men and women were called physicians and nurses of God. The reason for this is that when souls came to the Christians which were in a grossly irrational state, they lifted them up aright and like a physician they healed them of their illnesses and made them well. Or another reason was that because they sincerely served God with good conscience, they earned this name on account of their lives. But whether Philo first gave the Christians this name because of their works, or whether it was given by those who from the beginning lived according to the gospel before the Christians were spread throughout the world, is not significant. It is only important that the reading shows to whom this name fairly belonged. But Philo said that those who dedicate themselves to the teaching or philosophy of the Christians give over all their goods and possessions and escape from all the cares of this life. They avoid the cities and live in gardens and small farms and flee from unnecessary company. For they know that these things hinder those who desire to walk the narrow path of virtuous understanding.

Therefore it was said that those ones lived as those who first had that burning and glowing faith lived, that is (as we read in the Book of Acts), as they lived in Jerusalem and according to apostolic faith. They sold their possessions and laid the money at the feet of the apostles to be divided up and given to those in need. And they had no poverty among them. Philo wrote that this was also the case with believers in Alexandria. He also said that there were many places on earth where people of this kind could be found, in Greece and elsewhere. So there must have been many places where this use of possessions was practiced. There were especially many in such places as Egypt and the surrounding territory, above all in Alexandria. There are many faithful people there who came from many places and directions, just as the farmer goes to where he finds good land.

Clement wrote in the year 92 to his brother James in Jerusalem, the Lord's brother, saying that the common life is necessary for everyone, but particularly for those who without reproach struggle for God and desire to follow the life of the apostles and their disciples. For things should be held in common by all people in this world. But because of sin one says, "that is mine," while another says, "that is mine." And so dividing up does take place among people, but not according to the counsel of God. And that is why the wisest person among the Greeks recognized that this was how it should be, for he said that just as the sunshine cannot be divided up, or the air, so people should share all things in this life in common and not divide it up. Psalm 133 is an allegory of this, as is the practice of the first church in Jerusalem, that all things are given for the common use.

The old teacher Augustine (who lived some 370 years after Christ) heard also that there were to be found in his time those who held community. He wrote that a Christian is a distributor or manager of his possessions, not a lord over them. According to divine law all things should be held in common.

And elsewhere he wrote that only by human law, not by divine law, could one say, "this village is mine!"

John Chrysostom, who lived some 390 years after the birth of Christ, in his book on the Gospel of John wrote concerning the various sayings and teachings in the first chapter, "In what way may we become disciples of Christ? In that we use all things for the common good and not only for our private good. For Christ did not only gratify himself." And he said a number of such things. But they finally gave in to what is human and erred from the works of perfection. Again, concerning the first chapter of the Gospel of John he said, among other things, "We must labor with all our power to be disciples of Christ where he said that foxes have holes and birds have their nests, but the Son of man has nothing on which to lay his head." This I would demand of you, he said. Now perhaps many think this very difficult, which is why, on account of our short-sightedness, we have forsaken this perfection. But I do admonish you not to have your eyes on money, but rather do as I do in my own shortsightedness, to strive toward this as highest virtue. Therefore it is seemly for you that you also draw back from this greatest of evil—that you possess your wealth not as a servant but as a lord—and not be possessed by it.

The *German Theology* says in Chapter 51, "Were there no selfishness, there would be no private property. In heaven there is no private property and that is why there is contentment, joy and blessedness. And if anyone in heaven took something to be held privately, he would have to be thrown out into hell with the devil. Where one is selfishly willed, there is misfortune and misery." And so it is also with us. Again, where one possesses something for himself, or would like to possess something for himself, he is in fact himself a possession, that is, a possession of his own desires or longings. And the one who possesses nothing and has no desire to possess anything is free and liberated and the possession of no one.

Again, Christ said, "Follow me!" But whoever will follow him must leave everything behind just as he also left all behind. That is why he said: "Whoever will not renounce all that he has and take up the cross is not worthy of me; he is not my disciple and does not follow me."

148. Paul the apostle said, "I no longer live, but Christ lives in me" (Gal. 2:20); and elsewhere, "Christ is my life." Now, whoever does not live himself, but Christ lives in him, will demonstrate Christ in him by doing that which Christ did, namely, that Christ had community with his disciples. The one in whom Christ lives will say, "All that I have is yours and all that you have is mine." Indeed, the one in whom Christ lives will share the little loaves and few fishes he has and hold them in common with the four and five thousand.

✠

From Liechty, Early Anabaptist Spirituality, *139, 144–47, 190–96.*

Chapter 4
John Calvin

✠

Introduction

The prevailing image of John Calvin (1509–1564) continues to be that of the domineering tyrant, the utterly inflexible moralist, the humorless preacher, and the unrelenting dogmatist unshaken by even the slightest self-doubt. It must immediately be conceded that there is some warrant for this picture in the historical record. But historians today are increasingly aware that this portrait is far from complete, i.e., that it is a caricature. The other side of Calvin, only recently being uncovered, is his emotional side, his self-doubt, his vulnerability, his inner contradictions and struggles. In other words, what historians are discovering today is a far more human—and thus a far more interesting—John Calvin.

To begin to understand him, one needs to know first that his intellectually formative years were spent in the stimulating climate of French humanism. First at the University of Paris from 1521 to 1528, and then at schools of law in Bourges and Orleans till 1533, Calvin was deeply influenced by its foremost representatives: Jacques Lefèvre d'Etaples, Mathurin Cordier, Guillaume Budé, and above all the international humanist, Erasmus. To them he owed his life-long fascination with classical Latin, Hebrew, and Greek. From them he learned the importance of studying the church fathers and the Bible in their original languages. With them he turned in a reformist direction, calling for a church renewal on biblical foundations. Calvin learned from them, and utilized to the end, the principles of classical rhetoric. Only after 1533 did their paths diverge, and even then, by no means entirely.

The greater part of Calvin's working career was spent in exile, in Geneva (1536–1538, and 1541–1564). Here a good deal of his time and, judging by his complaints, an enormous amount of emotional energy were spent on what we might call church politics. Geneva had embraced the Reformation shortly before Calvin arrived in 1536. Immediately upon arrival, Calvin's forceful personality asserted itself and he assumed leadership of the church. Here began a lifetime of political struggles, almost all of which centered around his unceasing attempts to impose and enforce his conception of "godly living" on the populace. Genevans did not easily acquiesce, nor did political authorities cede power without a struggle. Thus, for instance, it was a continual thorn in Calvin's side that the power of excommunication and barring people from the sacraments for reasons of immorality rested with the magistrates. Only in 1555 did Calvin succeed in transferring this authority to church officials. In conflicts such as these, Calvin gave the impression, at least, of absolute moral certainty. And his opponents more often than not ended up being depicted as servants of Satan. Yet he acknowledged to friends again and again what an enormous emotional toll these struggles took on him. And in his last will and testament, the note of self-doubt was unmistakable: "I feel deficient in everything and everywhere," he wrote.

Calvin probably derived more personal satisfaction from another role that he played, that of pastor. After his return to Geneva, he averaged more than three sermons a week for the rest of his life. He performed numerous weddings and baptisms; he regularly administered Communion; and he counseled and advised, by letter and in person. All of these duties he seems to have taken with the utmost seriousness.

Above all, however, John Calvin understood himself as a theologian. And herein too lies his historical importance. The majority of his time, from 1541 until his death in 1564, was devoted to lectures on the Bible. These were delivered several times a week, in Latin, to pastors and students. While he sometimes prepared a written text for these lectures, more often they were given spontaneously, and taken down by students or secretaries. Calvin usually corrected these written versions, and they were then printed as commentaries on the various books of the Bible. In addition Calvin composed various polemical treatises in reply to attacks on his person and his reform program. What was to earn him the most fame, however, was his *Institutes of the Christian Religion,* written first in 1536 and then revised and expanded in later editions. Here was an authentic Protestant "Summa," easily the most powerfully systematic theological statement to emerge out of the first generation of reformers. Finally, it was also as a theologian that Calvin founded the Geneva Academy in 1559. By then the city had become truly international, taking in sympathetic refugees from England, Scotland, France, etc. Calvin now provided theological training, and it was here that the next generation of Reformed Protestant leaders was born.

If the sole criterion of "greatness" was the number of one's followers, we could say without hesitation that Calvin was the greatest of the Protestant reformers. For those who were in some way Calvin's disciples, whether they were known as "Calvinists" or "Reformed" or "Huguenots" or "Puritans," vastly outnumbered Luther's. What united these disciples was not so much loyalty to Calvin the person, but more a sharing in his obsessions: the glory of God as the purpose of all creation; the consistency between belief and ethical practice; the urgency of the call to personal sanctification; and the impulse toward transformation of the social order in the direction of holiness.

Calvin on Himself

48. Preface to the *Commentary on the Psalms* (1557)

In continuity with the medieval tradition, and especially with monastic spirituality, Calvin accorded enormous importance to the Psalms. Perhaps it was because this book spoke to him so personally that here, in his preface to his commentary, he could overcome his usual reticence and write about himself. The preface thus moves from commendation of the Psalms to autobiography to apologia.

✠ *(the Psalms)*

The varied and resplendent riches which are contained in this treasury it is no easy matter to express in words; so much so, that I well know that whatever I shall be able to say will be far from approaching the excellence of the subject. But as it is better to give to my readers some taste, however small, of the wonderful advantages they will derive from the study of this book, than to be entirely silent on the point, I may be permitted briefly to advert to a matter, the greatness of which does not admit of being fully unfolded. I have been accustomed to call this book, I think not inappropriately, *An Anatomy of All the Parts of the Soul;* for there is not an emotion of which anyone can be conscious that is not here represented as in a mirror. Or rather, the Holy Spirit has here drawn to the life all the griefs, sorrows, fears, doubts, hopes, cares, perplexities, in short, all the distracting emotions with which the minds of men are wont to be agitated. The other parts of Scripture contain the commandments which God enjoined his servants to announce to us. But here the prophets themselves, seeing they are exhibited to us as speaking to God, and laying open all their inmost thoughts and affections, call, or rather draw, each of us to the examination of himself in particular, in order that none of the many infirmities to which we are subject, and of the many vices with which we abound, may remain concealed. It is certainly a rare and singular advantage, when all lurking places are discovered, and the heart is brought into the light, purged from that most baneful infection, hypocrisy. In short, as calling upon God is one of the principal means of securing our safety, and as a better and more unerring rule for guiding us in this exercise cannot be found elsewhere than in the Psalms, it follows, that in proportion to the proficiency which a man shall have attained in understanding them, will be his knowledge of the most important part of celestial doctrine. Genuine and earnest prayer proceeds first from a sense of our need, and next, from faith in the promises of God. It is by perusing these inspired compositions, that men will be most effectually awakened to a sense of their maladies, and, at the same time, instructed in seeking remedies for their cure. In a word, whatever may serve to encourage us when we are about to pray to God, is taught us in this book. And not only are the promises of God presented to us in it, but oftentimes there is exhibited to us one standing, as it were, amidst the invitations of God on the one hand, and the impediments of the flesh on the other, girding and preparing himself for prayer: thus teaching us, if at any time we are agitated with a variety of doubts, to resist and fight against them, until the soul, freed and disentangled from all these impediments, rise up to God; and not only so, but even when in the midst of doubts, fears, and apprehensions, let us put forth our efforts in prayer, until we experience some consolation which may calm and bring contentment to our minds. Although distrust may shut the gate against our prayers, yet we must not allow ourselves to give way, whenever our hearts waver or are agitated with inquietude, but must persevere until faith finally come forth victorious from these conflicts. In many places we may perceive the exercise of the servants of God in prayer so fluctuating, that they are almost overwhelmed by the alternate hope of success and apprehension of failure, and gain the prize only by strenuous exertions. We see on the one hand, the flesh manifesting its infirmity; and on the other, faith putting forth its power; and if it is not so valiant and courageous as might be desired, it is at least prepared to fight until by degrees it acquire perfect strength.

But as those things which serve to teach us the true method of praying aright will be found scattered through the whole of this commentary, I will not now stop to treat of topics which it will be necessary afterwards to repeat, nor detain my readers from proceeding to the work itself. Only it appeared to me to be requisite to show in passing, that this book makes known to us this privilege, which is desirable above all others—that not only is there opened up to us familiar access to God, but also that we have permission and freedom granted us to lay open before him our infirmities, which we would be ashamed to confess before men. Besides, there is also here prescribed to us an infallible rule for directing us with respect to the right manner of offering to God the sacrifice of praise, which he declares to be most precious in his sight, and of the sweetest odor. There is no other book in which there is to be found more express and magnificent commendations, both of the unparalleled liberality of God towards his church, and of all his works;

there is no other book in which there are recorded so many deliverances, nor one in which the evidences and experiences of the fatherly providence and solicitude which God exercises towards us, are celebrated with such splendor of diction, and yet with the strictest adherence to truth; in short, there is no other book in which we are more perfectly taught the right manner of praising God, or in which we are more powerfully stirred up to the performance of this religious exercise. Moreover, although the Psalms are replete with all the precepts which serve to frame our life to every part of holiness, piety, and righteousness, yet they will principally teach and train us to bear the cross; and the bearing of the cross is a genuine proof of our obedience, since by doing this, we renounce the guidance of our own affections, and submit ourselves entirely to God, leaving him to govern us, and to dispose of our life according to his will, so that the afflictions which are the bitterest and most severe to our nature, become sweet to us, because they proceed from him. In one word, not only will we here find general commendations of the goodness of God, which may teach men to repose themselves in him alone, and to seek all their happiness solely in him; and which are intended to teach true believers with their whole hearts confidently to look to him for help in all their necessities; but we will also find that the free remission of sins, which alone reconciles God towards us, and procures for us settled peace with him, is so set forth and magnified, as that here there is nothing wanting which relates to the knowledge of eternal salvation.

Now, if my readers derive any fruit and advantage from the labor which I have bestowed in writing these commentaries, I would have them to understand that the small measure of experience which I have had by the conflicts with which the Lord has exercised me, has in no ordinary degree assisted me, not only in applying to present use whatever instruction could be gathered from these divine compositions, but also in more easily comprehending the design of each of the writers. And as David holds the principal place among them, it has greatly aided me in understanding more fully the complaints made by him of the internal afflictions which the church had to sustain through those who gave themselves out to be her members, that I had suffered the same or similar things from the domestic enemies of the church. For although I follow David at a great distance, and come far short of equalling him; or rather, although in aspiring slowly and with great difficulty to attain to the many virtues in which he excelled, I still feel myself tarnished with the contrary vices; yet if I have any things in common with him, I have no hesitation in comparing myself with him. In reading the instances of his faith, patience, fervor, zeal, and integrity, it has, as it ought, drawn from me unnumbered groans and sighs, that I am so far from approaching them; but it has, notwithstanding, been of very great advantage to me to behold in him as in a mirror, both the commencement of my calling, and the continued course of my function; so that I know the more assuredly, that whatever that most illustrious king and prophet suffered, was exhibited to me by God as an example for imitation. My condition, no doubt, is much inferior to his, and it is unnecessary for me to stay to show this. But as he was taken from the sheepfold, and elevated to the rank of supreme authority; so God having taken me from my originally obscure and humble condition, has reckoned me worthy of being invested with the honorable office of a preacher and minister of the gospel. When I was as yet a very little boy, my father had destined me for the study of theology. But afterwards, when he considered that the legal profession commonly raised those who followed it to wealth, this prospect induced him suddenly to change his purpose. Thus it came to pass, that I was withdrawn from the study of philosophy, and was put to the study of law. To this pursuit I endeavored faithfully to apply myself, in obedience to the will of my father; but God, by the secret guidance of his providence, at length gave a different direction to my course. And first, since I was too obstinately devoted to the superstitions of popery to be easily extricated from so profound an abyss of mire, God by a sudden conversion subdued and brought my mind to a teachable frame, which was more hardened in such matters than might have been expected from one at my early period of life. Having thus received some taste and knowledge of true godliness, I was immediately inflamed with so intense a desire to make progress therein, that although I did not altogether leave off other studies, I yet pursued them with less ardor.

I was quite surprised to find that before a year had elapsed, all who had any desire after purer doctrine were continually coming to me to learn, although I myself was as yet but a mere novice and tyro. Being of a disposition somewhat unpolished and bashful, which led me always to love the shade and retirement, I then began to seek some secluded corner where I might be withdrawn from the public view; but so far from being able to accomplish the object of my desire, all my retreats were like public schools. In short, whilst my one great object was to live in seclusion without being known, God so led me about through different turnings and changes, that he never permitted me to rest in any place, until, in spite of my natural disposition, he brought me forth to public notice. Leaving my native country, France, I in fact retired into Germany, expressly for the purpose of being able there to enjoy in some obscure corner the repose which I had always desired, and which had been so long denied me. But lo! whilst I lay hidden at Basel, and known only to a few people, many faithful and holy persons were burned alive in France; and the report of these burnings having reached foreign nations, they excited the strongest disapprobation among a great part of the Germans, whose indignation was kindled against the authors of such tyranny. In order to allay this indignation, certain wicked and lying pamphlets were circulated, stating, that none were treated with such cruelty but Anabaptists and seditious persons, who, by their perverse ravings and false opinions, were overthrowing not only religion but also all civil order. Observing that the object which these instruments of the court aimed at by their disguises, was not only that the disgrace of shedding so much innocent blood might remain buried under the false charges and calumnies which they brought against the holy martyrs after their death, but also, that afterwards they might be able to proceed to the utmost extremity in murdering the poor saints without exciting compassion towards them in the breasts of any, it appeared to me, that unless I opposed them to the utmost of my ability, my silence could not be vindicated from the charge of cowardice and treachery. This was the consideration which induced me to publish my *Institutes of the Christian Religion*. My objects were, first, to prove that these reports were false and calumnious, and thus to vindicate

my brethren, whose death was precious in the sight of the Lord; and next, that as the same cruelties might very soon after be exercised against many unhappy individuals, foreign nations might be touched with at least some compassion towards them and solicitude about them. When it was then published, it was not that copious and labored work which it now is, but only a small treatise containing a summary of the principal truths of the Christian religion; and it was published with no other design than that men might know what was the faith held by those whom I saw basely and wickedly defamed by those flagitious and perfidious flatterers. That my object was not to acquire fame, appeared from this, that immediately after I left Basel, and particularly from the fact that nobody there knew that I was the author.

Wherever else I have gone, I have taken care to conceal that I was the author of that performance; and I had resolved to continue in the same privacy and obscurity, until at length William Farel detained me at Geneva, not so much by counsel and exhortation, as by a dreadful imprecation, which I felt to be as if God had from heaven laid his mighty hand upon me to arrest me. As the most direct road to Strasbourg, to which I then intended to retire, was shut up by the wars, I had resolved to pass quickly by Geneva, without staying longer than a single night in that city. A little before this, popery had been driven from it by the exertions of the excellent person whom I have named, and Peter Viret; but matters were not yet brought to a settled state, and the city was divided into unholy and dangerous factions. Then an individual who now basely apostatized and returned to the papists, discovered me and made me known to others. Upon this, Farel, who burned with an extraordinary zeal to advance the gospel, immediately strained every nerve to detain me. And after having learned that my heart was set upon devoting myself to private studies, for which I wished to keep myself free from other pursuits, and finding that he gained nothing by entreaties, he proceeded to utter an imprecation that God would curse my retirement, and the tranquillity of the studies which I sought, if I should withdraw and refuse to give assistance, when the necessity was so urgent. By this imprecation I was so stricken with terror, that I desisted from the journey which I had undertaken; but sensible of my natural bashfulness and timidity, I would not bring myself under obligation to discharge any particular office. After that, four months had scarcely elapsed, when, on the one hand, the Anabaptists began to assail us, and, on the other, a certain wicked apostate, who being secretly supported by the influence of some of the magistrates of the city, was thus enabled to give us a great deal of trouble. At the same time, a succession of dissensions fell out in the city which strangely afflicted us. Being, as I acknowledge, naturally of a timid, soft, and pusillanimous disposition, I was compelled to encounter these violent tempests as part of my early training; and although I did not sink under them, yet I was not sustained by such greatness of mind, as not to rejoice more than it became me, when, in consequence of certain commotions, I was banished from Geneva.

By this means set at liberty and loosed from the tie of my vocation, I resolved to live in a private station, free from the burden and cares of any public charge, when that most excellent servant of Christ, Martin Bucer, employing a similar kind of remonstrance and protestation as that to which Farel had recourse before, drew me back to a new station. Alarmed by the example of Jonas which he set before me, I still continued in the work of teaching. And although I always continued like myself, studiously avoiding celebrity; yet I was carried, I know not how, as it were by force to the imperial assemblies, where, willing or unwilling, I was under the necessity of appearing before the eyes of many. Afterwards, when the Lord having compassion on this city, had allayed the hurtful agitations and broils which prevailed in it, and by his wonderful power had defeated both the wicked counsels and the sanguinary attempts of the disturbers of the republic, necessity was imposed upon me of returning to my former charge, contrary to my desire and inclination. The welfare of this church, it is true, lay so near my heart, that for its sake I would not have hesitated to lay down my life; but my timidity nevertheless suggested to me many reasons for excusing myself from again willingly taking upon my shoulders so heavy a burden. At length, however, a solemn and conscientious regard to my duty, prevailed with me to consent to return to the flock from which I had been torn; but with what grief, tears, great anxiety and distress I did this, the Lord is my best witness, and many godly persons who would have wished to see me delivered from this painful state, had it not been that that which I feared, and which made me give my consent, prevented them and shut their mouths.

Were I to narrate the various conflicts by which the Lord has exercised me since that time, and by what trials he has proved me, it would make a long history. But that I may not become tedious to my readers by a waste of words, I shall content myself with repeating briefly what I have touched upon a little before, that in considering the whole course

of the life of David, it seemed to me that by
his own footsteps he showed me the way, and
from this I have experienced no small consolation. As that holy king was harassed by the
Philistines and other foreign enemies with
continual wars, while he was much more
grievously afflicted by the malice and
wickedness of some perfidious men amongst
his own people, so I can say as to myself, that
I have been assailed on all sides, and have
scarcely been able to enjoy repose for a single
moment, but have always had to sustain
some conflict either from enemies without or
within the church. Satan has made many
attempts to overthrow the fabric of this
church; and once it came to this, that I, altogether feeble and timorous as I am, was compelled to break and put a stop to his deadly
assaults by putting my life in danger, and
opposing my person to his blows. Afterwards, for the space of five years, when some
wicked libertines were furnished with undue
influence, and also some of the common people, corrupted by the allurements and perverse discourse of such persons, desired to
obtain the liberty of doing whatever they
pleased, without control, I was under the
necessity of fighting without ceasing to
defend and maintain the discipline of the
church. To these irreligious characters and
despisers of the heavenly doctrine, it was a
matter of entire indifference, although the
church should sink into ruin, provided they
obtained what they sought—the power of
acting just as they pleased. Many, too,
harassed by poverty and hunger, and others
impelled by insatiable ambition or avarice
and a desire of dishonest gain, were become
so frantic, that they chose rather, by throw-
ing all things into confusion, to involve
themselves and us in one common ruin, than
to remain quiet by living peaceably and hon-

estly. During the whole of this lengthened
period, I think that there is scarcely any of
the weapons which are forged in the work-
shop of Satan, which has not been employed
by them in order to obtain their object. And
at length matters had come to such a state,
that an end could be put to their machinations in no other way than cutting them off
by an ignominious death; which was indeed
a painful and pitiable spectacle to me. They
no doubt deserved the severest punishment,
but I always rather desired that they might
live in prosperity, and continue safe and
untouched; which would have been the case
had they not been altogether incorrigible,
and obstinately refused to listen to wholesome admonition.

The trial of these five years was grievous
and hard to bear; but I experienced not less
excruciating pain from the malignity of
those who ceased not to assail myself and my
ministry with their envenomed calumnies. A
great proportion of them, it is true, are so
blinded by a passion for slander and detrac-
tion, that to their great disgrace, they betray
at once their impudence, while others, however crafty and cunning, cannot so cover or
disguise themselves as to escape being
shamefully convicted and disgraced; yet
when a man has been a hundred times found
innocent of a charge brought against him,
and when the charge is again repeated without any cause or occasion, it is an indignity
hard to bear. Because I affirm and maintain
that the world is managed and governed by
the secret providence of God, a multitude of
presumptuous men rise up against me, and
allege that I represent God as the author of
sin. This is so foolish a calumny, that it
would of itself quickly come to nothing, did
it not meet with persons who have tickled
ears, and who take pleasure in feeding upon

such discourse. But there are many whose minds are so filled with envy and spleen, or ingratitude, or malignity, that there is no falsehood, however preposterous, yea, even monstrous, which they do not receive, if it is spoken to them. Others endeavor to overthrow God's eternal purpose of predestination, by which he distinguishes between the reprobate and the elect; others take upon them to defend free will; and forthwith many throw themselves into their ranks, not so much through ignorance as by a perversity of zeal which I know not how to characterize. If they were open and avowed enemies, who brought these troubles upon me, the thing might in some way be borne. But that those who shroud themselves under the name of brethren, and not only eat Christ's sacred bread, but also administer it to others, that those, in short, who loudly boast of being preachers of the gospel, should wage such nefarious war against me, how detestable is it? In this matter I may very justly complain with David, "Yea, mine own familiar friend, in whom I trusted, who did eat of my bread, hath lifted up his heel against me" (Ps. 41:9). "For it was not an enemy that reproached me; but it was thou, a man mine equal, my guide, and mine acquaintance. We took sweet counsel together, and walked unto the house of God in company" (Ps. 55:12, 13, 14). Others circulated ridiculous reports concerning my treasures; others, of the extravagant authority and enormous influence which they say I possess; others speak of my delicacies and magnificence. But when a man is content with scanty food and common clothing, and does not require from the humblest more frugality than he shows and practices himself, shall it be said that such a one is too sumptuous, and lives in too high a style? As to the power and influence of which

they envy me, I wish I could discharge this burden upon them; for they estimate my power by the multitude of affairs, and the vast weight of labors with which I am overwhelmed. And if there are some whom I cannot persuade whilst I am alive that I am not rich, my death at length will prove it. I confess, indeed, that I am not poor; for I desire nothing more than what I have. All these are invented stories, and there is no color whatever for any one of them; but many nevertheless are very easily persuaded of their truth, and applaud them; and the reason is, because the greatest part judge that the only means of cloaking their enormities is to throw all things into disorder, and to confound black and white; and they think that the best and shortest way by which they can obtain full liberty to live with impunity just as they please, is to destroy the authority of Christ's servants.

In addition to these, there are "the hypocritical mockers in feasts," of whom David complains, (Ps. 35:16); and I mean by these not only lick-dish characters, who seek a meal to fill their belly, but all those who by false reports seek to obtain the favor of the great. Having been long accustomed to swallow such wrongs as these, I have become almost hardened; yet when the insolence of such characters increases, I cannot but sometimes feel my heart wounded with bitter pangs. Nor was it enough that I should be so inhumanly treated by my neighbors. In addition to this, in a distant country towards the frozen ocean, there was raised, I know not how, by the frenzy of a few, a storm which afterwards stirred up against me a vast number of persons, who are too much at leisure, and have nothing to do but by their bickering to hinder those who are laboring for the edification of the church. I am still speaking of the internal enemies of the church—of those who, boasting mightily of the gospel of Christ, nevertheless rush against me with greater impetuosity than against the open adversaries of the church, because I do not embrace their gross and fictitious notion concerning a carnal way of eating Christ in the sacrament; and of whom I may protest, after the example of David, "I am for peace; but when I speak, they are for war" (Ps. 120:7). Moreover, the cruel ingratitude of all of them is manifest in this, that they scruple not to assail both in flank and rear a man who strenuously exerts himself to maintain a cause which they have in common with him, and whom therefore they ought to aid and succor. Certainly, if such persons were possessed of even a small portion of humanity, the fury of the papists which is directed against me with such unbridled violence, would appease the most implacable animosity which they may bear towards me. But since the condition of David was such, that though he had deserved well of his own people, he was nevertheless bitterly hated by many without a cause, as he complains in Ps. 69:4, "I restored that which I took not away," it afforded me no small consolation when I was groundlessly assailed by the hatred of those who ought to have assisted and solaced me, to conform myself to the example of so great and so excellent a person. This knowledge and experience have been of much service in enabling me to understand the Psalms, so that in my meditations upon them, I did not wander, as it were, in an unknown region.

My readers, too, if I mistake not, will observe, that in unfolding the internal affections both of David and of others, I discourse upon them as matters of which I have familiar experience. Moreover, since I have labored faithfully to open up this treasure for the use of all the people of God, although what I have done has not been equal to my wishes, yet the attempt which I have made deserves to be received with some measure of favor. Still I only ask that each may judge of my labors with justice and candor, according to the advantage and fruit which he shall derive from them. Certainly, as I have said before, in reading these commentaries, it will be clearly seen that I have not sought to please, unless insofar as I might at the same time be profitable to others. And, therefore, I have not only observed throughout a simple style of teaching, but in order to be removed the farther from all ostentation, I have also generally abstained from refuting the opinions of others, although this presented a more favorable opportunity for plausible display, and of acquiring the applause of those who shall favor my book with a perusal. I have never touched upon opposite opinions, unless where there was reason to fear, that by being silent respecting them, I might leave my readers in doubt and perplexity. At the same time, I am sensible that it would have been much more agreeable to the taste of many, had I heaped together a great mass of materials which has great show, and acquires fame for the writer; but I have felt nothing to be of more importance than to have a regard to the edification of the church. May God, who has implanted this desire in my heart, grant by his grace that the success may correspond thereto!

Geneva, 22 July 1557

From J. Dillenberger, ed., John Calvin: Selections from His Writings *(New York: Doubleday, 1971), 23–33.*

49. Letter to Melanchthon (19 November 1558)

Personal friendships were important to Calvin, and in this context too he could reveal something of his human side. In this letter, his physical problems are described in detail.

I am aware, most distinguished sir and reverend brother, that as you are yourself an indolent correspondent, you very good-naturedly overlook a similar want of punctuality on the part of your friends. I had, therefore, determined to plead the excuse of bad health for not writing to you, but, that it gives me pleasure to pour into your bosom the annoyances, of which the burden weighs me down. As, thank God, I have up to these years never been visited by a quartan ague, it required a fourth attack to cure me of my ignorance of it, and reveal to me what kind of malady I had to deal with. Now, though I am ashamed of this indolence, you will perhaps be inclined to excuse me when you are made aware of what obstacles I had to contend with. At first, when the fit came upon me, as I was asleep or in a dozing mood, it was no difficult thing for it to steal a march on me without my perceiving it, especially as it was accompanied with very troublesome and acute pains, to which I am but too well accustomed from a long familiarity with them. But when the shivering fit once seized me, at supper time, I thought it quite sufficient to rid myself in my usual manner of my dyspepsia by a rigid fasting. The following day as I was lying with my strength quite prostrate, but relieved, however, and almost entirely delivered from the violence of my pain, I came to my fourth attack, still a novice and perfectly ignorant of the enemy I had to grapple with. Nearly six weeks have now elapsed since I became acquainted with the nature of my complaint, during which I have been in the hands of the doctors, who keep me shut up in my bedroom and pretty generally confine me to bed in which I am protected by a double coverlet, while every now and then they keep dinning in my ears the verse of Sophocles, "the belly has become so hard bound that it will not relax unless aided by a clyster [enema]," which is a state very alien to my usual habits. They prescribe to me all the best and most digestible kinds of food, none of which flatter my taste, so that my strength gets gradually more and more feeble. I struggle against my illness, nevertheless, and recruit my exhausted stomach with the most insipid of food, nor do I either allow my loathing to get the better of me, nor like most people, do I coax myself into an appetite by employing stimulants that are pernicious to my complaint. Nay, in everything I take care not to deviate one hairbreadth from the doctor's prescription, except that in my burning thirst I allow myself to drink a little more copiously. And even this excess I impute to their fault, for they most pointedly exact of me to drink burgundy wine, which I am not allowed to temper with water or any more common beverage. Nay, unless I had obstinately protested, they wanted to kill me outright with the heating fumes of malmsey and muscat wine. But as I know that they are men of no common skill in their profession, persons of sound good sense moreover, and experienced from a long practice of their art, I not only from motives of politeness pay implicit attention to their orders, but even willingly permit myself to be guided by such masters. They mix my wine with spleenwort or wormwood. They fortify my stomach by fomenting it with syrups of hyssop, or elecampane, or citron bark, at the same time applying to it a certain pressure, that the novelty of the sensation may give greater energy to the remedy and cause it to act more speedily. They only once attempted to expel the bilious humors from my spleen. But though I seem now to be abusing your leisure moments with too much indifference, and in dictating these details during the heat of the fever, I was not very judiciously consulting my own health; yet, as the issue of my complaint is still doubtful, I wished to assure you that I am now making it the principal subject of my meditation, how at a moment's warning I may be prepared to meet any lot which God intends for me. Meanwhile, that you may not be ignorant of what my dangers are, know that it is currently reported, that peace being concluded between the two kings, the whole brunt of the war will be directed against us, that whatever expiation has been judged necessary may be ratified by our blood. Know also, that we are not better protected, either by the distance of the localities or by fortifications, than if we had to engage in a conflict in the open field. Philip's territories are only two days' march from our gates. The king is still nearer, whose troops could reach our city in the space of half-an-hour. Whence you may conclude that we have not only exile to fear, but that all the most cruel varieties of death are impending over us, for in the cause of religion they will set no bounds to their barbarity. Wherefore your lot should appear to you less bitter if disciples, who ought to have repaid to your old age what they owed to you, now hostilely attack you, a man who had discharged with the highest fidelity and diligence the functions of a teacher, and also deserved the highest honors from the whole church; when you see that the treatment you experience is common to you with others, and particularly with myself; for it is scarcely to be believed how petulantly and unworthily certain brawlers assail me. The partisans of Westphal, though they hurl their darts from a distance, nevertheless, in their wickedness, take far more impudent liberties with me. I shall not for all that cease to press towards the mark at which I had begun to aim; in the controversy respecting the Lord's supper, not only your enemies traduce what they calumniously style your weakness, but your best friends also, and those who cherish you with the pious feelings which you deserve, would wish that the flame of your zeal burned more brightly, of which we behold but some feeble sparks, and thus it is that these pygmies strut like giants. Whatever happens, let us cultivate with sincerity a fraternal affection towards each other, of which no wiles of Satan shall ever burst asunder the ties. I confess, indeed, that about six months ago, when I read a letter of your acquaintance, Hubert Languet, I was slightly piqued because he reported you as having spoken in no friendly, or rather in a contemptuous manner of my doctrine. But it was his design to flatter Castalio, and to have his ravings approved of by your suffrage—ravings which are the greatest pest of our times. But by no slight shall my mind ever be alienated from that holy friendship and respect which I have vowed to you.

From Dillenberger, John Calvin, *69–72.*

Practical Matters

50. *Geneva Ordinances* (1547)

One of the things Calvin abhorred most was "disorderly living." Accordingly, when he returned to Geneva in 1541, he was more determined than ever to regulate every aspect of life in accordance with "God's law" (as he understood it). Immediately laws were passed reorganizing the Genevan church and attaching legal sanctions to breaches of "Christian" behavior. Calvin's attempt to thus "Christianize" the social order became a lifelong struggle in the face of considerable resistance. The following set of ordinances from 1547 give us an idea of what Calvin had in mind.

✠

Sermons

1. Everyone in each house is to come on Sundays, unless it be necessary to leave someone behind to take care of children or animals, under penalty of 3 sous.

2. If there be preaching any weekday, arranged with due notice, those that are able to go and have no legitimate excuse are to attend, at least one from each house, under penalty as above.

3. Those who have man- or maid-servants, are to bring them or have them conveyed when possible, so that they do not live like cattle without instruction.

4. Everyone is to be present at sermon when the prayer is begun, under penalty as above, unless he absent himself for legitimate reason.

5. Everyone is to pay attention during sermon, and there is to be no disorder or scandal.

6. No one is to leave or go out from the church until the prayer be made at the end of sermon, under penalty as above, unless he have legitimate cause.

Catechism

1. Because each preacher has two parishes, catechism is to take place each fortnight. Those who have children are to bring them, with the rest of their household who have not been to sermon, as above.

2. The same attention, honest and regular, is to be given to catechism as has been said for sermon.

Penalties

1. Those who fail in their duty of coming are to be admonished by the guardians, both themselves and their family.

2. If after intimation they continue to default, they are to be fined three groats, for each time. Of this one third will be applied to the guardians; the other two-thirds will be applied to the poor of the parish, and put into the funds of the church for distribution according to need as it becomes known.

3. If anyone come after sermon has begun, he is to be admonished, and if after this is done he does not amend, for each fault he is to be fined three sous, which will be applied as above.

4. If during sermon anyone make any disturbance or scandal, he is to be reported to the consistory to be cautioned, in order that procedure be in proportion to the fault; that is, if by carelessness he is to be well told off, if it happen by intended malice or rebelliousness he is to be reported to their lordships to be punished appropriately.

By Whom Fines Are to Be Exacted

1. The local lord, in conjunction with the ministers and the guardians, is to oblige the delinquents to pay the fines they have incurred, when they will not pay of their own free will. Legitimate excuses are to be admitted, but this is to be done without any formal procedure.

2. If there be any so rebellious that, despite the above fines, they do not at all amend, they are to be reported to the consistory with advice to the effect that their lordships punish them according to the seriousness of their obstinacy.

3. Fathers are to be responsible for their children, and, if there be a penalty, it is to be exacted from them.

Of Baptism

1. Baptism is to be administered any day, provided that there be sermon along with it. The ministers are always to exhort the people to link it up with the catechism.

2. Children are to be brought at the beginning of catechism or sermon.

3. Fathers are to be present, unless they have legitimate excuse of which cognizance will be taken by the consistory.

4. No godfather is to be admitted for presenting a child, unless he is of an age to make such a promise; that is, he must have passed fifteen years, be of the same confession as ourselves, and be duly instructed.

5. As to names, let their lordships' ordinances be careful both to avoid all superstition and idolatry and to remove from the church of God everything foolish and indecent.

6. If midwives usurp the office of baptism, they are to be reproved or chastised according to the measure of fault found, since no commission is given them in this matter, under penalty of being put on bread and water for three days and fined ten sous; and all who consent to their action or conceal it will be liable to the same penalty.

Of the Supper

1. No one is to be received at the supper unless he first have made confession of his faith. That is to say, he must declare before the minister that he desires to live according to the reformation of the gospel, and that he knows the creed, the Lord's Prayer and the commandments of God.

2. Those who wish to receive the supper are to come at the beginning of the service; those who come at the end are not to be received.

3. Other impediments are to be within the cognizance of the consistory, to deal with them, in accordance with what has been ordained.

4. All are to remain until the end, unless there be a legitimate excuse which is recognized as above.

Of Times of Meeting at Church

Buildings are to remain shut for the rest of the time, in order that no one outside the hours may enter for superstitious reasons. If anyone be found making any particular devotion inside or nearby, he is to be admonished: if it appear to be a superstition which he will not amend, he is to be chastised.

Faults Contravening the Reformation Besides Those Already Mentioned

First, Superstitions

1. Those found to have any paternosters or idols for adoration are to be brought before the consistory, and, besides the punishment imposed on them there, they are to be brought before their lordships.

2. Those who have been on pilgrimages or voyages the same.

3. Those who observe the papistical feasts or fastings are to be admonished only, unless they are obstinate in their rebellion.

4. Those who have attended mass, besides admonition, are to be brought before their lordships.

5. In such cases, their lordships will have the right of chastising by means of prison or otherwise, or of punishing by extraordinary fines, at their discretion.

In the case of fines, they are to apply some small portion of them to the guardians, if the delict was notified by them.

Blasphemies

1. Those who have blasphemed, swearing by the body or by the blood of our Lord, or suchlike, ought to do reverence for the first time; for the second a penalty of five sous; for the third ten sous; and for the last time put in the pillory for an hour.

2. Anyone who abjures or renounces God or his baptism is for the first time to be put

for ten days on bread and water; for the second and third time he is to be punished with some more rigorous corporal punishment, at the discretion of their lordships.

Contradiction of the Word

1. If there are any who contradict the Word of God, let them be brought before the consistory to be admonished, or be remanded to their lordships to receive chastisement according to the needs of the case.

2. If the contradiction or rebellion amount to scandal which demands prompter remedy, the local lord is to take a hand in the matter for the maintenance of the honor of the ministry and the magistracy.

Drunkenness

1. There is to be no treating of one another to drinks, under penalty of three sous.

2. The taverns are to be closed during service, under penalty that the taverner pay three sous and anyone entering them the same.

3. If anyone be found drunk, he is to pay for the first time three sous and be brought before the consistory; the second time he must pay the sum of five sous; and the third ten sous and be put in prison.

4. There are to be no carousings, under penalty of ten sous.

Songs and Dances

If anyone sing songs that are unworthy, dissolute or outrageous, or spin wildly round in the dance, or the like, he is to be imprisoned for three days, and then sent on to the consistory.

Usury

No one is to lend at interest or for profit greater than 5 percent, on pain of confiscation of the capital sum and of being required to make appropriate amends according to the needs of the case.

Brawling

1. No one is to cause noise or dispute on pain of being punished according to the needs of the case.

2. If there be any who causes sedition or assembling to make or support quarrels, he is to be punished with more rigorous penalties according to what he merits.

Complaints

If there be a complaint or dispute between two people, the minister, summoning the guardians, will do his duty to bring them to accord; and if he is unable to prevail, he will remand them to the consistory.

Games

No one is to play at games that are dissolute, or at games played for gold or silver or at excessive expense, on pain of five sous and loss of the sum staked.

Fornication

1. As to those who are caught in fornication, if it be an unmarried man with an unmarried woman, they are to be imprisoned for six days on bread and water, and pay sixty sous amends.

2. If it be adultery, one or the other being married, they are to be imprisoned for nine days on bread and water, and pay amends at the discretion of their lordships, as the crime is much more grave.

3. Those who are promised in marriage are not to cohabit as man and wife until the marriage be celebrated in church, otherwise they will be punished as for fornication.

Of the Election of Guardians

The local lord assembling the more responsible and better part of the parishioners, and duly advising them, election of guardians is to take place before them. They are to be men of substance and fearing God. He then brings the said guardians to the consistory, to be instructed in their office, and from there they will be brought before their lordships to take the oath.

For Remanding to the Consistory

The decision of the minister and the guardians or of one of them, the local lord, or in his absence one of the assistants, may remand delinquents to the consistory.

On May 16, 1547, the above ordinances were read, and then approved and accepted; and it is further declared that the penalties for offenses are to be applied in part to the guardians of the parishes, in part to the local lord and the municipal council, and in part to the poor of the parish and district.

By command of their lordships, the Syndics and Council of Geneva.

✠

From J. K. S. Reid, ed., Calvin: Theological Treatises *(Philadelphia: Westminster Press, 1954), 77–82.*

51. Letter Concerning a Pious Woman (22 July 1552)

Calvin frequently received requests for practical advice from people in difficult circumstances. This letter shows Calvin attempting to be realistic, firm, and yet not without compassion.

✠

At issue is a request from a pious woman who, because of her desire to follow the truth and pure religion, has been treated badly by her husband and subjected to cruel and harsh servitude. Thus she wishes to know if it is permissible to leave her husband and to come here or withdraw to another church where she might rest her conscience in peace. Accordingly, we offer the following advice.

First of all, with respect to her perplexity and agony, we are filled with pity and compassion for her and are drawn to pray that it will please God to give her such a sense of relief that she will be able to find the where-

withal to rejoice in him. Nevertheless, since she has asked for our counsel regarding what is permissible, our duty is to respond, purely and simply, on the basis of what God reveals to us in his Word, closing our eyes to all else. For this reason, we beg her not to take offense if our advice does not correspond with her hope. For it is necessary that she and we follow what the Master has ordained, without mingling our desires with it.

Now, with regard to the bond of marriage, one must remember that a believing party cannot, of his or her free will, divorce the unbeliever, as St. Paul makes clear in 1 Cor. 7:13. Without a doubt, St. Paul emphasizes this, fully knowing the suffering each party may be experiencing. For at that time the pagans and the Jews were no less poisoned against the Christian religion than the papists are today. But St. Paul commands the believing partner, who continues to persevere in the truth of God, not to leave the partner who resists God.

In brief, we ought so to prefer God and Jesus Christ to the whole world that fathers, children, husbands, and wives cease to constitute something we value. So much is this so, that if we cannot adhere to him and renounce all else, we ought to make ourselves do so. This does not mean that Christianity ought to abrogate the order of nature. Where the two parties consent, it is especially fitting for the Christian wife to double her efforts to be submissive to her husband—here regarded as an enemy of the truth—in order to win him if at all possible, as St. Peter advises in 1 Pet. 3:1.

Nevertheless, as matters stand today in the papal church, a believing wife ought not to relinquish her hope without striving and trying to direct her husband toward the road of salvation. No matter how great his obstinacy might be, she must not let herself be diverted from the faith; rather she must affirm it with constancy and steadfastness—whatever the dangers might be.

However, if the above party should be persecuted to the extent that she is in danger of denying her hope, then she is justified in fleeing. When a wife (or husband, as the case may be) has made her confession of faith and demonstrated how necessary it is not to consent to the abominations of the papacy, and if persecution arises against her for having done so and she is in grave peril, she may justly flee when God grants her an occasion to escape. For that does not constitute a willful divorce but occurs because of persecution.

Hence it is appropriate that the good lady who has sought our counsel endure until the above occurs. For according to her letters, she currently only holds her peace and quietly goes along; being required to taint herself before idols, she bows before them in condescension. For this reason she may not justify leaving her husband until she has amply declared her faith and resisted greater pressures than presently encountered. Therefore she needs to pray for God to strengthen her, then she needs to fight more valiantly than she has, drawing upon the power of the Holy Spirit, to show her husband her faith, doing so in gentleness and humility, explaining to him that she must not offend God for the sake of pleasing him.

We have also taken into consideration her husband's rudeness and cruelty, of which she has advised us. But that ought not to prevent her from taking heart to commend the matter to God. For whenever we are so preoccupied with fear that we are afraid to do what we ought, then we are guilty of infidelity. That is the foundation on which we should build.

If, after having attempted what we have advised, she should come into imminent peril, or her husband should persecute her to the point of death, then she is free to exercise that liberty which our Lord grants to all his own, i.e., to flee ravenous wolves.

From M. Beaty and B. Farley, eds., Calvin's Ecclesiastical Advice *(Louisville: Westminster/John Knox Press, 1991), 131–33.*

52. Letter on Usury (date unknown)

This example of Calvin's moral reasoning, on what was a major issue for all the churches in his time, belies many of the stereotypes. It pays careful attention to the Bible without being what we might call biblicist. It contextualizes the issue. It admits of gray areas and exceptions. It is humane. And it shows Calvin as cautious, even hesitant, about the rectitude of his own opinion.

From John Calvin to one of his friends.

I have not personally experienced this, but I have learned from the example of others how perilous it is to respond to the question for which you seek my counsel. For if we should totally prohibit the practice of usury, we would restrain consciences more rigidly than God himself. But if we permit it, then some, under this guise, would be content to act with unbridled license, unable to abide any limits.

If I were writing to you alone, I would have no fear of such a thing, for your prudence and the moderation of your heart are well known to me. But because you seek counsel for another, I fear that if I say anything he might permit himself more than I would prefer. Nonetheless, since I have no doubt that, in light of human nature and the matter at hand, you will thoughtfully consider the most expedient thing to do, I will share what I think.

First, there is no scriptural passage that totally bans all usury. For Christ's statement, which is commonly esteemed to manifest this, but which has to do with lending [Luke 6:35], has been falsely applied to usury. Furthermore, as elsewhere, when he rebukes the sumptuous guests and the ambitious invitations of the rich, he commands us to call instead the blind, the lame, and the other poor of the streets, who cannot repay. In so doing he corrects the world's vicious custom of lending money [only to those who can repay] and urges us, instead, to lend to those from whom no hope of repayment is possible.

Now we are accustomed to lending money where it will be safe. But we ought to help the poor, where our money will be at risk. For Christ's words far more emphasize our remembering the poor than our remembering the rich. Nonetheless, we need not conclude that all usury is forbidden.

The Law of Moses [Deut. 23: 19] is quite diplomatic, restraining us to act only within the bounds of equity and human reason. To be certain, it would be desirable if usurers were chased from every country, even if the practice were unknown. But since that is impossible, we ought at least to use it for the common good.

Passages in both the prophets and the psalms display the Holy Spirit's anger against usurers. There is a reference to a vile evil [Ps. 55:12, Vg.] that has been translated by the word *usura*. But since the Hebrew word *tok* can generally mean "defraud," it can be translated otherwise than "usury."

Even where the prophet specifically mentions usury, it is hardly a wonder that he mentions it among the other evil practices [Neh. 5:10]. The reason is that the more often usury is practiced with illicit license, the more often cruelty and other fraudulent activities arise.

What am I to say, except that usury almost always travels with two inseparable companions: tyrannical cruelty and the art of deception. This is why the Holy Spirit elsewhere advises all holy men, who praise and fear God, to abstain from usury, so much so that it is rare to find a good man who also practices usury.

The prophet Ezekiel [22:12] goes still further, for in citing the horrible case in which the vengeance of God has been kindled against the Jews, he uses the two Hebrew words *neshek* and *tarbith*—a form of usury so designated in Hebrew because of the manner in which it eats away at its victims. *Tarbith* means "to increase," or "add to," or "gain," and with good reason. For anyone interested in expanding his personal profit will take, or rather snatch, that gain from someone else. But undoubtedly the prophets only condemned usury as severely as they did because it was expressly prohibited for Jews to do. Hence when they rejected the clear commandment of God, they merited a still sterner rebuke.

Today, a similar objection against usury is raised by some who argue that since the Jews were prohibited from practicing it, we too, on the basis of our fraternal union, ought not to practice it. To that I respond that a political union is different. The situation in which God brought the Jews together, combined with other circumstances, made commerce without usury apt among them. Our situation is quite different. For that reason, I am unwilling to condemn it, so long as it is practiced with equity and charity.

The pretext that both St. Ambrose and Chrysostom cite is too frivolous in my judgment, that is, that money does not engender money. Does the sea or the earth [engender it]? I receive a fee from renting a house. Is that where money grows? Houses, in turn, are products of the trades, where money is also made. Even the value of a house can be exchanged for money. And what? Is money not more productive than merchandise or any other possession one could mention? Is it lawful to make money by renting a piece of ground, yet unlawful to make it from money? What? When you buy a field, is money not making money?

How do merchants increase their wealth? By being industrious, you answer. I readily admit what even children can see, that if you lock your money in a chest, it will not increase. Moreover, no one borrows money from others with the intention of hiding it or not making a profit. Consequently, the gain is not from the money but from profit.

We may therefore conclude that, although at first such subtleties appear convincing, upon closer examination they evaporate, since there is no substance to them. Hence, I conclude that we ought not to judge usury according to a few passages of scripture, but in accordance with the principle of equity.

An example ought to clarify the matter. Take a rich man whose wealth lies in possessions and rents but who has no money on hand. A second, whose wealth is somewhat more moderate—though less than the first—soon comes into money. If an opportunity should arise, the second person can easily buy what he wants, while the first will have to ask the latter for a loan. It is in the power of the second, under the rules of bargaining, to impose a fee on the first's goods until he repays, and in this manner the first's condition will be improved, although usury has been practiced.

Now, what makes a contract just and honest or unjust and dishonest? Has not the first fared better by means of an agreement involving usury by his neighbor than if the second had compelled him to mortgage or pawn his goods? To deny this is to play with God in a childish manner, preferring words over the truth itself. As if it were in our power, by changing words, to transform virtue into vice or vice into virtue. I certainly have no quarrel here.

I have said enough; you will be able to weigh this more diligently on your own. Nonetheless, I should hope that you will always keep in mind that what we must bring under judgment are not words but deeds themselves.

Now I come to the exceptions. For, as I said at the beginning, we must proceed with caution, as almost everyone is looking for some word to justify his intention. Hence, I must reiterate that when I approve of some usury, I am not extending my approval to all its forms. Furthermore, I disapprove of anyone engaging in usury as his form of occupation. Finally, I grant nothing without listing these additional exceptions.

The first is that no one should take interest [usury] from the poor, and no one, destitute by virtue of indigence or some affliction or calamity, should be forced into it. The second exception is that whoever lends should not be so preoccupied with gain as to neglect his necessary duties, nor, wishing to protect his money, disdain his poor brothers. The third exception is that no principle be followed that is not in accord with natural equity, for everything should be examined in the light of Christ's precept: Do unto others as you would have them do unto you. This precept is applicable every time. The fourth exception is that whoever borrows should make at least as much, if not more, than the amount borrowed. In the fifth place, we ought not to determine what is lawful by basing it on the common practice or in accordance with the iniquity of the world, but should base it on a principle derived from the Word of God. In the sixth place, we ought not to consider only the private advantage of those with whom we deal but should keep in mind what is best for the common good. For it is quite obvious that the interest a merchant pays is a public fee. Thus we should see that the contract will benefit all rather than hurt. In the seventh place, one ought not to exceed the rate that a country's public laws allow. Although this may not always suffice, for such laws quite often permit what they are able to correct or repress. Therefore one ought to prefer a principle of equity that can curtail abuse.

But rather than valuing my own opinion over yours, I desire only that you act in such a humane way that nothing more need be said on the matter. With that in mind, I have composed these thoughts more out of a desire to please you than out of any confidence of satisfying you. But owing to your kindness toward me, I know you will take to heart what I have offered.

[I commit you] to God, my most excellent and honored friend. May he preserve you and your family. Amen.

✠

From Beaty and Farley, Calvin's Ecclesiastical Advice, *139–43.*

The Servetus Affair

53. Letter from David Joris to Servetus' Judges (1553)

Michael Servetus (ca. 1511–1553), a Spanish physician with theological interests, was internationally notorious for his heretical views on the Trinity. In 1553 he escaped from the Roman Catholic Inquisition and showed up in Geneva where Calvin promptly had him arrested. On hearing of this, David Joris, an Anabaptist leader, issued the following appeal on Servetus' behalf.

Most noble, just, worthy, gracious, dear lords, now that I, your friend and brother in the Lord Jesus Christ, have heard what has happened to the good, worthy Servetus, how that he was delivered into your hands and power by no friendliness and love but through envy and hate, as will be made manifest in the days of judgment to those whose eyes are now blinded by cunning so that they cannot understand the ground of the truth. God give them to understand. The report has gone everywhere, and even to my ears, that the learned preachers or shepherds of souls have taken counsel and written to certain cities who have resolved to pass sentence to put him to death. This news has so stirred me that I can have no peace on behalf of our religion and the holy churches far and near, which stand fast in the love and unity of Christ, until I have raised my voice as a member of the body of Christ, until I have opened my heart humbly before your Highnesses and freed my conscience. I trust that the learned, perverted, carnal, and bloodthirsty may have no weight and make no impression on you, and if they should ingratiate themselves with you as did the scribes and Pharisees with Pilate in the case of our Lord Jesus, they will displease the King of kings and the teacher of all, Christ, who taught that no one should be crucified or put to death for his teaching. He himself was rather crucified and put to death. Yes, not only that, but he has severely forbidden persecution. Will it not then be a great perversion, blindness, evil, and darkness to indulge in impudent disobedience through hate and envy? They must first themselves have been deranged before they could bring a life to death, damn a soul forever, and hasten it to hell. Is that a Christian procedure or a true spirit? I say eternally no, however plausible it may appear. If the preachers are not of this mind and wish to avoid the sin against the Holy Spirit, let them be wary of seizing and killing men for their good intentions and belief according to their understanding, especially when these ministers stand so badly in other people's books that they dare not go out of their own city and land. Let them remember that they are called, sent, and anointed of God to save souls, to bring men to right and truth—that is, to make alive the dead, and not to destroy, offend, and corrupt, let alone to take life. This belongs to him alone to whom it is given, who was crucified, who died, and who suffered. . . .

Noble, wise, and prudent lords, consider what would happen if free rein were given to our opponents to kill heretics. How many men would be left on earth if each had this power over the other, inasmuch as each considers the other a heretic? The Jews so regard the Christians, so do the Saracens and the Turks, and the Christians reciprocate. The papists and the Lutherans, the Zwinglians and the Anabaptists, the Calvinists and the Adiaphorists, mutually ban each other. Because of these differences of opinion should men hate and kill each other? "Whoso sheddeth man's blood, by man shall his blood be shed," as Scripture says. Let us, then, not take the sword, and if anyone is of an erroneous and evil mind and understanding let us pray for him and awaken him to love, peace, and unity. . . .

And if the aforementioned Servetus is a heretic or a sectary before God, . . . we should inflict on him no harm in any of his members, but admonish him in a friendly way and at most banish him from the city, if he will not give up his obstinacy and stop disturbing the peace by his teaching . . . that he may come to a better mind and no longer molest your territory. No one should go beyond this. . . .

The Lord himself will judge of soul and spirit and will separate the good from the bad. . . . He "maketh his sun to rise on the evil and the good" and wills that we should imitate him in his long-suffering, graciousness, and mercy. He instructed the servants, who wished to anticipate the harvest as the apostles wished to call down fire from heaven, to leave the tares with the wheat. At the harvest he will send his angels who have knowledge and understanding to separate the good from the bad, the lies from the truth, the pure from the impure, for God's judgments are true and eternal and cannot fail . . . but great insufficiency shall be found in men when the day of light and the spirit of perfection shall appear. . . .

Those who have an evil spirit should be instructed, not put to death in the time of their ignorance and blindness similar to Paul's. That no one should assume judgment, the Lord has given us a new commandment in love that we do unto others as we would that they should do unto us. So be merciful, kind, and good, doing as it has been done to your Honors, and as the Lord wishes. "Judge not that ye be not judged." Condemn no man that ye be not condemned. Shed no blood and do no violence, my dear lords. Understand whose disciples you are, for nothing has the Lord punished more and forgiven less than the shedding of innocent blood and idolatry. Follow no one and believe in no one above God or Christ, who is Lord in spirit and truth. . . . Although I have withheld my name, you should not give this communication less consideration.

✝

From C. L. Manschreck, ed., A History of Christianity, Vol. 2: The Church from the Reformation to the Present (Grand Rapids: Baker Book House, 1964), 96–98.

54. Letters from Servetus to the Geneva Council (1553)

Languishing in prison since mid-August, Servetus wrote to the Geneva Council on 15 September, and then again on 10 October.

✝

I humbly beg that you [members of the council] cut short these long delays and deliver me from prosecution. You see that Calvin is at the end of his rope, not knowing what to say and for his pleasure wishes to make me rot in prison. The lice eat me alive. My clothes are torn and I have nothing for a change, neither jacket nor shirt, but a bad one. I have addressed to you another petition which was according to God and to impede it Calvin cites Justinian. He is in a bad way to quote against me what he does not himself credit, for he does not believe what Justinian has said about the holy church of bishops and priests and other matters of religion and knows well that the church was already degenerated. It is a great shame, the more so that I have been caged here for five weeks and he has not urged against me a single passage.

My lords, I have also asked you to give me a procurator or advocate as you did to my opponent, who was not in the same straits as I, who am a stranger and ignorant of the customs of the country. You permitted it to him,

but not to me, and you have liberated him from prison before knowing. I petition you that my case be referred to the Council of Two Hundred with my requests, and if I may appeal there I do so ready to assume all the cost, loss and interest of the law of an eye for an eye, both against the first accuser and against Calvin, who has taken up the case himself.

Done in your prisons of Geneva. September 15, 1553. Michael Servetus in his own cause.

Honored sirs, It is now three weeks that I have sought an audience and have been unable to secure one. I beg you for the love of Jesus Christ not to refuse me what you would not refuse to a Turk, who sought justice at your hands. I have some important and necessary matters to communicate to you.

As for what you commanded that something be done to keep me clean, nothing has been done and I am in a worse state than before. The cold greatly distresses me, because of my colic and rupture, causing other complaints which I should be ashamed to describe. It is great cruelty that I have not permission to speak if only to remedy my necessities. For the love of God, honored sirs, give your order whether for pity or duty.

Done in your prisons of Geneva, October 10, 1553. Michael Servetus.

From Manschreck, History of Christianity, vol. 2, 98–99.

55. Verdict and Sentence for Michael Servetus (1553)

The trial finally took place in late October. Calvin concurred of course with the verdict

and sentence, though he recommended a more humane form of execution, beheading. On 27 October Servetus was burned at the stake, as the sentence specified. Letters congratulating Calvin arrived from both Roman Catholic and Lutheran authorities.

✠

The sentence pronounced against Michael Servetus de Villeneufve of the Kingdom of Aragon in Spain who some twenty-three or twenty-four years ago printed a book at Hagenau in Germany against the Holy Trinity containing many great blasphemies to the scandal of the said churches of Germany, the which book he freely confesses to have printed in the teeth of the remonstrances made to him by the learned and evangelical doctors of Germany. In consequence he became a fugitive from Germany. Nevertheless he continued in his errors, and, in order the more to spread the venom of his heresy, he printed secretly a book in Vienne of Dauphiny full of the said heresies and horrible, execrable blasphemies against the Holy Trinity, against the Son of God, against the baptism of infants and the foundations of the Christian religion. He confesses that in this book he called believers in the Trinity Trinitarians and atheists. He calls this Trinity a diabolical monster with three heads. He blasphemes detestably against the Son of God, saying that Jesus Christ is not the Son of God from eternity. He calls infant baptism an invention of the devil and sorcery. His execrable blasphemies are scandalous against the majesty of God, the Son of God and the Holy Spirit. This entails the murder and ruin of many souls. Moreover he wrote a letter to one of our ministers in which, along with other numerous blasphemies, he declared our holy evangelical religion to be without faith and without God and that in place of God we have a three-headed Cerberus. He confesses that because of this abominable book he was made a prisoner at Vienne and perfidiously escaped. He has been burned there in effigy together with five bales of his books. Nevertheless, having been in prison in our city, he persists maliciously in his detestable errors and calumniates true Christians and faithful followers of the immaculate Christian tradition.

Wherefore we Syndics, judges of criminal cases in this city, having witnessed the trial conducted before us at the instance of our lieutenant against you "Michael Servetus de Villeneufve" of the Kingdom of Aragon in Spain, and having seen your voluntary and repeated confessions and your books, judge that you, Servetus, have for a long time promulgated false and thoroughly heretical doctrine, despising all remonstrances and corrections and that you have with malicious and perverse obstinacy sown and divulged even in printed books opinions against God the Father, the Son and the Holy Spirit, in a word against the fundamentals of the Christian religion, and that you have tried to make a schism and trouble the church of God by which many souls may have been ruined and lost, a thing horrible, shocking, scandalous and infectious. And you have had neither shame nor horror of setting yourself against the divine Majesty and the Holy Trinity, and so you have obstinately tried to infect the world with your stinking heretical poison. . . . For these and other reasons, desiring to purge the church of God of such infection and cut off the rotten member, having taken counsel with our citizens and having invoked the name of God to give just judgment . . . having God and the Holy Scriptures before our eyes, speaking in the name of the Father, Son and Holy Spirit, we now in writing give final sentence and condemn you, Michael Servetus, to be bound and taken to Champel and there attached to a stake and burned with your books to ashes. And so you shall finish your days and give an example to others who would commit the like.

✠

From Manschreck, History of Christianity, *2.99.*

Theology: *Institutes of the Christian Religion* (1559)

Calvin initially wrote this book in 1536 to instruct novices in the "new" faith, but partly also to clarify matters in his own mind. He dedicated it to the king of France who, he hoped, would see that this faith was not really new at all, but rather the original and authentic Christianity, and for that reason would put an end to the persecution of Calvin's French followers. In the following years, as his thought developed, Calvin continually revised and expanded the work. The book thus went through five major editions, all written in Latin and also translated by Calvin into French. The last Latin edition appeared in 1559.

Calvin's project in this work was inseparably related to his commentaries on Scripture. Its purpose, he said in the last edition, was to prepare church leaders for the study of the "sacred volume." It paves the way for such study by giving the reader an idea of what to look for in Scripture and organizing what is found there. Thus, Calvin believed, this book is an "indispensable prerequisite" if one wants to rightly and more easily understand the Bible.

If Luther was the polemical genius of the Reformation, Calvin was its systematic genius. His *Institutes* presents the reader with a theological "system." This means, first, that Calvin translates what he understands to be the revealed truths of the Bible from the alien thought-forms of the ancient Near East into thought-forms understandable to sixteenth-century Christians. It means that these truths are arranged into a logical and coherent pattern, and interpreted with a view to their internal consistency. And it means that the central and most fundamental belief of the Christian religion, as Calvin understands it, is allowed to "control" the interpretation of all the rest. The result is a supremely "systematic" statement of Christian belief, one that is fully deserving of a place alongside the great theological systems of Thomas Aquinas, Friedrich Schleiermacher and Karl Barth. A large part of Calvin's fame rests on this achievement.

The book is often heavy going for beginners. However, as many generations of theologians have found, it rewards patient study. It is divided into four sections. Book I deals with God as creator (included here are sections on the knowledge of God and Scripture); Book II treats God as redeemer (sections on original sin and Christ); Book III focuses on the grace of Christ (sections on the Holy Spirit, the Christian life, and predestination); and Book IV takes up the topic of the external means of grace (sections on the church, the Lord's Supper, and civil government). By including selections from each of the four parts, I hope to enable readers to glimpse the full scope of Calvin's system.

✠

56. Knowledge of God

Book I, The Knowledge of God the Creator

The Knowledge of God and That of Ourselves are Connected. How They Are Interrelated

1. Without Knowledge of Self There Is No Knowledge of God.

Nearly all the wisdom we possess, that is to say, true and sound wisdom, consists of two parts: the knowledge of God and of ourselves. But, while joined by many bonds, which one precedes and brings forth the other is not easy to discern. In the first place, no one can look upon himself without immediately turning his thoughts to the contemplation of God, in whom he "lives and moves" [Acts 17:28]. For, quite clearly, the mighty gifts with which we are endowed are hardly from ourselves; indeed, our very being is nothing but subsistence in the one God. Then, by these benefits shed like dew from heaven upon us, we are led as by rivulets to the spring itself. Indeed, our very poverty better discloses the infinitude of benefits reposing in God. The miserable ruin, into which the rebellion of the first man cast us, especially compels us to look upward. Thus, not only will we, in fasting and hungering, seek thence what we lack; but, in being aroused by fear, we shall learn humility. For, as a veritable world of miseries is to be found in mankind, and we are thereby despoiled of divine raiment, our shameful nakedness exposes a teeming horde of infamies. Each of us must, then, be so stung by the consciousness of his own unhappiness as to attain at least some knowledge of God. Thus, from the feeling of our own ignorance, vanity, poverty, infirmity, and—what is more—depravity and corruption, we recognize that the true light of wisdom, sound virtue, full abundance of every good, and purity of righteousness rest in the Lord alone. To this extent we are prompted by our own ills to contemplate the good things of God; and we cannot seriously aspire to him before we begin to become displeased with ourselves. For what man in all the world would not gladly remain as he is—what man does not remain as he is—so long as he does not know himself, that is, while content with his own gifts,

and either ignorant or unmindful of his own misery? Accordingly, the knowledge of ourselves not only arouses us to seek God, but also, as it were, leads us by the hand to find him.

2. Without Knowledge of God There Is No Knowledge of Self.

Again, it is certain that man never achieves a clear knowledge of himself unless he has first looked upon God's face, and then descends from contemplating him to scrutinize himself. For we always seem to ourselves righteous and upright and wise and holy—this pride is innate in all of us—unless by clear proofs we stand convinced of our own unrighteousness, foulness, folly, and impurity. Moreover, we are not thus convinced if we look merely to ourselves and not also to the Lord, who is the sole standard by which this judgment must be measured. For, because all of us are inclined by nature to hypocrisy, a kind of empty image of righteousness in place of righteousness itself abundantly satisfies us. And because nothing appears within or around us that has not been contaminated by great immorality, what is a little less vile pleases us as a thing most pure—so long as we confine our minds within the limits of human corruption. Just so, an eye which is shown nothing but black objects judges something dirty white or even rather darkly mottled to be whiteness itself. Indeed we can discern still more clearly from the bodily senses how much we are deluded in estimating the powers of the soul. For if in broad daylight we either look down upon the ground or survey whatever meets our view round about, we seem to ourselves endowed with the strongest and keenest sight; yet when we look up to the sun and gaze straight at it, that power of sight which was particularly strong on earth is at once blunted and confused by a great brilliance, and thus we are compelled to admit that our keenness in looking upon things earthly is sheer dullness when it comes to the sun. So it happens in estimating our spiritual goods. As long as we do not look beyond the earth, being quite content with our own righteousness, wisdom, and virtue, we flatter ourselves most sweetly, and fancy ourselves all but demigods. Suppose we but once begin to raise our thoughts to God, and to ponder his nature, and how completely perfect are his righteousness, wisdom, and power—the straightedge to which we must be shaped. Then, what masquerading earlier as righteousness was pleasing in us will soon grow filthy in its consummate wickedness. What wonderfully impressed us under the name of wisdom will stink in its very foolishness. What wore the face of power will prove itself the most miserable weakness. That is, what in us seems perfection itself corresponds ill to the purity of God.

3. Man before God's Majesty

Hence that dread and wonder with which Scripture commonly represents the saints as stricken and overcome whenever they felt the presence of God. Thus it comes about that we see men who in his absence normally remained firm and constant, but who, when he manifests his glory, are so shaken and struck dumb as to be laid low by the dread of death—are in fact overwhelmed by it and almost annihilated. As a consequence, we must infer that man is never sufficiently touched and affected by the awareness of his lowly state until he has compared himself with God's majesty. Moreover, we have numerous examples of this consternation both in the Book of Judges and in the prophets. So frequent was it that this expres-

sion was common among God's people: "We shall die, for the Lord has appeared to us" [Judg. 13:22; Isa. 6:5; Ezek. 2:1; 1:28; Judg. 6:22-23; and elsewhere]. The story of Job, in its description of God's wisdom, power, and purity, always expresses a powerful argument that overwhelms men with the realization of their own stupidity, impotence, and corruption [cf. Job 38:1ff.]. and not without cause: for we see how Abraham recognizes more clearly that he is earth and dust [Gen. 18:27] when once he had come nearer to beholding God's glory; and how Elijah, with uncovered face, cannot bear to await his approach, such is the awesomeness of his appearance [1 Kgs. 19:13]. And what can man do, who is rottenness itself [Job 13:28] and a worm [Job 7:5; Ps. 22:6], when even the very cherubim must veil their faces out of fear [Isa. 6:2]? It is this indeed of which the prophet Isaiah speaks: "The sun will blush and the moon be confounded when the Lord of Hosts shall reign" [Isa. 24:23]; that is, when he shall bring forth his splendor and cause it to draw nearer, the brightest thing will become darkness before it [Isa. 2:10, 19f.].

Yet, however the knowledge of God and of ourselves may be mutually connected, the order of right teaching requires that we discuss the former first, then proceed afterward to treat the latter. . . .

57. Scripture

Scripture Is Needed as Guide and Teacher for Anyone Who Would Come to God the Creator

1. God Bestows the Actual Knowledge of Himself upon Us Only in the Scriptures.

That brightness which is borne in upon the eyes of all men both in heaven and on earth is more than enough to withdraw all support from men's ingratitude—just as God, to involve the human race in the same guilt, sets forth to all without exception his presence portrayed in his creatures. Despite this, it is needful that another and better help be added to direct us aright to the very Creator of the universe. It was not in vain, then, that he added the light of his Word by which to become known unto salvation; and he regarded as worthy of this privilege those whom he pleased to gather more closely and intimately to himself. For because he saw the minds of all men tossed and agitated, after he chose the Jews as his very own flock, he fenced them about that they might not sink into oblivion as others had. With good reason he holds us by the same means in the pure knowledge of himself, since otherwise even those who seem to stand firm before all others would soon melt away. Just as old or bleary-eyed men and those with weak vision, if you thrust before them a most beautiful volume, even if they recognize it to be some sort of writing, yet can scarcely construe two words, but with the aid of spectacles will begin to read distinctly; so Scripture, gathering up the otherwise confused knowledge of God in our minds, having dispersed our dullness, clearly shows us the true God. This, therefore, is a special gift, where God, to instruct the church, not merely uses mute teachers but also opens his own most hallowed lips. Not only does he teach the elect to look upon a god, but also shows himself as the God upon whom they are to look. He has from the beginning maintained this plan for his church, so that besides these common proofs he also put forth his Word, which is a more direct and more certain mark whereby he is to be recognized.

There is no doubt that Adam, Noah, Abraham, and the rest of the patriarchs with this assistance penetrated to the intimate knowledge of him that in a way distinguished them from unbelievers. I am not yet speaking of the proper doctrine of faith whereby they had been illumined unto the hope of eternal life. For, that they might pass from death to life, it was necessary to recognize God not only as Creator but also as redeemer, for undoubtedly they arrived at both from the Word. First in order came that kind of knowledge by which one is permitted to grasp who that God is who founded and governs the universe. Then that other inner knowledge was added, which alone quickens dead souls, whereby God is known not only as the founder of the universe and the sole author and ruler of all that is made, but also in the person of the mediator as the redeemer. But because we have not yet come to the fall of the world and the corruption of nature, I shall now forego discussion of the remedy. My readers therefore should remember that I am not yet going to discuss that covenant by which God adopted to himself the sons of Abraham, or that part of doctrine which has always separated believers from unbelieving folk, for it was founded in Christ. But here I shall discuss only how we should learn from Scripture that God, the Creator of the universe, can by sure marks be distinguished from all the throng of feigned gods. Then, in due order, that series will lead us to the redemption. We shall derive many testimonies from the New Testament, and other testimonies also from the Law and the Prophets, where express mention is made of Christ. Nevertheless, all things will tend to this end, that God, the artificer of the universe, is made manifest to us in Scripture, and that what we ought to think of him is set forth there, lest we seek some uncertain deity by devious paths.

2. The Word of God as Holy Scripture

But whether God became known to the patriarchs through oracles and visions or by the work and ministry of men, he put into their minds what they should then hand down to their posterity. At any rate, there is no doubt that firm certainty of doctrine was engraved in their hearts, so that they were convinced and understood that what they had learned proceeded from God. For by his Word, God rendered faith unambiguous forever, a faith that should be superior to all opinion. Finally, in order that truth might abide forever in the world with a continuing succession of teaching and survive through all ages, the same oracles he had given to the patriarchs it was his pleasure to have recorded, as it were, on public tablets. With this intent the law was published, and the prophets afterward added as its interpreters. For even though the use of the law was manifold, as will be seen more clearly in its place, it was especially committed to Moses and all the prophets to teach the way of reconciliation between God and men, whence also Paul calls "Christ the end of the law" [Rom. 10:4]. Yet I repeat once more: besides the specific doctrine of faith and repentance that sets forth Christ as mediator, Scripture adorns with unmistakable marks and tokens the one true God, in that he has created and governs the universe, in order that he may not be mixed up with the throng of false gods. Therefore, however fitting it may be for man seriously to turn his eyes to contemplate God's works, since he has been placed in this most glorious theater to be a spectator of them, it is fitting that he prick up his ears to the Word, the better to profit. And it is therefore no wonder that those who were born in darkness become more and more hardened in their insensibility; for there are very few who, to contain themselves within bounds, apply themselves teachably to God's Word, but they rather exult in their own vanity. Now, in order that true religion may shine upon us, we ought to hold that it must take its beginning from heavenly doctrine and that no one can get even the slightest taste of right and sound doctrine unless he be a pupil of Scripture. Hence, there also emerges the beginning of true understanding when we reverently embrace what it pleases God there to witness of himself. But not only faith, perfect and in every way complete, but all right knowledge of God is born of obedience. And surely in this respect God has, by his singular providence, taken thought for mortals through all ages.

3. Without Scripture We Fall into Error.

Suppose we ponder how slippery is the fall of the human mind into forgetfulness of God, how great the tendency to every kind of error, how great the lust to fashion constantly new and artificial religions. Then we may perceive how necessary was such written proof of the heavenly doctrine, that it should neither perish through forgetfulness nor vanish through error nor be corrupted by the audacity of men. It is therefore clear that God has provided the assistance of the Word for the sake of all those to whom he has been pleased to give useful instruction because he foresaw that his likeness imprinted upon the most beautiful form of the universe would be insufficiently effective. Hence, we must strive onward by this straight path if we seriously aspire to the pure contemplation of God. We must come, I say, to the Word, where God is truly and vividly described to us from his works, while these very works are appraised not by our depraved judgment but by the rule of eternal truth. If we turn aside from the Word, as I have just now said, though we may strive with strenuous haste, yet, since we have got off the track, we shall never reach the goal. For we should so reason that the splendor of the divine countenance, which even the apostle calls "unapproachable" [1 Tim. 6:16], is for us like an inexplicable labyrinth unless we are conducted into it by the thread of the Word; so that it is better to limp along this path than to dash with all speed outside it. David very often, therefore, teaching that we ought to banish superstitions from the earth so that the pure religion may flourish, represented God as regnant [Ps. 93:1; 96:10; 97:1; 99:1; and the like]. Now he means by the word "regnant" not the power with which he is endowed, and which he exercises in governing the whole of nature, but the doctrine by which he asserts his lawful sovereignty. For the errors can never be uprooted from human hearts until true knowledge of God is planted therein.

4. Scripture Can Communicate to Us What the Revelation in the Creation Cannot.

Accordingly, the same prophet, after he states, "The heavens declare the glory of God, the firmament shows forth the works of his hands, the ordered succession of days and nights proclaims his majesty" [Ps. 19:1-2f.], then proceeds to mention his Word: "The law of the Lord is spotless, converting souls; the testimony of the Lord is faithful, giving wisdom to little ones; the righteous acts of the Lord are right, rejoicing hearts; the precept of the Lord is clear, enlightening eyes" [Ps. 18:8-9, Vg.; 19:7-8, EV]. For although he also includes other uses of the law, he means in general that, since God in vain calls all peoples to himself by the contemplation of heaven and earth, this is the very school of God's children. Psalm 29 looks to this same

end, where the prophet—speaking forth concerning God's awesome voice, which strikes the earth in thunder [v. 3], winds, rains, whirlwinds and tempests, causes mountains to tremble [v. 6], shatters the cedars [v. 5]—finally adds at the end that his praises are sung in the sanctuary because the unbelievers are deaf to all the voices of God that resound in the air [vv. 9-11]. Similarly, he thus ends another psalm where he has described the awesome waves of the sea: "Thy testimonies have been verified, the beauty and holiness of thy temple shall endure forevermore" [Ps. 93:5f.]. Hence, also, arises that which Christ said to the Samaritan woman, that her people and all other peoples worshipped they knew not what; that the Jews alone offered worship to the true God [John 4:22]. For, since the human mind because of its feebleness can in no way attain to God unless it be aided and assisted by his sacred Word, all mortals at that time—except for the Jews—because they were seeking God without the Word, had of necessity to stagger about in vanity and error.

Chapter 7, Scripture Must Be Confirmed by the Witness of the Spirit. Thus May Its Authority Be Established as Certain; and It Is a Wicked Falsehood That Its Credibility Depends on the Judgment of the Church.

1. Scripture Has Its Authority from God, Not from the Church.

Before I go any farther, it is worthwhile to say something about the authority of Scripture, not only to prepare our hearts to reverence it, but to banish all doubt. When that which is set forth is acknowledged to be the Word of God, there is no one so deplorably insolent—unless devoid also both of common sense and of humanity itself—as to dare impugn the credibility of him who speaks. Now daily oracles are not sent from heaven, for it pleased the Lord to hallow his truth to everlasting remembrance in the Scriptures alone [cf. John 5:39]. Hence the Scriptures obtain full authority among believers only when men regard them as having sprung from heaven, as if there the living words of God were heard. This matter is very well worth treating more fully and weighing more carefully. But my readers will pardon me if I regard more what the plan of the present work demands than what the greatness of this matter requires.

But a most pernicious error widely prevails that Scripture has only so much weight as is conceded to it by the consent of the church. As if the eternal and inviolable truth of God depended upon the decision of men! For they mock the Holy Spirit when they ask: Who can convince us that these writings came from God? Who can assure us that Scripture has come down whole and intact even to our very day? Who can persuade us to receive one book in reverence but to exclude another, unless the church prescribe a sure rule for all these matters? What reverence is due Scripture and what books ought to be reckoned within its canon depend, they say, upon the determination of the church. Thus these sacrilegious men, wishing to impose an unbridled tyranny under the cover of the church, do not care with what absurdities they ensnare themselves and others, provided they can force this one idea upon the simpleminded: that the church has authority in all things. Yet, if this is so, what will happen to miserable consciences seeking firm assurance of eternal life if all promises of it consist in and depend solely upon the judgment of men? Will they cease to vacillate and trem-

ble when they receive such an answer? Again, to what mockeries of the impious is our faith subjected, into what suspicion has it fallen among all men, if we believe that it has a precarious authority dependent solely upon the good pleasure of men!

2. The Church Is Itself Grounded upon Scripture.

But such wranglers are neatly refuted by just one word of the apostle. He testifies that the church is "built upon the foundation of the prophets and apostles" [Eph. 2:20]. If the teaching of the prophets and apostles is the foundation, this must have had authority before the church began to exist. Groundless, too, is their subtle objection that, although the church took its beginning here, the writings to be attributed to the prophets and apostles nevertheless remain in doubt until decided by the church. For if the Christian church was from the beginning founded upon the writings of the prophets and the preaching of the apostles, wherever this doctrine is found, the acceptance of it—without which the church itself would never have existed—must certainly have preceded the church. It is utterly vain, then, to pretend that the power of judging Scripture so lies with the church that its certainty depends upon churchly assent. Thus, while the church receives and gives its seal of approval to the Scriptures, it does not thereby render authentic what is otherwise doubtful or controversial. But because the church recognizes Scripture to be the truth of its own God, as a pious duty it unhesitatingly venerates Scripture. As to their question—How can we be assured that this has sprung from God unless we have recourse to the decree of the church?—it is as if someone asked: Whence will we learn to distinguish light from darkness, white from black, sweet from bitter?

Indeed, Scripture exhibits fully as clear evidence of its own truth as white and black things do of their color, or sweet and bitter things do of their taste.

3. Augustine Cannot Be Cited as Counterevidence.

Indeed, I know that statement of Augustine is commonly referred to, that he would not believe the gospel if the authority of the church did not move him to do so. But it is easy to grasp from the context how wrongly and deceptively they interpret this passage. Augustine was there concerned with the Manichees, who wished to be believed without controversy when they claimed, but did not demonstrate, that they themselves possessed the truth. Because in fact they used the gospel as a cloak to promote faith in their Mani, Augustine asks: "What would they do if they were to light upon a man who does not even believe in the gospel? By what kind of persuasion would they bring him around to their opinion?" Then he adds, "Indeed, I would not believe the gospel," etc., meaning that if he were alien to the faith, he could not be led to embrace the gospel as the certain truth of God unless constrained by the authority of the church. And what wonder if someone, not yet having known Christ, should have respect for men! Augustine is not, therefore, teaching that the faith of godly men is founded on the authority of the church; nor does he hold the view that the certainty of the gospel depends upon it. He is simply teaching that there would be no certainty of the gospel for unbelievers to win them to Christ if the consensus of the church did not impel them. And this he clearly confirms a little later, saying:

> When I praise what I believe, and laugh at what you believe, how do you think we are to judge, or what are we to do? Should we

not forsake those who invite us to a knowledge of things certain and then bid us believe things uncertain? Must we follow those who invite us first to believe what we are not yet strong enough to see, that, strengthened by this very faith, we may become worthy to comprehend what we believe [Col.1:4-11, 23]—with God himself, not men, now inwardly strengthening and illumining our mind?

These are Augustine's very words. From them it is easy for anyone to infer that the holy man's intention was not to make the faith that we hold in the Scriptures depend upon the assent or judgment of the church. He only meant to indicate what we also confess as true: those who have not yet been illumined by the Spirit of God are rendered teachable by reverence for the church, so that they may persevere in learning faith in Christ from the gospel. Thus, he avers, the authority of the church is an introduction through which we are prepared for faith in the gospel. For, as we see, he wants the certainty of the godly to rest upon a far different foundation. I do not deny that elsewhere, when he wishes to defend Scripture, which they repudiate, he often presses the Manichees with the consensus of the whole church. Hence, he reproaches Faustus for not submitting to the gospel truth—so firm, so stable, celebrated with such glory, and handed down from the time of the apostles through a sure succession. But it never occurs to him to teach that the authority which we ascribe to Scripture depends upon the definition or decree of men. He puts forward only the universal judgment of the church, in which he was superior to his adversaries, because of its very great value in this case. If anyone desires a fuller proof of this, let him read Augustine's little book *The Usefulness of Belief*. There he will find that the author recommends no other inducement to believe except what may provide us with an approach and be a suitable beginning for inquiry, as he himself says; yet we should not acquiesce in mere opinion, but should rely on sure and firm truth.

4. The Witness of the Holy Spirit: This Is Stronger Than All Proof.

We ought to remember what I said a bit ago: credibility of doctrine is not established until we are persuaded beyond doubt that God is its author. Thus, the highest proof of Scripture derives in general from the fact that God in person speaks in it. The prophets and apostles do not boast either of their keenness or of anything that obtains credit for them as they speak; nor do they dwell upon rational proofs. Rather, they bring forward God's holy name, that by it the whole world may be brought into obedience to him. Now we ought to see how apparent it is not only by plausible opinion but by clear truth that they do not call upon God's name heedlessly or falsely. If we desire to provide in the best way for our consciences—that they may not be perpetually beset by the instability of doubt or vacillation, and that they may not also boggle at the smallest quibbles—we ought to seek our conviction in a higher place than human reasons, judgments, or conjectures, that is, in the secret testimony of the Spirit. True, if we wished to proceed by arguments, we might advance many things that would easily prove—if there is any god in heaven—that the law, the prophets, and the gospel come from him. Indeed, ever-so-learned men, endowed with the highest judgment, rise up in opposition and bring to bear and display all their mental powers in this debate. Yet, unless they become hardened to the point of hopeless impudence, this confes-

sion will be wrested from them: that they see manifest signs of God speaking in Scripture. From this it is clear that the teaching of Scripture is from heaven. And a little later we shall see that all the books of Sacred Scripture far surpass all other writings. Yes, if we turn pure eyes and upright senses toward it, the majesty of God will immediately come to view, subdue our bold rejection, and compel us to obey.

Yet they who strive to build up firm faith in Scripture through disputation are doing things backwards. For my part, although I do not excel either in great dexterity or eloquence, if I were struggling against the most crafty sort of despisers of God, who seek to appear shrewd and witty in disparaging Scripture, I am confident it would not be difficult for me to silence their clamorous voices. And if it were a useful labor to refute their cavils, I would with no great trouble shatter the boasts they mutter in their lurking places. But even if anyone clears God's sacred Word from man's evil speaking, he will not at once imprint upon their hearts that certainty which piety requires. Since for unbelieving men religion seems to stand by opinion alone, they, in order not to believe anything foolishly or lightly, both wish and demand rational proof that Moses and the prophets spoke divinely. But I reply: the testimony of the Spirit is more excellent than all reason. For as God alone is a fit witness of himself in his Word, so also the Word will not find acceptance in men's hearts before it is sealed by the inward testimony of the Spirit. The same Spirit, therefore, who has spoken through the mouths of the prophets must penetrate into our hearts to persuade us that they faithfully proclaimed what had been divinely commanded. Isaiah very aptly expresses this connection in these words:

"My Spirit which is in you, and the words that I have put in your mouth, and the mouths of your offspring, shall never fail" [Isa. 59:21f.]. Some good folk are annoyed that a clear proof is not ready at hand when the impious, unpunished, murmur against God's Word. As if the Spirit were not called both "seal" and "guarantee" [2 Cor.1:22] for confirming the faith of the godly; because until he illumines their minds, they ever waver among many doubts!

5. Scripture Bears Its Own Authentication.

Let this point therefore stand: that those whom the Holy Spirit has inwardly taught truly rest upon Scripture, and that Scripture indeed is self-authenticated; hence, it is not right to subject it to proof and reasoning. And the certainty it deserves with us, it attains by the testimony of the Spirit. For even if it wins reverence for itself by its own majesty, it seriously affects us only when it is sealed upon our hearts through the Spirit. Therefore, illumined by his power, we believe neither by our own nor by anyone else's judgment that Scripture is from God; but above human judgment we affirm with utter certainty (just as if we were gazing upon the majesty of God himself) that it has flowed to us from the very mouth of God by the ministry of men. We seek no proofs, no marks of genuineness upon which our judgment may lean; but we subject our judgment and wit to it as to a thing far beyond any guesswork! This we do, not as persons accustomed to seize upon some unknown thing, which, under closer scrutiny, displeases them, but fully conscious that we hold the unassailable truth! Nor do we do this as those miserable men who habitually bind over their minds to the thralldom of superstition; but we feel that the undoubted

power of his divine majesty lives and breathes there. By this power we are drawn and inflamed, knowingly and willingly, to obey him, yet also more vitally and more effectively than by mere human willing or knowing!

God, therefore, very rightly proclaims through Isaiah that the prophets together with the whole people are witnesses to him; for they, instructed by prophecies, unhesitatingly held that God has spoken without deceit or ambiguity [Isa. 43:10]. Such, then, is a conviction that requires no reasons; such, a knowledge with which the best reason agrees—in which the mind truly reposes more securely and constantly than in any reasons; such, finally, a feeling that can be born only of heavenly revelation. I speak of nothing other than what each believer experiences within himself—though my words fall far beneath a just explanation of the matter.

I now refrain from saying more, since I shall have opportunity to discuss this matter elsewhere. Let us, then, know that the only true faith is that which the Spirit of God seals in our hearts. Indeed, the modest and teachable reader will be content with this one reason: Isaiah promised all the children of the renewed church that "they would be God's disciples" [Isa. 54:13f.]. God deems worthy of singular privilege only his elect, whom he distinguishes from the human race as a whole. Indeed, what is the beginning of true doctrine but a prompt eagerness to hearken to God's voice? But God asks to be heard through the mouth of Moses, as it is written: "Say not in your heart, who will ascend into heaven, or who will descend into the abyss: behold, the word is in your mouth" [conflation of Deut. 30:12, 14 and Ps. 107:26; 106:26, Vg.]. If God has willed this treasure of understanding to be hidden from his children, it is no wonder or absurdity that the multitude of men are so ignorant and stupid! Among the "multitude" I include even certain distinguished folk, until they become engrafted into the body of the church. Besides, Isaiah, warning that the prophetic teaching would be beyond belief, not only to foreigners but also to the Jews who wanted to be reckoned as members of the Lord's household, at the same time adds the reason: "The arm of God will not be revealed" to all [Isa. 53:1f.]. Whenever, then, the fewness of believers disturbs us, let the converse come to mind, that only those to whom it is given can comprehend the mysteries of God [cf. Matt. 13:11]. . . .

✠

58. Original Sin

Book II, The Knowledge of God the Redeemer in Christ, First Disclosed to the Fathers under the Law, and Then to Us in the Gospel

By the Fall and Revolt of Adam the Whole Human Race Was Delivered to the Curse, and Degenerated from Its Original Condition; the Doctrine of Original Sin

1. Wrong and Right Knowledge of Self

With good reason the ancient proverb strongly recommended knowledge of self to man. For if it is considered disgraceful for us not to know all that pertains to the business of human life, even more detestable is our ignorance of ourselves, by which, when making decisions in necessary matters, we miserably deceive and even blind ourselves!

But since this precept is so valuable, we ought more diligently to avoid applying it perversely. This, we observe, has happened to certain philosophers, who, while urging man to know himself, propose the goal of recog-

nizing his own worth and excellence. And they would have him contemplate in himself nothing but what swells him with empty assurance and puffs him up with pride [Gen. 1:27].

But knowledge of ourselves lies first in considering what we were given at creation and how generously God continues his favor toward us, in order to know how great our natural excellence would be if only it had remained unblemished; yet at the same time to bear in mind that there is in us nothing of our own, but that we hold on sufferance whatever God has bestowed on us. Hence we are ever dependent on him. Secondly, to call to mind our miserable condition after Adam's fall; the awareness of which, when all our boasting and self-assurance are laid low, should truly humble us and overwhelm us with shame. In the beginning God fashioned us after his image [Gen. 1:27] that he might arouse our minds both to zeal for virtue and to meditation upon eternal life. Thus, in order that the great nobility of our race (which distinguishes us from brute beasts) may not be buried beneath our own dullness of wit, it behooves us to recognize that we have been endowed with reason and understanding so that, by leading a holy and upright life, we may press on to the appointed goal of blessed immortality.

But that primal worthiness cannot come to mind without the sorry spectacle of our foulness and dishonor presenting itself by way of contrast, since in the person of the first man we have fallen from our original condition. From this source arise abhorrence and displeasure with ourselves, as well as true humility; and thence is kindled a new zeal to seek God, in whom each of us may recover those good things which we have utterly and completely lost.

2. Man by Nature Inclines to Deluded Self-Admiration.

Here, then, is what God's truth requires us to seek in examining ourselves: it requires the kind of knowledge that will strip us of all confidence in our own ability, deprive us of all occasion for boasting, and lead us to submission. We ought to keep this rule if we wish to reach the true goal of both wisdom and action. I am quite aware how much more pleasing is that principle which invites us to weigh our good traits rather than to look upon our miserable want and dishonor, which ought to overwhelm us with shame. There is, indeed, nothing that man's nature seeks more eagerly than to be flattered. Accordingly, when his nature becomes aware that its gifts are highly esteemed, it tends to be unduly credulous about them. It is thus no wonder that the majority of men have erred so perniciously in this respect. For, since blind self-love is innate in all mortals, they are most freely persuaded that nothing inheres in themselves that deserves to be considered hateful. Thus even with no outside support the utterly vain opinion generally obtains credence that man is abundantly sufficient of himself to lead a good and blessed life. But if any take a more modest attitude and concede something to God, so as not to appear to claim everything for themselves, they so divide the credit that the chief basis for boasting and confidence remains in themselves.

Nothing pleases man more than the sort of alluring talk that tickles the pride that itches in his very marrow. Therefore, in nearly every age, when anyone publicly extolled human nature in most favorable terms, he was listened to with applause. But however great such commendation of human excellence is that teaches man to be satisfied with himself, it does nothing but delight in its own sweetness; indeed, it so deceives as to drive those who assent to it into utter ruin. For what do we accomplish when, relying upon every vain assurance, we consider, plan, try, and undertake what we think is fitting; then—while in our very first efforts we are actually forsaken by and destitute of sane understanding as well as true virtue—we nonetheless rashly press on until we hurtle to destruction? Yet for those confident they can do anything by their own power, things cannot happen otherwise. Whoever, then, heeds such teachers as hold us back with thought only of our good traits will not advance in self-knowledge, but will be plunged into the worst ignorance.

3. The Two Chief Problems of Self-Knowledge

God's truth, therefore, agrees with the common judgment of all mortals, that the second part of wisdom consists in the knowledge of ourselves; yet there is much disagreement as to how we acquire that knowledge. According to carnal judgment, man seems to know himself very well, when, confident in his understanding and uprightness, he becomes bold and urges himself to the duties of virtue and, declaring war on vices, endeavors to exert himself with all his ardor toward the excellent and the honorable. But he who scrutinizes and examines himself according to the standard of divine judgment finds nothing to lift his heart to self-confidence. And the more deeply he examines himself, the more dejected he becomes, until, utterly deprived of all such assurance, he leaves nothing to himself with which to direct his life aright.

Yet God would not have us forget our original nobility, which he had bestowed upon our father Adam, and which ought truly to arouse in us a zeal for righteousness and goodness. For we cannot think upon either our first condition or to what purpose we were formed without being prompted to meditate upon immortality, and to yearn after the kingdom of God. That recognition, however, far from encouraging pride in us, discourages us and casts us into humility. For what is that origin? It is that from which we have fallen. What is that end of our creation? It is that from which we have been completely estranged, so that sick of our miserable lot we groan, and in groaning we sigh for that lost worthiness. But when we say that man ought to see nothing in himself to cause elation, we mean that he has nothing to rely on to make him proud.

Therefore, if it is agreeable, let us divide the knowledge that man ought to have of himself. First, he should consider for what purpose he was created and endowed with no mean gifts. By this knowledge he should arouse himself to meditation upon divine worship and the future life. Secondly, he should weigh his own abilities—or rather, lack of abilities. When he perceives this lack, he should lie prostrate in extreme confusion, so to speak, reduced to naught. The first consideration tends to make him recognize the nature of his duty; the second, the extent of his ability to carry it out. We shall discuss each as the order of teaching demands.

4. The History of the Fall Shows Us What Sin Is [Genesis 3]: Unfaithfulness.

Because what God so severely punished must have been no light sin but a detestable crime, we must consider what kind of sin there was in Adam's desertion that enkindled God's fearful vengeance against the whole of mankind. To regard Adam's sin as gluttonous intemperance (a common notion) is childish. As if the sum and head of all virtues lay in abstaining solely from one fruit, when all sorts of desirable delights abounded everywhere; and not only abundance but also magnificent variety was at hand in that blessed fruitfulness of earth!

We ought therefore to look more deeply. Adam was denied the tree of the knowledge of good and evil to test his obedience and prove that he was willingly under God's command. The very name of the tree shows the sole purpose of the precept was to keep him content with his lot and to prevent him from becoming puffed up with wicked lust. But the promise by which he was bidden to hope for eternal life so long as he ate from the tree of life, and, conversely, the terrible threat of death once he tasted of the tree of the knowledge of good and evil, served to prove and exercise his faith. Hence it is not hard to deduce by what means Adam provoked God's wrath upon himself. Indeed, Augustine speaks rightly when he declares that pride was the beginning of all evils. For if ambition had not raised man higher than was meet and right, he could have remained in his original state.

But we must take a fuller definition from the nature of the temptation which Moses describes. Since the woman through unfaithfulness was led away from God's Word by the serpent's deceit, it is already clear that disobedience was the beginning of the Fall. This Paul also confirms, teaching that all were lost through the disobedience of one man [Rom. 5:19]. Yet it is at the same time to be noted that the first man revolted from God's authority, not only because he was seized by Satan's blandishments, but also because, contemptuous of truth, he turned aside to falsehood. And surely, once we hold God's Word in contempt, we shake off all reverence for him. For, unless we listen attentively to him, his majesty will not dwell among us, nor his worship remain perfect.

Unfaithfulness, then, was the root of the Fall. But thereafter ambition and pride, together with ungratefulness, arose, because Adam by seeking more than was granted him shamefully spurned God's great bounty, which had been lavished upon him. To have been made in the likeness of God seemed a small matter to a son of earth unless he also attained equality with God—a monstrous wickedness! If apostasy, by which man withdraws from the authority of his maker—indeed insolently shakes off his yoke—is a foul and detestable offense, it is vain to extenuate Adam's sin. Yet it was not simple apostasy, but was joined with vile reproaches against God. These assented to Satan's slanders, which accused God of falsehood and envy and ill will. Lastly, faithlessness opened the door to ambition, and ambition was indeed the mother of obstinate disobedience; as a result, men, having cast off the fear of God, threw themselves wherever lust carried them. Hence Bernard rightly teaches that the door of salvation is opened to us when we receive the gospel today with our ears, even as death was then admitted by those same windows when they were opened to Satan [cf. Jer. 9:21]. For Adam would never have dared oppose God's authority unless he had disbelieved in God's Word. Here, indeed, was the best bridle to control all passions: the thought that nothing is better than to practice righteousness by obeying God's commandments; then, that the ultimate goal of the happy life is to be loved by him. Therefore Adam, carried away by the devil's blasphemies, as far as he was able extinguished the whole glory of God.

5. The First Sin As Original Sin

As it was the spiritual life of Adam to remain united and bound to his maker, so estrangement from him was the death of his soul. Nor is it any wonder that he consigned his race to ruin by his rebellion when he perverted the whole order of nature in heaven and on earth. "All creatures," says Paul, "are groaning" [Rom. 8:22], "subject to corruption, not of their own will" [Rom. 8:20]. If the cause is sought, there is no doubt that they are bearing part of the punishment deserved by man, for whose use they were created. Since, therefore, the curse, which goes about through all the regions of the world, flowed hither and yon from Adam's guilt, it is not unreasonable if it is spread to all his offspring. Therefore, after the heavenly image was obliterated in him, he was not the only one to suffer this punishment—that, in place of wisdom, virtue, holiness, truth, and justice, with which adornments he had been clad, there came forth the most filthy plagues, blindness, impotence, impurity, vanity, and injustice—but he also entangled and immersed his offspring in the same miseries.

This is the inherited corruption, which the church fathers termed "original sin," meaning by the word "sin" the depravation of a nature previously good and pure. There was much contention over this matter, inasmuch as nothing is farther from the usual view than for all to be made guilty by the guilt of one, and thus for sin to be made common. This seems to be the reason why the most ancient doctors of the church touched upon this subject so obscurely. At least they explained it less clearly than was fitting. Yet this timidity could not prevent Pelagius from rising up with the profane fiction that Adam sinned only to his own loss without harming his posterity. Through this subtlety Satan attempted to cover up the disease and thus to render it incurable. But when it was shown by the clear testimony of Scripture that sin was transmitted from the first man to all his posterity [Rom. 5:12], Pelagius quibbled that it was transmitted through imitation, not propagation. Therefore, good men (and Augustine above the rest) labored to show us that we are corrupted not by derived wickedness, but that we bear inborn defect from our mother's womb. To deny this was the height of shamelessness. But no man will wonder at the temerity of the Pelagians and Coelestians when he perceived from that holy man's warnings what shameless beasts they were in all other respects. Surely there is no doubt that David confesses himself to have been "begotten in iniquities, and conceived by his mother in sin" [Ps. 51:5f.]. There he does not reprove his father and mother for their sins; but, that he may better commend God's goodness toward himself, from his very conception he carries the confession of his own perversity. Since it is clear that this was not peculiar to David, it follows that the common lot of mankind is exemplified in him.

Therefore all of us, who have descended from impure seed, are born infected with the contagion of sin. In fact, before we saw the light of this life we were soiled and spotted in God's sight. "For who can bring a clean thing from an unclean? There is not one"—as the Book of Job says [Job 14:4, cf. Vg.].

6. Original Sin Does Not Rest Upon Imitation.

We hear that the uncleanness of the parents is so transmitted to the children that all without any exception are defiled at their begetting. But we will not find the beginning of this pollution unless we go back to the first parent of all, as its source. We must surely hold that Adam was not only the progenitor but, as it were, the root of human nature; and that therefore in his corruption mankind deserved to be vitiated. This the

apostle makes clear from a comparison of Adam with Christ. "As through one man sin came into the world and through sin death, which spread among all men when all sinned" [Rom. 5:12], thus through Christ's grace righteousness and life are restored to us [Rom. 5:17]. What nonsense will the Pelagians chatter here? That Adam's sin was propagated by imitation? Then does Christ's righteousness benefit us only as an example set before us to imitate? Who can bear such sacrilege! But if it is beyond controversy that Christ's righteousness, and thereby life, are ours by communication, it immediately follows that both were lost in Adam, only to be recovered in Christ; and that sin and death crept in through Adam, only to be abolished through Christ. These are no obscure words: "Many are made righteous by Christ's obedience as by Adam's disobedience they had been made sinners" [Rom. 5:19f.]. Here, then, is the relationship between the two: Adam, implicating us in his ruin, destroyed us with himself; but Christ restores us to salvation by his grace.

In such clear light of truth, I think that there is no need for longer or more laborious proof. In the first letter to the Corinthians, Paul wishes to strengthen the faith of the godly in the resurrection. Here he accordingly shows that the life lost in Adam is recovered in Christ [1 Cor. 15:22]. Declaring that all of us died in Adam, Paul at the same time plainly testifies that we are infected with the disease of sin. For condemnation could not reach those untouched by the guilt of iniquity. The clearest explanation of his meaning lies in the other part of the statement, in which he declares that the hope of life is restored in Christ. But it is well known that this occurs in no other way than that wonderful communication whereby Christ transfuses into us the power of his righteousness. As it is written elsewhere, "The Spirit is life to us because of righteousness" [Rom. 8:10f.]. There is consequently but one way for us to interpret the statement, "We have died in Adam": Adam, by sinning, not only took upon himself misfortune and ruin but also plunged our nature into like destruction. This was not due to the guilt of himself alone, which would not pertain to us at all, but was because he infected all his posterity with that corruption into which he had fallen.

Paul's statement that "by nature all are children of wrath" [Eph. 2:3] could not stand, unless they had already been cursed in the womb itself. Obviously, Paul does not mean "nature" as it was established by God, but as it was vitiated in Adam. For it would be most unfitting for God to be made the author of death. Therefore, Adam so corrupted himself that infection spread from him to all his descendants. Christ himself, our heavenly judge, clearly enough proclaims that all men are born wicked and depraved when he says that "whatever is born of flesh is flesh" [John 3:6], and therefore the door of life is closed to all until they have been reborn [John 3:5].

7. The Transmission of Sin from One Generation to Another

No anxious discussion is needed to understand this question, which troubled the Fathers not a little—whether the son's soul proceeds by derivation from the father's soul—because the contagion chiefly lies in it. With this we ought to be content: that the Lord entrusted to Adam those gifts which he willed to be conferred upon human nature. Hence Adam, when he lost the gifts received, lost them not only for himself but for us all. Who should worry about the derivation of the soul when he hears that Adam had received for us no less than for himself those gifts which he lost, and that they had not been given to one man but had been assigned to the whole human race? There is nothing absurd, then, in supposing that, when Adam was despoiled, human nature was left naked and destitute, or that when he was infected with sin, contagion crept into human nature. Hence, rotten branches came forth from a rotten root, which transmitted their rottenness to the other twigs sprouting from them. For thus were the children corrupted in the parent, so that they brought disease upon their children's children. That is, the beginning of corruption in Adam was such that it was conveyed in a perpetual stream from the ancestors into their descendants. For the contagion does not take its origin from the substance of the flesh or soul, but because it had been so ordained by God that the first man should at one and the same time have and lose, both for himself and for his descendants, the gifts that God had bestowed upon him.

But it is easy to refute the quibble of the Pelagians, who hold it unlikely that children should derive corruption from godly parents, inasmuch as the offspring ought rather to be sanctified by their parents' purity [cf. 1 Cor. 7:14]. For they descend not from their parents' spiritual regeneration but from their carnal generation. Hence, as Augustine says, whether a man is a guilty unbeliever or an innocent believer, he begets not innocent but guilty children, for he begets them from a corrupted nature. Now, it is a special blessing of God's people that they partake in some degree of their parents' holiness. This does not gainsay the fact that the universal curse of the human race preceded. For guilt is of nature, but sanctification, of supernatural grace.

8. The Nature of Original Sin

So that these remarks may not be made concerning an uncertain and unknown matter, let us define original sin. It is not my intention to investigate the several definitions proposed by various writers, but simply to bring forward the one that appears to me most in accordance with truth. Original sin, therefore, seems to be a hereditary depravity and corruption of our nature, diffused into all parts of the soul, which first makes us liable to God's wrath, then also brings forth in us those works which Scripture calls "works of the flesh" [Gal. 5:19]. And that is properly what Paul often calls sin. The works that come forth from it—such as adulteries, fornications, thefts, hatreds, murders, carousings—he accordingly calls "fruits of sin" [Gal. 5:19-21], although they are also commonly called "sins" in Scripture, and even by Paul himself.

We must, therefore, distinctly note these two things. First, we are so vitiated and perverted in every part of our nature that by this great corruption we stand justly condemned and convicted before God, to whom nothing is acceptable but righteousness, innocence, and purity. And this is not liability for another's transgression. For, since it is said that we became subject to God's judgment through Adam's sin, we are to understand it not as if we, guiltless and undeserving, bore the guilt of his offense but in the sense that, since we through his transgression have become entangled in the curse, he is said to have made us guilty. Yet not only has punishment fallen upon us from Adam, but a contagion imparted by him resides in us, which justly deserves punishment. For this reason, Augustine, though he often calls sin "another's" to show more clearly that it is distributed among us through propagation, nevertheless declares at the same time that it is peculiar to each. And the apostle himself most eloquently testifies that "death has spread to all because all have sinned" [Rom. 5:12]. That is, they have been enveloped in original sin and defiled by its stains. For that reason, even infants themselves, while they carry their condemnation along with them from the mother's womb, are guilty not of another's fault but of their own. For, even though the fruits of their iniquity have not yet come forth, they have the seed enclosed within them. Indeed, their whole nature is a seed of sin; hence it can be only hateful and abhorrent to God. From this it follows that it is rightly considered sin in God's sight, for without guilt there would be no accusation.

Then comes the second consideration: that this perversity never ceases in us, but continually bears new fruits—the works of the flesh that we have already described—just as a burning furnace gives forth flame and sparks, or water ceaselessly bubbles up from a spring. Thus those who have defined original sin as "the lack of the original righteousness, which ought to reside in us," although they comprehend in this definition the whole meaning of the term, have still not expressed effectively enough its power and energy. For our nature is not only destitute and empty of good, but so fertile and fruitful of every evil that it cannot be idle. Those who have said that original sin is "concupiscence" have used an appropriate word, if only it be added—something that most will by no means concede—that whatever is in man, from the understanding to the will, from the soul even to the flesh, has been defiled and crammed with this concupiscence. Or, to put it more briefly, the whole man is of himself nothing but concupiscence.

9. Sin Overturns the Whole Man.

For this reason, I have said that all parts of the soul were possessed by sin after Adam deserted the fountain of righteousness. For not only did a lower appetite seduce him, but unspeakable impiety occupied the very citadel of his mind, and pride penetrated to the depths of his heart. Thus it is pointless and foolish to restrict the corruption that arises thence only to what are called the impulses of the senses; or to call it the "kindling wood" that attracts, arouses, and drags into sin only that part which they term "sensuality." In this matter Peter Lombard has betrayed his complete ignorance. For, in seeking and searching out its seat, he says that it lies in the flesh, as Paul testifies; yet not intrinsically, but because it appears more in the flesh. As if Paul were indicating that only a part of the soul, and not its entire nature, is opposed to supernatural grace! Paul removes all doubt when he teaches that corruption subsists not in one part only, but that none of the soul remains pure or untouched by that mortal disease. For in his discussion of a corrupt nature Paul not only condemns the inordinate impulses of the appetites that are seen, but especially contends the mind is given over to blindness and the heart to depravity.

The whole third chapter of Romans is nothing but a description of original sin [vv. 1-20]. From the "renewal" that fact appears more clearly. For the Spirit, who is opposed to the old man and to the flesh, not only marks the grace whereby the lower or sensual part of the soul is corrected, but embraces the full reformation of all the parts. Consequently, Paul not only enjoins that brute appetites be brought to naught but bids us "be renewed in the spirit of our mind" [Eph. 4:23]; in another passage he similarly urges us to "be transformed in newness of mind" [Rom. 12: 2]. From this it follows that that part in which the excellence and nobility of the soul especially shine has not only been wounded, but so corrupted that it needs to be healed and to put on a new nature as well. We shall soon see to what extent sin occupies both mind and heart. Here I only want to suggest briefly that the whole man is overwhelmed—as by a deluge—from head to foot, so that no part is immune from sin and all that proceeds from him is to be imputed to sin. As Paul says, all turnings of the thoughts to the flesh are enmities against God [Rom. 8:7], and are therefore death [Rom. 8:6].

10. Sin Is Not Our Nature, but Its Derangement.

Now away with those persons who dare write God's name upon their faults, because we declare that men are vicious by nature! They perversely search out God's handiwork in their own pollution, when they ought rather to have sought it in that unimpaired and uncorrupted nature of Adam. Our destruction, therefore, comes from the guilt of our flesh, not from God, inasmuch as we have perished solely because we have degenerated from our original condition.

Let no one grumble here that God could have provided better for our salvation if he had forestalled Adam's fall. Pious minds ought to loathe this objection, because it manifests inordinate curiosity. Furthermore, the matter has to do with the secret of predestination, which will be discussed later in its proper place. Let us accordingly remember to impute our ruin to depravity of nature, in order that we may not accuse God himself, the author of nature. True, this deadly wound clings to nature, but it is a very important question whether the wound has been inflicted from outside or has been present from the beginning. Yet it is evident that the wound was inflicted through sin. We have, therefore, no reason to complain except against ourselves. Scripture has diligently noted this fact. For Ecclesiastes says: "This I know, that God made man upright, but they have sought out many devices." [Eccl. 7:29]. Obviously, man's ruin is to be ascribed to man alone; for he, having acquired righteousness by God's kindness, has by his own folly sunk into vanity.

11. "Natural" Corruption of the "Nature" Created by God

Therefore we declare that man is corrupted through natural vitiation, but a vitiation that did not flow from nature. We deny that it has flowed from nature in order to indicate that it is an adventitious quality which comes upon man rather than a substantial property which has been implanted from the beginning. Yet we call it "natural" in order that no man may think that anyone obtains it through bad conduct, since it holds all men fast by hereditary right. Our usage of the term is not without authority. The apostle states: "We are all by nature children of wrath" [Eph. 2:3]. How could God, who is pleased by the least of his works, have been hostile to the noblest of all his creatures? But he is hostile toward the corruption of his work rather than toward the work itself. Therefore if it is right to declare that man, because of his vitiated nature, is naturally abominable to God, it is also proper to say that man is naturally depraved and faulty. Hence Augustine, in view of man's corrupted nature, is not afraid to call "natural" those sins which necessarily reign in our flesh wherever God's grace is absent. Thus vanishes the foolish trifling of the Manichees, who, when

they imagined wickedness of substance in man, dared fashion another creator for him in order that they might not seem to assign the cause and beginning of evil to the righteous God. . . .

✠

59. Christh

To Know the Purpose for Which Christ Was Sent by the Father, and What He Conferred upon Us, We Must Look above All at Three Things in Him: the Prophetic Office, Kingship, and Priesthood

1. The Need of Understanding This Doctrine: Scriptural Passages Applicable to Christ's Prophetic Office

As Augustine rightly states, the heretics, although they preach the name of Christ, have herein no common ground with believers, but it remains the sole possession of the church. For if we diligently consider the things that pertain to Christ, we will find Christ among the heretics in name only, not in reality. So today the words "Son of God, redeemer of the world," resound upon the lips of the papists. Yet because they are satisfied with vain pretense of the name, and strip him of his power and dignity, Paul's words apply to them: "They do not hold fast to the Head" [Col. 2:19f.].

Therefore, in order that faith may find a firm basis for salvation in Christ, and thus rest in him, this principle must be laid down: the office enjoined upon Christ by the Father consists of three parts. For he was given to be prophet, king, and priest. Yet it would be of little value to know these names without understanding their purpose and use. The papists use these names, too, but coldly and rather ineffectually, since they do not know what each of these titles contains.

We have already said that although God, by providing his people with an unbroken line of prophets, never left them without useful doctrine sufficient for salvation, yet the minds of the pious had always been imbued with the conviction that they were to hope for the full light of understanding only at the coming of the Messiah. This expectation penetrated even to the Samaritans, though they never had known the true religion, as appears from the words of the woman: "When the Messiah comes, he will teach us all things" [John 4:25f.]. And the Jews did not rashly presume this in their minds; but, being taught by clear oracles, they so believed. Isaiah's saying is particularly well known: "Behold, I have made him a witness to the peoples, I have given him as a leader and commander for the peoples" [Isa. 55:4]. Elsewhere, Isaiah called him "messenger or interpreter of great counsel" [Isa. 9:6, conflated with Isa. 28:29 and Jer. 32:19]. For this reason, the apostle commends the perfection of the gospel doctrine, first saying: "In many and various ways God spoke of old to our fathers by the prophets" [Heb. 1:1]. Then he adds, "In these last days he has spoken to us through a beloved son" [Heb. 1:2f.]. But, because the task common to the prophets was to hold the church in expectation and at the same time to support it until the mediator's coming, we read that in their dispersion believers complained that they were deprived of that ordinary benefit: "We do not see our signs; there is no . . . prophet among us, . . . there is no one . . . who knows how long" [Ps. 74:9]. But when Christ was no longer far off, a time was appointed for Daniel "to seal both vision and prophet" [Dan. 9:24], not only that the prophetic utterance there mentioned might be authoritatively established, but also that believers

might patiently go without the prophets for a time because the fullness and culmination of all revelations was at hand.

2. The Meaning of the Prophetic Office for Us

Now it is to be noted that the title "Christ" pertains to these three offices: for we know that under the law prophets as well as priests and kings were anointed with holy oil. Hence the illustrious name of "Messiah" was also bestowed upon the promised mediator. As I have elsewhere shown, I recognize that Christ was called Messiah especially with respect to, and by virtue of, his kingship. Yet his anointings as prophet and as priest have their place and must not be overlooked by us. Isaiah specifically mentions the former in these words: "The Spirit of the Lord Jehovah is upon me, because Jehovah has anointed me to preach to the humble, . . . to bring healing to the brokenhearted, to proclaim liberation to the captives . . . , to proclaim the year of the Lord's good pleasure," etc. [Isa. 61:1-2; cf. Luke 4:18]. We see that he was anointed by the Spirit to be herald and witness of the Father's grace. And that not in the common way—for he is distinguished from other teachers with a similar office. On the other hand, we must note this: he received anointing, not only for himself that he might carry out the office of teaching, but for his whole body that the power of the Spirit might be present in the continuing preaching of the gospel. This, however, remains certain: the perfect doctrine he has brought has made an end to all prophecies. All those, then, who, not content with the gospel, patch it with something extraneous to it, detract from Christ's authority. The voice that thundered from heaven, "This is my beloved Son; . . . hear him" [Matt. 17:5; cf. Matt. 3:17], exalted him by a singular privilege beyond the rank of all others. Then this anointing was diffused from the Head to the members, as Joel had foretold: "Your sons shall prophesy and your daughters . . . shall see visions," etc. [Joel 2:28f.]. But when Paul says that he was given to us as our wisdom [1 Cor. 1:30], and in another place, "In him are hid all the treasures of knowledge and understanding" [Col. 2:3f.], he has a slightly different meaning. That is, outside Christ there is nothing worth knowing, and all who by faith perceive what he is like have grasped the whole immensity of heavenly benefits. For this reason, Paul writes in another passage: "I decided to know nothing precious . . . except Jesus Christ and him crucified" [1 Cor. 2:2f.]. This is very true, because it is not lawful to go beyond the simplicity of the gospel. And the prophetic dignity in Christ leads us to know that in the sum of doctrine as he has given it to us all parts of perfect wisdom are contained.

3. The Eternity of Christ's Dominion

I come now to kingship. It would be pointless to speak of this without first warning my readers that it is spiritual in nature. For from this we infer its efficacy and benefit for us, as well as its whole force and eternity. Now this eternity, which the angel in the Book of Daniel attributes to the person of Christ [Dan. 2:44], in the Gospel of Luke the angel justly applies to the salvation of the people [Luke 1:33]. But this eternity is also of two sorts or must be considered in two ways: the first pertains to the whole body of the church; the second belongs to each individual member. We must refer to the first kind the statement in the psalms: "Once for all I have sworn by my holiness; I will not lie to David. His line shall endure forever, his throne as long as the sun before me. Like the

moon, it shall be established forever; the witness of heaven is sure" [Ps. 89:35-37f.]. God surely promises here that through the hand of his Son he will be the eternal protector and defender of his church. We find the true fulfillment of this prophecy in Christ alone, inasmuch as immediately after Solomon's death the authority over the greater part of the kingdom was destroyed, and—to the shame of the family of David— was transferred to a private person [1 Kings 12]. Afterward it diminished more and more until it came to a sad and shameful end [2 Kings 24].

Isaiah's exclamation means the same thing: "As for his generation, who will tell it?" [Isa. 53:8f.]. For he declares that Christ will so survive death as to bind himself with his members. Therefore, whenever we hear of Christ as armed with eternal power, let us remember that the perpetuity of the church is secure in this protection. Hence, amid the violent agitation with which it is continually troubled, amid the grievous and frightful storms that threaten it with unnumbered calamities, it still remains safe. David laughs at the boldness of his enemies who try to throw off the yoke of God and his anointed, and says: "The kings and people rage in vain . . . , for he who dwells in heaven is strong enough to break their assaults" [Ps. 2:2, 4f.]. Thus he assures the godly of the everlasting preservation of the church, and encourages them to hope, whenever it happens to be oppressed. Elsewhere, speaking in the person of God, David says: "Sit at my right hand, till I make your enemies your footstool" [Ps. 110:1]. Here he asserts that, no matter how many strong enemies plot to overthrow the church, they do not have sufficient strength to prevail over God's immutable decree by which he appointed his Son eternal king.

Hence it follows that the devil, with all the resources of the world, can never destroy the church, founded as it is on the eternal throne of Christ.

Now with regard to the special application of this to each one of us—the same "eternity" ought to inspire us to hope for blessed immortality. For we see that whatever is earthly is of the world and of time, and is indeed fleeting. Therefore Christ, to lift our hope to heaven, declares that his "kingship is not of this world" [John 18:36]. In short, when any one of us hears that Christ's kingship is spiritual, aroused by this word let him attain to the hope of a better life; and since it is now protected by Christ's hand, let him await the full fruit of this grace in the age to come.

4. The Blessing of Christ's Kingly Office for Us

We have said that we can perceive the force and usefulness of Christ's kingship only when we recognize it to be spiritual. This is clear enough from the fact that, while we must fight throughout life under the cross, our condition is harsh and wretched. What, then, would it profit us to be gathered under the reign of the heavenly king, unless beyond this earthly life we were certain of enjoying its benefits? For this reason we ought to know that the happiness promised us in Christ does not consist in outward advantages—such as leading a joyous and peaceful life, having rich possessions, being safe from all harm, and abounding with delights such as the flesh commonly longs after. No, our happiness belongs to the heavenly life! In the world the prosperity and well-being of a people depend partly on an abundance of all good things and domestic peace, partly on strong defenses that protect them from outside attacks. In like manner, Christ enriches

his people with all things necessary for the eternal salvation of souls and fortifies them with courage to stand unconquerable against all the assaults of spiritual enemies. From this we infer that he rules—inwardly and outwardly—more for our own sake than his. Hence we are furnished, as far as God knows to be expedient for us, with the gifts of the Spirit, which we lack by nature. By these first fruits we may perceive that we are truly joined to God in perfect blessedness. Then, relying upon the power of the same Spirit, let us not doubt that we shall always be victorious over the devil, the world, and every kind of harmful thing. This is the purport of Christ's reply to the Pharisees: because the kingdom of God is within us, it will not come with observation [Luke 17:21, 20]. Probably because he professed himself king under whom God's highest blessing was to be expected, the Pharisees jestingly asked Christ to furnish his tokens. But he enjoined them to enter into their own consciences, because "the kingdom of God . . . is righteousness and peace and joy in the Holy Spirit" [Rom. 14:17]. This he did to prevent those otherwise too much inclined to things earthly from indulging in foolish dreams of pomp. These words briefly teach us what Christ's kingdom confers upon us. For since it is not earthly or carnal and hence subject to corruption, but spiritual, it lifts us up even to eternal life.

Thus it is that we may patiently pass through this life with its misery, hunger, cold, contempt, reproaches, and other troubles—content with this one thing: that our king will never leave us destitute, but will provide for our needs until, our warfare ended, we are called to triumph. Such is the nature of his rule, that he shares with us all that he has received from the Father. Now he arms and equips us with his power, adorns us with his beauty and magnificence, enriches us with his wealth. These benefits, then, give us the most fruitful occasion to glory, and also provide us with confidence to struggle fearlessly against the devil, sin, and death. Finally, clothed with his righteousness, we can valiantly rise above all the world's reproaches; and just as he himself freely lavishes his gifts upon us, so may we, in return, bring forth fruit to his glory.

5. The Spiritual Nature of His Kingly Office: The Sovereignty of Christ and of the Father

Therefore the anointing of the king is not with oil or aromatic unguents. Rather, he is called "Anointed" [*Christus*] of God because "the spirit of wisdom and understanding, the spirit of counsel and might . . . and of the fear of the Lord have rested upon him" [Isa. 11:2f.]. This is "the oil of gladness" with which the psalm proclaims he "was anointed above his fellows" [Ps. 45:7], for if such excellence were not in him, all of us would be needy and hungry. As has already been said, he did not enrich himself for his own sake, but that he might pour out his abundance upon the hungry and thirsty. The Father is said "not by measure to have given the Spirit to his Son" [John 3:34f.]. The reason is expressed as follows: "That from his fullness we might all receive grace upon grace" [John 1:16f.]. From this fountain flows that abundance of which Paul speaks: "Grace was given to each believer according to the measure of Christ's gift" [Eph. 4:7]. These statements quite sufficiently confirm what I have said: that Christ's kingdom lies in the Spirit, not in earthly pleasures or pomp. Hence we must forsake the world if we are to share in the kingdom.

A visible symbol of this sacred anointing was shown in Christ's baptism, when the Spirit hovered over him in the likeness of a dove [Luke 3:22; John 1:32]. It is nothing new, and ought not to seem absurd that the Spirit and his gifts are designated by the word "anointing" [1 John 2:20, 27]. For it is only in this way that we are invigorated. Especially with regard to heavenly life, there is no drop of vigor in us save what the Holy Spirit instills. For the Spirit has chosen Christ as his seat, that from him might abundantly flow the heavenly riches of which we are in such need. The believers stand unconquered through the strength of their king, and his spiritual riches abound in them. Hence they are justly called Christians.

Paul's statement does not detract from this eternity of which we have spoken: "Then . . . he will deliver the kingdom to his God and Father" [1 Cor. 15:24]. Likewise: "The Son himself will . . . be subjected . . . that God may be all in all" [1 Cor. 15:28; cf. Vg.]. He means only that in that perfect glory the administration of the kingdom will not be as it now is. The Father has given all power to the Son that he may by the Son's hand govern, nourish, and sustain us, keep us in his care, and help us. Thus, while for the short time we wander away from God, Christ stands in our midst, to lead us little by little to a firm union with God.

And surely, to say that he sits at the right hand of the Father is equivalent to calling him the Father's deputy, who has in his possession the whole power of God's dominion. For God mediately, so to speak, wills to rule and protect the church in Christ's person. Paul explains in the first chapter of the letter to the Ephesians that Christ was placed "at the right hand of the Father" to be the "Head of the church, . . . which is Christ's body" [vv. 20-23f.]. He means the same thing when he teaches in another place: "God . . . has bestowed upon him the name which is above every name, that at the name of Jesus every knee should bow . . . and every tongue confess what is to the glory of God the Father" [Phil. 2:9-11]. In these words Paul also commends the order in the Kingdom of Christ as necessary for our present weakness. Thus Paul rightly infers: God will then of himself become the sole Head of the church, since the duties of Christ in defending the church will have been accomplished. For the same reason, Scripture usually calls Christ "Lord" because the Father set Christ over us to exercise his dominion through his Son. Although there are many lordships celebrated in the world [cf. 1 Cor. 8:5], "for us there is one God, the Father, from whom are all things and we in him, and one Lord, Jesus Christ, through whom are all things and we through him" [1 Cor. 8:6; cf. Vg.], says Paul. From this we duly infer that he is the same God who through the mouth of Isaiah declared himself to be king and lawgiver of the church [Isa. 33:22]. For even though [the Son] consistently calls all the power he holds "the benefit and gift of the Father," he merely means that he reigns by divine power. Why did he take the person of the mediator? He descended from the bosom of the Father and from incomprehensible glory that he might draw near to us. All the more reason, then, is there that we should one and all resolve to obey, and to direct our obedience with the greatest eagerness to the divine will! Now Christ fulfills the combined duties of king and pastor for the godly who submit willingly and obediently; on the other hand, we hear that he carries a "rod of iron to break them and dash them all in pieces like a potter's vessel" [Ps. 2:9f.]. We also hear that "he will execute judgment among the Gentiles, so that he fills the earth with corpses, and strikes down every height that opposes him" [Ps. 110:6f.]. We see today several examples

of this fact, but the full proof will appear at the last judgment, which may also be properly considered the last act of his reign.

6. The Priestly Office: Reconciliation and Intercession

Now we must speak briefly concerning the purpose and use of Christ's priestly office: as a pure and stainless mediator he is by his holiness to reconcile us to God. But God's righteous curse bars our access to him, and God in his capacity as judge is angry toward us. Hence, an expiation must intervene in order that Christ as priest may obtain God's favor for us and appease his wrath. Thus Christ to perform this office had to come forward with a sacrifice. For under the law, also, the priest was forbidden to enter the sanctuary without blood [Heb. 9:7], that believers might know, even though the priest as their advocate stood between them and God, that they could not propitiate God unless their sins were expiated [Lev. 16:2-3]. The apostle discusses this point at length in the Letter to the Hebrews, from the seventh almost to the end of the tenth chapter. To sum up his argument: The priestly office belongs to Christ alone because by the sacrifice of his death he blotted out our own guilt and made satisfaction for our sins [Heb. 9:22]. God's solemn oath, of which he "will not repent," warns us what a weighty matter this is: "You are a priest forever after the order of Melchizedek" [Ps. 110:4; cf. Heb. 5:6; 7:15]. God undoubtedly willed in these words to ordain the principal point on which, he knew, our whole salvation turns. For, as has been said, we or our prayers have no access to God unless Christ, as our high priest, having washed away our sins, sanctifies us and obtains for us that grace from which the uncleanness of our transgressions and vices debars us. Thus we see that we must begin from the death of

Christ in order that the efficacy and benefit of his priesthood may reach us.

It follows that he is an everlasting intercessor: through his pleading we obtain favor. Hence arises not only trust in prayer, but also peace for godly consciences, while they safely lean upon God's fatherly mercy and are surely persuaded that whatever has been consecrated through the mediator is pleasing to God. Although God under the law commanded animal sacrifices to be offered to himself, in Christ there was a new and different order, in which the same one was to be both priest and sacrifice. This was because no other satisfaction adequate for our sins, and no man worthy to offer to God the only-begotten Son, could be found. Now, Christ plays the priestly role, not only to render the Father favorable and propitious toward us by an eternal law of reconciliation, but also to receive us as his companions in this great office [Rev. 1:6]. For we who are defiled in ourselves, yet are priests in him, offer ourselves and our all to God, and freely enter the heavenly sanctuary that the sacrifices of prayers and praise that we bring may be acceptable and sweet-smelling before God. This is the meaning of Christ's statement: "For their sake I sanctify myself" [John 17:19]. For we, imbued with his holiness insofar as he has consecrated us to the Father with himself, although we would otherwise be loathsome to him, please him as pure and clean—and even as holy. This is why the sanctuary was anointed, as mentioned in Daniel [Dan. 9:24]. We must note the contrast between this anointing and that shadow anointing which was then in use. It is as if the angel had said, "When the shadows have been dispelled the true priesthood will shine forth in Christ." The more detestable is the fabrication of those who, not content with Christ's priesthood, have presumed to sacrifice him anew! The papists attempt this each day, considering the mass as the sacrificing of Christ. . . .

✠

60. The Holy Spirit

Book III, The Way in Which We Receive the Grace of Christ: What Benefits Come to Us from It, and What Effects Follow

The Things Spoken Concerning Christ Profit us by the Secret Working of the Spirit

1. The Holy Spirit As the Bond That Unites Us to Christ

We must now examine this question. How do we receive those benefits which the Father bestowed on his only-begotten Son—not for Christ's own private use, but that he might enrich poor and needy men? First, we must understand that as long as Christ remains outside of us, and we are separated from him, all that he has suffered and done for the salvation of the human race remains useless and of no value for us. Therefore, to share with us what he has received from the Father, he had to become ours and to dwell within us. For this reason, he is called "our Head" [Eph. 4:15], and "the firstborn among many brethren" [Rom. 8:29]. We also, in turn, are said to be "engrafted into him" [Rom. 11:17], and to "put on Christ" [Gal. 3:27]; for, as I have said, all that he possesses is nothing to us until we grow into one body with him. It is true that we obtain this by faith. Yet since we see that not all indiscriminately embrace that communion with Christ which is offered through the gospel, reason itself teaches us to climb higher and to examine into the secret energy of the Spirit, by which we come to enjoy Christ and all his benefits.

Earlier I discussed the eternal deity and essence of the Spirit. Now let us be content with this particular point: that Christ so "came by water and blood" in order that the Spirit may witness concerning him [1 John 5:6-7], lest the salvation imparted through him escape us. For, as three witnesses in heaven are named—the Father, the Word, and the Spirit—so there are three on earth: the water, the blood, and the Spirit [1 John 5:7-8]. There is good reason for the repeated mention of the "testimony of the Spirit," a testimony we feel engraved like a seal upon our hearts, with the result that it seals the cleansing and sacrifice of Christ. For this reason, also, Peter says that believers have been "chosen in the sanctification of the Spirit unto obedience and sprinkling of the blood of Christ" [1 Pet. 1:2f.]. By these words he explains that, in order that the shedding of his sacred blood may not be nullified, our souls are cleansed by the secret watering of the Spirit. For the same reason, also, Paul, in speaking of cleansing and justification, says that we come to possess both, "in the name of . . . Jesus Christ and in the Spirit of our God" [1 Cor. 6:11]. To sum up, the Holy Spirit is the bond by which Christ effectually unites us to himself. To this, also, pertains what we taught in the previous book concerning his anointing.

2. How and Why Christ Was Endowed with the Holy Spirit

But, in order to get a clearer notion of this matter, so well worth investigating, we must bear in mind that Christ came endowed with the Holy Spirit in a special way: that is, to separate us from the world and to gather us unto the hope of the eternal inheritance. Hence he is called the "spirit of sanctification" [cf. Rom. 1:4; 2 Thess. 2:13; 1 Pet. 1:2] because he not only quickens and nour-

ishes us by a general power that is visible both in the human race and in the rest of the living creatures, but he is also the root and seed of heavenly life in us. To the kingdom of Christ, then, the prophets give the lofty title of the time when there will be a richer outpouring of the Spirit. There is a passage in Joel notable above all others: "And in that day I shall pour forth of my spirit upon all flesh" [Joel 2:28f.]. For even if the prophet seems to restrict the gifts of the Spirit to the prophetic office, under this figure he signifies that, in manifesting his Spirit, God will make disciples of those who were previously destitute and empty of heavenly doctrine.

Further, God the Father gives us the Holy Spirit for his Son's sake, and yet has bestowed the whole fullness of the Spirit upon the Son to be minister and steward of his liberality. For this reason, the Spirit is sometimes called the "Spirit of the Father," sometimes the "Spirit of the Son." Paul says: "You are not in the flesh, but in the spirit, if indeed the Spirit of God dwells in you. But if anyone does not have the Spirit of Christ, he is not his" [Rom. 8:9, cf. Vg.]. Hence, he arouses hope of a full renewal "because he who raised Christ from the dead will quicken our mortal bodies, because of his Spirit that dwells in us" [Rom. 8:11f.]. For there is nothing absurd in ascribing to the Father praise for those gifts of which he is the Author, and yet in ascribing the same powers to Christ, with whom were laid up the gifts of the Spirit to bestow upon his people. For this reason he invites unto himself all who thirst, that they may drink [John 7:37]. And Paul teaches that the Spirit is given to each "according to the measure of Christ's gift" [Eph. 4:7]. Also, we ought to know that he is called the "Spirit of Christ" not only because Christ, as eternal Word of God, is joined in the same Spirit with the Father, but also from his character as the mediator. For he would have come to us in vain if he had not been furnished with this power. In this sense he is called the "second Adam," given from heaven as "a life-giving spirit" [1 Cor. 15:45]. This unique life which the Son of God inspires in his own so that they become one with him, Paul here contrasts with that natural life which is common also to the wicked. Likewise, he asks "the grace of . . . Christ and the love of God" for believers, at the same time coupling with it "participation in the . . . Spirit" [2 Cor. 13:14], without which no one can taste either the fatherly favor of God or the beneficence of Christ; just as he also says in another passage, "The love of God has been poured into our hearts through the Holy Spirit, who has been given to us" [Rom. 5:5; cf. Vg.].

3. Titles of the Holy Spirit in Scripture

And here it is useful to note what titles are applied to the Holy Spirit in Scripture, when the beginning and the whole renewal of our salvation are under discussion.

First, he is called the "spirit of adoption" because he is the witness to us of the free benevolence of God with which God the Father has embraced us in his beloved only-begotten Son to become a Father to us; and he encourages us to have trust in prayer. In fact, he supplies the very words so that we may fearlessly cry, "Abba, Father!" [Rom. 8:15; Gal. 4:6].

For the same reason he is called "the guarantee and seal" of our inheritance [2 Cor. 1:22; cf. Eph. 1:14]. Because from heaven he so gives life to us, on pilgrimage in the world and resembling dead men, as to assure us that our salvation is safe in God's unfailing care. He is also called "life" because of righteousness [cf. Rom. 8:10].

By his secret watering the Spirit makes us fruitful to bring forth the buds of righteous-

ness. Accordingly, he is frequently called "water," as in Isaiah: "Come, all ye who thirst, to the waters" [Isa. 55:1]. Also, "I shall pour out my Spirit upon him who thirsts, and rivers upon the dry land" [Isa. 44:3]. To these verses Christ's statement, quoted above, corresponds: "If anyone thirst, let him come to me" [John 7:37]. Although sometimes he is so called because of his power to cleanse and purify, as in Ezekiel, where the Lord promises "clean water" in which he will "wash away the filth" of his people [Ezek. 36:25].

From the fact that he restores and nourishes unto vigor of life those on whom he has poured the stream of his grace, he gets the names "oil" and "anointing" [1 John 2:20, 27].

On the other hand, persistently boiling away and burning up our vicious and inordinate desires, he enflames our hearts with the love of God and with zealous devotion. From this effect upon us he is also justly called "fire" [Luke 3:16].

In short, he is described as the "spring" [John 4:14] whence all heavenly riches flow forth to us; or as the "hand of God" [Acts 11:21], by which he exercises his might. For by the inspiration of his power he so breathes divine life into us that we are no longer actuated by ourselves, but are ruled by his action and prompting. Accordingly, whatever good things are in us are the fruits of his grace; and without him our gifts are darkness of mind and perversity of heart [cf. Gal. 5:19-21].

As has already been clearly explained, until our minds become intent upon the Spirit, Christ, so to speak, lies idle because we coldly contemplate him as outside ourselves—indeed, far from us. We know, moreover, that he benefits only those whose "Head" he is [Eph. 4:15], for whom he is "the firstborn among brethren" [Rom. 8:29], and who, finally, "have put on him" [Gal.

3:27]. This union alone ensures that, as far as we are concerned, he has not unprofitably come with the name of Savior. The same purpose is served by that sacred wedlock through which we are made flesh of his flesh and bone of his bone [Eph. 5:30], and thus one with him. But he unites himself to us by the Spirit alone. By the grace and power of the same Spirit we are made his members, to keep us under himself and in turn to possess him.

4. Faith as the Work of the Spirit

But faith is the principal work of the Holy Spirit. Consequently, the terms commonly employed to express his power and working are, in large measure, referred to it because by faith alone he leads us into the light of the gospel, as John teaches: to believers in Christ is given the privilege of becoming children of God, who are born not of flesh and blood, but of God [John 1:12-13]. Contrasting God with flesh and blood, he declares it to be a supernatural gift that those who would otherwise remain in unbelief receive Christ by faith. Similar to this is that reply of Christ's: "Flesh and blood have not revealed it to you, but my Father, who is in heaven" [Matt. 16:17]. I am now touching briefly upon these things because I have already treated them at length elsewhere. Like this, too, is the saying of Paul's that the Ephesians had been "sealed with the Holy Spirit of promise" [Eph. 1:13]. Paul shows the Spirit to be the inner teacher by whose effort the promise of salvation penetrates into our minds, a promise that would otherwise only strike the air or beat upon our ears. Similarly, where he says that the Thessalonians have been chosen by God "in sanctification of the Spirit and belief in the truth" [2 Thess. 2:13], he is briefly warning us that faith itself has no other source than the Spirit. John explains this more clearly: "We know

that he abides in us from the Spirit whom he has given us" [1 John 3:24]. Likewise, "From this we know that we abide in him and he in us, because he has given us of his Spirit" [1 John 4:13]. Therefore, Christ promised to his disciples "the Spirit of truth that the world cannot receive" [John 14:17] that they might be capable of receiving heavenly wisdom. And, as the proper office of the Spirit, he assigned the task of bringing to mind what he had taught by mouth. For light would be given the sightless in vain had that Spirit of discernment [Job 20:3] not opened the eyes of the mind. Consequently, he may rightly be called the key that unlocks for us the treasures of the kingdom of Heaven [cf. Rev. 3:7]; and his illumination, the keenness of our insight. Paul so highly commends the "ministry of the Spirit" [2 Cor. 3:6] for the reason that teachers would shout to no effect if Christ himself, inner schoolmaster, did not by his Spirit draw to himself those given to him by the Father [cf. John 6:44; 12:32; 17:6]. We have said that perfect salvation is found in the person of Christ. Accordingly, that we may become partakers of it "he baptizes us in the Holy Spirit and fire" [Luke 3:16], bringing us into the light of faith in his gospel and so regenerating us that we become new creatures [cf. 2 Cor. 5:17]; and he consecrates us, purged of worldly uncleanness, as temples holy to God [cf. 1 Cor. 3:16-17; 6:19; 2 Cor. 6:16; Eph. 2:21]. . . .

✠

61. The Christian Life

The Sum of the Christian Life: The Denial of Ourselves

1. We Are Not Our Own Masters, but Belong to God.

Even though the law of the Lord provides the finest and best-disposed method of ordering a man's life, it seemed good to the heavenly teacher to shape his people by an even more explicit plan to that rule which he had set forth in the law. Here, then, is the beginning of this plan: the duty of believers is "to present their bodies to God as a living sacrifice, holy and acceptable to him," and in this consists the lawful worship of him [Rom. 12:1]. From this is derived the basis of the exhortation that "they be not conformed to the fashion of this world, but be transformed by the renewal of their minds, so that they may prove what is the will of God" [Rom. 12:2]. Now the great thing is this: we are consecrated and dedicated to God in order that we may thereafter think, speak, meditate, and do nothing except to his glory. For a sacred thing may not be applied to profane uses without marked injury to him.

If we, then, are not our own [cf. 1 Cor. 6:19] but the Lord's, it is clear what error we must flee, and whither we must direct all the acts of our life.

We are not our own: let not our reason nor our will, therefore, sway our plans and deeds. We are not our own: let us therefore not set it as our goal to seek what is expedient for us according to the flesh. We are not our own: insofar as we can, let us therefore forget ourselves and all that is ours.

Conversely, we are God's: let us therefore live for him and die for him. We are God's: let his wisdom and will therefore rule all our actions. We are God's: let all the parts of our life accordingly strive toward him as our only lawful goal [Rom. 14:8; cf. 1 Cor. 6:19]. O, how much has that man profited who, having been taught that he is not his own, has taken away dominion and rule from his own reason that he may yield it to God! For, as consulting our self-interest is the pestilence that most effectively leads to our destruction, so

the sole haven of salvation is to be wise in nothing and to will nothing through ourselves but to follow the leading of the Lord alone.

Let this therefore be the first step, that a man depart from himself in order that he may apply the whole force of his ability in the service of the Lord. I call "service" not only what lies in obedience to God's Word but what turns the mind of man, empty of its own carnal sense, wholly to the bidding of God's Spirit. While it is the first entrance to life, all philosophers were ignorant of this transformation, which Paul calls "renewal of the mind" [Eph. 4:23]. For they set up reason alone as the ruling principle in man, and think that it alone should be listened to; to it alone, in short, they entrust the conduct of life. But the Christian philosophy bids reason give way to, submit and subject itself to, the Holy Spirit so that the man himself may no longer live but hear Christ living and reigning within him [Gal. 2:20].

2. Self-Denial through Devotion to God

From this also follows this second point: that we seek not the things that are ours but those which are of the Lord's will and will serve to advance his glory. This is also evidence of great progress: that, almost forgetful of ourselves, surely subordinating our self-concern, we try faithfully to devote our zeal to God and his commandments. For when Scripture bids us leave off self-concern, it not only erases from our minds the yearning to possess, the desire for power, and the favor of men, but it also uproots ambition and all craving for human glory and other more secret plagues. Accordingly, the Christian must surely be so disposed and minded that he feels within himself it is with God he has to deal throughout his life. In this way, as he will refer all he has to God's decision and judgment, so will he refer his whole intention of mind scrupulously to him. For he who has learned to look to God in all things that he must do, at the same time avoids all vain thoughts. This, then, is that denial of self which Christ enjoins with such great earnestness upon his disciples at the outset of their service [cf. Matt. 16:24]. When it has once taken possession of their hearts, it leaves no place at all first either to pride, or arrogance, or ostentation; then either to avarice, or desire, or lasciviousness, or effeminacy, or to other evils that our self-love spawns [cf. 2 Tim. 3:2-5]. On the other hand, wherever denial of ourselves does not reign, there either the foulest vices rage without shame or if there is any semblance of virtue, it is vitiated by depraved lusting after glory. Show me a man, if you can, who, unless he has according to the commandment of the Lord renounced himself, would freely exercise goodness among men. For all who have not been possessed with this feeling have at least followed virtue for the sake of praise. Now those of the philosophers who at any time most strongly contended that virtue should be pursued for its own sake were puffed up with such great arrogance as to show they sought after virtue for no other reason than to have occasion for pride. Yet God is so displeased, both with those who court the popular breeze and with such swollen souls, as to declare that they have received their reward in this world [Matt. 6:2, 5, 16], and to make harlots and publicans nearer to the kingdom of heaven than are they [Matt. 21:31]. Yet we have still not clearly explained how many and how great are the obstacles that hinder man from a right course so long as he has not denied himself. For it was once truly said: "A world of vices is hidden in the soul of man." And you can find no other remedy than in denying yourself and giving up concern for yourself, and in turning your mind wholly to seek after those things which the Lord requires of you, and to seek them only because they are pleasing to him.

3. Self-Renunciation According to Titus, Chapter 2

In another place, Paul more clearly, although briefly, delineates the individual parts of a well-ordered life.

> The grace of God has appeared, bringing salvation to all men, training us to renounce irreligion and worldly passions and to live sober, upright, and godly lives, in the present age; awaiting our blessed hope, and the appearing of the glory of our great God and of our Savior Jesus Christ, who gave himself for us to redeem us from all iniquity and to purify for himself a people of his own who are zealous for good deeds [Titus 2:11-14].

For, after he proffered the grace of God to hearten us, in order to pave the way for us to worship God truly he removed the two obstacles that chiefly hinder us: namely, ungodliness, to which by nature we are too much inclined; and second, worldly desires, which extend more widely. And by ungodliness, indeed, he not only means superstition but includes also whatever contends against the earnest fear of God. Worldly lusts are also equivalent to the passions of the flesh [cf. Gal. 5:16; Eph. 2:3; 2 Pet. 2:18; 1 John 2:16; etc.]. Thus, with reference to both Tables of the Law, he commands us to put off our own nature and to deny whatever our reason and will dictate. Now he limits all actions of life to three parts: soberness, righteousness, and godliness. Of these, soberness doubtless denotes chastity and temperance as well as a pure and frugal use of temporal goods, and patience in poverty. Now righteousness embraces all the duties of equity in order that to each one be rendered what is his own [cf. Rom. 13:7]. There follows godliness, which joins us in true holiness with God when we are separated from the iniquities of the world. When these things are joined together by an inseparable bond, they bring about complete perfection. But, nothing is more difficult than, having bidden farewell to the reason of the flesh and having bridled our desires—nay, having put them away—to devote ourselves to God and our brethren, and to meditate, amid earth's filth, upon the life of the angels. Consequently, Paul, in order to extricate our minds from all snares, recalls us to the hope of blessed immortality, reminding us that we strive not in vain [cf. 1 Thess. 3:5]. For, as Christ our redeemer once appeared, so in his final coming he will show the fruit of the salvation brought forth by him. In this way he scatters all the allurements that becloud us and prevent us from aspiring as we ought to heavenly glory. Nay, he teaches us to travel as pilgrims in this world that our celestial heritage may not perish or pass away.

4. Self-Denial Gives Us the Right Attitude toward Our Fellow Men.

Now in these words we perceive that denial of self has regard partly to men, partly, and chiefly, to God.

For when Scripture bids us act toward men so as to esteem them above ourselves [Phil. 2:3], and in good faith to apply ourselves wholly to doing them good [cf. Rom. 12:10], it gives us commandments of which our mind is quite incapable unless our mind be previously emptied of its natural feeling. For, such is the blindness with which we all rush into self-love that each one of us seems to himself to have just cause to be proud of himself and to despise all others in comparison. If God has conferred upon us anything of which we need not repent, relying upon it we immediately lift up our minds, and are not only puffed up but almost burst with pride. The very vices that infest us we take pains to hide from others, while we flatter ourselves with the pretense that they are slight and insignificant, and even sometimes embrace them as virtues. If others manifest the same endowments we admire in ourselves, or even superior ones, we spitefully belittle and revile these gifts in order to avoid yielding place to such persons. If there are any faults in others, not content with noting them with severe and sharp reproach, we hatefully exaggerate them. Hence arises such insolence that each one of us, as if exempt from the common lot, wishes to tower above the rest, and loftily and savagely abuses every mortal man, or at least looks down upon him as an inferior. The poor yield to the rich; the common folk, to the nobles; the servants, to their masters; the unlearned, to the educated. But there is no one who does not cherish within himself some opinion of his own preeminence.

Thus, each individual, by flattering himself, bears a kind of kingdom in his breast. For claiming as his own what pleases him, he censures the character and morals of others. But if this comes to the point of conflict, his venom bursts forth. For many obviously display some gentleness so long as they find everything sweet and pleasant. But just how many are there who will preserve this even tenor of modesty when they are pricked and irritated? There is no other remedy than to tear out from our inward parts this most deadly pestilence of love of strife and love of self, even as it is plucked out by scriptural teaching. For thus we are instructed to remember that those talents which God has bestowed upon us are not our own goods but the free gifts of God; and any persons who become proud of them show their ungratefulness. "Who causes you to excel?" Paul asks. "If you have received all things, why do you boast as if they were not given to you?" [1 Cor. 4:7].

Let us, then, unremittingly examining our faults, call ourselves back to humility. Thus nothing will remain in us to puff us up; but there will be much occasion to be cast down. On the other hand, we are bidden so to esteem and regard whatever gifts of God we see in other men that we may honor those men in whom they reside. For it would be great depravity on our part to deprive them of that honor which the Lord has bestowed upon them. But we are taught to overlook their faults, certainly not flatteringly to cherish them; but not on account of such faults to revile men whom we ought to cherish with good will and honor. Thus it will come about that, whatever man we deal with, we shall treat him not only moderately and modestly but also cordially and as a friend. You will never attain true gentleness except by one path: a heart imbued with lowliness and with reverence for others.

5. Self-Renunciation Leads to Proper Helpfulness toward Our Neighbors.

Now, in seeking to benefit one's neighbor, how difficult it is to do one's duty! Unless you give up all thought of self and, so to speak, get out of yourself, you will accomplish nothing here. For how can you perform those works which Paul teaches to be the works of love, unless you renounce yourself, and give yourself wholly to others? "Love," he says, "is patient and kind, not jealous or boastful, is not envious or puffed up, does

not seek its own, is not irritable," etc. [1 Cor. 13: 4-5f.]. If this is the one thing required—that we seek not what is our own—still we shall do no little violence to nature, which so inclines us to love of ourselves alone that it does not easily allow us to neglect ourselves and our possessions in order to look after another's good, nay, to yield willingly what is ours by right and resign it to another. But Scripture, to lead us by the hand to this, warns that whatever benefits we obtain from the Lord have been entrusted to us on this condition: that they be applied to the common good of the church. And therefore the lawful use of all benefits consists in a liberal and kindly sharing of them with others. No surer rule and no more valid exhortation to keep it could be devised than when we are taught that all the gifts we possess have been bestowed by God and entrusted to us on condition that they be distributed for our neighbors' benefit [cf. 1 Pet. 4:10].

But Scripture goes even farther by comparing them to the powers with which the members of the human body are endowed [1 Cor. 12:12ff.]. No member has this power for itself nor applies it to its own private use; but each pours it out to the fellow members. Nor does it take any profit from its power except what proceeds from the common advantage of the whole body. So, too, whatever a godly man can do he ought to be able to do for his brothers, providing for himself in no way other than to have his mind intent upon the common upbuilding of the church. Let this, therefore, be our rule for generosity and beneficence: We are the stewards of everything God has conferred on us by which we are able to help our neighbor, and are required to render account of our stewardship. Moreover, the only right stewardship is that which is tested by the rule of love. Thus it will come about that we shall not only join zeal for another's benefit with care for our own advantage, but shall subordinate the latter to the former.

And lest perhaps we should not realize that this is the rule for the proper management of all gifts we have received from God, he also in early times applied it to the least gifts of his generosity. For he commanded that the first fruits be brought to him by which the people were to testify that it was unlawful to accept for themselves any enjoyment of benefits not previously consecrated to him [Exod. 23:19; cf. 22:29, Vg.]. But if the gifts of God are only thus sanctified to us when we have dedicated them by our hand to the author himself, that which does not savor of such dedication is clearly a corrupt abuse. Yet you wish to strive in vain to enrich the Lord by sharing your possessions; since, then, your generosity cannot extend to him, you must, as the prophet says, practice it toward the saints on earth [Ps. 16:2-3]. And alms are compared to holy sacrifices so as to correspond now to those requirements of the law [Heb. 13:16].

6. Love of Neighbor Is Not Dependent upon Manner of Men but Looks to God.

Furthermore, not to grow weary in well doing [Gal. 6:9], which otherwise must happen immediately, we ought to add that other idea which the apostle mentions: "Love is patient . . . and is not irritable" [1 Cor. 13:4-5]. The Lord commands all men without exception "to do good" [Heb. 13:16]. Yet the great part of them are most unworthy if they be judged by their own merit. But here Scripture helps in the best way when it teaches that we are not to consider that men merit of themselves but to look upon the image of God in all men, to which we owe all

honor and love. However, it is among members of the household of faith that this same image is more carefully to be noted [Gal. 6:10], insofar as it has been renewed and restored through the Spirit of Christ. Therefore, whatever man you meet who needs your aid, you have no reason to refuse to help him. Say, "He is a stranger"; but the Lord has given him a mark that ought to be familiar to you, by virtue of the fact that he forbids you to despise your own flesh [Isa. 58:7, Vg.]. Say, "He is contemptible and worthless"; but the Lord shows him to be one to whom he has deigned to give the beauty of his image. Say that you owe nothing for any service of his; but God, as it were, has put him in his own place in order that you may recognize toward him the many and great benefits with which God has bound you to himself. Say that he does not deserve even your least effort for his sake; but the image of God, which recommends him to you, is worthy of your giving yourself and all your possessions. Now if he has not only deserved no good at your hand, but has also provoked you by unjust acts and curses, not even this is just reason why you should cease to embrace him in love and to perform the duties of love on his behalf [Matt. 6:14; 18:35; Luke 17:3]. You will say, "He has deserved something far different of me." Yet what has the Lord deserved? While he bids you forgive this man for all sins he has committed against you, he would truly have them charged against himself. Assuredly there is but one way in which to achieve what is not merely difficult but utterly against human nature: to love those who hate us, to repay their evil deeds with benefits, to return blessings for reproaches [Matt. 5:44]. It is that we remember not to consider men's evil intention but to look upon the image of God in them, which cancels and effaces their transgressions, and with its beauty and dignity allures us to love and embrace them.

7. The Outward Work of Love Is Not Sufficient, but It Is Intention That Counts!

This mortification, then, will take place in us only if we fulfill the duties of love. Now he who merely performs all the duties of love does not fulfill them, even though he overlooks none; but he, rather, fulfills them who does this from a sincere feeling of love. For it can happen that one who indeed discharges to the full all his obligations as far as outward duties are concerned is still all the while far away from the true way of discharging them. For you may see some who wish to seem very liberal and yet bestow nothing that they do not make reprehensible with a proud countenance or even insolent words. And in this tragic and unhappy age it has come to this pass, that most men give their alms contemptuously. Such depravity ought not to have been tolerable even among the pagans; of Christians something even more is required than to show a cheerful countenance and to render their duties pleasing with friendly words. First, they must put themselves in the place of him whom they see in need of their assistance, and pity his ill fortune as if they themselves experienced and bore it, so that they may be impelled by a feeling of mercy and humaneness to go to his aid just as to their own.

He who, thus disposed, proceeds to give help to his brethren will not corrupt his own duties by either arrogance or upbraiding. Furthermore, in giving benefits he will not despise his needy brother or enslave him as one indebted to himself. This would no more be reasonable than that we should either chide a sick member that the rest of the body labors to revive or consider it especially obligated to the remaining members because it has drawn more help to itself than it can repay. Now the sharing of tasks among members is believed to have nothing gratuitous about it but, rather, to be a payment of that which, due by the law of nature, it would be monstrous to refuse. Also, in this way it will come about that he who has discharged one kind of task will not think himself free, as commonly happens when a rich man, after he has given up something of his own, delegates to other men other burdens as having nothing at all to do with him. Rather, each man will so consider with himself that in all his greatness he is a debtor to his neighbors, and that he ought in exercising kindness toward them to set no other limit than the end of his resources; these, as widely as they are extended, ought to have their limits set according to the rule of love.

8. Self-Denial toward God: Devotion to His Will!

Let us reiterate in fuller form the chief part of self-denial, which, as we have said, looks to God. And indeed, many things have been said about this already that it would be superfluous to repeat. It will be enough to show how it forms us to fair-mindedness and tolerance.

To begin with, then, in seeking either the convenience or the tranquillity of the present life, Scripture calls us to resign ourselves and all our possessions to the Lord's will, and to yield to him the desires of our hearts to be tamed and subjugated. To covet wealth and honors, to strive for authority, to heap up riches, to gather together all those follies which seem to make for magnificence and pomp, our lust is mad, our desire boundless. On the other hand, wonderful is our fear, wonderful our hatred, of poverty, lowly birth, and humble condition! And we are spurred to rid ourselves of them by every means. Hence we can see how uneasy in mind all those persons are who order their lives according to their own plan. We can see how artfully they strive—to the point of weariness—to obtain the goal of their ambition or avarice, while, on the other hand, avoiding poverty and a lowly condition.

In order not to be caught in such snares, godly men must hold to this path. First of all, let them neither desire nor hope for, nor contemplate, any other way of prospering than by the Lord's blessing. Upon this, then, let them safely and confidently throw themselves and rest. For however beautifully the flesh may seem to suffice unto itself, while it either strives by its own effort for honors and riches or relies upon its diligence, or is aided by the favor of men, yet it is certain that all these things are nothing; nor will we benefit at all, either by skill or by labor, except insofar as the Lord prospers them both. On the contrary, however, his blessing alone finds a way, even through all hindrances, to bring all things to a happy and favorable outcome for us; again, though entirely without it, to enable us to obtain some glory and opulence for ourselves (as we daily see impious men amassing great honors and riches), yet, inasmuch as those upon whom the curse of God rests taste not even the least particle of happiness, without this blessing we shall obtain nothing but what turns to our misfortune. For we ought by no means to desire what makes men more miserable.

9. Trust in God's Blessing Only

Therefore, suppose we believe that every means toward a prosperous and desirable outcome rests upon the blessing of God alone; and that, when this is absent, all sorts of misery and calamity dog us. It remains for us not greedily to strive after riches and honors—whether relying upon our own dexterity of wit or our own diligence, or depending upon the favor of men, or having confidence in vainly imagined fortune—but for us always to look to the Lord so that by his guidance we may be led to whatever lot he has provided for us. Thus it will first come to pass that we shall not dash out to seize upon riches and usurp honors through wickedness and by stratagems and evil arts, or greed, to the injury of our neighbors; but pursue only those enterprises which do not lead us away from innocence.

Who can hope for the help of a divine blessing amidst frauds, robberies, and other wicked arts? For as that blessing follows only him who thinks purely and acts rightly, thus it calls back from crooked thoughts and wicked actions all those who seek it. Then will a bridle be put on us that we may not burn with an immoderate desire to grow rich or ambitiously pant after honors. For with what shamelessness does a man trust that he will be helped by God to obtain those things which he desires contrary to God's Word? Away with the thought that God would abet with his blessing what he curses with his mouth! Lastly, if things do not go according to our wish and hope, we will still be restrained from impatience and loathing of our condition, whatever it may be. For we shall know that this is to murmur against God, by whose will riches and poverty, contempt and honor, are dispensed. To sum up, he who rests solely upon the blessing of God, as it has been here expressed, will neither strive with evil arts after those things which men customarily madly seek after, which he realizes will not profit him, nor will he, if things go well, give credit to himself or even to his diligence, or industry, or fortune. Rather, he will give God the credit as its author. But if, while other men's affairs flourish, he makes but slight advancement, or even slips back, he will still bear his low estate with greater equanimity and moderation of mind than some profane person would bear a moderate success which merely does not correspond with his wish. For he indeed possesses a solace in which he may repose more peacefully than in the highest degree of wealth or power. Since this leads to his salvation, he considers that his affairs are ordained by the Lord. We see that David was so minded; while he follows God and gives himself over to his leading, he attests that he is like a child weaned from his mother's breast, and that he does not occupy himself with things too deep and wonderful for him [Ps. 131:1-2].

10. Self-Denial Helps Us Bear Adversity.

And for godly minds the peace and forbearance we have spoken of ought not to rest solely in this point; but it must also be extended to every occurrence to which the present life is subject. Therefore, he alone has duly denied himself who has so totally resigned himself to the Lord that he permits every part of his life to be governed by God's will. He who will be thus composed in mind, whatever happens, will not consider himself miserable nor complain of his lot with ill will toward God. How necessary this disposition is will appear if you weigh the many chance happenings to which we are subject. Various diseases repeatedly trouble us: now plague rages; now we are cruelly beset by the calamities of war; now ice and hail, consuming the year's expectation, lead to barrenness, which reduces us to poverty; wife, parents, children, neighbors, are snatched away by

death; our house is burned by fire. It is on account of these occurrences that men curse their life, loathe the day of their birth, abominate heaven and the light of day, rail against God, and as they are eloquent in blasphemy, accuse him of injustice and cruelty. But in these matters the believer must also look to God's kindness and truly fatherly indulgence. Accordingly, if he sees his house reduced to solitude by the removal of his kinsfolk, he will not indeed even then cease to bless the Lord, but rather will turn his attention to this thought: nevertheless, the grace of the Lord, which dwells in my house, will not leave it desolate. Or, if his crops are blasted by frost, or destroyed by ice, or beaten down with hail, and he sees famine threatening, yet he will not despair or bear a grudge against God, but will remain firm in this trust [cf. Ps. 78:47]: "Nevertheless we are in the Lord's protection, sheep brought up in his pastures" [Ps. 79:13]. The Lord will therefore supply food to us even in extreme barrenness. If he shall be afflicted by disease, he will not even then be so unmanned by the harshness of pain as to break forth into impatience and expostulate with God; but, by considering the righteousness and gentleness of God's chastening, he will recall himself to forbearance. In short, whatever happens, because he will know it ordained of God, he will undergo it with a peaceful and grateful mind so as not obstinately to resist the command of him into whose power he once for all surrendered himself and his every possession.

Especially let that foolish and most miserable consolation of the pagans be far away from the breast of the Christian man; to strengthen their minds against adversities, they charged these to fortune. Against fortune they considered it foolish to be angry because she was blind and unthinking, with unseeing eyes wounding the deserving and the undeserving at the same time. On the contrary, the rule of piety is that God's hand alone is the judge and governor of fortune, good or bad, and that it does not rush about with heedless force, but with most orderly justice deals out good as well as ill to us. . . .

62. Predestination

Eternal Election by Which God Has Predestined Some to Salvation, Others to Destruction

1. Necessity and Beneficial Effect of the Doctrine of Election; Danger of Curiosity

In actual fact, the covenant of life is not preached equally among all men, and among those to whom it is preached, it does not gain the same acceptance either constantly or in equal degree. In this diversity the wonderful depth of God's judgment is made known. For there is no doubt that this variety also serves the decision of God's eternal election. If it is plain that it comes to pass by God's bidding that salvation is freely offered to some while others are barred from access to it, at once great and difficult questions spring up, explicable only when reverent minds regard as settled what they may suitably hold concerning election and predestination. A baffling question this seems to many. For they think nothing more inconsistent than that out of the common multitude of men some should be predestined to salvation, others to destruction. But how mistakenly they entangle themselves will become clear in the following discussion. Besides, in the very darkness that frightens them not only is the usefulness of this doctrine made known but also its very sweet fruit. We shall never be clearly persuaded, as we ought to be, that our salvation flows from the wellspring of God's

free mercy until we come to know his eternal election, which illumines God's grace by this contrast: that he does not indiscriminately adopt all into the hope of salvation but gives to some what he denies to others.

How much the ignorance of this principle detracts from God's glory, how much it takes away from true humility, is well known. Yet Paul denies that this which needs so much to be known can be known unless God, utterly disregarding works, chooses those whom he has decreed within himself. "At the present time," he says, "a remnant has been saved according to the election of grace. But if it is by grace, it is no more of works; otherwise grace would no more be grace. But if it is of works, it is no more of grace; otherwise work would not be work" [Rom. 11:5-6]. If—to make it clear that our salvation comes about solely from God's mere generosity—we must be called back to the course of election, those who wish to get rid of all this are obscuring as maliciously as they can what ought to have been gloriously and vociferously proclaimed, and they tear humility up by the very roots. Paul clearly testifies that, when the salvation of a remnant of the people is ascribed to the election of grace, then only is it acknowledged that God of his mere good pleasure preserves whom he will, and moreover that he pays no reward, since he can owe none.

They who shut the gates that no one may dare seek a taste of this doctrine wrong men no less than God. For neither will anything else suffice to make us humble as we ought to be nor shall we otherwise sincerely feel how much we are obliged to God. And as Christ teaches, here is our only ground for firmness and confidence: in order to free us of all fear and render us victorious amid so many dangers, snares, and mortal struggles, he promises that whatever the Father has entrusted into his keeping will be safe [John 10:28-29]. From this we infer that all those who do not know that they are God's own will be miserable through constant fear. Hence, those who by being blind to the three benefits we have noted would wish the foundation of our salvation to be removed from our midst, very badly serve the interests of themselves and of all other believers. How is it that the church becomes manifest to us from this, when, as Bernard rightly teaches, "it could not otherwise be found or recognized among creatures, since it lies marvelously hidden . . . both within the bosom of a blessed predestination and within the mass of a miserable condemnation?"

But before I enter into the matter itself, I need to mention by way of preface two kinds of men.

Human curiosity renders the discussion of predestination, already somewhat difficult of itself, very confusing and even dangerous. No restraints can hold it back from wandering in forbidden bypaths and thrusting upward to the heights. If allowed, it will leave no secret to God that it will not search out and unravel. Since we see so many on all sides rushing into this audacity and impudence, among them certain men not otherwise bad, they should in due season be reminded of the measure of their duty in this regard.

First, then, let them remember that when they inquire into predestination, they are penetrating the sacred precincts of divine wisdom. If anyone with carefree assurance breaks into this place, he will not succeed in satisfying his curiosity and he will enter a labyrinth from which he can find no exit. For it is not right for man unrestrainedly to search out things that the Lord has willed to be hid in himself, and to unfold from eter-

nity itself the sublimest wisdom, which he would have us revere but not understand that through this also he should fill us with wonder. He has set forth by his Word the secrets of his will that he has decided to reveal to us. These he decided to reveal insofar as he foresaw that they would concern us and benefit us.

2. Doctrine of Predestination to Be Sought in Scripture Only

"We have entered the pathway of faith," says Augustine, "let us hold steadfastly to it. It leads us to the king's chamber, in which are hid all treasures of knowledge and wisdom. For the Lord Christ himself did not bear a grudge against his great and most select disciples when he said: 'I have . . . many things to say to you, but you cannot bear them now' [John 16:12]. We must walk, we must advance, we must grow, that our hearts may be capable of those things which we cannot yet grasp. But if the last day finds us advancing, there we shall learn what we could not learn here."

If this thought prevails with us, that the Word of the Lord is the sole way that can lead us in our search for all that it is lawful to hold concerning him, and is the sole light to illumine our vision of all that we should see of him, it will readily keep and restrain us from all rashness. For we shall know that the moment we exceed the bounds of the Word, our course is outside the pathway and in darkness, and that there we must repeatedly wander, slip, and stumble. Let this, therefore, first of all be before our eyes: to seek any other knowledge of predestination than what the Word of God discloses is not less insane than if one should purpose to walk in a pathless waste [cf. Job 12:24], or to see in darkness. And let us not be ashamed to be ignorant of something in this matter, wherein there is a certain learned ignorance. Rather, let us willingly refrain from inquiring into a kind of knowledge, the ardent desire for which is both foolish and dangerous, nay, even deadly. But if a wanton curiosity agitates us, we shall always do well to oppose to it this restraining thought: just as too much honey is not good, so for the curious the investigation of glory is not turned into glory [Prov. 25:27; cf. Vg.]. For there is good reason for us to be deterred from this insolence which can only plunge us into ruin.

3. The Second Danger: Anxious Silence about the Doctrine of Election

There are others who, wishing to cure this evil, all but require that every mention of predestination be buried; indeed, they teach us to avoid any question of it, as we would a reef. Even though their moderation in this matter is rightly to be praised, because they feel that these mysteries ought to be discussed with great soberness, yet because they descend to too low a level, they make little progress with the human understanding, which does not allow itself to be easily restrained. Therefore, to hold to a proper limit in this regard also, we shall have to turn back to the Word of the Lord, in which we have a sure rule for the understanding. For Scripture is the school of the Holy Spirit, in which, as nothing is omitted that is both necessary and useful to know, so nothing is taught but what is expedient to know. Therefore we must guard against depriving believers of anything disclosed about predestination in Scripture, lest we seem either wickedly to defraud them of the blessing of their God or to accuse and scoff at the Holy Spirit for having published what it is in any way profitable to suppress.

Let us, I say, permit the Christian man to open his mind and ears to every utterance of God directed to him, provided it be with such restraint that when the Lord closes his holy lips, he also shall at once close the way to inquiry. The best limit of sobriety for us will be not only to follow God's lead always in learning but, when he sets an end to teaching, to stop trying to be wise. The fact that they fear danger is not sufficiently important that we should on that account turn away our minds from the oracles of God. Solomon's saying is familiar: "It is the glory of God to conceal the word" [Prov. 25:2, Vg.]. But since piety and common sense show that this is not to be understood indiscriminately of everything, we must seek a distinction, lest under the pretense of modesty and sobriety we are satisfied with brutish ignorance. Moses clearly expresses this in a few words: "The secret things," he says, "belong to . . . our God, but he has manifested them to us and to our children" [Deut. 29:29, cf. Vg.]. We see how he urges the people to study the teaching of the law only on the ground of a heavenly decree, because it pleased God to publish it; and how he held the same people within these bounds for this reason alone: that it is not lawful for mortal men to intrude upon the secrets of God.

4. The Alleged Peril in the Doctrine Dismissed

Profane men, I admit, in the matter of predestination abruptly seize upon something to carp, rail, bark, or scoff at. But if their shamelessness deters us, we shall have to keep secret the chief doctrines of the faith, almost none of which they or their like leave untouched by blasphemy. An obstinate person would be no less insolently puffed up on hearing that within the essence of God there are three persons than if he were told that

God foresaw what would happen to man when he created him. And they will not refrain from guffaws when they are informed that but little more than five thousand years have passed since the creation of the universe, for they ask why God's power was idle and asleep for so long. Nothing, in short, can be brought forth that they do not assail with their mockery. Should we, to silence these blasphemies, forbear to speak of the deity of Son and Spirit? Must we pass over in silence the creation of the universe? No! God's truth is so powerful, both in this respect and in every other, that it has nothing to fear from the evilspeaking of wicked men.

So Augustine stoutly maintains in his little treatise *The Gift of Perseverance.* For we see that the false apostles could not make Paul ashamed by defaming and accusing his true doctrine. They say that this whole discussion is dangerous for godly minds—because it hinders exhortations, because it shakes faith, because it disturbs and terrifies the heart itself—but this is nonsense! Augustine admits that for these reasons he was frequently charged with preaching predestination too freely, but, as it was easy for him, he overwhelmingly refuted the charge. We, moreover, because many and various absurdities are obtruded at this point, have preferred to dispose of each in its own place. I desire only to have them generally admit that we should not investigate what the Lord has left hidden in secret, that we should not neglect what he has brought into the open, so that we may not be convicted of excessive curiosity on the one hand, or of excessive ingratitude on the other. For Augustine also skillfully expressed this idea: we can safely follow Scripture, which proceeds at the pace of a mother stooping to her child, so to speak, so as not to leave us behind in our

weakness. But for those who are so cautious or fearful that they desire to bury predestination in order not to disturb weak souls—with what color will they cloak their arrogance when they accuse God indirectly of stupid thoughtlessness, as if he had not foreseen the peril that they feel they have wisely met? Whoever, then, heaps odium upon the doctrine of predestination openly reproaches God, as if he had unadvisedly let slip something hurtful to the church.

5. Predestination and Foreknowledge of God; the Election of Israel

No one who wishes to be thought religious dares simply deny predestination, by which God adopts some to hope of life, and sentences others to eternal death. But our opponents, especially those who make foreknowledge its cause, envelop it in numerous petty objections. We, indeed, place both doctrines in God, but we say that subjecting one to the other is absurd.

When we attribute foreknowledge to God, we mean that all things always were, and perpetually remain, under his eyes, so that to his knowledge there is nothing future or past, but all things are present. And they are present in such a way that he not only conceives them through ideas, as we have before us those things which our minds remember, but he truly looks upon them and discerns them as things placed before him. And this foreknowledge is extended throughout the universe to every creature. We call predestination God's eternal decree, by which he compacted with himself what he willed to become of each man. For all are not created in equal condition; rather, eternal life is foreordained for some, eternal damnation for others. Therefore, as any man has been created to one or the other of these ends, we speak of him as predestined to life or to death.

God has attested this not only in individual persons but has given us an example of it in the whole offspring of Abraham, to make it clear that in his choice rests the future condition of each nation. "When the most high divided the nations, and separated the sons of Adam . . . the people of Israel were his portion, . . . the cord of his inheritance" [Deut. 32:8-9f.; cf. Vg.]. The separation is apparent to all men: in the person of Abraham, as in a dry tree trunk, one people is peculiarly chosen, while the others are rejected; but the cause does not appear except that Moses, to cut off from posterity any occasion to boast, teaches that they excel solely by God's freely given love. For he declares this the cause of their deliverance: that God loved the patriarchs, "and chose their seed after them" [Deut. 4:37].

More explicitly, in another chapter: "Not because you surpassed all other peoples in number did he take pleasure in you to choose you, . . . but because he loved you" [Deut. 7:7-8f.; cf. Vg.]. Moses quite frequently repeats the same declaration: "Behold, to the Lord your God belong heaven, . . . earth, and all that is in them. Only he delighted in your fathers and loved them, and chose you their seed" [Deut. 10:14-15; cf. Vg.]. Likewise, elsewhere, sanctification is enjoined upon them because they have been chosen as his "special people" [Deut. 7:6]. And in another passage love is again declared the reason for his protection [Deut. 23:5]. Believers also proclaim this with one voice: "He chooses our heritage for us, the glory of Jacob, whom he has loved" [Ps. 47:4]. For all who have been adorned with gifts by God credit them to his freely given love because they knew not only that they had not merited them but

that even the holy patriarch himself was not endowed with such virtue as to acquire such a high honor for himself and his descendants. And in order more effectively to crush all pride, he reproaches them as deserving no such thing, since they were a stubborn and stiff-necked people [Exod. 32:9; cf. Deut. 9:6]. Also, the prophets often confront the Jews with this election, to the latter's displeasure and by way of reproach, since they had shamefully fallen away from it [cf. Amos 3:2].

Be this as it may, let those now come forward who would bind God's election either to the worthiness of men or to the merit of works. Since they see one nation preferred above all others, and hear that God was not for any reason moved to be more favorably inclined to a few, ignoble—indeed, even wicked and stubborn—men, will they quarrel with him because he chose to give such evidence of his mercy? But they shall neither hinder his work with their clamorous voices nor strike and hurt his righteousness by hurling the stones of their insults toward heaven. Rather, these will fall back on their own heads! Also, the Israelites are recalled to this principle of a freely given covenant when thanks are to be given to God, or when hope is to be aroused for the age to come. "He has made us and not we ourselves," says the prophet, "we are his people and the sheep of his pastures" [Ps. 100:3; cf. Ps. 99:3, Vg.]. The negative, which is added to exclude "ourselves," is not superfluous, since by it they may know that God is not only the Author of all good things in which they abound but has derived the cause from himself, because nothing in them was worthy of so great honor.

He also bids them be content with God's mere good pleasure, in these words: "O seed of Abraham his servant, sons of Jacob, his chosen ones!" [Ps. 105:6; 104:6, Vg.]. And after having recounted the continuing benefits of God as the fruit of election, he finally concludes that he acted so generously because "he remembered his covenant" [Ps. 105:42]. With this doctrine the song of the whole church is in accord: "Thy right hand . . . and the light of thy countenance gave the land to our fathers, for thou didst delight in them" [Ps. 44:3]. Now we must note that where "land" is mentioned, it is a visible symbol of the secret separation that includes adoption. David elsewhere urges the people to the same gratitude: "Blessed is the nation whose God is Jehovah, the people whom he has chosen as his heritage!" [Ps. 33:12]. And Samuel arouses them to good hope: "For God will not forsake you for his great name's sake, since it has pleased him to create you a people for himself" [1 Sam. 12:22f.]. In this way, David also arms himself for battle when his faith is assailed: "The blessed one whom thou hast elected . . . will dwell in thy courts" [Ps. 65:4; cf. 64:5 Vg.]. Moreover, because the election, being hidden in God, was confirmed by the first liberation, as well as by the second and other intermediate benefits, the word "to elect" is applied to this effect in Isaiah: "God will have mercy on Jacob and will yet elect out of Israel" [Isa. 14:1f.]. In describing the time to come, the prophet says that the gathering together of the remnant of the people, whom he had seemed to forsake, will be a sign of the stability and firmness of his election, which at that very moment had seemingly failed. When he also says in another place, "I have elected you and not cast you off" [Isa. 41:9], he emphasizes the ceaseless course of the remarkable generosity of his fatherly benevolence. The angel in Zechariah expresses this more clearly: "God . . . will yet elect Jerusalem"

[Zech. 2:12]. It is as though he, by more harshly chastening, had rejected her, or as though the exile had been an interruption of election. Yet election remains inviolable, although its signs do not always appear.

6. The Second Stage: Election and Reprobation of Individual Israelites

We must now add a second, more limited degree of election, or one in which God's more special grace was evident, that is, when from the same race of Abraham God rejected some but showed that he kept others among his sons by cherishing them in the church. Ishmael had at first obtained equal rank with his brother, Isaac, for in him the spiritual covenant had been equally sealed by the sign of circumcision. Ishmael is cut off; then Esau; afterward, a countless multitude, and well-nigh all Israel. In Isaac the seed was called; the same calling continued in Jacob. God showed a similar example in rejecting Saul. This is also wonderfully proclaimed in the psalm: "He rejected the tribe of Joseph, and chose not the tribe of Ephraim but chose the tribe of Judah" [Ps. 78:67-68; cf. LXX and Ps. 77:67-68, Vg.]. This is several times repeated in the sacred history, the better to reveal in this change the marvelous secret of God's grace. By their own defect and guilt, I admit, Ishmael, Esau, and the like were cut off from adoption. For the condition had been laid down that they should faithfully keep God's covenant, which they faithlessly violated. Yet this was a singular benefit of God, that he had deigned to prefer them to the other nations, as the psalm says: "He has not dealt thus with any other nations, and has not shown them his judgments" [Ps. 147:20, cf. LXX].

But I had good reason to say that here we must note two degrees, for in the election of a whole nation God has already shown that in his mere generosity he has not been bound by any laws but is free, so that equal apportionment of grace is not to be required of him. The very inequality of his grace proves that it is free. For this reason, Malachi emphasizes Israel's ungratefulness because, while not only chosen from the whole human race but also separated out of a holy house as his own people, they faithlessly and impiously despise God, their beneficent Father. "Was not Esau Jacob's brother?" he asks. "Yet I have loved Jacob, but I have hated Esau" [Mal. 1:2-3; Rom. 9:13]. For God takes it for granted that, as both had been begotten of a holy father, were successors of the covenant, and in short, were branches of a sacred root, the children of Jacob were now under extraordinary obligation, having been received into that dignity; but after the firstborn, Esau, had been rejected, and their father, who was inferior by birth, had been made heir, God accuses them of being doubly thankless, and complains that they were not held by that double bond.

7. The Election of Individuals as Actual Election

Although it is now sufficiently clear that God by his secret plan freely chooses whom he pleases, rejecting others, still his free election has been only half explained until we come to individual persons, to whom God not only offers salvation but so assigns it that the certainty of its effect is not in suspense or doubt. These are reckoned among the unique offspring mentioned by Paul [cf. Rom. 9:7-8; Gal. 3:16ff.]. The adoption was put in Abraham's hands. Nevertheless, because many of his descendants were cut off as rotten members, we must, in order that election may be effectual and truly enduring, ascend to the Head, in whom the heavenly Father

has gathered his elect together, and has joined them to himself by an indissoluble bond. So, indeed, God's generous favor, which he has denied to others, has been displayed in the adoption of the race of Abraham; yet in the members of Christ a far more excellent power of grace appears, for, engrafted to their Head, they are never cut off from salvation. Therefore Paul skillfully argues from the passage of Malachi that I have just cited that where God has made a covenant of eternal life and calls any people to himself, a special mode of election is employed for a part of them, so that he does not with indiscriminate grace effectually elect all [Rom. 9:13]. The statement "I have loved Jacob" [Mal. 1:2] applies to the whole offspring of the patriarch, whom the prophet there contrasts to the posterity of Esau. Still this does not gainsay the fact that there was set before us in the person of one man an example of election that cannot fail to accomplish its purpose. Paul with good reason notes that they are called the "remnant" [Rom. 9:27; 11:5; cf. Isa. 10:22-23]. For experience shows that of the great multitude many fall away and disappear, so that often only a slight portion remains.

It is easy to explain why the general election of a people is not always firm and effectual: to those with whom God makes a covenant, he does not at once give the spirit of regeneration that would enable them to persevere in the covenant to the very end. Rather, the outward change, without the working of inner grace, which might have availed to keep them, is intermediate between the rejection of mankind and the election of a meager number of the godly. The whole people of Israel has been called "the inheritance of God" [Deut. 32:9; 1 Kgs. 8:51; Ps. 28:9; 33:12; etc.], yet many of them were foreigners. But because God has not pointlessly covenanted that he would become their Father and redeemer, he sees to his freely given favor rather than to the many who treacherously desert him. Even through them his truth was not set aside, for where he preserved some remnant for himself, it appeared that his calling was "without repentance" [Rom. 11:29]. For the fact that God was continually gathering his church from Abraham's children rather than from profane nations had its reason in his covenant, which, when violated by that multitude, he confined to a few that it might not utterly cease. In short, that adoption of Abraham's seed in common was a visible image of the greater benefit that God bestowed on some out of the many. This is why Paul so carefully distinguishes the children of Abraham according to the flesh from the spiritual children who have been called after the example of Isaac [Gal. 4:28]. Not that it was a vain and unprofitable thing simply to be a child of Abraham; such could not be said without dishonoring the covenant! No, God's unchangeable plan, by which he predestined for himself those whom he willed, was in fact intrinsically effectual unto salvation for these spiritual offspring alone. But I advise my readers not to take a prejudiced position on either side until, when the passages of Scripture have been adduced, it shall be clear what opinion ought to be held.

Summary Survey of the Doctrine of Election

As Scripture, then, clearly shows, we say that God once established by his eternal and unchangeable plan those whom he long before determined once for all to receive into salvation, and those whom, on the other hand, he would devote to destruction. We assert that, with respect to the elect, this

plan was founded upon his freely given mercy, without regard to human worth; but by his just and irreprehensible but incomprehensible judgment he has barred the door of life to those whom he has given over to damnation. Now among the elect we regard the call as a testimony of election. Then we hold justification another sign of its manifestation, until they come into the glory in which the fulfillment of that election lies. But as the Lord seals his elect by call and justification, so, by shutting off the reprobate from knowledge of his name or from the sanctification of his Spirit, he, as it were, reveals by these marks what sort of judgment awaits them. Here I shall pass over many fictions that stupid men have invented to overthrow predestination. They need no refutation, for as soon as they are brought forth they abundantly prove their own falsity. I shall pause only over those which either are being argued by the learned or may raise difficulty for the simple, or which impiety speciously sets forth in order to assail God's righteousness. . . .

63. The Church

Book IV, The External Means or Aims by Which God Invites Us into the Society of Christ and Holds Us Therein

A Comparison of the False and True Church

1. The Basic Distinction

It has already been explained how much we ought to value the ministry of the Word and sacraments, and how far our reverence for it should go, that it may be to us a perpetual token by which to distinguish the church. That is, wherever the ministry remains whole and uncorrupted, no moral faults or diseases prevent it from bearing the name "church." Secondly, it is not so weakened by trivial errors as not to be esteemed lawful. We have, moreover, shown that the errors which ought to be pardoned are those which do not harm the chief doctrine of religion, which do not destroy the articles of religion on which all believers ought to agree; and with regard to the sacraments, those which do not abolish or throw down the lawful institution of the author. But, as soon as falsehood breaks into the citadel of religion and the sum of necessary doctrine is overturned and the use of the sacraments is destroyed, surely the death of the church follows—just as a man's life is ended when his throat is pierced or his heart mortally wounded. And that is clearly evident from Paul's words when he teaches that the church is founded upon the teaching of the apostles and prophets, with Christ himself the chief cornerstone [Eph. 2:20]. If the foundation of the church is the teaching of the prophets and apostles, which bids believers entrust their salvation to Christ alone—then take away that teaching, and how will the building continue to stand? Therefore, the church must tumble down when that sum of religion dies which alone can sustain it. Again, if the true church is the pillar and foundation of truth [1 Tim. 3: 15], it is certain that no church can exist where lying and falsehood have gained sway.

2. The Roman Church and Its Claim

Since conditions are such under popery, one can understand how much of the church remains there. Instead of the ministry of the Word, a perverse government compounded of lies rules there, which partly extinguishes the pure light, partly chokes it. The foulest sacrilege has been introduced in place of the Lord's supper. The worship of God has been deformed by a diverse and unbearable mass of superstitions. Doctrine (apart from which Christianity cannot stand) has been entirely buried and driven out. Public assemblies have become schools of idolatry and ungodliness. In withdrawing from deadly participation in so many misdeeds, there is accordingly no danger that we be snatched away from the church of Christ. The communion of the church was not established on the condition that it should serve to snare us in idolatry, ungodliness, ignorance of God, and other sorts of evils, but rather to hold us in the fear of God and obedience to truth.

They indeed gloriously extol their church to us to make it seem that there is no other in the world. Thereupon, as if the matter were settled, they conclude that all who dare withdraw from the obedience with which they adorn the church are schismatics; that all who dare mutter against its doctrine are heretics. But what are their reasons to prove that they have the true church? From ancient chronicles they allege what once took place in Italy, France, and Spain. They claim to take their origin from those holy men who with sound doctrine founded and raised up churches, and by their blood established the very doctrine and upbuilding of the church. Moreover, they say that the church was so consecrated both by spiritual gifts and by the blood of martyrs among them, and preserved by an unending succession of bishops, in order that it should not perish. They recall how much Irenaeus, Tertullian, Origen, Augustine, and others made of this succession.

But I shall easily enable those willing to consider these claims for a moment with me to understand how trifling and plainly ludicrous they are. Indeed, I would urge them also to give serious attention to this, if I were confident that I could benefit them by so teaching. But since their one purpose is to defend their own cause in any way they can without regard for truth, I shall say only a few things by which good men and those zealous for truth can extricate themselves from their deceits.

First, I ask them why they do not mention Africa, Egypt, and all Asia. The reason is that in all these districts this sacred succession of bishops, by virtue of which they boast that the churches have been maintained, has ceased to be. They therefore revert to the point that they have the true church because from its beginning it has not been destitute of bishops, for one has followed another in unbroken succession. But what if I confront them with Greece? I therefore ask them once more why they say that the church perished among the Greeks, among whom the succession of bishops (in their opinion the sole custodian and preserver of the church) has never been interrupted. They make the Greeks schismatics; with what right? Because in withdrawing from the apostolic see, they lost their privilege. What? Would not they who fall away from Christ deserve to lose it much more? It therefore follows that this pretense of succession is vain unless their descendants conserve safe and uncorrupted the truth of Christ which they have received at their fathers' hands, and abide in it.

3. The False Church, Despite Its High Pretensions, Shows That It Does Not Hear God's Word.

The Romanists, therefore, today make no other pretension than what the Jews once apparently claimed when they were reproved for blindness, ungodliness, and idolatry by the Lord's prophets. For like the Romanists, they boasted gloriously of temple, ceremonies, and priestly functions, and measured the church very convincingly, as it seemed to

them, by these. So in place of the church the Romanists display certain outward appearances which are often far removed from the church and without which the church can very well stand. Accordingly, we are to refute them by the very argument with which Jeremiah combatted the stupid confidence of the Jews. That is, "Let them not boast in lying words, saying, 'This is the temple of the Lord, the temple of the Lord, the temple of the Lord'" [Jer. 7:4]. For the Lord nowhere recognizes any temple as his save where his Word is heard and scrupulously observed. So, although the glory of God sat between the cherubim in the sanctuary [Ezek. 10:4], and he promised his people that this would be his abiding seat; when the priests corrupt his worship with wicked superstitions, he moves elsewhere and strips the place of holiness. If that temple, which seemed consecrated as God's everlasting abode, could be abandoned by God and become profane, there is no reason why these men should pretend to us that God is so bound to persons and places, and attached to external observances, that he has to remain among those who have only the title and appearance of the church [Rom. 9:6].

And this is Paul's contention in chapters 9 to 12 of the Letter to the Romans [Romans 9–11]. For this fact sorely troubled weak consciences, that, while the Jews seemed to be God's people, they not only rejected the teaching of the gospel but also persecuted it. Accordingly, after Paul has expounded the doctrine, he disposes of this difficulty, denying those Jews (as enemies of truth) to be the church, even though they lacked nothing which could otherwise be desired for the outward form of the church. He denies it, then, because they would not embrace Christ. He speaks somewhat more explicitly in the Letter to the Galatians, where, in comparing Ishmael with Isaac, he states that many have a place in the church to whom the inheritance does not apply, for they are not the offspring of a free mother [Gal. 4:22ff.]. From this, Paul goes on to the comparison of the two Jerusalems. For just as the law was given on Mt. Sinai, so the gospel came forth from Jerusalem. Thus, many born and brought up as slaves boast without hesitation that they are children of God and of the church. Indeed, they haughtily despise God's real children, even though they themselves are bastards. We also, on the contrary, while we once heard it declared from heaven, "Cast out this slave woman with her son" [Gen. 21:10], rely on this inviolable decree and stoutly reject their insipid boastings. For if they boast of outward profession, Ishmael also was circumcised; if they contend for antiquity, he was the firstborn: yet we see him repudiated. If a reason be sought, Paul points out that only those born of the pure and lawful seed of doctrine are accounted God's children [Rom. 9:6-9].

According to this reasoning, God denies that he is bound to wicked priests by the fact that he covenanted with their father Levi to be his angel or interpreter. Indeed, he turns back upon them that false glorying with which they habitually rose up against the prophets—that the dignity of the priesthood was to be held in peculiar esteem. God willingly admits this and disputes with them on the ground that he is ready to keep the covenant, but that when they do not reciprocate, they deserve to be repudiated. See what value this succession has, unless it also include a true and uninterrupted emulation on the part of the successors! For they, as soon as they are convicted of degenerating from their origin, are deprived of all honor [Mal. 2:1-9]. Unless, perhaps, because Caiaphas

succeeded many devout priests (indeed, from Aaron to him there was an unbroken succession), that wicked assembly deserved the name "church"! Yet not even in earthly dominions was it tolerable that the tyranny of Caligula, Nero, Heliogabalus, or the like should be considered a true state of the commonwealth just because they succeeded a Brutus, a Scipio, or a Camillus. But especially in the organization of the church nothing is more absurd than to lodge the succession in persons alone to the exclusion of teaching.

Nothing was farther from the minds of the holy doctors (whom they falsely thrust upon us) than to prove absolutely, as if by right of inheritance, that the church exists wherever bishops succeed one another. But while it was uncontroverted that no change in doctrine had occurred from the beginning down to that age, they adopted this principle as sufficient to guard against all new errors; that is, they opposed them with the teaching firmly and with unanimous agreement maintained since the time of the apostles. Accordingly, there is no reason why men should any longer endeavor to deceive in the name of the church, which we reverently honor as we ought. But when they come to the definition of it, not only does water (as the saying goes) cleave to them, but they are stuck in their mire, for they put a foul harlot in place of Christ's sacred bride. That this substitution may not deceive us, let this admonition of Augustine's (besides others) come to mind. Speaking of the church, he says, "She herself is sometimes obscured, as if beclouded by a multitude of scandals; sometimes appears quiet and free in a time of tranquillity; sometimes is covered and tossed by waves of tribulations and temptations." He brings forward examples to show that often the strongest pillars valiantly suffered exile for the faith, or lay in hiding throughout the world.

4. The Church Is Founded upon God's Word.

In this same way the Romanists vex us today and frighten the uneducated with the name of the church, even though they are Christ's chief adversaries. Therefore, although they put forward temple, priesthood, and the rest of the outward shows, this empty glitter which blinds the eyes of the simple ought not to move us a whit to grant that the church exists where God's Word is not found. For this is the abiding mark with which our Lord has sealed his own: "Everyone who is of the truth hears my voice" [John 18:37]. Likewise: "I am the good shepherd; I know my sheep, and they know me" [John 10:14]. "My sheep hear my voice, and I know them, and they follow me" [John 10:27]. But a little before, he had said: "The sheep follow their shepherd, for they know his voice. A stranger they do not follow but flee from him, for they do not know the voice of strangers" [John 10:4-5]. Why do we willfully act like madmen in searching out the church when Christ has marked it with an unmistakable sign, which, wherever it is seen, cannot fail to show the church there; while where it is absent, nothing remains that can give the true meaning of the church? Paul reminds us that the church was founded not upon men's judgments, not upon priesthoods, but upon the teaching of apostles and prophets [Eph. 2:20]. Nay, Jerusalem is to be distinguished from Babylon, Christ's church from Satan's cabal, by the very difference with which Christ distinguishes between them. He says: "He who is of God hears the words of God. The reason why you do not hear them is that you are not of God" [John 8:47].

To sum up, since the church is Christ's kingdom, and he reigns by his Word alone, will it not be clear to any man that those are lying words [cf. Jer. 7:4] by which the king-dom of Christ is imagined to exist apart from his scepter (that is, his most holy Word)?

5. Defense against the Charge of Schism and Heresy

Now they treat us as persons guilty of schism and heresy because we preach a doctrine unlike theirs, do not obey their laws, and hold our separate assemblies for prayers, baptism and the celebration of the supper, and other holy activities.

This is indeed a very grave accusation but one that needs no long and labored defense. Those who, by making dissension, break the communion of the church are called heretics and schismatics. Now this communion is held together by two bonds, agreement in sound doctrine and brotherly love. Hence, between heretics and schismatics Augustine makes this sort of distinction: heretics corrupt the sincerity of the faith with false dogmas; but schismatics, while sometimes even of the same faith, break the bond of fellowship.

But it must also be noted that this conjunction of love so depends upon unity of faith that it ought to be its beginning, end, and, in fine, its sole rule. Let us therefore remember that whenever church unity is commended to us, this is required: that while our minds agree in Christ, our wills should also be joined with mutual benevolence in Christ. Paul, therefore, while urging us to it, takes it as his foundation that "there is . . . one God, one faith, and one baptism" [Eph. 4:5]. Indeed, wherever Paul teaches us to feel the same and will the same, he immediately adds, "in Christ" [Phil. 2:1, 5] or "according to Christ" [Rom. 15:5]. He means that apart from the Lord's Word there is not an agreement of believers but a faction of wicked men.

6. Christ's Headship the Condition of Unity

Cyprian, also following Paul, derives the source of concord of the entire church from Christ's episcopate alone. Afterward he adds:

The church is one, which is spread abroad far and wide into a multitude by an increase of fruitfulness. As there are many rays of the sun but one light, and many branches of a tree but one strong trunk grounded in its tenacious root, and since from one spring flow many streams, although a goodly number seem outpoured from their bounty and superabundance, still, at the source unity abides. Take a ray from the body of the sun; its unity undergoes no division. Break a branch from a tree; the severed branch cannot sprout. Cut off a stream from its source; cut off, it dries up. So also the church, bathed in the light of the Lord, extends over the whole earth: yet there is one light diffused everywhere.

Nothing more fitting could be said to express this indivisible connection which all members of Christ have with one another. We see how he continually calls us back to the Head himself. Accordingly, Cyprian declares that heresies and schisms arise because men return not to the source of truth, seek not the Head, keep not the teaching of the heavenly Master.

Now let them go and shout that we who have withdrawn from their church are heretics, since the sole cause of our separation is that they could in no way bear the pure profession of truth. I forbear to mention that they have expelled us with anathemas and curses—more than sufficient reason to absolve us, unless they wish to condemn the apostles also as schismatics, whose case was like our own. Christ, I say, forewarned his apostles that they would be cast out of the synagogues for his name's sake [John 16:2]. Now those synagogues of which he speaks were then considered lawful churches. Since, therefore, it is clear that we have been cast out, and we are ready to show that this happened for Christ's sake, surely the case ought to be investigated before any decision is made about us, one way or the other. But I willingly grant them this point, if they so desire. For it is enough for me that it behooved us to withdraw from them that we might come to Christ.

7. The Condition of the Roman Church Resembles That of Israel under Jeroboam.

But it will appear even more clearly how we ought to esteem all the churches which are in subjection to that Roman idol's tyranny if they be compared with the ancient church of Israel, described by the prophets. The true church existed among the Jews and Israelites when they kept the laws of the covenant. That is, by God's beneficence they obtained those things by which the church is held together. They had the doctrine of truth in the law; its ministry was in the hands of priests and prophets. They were initiated into religion by the sign of circumcision; for the strengthening of their faith they were exercised in the other sacraments. There is no doubt that the titles with which the Lord honored his church applied to their society. Afterward, having forsaken the law of the Lord, they sank into idolatry and superstition and partly lost that privilege. For who has dared to take the name of church away from those among whom God entrusted the preaching of his Word and the observance of his sacraments? Again, who has without exception dared to call that assembly "church" where the Lord's Word is openly and with impunity trodden underfoot? where his ministry, the church's chief sinew, indeed its very soul, is destroyed?

8. Despite the Idolatry of the Jews, Their Church Remained.

What, then, someone will ask—did, therefore, no trace of the church remain among the Jews after they fell away into idolatry? The answer is easy. First, I say that in falling away there were certain degrees. For we shall not say that there was the same decline in Israel as in Judah at the time when both first turned aside from the pure worship of God. Jeroboam, when he first fashioned calves against God's express prohibition, and dedicated an unlawful place for worship, utterly corrupted religion [1 Kgs. 12:28ff.]. The people of Judah contaminated themselves with wicked and superstitious customs before they falsified the outward form of their religion. For although under Rehoboam they had already commonly adopted many perverted rites, still because the teaching of the law, the priestly order, and such rites as God had ordained continued in Jerusalem, the godly there had a church in passable condition. Among the Israelites, to Ahab's reign things got not a whit better, and then got even worse. The kings who came after, until the destruction of the kingdom, were partly like Ahab, partly (when they wanted to be a little better) followed the example of Jeroboam. But all without exception were ungodly and idolaters. In Judah, there were from time to time various changes: while some kings perverted the worship of God with false and contrived superstitions, others restored the decadent religion. Finally, even the priests themselves befouled God's temple with profane and loathsome ceremonies.

9. The Papal Church Corrupt and to Be Repudiated

Come now, let the papists deny if they can—however much they extenuate their faults—that the condition of religion among them is as corrupt and debased as it was in the kingdom of Israel under Jeroboam. But they have a grosser idolatry. And in doctrine they are not one droplet purer, but actually even more impure in this! God, and indeed all men endowed with average judgment, will be my witnesses; and even the thing itself declares that I am not exaggerating here.

Now when they wish to constrain us to the communion of their church, they demand two things of us. The first is that we should participate in all their prayers, sacraments, and ceremonies. The second, that we should grant to their church every honor, power, and jurisdiction that Christ gives to his church.

As to the first point, I admit that all the prophets who were at Jerusalem when things were absolutely corrupt neither sacrificed privately nor had separate assemblies from the others for prayer. For they had God's command by which they were bidden to assemble in Solomon's Temple [Deut. 12:11, 13]. They knew that the Levitical priests, although unworthy of that office, because ordained ministers of sacred rites by the Lord [Exod. 29:9] and not yet deposed, still held that office by right. But—the chief point of the whole question—they were not compelled to any superstitious worship; indeed, they were obligated to nothing that had not been instituted by God.

But among these men—I mean the papists—where is the resemblance? For we can scarcely have any meeting with them in which we do not pollute ourselves with manifest idolatry. Surely, their chief bond of communion is in the mass, which we abominate as the greatest sacrilege. And whether we do this rightly or recklessly will appear elsewhere. Now it is enough to show that in this respect our case is different from that of the prophets, who, although present at the ceremonies of the wicked, were compelled neither to look at nor to take part in any rites save those established by God.

And, if we wish to have an example parallel in every respect, let us take it from the Israelite kingdom. According to Jeroboam's decree, circumcision remained, sacrifices were offered, the holy law was observed, the God whom their fathers had received was invoked; but, because of counterfeit and forbidden forms of worship, God disapproved and condemned whatever was done there [1 Kgs. 12:31]. Let anyone show me one prophet or any godly man who once worshiped or sacrificed in Bethel. For they knew that they could not do it without contaminating themselves with some sacrilege. We therefore conclude that among the godly the communion of the church ought not to extend so far that, if it degenerates into profane and corrupted rites, they have to follow it headlong.

10. Why We Must Separate from the Corrupted Church

Over the second point, however, we contend even more. For if we think of the church in this way—that we should reverence its judgment, defer to its authority, obey its warnings, be moved by its chastisements, and keep its communion scrupulously in all respects—then we cannot admit that they have a church without the necessity of subjection and obedience to it awaiting us. Yet we shall willingly concede to them what the prophets granted to the Jews and Israelites of their own age, when equal or even better conditions prevailed there. But we see how the prophets again and again proclaim that their assemblies are profane [Isa. 1:14], and

that it was no more lawful to consent to them than to deny God. And surely if those were churches, it follows that in Israel, Elijah, Micah, and the like, and in Judah, Isaiah, Jeremiah, Hosea, and others of that mark (whom the prophets, priests, and people of their age hated and cursed as worse than the uncircumcised) were strangers to the church of God. If those were churches, then the church is not the pillar of truth [1 Tim. 3:15], but the prop of falsehood; not the tabernacle of the living God, but a receptacle of idols. The prophets, then, had to depart from agreement with those assemblies, which were nothing but a wicked conspiracy against God.

In the same way if anyone recognizes the present congregations—contaminated with idolatry, superstition, and ungodly doctrine—as churches (in full communion of which a Christian man must stand—even to the point of agreeing in doctrine), he will gravely err. For if they are churches, the power of the keys is in their hands; but the keys have an indissoluble bond with the Word, which has been destroyed from among them. Again, if they are churches, Christ's promise prevails among them; "Whatever you bind," etc. [Matt. 16:19; 18:18; John 20:23]. But on the contrary, they disown from their communion all that genuinely profess themselves servants of Christ. Accordingly, either Christ's promise is vain, or they are not, at least in this regard, churches. Finally, instead of the ministry of the Word, they have schools of ungodliness and a sink of all kinds of errors. Consequently, by this reckoning either they are not churches or no mark will remain to distinguish the lawful congregations of believers from the assemblies of Turks.

11. Vestiges of the Church under the Papacy

Of old, certain peculiar prerogatives of the church remained among the Jews. In like manner, today we do not deprive the papists of those traces of the church which the Lord willed should among them survive the destruction. God had once for all made his covenant with the Jews, but it was not they who preserved the covenant; rather, leaning upon its own strength, it kept itself alive by struggling against their impiety. Therefore—such was the certainty and constancy of God's goodness—the Lord's covenant abode there. Their treachery could not obliterate his faithfulness, and circumcision could not be so profaned by their unclean hands as to cease to be the true sign and sacrament of his covenant. Whence the Lord called the children born to them his children [Ezek. 16:20-21], when these belonged to him only by a special blessing. So it was in France, Italy, Germany, Spain, and England after the Lord established his covenant there. When those countries were oppressed by the tyranny of Antichrist, the Lord used two means to keep his covenant inviolable. First, he maintained baptism there, a witness to this covenant; consecrated by his own mouth, it retains its force despite the impiety of men. Secondly, by his own providence he caused other vestiges to remain, that the church might not utterly die. And just as often happens when buildings are pulled down the foundations and ruins remain, so he did not allow his church either to be destroyed to the very foundations by Antichrist or to be leveled to the ground, even though to punish the ungratefulness of men who had despised his word he let it undergo frightful shaking and shattering, but even after this very destruction willed that a half-demolished building remain.

12. The Sound Elements Do Not Make the Corrupted Church a True Church.

However, when we categorically deny to the papists the title of the church, we do not for this reason impugn the existence of churches among them. Rather, we are only contending about the true and lawful constitution of the church, required in the communion not only of the sacraments (which are the signs of profession) but also especially of doctrine. Daniel [Dan. 9:27] and Paul [2 Thess. 2:4] foretold that Antichrist would sit in the temple of God. With us, it is the Roman pontiff we make the leader and standard-bearer of that wicked and abominable kingdom. The fact that his seat is placed in the temple of God signifies that his reign was not to be such as to wipe out either the name of Christ or of the church. From this it therefore is evident that we by no means deny that the churches under his tyranny remain churches. But these he has profaned by his sacrilegious impiety, afflicted by his inhuman domination, corrupted and well-nigh killed by his evil and deadly doctrines, which are like poisoned drinks. In them Christ lies hidden, half buried, the gospel overthrown, piety scattered, the worship of God nearly wiped out. In them, briefly, everything is so confused that there we see the face of Babylon rather than that of the holy city of God. To sum up, I call them churches to the extent that the Lord wonderfully preserves in them a remnant of his people, however woefully dispersed and scattered, and to the extent that some marks of the church remain—especially those marks whose effectiveness neither the devil's wiles nor human depravity can destroy. But on the other hand, because in them those marks have been erased to which we should pay particular regard in this discourse, I say that every one of their congregations and their whole body lack the lawful form of the church. . . .

64. The Lord's Supper

The Sacred Supper of Christ, and What It Brings to Us

1. Sign and Thing

God has received us, once for all, into his family, to hold us not only as servants but as sons. Thereafter, to fulfill the duties of a most excellent Father concerned for his offspring, he undertakes also to nourish us throughout the course of our life. And not content with this alone, he has willed, by giving his pledge, to assure us of this continuing liberality. To this end, therefore, he has, through the hand of his only-begotten Son, given to his church another sacrament, that is, a spiritual banquet, wherein Christ attests himself to be the life-giving bread, upon which our souls feed unto true and blessed immortality [John 6:51].

The knowledge of this high mystery is very necessary, and in view of its very greatness it demands a careful explanation. Furthermore, Satan, to deprive the church of this inestimable treasure, has long since spread clouds, and afterward, to obscure this light, has raised quarrels and conflicts to estrange the minds of simple folk from a taste for this sacred food, and also has tried the same trick in our own day. For these reasons, after summarizing the matter in a way intelligible to the unlearned, I shall resolve those difficulties with which Satan has tried to ensnare the world.

First, the signs are bread and wine, which represent for us the invisible food that we receive from the flesh and blood of Christ. For as in baptism, God, regenerating us, engrafts us into the society of his church and makes us his own by adoption, so we have said, that he discharges the function of a provident householder in continually supplying to us the food to sustain and preserve us in that life into which he has begotten us by his Word.

Now Christ is the only food of our soul, and therefore our heavenly Father invites us to Christ, that, refreshed by partaking of him, we may repeatedly gather strength until we shall have reached heavenly immortality.

Since, however, this mystery of Christ's secret union with the devout is by nature incomprehensible, he shows its figure and image in visible signs best adapted to our small capacity. Indeed, by giving guarantees and tokens he makes it as certain for us as if we had seen it with our own eyes. For this very familiar comparison penetrates into even the dullest minds: just as bread and wine sustain physical life, so are souls fed by Christ. We now understand the purpose of this mystical blessing, namely, to confirm for us the fact that the Lord's body was once for all so sacrificed for us that we may now feed upon it, and by feeding feel in ourselves the working of that unique sacrifice; and that his blood was once so shed for us in order to be our perpetual drink. And so speak the words of the promise added there: "Take, this is my body which is given for you" [1 Cor. 11:24; cf. Matt. 26:26; Mark 14:22; Luke 22:19]. We are therefore bidden to take and eat the body which was once for all offered for our salvation, in order that when we see ourselves made partakers in it, we may assuredly conclude that the power of his life-giving death will be efficacious in us. Hence, he also calls the cup "the covenant in his blood" [Luke 22:20; 1 Cor. 11:25]. For he in some measure renews, or rather continues, the covenant which he once for all ratified with his blood (as far as it pertains to the strengthening of our faith) whenever he proffers that sacred blood for us to taste.

2. Union with Christ as the Special Fruit of the Lord's Supper

Godly souls can gather great assurance and delight from this sacrament; in it they have a witness of our growth into one body with Christ such that whatever is his may be called ours. As a consequence, we may dare assure ourselves that eternal life, of which he is the heir, is ours; and that the kingdom of Heaven, into which he has already entered, can no more be cut off from us than from him; again, that we cannot be condemned for our sins, from whose guilt he has absolved us, since he willed to take them upon himself as if they were his own. This is the wonderful exchange which, out of his measureless benevolence, he has made with us; that, becoming Son of man with us, he has made us sons of God with him; that, by his descent to earth, he has prepared an ascent to heaven for us; that, by taking on our mortality, he has conferred his immortality upon us; that, accepting our weakness, he has strengthened us by his power; that, receiving our poverty unto himself, he has transferred his wealth to us; that, taking the weight of our iniquity upon himself (which oppressed us), he has clothed us with his righteousness.

3. The Spiritual Presence of Christ

In this sacrament we have such full witness of all these things that we must certainly consider them as if Christ here present were himself set before our eyes and touched by our hands. For his word cannot lie or deceive us: "Take, eat, drink: this is my body, which is given for you; this is my blood, which is shed for forgiveness of sins" [Matt. 26:26-28,

conflated with 1 Cor. 11:24; cf. Mark 14:22-24; Luke 22:19-20]. By bidding us take, he indicates that it is ours; by bidding us eat, that it is made one substance with us; by declaring that his body is given for us and his blood shed for us, he teaches that both are not so much his as ours. For he took up and laid down both, not for his own advantage but for our salvation.

And, indeed, we must carefully observe that the very powerful and almost entire force of the sacrament lies in these words: "which is given for you," "which is shed for you." The present distribution of the body and blood of the Lord would not greatly benefit us unless they had once for all been given for our redemption and salvation. They are therefore represented under bread and wine so that we may learn not only that they are ours but that they have been destined as food for our spiritual life.

And so as we previously stated, from the physical things set forth in the sacrament we are led by a sort of analogy to spiritual things. Thus, when bread is given as a symbol of Christ's body, we must at once grasp this comparison: as bread nourishes, sustains, and keeps the life of our body, so Christ's body is the only food to invigorate and enliven our soul. When we see wine set forth as a symbol of blood, we must reflect on the benefits which wine imparts to the body, and so realize that the same are spiritually imparted to us by Christ's blood. These benefits are to nourish, refresh, strengthen, and gladden. For if we sufficiently consider what value we have received from the giving of that most holy body and the shedding of that blood, we shall clearly perceive that those qualities of bread and wine are, according to such an analogy, excellently adapted to express those things when they are communicated to us.

4. The Meaning of the Promise of the Lord's Supper

It is not, therefore, the chief function of the sacrament simply and without higher consideration to extend to us the body of Christ. Rather, it is to seal and confirm that promise by which he testifies that his flesh is food indeed and his blood is drink [John 6:56], which feed us unto eternal life [John 6:55]. By this he declares himself to be the bread of life, of which he who eats will live forever [John 6:48, 50]. And to do this, the sacrament sends us to the cross of Christ, where that promise was indeed performed and in all respects fulfilled. For we do not eat Christ duly and unto salvation unless he is crucified, when in living experience we grasp the efficacy of his death. In calling himself the bread of life, he did not borrow that name from the sacrament, as some wrongly interpret. Rather, he had been given as such to us by the Father and showed himself as such when, being made a sharer in our human mortality, he made us partakers in his divine immortality; when, offering himself as a sacrifice, he bore our curse in himself to imbue us with his blessing; when, by his death, he swallowed up and annihilated death [cf. 1 Pet. 3:22, Vg., and 1 Cor. 15:54]; and when, in his resurrection, he raised up this corruptible flesh of ours, which he had put on, to glory and incorruption [cf. 1 Cor. 15:53-54]. . . .

65. Civil Government

On Civil Government

1. Differences between Spiritual and Civil Government

Now, since we have established above that man is under a twofold government, and since we have elsewhere discussed at sufficient length the kind that resides in the soul or inner man and pertains to eternal life, this is the place to say something also about the other kind, which pertains only to the establishment of civil justice and outward morality.

For although this topic seems by nature alien to the spiritual doctrine of faith which I have undertaken to discuss, what follows will show that I am right in joining them, in fact, that necessity compels me to do so. This is especially true since, from one side, insane and barbarous men furiously strive to overturn this divinely established order; while, on the other side, the flatterers of princes, immoderately praising their power, do not hesitate to set them against the rule of God himself. Unless both these evils are checked, purity of faith will perish. Besides, it is of no slight importance to us to know how lovingly God has provided in this respect for mankind, that greater zeal for piety may flourish in us to attest our gratefulness.

First, before we enter into the matter itself, we must keep in mind that distinction which we previously laid down so that we do not (as commonly happens) unwisely mingle these two, which have a completely different nature. For certain men, when they hear that the gospel promises a freedom that acknowledges no king and no magistrate among men, but looks to Christ alone, think that they cannot benefit by their freedom so long as they see any power set up over them. They therefore think that nothing will be safe unless the whole world is reshaped to a new form, where there are neither courts, nor laws, nor magistrates, nor anything which in their opinion restricts their freedom. But whoever knows how to distinguish between body and soul, between this present fleeting life and that future eternal life, will without difficulty know that Christ's spiritual kingdom and the civil jurisdiction are things completely distinct. Since, then, it is a Jewish vanity to seek and enclose Christ's kingdom within the elements of this world, let us rather ponder that what Scripture clearly teaches is a spiritual fruit, which we gather from Christ's grace; and let us remember to keep within its own limits all that freedom which is promised and offered to us in him. For why is it that the same apostle who bids us stand and not submit to the "yoke of bondage" [Gal. 5:1] elsewhere forbids slaves to be anxious about their state [1 Cor. 7:21], unless it be that spiritual freedom can perfectly well exist along with civil bondage? These statements of his must also be taken in the same sense: In the kingdom of God "there is neither Jew nor Greek, neither male nor female, neither slave nor free" [Gal. 3:28, Vg.]. And again, "there is not Jew nor Greek, uncircumcised and circumcised, barbarian, Scythian, slave, freeman; but Christ is all in all" [Col. 3:11f.]. By these statements he means that it makes no difference what your condition among men may be or under what nation's laws you live, since the kingdom of Christ does not at all consist in these things.

2. The Two "Governments" Are Not Antithetical.

Yet this distinction does not lead us to consider the whole nature of government a thing polluted, which has nothing to do with Christian men. That is what, indeed, certain fanatics who delight in unbridled license shout and boast: after we have died through Christ to the elements of this world [Col. 2:20], are transported to God's kingdom, and sit among heavenly beings, it is a thing unworthy of us and set far beneath our excellence to be occupied with those vile and worldly cares which have to do with business foreign to a Christian man. To what purpose, they ask, are there laws without trials and

tribunals? But what has a Christian man to do with trials themselves? Indeed, if it is not lawful to kill, why do we have laws and trials? But as we have just now pointed out that this kind of government is distinct from that spiritual and inward kingdom of Christ, so we must know that they are not at variance. For spiritual government, indeed, is already initiating in us upon earth certain beginnings of the heavenly kingdom, and in this mortal and fleeting life affords a certain forecast of an immortal and incorruptible blessedness. Yet civil government has as its appointed end, so long as we live among men, to cherish and protect the outward worship of God, to defend sound doctrine of piety and the position of the church, to adjust our life to the society of men, to form our social behavior to civil righteousness, to reconcile us with one another, and to promote general peace and tranquillity. All of this I admit to be superfluous, if God's kingdom, such as it is now among us, wipes out the present life. But if it is God's will that we go as pilgrims upon the earth while we aspire to the true fatherland, and if the pilgrimage requires such helps, those who take these from man deprive him of his very humanity. Our adversaries claim that there ought to be such great perfection in the church of God that its government should suffice for law. But they stupidly imagine such a perfection as can never be found in a community of men. For since the insolence of evil men is so great, their wickedness so stubborn, that it can scarcely be restrained by extremely severe laws, what do we expect them to do if they see that their depravity can go scot-free—when no power can force them to cease from doing evil?

3. The Chief Tasks and Burdens of Civil Government

But there will be a more appropriate place to speak of the practice of civil government. Now we only wish it to be understood that to think of doing away with it is outrageous barbarity. Its function among men is no less than that of bread, water, sun, and air; indeed, its place of honor is far more excellent. For it does not merely see to it, as all these serve to do, that men breathe, eat, drink, and are kept warm, even though it surely embraces all these activities when it provides for their living together. It does not, I repeat, look to this only, but also prevents idolatry, sacrilege against God's name, blasphemies against his truth, and other public offenses against religion from arising and spreading among the people; it prevents the public peace from being disturbed; it provides that each man may keep his property safe and sound; that men may carry on blameless intercourse among themselves; that honesty and modesty may be preserved among men. In short, it provides that a public manifestation of religion may exist among Christians, and that humanity be maintained among men.

Let no man be disturbed that I now commit to civil government the duty of rightly establishing religion, which I seem above to have put outside of human decision. For, when I approve of a civil administration that aims to prevent the true religion which is contained in God's law from being openly and with public sacrilege violated and defiled with impunity, I do not here, any more than before, allow men to make laws according to their own decision concerning religion and the worship of God.

But my readers, assisted by the very clarity of the arrangement, will better understand what is to be thought of the whole subject of civil government if we discuss its parts separately. These are three: the magistrate, who is the protector and guardian of the laws; the laws, according to which he governs; the people, who are governed by the laws and obey the magistrate.

Let us, then, first look at the office of the magistrate, noting whether it is a lawful calling approved of God; the nature of the office; the extent of its power; then, with what laws a Christian government ought to be governed; and finally, how the laws benefit the people, and what obedience is owed to the magistrate. . . .

✠

From J. T. McNeill, ed., and F. L. Battles, trans., Calvin: Institutes of the Christian Religion, 2 vols. *(Philadelphia: Westminster Press, 1955), 35–39, 69–81, 241–55, 494–503, 537–42, 689–701, 920–32, 1041–53, 1359–64, 1485–89.*

Chapter 5
The Reformation in England

✠

Introduction

The sixteenth-century transition from Roman Catholicism to Protestantism in England was a long and extremely complex process which even today generates heated controversy among historians. Many of the most important questions have been recently reopened. Was the late medieval Roman Catholic Church a decadent institution, perceived by the masses as oppressive and unresponsive to their needs? Or was it a vibrant, flourishing institution in which most people found spiritual fulfillment and to which they remained loyal? Was the Reformation eagerly embraced by the vast majority, or was it imposed by political authority on an unenthusiastic and indifferent populace? And was the institutional result, the Church of England, a middle way between Rome and Geneva, or was its leadership solidly committed to the Reformed perspective? These complex questions, while they admit of no easy answers, must be kept in mind while studying the basic texts which follow.

What can be said with relative certainty is that the English church on the eve of the Reformation was not in crisis. True, the Lollard heresy claimed some support in its challenge to the established church. The wealth of the church and the lavish lifestyle of some of its officials attracted a certain amount of criticism. The legal privileges of the clergy caused some resentment. But none of this seems to have amounted to widespread discontent. Protestant ideas from the continent had some adherents in the 1520s, but nothing resembling a mass movement. These things could be seen as warning signs, perhaps, but not as smoldering embers about to burst into flame.

The decisive impetus came of course during the reign of Henry VIII (1509–1547), and it involved church-political change rather than religious reform. Essentially Henry had to have himself declared head of the church in England in order to have his marriage to Catherine of Aragon annulled. Outspoken opponents of royal supremacy were now eliminated. But Henry also wished to remain faithful to traditional Roman Catholic doctrine, and so outspoken sympathizers with Protestant beliefs also became victims. Others like Thomas Cranmer, who was archbishop of Canterbury from 1533 to 1553, clearly had Protestant sympathies but remained discreet about these and thus prolonged their earthly sojourn.

When Edward VI, a sickly child of nine, inherited the throne in 1547, leaders such as Cranmer felt at greater liberty to express and promote their Protestant leanings. Now a full-scale religious Reformation was soon under way. A *Book of Common Prayer* was approved in 1549 (and then a revised one in 1552), standardizing distinctively Protestant forms of worship. Priests were allowed to marry. Cranmer's *Forty-two Articles* of 1553 summarized an unmistakably Protestant church doctrine. But none of this meant that the masses were eagerly embracing the new faith. Some actively resisted it, others enthusiastically promoted it, but most perhaps simply acquiesced.

A great reversal set in, of course, when the fervently Catholic Mary succeeded to the throne in 1553. Now, insofar as it was possible, the old regime was restored. To begin with, Mary had much popular support, but her ruthlessness in burning Protestants (including Cranmer) at the stake seems to have helped turn public opinion against her and prepare the way for the restoration of Protestantism when Elizabeth I became queen in 1558.

Under Elizabeth, the *Acts of Supremacy* and *Uniformity* (1559), and the *Thirty-nine Articles* (1563) provided the legal foundation for a return to Protestantism and for a uniquely English church. Protestant leaders, exiled under Mary, now returned. Clergy with Protestant sympathies who had remained in England and suppressed these instincts during Mary's reign joined them in promoting religious reform known as the Elizabethan Settlement. By perhaps the 1580s then, one can begin to speak of a Protestant England, in the sense that many lay people accepted the reform, albeit still with varying degrees of enthusiasm. Already at this stage, however, dissident elements refused to accept the settlement. For Roman Catholic "recusants" on the one hand, Elizabeth's church was too Protestant, and for "Puritans" on the other hand, it was still too Catholic. Nevertheless, by the time Elizabeth died in 1603, her "middle way" dominated religious life in England.

The following documents illustrate the major features of this development.

Origins: Henry VIII

66. Act of Supremacy (1534)

After long and complex maneuvering to solve Henry's marital problems, an English ecclesiastical court annulled his marriage to Catherine of Aragon in 1533. The pope thereupon excommunicated Henry, who responded in 1534 with this act of parliament. This legal repudiation of papal authority capitalized on existing anti-Roman sentiment and required a loyalty oath to the king. Refusal to sign meant the death penalty for church leaders like Thomas More.

✠

Albeit the King's Majesty justly and rightfully is and oweth to be the supreme head of the Church of England, and so is recognized by the clergy of this realm in their convocations, yet nevertheless for corroboration and confirmation thereof, and for increase of virtue in Christ's religion within this realm of England, and to repress and extirp all errors, heresies, and other enormities and abuses heretofore used in the same; be it enacted by authority of this present Parliament, that the King our sovereign lord, his heirs and successors, Kings of this realm, shall be taken, accepted, and reputed the only supreme head on earth of the Church of England, called *Anglicana Ecclesia*, and shall have and enjoy, annexed and united to the imperial crown of this realm, as well the style and title thereof, as all honors, dignities, preeminences, jurisdictions, privileges, authorities, immunities, profits, and commodities, to the said dignity of supreme head of the same Church belonging and appertaining; and that our said sovereign lord, his heirs and successors, Kings of this realm, shall have full power and authority from time to time to visit, repress, redress, reform, order, correct, restrain, and amend all such errors, heresies, abuses, offenses, contempts, and enormities, whatsoever they be, which by any manner spiritual authority or jurisdiction ought or may lawfully be reformed, repressed, ordered, redressed, corrected, restrained, or amended, most to the pleasure of almighty God, the increase of virtue in Christ's religion, and for the conservation of the peace, unity and tranquillity of this realm; any usage, custom, foreign laws, foreign authority, prescription, or any other thing or things to the contrary hereof notwithstanding.

✠

From G. Bray, ed., Documents of the English Reformation *(Minneapolis: Fortress Press, 1994), 113–14.*

67. Act of Six Articles (1539)

Henry did not intend for there to be a Reformation in England along the lines of the continental Reformations. This became clear in his Act of Six Articles, which reaffirmed traditional Roman Catholic teaching and practice, and repudiated typically "Protestant" innovations. The Act attached very severe penalties for dissenters, some of which were soon relaxed.

✠

1. Where the King's most excellent Majesty is, by God's law, supreme head immediately under him of this whole Church and Congregation of England, intending the conservation of this same church and congregation in a true, sincere and uniform doctrine of Christ's religion, calling also to his most blessed and gracious remembrance as well the great and quiet assurance, prosperous

increase and other innumerable commodities, which have ever ensued, come and followed, of concord, agreement and unity in opinions, as also the manifold perils, dangers and inconveniences which have heretofore, in many places and regions, grown, sprung and arisen, of the diversities of minds and opinions especially of matters of Christian religion, and therefore desiring that such a unity might and should be charitably established in all things touching and concerning the same, as the same, so being established, might chiefly be to the honor of almighty God, the very author and fountain of all true unity and sincere concord, and consequently redound to the common wealth of this his Highness's most noble realm, and of all his loving subjects, and other residents or inhabitants of or in the same; hath therefore caused and commanded that this his most high court of Parliament, for sundry and many urgent causes and considerations, to be at this time summoned, and also a synod and convocation of all the archbishops, bishops and other learned men of the clergy of this his realm, to be in like manner assembled.

And for as much as in the said Parliament, synod and convocation, there were certain articles, matters and questions proponed and set forth touching Christian religion, that is to say:

First, whether in the most blessed Sacrament of the Altar remaineth after consecration the substance of bread and wine or not;

Secondly, whether it be necessary by God's law that all men should be communicated with both kinds or not;

Thirdly, whether priests, (that is to say, men dedicated to God by priesthood), may by the law of God marry after, or not;

Fourthly, whether vows of chastity or widowhood made to God advisedly by man or woman, be by the law of God to be observed or not;

Fifthly, whether private masses stand with the law of God and be to be used and continued in the Church and Congregation of England, as things whereby good Christian people may and do receive both godly consolation and wholesome benefit or not;

Sixthly, whether auricular confession is necessary to be retained, continued, used and frequented in the church, or not;

The King's most royal Majesty, most prudently pondering and considering, that by occasion of variable and sundry opinions and judgments of the said articles, great discord and variance has arisen, as well amongst the clergy of this his realm, as amongst a great number of vulgar people, his loving subjects of the same, and being in a full hope and trust that a full and perfect resolution of the said articles should make a perfect concord and unity generally amongst all his loving and obedient subjects, of his most excellent goodness, not only commanded that the said articles should deliberately and advisedly, by his said archbishops, bishops and other learned men of his clergy, be debated, argued and reasoned, and their opinions therein to be understood, declared and known, but also most graciously vouchsafed, in his own princely person, to descend and come into his said high court of Parliament and council, and there, like a prince of most high prudence and no less learning, opened and declared many things of high learning and great knowledge, touching the said articles, matters and questions, for a unity to be had in the same; whereupon, after a great and long, deliberate and advised disputation and consultation had and made concerning the said articles, as well by the consent of the King's Highness, as by the assent of the

Lords spiritual and temporal, and other learned men of his clergy in their convocation, and by the consent of the Commons in this present Parliament assembled, it was and is finally resolved, accorded and agreed in manner and form following, that is to say:

First, that in the most blessed Sacrament of the Altar, by the strength and efficacy of Christ's mighty word (it being spoken by the priest), is present really, under the form of bread and wine, the natural body and blood of our Savior Jesus Christ, conceived of the Virgin Mary; and that after the consecration there remaineth no substance of bread and wine, nor any other substance, but the substance of Christ, God and man.

Secondly, that communion in both kinds is not necessary *ad salutem,* by the law of God, to all persons; and that it is to be believed, and not doubted of, but that in the flesh, under the form of bread, is the very blood; and with the blood, under the form of wine, is the very flesh; as well apart, as though they were both together;

Thirdly, that priests after the order of priesthood received, as afore, may not marry, by the law of God.

Fourthly, that vows of chastity or widowhood, by man or woman made to God advisedly, ought to be observed by the law of God; and that it exempts them from other liberties of Christian people, which without that they might enjoy.

Fifthly, that it is meet and necessary that private masses be continued and admitted in this the King's English Church and Congregation, as whereby good Christian people, ordering themselves accordingly, do receive both godly and goodly consolations and benefits; and it is agreeable also to God's law.

Sixthly, that auricular confession is expedient and necessary to be retained and continued, used and frequented in the church of God.

For the which most godly study, travail and pain of his Majesty, and determination and resolution of the premises, his most humble and obedient subjects, the Lords spiritual and temporal and the Commons in this present Parliament assembled, not only render and give unto his Highness their most high and hearty thanks, and think themselves most bounden to pray for the long continuance of his Grace's most royal estate, but also being desirous that his most godly enterprise may be well accomplished, and brought to a full end and perfection, and so established that the same might be to the honor of God, and after to the common quiet, unity and concord to be had in the whole body of this realm for ever, most humbly beseech his royal Majesty, that the resolution and determination above written of the said articles may be established, and perpetually perfected, by authority of this present Parliament:

It is therefore ordained and enacted by the King our sovereign lord, the Lords spiritual and temporal, and the Commons in this present Parliament assembled, and by the authority of the same, that if any person or persons within this realm of England, or any other the King's dominions, after the twelfth of July next coming (12 July 1539), by word, writing, printing, ciphering or in any other wise do publish, preach, teach, say, affirm, declare, dispute, argue or hold any opinion, that in the blessed Sacrament of the Altar, under the form of bread and wine, after the consecration therefore, there is not present really the natural body and blood of our Savior Jesus Christ, conceived of the Virgin Mary; or that after the said consecration there remaineth any substance of bread and wine, or any other substance but the substance of Christ, God and man; or after the time above said, publish, preach, teach, say, affirm, declare, dispute, argue, or hold opinion, that in the flesh under form of bread, is not the very blood of Christ, or that with the blood under form of wine is not the very flesh of Christ, as well apart as though they were both together, or by any of the means above-said or otherwise preach, teach, declare or affirm the said sacrament to be of other sub-stance than is abovesaid, or by any means contempt, deprave or despise the said blessed sacrament, that then every such person and persons so offending, their aiders, com-forters, counselors, consenters and abettors therein, being thereof convicted in form underwritten, by the authority abovesaid, shall be deemed and adjudged heretics, and that every such offense shall be judged man-ifest heresy, and that every such offender and offenders shall therefore have and suffer judgment, execution, pain and pains of death by way of burning, without any abjuration, clergy or sanctuary to be therefore permitted, had, allowed, admitted, or suffered; and also shall therefore forfeit and lose to the King's Highness, his heirs and successors, all his or their honors, manors, castles, lands, tenan-cies, rents, revisions, services, possessions and all other his or their hereditaments, goods and chattels, terms and freeholds whatsoever they be, which any such offender or offenders shall have, at the time of any such offense or offenses committed or done at any time after, as in cases of high treason.

2. And furthermore, be it enacted by the authority of this present Parliament, that if any person or persons, after the said twelfth day of July (12 July 1539), preach in any ser-mon or collation openly made to the King's people, or teach in any common school or to other congregation of people, or being called before such judges and according to such form of the law as hereafter shall be declared, do obstinately affirm, uphold, maintain or defend that the communion of the said blessed sacrament in both kinds, that is to say, in form of bread and also of wine, is nec-essary for the health of man's soul to be given or ministered to any person in both kinds, or that it is necessary so to be received or taken by any person, other than by priests being at mass and consecrating the same; or that any man, after the order of priesthood received as aforesaid, may marry or contract matrimony; or that private masses be not lawful or not laudable or should not be celebrated, had nor used in this realm, nor be not agreeable to the laws of God; or that auricular confession is not expedient and necessary to be retained and continued, used and frequented in the church of God; or if any priest, after the said twelfth day of July (12 July 1539), or any other man or woman which advisedly hath vowed or after the said day advisedly do vow chastity or widowhood, do actually marry or contract matrimony with any person, that then all and every person and persons so preaching, teaching, obstinately affirming, upholding, maintaining or defending, or making marriage or contract of matrimony as above specified, be and shall be by author-ity above written, deemed and adjudged a felon and felons; and that every offender in the same being duly convicted or attainted by the laws underwritten, shall therefore suf-fer pains of death as in cases of felony without any benefit of clergy or privilege of church or sanctuary to him or her to be allowed in that behalf, and shall forfeit all his or her lands and goods as in cases of felony; and that it shall be lawful to the patron or patrons, of any manner of benefice which any such

offender at the time of his said conviction or attainder had, to present one other incumbent thereunto, as if the same person so convicted or attainted had been bodily deceased.

3. Also be it enacted by the authority aforesaid that if any person or persons, after the said twelfth of July (12 July 1539) by word, writing, printing, ciphering or otherwise than is above rehearsed, publish, declare or hold opinion that the said communion of the blessed sacrament in both kinds aforesaid is necessary for the health of man's soul to be given or ministered in both kinds, and so ought or should be given or ministered to any person, or ought or should be so in both kinds received or taken by any person other than by priests, being at mass and consecrating the same as is aforesaid; or that any man after the order of priesthood received as is aforesaid, may marry or may make contract of matrimony; or that any man or woman which advisedly hath made or shall make a vow to God of chastity or widowhood, may marry or may make contract of matrimony; or that private masses be not lawful or not laudable or should not be celebrated, had nor used, nor be agreeable to the laws of God; or that auricular confession is not expedient and necessary to be retained and continued, used and frequented in the church of God; every person being for every such offense duly convicted and attainted, by the laws underwritten, shall forfeit and lose to the King our sovereign lord, all his goods and chattels for ever, and also the profits of all his lands, tenancies, annuities, fees and offices during his life, and all his benefices and spiritual promotions shall be utterly void; and also shall suffer imprisonment of his body at the will and pleasure of our said sovereign lord the King; and if any such person or persons, being once convicted of any of the offenses

mentioned in this article as is abovesaid, do afterwards eftsones [i.e., again, *Ed.*] offend in any of the same and be thereof accused, indicted or presented and convicted again by the authority of the laws underwritten, that then every such person and persons so being twice convicted and attainted of the said offenses or of any of them, shall be adjudged a felon and felons; and shall suffer judgment, execution and pains of death, loss and forfeiture of lands and goods as in cases of felony, without any privilege of clergy or sanctuary to be in any wise permitted, admitted or allowed in that behalf.

4. Be it further enacted by the authority abovesaid, that if any person which is or hath been a priest, before this present Parliament or during the time of session of the same, hath married and hath made any contract of matrimony with any woman, or that any man or woman, which before the making of this Act advisedly hath vowed chastity or widowhood before this present Parliament or during the session of the same, hath married or contracted matrimony with any person; that then every such marriage and contract of matrimony shall be utterly void and of none effect; and that the ordinaries within whose diocese or jurisdiction the person or persons so married or contracted is to be resident or abiding, shall from time to time make separation and divorces of the said marriages and contracts.

5. And further be it enacted by the authority abovesaid, that if any man which is or hath been a priest, as is aforesaid, at any time from and after the said twelfth day of July next coming (12 July 1539) do carnally keep or use any woman, to whom he is or hath been married, or with whom he hath contracted matrimony, or openly been conversant, nay kept company and familiarity with

any such woman to the evil example of other persons, every carnal use, copulation, open conversation, keeping of company and familiarity be and shall be deemed and adjudged felony, as well against the man as the woman; and that every such person so offending shall be inquired of, tried, punished, suffer, lose and forfeit all and every thing and things as other felons made and declared by this Act, and as in case of felony as is aforesaid.

6. And be it further enacted by authority abovesaid, that if any person or persons at any time hereafter contemn or contemptuously refuse, deny or abstain to be confessed, at the time commonly accustomed within this realm and Church of England, or contemn and contemptuously refuse, deny or abstain to receive the holy and blessed sacrament abovesaid at the time commonly used and accustomed for the same, that then every such offender being thereof duly convicted or attainted, by the laws underwritten, shall suffer such imprisonment and make such fine and ransom to the King our sovereign lord and his heirs as by his Highness or by his or their council shall be ordered or adjudged in that behalf; and if any such offender or offenders at any time or times after the said conviction or attainder so had, do eftsones [i.e., again, *Ed.*] contemn or contemptuously refuse, deny or abstain to be confessed or to be communicated in manner and form above written, and be thereof duly convicted or attainted by the laws underwritten, that then every such offense shall be deemed and adjudged felony and the offender or offenders therein shall suffer pains of death and lose and forfeit all his and their goods, lands and tenancies, as in cases of felony.

7. And for full and effectual execution of the premises before devised, ordered and enacted by this Act, be if further enacted by the authority of this present Parliament, that immediately after the said twelfth day of July next coming (12 July 1539), sundry commissions shall be made from time to time into every shire of this realm and Wales, and in and to such other places within the King's dominions as shall please his Majesty, to be directed to the archbishop or bishop of the diocese and to his chancellor or commissary, and to such other persons as shall be named by his Highness, or by such other as his Majesty at his pleasure shall appoint to name the same, which archbishop or bishop or his chancellor or commissary to be one, should hold and keep their sessions within the limits of their commission four several times of the year at the least, or oftener if they shall think it expedient by their discretions, and shall have power and authority by virtue of this Act and their said commission, as well to take information and accusation by the oaths and depositions of two able and lawful persons at the least, as to inquire by oaths of twelve men of all and singular the heresies, felonies, contempts and other offenses above written, committed, done or perpetrated within the limits of their commission; and that every such accusation and information containing the matter, names and surnames and dwelling places of the offenders and the day, year, place and county when and wherein their offenses were committed, shall be of as good force and effect in the law as if the matter therein contained had been presented by verdicts of twelve men.

8. And nevertheless it is further enacted that every of the said archbishops and bishops, and every of their chancellors, commissaries, archdeacons and other ordinaries, having any peculiar ecclesiastical jurisdiction within this realm or in Wales, or in any other

the King's dominions, shall have full power and authority by virtue of this Act as well to inquire in their visitations and senys [possibly: synods, *Ed.*], as there and elsewhere within their jurisdictions at any other time or place, to take accusations and informations as is aforesaid of the heresies, felonies, contempts and offenses above mentioned, done, committed or perpetrated within the limits of their jurisdictions and authorities; and that every such accusation, information and presentment so taken or had as is aforesaid, shall be of as good force and effect as if the matter therein contained had been presented before the justices of peace in their sessions; and also that justices of peace in their sessions, and every steward, understeward or deputy of steward of any leet or lawday in their leet or lawday, shall have like power and authority by virtue of this Act to inquire by the oaths of twelve lawful men of all and singular the heresies, felonies, contempts and other offenses above written, done, perpetrated or committed within the limits of their commissions and authorities.

9. And it is also enacted by the authority aforesaid, that every such person or persons, after whom any presentment, information or accusation shall be made or taken as is aforesaid, shall examine the accusers what other witness were by and present at the time of doing and committing of the offense whereof the information, accusation or presentment shall be made, and how many others than the accusers have knowledge thereof; and shall have power and authority to bind by recognizance to be taken afore them, as well the said accusers as all such other persons whom the same accusers shall declare to have knowledge of the offenses by them presented or informed, every of them in five pounds to the King our sovereign lord, to appear before

the commissioners afore whom the offender or offenders shall be tried at the day of the trial of such offenders; and that all and singular indictments, presentments, accusations, informations and recognizances taken and had as is aforesaid, within twenty days next after the taking of the same shall be certified in due form by writing upon parchment by the taker or takers thereof under his or their seals, unto any one of the said commissioners to be appointed as is aforesaid, within the limits of whose commission the heresies, felonies, contempts and offenses, whereof any such presentment, indictment, information or accusation shall be taken or had as is above written, shall be committed, done or perpetrated; and if any person or persons, which hereafter shall happen to take any such accusation, information, presentment or recognizances as is above said, do make default of the certificate thereof contrary to the form above rehearsed, that then every person and persons so offending shall forfeit to our sovereign lord the King of every such default ten pounds.

10. And it is further enacted by the authority abovesaid, that the said commissioners or three of them at the least, as is aforesaid by virtue of this Act, and their commission shall have full power and authority to make like process against every person and persons indicted, presented or accused in form as is above remembered, as is used and accustomed in case of felony, and that as well within the limits of their commission as into all other shires and places of the realm, Wales and other the King's dominions, as well within liberties as without, and the same process to be good and effectual in the law as in cases of felony; and upon the appearance of any of the offenders shall have full power and authority by virtue

of this Act and the said commission to hear and determine the aforesaid heresies, felonies, contempts and other offenses according to the laws of this realm and the effects of this Act.

11. And it is also enacted by the authority abovesaid, that every of the said commissioners, upon any such accusation, presentment or information, shall endeavor himself effectually, without affection, dread or corruption, to apprehend and take the offenders, and after the apprehension of any such offender or offenders, shall have full power and authority to let any person or persons so accused or presented upon sufficient sureties by their discretion to bail for their appearance, to be tried according to the tenor, form and effect of this Act.

12. And further it is enacted by the authority abovesaid that if any person or persons which hereafter shall be named and assigned to be commissioner or commissioners as is abovesaid, be accused, indicted or presented of or for any of the offenses above written, that then all and every such commissioner or commissioners so accused, indicted and presented, shall be examined, put to answer and tried of and upon any such offense according to the tenor and effect of this Act, before such other person or persons as it shall please the King's Highness to name, assign and appoint by his Grace's commission, to hear and determine the same.

13. And it is further enacted by authority abovesaid, that no person or persons which at any time hereafter shall be accused, indicted or presented, as is abovesaid, shall be admitted to the challenge of any person or persons, which shall be empanelled for the trial of his or their offense, for any matter or cause other than for malice or enmity, which challenge shall forthwith be tried in like manner as

other challenges be used to be tried in cases of felony.

14. And it is further enacted by the authority abovesaid, that all foreign pleas triable by the country, which at any time hereafter shall be pleaded by any person or persons hereafter to be arraigned, or put to answer upon any accusation, indictment or presentment, of or for any of the offenses above specified or of or for any of them, shall be tried before the same commissioners afore whom such person or persons shall be arraigned or put to answer, and by the jurors that shall try the said offense or offenses without any further respite or delay.

15. And it is further enacted by the authority abovesaid, that all mayors, sheriffs, stewards, bailiffs of liberties, jailers and other officers and ministers, of what name, degree or condition soever they be, and every of them, shall from time to time truly and diligently receive and serve all and all manner the process, precepts and commandments to them or any of them by the said commissioners or any of them to be made, given or directed touching or concerning the premises or any parcel thereof; and shall also from time to time be obedient and attendant unto the said commissioners for the time being for the due execution of this present Act or of anything therein contained.

16. And it is also enacted that every person which shall be named to be commissioner in the said commission, after that he hath knowledge thereof, shall effectually put his diligence and attendance in and about the execution of the said commission; and before he shall take upon him the execution of the said commission, shall take a corporal oath before the lord chancellor of England for the time being, or before him or them to whom the said lord chancellor shall direct the

King's writ of *Dedimus potestatem* to take the same, the tenor of which oath hereafter ensueth: "Ye shall swear that ye to your cunning, wit and power shall truly and indifferently execute the authority to you given by the King's commission made for correction of heretics and other offenders mentioned in the same commission, without any favor, affection, corruption, dread or malice to be borne to any person or persons, as God your help and all saints." And in case that any of the said persons named to be commissioners refuse to take the said oath, or willingly absent or eloign [i.e. distance, *Ed.*] himself from the taking of the said oath, then every such person so offending, and the same offense estreated and certified into the King's exchequer by the said lord chancellor, or by him or them to whom any such writ of *Dedimus potestatem* as is aforesaid shall be directed, shall forfeit and lose to our said sovereign lord the King for every time so offending, five marks of lawful money.

17. And it is also enacted by the authority abovesaid, that the said commissioners and every of them, shall from time to time have full power and authority by virtue of this Act to take into his or their keeping or possession all and all manner of books, which be or have been or hereafter shall be set forth, read or declared within this realm or other the King's dominions, wherein is or be contained or comprised any clause, article, matter or sentence repugnant or contrary to the tenor, form or effect of this present Act, or any of the articles contained in the same; and the said commissioners, or three of them at the least, to burn or otherwise destroy the said books or any part of them, as unto the said commissioners or unto three of them at the least shall be thought expedient by their discretions.

18. And it is also enacted by the authority abovesaid, that every parson, vicar, curate or parish priest of every parish church within this realm or other the King's dominions, or his or their deputy, upon the Sunday next after the first day of September next ensuing (7 September 1539), and so from thenceforth once in every quarter of the year at the least, shall openly, plainly and distinctly read this present Act in the parish church where he is parson, vicar, curate, parish priest or deputy, unto his or their parishioners then assembled together to hear divine service; and that every such parson, vicar, curate, or parish priest making default of reading this Act, contrary to the form aforesaid, shall forfeit unto our said sovereign lord, his heirs or successors, for every such default, forty shillings sterling.

19. Saving to all and singular person and persons, bodies politic and corporate, their heirs and successors, and to the heirs and successors of every of them, other than all and singular such person and persons that shall be hereafter convicted or attainted of or for any of the offenses or contempts above specified, their heirs and successors, and the heirs and successors of every of them, all such right, title, claim, interest, entry, possessions, rents, reversion, fees, annuities, commons, offices, profits and demands whatsoever as they or any of them have, or then at the time of the said conviction or attainder had, shall have, of, in or to any honors, castles, lordships, manors, lands, tenancies, liberties, franchises, advowsons [rights to church benefices] and other hereditaments, which any such person or persons being so convicted or attainted as is aforesaid, had or were entitled to have at the time of their offense or offenses committed or at any time after, and that in as ample manner,

form and condition to all intents, construc-
tions and purposes as if this Act had never
been had nor made; anything contained in
this Act to the contrary in any wise notwithstanding. Provided always that the Lords
shall not have nor claim any escheats of any
offender or offenders that shall be judged to
be burned by authority of this Act.

20. Be it also further enacted by the
authority aforesaid, not giving advantage or
detriment to any article aforesaid, that if any
man, which is or hath been priest or hereafter
shall be, at any time after the said twelfth
day of July (12 July 1539), do carnally use
and accustom any woman, or keep her as his
concubine, as by paying for her board, maintaining her with money, array or any other
gifts or means, to the evil example of other
persons, that then every such offender being
thereof duly convicted or attainted by the
laws mentioned in this Act, shall forfeit and
lose all his goods and chattels, benefices,
prebends and other spiritual promotions and
dignities, and also shall have and suffer
imprisonment of his body at the King's will
and pleasure; and that every of the said
benefices, prebends and other promotions
and dignities shall be to all intents and purposes utterly void as if the said offender had
resigned or permuted; and if any such
offender or offenders, at any time after the
said conviction or attainder, eftsones [i.e.,
again, *Ed.*] commit, do or perpetrate the said
offenses or any of them next afore rehearsed,
and be thereof duly convicted or attainted by
the laws aforesaid, that then all and every
such offense and offenses shall be deemed and
adjudged felony, and the offender and offenders therein shall suffer pains of death and lose
and forfeit all his and their goods, lands and
tenancies as in cases of felony, without having any benefit of clergy or sanctuary.

21. And be it further enacted by the authority aforesaid, that those women with whom all
or singular of the foresaid priests shall in any
of the foresaid ways have to do with or carnally know as is aforesaid, shall have like
punishment as the priest.

22. And because disputations and doubts
might perhaps arise hereafter upon these
words in this Act, that is to say, "advisedly
made to God," be it therefore provided and
enacted by authority aforesaid, that these
words in the Act, that is to say, "advisedly
made to God," for vows of chastity or widowhood, shall be alonely taken, expounded or
interpreted to bind such person or persons
and none other (saving priests) to and by the
same, which at the time of any of their so
vowing, being thereto admitted, were or
shall be of the age of twenty-one years or
above, and then did or do consent, submit
themselves or condescend to the same, and
continue or continued in observation of it
any while after; unless any such person or
persons do or can duly prove any unlawful
coercion or compulsion done to them or any
of them, for making of any such vow.

✠

From Bray, Documents of the English Reformation, *222–32.*

The Explicator: Thomas Cranmer

68. Preface to the Great Bible (1540)

Thomas Cranmer (1489–1556) had been
made archbishop of Canterbury by Henry in
1533. He, along with Thomas Cromwell, persuaded the king in 1538 to have an English
Bible placed in every church. Cranmer wrote
a preface for a recent translation, which soon
became known as the "Great Bible." In this
preface, the most important and influential

theologian of the Henrician and Edwardian periods sets forth what was to become the typically English understanding of the Reformation *sola scriptura* principle.

✠

1. For two sundry sorts of people, it seemeth much necessary that something be said in the entry of this book, by the way of a preface or prologue; whereby hereafter it may be both the better accepted of them which hitherto could not well bear it, and also the better used of them which heretofore have misused it. For truly some there are that be too slow, and need the spur; some other seem too quick, and need more of the bridle: some lose their game by short shooting, some by overshooting: some walk too much on the left hand, some too much on the right. In the former sort be all they that refuse to read, or to hear read the Scripture in the vulgar tongues; much worse they that also let or discourage the other from the reading thereof. In the latter sort be they, which by their inordinate reading, indiscreet speaking, contentious disputing, or otherwise, by their licentious living, slander and hinder the Word of God most of all other, whereof they would seem to be greatest furtherers. These two sorts, albeit they be most far unlike the one to the other, yet they both deserve in effect like reproach. Neither can I well tell whether of them I may judge the more offender, him that doth obstinately refuse so godly and goodly knowledge, or him that so ungodly and so ungoodly doth abuse the same.

2. And as touching the former, I would marvel much that any man should be so mad as to refuse in darkness, light; in hunger, food; in cold, fire: for the Word of God is light: *lucerna pedibus meis Verbum tuum* (Thy Word is a light unto my feet); food, *non in solo pane vivit homo, sed in omni Verbo Dei* (not on bread alone does man live, but in the whole Word of God); fire, *ignem veni mittere in terram, et quid volo, nisi ut ardeat?* (I have come to put fire in the earth, and what do I desire, except that it burn?) I would marvel (I say) at this, save that I consider how much custom and usage may do. So that if there were a people, as some write, *De Cimmeriis,* which never saw the sun by reason that they be situated far toward the North Pole, and be enclosed and overshadowed with high mountains; it is credible and like enough that if, by the power and will of God, the mountains should sink down and give place, that the light of the sun might have entrance to them, at the first some of them might be offended therewith. And the old proverb affirmeth, that after tillage of corn was first found, many delighted more to feed of mast and acorns, wherewith they had been accustomed, than to eat bread made of good corn. Such is the nature of custom, that it causeth us to bear all things well and easily, wherewith we have been accustomed, and to be offended with all things thereunto contrary. And therefore I can well think them worthy pardon, which at the coming abroad of Scripture doubted and drew back. But such as will persist still in their willfulness, I must needs judge, not only foolish, froward and obstinate, but also peevish, perverse and indurate.

3. And yet, if the matter should be tried by custom, we might also allege custom for the reading of the Scripture in the vulgar tongues, and prescribe the more ancient custom. For it is not much above one hundred years ago, since Scripture hath not been accustomed to be read in the vulgar tongues within this realm; and many hundred years before that it was translated and read in the

Saxons' tongue, which at that time was our mother's tongue; whereof there remaineth yet diverse copies found lately in old abbeys, of such antique manners of writing and speaking, that few men now be able to read and understand them. And when this language waxed old and out of common usage, because folk should not lack the fruit of reading, it was again translated in the newer language. Whereof yet also many copies remain and be daily found.

4. But now to let pass custom, and to weigh, as wise men ever should, the thing in his own nature: let us here discuss, what availeth Scripture to be had and read of the lay and vulgar people. And to this question I intend here to say nothing but that was spoken and written by the noble doctor and most moral divine, St. John Chrysostom, in his third sermon, *De Lazoro:* albeit I will be something shorter, and gather the matter into fewer words and less room than he doth there, because I would not be tedious. He exhorteth there his audience, that every man should read by himself at home in the mean days and time, between sermon and sermon, to the intent they might both more profoundly fix in their minds and memories that he had said before upon such texts, whereupon he had already preached; and also that they might have their minds the more ready and better prepared to receive and perceive that which he should say from thenceforth in his sermons, upon such texts as he had not yet declared and preached upon: therefore saith he there: "My common usage is to give you warning before, what matter I intend after to entreat upon, that you yourselves, in the mean days, may take the book in hand, read, weigh and perceive the sum and effect of the matter, and mark what hath been declared, and what remaineth yet to be declared: so that thereby your mind may be the more furnished, to hear the rest that shall be said. And that I exhort you," saith he, "and ever have and will exhort you, that ye (not only here in the church) give ear to that that is said by the preacher, but that also, when ye be at home in your houses, ye apply yourselves from time to time to the reading of Holy Scriptures, which thing also I never linn [i.e., cease, *Ed.*] to beat into the ears of them that be my familiars, and with whom I have private acquaintance and conversation. Let no man make excuse and say," saith he, "'I am busied about matters of the commonwealth,' 'I bear this office or that,' 'I am a craftsman, I must apply mine occupation,' 'I have a wife, my children must be fed, my household must I provide for,' briefly, 'I am a man of the world, it is not for me to read the Scriptures, that belongeth to them that hath bidden the world farewell, which live in solitariness and contemplation, that hath been brought up and continually nosylled [i.e., nurtured, *Ed.*] in learning and religion.'"

5. To this answering, "What sayest thou, man?" saith he: "Is it not for thee to study and to read the Scripture, because thou art encumbered and distract with cures and business? So much the more it is behoveful [helpful] for thee to have defense of Scriptures, how much thou art the more distressed in worldly dangers. They that be free and far from trouble and intermeddling of worldly things, liveth in safeguard and tranquillity, and in the calm, or within a sure haven. Thou art in the midst of the sea of worldly wickedness, and therefore thou needest the more of ghostly succor and comfort; they sit far from the strokes of battle, and far out of gunshot, and therefore they be but seldom wounded; thou that standest in the forefront of the host and nighest to thine enemies, must needs

take now and then many strokes, and be grievously wounded. And therefore thou hast more need to have thy remedies and medicines at hand. Thy wife provoketh thee to anger, thy child giveth thee occasion to take sorrow and pensiveness, thine enemies lieth in wait for thee, thy friend (as thou takest him) sometime envieth thee, thy neighbor misreporteth thee, or pricketh quarrels against thee, thy mate or partner undermineth thee, thy lord judge or justice threateneth thee, poverty is painful unto thee, the loss of thy dear and well-beloved causeth thee to mourn; prosperity exalteth thee, adversity bringeth thee low. Briefly, so diverse and so manifold occasions of cares, tribulations and temptations besetteth thee and besiegeth thee round about. Where canst thou have armor or fortress against thine assaults? Where canst thou have salve for thy sores, but of Holy Scripture? Thy flesh must needs be prone and subject to fleshly lusts, which daily walkest and art conversant amongst women, seest their beauties set forth to the eye, hearest their nice and wanton words, smellest their balm, civet and musk, with other like provocations and stirrings, except thou hast in a readiness wherewith to suppress and avoid them, which cannot elsewhere be had, but only out of the Holy Scriptures. Let us read and seek all remedies that we can, and all shall be little enough. How shall we then do, if we suffer and take daily wounds, and when we have done, will sit still and search for no medicines? Dost thou not mark and consider how the smith, mason or carpenter, or any other handy-craftsman, what need soever he be in, what other shift soever he make, he will not sell nor lay pledge the tools of his occupation; for then how should he work his feat, or get a living thereby? Of like mind and affec-

tion ought we to be towards Holy Scripture; for as mallets, hammers, saws, chisels, axes and hatchets be the tools of their occupation, so be the books of the prophets and apostles, and all Holy Writ inspired by the Holy Spirit, the instruments of our salvation. Wherefore, let us not stick to buy and provide us the Bible, that is to say, the books of Holy Scripture. And let us think that to be a better jewel in our house than either gold or silver. For like as thieves be loath to assault a house where they know to be good armor and artillery; so wheresoever these holy and ghostly books be occupied, there neither the devil nor none of his angels dare come near. And they that occupy them be in much safeguard, and having great consolation, and be the readier unto all goodness, the slower to all evil; and if they have done anything amiss, anon, even by the sight of the books, their consciences be admonished, and they wax sorry and ashamed of the fact."

6. Peradventure they will say unto me, "How and if we understand not that we read that is contained in the books?" What then? Suppose thou understand not the deep and profound mysteries of Scripture; yet can it not be but that much fruit and holiness must come and grow unto thee by the reading: for it cannot be that thou shouldest be ignorant in all things alike. For the Holy Spirit hath so ordered and attempered the Scriptures, that in them as well publicans, fishers and shepherds may find their edification, as great doctors their erudition: for those books were not made to vainglory, like as were the writings of the gentile philosophers and rhetoricians, to the intent the makers should be had in admiration for their high styles and obscure manner of writing, whereof nothing can be understand [*sic*] without a master or an expositor. But the apostles and prophets

wrote their books so that their special intent and purpose might be understood [sic] and perceived of every reader, which was nothing but the edification or amendment of the life of them that readeth or heareth it. Who is that reading or hearing read in the gospel "Blessed are they that be meek, blessed are they that be merciful, blessed are they that be of clean heart," and such other like places, can perceive nothing, except he have a master to teach him what it meaneth? Likewise the signs and miracles with all other histories of the doings of Christ or his apostles, who is there of so simple wit and capacity, but he may be able to perceive and understand them? These be but excuses and cloaks for the rain, and coverings of their own idle slothfulness. "I cannot understand it." What marvel? How shouldest thou understand, if thou wilt not read nor look upon it? Take the books into thine hands, read the whole story, and that thou understandest keep it well in memory; thou that understandest not, read it again and again: if thou can neither so come by it, counsel with some other that is better learned. Go to thy curate and preacher; show thyself to be desirous to know and learn: and I doubt not but God, seeing thy diligence and readiness (if no man else teach thee), will himself vouchsafe with his Holy Spirit to illuminate thee, and to open unto thee that which was locked from thee.

7. "Remember the eunuch of Candace, Queen of Ethiopia, which, albeit he was a man of a wild and barbarous country, and one occupied with worldly cures and business, yet riding in his chariot, he was reading the Scripture. Now consider, if this man passing in his journey, was so diligent as to read the Scripture, what thinkest thou of like was he wont to do sitting at home? Again, he that letted [failed] not to read, albeit he did not understand, what did he then, trowest [i.e.,

believest, Ed.] thou, after that, when he had learned and gotten understanding? For that thou may well know that he understood not what he read, hearken what Philip there saith unto him: 'Understandest thou what thou readest?' And he, nothing ashamed to confess his ignorance, answereth, 'How should I understand, having nobody to show me the way?' Lo, when he lacked one to show him the way and to expound to him the Scriptures, yet did he read; and therefore God the rather provided for him a guide of the way, that taught him to understand it. God perceived his willing and toward mind; and therefore he sent him a teacher by and by. Therefore let no man be negligent about his own health and salvation: though thou have not Philip always when thou wouldest, the Holy Spirit, which then moved and stirred up Philip, will be ready and not to fail thee if thou do thy diligence accordingly. All these things be written to us to our edification and amendment, which be born towards the latter end of the world. The reading of Scriptures is a great and strong bulwark or fortress against sin; the ignorance of the same is the greater ruin and destruction of them that will not know it. That is the thing that bringeth in heresies, that it is that causeth all corrupt and perverse living; that it is that bringeth all things out of good order."

8. Hitherto, all that I have said, I have taken and gathered out of the foresaid sermon of this holy doctor, St. John Chrysostom. Now if I should in like manner bring forth what the selfsame doctor speaketh in other places, and what other doctors and writers say concerning the same purpose, I might seem to you to write another Bible rather than to make a preface to the Bible. Wherefore, in few words to comprehend the largeness and utility of the Scripture, how it containeth fruitful instruction and erudition

for every man; if any things be necessary to be learned, of the Holy Scripture we may learn it. If falsehood shall be reproved, thereof we may gather wherewithal. If anything be to be corrected and amended, if there need any exhortation or consolation, of the Scripture we may well learn. In the Scriptures be the fat pastures of the soul; therein is no venomous meat, no unwholesome thing; they be the very dainty and pure feeding. He that is ignorant shall find there what he should learn. He that is a perverse sinner shall there find his damnation to make him to tremble for fear. He that laboreth to serve God shall find there his glory, and the promissions of eternal life, exhorting him more diligently to labor. Herein may princes learn how to govern their subjects; subjects, obedience, love and dread to their princes; husbands, how they should behave them unto their wives; how to educate their children and servants; and contrary the wives, children and servants may know their duty to their husbands, parents and masters. Here may all manner of persons, men, women, young, old, learned, unlearned, rich, poor, priests, laymen, lords, ladies, officers, tenants, and mean men, virgins, wives, widows, lawyers, merchants, artificers, husbandmen, and all manner of persons, of what estate or condition soever they be, may in this book learn all things what they ought to believe, what they ought to do, and what they should not do, as well concerning almighty God, as also concerning themselves and all other. Briefly, to the reading of the Scripture none can be enemy, but that either be so sick that they love not to hear of any medicine, or else that be so ignorant that they know not Scripture to be the most healthful medicine.

9. Therefore, as touching this former part, I will here conclude and take it as a conclusion sufficiently determined and approved, that it is convenient and good the Scripture to be read of all sorts and kinds of people, and in the vulgar tongue, without further allegations and probations for the same; which shall not need, since that this one place of John Chrysostom is enough and sufficient to persuade all of them that be not frowardly and perversely set in their own willful opinion; specially now that the King's Highness, being supreme head next under Christ of this Church of England, hath approved with his royal assent the setting forth hereof, which only to all true and obedient subjects ought to be a sufficient reason for the allowance of the same, without farther delay, reclamation or resistance, although there were no preface nor other reason herein expressed.

10. Therefore now to come to the second and latter part of my purpose. There is nothing so good in this world, but it may be abused, and turned from fruitful and wholesome to hurtful and noisome. What is there above better than the sun, the moon, the stars? Yet was there that took occasion by the great beauty and virtue of them to dishonor God, and to defile themselves with idolatry, giving the honor of the living God and Creator of all things to such things as he had created. What is there here beneath better than fire, water, meats, drinks, metals of gold, silver, iron and steel? Yet we see daily great harm and much mischief done by every one of these, as well for lack of wisdom and providence of them that suffer evil, as by the malice of them that worketh the evil. Thus to them that be evil of themselves everything setteth forward and increaseth their evil, be it of his own nature a thing never so good; like as contrarily, to them that studieth and endeavoreth themselves to goodness, everything prevaileth them and profiteth unto good, be it of his own nature a thing never so bad. As St. Paul saith: *His qui diligant Deum,*

omnia cooperantur in bonum (To them that love God, everything works together for good); even as out of most venomous worms is made treacle, the most sovereign medicine for the preservation of man's health in time of danger. Wherefore I would advise you all, that cometh to the reading or hearing of this book, which is the Word of God, the most precious jewel, and most holy relic that remaineth upon earth, that ye bring with you the fear of God, and that ye do it with all due reverence, and use your knowledge thereof, not to vainglory of frivolous disputation, but to the honor of God, increase of virtue and edification both of yourselves and other.

11. And to the intent that my words may be the more regarded, I will use in this part the authority of St. Gregory Nazianzene, like as in the other I did of St. John Chrysostom. It appeareth that in his time there were some (as I fear me, there be also now at these days a great number) which were idle babblers and talkers of the Scripture out of season and all good order, and without any increase of virtue or example of good living. To them he writeth all his first book, *De theologia* [Orat. 27, *Ed*]; whereof I shall briefly gather the whole effect, and recite it here unto you. "There be some," saith he, "whose not only ears and tongues, but also their fists, be whetted and ready bent all to contention and unprofitable disputation; whom I would wish, as they be vehement and earnest to reason the matter with tongue, so they were also ready and practive [willing] to do all good deeds. But forasmuch as they, subverting the order of all godliness, have respect only to this thing, how they may bind and loose subtle questions, so that now every marketplace, every alehouse and tavern, every feast-house, briefly, every company of men, every assembly of women, is filled with such talk; since

the matter is so," saith he, "and that our faith and holy religion of Christ beginneth to wax nothing else, but as were a sophistry or a talking-craft, I can no less do but say something thereunto. It is not fit," saith he, "for every man to dispute the high questions of divinity, neither is it to be done at all times, neither in every audience must we discuss every doubt; but we must know when, to whom, and how far we ought to enter into such matters."

12. "First, it is not for every man, but it is for such as be of exact and exquisite judgments, and such as have spent their time before in study and contemplation; and such as before have cleansed themselves as well in soul and body, or at the least, endeavored themselves to be made clean. For it is dangerous," saith he, "for the unclean to touch that thing that is most clean; like as the sore eye taketh harm by looking upon the sun. Secondarily, not at all times, but when we be reposed and at rest from all outward dregs and trouble, and when that our heads be not encumbered with other worldly and wandering imaginations: as if a man should mingle balm and dirt together. For he that shall judge and determine such matters and doubts of Scriptures, must take his time when he may apply his wits thereunto, that he may thereby the better see and discern what is truth. Thirdly, where, and in what audience? There and among those that be studious to learn, and not among such as have pleasure to trifle with such matters as with other things of pastime, which repute for their chief delicates the disputation of high questions, to show their wits, learning and eloquence in reasoning of high matters."

13. "Fourthly, it is to be considered how far to wade in such matters of difficulty. No further," saith he, "but as every man's own

capacity will serve him; and again, no further than the weakness or intelligence of the other audience may bear. For like as too great noise hurteth the ear, too much meat hurteth a man's body, too heavy burdens hurteth the bearers of them, too much rain doth more hurt than good to the ground; briefly, in all things too much is noyous [i.e., harmful, Ed.]; even so weak wits and weak consciences may soon be oppressed with over-hard questions. I say not this to dissuade men from the knowledge of God, and reading or studying of the Scripture. For I say that it is as necessary for the life of man's soul, as for the body to breathe. And if it were possible so to live, I would think it good for a man to spend all his life in that, and to do no other thing. I commend the law which biddeth to meditate and study the Scriptures always, both night and day, and sermons and preachings to be made both morning, noon and eventide; and God to be lauded and blessed in all times, to bedward, from bed, in our journeys and all our other works. I forbid not to read, but I forbid to reason. Neither forbid I to reason so far as is good and godly. But I allow not that this is done out of season, and out of measure and good order. A man may eat too much of honey, be it never so sweet, and there is time for everything; and that thing that is good is not good, if it be ungodly done; even as a flower in winter is out of season and as a woman's apparel becometh not a man, neither contrarily, the man's the woman; neither is weeping convenient at a bridal, neither laughing at burial. Now if we can observe and keep that is comely and timely in all other things, shall not we then the rather do the same in the Holy Scriptures? Let us not run forth as it were wild horse, that can suffer neither bridle in their mouths nor sitter on their backs. Let us keep us in our bounds,

and neither let us go too far on the one side, lest we return into Egypt, neither too far over the other, lest we be carried away to Babylon. Let us not sing the song of our Lord in a strange land; that is to say, let us not dispute the Word of God at all adventures, as well where it is not to be reasoned as where it is, and as well in the ears of them that be not fit therefore as of them that be. If we can in no wise forbear but that we must needs dispute, let us forbear thus much at the least, to do it out of time and place convenient. And let us entreat of those things which be holy holily; and upon those things that be mystical, mystically; and not to utter the divine mysteries in the ears unworthy to hear them; but let us know what is comely as well in our silence and talking, as in our garments' wearing, in our feeding, in our gesture, in our goings and in all our other behaving. This contention and debate about Scriptures and doubts thereof (specially when such as pretend to be the favorers and students thereof cannot agree within themselves) dost most hurt to ourselves, and to the furthering of the cause and quarrels that we would have furthered above all things. And we in this," saith he, "be not unlike to them that, being mad, set their own houses on fire, and that slay their own children, or beat their own parents. I marvel much," saith he, "to recount whereof cometh all this desire of vainglory, whereof cometh all this tongue-itch, that we have so much delight to talk and clatter? And wherein is our communication? Not in the commendations and virtuous and good deeds of hospitality, of love between Christian brother and brother, of love between man and wife, of virginity and chastity, and of alms towards the poor; not in psalms and godly songs, not in lamenting for our sins, not in repressing the affections of the body, not in prayers to God. We talk of Scripture, but in the meantime we subdue not our flesh by fasting, waking and weeping; we make not this life a meditation of death; we do not strive to be lords of our appetites and affections; we go not about to pull down our proud and high minds, to abate our furnish and rancorous stomachs, to restrain our lusts and bodily delectations, our indiscreet sorrows, our lascivious mirth, our inordinate looking, our insatiable hearing of vanities, our speaking without measure, our inconvenient thoughts, and briefly, to reform our life and manners. But all our holiness consisteth in talking. And we pardon each other from all good living, so that we may stick fast together in argumentation; as though there were no more ways to heaven but this alone, the way of speculation and knowledge (as they take it); but in very deed it is rather the way of superfluous contention and sophistication."

14. Hitherto have I recited the mind of Gregory Nazianzene in that book which I spake of before. The same author saith also in another place [*Orat.* 39], that "the learning of a Christian man ought to begin of the fear of God, to end in matters of high speculation; and not contrarily, to begin with speculation, and to end in fear. For speculation," saith he, "either high cunning or knowledge, if it be not stayed with the bridle of fear to offend God, is dangerous and enough to tumble a man headlong down the hill. Therefore," saith he, "the fear of God must be the first beginning, and as it were an ABC, or an introduction to all them that shall enter to the very true and most fruitful knowledge of Holy Scriptures. Where as is the fear of God, there is," saith he, "the keeping of the commandments, there is the cleansing of the flesh, which flesh is a cloud before the soul's eye, and suffereth it not purely to see the beam of the heavenly light. Where as is the cleansing of the flesh, there is the illumination of the Holy Spirit, the end of all our desires, and the very light whereby the verity of Scriptures is seen and perceived." This is the mind and almost the words of Gregory Nazianzene, doctor of the Greek Church, of whom St. Jerome saith, that unto his time the Latin church had no writer able to be compared and to make an even match with him.

15. Therefore, to conclude this latter part, every man that cometh to the reading of this holy book ought to bring with him first and foremost this fear of almighty God, and then next a firm and stable purpose to reform his own self according thereunto; and so to continue, proceed, and prosper from time to time, showing himself to be a sober and fruitful hearer and learner. Which if he do, he shall prove at the length well able to teach, though not with his mouth, yet with his living and good example, which is sure the most lively and most effectuous form and manner of teaching. He that otherwise intermeddleth with this book, let him be assured at once he shall make account therefore, when he shall have said to him, as it is written in the prophet David, *Peccatori dicit Deus etc.* [Ps. 50:16-23]: "Unto the ungodly saith God, Why dost thou preach my laws, and takest my testament in thy mouth? Whereas thou hatest to be reformed, and hast been partakers with advoutrers [i.e., adulterers, *Ed.*]. Thou hast let thy mouth speak wickedness, and with thy tongue thou hast set forth deceit. Thou sattest and spakest against thy brother; and hast slandered thine own mother's son. These things hast thou done, and I held my tongue, and thou thoughtedst (wickedly) that I am even such a one as thyself. But I will reprove thee, and set before

thee the things that thou hast done. O consider this, ye that forget God; lest I pluck you away, and there be none to deliver you. Whoso offereth me thanks and praise, he honoreth me: and to him that ordereth his conversation right will I show the salvation of God."

God save the King.

✠

From Bray, Documents of the English Reformation, *234–43.*

69. A Sermon of the Salvation of Mankind (1547)

It was during the reign of Edward VI that the foundations for the edifice of English Protestantism were laid. The chief architect was undoubtedly Thomas Cranmer. Whether his thinking now veered in a more Protestant direction, or whether he could now express the sentiments he had harbored all along, these were crystallized in the *Book of Common Prayer* **(1549; revised in 1552), and in the doctrinal formulations of the** *Forty-two Articles* **(1553). In a series of** *Edwardian Homilies,* **which were to be read in every local church, Cranmer explained his theological views. The one printed here, thought by some to be one of the finest among English theological writings, allows us to gauge the depth of Cranmer's "Protestantism" on justification, the central issue in Luther's Reformation.**

✠

Because all men be sinners and offenders against God, and breakers of his law and commandments, therefore can no man by his own acts, works, and deeds (seem they never so good) be justified, and made righteous before God: But every man of necessity is constrained to seek for another righteousness or justification, to be received at God's own hands, that is to say, the forgiveness of his sins and trespasses, in such things as he hath offended. And this justification or righteousness, which we so receive of God's mercy and Christ's merits, embraced by faith, is taken, accepted, and allowed of God, for our perfect and full justification. For the more full understanding hereof, it is our parts and duties ever to remember the great mercy of God, how that (all the world being wrapped in sin by breaking of the law) God sent his only son our Savior Christ, into this world, to fulfill the law for us, and, by shedding of his most precious blood, to make a sacrifice and satisfaction, or (as it may be called) amends to his Father for our sins, to assuage his wrath and indignation conceived against us for the same.

Insomuch that infants, being baptized and dying in their infancy, are by this sacrifice washed from their sins, brought to God's favor, and made his children, and inheritors of his kingdom of heaven. And they, which in act or deed do sin after their baptism, when they turn again to God unfeignedly, they are likewise washed by this sacrifice from their sins, in such sort, that there remaineth not any spot of sin, that shall be imputed to their damnation. This is that justification or righteousness which St. Paul speaketh of, when he saith, "No man is justified by the works of the law, but freely by faith in Jesus Christ." And again he saith, "We believe in Jesus Christ, that we be justified freely by the faith of Christ, and not by the works of the law, because that no man shall be justified by the works of the law." And although this justification be free unto us, yet it cometh not so freely unto us, that there is no ransom paid therefore at all. But here may man's reason be astonied [astonished], reasoning after this fashion: if a ransom be paid for our redemption, then is it not given us freely? For a prisoner that paid his ransom is not let go freely; for if he go freely, then he goeth without ransom: for what is it else to go freely, than to be set at liberty without paying of ransom? This reason is satisfied by the great wisdom of God in this mystery of our redemption, who hath so tempered his justice and mercy together, that he would neither by his justice condemn us unto the everlasting captivity of the devil, and his prison of hell, remediless forever without mercy, nor by his mercy deliver us clearly, without justice, or payment of a just ransom: but with his endless mercy he joined his most upright and equal justice. His great mercy he shewed unto us in delivering us from our former captivity, without requiring of any ransom to be paid, or amends to be made upon our parts, which thing by us had been impossible to be done. And whereas it lay not in us that to do, he provided a ransom for us, that was, the most precious body and blood of his own most dear and best beloved son Jesus Christ, who, besides this ransom, fulfilled the law for us perfectly. And so the justice of God and his mercy did embrace together, and fulfilled the mystery of our redemption. And of this justice and mercy of God, knit together, speaketh St. Paul in the third chapter to the Romans, "All have offended, and have need of the glory of God; but are justified freely by his grace, by redemption which is in Jesus Christ, whom God hath set forth to us for a reconciler and peace-maker, through faith in his blood, to shew his righteousness." And in the tenth chapter, "Christ is the end of the law, unto righteousness, to every man that believeth." And in the eighth chapter, "That which was

impossible by the law, inasmuch as it was weak by the flesh, God sending his own son in the similitude of sinful flesh, by sin damned sin in the flesh, that the righteousness of the law might be fulfilled in us, which walk not after the flesh, but after the Spirit." In these foresaid places, the apostle toucheth specially three things, which must go together in our justification. Upon God's part, his great mercy and grace; upon Christ's part, justice, that is, the satisfaction of God's justice, or the price of our redemption, by the offering of his body, and shedding of his blood, with fulfilling of the law perfectly and thoroughly; and upon our part, true and lively faith in the merits of Jesus Christ, which yet is not ours, but by God's working in us: so that in our justification, is not only God's mercy and grace, but also his justice, which the apostle calleth the justice of God, and it consisteth in paying our ransom, and fulfilling of the law: and so the grace of God doth not shut out the justice of God in our justification, but only shutteth out the justice of man, that is to say, the justice of our works, as to be merits of deserving our justification. And therefore St. Paul declareth here nothing upon the behalf of man concerning his justification, but only a true and lively faith, which nevertheless is the gift of God, and not man's only work, without God. And yet that faith doth not shut out repentance, hope, love, dread, and the fear of God, to be joined with faith in every man that is justified; but it shutteth them out from the office of justifying. So that, although they be all present together in him that is justified, yet they justify not altogether. Nor the faith also doth not shut out the justice of our good works, necessarily to be done afterwards of duty towards God; (for we are most bounden to serve God, in doing good deeds, commanded by him in his Holy Scripture, all the days of our life) but it excludeth them, so that we may not do them to this intent, to be made good by doing them. For all the good works that we can do be imperfect, and therefore not able to deserve our justification: but our justification doth come freely by the mere mercy of God, and of so great and free mercy, that, whereas all the world was not able of themselves to pay any part towards their ransom, it pleased our heavenly Father of his infinite mercy, without any our desert or deserving, to prepare for us the most precious jewels of Christ's body and blood, whereby our ransom might be fully paid, the law fulfilled, and his justice fully satisfied. So that Christ is now the righteousness of all them that truly do believe in him. He for them paid their ransom by his death. He for them fulfilled the law in his life. So that now in him, and by him, every true Christian man may be called a fulfiller of the law; forasmuch as that which their infirmity lacked, Christ's justice hath supplied.

The Second Part of the Sermon of Salvation

Ye have heard, of whom all men ought to seek their justification and righteousness, and how also this righteousness cometh unto men by Christ's death and merits: ye heard also, how that three things are required to the obtaining of our righteousness, that is, God's mercy, Christ's justice, and a true and lively faith, out of the which faith springeth good works. Also before was declared at large, that no man can be justified by his own good works, that no man fulfilleth the law, according to the full request of the law.

And St. Paul in his Epistle to the Galatians proveth the same, saying thus: "If there had been any law given, which could have justified, verily righteousness should have been by the law." And again he saith, "If

righteousness be by the law, then Christ died in vain." And again he saith, "You that are justified by the law are fallen away from grace." And furthermore, he writeth to the Ephesians on this wise, "By grace are ye saved through faith, and that not of yourselves, for it is the gift of God, and not of works, lest any man should glory." And, to be short, the sum of all Paul's disputation is this; that if justice come of works, then it cometh not of grace; and if it come of grace, then it cometh not of works. And to this end tendeth all the prophets, as St. Peter saith in the tenth of the Acts: "Of Christ all the prophets," saith St. Peter, "do witness, that through his name, all they that believe in him shall receive the remission of sins." And after this wise to be justified only by this true and lively faith in Christ, speaketh all the old and ancient authors, both Greeks and Latins; of whom I will specially rehearse three, Hilary, Basil, and Ambrose. St. Hilary saith these words plainly in the ninth canon upon Matthew; "Faith only justifieth." And St. Basil, a Greek author, writeth thus; "This is a perfect and whole rejoicing in God, when a man advanceth not himself for his own righteousness, but knowledgeth himself to lack true justice and righteousness, and to be justified by the only faith in Christ. And Paul," saith he, "doth glory in the contempt of his own righteousness, and that he looketh for the righteousness of God by faith."

These be the very words of St. Basil; and St. Ambrose, a Latin author, saith these words; "This is the ordinance of God, that they which believe in Christ should be saved without works, by faith only, freely receiving remission of their sins." Consider diligently these words, without works, by faith only, freely we receive remission of our sins. What can be spoken more plainly, than to say, that freely without works, by faith only, we obtain remission of our sins? These and other like sentences, that we be justified by faith only, freely, and without works, we do read ofttimes in the most and best ancient writers: as, beside Hilary, Basil, and St. Ambrose, before rehearsed, we read the same in Origen, St. Chrysostom, St. Cyprian, St. Augustine, Prosper, Œcumenius, Photius, Bernardus, Anselm, and many other authors, Greek and Latin. Nevertheless, this sentence, that we be justified by faith only, is not so meant of them, that the said justifying faith is alone in man, without true repentance, hope, charity, dread, and the fear of God, at any time and season. Nor when they say, that we be justified freely, they mean not that we should or might afterwards be idle, and that nothing should be required on our parts afterward: neither they mean not so to be justified without good works, that we should do no good works at all, like as shall be more expressed at large hereafter. But this saying, that we be justified by faith only, freely, and without works, is spoken for to take away clearly all merit of our works, as being unable to deserve our justification at God's hands, and thereby most plainly to express the weakness of man, and the goodness of God; the great infirmity of ourselves, and the might and power of God; the imperfectness of our own works, and the most abundant grace of our Savior Christ; and therefore wholly to ascribe the merit and deserving of our justification unto Christ only, and his most precious bloodshedding. This faith the Holy Scripture teacheth us; this is the strong rock and foundation of Christian religion; this doctrine all old and ancient authors of Christ's church do approve; this doctrine advanceth and setteth forth the true glory of Christ, and beateth down the vainglory of man; this whosoever

denieth, is not to be accounted for a Christian man, nor for a setter-forth of Christ's glory; but for an adversary to Christ and his gospel, and for a setter-forth of men's vainglory. And although this doctrine be never so true (as it is most true indeed), that we be justified freely, without all merit of our own good works (as St. Paul doth express it), and freely, by this lively and perfect faith in Christ only (as the ancient authors use to speak it), yet this true doctrine must be also truly understood, and most plainly declared, lest carnal men should take unjustly occasion thereby to live carnally, after the appetite and will of the world, the flesh, and the devil. And because no man should err by mistaking of this doctrine, I shall plainly and shortly so declare the right understanding of the same, that no man shall justly think that he may thereby take any occasion of carnal liberty, to follow the desires of the flesh, or that thereby any kind of sin shall be committed, or any ungodly living the more used.

First, you shall understand, that in our justification by Christ it is not all one thing, the office of God unto man, and the office of man unto God. Justification is not the office of man, but of God; for man cannot make himself righteous by his own works, neither in part, nor in the whole; for that were the greatest arrogance and presumption of man that Antichrist could set up against God, to affirm that a man might by his own works take away and purge his own sins, and so justify himself. But justification is the office of God only, and is not a thing which we render unto him, but which we receive of him; not which we give to him, but which we take of him, by his free mercy, and by the only merits of his most dearly beloved Son, our only redeemer, Savior, and justifier, Jesus Christ: so that the true understanding of this doctrine, we be justified freely by faith without works, or that we be justified by faith in Christ only, is not, that this our own act to believe in Christ, or this our faith in Christ, which is within us, doth justify us, and deserve our justification unto us (for that were to count ourselves to be justified by some act or virtue that is within ourselves); but the true understanding and meaning thereof is, that although we hear God's word, and believe it; although we have faith, hope, charity, repentance, dread, and fear of God within us, and do never so many works thereunto; yet we must renounce the merit of all our said virtues, of faith, hope, charity, and all other virtues and good deeds, which we either have done, shall do, or can do, as things that be far too weak and insufficient, and imperfect, to deserve remission of our sins, and our justification; and therefore we must trust only in God's mercy, and that sacrifice which our high priest and Savior Christ Jesus, the Son of God, once offered for us upon the cross, to obtain thereby God's grace and remission, as well of our original sin in baptism, as of all actual sin committed by us after our baptism, if we truly repent, and turn unfeignedly to him again. So that, as St. John the Baptist, although he were never so virtuous and godly a man, yet in this matter of forgiving of sin, he did put the people from him, and appointed them unto Christ, saying thus unto them, "Behold, yonder is the lamb of God, which taketh away the sins of the world"; even so, as great and as godly a virtue as the lively faith is, yet it putteth us from itself, and remitteth or appointeth us unto Christ, for to have only by him remission of our sins, or justification. So that our faith in Christ (as it were) saith unto us thus: It is not I that take away your sins, but it is Christ only; and to him only I send you for

that purpose, forsaking therein all your good virtues, words, thoughts, and works, and only putting your trust in Christ.

The Third Part of the Sermon of Salvation

It hath been manifestly declared unto you, that no man can fulfill the law of God; and therefore by the law all men are condemned: whereupon it followeth necessarily, that some other thing should be required for our salvation than the law; and that is, a true and a lively faith in Christ; bringing forth good works, and a life according to God's commandments. And also you heard the ancient authors' minds of this saying, Faith in Christ only justifieth man, so plainly declared, that you see, that the very true meaning of this proposition or saying, We be justified by faith in Christ only (according to the meaning of the old ancient authors) is this: We put our faith in Christ, that we be justified by him only, that we be justified by God's free mercy, and the merits of our Savior Christ only, and by no virtue or good works of our own that is in us, or that we can be able to have, or to do, for to deserve the same; Christ himself only being the cause meritorious thereof.

Here you perceive many words to be used to avoid contention in words with them that delight to brawl about words, and also to shew the true meaning to avoid evil taking and misunderstanding; and yet peradventure all will not serve with them that be contentious; but contenders will ever forge matters of contention, even when they have none occasion thereto. Notwithstanding, such be the less to be passed upon, so that the rest may profit, which will be more desirous to know the truth, than (when it is plain enough) to contend about it, and with contentious and captious cavillation, to obscure and darken it. Truth it is, that our own works do not justify us, to speak properly of our justification; that is to say, our works do not merit or deserve remission of our sins, and make us, of unjust, just before God: but God of his own mercy, through the only merits and deserving of his Son Jesus Christ, doth justify us. Nevertheless, because faith doth directly send us to Christ for remission of our sins, and that, by faith given us of God, we embrace the promise of God's mercy, and of the remission of our sins (which thing none other of our virtues or works properly doth), therefore Scripture useth to say, that faith without works doth justify. And forasmuch that it is all one sentence in effect, to say, faith without works, and only faith, doth justify us; therefore the old ancient Fathers of the church from time to time have uttered our justification with this speech; Only faith justifieth us; meaning none other thing than St. Paul meant, when he said, "Faith without works justifieth us." And because all this is brought to pass through the only merits and deservings of our Savior Christ, and not through our merits, or through the merit of any virtue that we have within us, or of any work that cometh from us; therefore, in that respect of merit and deserving, we forsake, as it were, altogether again, faith, works, and all other virtues. For our own imperfection is so great, through the corruption of original sin, that all is imperfect that is within us, faith, charity, hope, dread, thoughts, words, and works, and therefore not apt to merit and deserve any part of our justification for us. And this form of speaking use we, in the humbling of ourselves to God, and to give all the glory to our Savior Christ, which is best worthy to have it.

Here you have heard the office of God in our justification, and how we receive it of him freely, by his mercy, without our deserts, through true and lively faith. Now you shall

hear the office and duty of a Christian man unto God, what we ought on our part to render unto God again for his great mercy and goodness. Our office is, not to pass the time of this present life unfruitfully and idly, after that we are baptized or justified, not caring how few good works we do, to the glory of God, and profit of our neighbors: much less is it our office, after that we be once made Christ's members, to live contrary to the same; making ourselves members of the devil, walking after his enticements, and after the suggestions of the world and the flesh, whereby we know that we do serve the world and the devil, and not God. For that faith which bringeth forth (without repentance) either evil works, or no good works, is not a right, pure, and lively faith, but a dead, devilish, counterfeit, and feigned faith, as St. Paul and St. James call it. For even the devils know and believe that Christ was born of a virgin; that he fasted forty days and nights without meat and drink; that he wrought all kind of miracles, declaring himself very God: they believe also, that Christ for our sakes suffered most painful death, to redeem us from everlasting death, and that he rose again from death the third day: they believe that he ascended into heaven, and that he sitteth on the right hand of the Father, and at the last end of this world shall come again, and judge both the quick and the dead. These articles of our faith the devils believe, and so they believe all things that be written in the New and Old Testament to be true: and yet for all this faith they be but devils, remaining still in their damnable estate, lacking the very true Christian faith. For the right and true Christian faith is, not only to believe that Holy Scripture, and all the foresaid articles of our faith are true; but also to have a sure trust and confidence in God's merciful promises, to be saved from everlasting damnation by Christ: whereof doth follow a loving heart to obey his commandments. And this true Christian faith neither any devil hath, nor yet any man, which in the outward profession of his mouth, and in his outward receiving of the sacraments, in coming to the church, and in all other outward appearances, seemeth to be a Christian man, and yet in his living and deeds sheweth the contrary. For how can a man have this true faith, this sure trust and confidence in God, that by the merits of Christ his sins be forgiven, and he reconciled to the favor of God, and to be partaker of the kingdom of heaven by Christ, when he liveth ungodly, and denieth Christ in his deeds? Surely no such ungodly man can have this faith and trust in God. For as they know Christ to be the only Savior of the world; so they know also that wicked men shall not enjoy the kingdom of God. They know that God hateth unrighteousness; that he will destroy all those that speak untruly; that those which have done good works (which cannot be done without a lively faith in Christ) shall come forth into the resurrection of life, and those that have done evil shall come unto the resurrection of judgment. Very well they know also, that to them that be contentious, and to them that will not be obedient unto the truth, but will obey unrighteousness, shall come indignation, wrath, and affliction, etc. Therefore, to conclude, considering the infinite benefits of God, shewed and given unto us mercifully without our deserts, who hath not only created us of nothing, and from a piece of vile clay, of his infinite goodness hath exalted us, as touching our soul, unto his own similitude and likeness; but also, whereas we were condemned to hell and death everlasting, hath given his own natural Son, being God eternal, immortal, and equal unto himself in power and glory, to be incarnated, and to take our mortal nature upon him, with the infirmities of the same, and in the same nature to suffer most shameful and painful death for our offenses, to the intent to justify us, and to restore us to life everlasting: so making us also his dear children, brethren unto his only Son our Savior Christ, and inheritors forever with him of his eternal kingdom of heaven.

These great and merciful benefits of God, if they be well considered, do neither minister unto us occasion to be idle, and to live without doing any good works, neither yet stirreth us up by any means to do evil things; but contrariwise, if we be not desperate persons, and our hearts harder than stones, they move us to render ourselves unto God wholly, with all our will, hearts, might, and power, to serve him in all good deeds, obeying his commandments during our lives, to seek in all things his glory and honor, not our sensual pleasures and vainglory; evermore dreading willingly to offend such a merciful God and loving redeemer, in word, thought, or deed. And the said benefits of God, deeply considered, move us for his sake also to be ever ready to give ourselves to our neighbors, and, as much as lieth in us, to study with all our endeavor to do good to every man. These be the fruits of true faith, to do good as much as lieth in us to every man, and, above all things, and in all things, to advance the glory of God, of whom only we have our sanctification, justification, salvation, and redemption: to whom be ever glory, praise, and honor, world without end. Amen.

✠

From J. H. Leith, ed., Creeds of the Churches *(Richmond, Va.: John Knox Press, 1973), 239–51.*

Return to the Fold: Mary

70. The Marian Injunctions (1554)

The accession of Mary to the throne brought with it an attempt to restore the English church to Roman obedience. Mary's Parliament repealed the religious laws enacted under Edward and Henry's *Act of Supremacy*. The following set of injunctions from 1554 indicates the depth of Mary's traditionalism when it came to ecclesiastical affairs.

✠

1. That every bishop and his officers, with all others having ecclesiastical jurisdiction, shall with all speed and diligence, and all manner of ways to them possible, put in execution all such canons and ecclesiastical laws heretofore in the time of King Henry VIII used within this realm of England, and the dominions of the same, not being direct and expressly contrary to the laws and statutes of this realm.

2. That no bishop or any his officer, or other person aforesaid, hereafter in any of their ecclesiastical writings in process, or other extra-judicial acts, do use to put in this clause or sentence: *regia auctoritate fulcitus* (sanctioned by royal authority).

3. That no bishop or any of his officers or other person aforesaid, do hereafter exact or demand in the admission of any person to any ecclesiastical promotion, order or office, any oath touching the primacy or succession, as of late, in few years past, has been accustomed and used.

4. That every bishop and his officers, with all other persons aforesaid, have a vigilant eye and use special diligence and foresight, that no person be admitted or received to any ecclesiastical function, benefice or office, being a sacramentary, infected or defamed with any notable kind of heresy or other great crime; and that the said bishop do stay and cause to be stayed, as much as lieth in him, that benefices and ecclesiastical promotions do not notably decay, or take hindrance, by passing or confirming of unreasonable leases.

5. That every bishop and all other persons aforesaid do diligently travail for the repressing of heresies and notable crimes, especially in the clergy, duly correcting and punishing the same.

6. That every bishop and all other persons aforesaid do likewise travail for the condemning and repressing of corrupt and naughty opinions, unlawful books, ballads and other pernicious and hurtful devices, engendering hatred among the people and discord among the same; and that schoolmasters, preachers and teachers do exercise and use their offices and duties without teaching, preaching or setting forth any evil or corrupt doctrine; and that, doing the contrary, they may be, by the bishop and his said officers, punished and removed.

7. That every bishop and all other persons aforesaid, proceeding summarily, and with all celerity and speed, may and shall deprive, or declare deprived, and amove [remove], according to their learning and discretion, all such persons from their benefices and ecclesiastical promotions who, contrary to the state of their order and the laudable custom of the church, have married and used women as their wives, or otherwise notably and slanderously disordered or abused themselves; sequestering also, during the said process, the fruits and profits of the said benefices and ecclesiastical promotions.

8. That the said bishop and all other persons aforesaid, do use more lenity and clemency with such as have married, whose wives be dead, than with others whose women do yet remain in life; and likewise such priests as, with the consents of their

wives or women, openly in the presence of the bishop do profess to abstain, to be used the more favorably; in which case, after penance effectually done, the bishop, according to his discretion and wisdom, may, upon just consideration, receive and admit them again to their former administration, so it be not in the same place; appointing them such a portion to live upon, to be paid out of their benefice, whereof they be deprived, by discretion of the said bishop, or his officers, as they shall think they may be spared of the said benefice.

9. That every bishop and all persons aforesaid, do foresee that they suffer not any religious man, having solemnly professed chastity, to continue with his woman or wife; but that all such persons, after deprivation of their benefice or ecclesiastical promotion, be also divorced every one from his said woman, and due punishment otherwise taken for the offense therein.

10. That every bishop and all other persons aforesaid do take order and direction with the parishioners of every benefice where priests do want [i.e., are lacking, *Ed.*], to repair to the next parish for divine service; or to appoint for a convenient time, till other better provision may be made, one curate to serve (alternately) in diverse parishes, and to allot to the said curate for his labor some portion of the benefice that he so serves.

11. That all and all manner of processions of the church be used, frequented and continued after the old order of the church, in the Latin tongue.

12. That all such holy days and fasting days be observed and kept, as were observed and kept in the latter time of Henry VIII.

13. That the laudable and honest ceremonies which were wont to be used, frequented and observed in the church be also hereafter used, frequented and observed.

14. That children be christened by the priest, and confirmed by the bishops, as heretofore hath been accustomed and used.

15. Touching such persons as were heretofore promoted to any orders after the new sort and fashion of order, considering they were not ordered in very deed, the bishop of the diocese finding otherwise sufficiency and ability in these men, may supply that thing which wanted in them before; and then, according to his discretion, admit them to minister.

16. That by the bishop of the diocese, a uniform doctrine be set forth by homilies or otherwise, for the good instruction and teaching of all people; and that the said bishop and other persons aforesaid, do compel the parishioners to come to their several churches and there devoutly to hear divine service, as of reason they ought.

17. That they examine all schoolmasters and teachers of children, and finding them suspect in any wise, to remove them and place Catholic men in their rooms, with a special commandment to instruct their children, so as they may be able to answer the priest at the mass and so help the priest to mass as has been accustomed.

18. That the said bishop and all other persons aforesaid have such regard, respect and consideration of and for the setting forth of the premises with all kind of virtue, godly living and good example, with repressing also and keeping under of vice and unthriftiness, as they and every of them may be seen to favor the restitution of true religion; and also to make an honest account and reckoning of their office and cure to the honor of God, our good contentation [contentment], and the profit of this realm and dominions of the same.

From Bray, **Documents of the English Reformation,** *315–17.*

The Final Split: Elizabeth I

71. Act of Supremacy (1559)

Soon after Elizabeth came to the throne in 1558, Parliament repealed the religious laws made under Mary, and restored ultimate jurisdiction over the church to the monarch. What follows is an excerpt from this act, and the oath that was now to be required of church and government officials.

✠

And to the intent that all usurped and foreign power and authority, spiritual and temporal, may forever be clearly extinguished, and never to be used or obeyed within this realm, or any other your Majesty's dominions or countries, may it please your Highness that it may be further enacted by the authority aforesaid, that no foreign prince, person, prelate, state or potentate, spiritual or temporal, shall at any time after the last day of this session of Parliament (8 May 1559), use, enjoy or exercise any manner of power, jurisdiction, superiority, authority, pre-eminence or privilege, spiritual or ecclesiastical, within this realm, or within any other your Majesty's dominions or countries that now be, or hereafter shall be, but from thenceforth the same shall be clearly abolished out of this realm, and all other your Highness's dominions for ever; any statute, ordinance, custom, constitutions or any other matter or cause whatsoever to the contrary in any wise notwithstanding.

And that also it may likewise please your Highness, that it may be established and enacted by the authority aforesaid, that such jurisdictions, privileges, superiorities and pre-eminences, spiritual and ecclesiastical, as by any spiritual or ecclesiastical power or authority have heretofore been, or may lawfully be exercised or used for the visitation of the ecclesiastical state and persons, and for reformation, order and correction of the same, and of all manner of errors, heresies, schisms, abuses, offenses, contempts and enormities, shall for ever, by authority of this present Parliament, be united and annexed to the imperial crown of this realm. . . .

And for the better observation and maintenance of this Act, may it please your Highness, that it may be further enacted by the authority aforesaid, that all and every archbishop, bishop, and all and every other ecclesiastical person, and other ecclesiastical officer and minister, of what estate, dignity, pre-eminence or degree soever he or they be or shall be, and all and every temporal judge, justice, mayor and other lay and temporal officer and minister, and every other person having your Highness's fee or wages, within this realm, or any your Highness's dominions, shall make, take and receive a corporal oath upon the evangelist, before such person or persons as shall please your Highness, your heirs or successors, under the great seal of England to assign and name, to accept and to take the same according to the tenor and effect hereafter following, that is to say:

I, A.B., do utterly testify and declare in my conscience, that the queen's Highness is the only supreme governor of this realm and of all other her Highness's dominions and countries, as well in all spiritual or ecclesiastical things or causes, as temporal, and that no foreign prince, person, prelate, state or potentate has, or ought to have, any jurisdiction, power, superiority, preeminence or authority ecclesiastical or spiritual, within this realm; and therefore I do utterly renounce and forsake all foreign jurisdictions, powers, superiorities and authorities, and do promise that from henceforth I shall bear faith and true allegiance to the queen's Highness, her heirs and lawful successors, and to my power shall assist and defend all jurisdictions, pre-eminences, privileges and authorities granted or belonging to the queen's Highness, her heirs and successors, or united and annexed to the imperial crown of this realm. So help me God, and by the contents of this book.

✠

From Bray, Documents of the English Reformation, *321–23.*

72. Act of Uniformity (1559)

One aspect of Elizabeth's strategy was to standardize worship in the Church of England. This act reinstated the *Book of Common Prayer,* mandated its use in all churches, and attached stiff penalties for those who refused.

✠

Where at the death of our late sovereign lord King Edward the Sixth, there remained one uniform order of common service and prayer and of the administration of sacraments, rites and ceremonies in the Church of England, which was set forth in one book entitled the *Book of Common Prayer and Administration of Sacraments and Other Rites and Ceremonies in the Church of England,* authorized by Act of Parliament holden in the fifth and sixth years of our said late sovereign lord King Edward the Sixth, entitled *An Act for the Uniformity of Common Prayer and Administration of the Sacraments*, the which was repealed and taken away by Act of Parliament in the first year of the reign of our late sovereign lady Queen Mary, to the great decay of the due honor of God and discomfort to the professors of the truth of Christ's religion:

Be it therefore enacted by the authority of this present Parliament that the said Statute of Repeal and everything therein contained, only concerning the said book and service, administration of sacraments, rites and ceremonies contained or appointed in or by the said book, shall be void and of none effect from and after the feast of the nativity of St. John the Baptist next coming (24 June 1559), and that the said book, with the order of service and of the administration of sacraments, rites and ceremonies, with the alterations and additions therein added and appointed by this statute, shall stand and be from and after the said feast of the nativity of St. John the Baptist in full force and effect according to the tenor and effect of this statute, anything in the aforesaid statute of repeal to the contrary notwithstanding.

And further be it enacted by the Queen's Highness with the assent of the Lords and Commons in this present Parliament assembled, and by the authority of the same, that all and singular ministers in any cathedral or parish church or other place within this realm of England, Wales, and the marches of the same, or other the Queen's dominions, shall from and after the feast of the nativity of St. John the Baptist next coming (24 June 1559), be bound to say and use the Matins, Evensong, celebration of the Lord's supper, and administration of each of the sacraments, and all their common and open prayer, in such order and form as is mentioned in the said book so authorized by Parliament in the said fifth and sixth year of the reign of King Edward the Sixth, with one alteration or addition of certain lessons to be used on every Sunday in the year, and the form of the litany altered and corrected, and two sentences only added in the delivery of the sacrament to the communicants, and none other or otherwise; and that if any manner of parson, vicar or other whatsoever minister, that ought or should sing or say common prayer mentioned in the said book, or minister the sacraments, shall after the said feast of the nativity of St. John the Baptist next coming (24 June 1559) refuse to use the said common prayers, or to minister the sacraments in such cathedral or parish church or other places as he should use to minister the same, in such order and form as they be mentioned and set forth in the said book; or shall use, willfully or obstinately standing in the same, any other rite, ceremony, order, form or manner of mass openly or privately, or Matins, Evensong, administration of the sacraments, or other open prayer than is mentioned and set forth in the said book (open prayer in and throughout this Act, is meant that prayer which is for other to come unto or hear, either in common churches or private chapels or oratories, commonly called the service of the church); or shall preach, declare or speak anything in the derogation or depraving of the said book, or anything therein contained, or of any part thereof, and shall be thereof lawfully convicted according to the laws of this realm, by verdict of twelve men, or by his own confession, or by the notorious evidence of the fact, shall lose and forfeit to the queen's Highness, her heirs and successors, for his first offense, the profit of all his spiritual benefices or promotions coming and arising in one whole year after his conviction; and also that the same person so convicted shall for the same offense suffer imprisonment by the space of six months, without bail or mainprise; and if any such person, once convicted of any offense concerning the premises, shall after his first conviction eftsones [i.e., again, *Ed.*] offend, and be thereof in form aforesaid lawfully convicted, that

then the same person shall for his second offense suffer imprisonment by the space of one whole year, and also shall therefore be deprived ipso facto of all his spiritual promotions; and that it shall be lawful to all patrons, donors and grantees of all and singular the same spiritual promotions to present to the same any other able clerk, in like manner and form as though the party so offending were dead; and that if any such person or persons, after he shall be twice convicted in form aforesaid, shall offend against any of the premises the third time shall be deprived ipso facto of all his spiritual promotions and also shall suffer imprisonment during his life; and if the person that shall offend or be convicted in form aforesaid, concerning any of the premises, shall not be beneficed nor have any spiritual promotion, that then the same person so offending and convicted shall for the first offense suffer imprisonment during one whole year next after his conviction without bail or mainprise; and that if any such person not having any spiritual promotion after his first conviction shall eftsones offend in anything concerning the premises, and shall in form aforesaid be lawfully convicted, that then the same person shall for his second offence suffer imprisonment during his life. . . .

✠

From Bray, Documents of the English Reformation, *329–31.*

73. The Elizabethan Injunctions (1559)

Elizabeth also issued a lengthy set of rules governing almost every aspect of church life. They reveal her interest in the particulars as well as just how "Protestant" she intended her church to be.

✠

1. The first is that all deans, archdeacons, parsons, vicars and other ecclesiastical persons shall faithfully keep and observe, and as far as in them may be, shall cause to be observed and kept of other, all and singular laws and statutes made for the restoring to the crown the ancient jurisdiction over the state ecclesiastical, and abolishing of all foreign power repugnant to the same. And furthermore, all ecclesiastical persons having cure of soul, shall to the uttermost of their wit, knowledge and learning, purely and sincerely, and without any color or dissimulation, declare, manifest and open, four times every year at the least, in their sermons and other collations, that all usurped and foreign power, having no establishment nor ground by the law of God, was of most just causes taken away and abolished, and that therefore no manner of obedience or subjection within her Highness's realms and dominions is due unto any such foreign power. And that the queen's power within her realms and dominions is the highest power under God, to whom all men within the same realms and dominions, by God's laws owe most loyalty and obedience, afore and above all other powers and potentates in earth. . . .

3. Item, that they, the persons above rehearsed, shall preach in their churches, and every other cure they have, one sermon, every quarter of the year at the least, wherein they shall purely and sincerely declare the Word of God, and in the same, exhort their hearers to the works of faith, mercy and charity specially prescribed and commanded in Scripture, and that works devised by men's fantasies, besides Scripture, as wandering to pilgrimages, offering of money, candles or tapers to relics, or images, or kissing and

licking of the same, praying upon beads, or such like superstition, have not only no promise of reward in Scripture, for doing of them, but contrariwise, great threats and maledictions of God, for that they be things tending to idolatry and superstition, which of all other offenses God almighty doth most detest and abhor, for that the same diminish his honor and glory. . . .

7. Also, the said ecclesiastical persons shall in no wise at any unlawful time, nor for any other cause than their honest necessity, haunt or resort to any taverns or alehouses. And after their dinner and supper, they shall not give themselves to drinking or riot, spending their time idly, by day or by night, at dice, cards or tables playing, or any other lawful game, but at all times as they shall have leisure, they shall hear or read somewhat of Holy Scripture, or shall occupy themselves with some other honest exercise, and that they always do the things which appertain to honesty, with endeavor to profit the common weal, having always in mind that they ought to excel all others in purity of life and should be examples to the people, to live well and Christianly. . . .

12. And to the intent that learned men may hereafter spring the more for the execution of the premises, every parson, vicar, clerk or beneficed man within this deanery, having yearly to dispend, in benefices and other promotions of the church an hundred pounds, shall give competent exhibition to one scholar, and for as many hundred pounds more as he may dispend, to so many scholars more shall give like exhibition in the University of Oxford or Cambridge, or some grammar school, which, after they have profited in good learning, may be partners of their patron's cure and charge, as well in preaching as otherwise in the execution of

their offices, or may, when need shall be, otherwise profit the commonwealth with their counsel and wisdom. . . .

17. Also, that this vice of damnable despair may be clearly taken away and firm belief and steadfast hope surely conceived of all their parishioners, being in any danger, they shall learn, and have always in a readiness, such comfortable places and sentences of Scripture as do set forth the mercy, benefits and goodness of almighty God, towards all penitent and believing persons, that they may at all times, when necessity shall require, promptly comfort their flock with the lively Word of God, which is the only stay of man's conscience. . . .

23. Also that they shall take away, utterly extinct and destroy all shrines, covering of shrines, all tables and candlesticks, trundles or rolls of ware, pictures, paintings and all other monuments of feigned miracles, pilgrimages, idolatry and superstition, so that there remain no memory of the same in walls, glasses, windows or elsewhere within their churches or houses. And they shall exhort all their parishioners to do the like within their several houses. . . .

29. Item, although there be no prohibition by the Word of God, nor any example of the primitive church, but that the priests and ministers of the church may lawfully, for the avoiding of fornication, have an honest and sober wife . . . yet because there hath grown offense and some slander to the church by lack of discreet and sober behavior in many ministers of the church, both in choosing of their wives and in indiscreet living with them, the remedy whereof is necessary to be sought. It is thought therefore very necessary that no manner of priest or deacon shall hereafter take to his wife any manner of woman, without the advice and allowance first had

upon good examination by the bishop of the same diocese, and two justices of the peace of the same shire, dwelling next to the place where the same woman hath made her most abode before her marriage, nor without the good will of the parents of the said woman, if she have any living, or two of the next of her kinfolks, or for lack of knowledge of such, of her master or masters where she serveth. . . .

44. Item, every parson, vicar and curate shall upon every holy day and every second Sunday in the year, hear and instruct all the youth of the parish for half an hour at the least, before Evening Prayer, in the Ten Commandments, the Articles of the Belief, and in the Lord's Prayer, and diligently examine and teach the catechism set forth in the Book of Public [Common] Prayer. . . .

50. Item, because in all alterations and specially in rites and ceremonies, there happeneth discord among the people, and thereupon slanderous words and railings whereby charity, the knot of all Christian society, is loosed. The queen's Majesty being most desirous of all other earthly things, that her people should live in charity both towards God and man, and therein abound in good works, willeth and straightly commandeth all manner her subjects to forbear all vain and contentious disputations in matters of religion, and not to use in despite or rebuke of any person, these convicious words: papist, or papistical heretic, schismatic or sacramentary, or any suchlike words of reproach. But if any manner of person shall deserve the accusation of such, that first he be charitably admonished thereof. And if that shall not amend him, then to denounce the offenders to the ordinary or to some higher power having authority to correct the same. . . .

52. Item, although almighty God is at all times to be honored with all manner of rev-

erence that may be devised, yet of all other times, in time of common prayer the same is most to be regarded. Therefore it is to be necessarily received, that in time of the litany, and of all other collects and common supplications to almighty God, all manner of people shall devoutly and humbly kneel upon their knees, and give ear thereunto. And that whensoever the name of Jesus shall be in any lesson, sermon or otherwise in the church pronounced, that due reverence be made of all persons, young and old, with lowliness of curtsy, and uncovering of heads of the men kind, as thereunto doth necessarily belong, and heretofore hath been accustomed. . . .

✠

From Bray, Documents of the English Reformation, *335–46.*

74. The Thirty-nine Articles (1563)

This revision of Edward's Forty-two Articles of 1553 became the most important statement of what was to be believed in the Church of England. With its moderate tone and masterful ambiguity, it was a key plank in Elizabeth's policy of comprehension.

✠

Articles whereupon it was agreed by the archbishops and bishops of both provinces and the whole clergy, in the convocation holden at London in the year of our Lord God 1562, according to the computation of the Church of England, for the avoiding of the diversities of opinions, and for the establishing of consent touching true religion.

1. Of Faith in the Holy Trinity

There is but one living and true God, everlasting, without body, parts or passions, of infinite power, wisdom and goodness, the maker and preserver of all things both visible and invisible. And in unity of this Godhead there be three persons, of one substance, power and eternity, the Father, the Son and the Holy Spirit.

2. That of the Word or Son of God, Which Was Made Very Man

The Son, which is the Word of the Father, begotten from everlasting of the Father, the very and eternal God, of one substance with the Father, took man's nature in the womb of the Blessed Virgin, of her substance: so that two whole and perfect natures, that is to say the godhead and manhood, were joined together in one person, never to be divided, whereof is one Christ, very God and very man, who truly suffered, was crucified, dead and buried, to reconcile his Father to us and to be a sacrifice not only for original guilt but also for all actual sins of men.

3. Of the Going Down of Christ into Hell

As Christ died for us, and was buried, so also it is to be believed, that he went down into hell.

4. Of the Resurrection of Christ

Christ did truly arise again from death, and took again his body, with flesh, bones and all things appertaining to the perfection of man's nature, wherewith he ascended into heaven, and there sitteth, until he return to judge all men at the last day.

5. Of the Holy Spirit

The Holy Spirit, proceeding from the Father and the Son, is of one substance, majesty and glory with the Father and the Son, very and eternal God.

6. Of the Sufficiency of the Holy Scriptures for Salvation

Holy Scripture containeth all things necessary to salvation: so that whatsoever is not read therein, nor may be proved thereby, is not to be required of any man, that it should be believed as an article of the faith, or be thought requisite as necessary to salvation.

In the name of Holy Scripture we do understand those canonical books of the Old and New Testament, of whose authority was never any doubt in the church.

7. Of the Old Testament

The Old Testament is not contrary to the New, for both in the Old and New Testament everlasting life is offered to mankind by Christ, who is the only Mediator between God and man, being both God and man. Wherefore they are not to be heard which feign that the old Fathers did look only for transitory promises. Although the law given from God by Moses, as touching ceremonies and rites, do not bind Christian men, nor the civil precepts thereof, ought of necessity to be received in any commonwealth; yet notwithstanding, no Christian man whatsoever is free from the obedience of the commandments which are called moral.

8. Of the Three Creeds

The three Creeds, Nicene Creed, Athanasius' Creed, and that which is commonly called the Apostles' Creed, ought thoroughly to be received and believed, for they may be proved by most certain warrants of Holy Scripture.

9. Of Original, or Birth Sin

Original sin standeth not in the following of Adam, as the Pelagians do vainly talk, but it is the fault and corruption of the nature of every man, that naturally is engendered of the offspring of Adam, whereby man is very far gone from original righteousness, and is of his own nature inclined to evil, so that the flesh lusteth always contrary to the spirit, and therefore in every person born into this world, it deserveth God's wrath and damnation. And this infection of nature doth remain, yea in them that are regenerated, whereby the lust of the flesh, called in Greek *phronema sarkos,* which some do expound the wisdom, some sensuality, some the affection, and some the desire of the flesh, is not subject to the law of God. And although there is no condemnation for them that believe and are baptized, yet the apostle doth confess that concupiscence and lust hath of itself the nature of sin.

10. Of Free Will

The condition of man after the fall of Adam is such that he cannot turn and prepare himself by his own natural strength and good works to faith and calling upon God; wherefore we have no power to do good works pleasant and acceptable to God, without the grace of God preventing us, that we may have a good will, and working with us, when we have that good will.

11. Of the Justification of Man

We are accounted righteous before God only for the merit of our Lord and Savior Jesus Christ by faith, and not for our own works or deservings. Wherefore, that we are justified by faith only, is a most wholesome doctrine, and very full of comfort, as more largely is expressed in the Homily of Justification.

12. Of Good Works

Albeit that good works, which are the fruits of faith, and follow after justification, cannot put away our sins, and endure the severity of God's judgment; yet are they pleasing and acceptable to God in Christ, and do spring out necessarily of a true and lively faith, insomuch that by them a lively faith may be as evidently known, as a tree discerned by the fruit.

13. Of Works before Justification

Works done before the grace of Christ, and the inspiration of his Spirit, are not pleasant to God, forasmuch as they spring not of faith in Jesus Christ, neither do they make men meet to receive grace, or as the school authors say, deserve grace of congruity; yet rather for that they are not done as God hath willed and commanded them to be done, we doubt not but they have the nature of sin.

14. Of Works of Supererogation

Voluntary works besides, over and above God's commandments, which they call works of supererogation, cannot be taught without arrogance and impiety. For by them men do declare that they do not only render unto God as much as they are bound to do, but that they do more for his sake than of bounden duty is required; whereas Christ saith plainly: "When ye have done all that are commanded to you, say: We be unprofitable servants."

15. Of Christ Alone without Sin

Christ in the truth of our nature, was made like unto us in all things, sin only except, from which he was clearly void, both in his flesh and in his spirit. He came to be the lamb without spot, who by the sacrifice of himself once made, should take away the sins of the world; and sin, as St. John saith, was not in him. But all we the rest, although baptized and born again in Christ, yet offend in many things, and if we say we have no sin, we deceive ourselves and the truth is not in us.

16. Of Sin after Baptism

Not every deadly sin willingly committed after baptism is sin against the Holy Spirit, and unpardonable. Wherefore the grant of repentance is not to be denied to such as fall into sin after baptism. After we have received the Holy Spirit, we may depart from grace given and fall into sin, and by the grace of God we may arise again and amend our lives. And therefore they are to be condemned, which say they can no more sin as long as

they live here, or deny the place of forgiveness to such as truly repent.

17. Of Predestination and Election

Predestination to life is the everlasting purpose of God, whereby before the foundations of the world were laid, he hath constantly decreed by his counsel secret to us, to deliver from curse and damnation those whom he hath chosen in Christ out of mankind, and to bring them by Christ to everlasting salvation, as vessels made to honor. Wherefore they which be imbued with so excellent a benefit of God be called according to God's purpose by his Spirit, working in due season; they through grace obey the calling; they be justified freely; they be made sons of God by adoption; they be made like the image of his only-begotten Son Jesus Christ; they walk religiously in good works and at length by God's mercy, they attain to everlasting felicity.

As the godly consideration of predestination, and our election in Christ is full of sweet, pleasant and unspeakable comfort to godly persons, and such as feel in themselves the working of the spirit of Christ, mortifying the works of the flesh and their earthly members, and drawing up their mind to high and heavenly things, as well because it doth greatly establish and confirm their faith of eternal salvation to be enjoyed through Christ, as because it doth fervently kindle their love towards God; so for curious and carnal persons, lacking the spirit of Christ, to have continually before their eyes the sentence of God's predestination, is a most dangerous downfall, whereby the devil doth thrust them either into desperation, or into recklessness of most unclean living, no less perilous than desperation.

Furthermore, we must receive God's promises in such wise as they be generally set forth to us in Holy Scripture; and in our doings that will of God is to be followed which we have, expressly declared to us in the Word of God.

18. Of Obtaining Eternal Salvation, Only by the Name of Christ

They also are to be had accursed that presume to say that every man shall be saved by the law or sect which he professeth, so that he be diligent to frame his life according to that law, and the light of nature. For Holy Scripture doth set out unto us only the name of Jesus Christ, whereby men must be saved.

19. Of the Church

The visible church of Christ is a congregation of faithful men in which the pure Word of God is preached and the sacraments be duly administered, according to Christ's ordinance in all those things that of necessity are requisite to the same.

As the church of Jerusalem, Alexandria and Antioch have erred, so also the church of Rome hath erred, not only in their living and manner of ceremonies, but also in matters of faith.

20. Of the Authority of the Church

The church hath power to decree rites and ceremonies, and authority in controversies of faith; and yet it is not lawful for the church to ordain anything that is contrary to God's Word written, neither may it so expound one place of Scripture that it is repugnant to another. Wherefore, although the church be a witness and a keeper of Holy Writ; yet as it ought not to decree anything against the same, so besides the same, ought it not to enforce anything to be believed for necessity of salvation.

21. Of the Authority of General Councils

General councils may not be gathered together without the commandment and will of princes. And when they be gathered together, forasmuch as they shall be an assembly of men, whereof all be not governed with the Spirit and Word of God, they may err, and sometimes have erred, even in things pertaining unto God. Wherefore things ordained by them as necessary to salvation have neither strength nor authority, unless it may be declared that they be taken out of Holy Scripture.

22. Of Purgatory

The Romish doctrine concerning purgatory, pardons, worshipping and adoration as well of images as of relics, and also invocation of saints, is a fond thing vainly invented, and grounded upon no warranty of Scripture, but rather repugnant to the Word of God.

23. Of Ministering in the Congregation

It is not lawful for any man to take upon him the office of public preaching, or ministering the sacraments in the congregation, before he be lawfully called and sent to execute the same. And those we ought to judge lawfully called to this work by men, who have public authority given unto them in the congregation, to call and send ministers into the Lord's vineyard.

24. Of speaking in the Congregation in Such a Tongue as the People Understandeth

It is a thing plainly repugnant to the Word of God and the custom of the primitive church to have public prayer in the church, or to minister the sacraments in a tongue not understood of the people.

25. Of the Sacraments

Sacraments ordained of Christ, be not only badges or tokens of Christian men's profession; but rather they be certain sure witnesses and effectual signs of grace towards us, by the which he doth work invisibly in us, and doth not only quicken, but also strengthen and confirm our faith in him.

There are two sacraments ordained of Christ our Lord in the gospel, that is to say, baptism and the supper of the Lord.

Those five, commonly called sacraments, that is to say, confirmation, penance, orders, matrimony and extreme unction, are not to be counted for sacraments of the gospel, being such as have grown partly of the corrupt following of the apostles, partly are states of life allowed in the Scriptures; but yet have not like nature of sacraments with baptism and the Lord's supper, for that they have not any visible sign or ceremony ordained of God.

26. Of the Unworthiness of the Ministers, Which Hinders Not the Effect of the Sacraments

Although in the visible church the evil be ever mingled with the good, and sometime the evil have chief authority in the ministration of the Word and sacraments; yet forasmuch as they do not the same in their own name but in Christ's, and do minister by his commission and authority; we may use their ministry both in hearing the Word of God, and in the receiving of the sacraments. Neither is the effect of Christ's ordinances taken away by their wickedness, nor the grace of God's gifts diminished from such as by faith and rightly do receive the sacraments ministered unto them, which be effectual because of Christ's institution and promise, although they be ministered by evil men. Nevertheless it appertaineth to the discipline of the church, that inquiry be made of evil ministers, and that they be accused by those that have knowledge of their offenses, and finally, being found guilty by just judgment, be deposed.

27. Of Baptism

Baptism is not only a sign of profession and mark of difference, whereby Christian men are discerned from other that be not christened; but is also a sign of regeneration or new birth, whereby as by an instrument, they that receive baptism rightly are grafted into the church; the promises of the forgiveness of sin, and of our adoption to be the sons of God, by the Holy Spirit, are visibly signed and sealed; faith is confirmed; and grace increased by virtue of prayer unto God. The baptism of young children is in any wise to be retained in the church as most agreeable with the institution of Christ.

28. Of the Lord's Supper

The supper of the Lord is not only a sign of the love Christians ought to have among themselves to one another; but rather it is a sacrament of our redemption by Christ's death. Insomuch that to such as rightly, worthily and with faith receive the same, the bread which we break is a partaking of the body of Christ, and likewise the cup of blessing is a partaking of the blood of Christ.

Transubstantiation, or the change of the substance of the bread and wine into the substance of Christ's body and blood in the supper of the Lord, cannot be proved by Holy Writ, but is repugnant to the plain words of Scripture, overthroweth the nature of a sacrament, and hath given occasion to many superstitions.

The body of Christ is given, taken and eaten in the supper only after an heavenly and spiritual manner; and the mean whereby the body of Christ is received and eaten in the supper is faith.

The sacrament of the Lord's supper was not by Christ's ordinance reserved, carried about, lifted up or worshipped.

29. Of the Wicked Which Do Not Eat the Body of Christ in the Use of the Lord's Supper

The wicked, and such as be void of a lively faith, although they do carnally and visibly press with their teeth, as St. Augustine saith, the sacrament of the body and blood of Christ; yet in no wise are they partakers of Christ, but rather to their condemnation do eat and drink the sign or sacrament of so great a thing.

30. Of Both Kinds

The cup of the Lord is not to be denied to the lay people. For both the parts of the Lord's sacrament, by Christ's ordinance and commandment, ought to be ministered to all Christian men alike.

31. Of the One Oblation of Christ Finished upon the Cross

The offering of Christ once made, is the perfect redemption, propitiation, and satisfaction for all the sins of the whole world, both original and actual, and there is none other satisfaction for sin but that alone. Wherefore the sacrifices of masses, in the which it was commonly said that the priests did offer Christ for the quick and the dead, to have remission of pain or guilt, were blasphemous fables and dangerous deceits.

32. Of the Marriage of Priests

Bishops, priests and deacons are not commanded by God's law to vow the estate of single life, or to abstain from marriage. Therefore it is lawful also for them, as for all other Christian men, to marry at their own discretion, as they shall judge the same to serve better godliness.

33. Of Excommunicate Persons, How They Are to Be Avoided

That person, which by open denunciation of the church is rightly cut off from the unity of the church and excommunicated, ought to be taken of the whole multitude of the faithful as an heathen and publican, until he be openly reconciled by penance, and received into the Church by a judge that hath authority thereto.

34. Of the Traditions of the Church

It is not necessary that traditions and ceremonies be in all places one or utterly like, for at all times they have been diverse, and may be changed according to the diversity of countries, times and men's manners, so that nothing be ordained against God's Word.

Whosoever through his private judgment willingly and purposely doth openly break the traditions and ceremonies of the church, which be not repugnant to the Word of God and be ordained and approved by common authority, ought to be rebuked openly, that other may fear to do the like, as he that offendeth against the common order of the church and hurteth the authority of the magistrate, and woundeth the consciences of the weak brethren.

Every particular or national church hath authority to ordain, change and abolish ceremonies, or rites of the church ordained only by man's authority, so that all things be done to edifying.

35. Of Homilies

The second Book of Homilies, the several titles whereof we have joined under this Article, doth contain a godly and wholesome doctrine, and necessary for these times, as doth the former Book of Homilies, which were set forth in the time of King Edward the Sixth; and therefore we judge them to be read in churches by the ministers diligently and distinctly, that they may be understood of the people. . . .

36. Of Consecration of Bishops and Ministers

The book of consecration of archbishops and bishops, and ordering of priests and deacons, lately set forth in the time of Edward the Sixth, and confirmed at the same time by authority of Parliament, doth contain all things necessary to such consecration and ordering; neither hath it anything that of itself is superstitious or ungodly. And therefore, whosoever are consecrate or ordered according to the rites of that book, since the second year of the aforenamed King Edward, unto this time, or hereafter shall be consecrated or ordered according to the same rites we decree all such to be rightly, orderly and lawfully consecrated and ordered.

37. Of the Civil Magistrates

The Queen's Majesty hath the chief power in this realm of England, and other her dominions, unto whom the chief government of all estates of this realm, whether they be ecclesiastical or civil, in all causes doth appertain, and is not, nor ought to be subject to any foreign jurisdiction.

Where we attribute to the Queen's Majesty the chief government, by which titles we understand the minds of some slanderous folk to be offended; we give not to our princes the ministering either of God's Word or of sacraments, the which thing the injunctions also lately set forth by Elizabeth our queen doth most plainly testify; but that only prerogative which we see to have been given always to all godly princes in Holy Scriptures by God himself, that is, that they should rule all estates and degrees committed to their charge by God, whether they be ecclesiastical or temporal, and restrain with the civil sword the stubborn and evildoers.

The bishop of Rome hath no jurisdiction in this realm of England.

The laws of the realm may punish Christian men with death for heinous and grievous offenses. It is lawful for Christian men, at the commandment of the magistrate, to wear weapons and to serve in the wars.

38. Of Christian Men's Goods, Which Are Not Common

The riches and goods of Christians are not common, as touching the right title and possession of the same, as certain Anabaptists do falsely boast; notwithstanding, every man ought of such things as he possesseth, liberally to give alms to the poor, according to his ability.

39. Of a Christian Man's Oath

As we confess that vain and rash swearing is forbidden Christian men by our Lord Jesus Christ, and James his apostle; so we judge that Christian religion doth not prohibit, but that a man may swear when the magistrate requireth, in a cause of faith and charity, so it be done, according to the prophet's teaching, in justice, judgment and truth.

These Articles of the Christian faith, containing in all nineteen pages in the original, which is kept by the most reverend father in Christ, Matthew Archbishop of Canterbury, Primate of all England and Metropolitan, the archbishops and bishops of each province of the realm of England, gathered lawfully in the holy provincial synod, receive with one voice and confess, and by the subscription of their own hands approve as true and orthodox, the twenty-ninth day of the month of January, in the year of our Lord, according to the reckoning of the Church of England, one thousand five hundred and sixty-two. And the whole clergy of the lower house has likewise received and confessed them with one voice, as is clear from the subscriptions of their own hands, which subscriptions the clergy have presented and deposited with the same most reverend archbishop of Canterbury, the fifth day of February in the aforesaid year.

To all which Articles, the most sovereign princess Elizabeth, by the grace of God of England, France and Ireland, Queen, Defender of the Faith etc., having herself carefully read and examined them beforehand, has given her royal assent.

✠

From Bray, **Documents of the English Reformation,** *285–311.*

Chapter 6
The Counter/Catholic Reformation

✠

Introduction

The Reformation of the sixteenth century can be seen as the disintegration of Western Christendom, a process which recent historians have called "confessionalization." Whereas the Catholic Church had held a monopoly over religious life in the pre-Reformation period, it now became one "confession" among many. It was no longer simply "catholic," a term which meant "universal" and which Protestant confessions claimed as well. It was now specifically "Roman" Catholic. It claimed continuity, of course, with the Catholic tradition, but there was also change. And the nature of this change is still debated by historians.

The primary difficulty historians face in assessing this change is reflected in the title of this chapter. Should the era into which the Roman Catholic Church now entered be seen in the first instance as a Counter-Reformation or as primarily a Catholic Reformation? Conventionally the term "Counter-Reformation" has carried the day. It implies of course a reactionary traditionalism, a reaffirmation of long-held teachings and practices in the face of Protestant criticism, a blanket condemnation of all that seemed new, in short a kind of anti-Reformation. For half a century now, this view has come under criticism. For it seems to ignore the considerable impetus toward self-reform, the attempt to preserve the best of the medieval heritage while eliminating abuses, the renewal of church discipline, the curbing of immorality and the reinvigorating of personal piety—all of which were also realities. If this is what predominated, then, say some more recent historians, the term "Catholic Reformation" is more appropriate.

The fact is there is evidence to support both of these labels. Some of the texts in this chapter point in the direction of "Counter-Reformation" while others speak for "Catholic Reformation." Thus we are left with the complex task of weighing the evidence, without foreclosing the question prematurely.

To begin with, it is important to take into consideration that there were significant reform impulses in the Catholic Church that predate the Protestant reforms. Already at the Council of Constance (1414–1418) a call was issued for the reform of the church "in head and members." From then until the Fifth Lateran Council (1512–1517), protests against simony, plurality of benefices, nonresident bishops, nepotism, and so forth, were frequent. While these reform impulses were, for the most part, miserable failures, new efforts to deepen lay piety were not. Movements such as the Modern Devotion, lay confraternities, and the religious societies known as "oratories" had a lasting impact. Also, the establishment of new religious orders and the reform of old ones were attempts to deepen the spiritual lives of monks, nuns, and friars.

Internal calls for reform are of course implicit critiques of the existing reality. As such, they understandably receded into the background as Luther's movement gathered strength. Self-criticism, though not entirely absent, became muted as condemnations and anathemas rose to the fore. And popes of course played a major role. Here again distinctions must be made.

Whereas some like Leo X (1513–1521), obsessed with preserving the church's power, simply issued blanket denunciations of the Protestant "novelties," others like the saintly Adrian VI (1522–1523) were determined above all to set their own house in order. Paul III (1534–1549), on the other hand, seemed to embody contradictions: while he had a mistress and four children and was guilty of nepotism, yet he appointed a good number of reform-minded cardinals. Paul IV (1555–1559), who as a cardinal had been a vociferous advocate of reform, became something of a paranoid fanatic when he was made pope. Thus the question of whether the papacy in the sixteenth century stood on the side of Catholic reform or anti-Reformation is complex.

The Council of Trent (1545–1563) itself pointed in both directions as well. In its decrees, it laid out for the faithful an authoritative version of what it considered to be genuinely Catholic teaching on all the controverted issues, much of which had previously been unclear. And it appended to these decrees canons condemning many aspects of what it understood to be the Protestant heresy. But it also promulgated reform decrees aimed at correcting the church's shortcomings and abuses.

It is also not easy to say whether the new Jesuit order (approved in 1540) stood on the side of Catholic reform or counter-reform. It combined in itself a certain internal flexibility with a hierarchical authoritarianism. It played an enormous role in the renewal and deepening of Catholic spirituality, and yet it reaffirmed what the Protestants saw as the worst symptoms of a deformed spirituality—indulgences, relics, and so on. It injected new vigor into intellectual life by its astonishingly successful educational ventures, but in the end subjected rational inquiry to church dogma.

Theologically, the Counter/Catholic Reformation brought a retrenchment and a narrowing of horizons. We recall the exuberant pluralism of Catholic theology on the eve of the Reformation. Augustinians, Thomists, Scotists, Occamists, and other "schools" vied for influence. Now, out of this struggle, it was Thomism which emerged triumphant, eventually exercising a virtual hegemony over Roman Catholic theological thought. Luther's most prominent literary opponents were largely Thomists. This same school dominated at the Council of Trent. The new Jesuit order named Thomas as its official teacher. And in 1567 Pius V declared him a "doctor" of the universal church. Of course, in this era intra-Catholic theological argument did not come to an end. But now all Catholic theologians appealed to Thomas as the highest authority to support their own views.

When did the Counter/Catholic Reformation end? Here again historians leave us with more questions than answers. Did it end in 1648, as tradition has it, when the great wars of religion which engulfed most of Europe gave way to a kind of "cold war" between Roman Catholics and Protestants? Or did it end in 1962 when the Second Vatican Council flung the windows and doors of the church open to modernity, abandoned its defensive posture, embraced some of the very things the Protestant reformers had advocated, and took some initial steps to democratize the institution? Or was it really a sixteenth-century movement functioning in tandem with the Protestant Reformation to effectively "Christianize" the European masses for the first time, with both movements then falling victim to the Enlightenment? These larger questions take us beyond the scope of this book. What we can say about the sixteenth century is that it was in this period that the Roman Catholic Church really became what it was henceforth to be throughout most of the modern era.

Early Reactions

75. Leo X, *Exsurge Domine* (1520)

Pope Leo X (1513–1521) had been made a cardinal in 1489 at the age of fourteen. He was elected pope in 1513 and subsequently ordained to the priesthood. In 1520, alarmed by the furor in Germany, and distracted by it from his main preoccupations of hunting, music, and art, Leo issued this bull, hoping thereby to stifle a potentially dangerous movement. It censured forty-one statements as "heretical, scandalous, erroneous, offensive to pious ears, misleading to simple minds, and contradictory to Catholic teaching." If Luther did not recant in sixty days, he would be excommunicated. The list shows that at this stage there was in Rome considerable confusion over what Luther actually taught.

✠

Arise O Lord and judge thy cause. . . . Arise O Peter, and in the name of the pastoral charge committed to thee from on high, put forth thy strength in the cause of the holy Roman Church, the mother of all churches, the mistress of the faith. . . . Arise thou also, O Paul, we beg thee, who hast enlightened her with thy teaching. . . . In a word, let every saint arise and the whole remaining universal church. . . . Let intercession be made to almighty God, that his sheep may be purged of their errors and every heresy be expelled from the confines of the faithful, and that God may deign to preserve the peace and unity of his holy church. . . .

For some time we have been hearing of, or rather, alas!, seeing and reading with our own eyes, many different errors which, although in part condemned aforetimes by councils and decisions of our predecessors . . . have been stirred up afresh, and latterly . . . sown abroad in the renowned nation of Germany. . . . We cannot, in view of our pastoral office, laid on us by divine grace, any longer tolerate the poisonous virus of these errors. . . .[A partial list follows.]

1. It is an heretical but commonly held opinion that the sacraments of the new law give justifying grace to those who place no obstacle in their way.

2. To deny that sin remains in a child after baptism is to trample on [the teachings of] Paul and Christ alike.

3. The capacity of sinning [*fomes peccati,* literally the "tinder of sin"], even where no actual sin is present, hinders the soul, as it leaves the body, from entering heaven.

4. The imperfect love of a dying man cannot but produce a great fear, which of itself is enough to constitute the penalty of purgatory; and this hinders entrance into the kingdom.

5. The threefold division of penitence into contrition, confession and satisfaction, is based neither on Holy Scripture nor the writings of the ancient and holy Christian doctors.

6. The contrition which results from discussion, comparison and detestation of one's sins, and with which one reviews one's past years in bitterness of soul, weighing the gravity, multitude, hideousness of the sins— the forfeiting of eternal blessedness, the procuring of eternal damnation—such contrition makes of one a hypocrite and a worse sinner than before.

7. Truest of all, and worth more than all that has been taught to date about contrition, is the proverb: "Penitence at its highest is not to do it again; penitence at its best is— a new life."

8. You must not in the least presume to confess venial sins—nor all your mortal sins, either, for you cannot possibly have cognizance

of them all. This is why in the primitive church the only mortal sins confessed were those committed for all to see.

9. Our purpose to make pure confession of everything really only means that we want there to be nothing left for the divine mercy to pardon.

10. No sins are remitted unless, when the priest pronounces absolution, a man *believes* that they are remitted; . . .

11. You are on no account to believe that absolution is due to your contrition, but rather to the Word of Christ ("Whatsoever ye shall loose . . ." [Matt. 16:19]). . . .

12. If, to take an impossible case, the one confessing were not contrite, or the priest were not serious but joking in his absolution, nevertheless if he believes he is absolved, then absolved he is in very truth.

13. In the sacrament of penance or the remission of guilt, the pope or the bishop does no more than the lowliest priest; indeed, when there is no priest, any Christian—even a woman or child—could do the same.

14. No one is bound to reply to the priest that he is contrite, nor the priest to ask it.

15. They are greatly in error who approach the Eucharist relying on their confession of sin, on their consciousness of no mortal sin, or their due performance of prayers and preparations: all such eat and drink to their own judgment. But if they believe and trust that there they will find grace, this faith alone (*sola fides*) makes them pure and worthy.

16. It is apparently agreed that the church should decree by a general council that the laity should be communicated in both kinds: the Bohemians, who follow this practice, are not heretics—merely schismatics.

17. The treasures of the church, whence the pope grants indulgences, are *not* the merits of Christ and the saints. . . .

19. Indulgences, even when sincerely sought, have no power for the remission of the punishment which divine justice awards actual sins. . . .

21. Indulgences are only necessary for public crimes, and are properly granted only to hardened and unfeeling offenders. . . .

23. Excommunication is a mere external penalty; it does not deprive a man of the common spiritual prayers of the church. . . .

25. The Roman Pontiff, the successor of Peter, is *not* the vicar of Christ over all the churches in the whole world, appointed as such by Christ himself in blessed Peter.

26. The word of Christ to Peter: "Whatsoever thou loosest on earth" etc. [Matt. 16:19] applies only to Peter's own binding (and loosing).

27. It is certain that it is not in the power of the church or pope to fix articles of faith, or even laws of conduct or good works.

28. If the pope, supported by a large part of the church, expresses this or that opinion—and a correct one at that: even so, it is neither sin nor heresy to disagree, especially if the matter is not one necessary to salvation, until a universal council has approved the one view and condemned the other.

29. It is open to us to weaken the authority of councils, freely to contradict their findings, to sit in judgment on their decrees, and to confess with boldness whatever appears to us to be true, whether any council has approved or condemned it.

30. Certain articles of John Huss, condemned by the Council of Constance, are most Christian, true, and evangelical; the universal church could not possibly condemn them.

31. In every good work a righteous man sins.

32. A good work perfectly executed is—a venial sin.

33. To burn heretics is contrary to the will of the Spirit.

34. To fight the Turks is to resist God, who is visiting our sins upon us through them.

35. No one can be sure that he is not always sinning mortally, because of the hidden and secret vice of pride.

36. Free will after sin is a mere name; while it does what in it lies, it sins mortally.

37. Purgatory cannot be proved by the canonical Sacred Scriptures.

38. Souls in purgatory have no assurance of their salvation—at least, not all of them.
. . .

39. Souls in purgatory sin without intermission as long as they look for rest and recoil from punishment.

40. Souls released from purgatory receive less blessing from the intercessions of the living than if they had given satisfaction of themselves. . . .

☩

From E. G. Rupp and B. Drewery, eds., Martin Luther (London: Edward Arnold; New York.: St. Martin's Press, 1970), 36–40.

76. Leo X, *Decet Romanum* (1521)

Luther and his colleagues burned the bull *Exsurge Domine*, together with books of canon law and scholastic theology, on 10 December 1520, in Wittenberg. On 3 January 1521, Leo issued the bull *Decet Romanum* officially excommunicating Luther.

☩

Through the power given him from God, the Roman Pontiff has been appointed to administer spiritual and temporal punishments as each case severally deserves. The purpose of this is the repression of the wicked designs of misguided men, who have been so captivated by the debased impulse of their evil purposes as to forget the fear of the Lord, to set aside with contempt canonical decrees and apostolic commandments, and to dare to formulate new and false dogmas and to introduce the evil of schism into the church of God—or to support, help and adhere to such schismatics, who make it their business to cleave asunder the seamless robe of our redeemer and the unity of the orthodox faith. Hence it befits the Pontiff, lest the vessel of Peter appear to sail without pilot or oarsman, to take severe measures against such men and their followers, and by multiplying punitive measures and by other suitable remedies to see to it that these same overbearing men, devoted as they are to purposes of evil, along with their adherents, should not deceive the multitude of the simple by their lies and their deceitful devices, nor drag them along to share their own error and ruination, contaminating them with what amounts to a contagious disease. It also befits the Pontiff, having condemned the schismatics, to ensure their still greater confounding by publicly showing and openly declaring to all faithful Christians how formidable are the censures and punishments to which such guilt can lead; to the end that by such public declaration they themselves may return, in confusion and remorse, to their true selves, making an unqualified withdrawal from the prohibited conversation, fellowship and (above all) obedience to such accursed excommunicates; by this means they may escape divine vengeance and any degree of participation in their damnation. . . .

[Here the Pope recounts his previous bull *Exsurge Domine* and continues.]

We have been informed that after this previous missive had been exhibited in public and the interval or intervals it prescribed had elapsed—and we hereby give solemn notice to all faithful Christians that these intervals have and are elapsed—many of those who had followed the errors of Martin took cognizance of our missive and its warnings and injunctions; the spirit of a saner counsel brought them back to themselves, they confessed their errors and abjured the heresy at our instance, and by returning to the true Catholic faith obtained the blessing of absolution with which the self-same messengers had been empowered; and in several states and localities of the said Germany the books and writings of the said Martin were publicly burned, as we had enjoined.

Nevertheless Martin himself—and it gives us grievous sorrow and perplexity to say this—the slave of a depraved mind, has scorned to revoke his errors within the prescribed interval and to send us word of such revocation, or to come to us himself; nay, like a stone of stumbling, he has feared not to write and preach worse things than before against us and this holy see and the Catholic faith, and to lead others on to do the same.

He has now been declared a heretic; and so also others, whatever their authority and rank, who have recked naught of their own salvation but publicly and in all men's eyes become followers of Martin's pernicious and heretical sect, and given him openly and publicly their help, counsel and favor, encouraging him in their midst in his disobedience and obstinacy, or hindering the publication of our said missive: such men have incurred the punishments set out in that missive, and are to be treated rightfully as heretics and avoided by all faithful Christians, as the apostle says [Titus 3:10-11].

Our purpose is that such men should rightfully be ranked with Martin and other accursed heretics and excommunicates, and that even as they have ranged themselves with the obstinacy in sinning of the said Martin, they shall likewise share his punishments and his name, by bearing with them everywhere the title "Lutheran" and the punishments it incurs.

Our previous instructions were so clear and so effectively publicized and we shall adhere so strictly to our present decrees and declarations, that they will lack no proof, warning or citation.

Our decrees which follow are passed against Martin and others who follow him in the obstinacy of his depraved and damnable purpose, as also against those who defend and protect him with a military bodyguard, and do not fear to support him with their own resources or in any other way, and have and do presume to offer and afford help, counsel and favor toward him. All their names, surnames and rank—however lofty and dazzling their dignity may be—we wish to be taken as included in these decrees with the same effect as if they were individually listed and could be so listed in their publication, which must be furthered with an energy to match their contents.

On all these we decree the sentences of excommunication, of anathema, of our perpetual condemnation and interdict; of privation of dignities, honors and property on them and their descendants, and of declared unfitness for such possessions; of the confiscation of their goods and of the crime of treason; and these and the other sentences, censures and punishments which are inflicted by canon law on heretics and are set out in our aforesaid missive, we decree to have fallen on all these men to their damnation.

We add to our present declaration, by our apostolic authority, that states, territories, camps, towns and places in which these men have temporarily lived or chanced to visit, along with their possessions—cities which house cathedrals and metropolitans, monasteries and other religious and sacred places, privileged or unprivileged—one and all are placed under our ecclesiastical interdict. While this interdict lasts, no pretext of apostolic indulgence (except in cases the law allows, and even there as it were with the doors shut and those under excommunication and interdict excluded) shall avail to allow the celebration of mass and other divine offices. We prescribe and enjoin that the men in question are everywhere to be denounced publicly as excommunicated, accursed, condemned, interdicted, deprived of possessions and incapable of owning them. They are to be strictly shunned by all faithful Christians.

We would make known to all the small store that Martin, his followers and the other rebels have set on God and his church by their obstinate and shameless temerity. We would protect the herd from one infectious animal, lest its infection spread to the healthy ones. Hence we lay the following injunction on each and every patriarch, archbishop, bishop, on the prelates of patriarchal, metropolitan, cathedral and collegiate churches, and on the religious of every order—even the mendicants—privileged or unprivileged, wherever they may be stationed: that in the strength of their vow of obedience and on pain of the sentence of excommunication, they shall, if so required in the execution of these presents, publicly announce and cause to be announced by others in their churches, that this same Martin and the rest are excommunicate, accursed, condemned, heretics, hardened, interdicted, deprived of possessions and incapable of

owning them, and so listed in the enforcement of these presents. Three days will be given: we pronounce canonical warning and allow one day's notice on the first, another on the second, but on the third peremptory and final execution of our order. This shall take place on a Sunday or some other festival, when a large congregation assembles for worship. The banner of the cross shall be raised, the bells rung, the candles lit and after a time extinguished, cast on the ground and trampled under foot, and the stones shall be cast forth three times, and the other ceremonies observed which are usual in such cases. The faithful Christians, one and all, shall be enjoined strictly to shun these men.

We would occasion still greater confounding on the said Martin and the other heretics we have mentioned, and on their adherents, followers and partisans: hence, on the strength of their vow of obedience we enjoin each and every patriarch, archbishop and all other prelates, that even as they were appointed on the authority of Jerome to allay schisms, so now in the present crisis, as their office obliges them, they shall make themselves a wall of defense for their Christian people. They shall not keep silence like dumb dogs that cannot bark, but incessantly cry and lift up their voice, preaching and causing to be preached the Word of God and the truth of the Catholic faith against the damnable articles and heretics aforesaid.

To each and every rector of the parish churches, to the rectors of all the orders, even the mendicants, privileged or unprivileged, we enjoin in the same terms, on the strength of their vow of obedience, that appointed by the Lord as they are to be like clouds, they shall sprinkle showers on the people of God, and have no fear in giving the widest publicity to the condemnation of the aforesaid articles, as their office obliges them. It is written that perfect love casteth out fear. Let each and every one of you take up the burden of such a meritorious duty with complete devotion; show yourselves so punctilious in its execution, so zealous and eager in word and deed, that from your labors, by the favor of divine grace, the hoped-for harvest will come in, and that through your devotion you will not only earn that crown of glory which is the due recompense of all who promote religious causes, but also attain from us and the said holy see the unbounded commendation that your proved diligence will deserve.

However, since it would be difficult to deliver the present missive, with its declarations and announcements, to Martin and the other declared excommunicates in person, because of the strength of their faction, our wish is that the public nailing of this missive on the doors of two cathedrals—either both metropolitan, or one cathedral and one metropolitan of the churches in the said Germany—by a messenger of ours in those places, shall have such binding force that Martin and the others we have declared shall be shown to be condemned at every point as decisively as if the missive had been personally made known and presented to them.

It would also be difficult to transmit this missive to every single place where its publication might be necessary. Hence our wish and authoritative decree is that copies of it, sealed by some ecclesiastical prelate or by one of our aforesaid messengers, and countersigned by the hand of some public notary, should everywhere bear the same authority as the production and exhibition of the original itself.

No obstacle is afforded to our wishes by the apostolic constitutions and orders, or by anything in our aforesaid earlier missive

which we do not wish to stand in the way, or by any other pronouncements to the contrary.

No one whatsoever may infringe this our written decision, declaration, precept, injunction, assignation, will, decree; or rashly contravene it. Should anyone dare to attempt such a thing, let him know that he will incur the wrath of almighty God and of the blessed apostles Peter and Paul.

Written at St. Peter's, Rome, on the third of January 1521, during the eighth year of our pontificate.

✠

From Rupp and Drewery, Martin Luther, 63–67.

77. Adrian VI to the Diet of Nuremberg (1523)

Pope Adrian VI (1522–1523) differed from his immediate predecessors in that he was Dutch, a theologian by training, and deeply concerned about the church's spiritual welfare. His memorandum to German authorities in 1523 shows that the spirit of self-criticism and reform was by no means dead in the Catholic Church. Had he lived longer, we could speculate, things might have turned out differently.

✠

God has allowed this punishment [the fall of Belgrade and Rhodes to the Turks] to overtake his church because of the sins of men, especially those of priests and prelates. . . . There have been great spiritual abominations and abuses in the holy see for many years. Perversion has grown everywhere and it is hardly surprising that the sickness has spread from the head to the members. Every single one of us has fallen victim. Not even one of us has done good. . . . We will do everything in our power to reform first this see, from which the powerful evil advanced so that, even as corruption passed from Rome to every other part, so healing will spread from Rome. The whole world eagerly desires reform and we are definitely responsible. . . . Be patient. Every error and abuse will not be swept away at once; the disease is well established. Therefore progress must be made step by step . . . lest everything become still more chaotic. . . .

✠

From M. Jones, ed., The Counter Reformation: Religion and Society in Early Modern Europe *(New York: Cambridge University Press, 1995), 45.*

78. Cajetan, *On Faith and Works* (1532)

Of the many Roman Catholic theologians who took up the pen against Luther, Cardinal Cajetan (1468–1534) ranks among the best. This Thomist, who had met with Luther in Augsburg in 1518, was one of the few in the next decade who recognized the issue that was at the heart of Luther's attack on the church. His careful response to it in this essay allows us to compare Luther's theology of justification with a contemporary and indisputably Roman Catholic perspective on the issue.

✠

To the Supreme Pontiff, Clement VII:

Obedience to the commands of your Holiness is always due, but now it is for me a delight since I was wanting to refute the poisonous Lutheran views on faith and works. Fearing these were infecting even the hearts of the faithful, I had shortly before receiving your Holiness' command felt called to write this treatise. This is consequently an agreeable act of obedience which I hope proves fruitful for Christ's faithful and pleasing to your Holiness, whose office it is also to judge this short work.

1. The Lutheran Doctrine of Faith

The Lutherans exalt the evangelical doctrine of man's eternal salvation through faith in Jesus Christ, our human Mediator between God and man. They teach that men attain the forgiveness of sins through faith in Jesus Christ, but they enlarge the term "faith" so as to include that conviction by which the sinner approaching the sacrament believes he is justified by the divine mercy through the intercession of Jesus Christ. They assign such great value to this conviction that they say it attains the forgiveness of sins through the divine promise. They affirm that unless one has this firm conviction about the Word of God, one is despising the divine Word by not believing the divine promise. But if in receiving the sacrament one firmly believes he is justified, then he is truly justified. Otherwise the divine promise would not be true and effective.

Some Lutherans so extol this kind of faith that they teach it attains the forgiveness of sins before the sinner has charity. They base this on extended texts of the apostle Paul which distinguish justifying faith from the law. Charity, they hold, is included under the law, since the first and greatest commandment of the law is to love God with one's whole heart, and so on, as our Lord said in the gospel, in Matthew 22[:37].—These views make up the heart of Lutheran teaching concerning faith.

2. A First Error: Equivocal Use of the Term "Faith"

"Faith" means one thing when Holy Scripture refers to that which justifies men, and means something else when it refers to that conviction by which one believes he is justified by Christ and the sacraments. Justifying faith is that which Hebrews 11 [:1] defines: "Faith is the substance of things hoped for, and the conviction of things not seen." Taken in this sense, faith is one of the three theological virtues referred to by Paul, "Now faith, hope, and charity remain" [1 Cor. 13:13]. Taken in this sense faith is the gift of God, as written in Ephesians 2 [:8], by which we are saved and without which it is impossible to please God. By such faith we believe all the articles of faith and whatever is to be believed as necessary to salvation.

But faith, taken as a conviction by which a person believes he is justified as he here and now receives this sacrament by the merit of Christ, is much different from faith taken in the first way. As a first indication of this, consider what is believed. Now faith cannot hold to something false, but this conviction can be deceived, since it concerns a particular effect here and now. This conviction arises in part from the faith that is necessary for salvation and in part from human conjecture. Concerning the merit of Christ and the sacraments, it is faith that calls for such a conviction; but concerning the effect here and now in one's own case, it is human conjecture that gives rise to the conviction.

It is a matter of Christian faith that anyone trusting in the merit of Christ and inwardly and outwardly receiving the sacrament correctly is justified by divine grace. But Christian faith does not extend to the belief that I am at this moment inwardly and outwardly receiving the sacrament correctly. Similarly I am held by Christian faith to believe that the true body of Christ is in a correctly consecrated host, but Christian faith does not extend to the belief that the host consecrated at this moment by this particular celebrant on this altar is the body of Christ, since this latter can for various reasons be false.

A second consideration is that all Christians share in one and the same faith, according to Ephesians 4 [:5], "One Lord, one faith." Obviously, my own faith does not entail believing that this man who is receiving the sacrament is here and now justified or that the body of Christ is in a particular host. Consequently no one's "faith" entails believing this particular effect of this sacrament in the case of this individual. Therefore, the unity of faith brings to light the second difference between faith and the conviction described.

Hence the first error of the Lutherans in this matter is that they attribute to this conviction what Holy Scripture attributes to faith. When they teach this conviction they constantly cite texts of Holy Scripture on faith, such as, "As justified by faith, we have peace with God" [Rom. 5:1], and "by faith purifying their hearts" [Acts 15:9] and countless texts like these.

3. The Second Error: Teaching That This Conviction Attains Forgiveness of Sins

Their assertion that a conviction of this type attains the forgiveness of sins can be said and understood both rightly and wrongly. If it is said and understood that this conviction informed by faith and charity attains forgiveness of sins, this is true. But if the informing influence of charity is excluded, then it is false. As Augustine says in *De Trinitate*, Book XV, Chapter 18, there is no more excellent gift of God than charity, which alone distinguishes the sons of the eternal kingdom from the sons of eternal perdition.

One should know that this conviction is in fact shared by all who devoutly approach the sacraments. A person devoutly approaching any sacrament does believe that by receiving it he is justified by the merits of the passion and death of Christ, or else he would not so approach. But this conviction is not the same in all, since one person may believe more than another that he is justified. Generally the devout join to this conviction a doubt, namely, that the contrary may be the case. They do this since no text of Scripture and no document of the church teaches us that we must hold this conviction against all doubt. The reason for doubt is that generally no one knows whether on his part something impedes reception of the gift of forgiveness of sins. Generally, one does not know whether he is lacking the grace of God. Hence such a doubt entails no despising of the divine promise. One is not doubting about God, not about the merit of Christ, and not about the sacrament, but one is doubting about himself. It is written [Ps. 18:13], "Who understands his own sins?" Further evidence for this ordinary doubt about a particular effect of the divine mercy, that is, the forgiveness of sins of an individual now devoutly turning to God, is found in chapter 2 of the prophet Joel. After speaking of those who had turned to God with their whole heart in fasting, weeping, and lament, and after referring to the greatness of God's mercy toward sinners, the prophet added [Joel 2:14], "Who knows whether God will turn and forgive?" Thus no one among those who were converted was certain, but each had some doubt whether God forgave them.

A confirmation of this lies in the fact that the doubt affecting this conviction would only be justifiably removed by one of three causes. First, divine revelation could bring this about, but this is not to the point here, since although God has revealed that all do attain forgiveness who inwardly and outwardly trust correctly that they attain this, he has not revealed that this person is now correctly turning to God inwardly and outwardly. This particular effect is not included in the revelation on which Christian faith is based. Second, a sufficient number of testimonies can motivate one to believe in a particular fact. For instance, a sufficient number of testimonies can bring one who has never left Rome to believe that the island of Calicut or Taproban does exist. But obviously in the case of the conviction by which one believes he is justified there do not occur any testimonies that bring the mind to be convinced about this effect now in oneself. Third, the special competence of witnesses could remove the doubt, for instance, if they were beyond all objection, as in Romans 8 [:16] where the apostle writes that the Holy Spirit bears witness to our spirit that we are sons of God. This witness presupposes that the forgiveness of sins has been conferred, because it presupposes that the one about whom witness is given is in fact a son of God, as the text clearly indicates. But the conviction asserted by the Lutherans does not presuppose in one the forgiveness of sins, but is itself the way of attaining this, as a prior reality attains what follows.

Hence it is to posit an arbitrary dogma to say that this sort of conviction about the word of Christ, based on the merit of his passion, and so on, infallibly attains the forgiveness of sins. Consequently Leo X included the following among the condemned articles of Luther:

> Sins are not forgiven unless when the priest forgives one believes they are forgiven; in fact, sins remain unless one believes he is forgiven. It is not sufficient that sins be forgiven and grace be given; one must also

believe he is forgiven. . . . You should in no wise trust you are absolved because of your contrition, but because of the words of Christ, "Whatever you loose. . . ." Rely on these if you receive the priest's absolution; firmly believe you are absolved, and you will truly be absolved, however it might be with your contrition. . . . If perchance, as could not occur, one is not contrite when he confesses, or if the priest gives absolution in jest and not seriously, still if one believes he is absolved, he is in fact truly absolved.

4. The Third Error: Forgiveness of Sins Preceding Charity

It is intolerable that one's sins would be forgiven before charity is infused in the person forgiven, as the following will convincingly show. An enemy cannot be made a friend unless he have the attitude of friendship. A friend devoid of the quality of friendship would be incomprehensible, just as something white is incomprehensible without whiteness. But when the unrighteous man is made righteous through Christ, an enemy of God is transformed into a friend of God, as the apostle says in Romans 5[:10], "When we were enemies we were reconciled to God by the death of his Son." Reconciliation makes the reconciled person a friend. Hence it is impossible and incomprehensible that a sinner be justified in the absence of friendship toward God. Charity is this friendship between man and God, being both man's love of friendship toward God and God's toward man. "God is love, and he who abides in love abides in God, and God in him" [1 John 4:16]. We read in the same epistle, "We love God, because he first loved us" [4:19].

Since friendship consists in mutual love, the forgiveness of sins takes place essentially through charity. Hence what we call the righteousness of faith is identical with charity. We speak of the righteousness of faith, since

by it a person is righteous before God, conformable to the divine realities and deeds in which we believe. The sense appetites are subject to the will, the will to right reason, and right reason is subject to God in conformity to what we accept in faith about him and about our heavenly homeland. We call the same thing charity since it also involves the love of friendship toward the God who is granting us citizenship in the heavenly homeland. Philippians 3[:20] says, "Our citizenship is in heaven." And Ephesians 2[:19], "You are no longer guests and strangers, but citizens with the saints and members of God's household." Also, in the Canticle, "My beloved is mine, and I am his" [2:16].

This reasoning suffices in itself to convince the mind, but it is further supported by the authority of Christ, and of Peter, John, and Paul, all of whom attribute the forgiveness of sins to both faith and charity. In Luke 7[:50], Christ said to the sinful woman, "Your faith has saved you." But he also said about her: "Many sins are forgiven her, because she has loved much" [7:47]. In this text the conjunction "because" shows that love is the proximate cause of the forgiveness of sins, that is, "because she has loved." Faith is the cause inchoatively, but charity is the cause completing the forgiveness of sins.

Peter the apostle said in Acts 10 [:43], "To him all the prophets bear witness that everyone receives forgiveness of sins who believes in his name." Then in his First Epistle, chapter 4 [:8], he wrote, "Charity covers a multitude of sins."

In a similar way the apostle John wrote in chapter 5 of his First Epistle, "Everyone who believes that Jesus is the Christ is born of God" [5:1]. And in chapter 3, "We know that we have passed from death to life, because we love the brethren. One who does not love remains in death" [3:14]. Granted that John wrote specifically about love of the neighbor, but this does not disprove our point, since obviously the charity by which we love God for his own sake is identical with that by which we love the neighbor for the sake of God. John's First Epistle says this in chapter 4 [:7-12] and finds evidence for the passage from death to life only in such love of the neighbor [3:14].

Finally, the apostle Paul, in Romans 5[:1], wrote, "Justified by faith, we have peace with God." But in 1 Corinthians 13[:2], "If I have all faith, so as to move mountains, but have not charity, I am nothing," nothing, that is, in the spiritual realm where we are made children of God. In Galatians 5[:6] he wrote, "In Christ Jesus neither circumcision nor uncircumcision avails anything, but rather faith working through love." What avails in Christ is evidently not just any kind of faith but that working through love.

It is evident therefore that the ordinary teaching of the church is true: that the forgiveness of sins occurs not by uninformed faith but by faith informed by charity. The normative texts teaching that we are made righteous by faith are consequently to be understood in the precise sense of faith informed by that friendship toward God, which we call charity.

Now it was objected that faith is made distinct from and opposed to the law, and that charity is included under the law. We answer that when Christ spoke of the first and greatest commandment of the law, he used "law" in a different sense than did the apostle in distinguishing faith from the law [Matt. 22:37f.]. Christ used "law" to indicate all the divine commandments written in the books of Moses. But the apostle spoke of "law" in a narrower sense, as embracing moral, ceremonial, and juridical precepts.

I have not invented this distinction, but have taken it from Scripture itself, so that even the adversaries should accept it. The fact that Christ used "law" in a broad sense is proven by the text of Deuteronomy 6 from which he cited the precept concerning love of God [6:5]. Immediately before this, there is a precept concerning faith, where it says, "Hear O Israel: the Lord our God is one Lord" [6:4]. In the same passage of the law there is laid down a precept of faith, believing God is only one, and a precept of loving the same God. We are to understand that a precept concerning charity is no less included in the law than a precept concerning faith, when we take "law" in a broad sense. Hence it is also clear that just as the apostle distinguishes faith from the law, one can equally well distinguish charity from the same law.

But the fact that the apostle speaks of the law in a manner excluding the elements of faith and charity is obvious when he calls it the "law of works" [Rom. 3:27, Vg.], and says that the gentiles observe it by nature, as in Romans 2 [:14], "the gentiles who do not have the law do by nature what the law requires." It is certain that they do not do by nature what charity requires.

Since this objection equivocates in speaking of "law," it consequently is of no worth. Love of God is not embraced by the law of works which is distinguished against faith, but is under the same law that includes faith, as in Deuteronomy 6 where precepts of faith and love of God occur together. Answers to the other objections of the Lutherans are obvious from what has been said.—This is sufficient treatment of faith.

5. The Lutheran Teaching on Works

The Lutherans teach that our works are neither meritorious of grace and eternal life, nor do these works make satisfaction for sins.

They argue that since Christ has superabundantly merited for us both the grace of forgiveness of sins and eternal life, and since he satisfied superabundantly for all, it is consequently perverse to attribute to our works the merit of grace (or of forgiveness of sins) and of eternal life, and to say our works satisfy for our sins. Such teaching is said to insult Christ, since it is blasphemy to attribute to ourselves what is Christ's own work. If there is need of our merits and satisfaction, this detracts from the merit and satisfaction of Christ, implying they are inadequate.

These denials are made on the basis of many texts of Scripture, beginning with those asserting that we do not merit by our works the forgiveness of sins. This is proven by Paul's demonstration in Romans and Galatians that we are justified not by works but by faith. He cited Habakkuk 2[:4], "The man righteous by faith will live" [Rom. 1:17; Gal. 3:11]. Paul wrote to Titus, "Not by works of righteousness that we did, but through his mercy, he saved us" [3:5]. Also, in Ephesians 2[:8f.], "By grace you have been saved through faith, not of your own doing, but by the gift of God, and not because of works, lest one should boast."

The fact that we do not merit eternal life through works, but attain it by the gift of God, is shown in Romans 6[:23], "The wages of sin is death, but the gift of God is eternal life." Luke 17[:10] is cited to prove the same point and at the same time to demonstrate that no matter how righteous we may be, our works do not make satisfaction for sins: "When you have done all that I command you, say, 'We have done what we ought, we are unworthy servants.'" If they are unworthy servants who have kept all the commandments of Christ, then clearly the reward is not merited. Those then who have not kept all the commandments, and so need to make satisfaction, are much more unworthy and incapable of making satisfaction.

I can omit the texts proving the sufficiency of Christ's merit and satisfaction on our behalf. About this there is no controversy.

The Lutherans therefore teach that good works are to be done, because they are commanded by God as the fruit of justifying faith, but not because they are meritorious of eternal life and satisfactory for sins.

6. The Meaning of Merit in This Context

Before determining whether our works are meritorious or not, we must first briefly examine what is meant by merit and how theologians understand it in this context concerning our works.

Merit is said of a voluntary work, whether interior or external, to which by right a payment or reward is due. The apostle says in Romans 4[:4], "To one who works payment is not accounted as a grace, but as his due." Hence four elements go together to constitute merit: the person meriting, the voluntary work of merit, the payment due for the merit, and the person rendering payment. The last is essential, since it would be pointless to merit unless it be from some person rendering one payment.

Since we are discussing our merit before God, we must explain how men can merit from God a reward for their works. It appears problematical that God would by right render payment for our work, since between ourselves and God there is no right, strictly and absolutely speaking. Scripture says, "Enter not in judgment with your servant, Lord" [Ps. 142:2]. There is only a derived kind of right, which is much less than the right of a son toward his father and of a slave toward his master. How much less are we in relation to God than a man who is slave in relation to the man who is his master, and than a son in relation to the earthly father who begot him. So, if as is written in Book V of the *Ethics,* there is no right strictly and absolutely speaking, but only a derivative kind of right between slave and master and between father and son, then much less is there a right between ourselves and God.

All that the slave is belongs to the master. A son cannot render as much to his father as he received. Hence a right, strictly and absolutely considered, cannot exist between master and slave and between father and son. It is true to a much greater extent that all that a man is belongs to God and that man cannot render as much to God as he received. Hence man cannot merit something from God that would be due him by right, unless this be a right so weakened that it be far less than the right between master and slave and father and son. Even such a weakened right is not, absolutely speaking, found between man and God, because absolutely speaking man's every voluntary good action is due to God. In fact, the more and the better a man's interior and outward works, so much more does he owe to God, since it is God who works in us both to will and to complete our every action [Phil. 2:13]. This weakened right is found between man and God by reason of the divine ordination by which God ordained our works to be meritorious before himself.

When man merits anything before God, God never becomes man's debtor, but rather his own. If even this weakened debt were given in an absolute sense between man and God, then God would owe man the payment he earned. But it is obvious that God is in debt to no one, as Paul says in Romans 12 [*sic* = Rom. 11:35], "He who has given the gift, shall he then reward this?" God is there-

fore indebted to himself alone, that he should carry out his own will by which he granted that human works would be meritorious so he would render to man the reward for his work.

This is undoubtedly true about the simple and absolute sense of merit. In other cases, an agreement is presupposed between God and man on some matter, as among men when a master makes a pact of some kind with his slave. In this case a right can arise between master and slave. Thus if God deigns to make a pact with man, a right can arise between man and God with reference to the matter of the agreement. We often read in the Old Testament that God deigned to enter covenants with men. Genesis 9[:9-16] records God's covenant to never again permit a flood over the whole world. Genesis 15 [:18-21] describes God's covenant with Abraham concerning the land of Canaan which was to be given to his offspring. Genesis 17 [:1-11] tells of the covenant of circumcision. In Exodus 24[:8] Moses says, "This is the blood of the covenant. . . ." In Jeremiah 31[:31-34] God speaks explicitly of the covenants of the old and new law. In the New Testament our Savior reveals God under the form of the householder hiring workmen for his vineyard for a day's wages, in Matthew 20[:1-16]. "After making an agreement for a denarius a day, he sent them into his vineyard" [20:2]. Further on [20:13], "Did you not enter into an agreement with me?"

These texts make it clear that there can be in our works an element of merit even by right, with reference to the reward concerning which an agreement has been made with God.

Keep in mind though that to whatever extent there is a pact between God and man concerning a reward, still God never falls into our debt, but is only in debt to himself. For in view of the agreement made, there is due to our works the reward on which was agreed. God does not thereby become indebted to us regarding this reward, but rather indebted to his own prior determination by which he deigned to enter a pact with us. Consequently we profess in full truth that God is indebted to no one but to himself. One can therefore ascertain a double aspect of merit before God in our works. There is first the weakened right, and second the agreement. But never is God indebted to us.— These, then, are the initial considerations for a right understanding of the terms used in treating our merits before God.

7. Human Works Merit Something from God

God has revealed in Holy Scripture that human works have some merit with himself. To avoid becoming occupied in explaining each text of Holy Scripture on this point, we should realize that whenever God promises man a reward, merit is to be understood as entailed, since reward and merit are correlative to each other. Merit is merit of a reward and a reward is reward for merit.

Consequently, whenever you read in Holy Scripture that God promises man a reward, no further explanation is required for you to conclude that man can have merit with respect of the reward God will render. But in both testaments God openly promises men rewards. In Genesis 15 [:1] he said to Abraham, "I shall be your own great reward." Isaiah 40 [:10] says, "Behold, the Lord will come; behold, his reward is with him." In Ezekiel 29 [:18] God says, "Son of man, Nebuchadnezzar, king of Babylon, made his army labor greatly against Tyre . . . but no payment was given him." Then he

added, "The land of Egypt shall be his army's payment" [29:20]. In Matthew 20[:8] God says, "Call the workmen and pay them their wages." Also, in Revelation 22[:12], "Behold, I am coming soon, bringing my reward, to render to each one according to his works."

In these texts there is clear evidence that not only the works of the saints are meritorious of some benefit from God, but also the works of evil men and even of pagans such as the king of Babylon and his army. The latter besieged Tyre without any intention of serving God, but nonetheless God bore witness that they have merited a reward as he decreed that Egypt shall be given them as this reward. Hence we are to understand that the divine goodness is so generous as even to bring the wars of mankind into his service and to rejoice in admitting even evil actions as meritorious of some benefit from himself. From this we have impressive evidence that God is by far more willing to admit the good deeds of men as meritorious of some reward from himself.

8. Eternal Life Merited by Living Members of Christ

Many agree that human works are meritorious of some benefit from God, but not of eternal life. Therefore we must show specifically that the works of the living members of Christ are meritorious of eternal life. Our Savior said in Matthew 5[:12], "Rejoice and be glad for your reward is great in heaven." Thus the heavenly reward of those who suffer for Christ's sake entails first of all beatitude, or eternal life. When Matthew 20[:9f.] describes the payment given the workmen, saying they received a denarius, it is obvious that the payment given to all the workers in the Lord's vineyard is eternal life.

Paul wrote in Timothy 4[:7f.], "I have fought the good fight, completed the course, and have kept faith. For the rest, there is laid up for me a crown of righteousness which the Lord, the just judge, will grant me." Clearly the crown given Paul is first of all beatitude. Also, unless the reward was due by reason of his previous works, it would not be true that God is giving him the crown precisely as the just judge. Paul obviously teaches that eternal life is due to him by right because of the works he referred to. Our Lord made the same thing clear in describing how in judging the world he will give eternal life in return for the works of mercy. "I was hungry and you fed me . . ." [Matt. 25:35]. This scene ends: "These go away for eternal punishment, but the righteous enter eternal life" [25:46]. The judge determines this by reason of the diversity of works, as the works merit; otherwise, he would not have given the reasons on each side.

According to Holy Scripture, therefore, the works of some men are clearly meritorious of eternal life. What is more, according to Matthew 20, the workmen merit this by reason of an agreement. Origen, Jerome, Augustine, Gregory, and Chrysostom all explain the denarius given to each as the beatitude in which the blessed share.

9. How Our Works Merit Eternal Life

Theologians say that our works are meritorious of eternal life, because they arise from charity, from sanctifying grace, and from the Holy Spirit dwelling within us. Human works, as proceeding from our free choice, are not meritorious of eternal life, except by a certain kind of fittingness, by which it would be proper for God to reward out of the abundance of his grace a man who uses his free choice rightly in the things pertaining to God. However, insofar as these works stem from the Spirit dwelling in a person through grace and charity, they are meritorious of eternal life.

Grace, or charity, is comparable to the seed of God mentioned in 1 John 3[:9], whose power extends to producing fruit, so that just as the fruit is due by natural right to the action of the seed, so the fruit of eternal life is due to the actions of divine grace in the soul. Also, divine grace, as our Lord said in John 4[:14], becomes in the man having it a spring of water welling up unto eternal life. This clearly indicates the efficacy of grace in us to attain to eternal life. By saying that the grace given wells up unto eternal life, he teaches that the attaining takes place by an intervening activity, since what occurs in me after accepting grace occurs with my cooperation. Especially, the power of the Holy Spirit dwelling in a person is adequate for attaining eternal life and for bringing it about that eternal life is due to his works in us.

A more manifest and convincing reason for merit of this kind can be seen in the fact that meriting eternal life is less our own action than the action of Christ who is Head in us and through us. When we begin with the apostle's teaching, in Romans 12[:4f.], Ephesians 4[:15f.], and Colossians 2[:19], then persons in grace are living members of Christ the Head. Christ the Head and the persons who are his living members do not make up a body of a political type, like the body of citizens in a well-governed state. Rather they constitute a body like a single natural body, since Christ the Head gives life to his members by his own Spirit. As is clear in Paul's texts, he unites the members of the body by spiritual bonds and ligaments. Going on from this, we find that Holy Scripture also teaches that the sufferings and deeds of Christ's living members are the sufferings and deeds of Christ the Head. Christ himself gives evidence concerning the sufferings in Acts 9[:4], "Saul, Saul, why are you persecuting me?" But Saul was persecuting his members. In Galatians 4[=3:1, Vg.] Paul reminds the Galatians that Christ had been crucified in them, no doubt referring to the sufferings they had undergone for Christ. Concerning actions, Paul said in 2 Corinthians 13[:3], "Do you desire proof of him who speaks in me, that is, Christ?" He said in an all-embracing manner in Galatians 2[:20], "I live, now not I, but Christ lives in me." Hence I can most truly say, "I merit, now not I, but Christ merits in me; I fast, now not I, but Christ fasts in me," and so on, about the other voluntary actions carried out for God by Christ's living members. In this way the merit of eternal life is not so much attributed to our works as to the works of Christ the Head in us and through us.

Consequently we discern a difference between the merit of eternal life by baptized infants and by adults advancing in God's grace. Eternal life is due the infants solely by the merit Christ gained as he lived, suffered, and died in this mortal life. But to adults progressing in grace eternal life is due in a twofold manner, first by right of the merit Christ gained in his own person and then by right of the merit of Christ working meritoriously as the head in and through this adult person. It is appropriate to the divine munificence to grant the merit of eternal life in both manners to adults who are God's sons and daughters. As we read in Romans 8 [:29], "He predestined them to be conformed to the image of his son." Those however are more conformed to Christ who have merit of eternal life in both manners rather than only

in the first. Christ's own glory was due him by a twofold right. First it was his by right of the grace of personal union by which the Word was made flesh, a right devolving on Christ without his meriting. Second, the same glory was due Christ by the merit of his obedience unto death, as Paul says in Philippians 2[:8f.], "He became obedient unto death, death on the cross. Therefore God has exalted him. . . ." Hence Christ has glory by a twofold right, and we are made conformed to him by attaining eternal life by a twofold right, namely without our own meriting but through the merit of Christ in his own person, and with our meriting through the merit of Christ the Head in and through us.

As it pertained to Christ's excellence also to gain eternal life for his body, glory for his name, and the like, by his own merit, so it belongs to the dignity of a member of Christ to cooperate with his Head in attaining eternal life. "The most divine thing of all is to become a cooperator with God," says Dionysius in the *Heavenly Hierarchies*, chapter 3. Thus, you see it is not superfluous for us to merit eternal life, for this is to make eternal life our due in another manner or by an additional right, just as Christ merited his exaltation, making it due to himself by an additional right.—We will respond below to the objections urged against this.

10. Works Performed in Mortal Sin

We agree that the works performed by persons in mortal sin are neither meritorious of eternal life nor of the forgiveness of sins. Nonetheless they are of considerable importance for a man caught in mortal sin, since Holy Scripture says they lead to attaining forgiveness of sins. Although these works have no power to merit forgiveness of sins, they do have power to impetrate this forgiveness, since in the manner of a supplication they are of great value in attaining from the divine goodness the forgiveness of sins. Our Savior bears witness that prayer is of considerable importance toward gaining forgiveness of sins, when in Luke 18[:13] he described the publican as praying, "God, be merciful to me a sinner." Thereby he obtained mercy. Joel witnesses to the value of fasting when he speaks in God's stead, "Turn to me with all your heart, in fasting, weeping and lament" [2:12]. The remark follows [2:14], "Who knows whether God will turn and forgive?" The value of alms is shown by Daniel in chapter 4 [:24], where he counsels King Nebuchadnezzar, "Redeem your sins by alms." Hebrews 13[:16] says, "Forget not giving aid and sharing what you have; by such offerings God is appeased." The same can be affirmed concerning pilgrimages, hardships, continence and other acts of this kind.

Over and above this power of supplication, Holy Scripture points to a greater power of impetration in the observance of all the commandments of God. Ezekiel 18 teaches us that the conversion of the sinner to keeping the commandments of the law leads eventually to the forgiveness of sins. The text reads:

> You say, "the way of the Lord is not just." But hear now, house of Israel. Is my way not just? Is it not your ways that are not just? When a righteous person turns from his righteousness and commits sin, he shall die in the sin he committed. When an evil person turns away from the sin he committed and lives righteously, he will gain life for his soul. Because he took thought and turned away from all the sins he committed, he shall live and not die. [Ezek. 18:25-28]

This text indicates that the justice of God's ways consists in this, that just as the turning of a righteous person from righteousness to sinful deeds leads to the death of the soul, so the conversion of a sinner to good deeds leads to life for his soul. It was revealed to the prophet that the conversion of a sinner with regard to works (that is, from evil works to good works for God's sake) is so pleasing to God that he no longer considers all his previous sins. This is the same as granting forgiveness of sins and the life of grace.

God revealed a yet greater power of impetration in works of this kind by men caught in sin in a passage of Isaiah: "Wash yourselves, make yourselves clean, remove the evil of your thoughts from my sight, cease to act wickedly; learn to do good and seek what is right, aiding the oppressed, defending the orphan, and taking the part of the widow, and we can reason together, says the Lord. If your sins are like scarlet, they will become white like snow; if red like crimson, they will become like white wool" [Isa. 1:16-18].

From this we learn that God's largess is so great that to those converted from wickedness to works of righteousness and mercy God presents himself as arguing their case if he has not forgiven their past sins.

We have therefore gained this from divine revelation: the good works of sinners are not only of importance toward the forgiveness of sins, but when they stem from the heart of one turning to God, God's generous love so accompanies them that they do lead to forgiveness of sins and impetrate this as if an agreement had been made. God is truly generous toward us, arranging that in spite of our inability in the state of sin to merit the forgiveness of sins, we are capable of impetrating this by prayer, fasting, alms, and other good works.

God's immense love for sinners and desire of their salvation is shown in his deigning to grant the power of impetrating forgiveness of sins to our good works even done in sin. In addition, as we showed in chapter 7 from the text of Ezekiel, these works are meritorious of certain temporal benefits from God. Consequently sinners should be urged to perform good works, since they are in fact of value in impetrating and attaining the forgiveness of sins, when done devoutly.

11. Works Satisfying for Sin

Since the Lutherans deny any element of satisfaction in our works, we must indicate the mind of the church on this topic. One must first distinguish according to the state in which the works are performed, whether in mortal sin or in the state of grace. Also one must distinguish concerning satisfaction for sins between guilt and punishment.

We say first that none of our works satisfies for the guilt of our sins, since no deed done in the state of mortal sin satisfies God for our offenses, as is clear. Our deeds in the state of grace presuppose the removal of the guilt or the offense by divine grace through the satisfaction Christ made to God for our offenses against God, when he offered up his life to God on the altar of the cross.

We say secondly that none of our works done in mortal sin satisfy God for the punishment due for our sins, even if these were forgiven previously in the sacrament of penance. The reason for this is quite clear, since when God forgives the offense of sin, the sinner is changed from being an enemy to being a friend of God. Consequently he is no longer subject to punishment in a hostile manner as in the punishment of hell. But if with forgiveness of guilt the gift of grace is not given so abundantly that all punishment is remitted, one remains bound to fulfilling the rest of the punishment in a

loving manner. If one in this latter condition falls back into sin and again becomes an enemy of God before he has completed the rest of the punishment, his works are then done in a state of hostility, not a state of friendship, and so they cannot satisfy for the previous punishment.

We say thirdly that the works of one continuing to love God are in no way prevented from being satisfactory for the punishment that may remain. On this point the Lutherans err in a twofold way. They first teach that when the guilt of sin is forgiven all punishment is remitted as well. One who has attained mercy from God upon his sin is no longer bound to any punishment. This is patently contrary to Holy Scripture, which teaches in 2 Samuel 12 that even though David gained the forgiveness of sins when he said, "I have sinned against the Lord" [12:13], still he did not attain remission of all punishment but remained bound to many punishments, as Scripture bears witness. The second Lutheran error is denying the satisfactory power of the works of Christ's living members regarding punishments not yet remitted. This is contrary to the effectiveness in us of Christ the Head, since "I satisfy, now not I, but Christ satisfies in me." It is also against the practice of the Catholic Church by which salutary acts of satisfaction are customarily imposed through the ministry of priests upon those who truly repent and confess.

12. Response to Objections

It remains for us to answer the objections. The first arose from the sufficiency of the merit and satisfaction of Christ. We answer that the merit of Christ was completely and utterly sufficient, and that this satisfaction was more than adequate for our sins and for the sins of the whole world, including original sin, mortal sins, and venial sins, as 1 John 2 [:2] teaches. Therefore it is not because of an inadequacy in the merit and satisfaction of Christ that we attribute merit and satisfaction to the works of Christ's living members, but rather because of the excessive riches of Christ's merit which he shares with his living members so that their works as well may be meritorious and satisfactory. A greater grace is conferred on us by Christ, when he our head merits and satisfies in and through us his members than if we were only to share in the merit Christ gained in his own person.

To the objection that what is proper to Christ must not be attributed to us, we answer that it should not be attributed to us in the manner in which it is proper to Christ. It can be attributed to us in another manner, namely by participation. Something proper to God can be attributed to no one in that manner proper to God, but it can be shared by others by participation. For instance, the vision of the divine essence is proper to God, and no creature can see God as he is, since he alone by his own nature sees himself. But God can by grace grant a share in the vision of God, and this he does to all the blessed. In the present case merit of eternal life is proper to Christ, when this is understood as merit by one's own power. But this can be granted to his living members, not that they merit by their own power, but that they merit by the power of Christ the Head. The same thing can be understood concerning satisfaction.

There is no need to respond concerning the forgiveness of sins, since we already said that this is not granted to Christ's living members, because their good works presuppose that their sins have been forgiven. No one merits that which he already has. Merit is gained concerning something not had. For this reason Christ apportions to his members the merit of an increase in grace and of heavenly beatitude. He does not apportion to them merit of forgiveness of sins. Eternal beatitude is something lacking to Christ's members in this life, while they do have forgiveness of sins by the very fact of becoming members of Christ. No one merits what he has but what he hopes to attain. This makes it clear that our merits and satisfactions in no way detract from the merit and satisfaction of Christ, but rather that the grace of merit and satisfaction Christ gained in his own person is extended to himself as Head working in and through his members.

All the texts cited as showing that we do not by our works merit the forgiveness of sins require no answer, since we agree with this conclusion. But we must respond to the texts cited to prove that we do not merit eternal life by our works. To the text of the apostle from Romans, "The gift of God is eternal life" [6:23], we answer that we indeed say and teach this, since it is by God's gift of sanctifying grace that we are members of Christ, and by the power in us of Christ the Head that we merit eternal life. We do not say that we merit eternal life through our works specifically as ours, but in so far as they are in us and through us from Christ.

We propose the same distinction in answer to the objection raised from Christ's words, "Say, 'we are unworthy servants'" [Luke 17:10]. However much we might fulfill all the commandments of Christ, to the extent we fulfill them by our own free choice, we are unworthy servants regarding our Father's heavenly household. We are unworthy of our homeland in heaven and whatever concerns it, such as the forgiveness of sins, the grace of the Holy Spirit, charity, and other things proper to God's children. The reason is obvious, since when we act on our own we are too weak to reach the higher order in which are conferred the proper goods of God's children. This goes together with the other truth, namely, that insofar as our deeds proceed from the influence in us of Christ the Head in his living members, we can contribute much through our works to gaining the heavenly homeland and our Father's household. As his members, we are raised to the order of God's children, not to be unworthy servants, but worthy members of our Father's household and the heavenly homeland.

An argument can be made from these words of Christ against the capability of good works done in the state of mortal sin to impetrate the forgiveness of sins. . . . If the argument is made that our good works have no usefulness in impetrating the forgiveness of sins, we answer that insofar as prayer, fasting, alms, and other good works arise from them as sinners they are not capable of impetrating forgiveness of sins. But insofar as the divine goodness orders them to impetrating forgiveness of sins, they are highly effective for impetrating this. Consequently, in Ezekiel these works are called "the ways of God" and not "our ways" [18:29]. The divine goodness has arranged that we impetrate many things we never merit. As Christ, Isaiah, Ezekiel, and the apostle (in Hebrews) bear witness, the divine goodness has conferred on the good works of persons returning to God the power of impetrating the forgiveness of sins from the divine mercy through the merit of Christ. Because of this, the fasting, prayers, alms, and other righteous works of sinners are beneficial, not for meriting, nor for satisfying, but for impetrating forgiveness of their sins.

This, I believe will suffice to explain these questions about faith and works. May it bring glory to almighty God and consolation to the devout.

Rome, May 13, 1532.

✝

From J. Wicks, ed. and trans., Cajetan Responds: A Reader in Reformation Controversy *(Washington, D.C.: Catholic University of America Press, 1978), 219–39.*

79. Contarini and Carafa, *Consilium de emendanda ecclesiae* (1537)

In 1536 Pope Paul III (1534–1549) called for a general council and appointed a commission to prepare a report on the state of the church. Two cardinals, Contarini and Carafa (who was later to become the fanatical Pope Paul IV), drafted the "Consilium" in 1537. Its frank admission of appalling abuses again illustrates the strength of reform impulses within the church.

✝

The spirit of God decrees that Christ's church, almost collapsed, should be restored to its early glory. . . . Your Holiness knows that these evils arose from the willfulness of several previous popes . . . [and their belief] that the pope, being lord of all benefices, can sell his own and cannot therefore be guilty of simony. . . . From this, as the Trojan horse, burst forth into God's church so many grave ills . . . [which] obeying your command we have examined and here make known to you. . . .

Concerning ordination: no care is taken. Whoever they are (uneducated, of appalling morals, under age), they are routinely admitted to the holy order from which came so many scandals and a contempt for the church. Reverence for divine service is so much diminished as now to be virtually extinct. . . . Your Holiness should order every bishop to take the greatest care in this and, observing the laws, appoint a professor to instruct their clergy in letters and in morals. . . . [Eleven paragraphs detail abuses relating to benefices.]

Another common abuse is the conferring of bishoprics on the most reverend cardinals. These offices are incompatible. Cardinals should assist your Holiness in Rome whereas bishops must care for their flocks and so be resident with them as the shepherd. This sets a particularly harmful example for how can the holy see correct the abuses of others if abuse is tolerated in its own senior ranks? And as they are cardinals they have not greater freedom to break the law but far less. Their life should be as a law to all others . . . yet what can they encourage in others but greed? . . . Heavy penalties should be imposed, especially withholding of income. . . .

Concerning the government of the Christian faithful, the most fundamental abuse in need of reformation is that bishops and priests must not be absent from their churches, but must be resident for they are entrusted with their care. What sight can be more piteous than deserted churches? Almost all the shepherds have deserted their flocks or abandoned them to hirelings. A heavy penalty must be imposed, not only censures but the withholding of income . . . [on all] absent for more than three Sundays per year. . . .

An intolerable abuse lies in the impediments put in the way of bishops ruling their flocks. Many evildoers are exempt from their jurisdiction. . . . Among these, none are more blatant than the monastic orders, who are become so deformed that they do grave harm by example. All conventuals should be done away with, by the prohibition of admitting novices. . . . [Ten paragraphs detail the evils of dispensations and indulgences.]

Concerning Rome: honest manners should flourish in this city and church, mother and teacher of other churches . . . [yet] whores perambulate like matrons or ride on muleback, with whom noblemen, cardinals and priests consort in broad daylight. . . .

From Jones, Counter Reformation, *45–46*.

80. Paul III, *Licet ab initio* (1542)

Along with the *Index of Prohibited Books* (the longevity of which extended from 1559 to 1966), the establishment of the Roman Inquisition was the most direct and repressive measure taken by the Roman Catholic Church to check the growth of Protestantism. With roots reaching back to the thirteenth century, this institution was reconstituted by Pope Paul III in this bull of 1542, at the urging of the zealous Carafa.

From the beginning of our assumption of the apostolic office we have been concerned for the flourishing of the Catholic faith and the purging of heresy. Those seduced by diabolical wiles should then return to the fold and unity of the church. Those who persist in their damnable course should be removed and their punishment serve as an example to others. Nevertheless we hope that the mercy of God, the prayers of the faithful and the preaching of the learned would cause them to recognize their errors and come back to the holy Catholic Church. If any delayed they should be induced by the authority of the sacred, ecumenical and general council, which we hope speedily to convene; therefore we deferred the establishment of the Inquisition of Heretical Pravity. But now, for a variety of reasons, the council has not met and the enemy of the human race has disseminated even more heresy among the faithful and the robe of Christ is torn. . . :

Lest things grow worse while waiting for a council, we have appointed our beloved son, Giovanni Pietro Carafa, Inquisitor General with jurisdiction throughout Christendom including Italy and the Roman Curia. . . . [He and his subordinates] are to investigate by way of inquisition all and single who wander from the way of the Lord and the Catholic faith, as well as those suspected of heresy, together with their followers and abettors, public or private, direct or indirect. The guilty and the suspects are to be imprisoned and proceeded against up to the final sentence. Those judged guilty are to be punished in accord with canonical penalties. After the infliction of death their property may be sold. The aid of the civil arm may be invoked to implement whatever measures are deemed necessary. Anyone who dares to impede this will incur the anger of almighty God and of the blessed apostles, Peter and Paul.

✠

From R. E. Van Voorst, ed., Readings in Christianity *(New York: Wadsworth Publishing Co., 1997), 183–84.*

The Council of Trent (1545–1563)

Though the Council was originally summoned by Paul III in 1537, it did not actually convene until 1545. The delay was due to political factors, but also to the pope's hesitations over the possibility of a resurgence of conciliarism and the Curia's fear that its prerogatives and privileges might be limited by reform. When it finally began, the Council's charge was "the uprooting of heresy, the restoring of peace and unity, and the reformation of ecclesiastical discipline and morals."

With regard to the first, heresy, the Council in its decrees and canons responded to most of the Protestant "innovations," clarifying official church teaching, closing theological questions which were hitherto open, and reining in the exuberant theological pluralism of the late medieval period. As for the second goal, the restoration of unity, it was much too late for this: the confessional lines had hardened and an entire generation of Christians had grown accustomed to living in a religiously fragmented world. Finally, the Council of Trent's reform of church discipline, though implemented slowly, eventually had a profound impact in shaping church life throughout the period which came to be called "Tridentine Catholicism."

Interrupted by politics and war, the Council met in three periods. The first, presided over by Paul III with only twenty-nine bishops present, lasted from 1545 to 1547, and took up the controverted issues of Scripture, original sin, and justification. The second period, 1551–1552, was under the leadership of Pope Julius III. A few Protestant representatives who had been invited now showed up. But since their demand to revisit the topics of the first period was denied, they soon left in disillusionment. Now the sacraments of the Eucharist, penance, and extreme unction dominated the agenda.

The final period of the council, 1561–1563, was led by Pope Pius IV and attended by over two hundred bishops. Decrees and canons were now formulated on such matters as the sacrificial nature of the Eucharist, orders, matrimony, purgatory, indulgences, and the saints. Moreover, the most important disciplinary reform decrees were agreed on in this period. Pius IV then quickly approved and officially promulgated the Council's decisions. A few of the more important texts follow.

81. Decree and Canons on Justification (1547)

Introduction

Since there is being disseminated at this time, not without the loss of many souls and grievous detriment to the unity of the church, a certain erroneous doctrine concerning justification, the holy, ecumenical and general Council of Trent, lawfully assembled in the Holy Spirit, the most reverend John Maria, bishop of Praeneste de Monte, and Marcellus, priest of the Holy Cross in Jerusalem, cardinals of the holy Roman Church and legates Apostolic *a latere,* presiding in the name of our most holy Father and Lord in Christ, Paul III, by the providence of God, pope, intends, for the praise and glory of almighty God, for the tranquillity of the church and the salvation of souls, to expound to all the faithful of Christ the true and salutary doctrine of justification, which the Sun of justice, Jesus Christ, "the author and finisher of our faith taught" [Heb. 12:2], which the apostles transmitted and which the Catholic Church under the inspiration of the Holy Spirit has always retained; strictly forbidding that anyone henceforth presume to believe, preach or teach otherwise than is defined and declared in the present decree.

The Impotency of Nature and the Law to Justify Man

The holy council declares first, that for a correct and clear understanding of the doctrine of justification, it is necessary that each one

recognize and confess that since all men had lost innocence in the prevarication of Adam, having become unclean, and, as the apostle says, "by nature children of wrath" [Eph. 2:3], as has been set forth in the decree on original sin, they were so far the servants of sin and under the power of the devil and of death, that not only the Gentiles by the force of nature, but not even the Jews by the very letter of the law of Moses, were able to be liberated or to rise therefrom, though free will, weakened as it was in its powers and downward bent, was by no means extinguished in them.

The Dispensation and Mystery of the Advent of Christ

Whence it came to pass that the heavenly Father, "the Father of mercies and the God of all comfort, when the blessed fullness of the time was come" [Gal. 4:4], sent to men Jesus Christ, his own Son, who had both before the law and during the time of the law been announced and promised to many of the holy fathers, "that he might redeem the Jews who were under the law" [Gal. 4:5], and "that the Gentiles who followed not after justice" [Rom. 9:30] might attain to justice, and that all men might receive the adoption of sons. Him has God proposed as a propitiator "through faith in his blood for our sins, and not for our sins only, but also for those of the whole world" [Rom. 3:25; 1 John 2:2].

Who Are Justified Through Christ

But though He died for all, yet all do not receive the benefit of His death, but those only to whom the merit of His passion is communicated; because as truly as men would not be born unjust, if they were not born through propagation of the seed of

Adam, since by that propagation they contract through him, when they are conceived, injustice as their own, so if they were not born again in Christ, they would never be justified, since in that new birth there is bestowed upon them, through the merit of his passion, the grace by which they are made just. For this benefit the apostle exhorts us always "to give thanks to the Father, who hath made us worthy to be partakers of the lot of the saints in light, and hath delivered us from the power of darkness, and hath translated us into the kingdom of the Son of his love, in whom we have redemption and remissions of sins" [Col. 1:12-14].

A Brief Description of the Justification of the Sinner and Its Mode in the State of Grace

In which words is given a brief description of the justification of the sinner, as being a translation from that state in which man is born a child of the first Adam, to the state of grace and of the adoption of the sons of God through the second Adam, Jesus Christ, our Savior. This translation however cannot, since the promulgation of the gospel, be effected except through the laver of regeneration or its desire, as it is written: "Unless a man be born again of water and the Holy Spirit, he cannot enter into the kingdom of God" [John 3:5].

The Necessity of Preparation for Justification in Adults, and Whence It Proceeds

It is furthermore declared that in adults the beginning of that justification must proceed from the predisposing grace of God through Jesus Christ, that is, from his vocation, whereby, without any merits on their part, they are called; that they who by sin had been cut off from God, may be disposed through his quickening and helping grace to convert themselves to their own justification by freely assenting to and cooperating with that grace; so that, while God touches the heart of man through the illumination of the Holy Spirit, man himself neither does absolutely nothing while receiving that inspiration, since he can also reject it, nor yet is he able by his own free will and without the grace of God to move himself to justice in his sight. Hence, when it is said in the sacred writings: "Turn ye to me, and I will turn to you" [Zech. 1:3], we are reminded of our liberty; and when we reply: "Convert us, O Lord, to thee, and we shall be converted" [Lam. 5:21], we confess that we need the grace of God.

The Manner of Preparation

Now, they [the adults] are disposed to that justice when, aroused and aided by divine grace, receiving faith by hearing, they are moved freely toward God, believing to be true what has been divinely revealed and promised, especially that the sinner is justified by God "by his grace, through the redemption that is in Christ Jesus" [Rom. 3:24]; and when, understanding themselves to be sinners, they, by turning themselves from the fear of divine justice, by which they are salutarily aroused, to consider the mercy of God, are raised to hope, trusting that God will be propitious to them for Christ's sake; and they begin to love him as the fountain of all justice, and on that account are moved against sin by a certain hatred and detestation, that is, by that repentance that must be performed before baptism; finally, when they resolve to receive baptism, to begin a new life and to keep the commandments of God. Because of this disposition it is written: "He that cometh to God, must believe that he is, and is a rewarder to them that seek him"

[Heb. 11:6]; and, "Be of good faith, son, thy sins are forgiven thee" [Matt. 9:2]; and, "The fear of the Lord driveth out sin" [Ecclus. 1:27]; and, "Do penance, and be baptized every one of you in the name of Jesus Christ, for the remission of your sins, and you shall receive the gift of the Holy Spirit" [Acts 2:38]; and, "Going, therefore, teach ye all nations, baptizing them in the name of the Father, and of the Son, and of the Holy Spirit, teaching them to observe all things whatsoever I have commanded you" [Matt. 28:19f.]; finally, "Prepare your hearts unto the Lord" [1 Kings 7:3].

In What the Justification of the Sinner Consists, and What Are Its Causes

This disposition or preparation is followed by justification itself, which is not only a remission of sins but also the sanctification and renewal of the inward man through the voluntary reception of the grace and gifts whereby an unjust man becomes just and from being an enemy becomes a friend, that he may be "an heir according to hope of life everlasting" [Titus 3:7]. The causes of this justification are: the final cause is the glory of God and of Christ and life everlasting; the efficient cause is the merciful God who washes and sanctifies gratuitously, signing and anointing "with the Holy Spirit of promise, who is the pledge of our inheritance" [Eph. 1:13f.], the meritorious cause is his most beloved only-begotten, our Lord Jesus Christ, who, when we were enemies, "for the exceeding charity wherewith he loved us" [Eph. 2:4], merited for us justification by his most holy passion on the wood of the cross and made satisfaction for us to God the Father, the instrumental cause is the sacrament of baptism, which is the sacrament of faith, without which no man was ever justified. Finally,

the single formal cause is the justice of God, not that by which he himself is just, but that by which he makes us just, that, namely, with which we being endowed by him, are "renewed in the spirit of our mind" [Eph. 4:23], and not only are we reputed but we are truly called and are just, receiving justice within us, each one according to his own measure, which the Holy Spirit distributes to everyone as he wills, and according to each one's disposition and cooperation. For though no one can be just except he to whom the merits of the passion of our Lord Jesus Christ are communicated, yet this takes place in that justification of the sinner, when by the merit of the most holy passion, "the charity of God is poured forth by the Holy Spirit in the hearts" [Rom. 5:5] of those who are justified and inheres in them; whence man through Jesus Christ, in whom he is ingrafted, receives in that justification, together with the remission of sins, all these infused at the same time, namely, faith, hope and charity. For faith, unless hope and charity be added to it, neither unites man perfectly with Christ nor makes him a living member of his body. For which reason it is most truly said that "faith without works is dead" [James 2:17, 20] and of no profit, and "in Christ Jesus neither circumcision availeth anything nor uncircumcision, but faith that worketh by charity" [Gal. 5:6; 6:15]. This faith, conformably to apostolic tradition, catechumens ask of the church before the sacrament of baptism, when they ask for the faith that gives eternal life, which without hope and charity faith cannot give. Whence also they hear immediately the word of Christ: "If thou wilt enter into life, keep the commandments" [Matt. 19:17]. Wherefore, when receiving true and Christian justice, they are commanded, immediately on being born again, to preserve it pure and spotless, as the first robe given them through Christ Jesus in place of that which Adam by his disobedience lost for himself and for us, so that they may bear it before the tribunal of our Lord Jesus Christ and may have life eternal.

How the Gratuitous Justification of the Sinner by Faith Is to Be Understood

But when the apostle says that man is justified by faith and freely, these words are to be understood in that sense in which the uninterrupted unanimity of the Catholic Church has held and expressed them, namely, that we are therefore said to be justified by faith, because faith is the beginning of human salvation, the foundation and root of all justification, "without which it is impossible to please God" [Heb. 11:6] and to come to the fellowship of his sons; and we are therefore said to be justified gratuitously, because none of those things that precede justification, whether faith or works, merit the grace of justification. For, "if by grace, it is not now by works, otherwise, as the apostle says, grace is no more grace" [Rom. 11:6].

Against the Vain Confidence of Heretics

But though it is necessary to believe that sins neither are remitted nor ever have been remitted except gratuitously by divine mercy for Christ's sake, yet it must not be said that sins are forgiven or have been forgiven to anyone who boasts of his confidence and certainty of the remission of his sins, resting on that alone, though among heretics and schismatics this vain and ungodly confidence may be and in our troubled times indeed is found and preached with untiring fury against the Catholic Church. Moreover, it must not be maintained, that they who are truly justified must needs, without any doubt whatever, convince themselves that

they are justified, and that no one is absolved from sins and justified except he that believes with certainty that he is absolved and justified, and that absolution and justification are effected by this faith alone, as if he who does not believe this, doubts the promises of God and the efficacy of the death and resurrection of Christ. For as no pious person ought to doubt the mercy of God, the merit of Christ and the virtue and efficacy of the sacraments, so each one, when he considers himself and his own weakness and indisposition, may have fear and apprehension concerning his own grace, since no one can know with the certainty of faith, which cannot be subject to error, that he has obtained the grace of God.

The Increase of the Justification Received

Having, therefore, been thus justified and made the friends and domestics of God, advancing from virtue to virtue, they are "renewed," as the apostle says, "day by day" [2 Cor. 4:16], that is, "mortifying the members" [Col. 3:5] of their flesh, and presenting them as instruments of justice unto sanctification, they, through the observance of the commandments of God and of the church, faith cooperating with good works, increase in that justice received through the grace of Christ and are further justified, as it is written: "He that is just, let him be justified still" [Rev. 22:11]; and, "Be not afraid to be justified even to death" [Ecclus. 18:22]; and again, "Do you see that by works a man is justified, and not by faith only?" [James 2:24]. This increase of justice holy church asks for when she prays: "Give unto us, O Lord, an increase of faith, hope and charity."

The Observance of the Commandments and the Necessity and Possibility Thereof

But no one, however much justified, should consider himself exempt from the observance of the commandments; no one should use that rash statement, once forbidden by the Fathers under anathema, that the observance of the commandments of God is impossible for one that is justified. For God does not command impossibilities, but by commanding admonishes thee to do what thou canst and to pray for what thou canst not, and aids thee that thou mayest be able. "His commandments are not heavy" [1 John 5:3], and "his yoke is sweet and burden light" [Matt. 11:30]. For they who are the sons of God love Christ, but they who love him, keep his commandments, as he himself testifies; which, indeed, with the divine help they can do. For though during this mortal life, men, however holy and just, fall at times into at least light and daily sins, which are also called venial, they do not on that account cease to be just, for that petition of the just, "forgive our trespasses" [Matt. 6:12], is both humble and true; for which reason the just ought to feel themselves the more obliged to walk in the way of justice, for "being now freed from sin and made servants of God" [Rom. 6:18, 22], they are able, "living soberly, justly and godly" [Titus 2:12], to proceed onward through Jesus Christ, by whom they have access unto this grace. For God does not forsake those who have been once justified by his grace, unless he be first forsaken by them. Wherefore, no one ought to flatter himself with faith alone, thinking that by faith alone he is made an heir and will obtain the inheritance, even though "he suffer" not "with Christ, that he may be also glorified with him" [Rom. 8:17]. For even Christ Himself, as the apostle says, "whereas he was the Son of God, he learned obedience by the things which he suffered, and being consummated, he became to all who obey him the cause of eternal salvation" [Heb. 5:8f.]. For which reason the same apostle admonished those

justified, saying: "Know you not that they who run in the race, all run indeed, but one receiveth the prize? So run that you may obtain. I therefore so run, not as at an uncertainty; I so fight, not as one beating the air, but I chastise my body and bring it into subjection; lest perhaps when I have preached to others, I myself should become a castaway" [1 Cor. 9:24, 26f.].

So also the prince of the apostles, Peter: "Labor the more, that by good works you may make sure your calling and election. For doing these things, you shall not sin at any time" [2 Pet. 1:10]. From which it is clear that they are opposed to the orthodox teaching of religion who maintain that the just man sins, venially at least, in every good work; or, what is more intolerable, that he merits eternal punishment; and they also who assert that the just sin in all works, if, in order to arouse their sloth and to encourage themselves to run the race, they, in addition to this, that above all God may be glorified, have in view also the eternal reward, since it is written: "I have inclined my heart to do thy justifications on account of the reward" [Ps. 118:112]; and of Moses the apostle says that "he looked unto the reward" [Heb. 11:26].

Rash Presumption of Predestination Is to Be Avoided

No one, moreover, so long as he lives this mortal life, ought in regard to the sacred mystery of divine predestination, so far presume as to state with absolute certainty that he is among the number of the predestined, as if it were true that the one justified either cannot sin any more, or, if he does sin, that he ought to promise himself an assured repentance. For except by special revelation, it cannot be known whom God has chosen to himself.

The Gift of Perseverance

Similarly with regard to the gift of perseverance, of which it is written, "He that shall persevere to the end, he shall be saved" [Matt. 10:22; 24:13], which cannot be obtained from anyone except from him who is able to make him stand who stands, that he may stand perseveringly, and to raise him who falls, let no one promise himself herein something as certain with an absolute certainty, though all ought to place and repose the firmest hope in God's help. For God, unless men themselves fail in his grace, "as he has begun a good work, so will he perfect it, working to will and to accomplish" [Phil. 1:6; 2:13]. Nevertheless, let those who think themselves to stand, take heed lest they fall, and with fear and trembling work out their salvation, in labors, in watchings, in almsdeeds, in prayer, in fastings and chastity. For knowing that they are born again unto the hope of glory, and not as yet unto glory, they ought to fear for the combat that yet remains with the flesh, with the world and with the devil, in which they cannot be victorious unless they be with the grace of God obedient to the apostle who says: "We are debtors, not to the flesh, to live according to the flesh; for if you live according to the flesh, you shall die, but if by the spirit you mortify the deeds of the flesh, you shall live" [Rom. 8:12f.].

The Fallen and Their Restoration

Those who through sin have forfeited the received grace of justification, can again be justified when, moved by God, they exert themselves to obtain through the sacrament of penance the recovery, by the merits of Christ, of the grace lost. For this manner of justification is restoration for those fallen, which the holy Fathers have aptly called a second plank after the shipwreck of grace lost. For on behalf of those who fall into sins after baptism, Christ Jesus instituted the sacrament of penance when He said: "Receive ye the Holy Spirit, whose sins you shall forgive, they are forgiven them, and whose sins you shall retain, they are retained" [John 20:22f.]. Hence, it must be taught that the repentance of a Christian after his fall is very different from that at his baptism, and that it includes not only a determination to avoid sins and a hatred of them, or a contrite and humble heart, but also the sacramental confession of those sins, at least in desire, to be made in its season, and sacerdotal absolution, as well as satisfaction by fasts, alms, prayers and other devout exercises of the spiritual life, not indeed for the eternal punishment, which is, together with the guilt, remitted either by the sacrament or by the desire of the sacrament, but for the temporal punishment which, as the sacred writings teach, is not always wholly remitted, as is done in baptism, to those who, ungrateful to the grace of God which they have received, have grieved the Holy Spirit and have not feared to violate the temple of God. Of which repentance it is written: "Be mindful whence thou art fallen; do penance, and do the first works" [Rev. 2:5]; and again, "The sorrow that is according to God worketh penance, steadfast unto salvation" [2 Cor. 7:10]; and again, "Do penance, and bring forth fruits worthy of penance" [Matt. 3:2; 4:17].

By Every Mortal Sin Grace Is Lost, but Not Faith

Against the subtle wits of some also, who "by pleasing speeches and good words seduce the hearts of the innocent" [Rom. 16:18], it must be maintained that the grace of justification once received is lost not only by infidelity, whereby also faith itself is lost, but also by every other mortal sin, though in this case faith is not lost; thus defending the teaching of the divine law which excludes from the kingdom of God not only unbelievers, but also the faithful [who are] "fornicators, adulterers, effeminate, liers with mankind, thieves, covetous, drunkards, railers, extortioners" [1 Cor. 6:9f.], and all others who commit deadly sins, from which with the help of divine grace they can refrain, and on account of which they are cut off from the grace of Christ.

The Fruits of Justification, That Is, the Merit of Good Works, and the Nature of That Merit

Therefore, to men justified in this manner, whether they have preserved uninterruptedly the grace received or recovered it when lost, are to be pointed out the words of the apostle: "Abound in every good work, knowing that your labor is not in vain in the Lord" [1 Cor. 15:58]. "For God is not unjust, that he should forget your work, and the love which you have shown in his name" [Heb. 6:10]; and, "Do not lose your confidence, which hath a great reward" [Heb. 10:35]. Hence, to those who work well unto the end and trust in God, eternal life is to be offered, both as a grace mercifully promised to the sons of God through Christ Jesus, and as a reward promised by God himself, to be faithfully given to their good works and merits. For this is the crown of justice which after his fight and course the apostle declared was laid up for him, to be rendered to him by the just judge, and not only to him, but also to all that love his coming. For since Christ Jesus himself, as the head into the members and the vine into the branches, continually infuses strength into those justified, which strength always precedes, accompanies and follows their good works, and without which

they could not in any manner be pleasing and meritorious before God, we must believe that nothing further is wanting to those justified to prevent them from being considered to have, by those very works which have been done in God, fully satisfied the divine law according to the state of this life and to have truly merited eternal life, to be obtained in its [due] time, provided they depart [this life] in grace, since Christ our Savior says: "If anyone shall drink of the water that I will give him, he shall not thirst forever; but it shall become in him a fountain of water springing up unto life everlasting" [John 4:13f.]. Thus, neither is our own justice established as our own from ourselves, nor is the justice of God ignored or repudiated, for that justice which is called ours, because we are justified by its inherence in us, that same is [the justice] of God, because it is infused into us by God through the merit of Christ. Nor must this be omitted, that although in the sacred writings so much is attributed to good works, that even "he that shall give a drink of cold water to one of his least ones," Christ promises, "shall not lose his reward" [Matt. 10:42]; and the apostle testifies that, "That which is at present momentary and light of our tribulation, worketh for us above measure exceedingly an eternal weight of glory" [2 Cor. 4:17]; nevertheless, far be it that a Christian should either trust or glory in himself and not in the Lord, whose bounty toward all men is so great that he wishes the things that are his gifts to be their merits. And since "in many things we all offend" [James 3:2], each one ought to have before his eyes not only the mercy and goodness but also the severity and judgment [of God]; neither ought anyone to judge himself, even though he be not conscious to himself of anything; because the whole life of man is to be examined and judged not by the judgment of man but of God, "who will bring to light the hidden things of darkness, and will make manifest the counsels of the hearts, and then shall every man have praise from God" [1 Cor. 4:5], who, as it is written, "will render to every man according to his works" [Matt. 16:27].

After this Catholic doctrine on justification, which whosoever does not faithfully and firmly accept cannot be justified, it seemed good to the holy council to add these canons, that all may know not only what they must hold and follow, but also what to avoid and shun.

Canon 1. If anyone says that man can be justified before God by his own works, whether done by his own natural powers or through the teaching of the law, without divine grace through Jesus Christ, let him be anathema.

Canon 2. If anyone says that divine grace through Christ Jesus is given for this only, that man may be able more easily to live justly and to merit eternal life, as if by free will without grace he is able to do both, though with hardship and difficulty, let him be anathema.

Canon 3. If anyone says that without the predisposing inspiration of the Holy Spirit and without his help, man can believe, hope, love or be repentant as he ought, so that the grace of justification may be bestowed upon him, let him be anathema.

Canon 4. If anyone says that man's free will moved and aroused by God, by assenting to God's call and action, in no way cooperates toward disposing and preparing itself to obtain the grace of justification, that it cannot refuse its assent if it wishes, but that, as something inanimate, it does nothing whatever and is merely passive, let him be anathema.

Canon 5. If anyone says that after the sin of Adam man's free will was lost and destroyed, or that it is a thing only in name, indeed a name without a reality, a fiction introduced into the church by Satan, let him be anathema.

Canon 6. If anyone says that it is not in man's power to make his ways evil, but that the works that are evil as well as those that are good God produces, not permissively only but also *proprie et per se,* so that the treason of Judas is no less his own proper work than the vocation of St. Paul, let him be anathema.

Canon 7. If anyone says that all works done before justification, in whatever manner they may be done, are truly sins, or merit the hatred of God; that the more earnestly one strives to dispose himself for grace, the more grievously he sins, let him be anathema.

Canon 8. If anyone says that the fear of hell, whereby, by grieving for sins, we flee to the mercy of God or abstain from sinning, is a sin or makes sinners worse, let him be anathema.

Canon 9. If anyone says that the sinner is justified by faith alone, meaning that nothing else is required to cooperate in order to obtain the grace of justification, and that it is not in any way necessary that he be prepared and disposed by the action of his own will, let him be anathema.

Canon 10. If anyone says that men are justified without the justice of Christ, whereby he merited for us, or by that justice are formally just, let him be anathema.

Canon 11. If anyone says that men are justified either by the sole imputation of the justice of Christ or by the sole remission of sins, to the exclusion of the grace and "the charity which is poured forth in their hearts by the Holy Spirit" [Rom. 5:5], and remains in them, or also that the grace by which we are justified is only the good will of God, let him be anathema.

Canon 12. If anyone says that justifying faith is nothing else than confidence in divine mercy, which remits sins for Christ's sake, or that it is this confidence alone that justifies us, let him be anathema.

Canon 13. If anyone says that in order to obtain the remission of sins it is necessary for every man to believe with certainty and without any hesitation arising from his own weakness and indisposition that his sins are forgiven him, let him be anathema.

Canon 14. If anyone says that man is absolved from his sins and justified because he firmly believes that he is absolved and justified, or that no one is truly justified except him who believes himself justified, and that by this faith alone absolution and justification are effected, let him be anathema.

Canon 15. If anyone says that a man who is born again and justified is bound *ex fide* to believe that he is certainly in the number of the predestined, let him be anathema.

Canon 16. If anyone says that he will for certain, with an absolute and infallible certainty, have that great gift of perseverance even to the end, unless he shall have learned this by a special revelation, let him be anathema.

Canon 17. If anyone says that the grace of justification is shared by those only who are predestined to life, but that all others who are called are called indeed but receive not grace, as if they are by divine power predestined to evil, let him be anathema.

Canon 18. If anyone says that the commandments of God are, even for one that is justified and constituted in grace, impossible to observe, let him be anathema.

Canon 19. If anyone says that nothing besides faith is commanded in the gospel,

that other things are indifferent, neither commanded nor forbidden, but free; or that the ten commandments in no way pertain to Christians, let him be anathema.

Canon 20. If anyone says that a man who is justified and however perfect is not bound to observe the commandments of God and the church, but only to believe, as if the gospel were a bare and absolute promise of eternal life without the condition of observing the commandments, let him be anathema.

Canon 21. If anyone says that Christ Jesus was given by God to men as a redeemer in whom to trust, and not also as a legislator whom to obey, let him be anathema.

Canon 22. If anyone says that the one justified either can without the special help of God persevere in the justice received, or that with that help he cannot, let him be anathema.

Canon 23. If anyone says that a man once justified can sin no more, nor lose grace, and that therefore he that falls and sins was never truly justified; or on the contrary, that he can during his whole life avoid all sins, even those that are venial, except by a special privilege from God, as the church holds in regard to the Blessed Virgin, let him be anathema.

Canon 24. If anyone says that the justice received is not preserved and also not increased before God through good works, but that those works are merely the fruits and signs of justification obtained, but not the cause of its increase, let him be anathema.

Canon 25. If anyone says that in every good work the just man sins at least venially, or, what is more intolerable, mortally, and hence merits eternal punishment, and that he is not damned for this reason only, because God does not impute these works unto damnation, let him be anathema.

Canon 26. If anyone says that the just ought not for the good works done in God to expect and hope for an eternal reward from God through his mercy and the merit of Jesus Christ, if by doing well and by keeping the divine commandments they persevere to the end, let him be anathema.

Canon 27. If anyone says that there is no mortal sin except that of unbelief, or that grace once received is not lost through any other sin however grievous and enormous except by that of unbelief, let him be anathema.

Canon 28. If anyone says that with the loss of grace through sin faith is also lost with it, or that the faith which remains is not a true faith, though it is not a living one, or that he who has faith without charity is not a Christian, let him be anathema.

Canon 29. If anyone says that he who has fallen after baptism cannot by the grace of God rise again, or that he can indeed recover again the lost justice but by faith alone without the sacrament of penance, contrary to what the holy Roman and universal Church, instructed by Christ the Lord and his apostles, has hitherto professed, observed and taught, let him be anathema.

Canon 30. If anyone says that after the reception of the grace of justification the guilt is so remitted and the debt of eternal punishment so blotted out to every repentant sinner, that no debt of temporal punishment remains to be discharged either in this world or in purgatory before the gates of heaven can be opened, let him be anathema.

Canon 31. If anyone says that the one justified sins when he performs good works with a view to an eternal reward, let him be anathema.

Canon 32. If anyone says that the good works of the one justified are in such manner the gifts of God that they are not also the good merits of him justified; or that the one justified by the good works that he performs by the grace of God and the merit of Jesus Christ, whose living member he is, does not truly merit an increase of grace, eternal life, and in case he dies in grace, the attainment of eternal life itself and also an increase in glory, let him be anathema.

Canon 33. If anyone says that the Catholic doctrine of justification as set forth by the holy council in the present decree, derogates is some respect from the glory of God or the merits of our Lord Jesus Christ, and does not rather illustrate the truth of our faith and no less the glory of God and of Christ Jesus, let him be anathema.

From H. J. Schroeder, trans., Canons and Decrees of the Council of Trent *(Rockford, Ill.: Tan Books, 1978), 29–46.*

82. Canons on the Sacraments in General (1547)

Foreword

For the completion of the salutary doctrine on justification, which was promulgated with the unanimous consent of the Fathers in the last session, it has seemed proper to deal with the most holy sacraments of the church, through which all true justice either begins, or being begun is increased, or being lost is restored. Wherefore, in order to destroy the errors and extirpate the heresies that in our stormy times are directed against the most holy sacraments, some of which are a revival of heresies long ago condemned by our Fathers, while others are of recent origin, all of which are exceedingly detrimental to the purity of the Catholic Church and the salvation of souls, the holy, ecumenical and general Council of Trent, lawfully assembled in the Holy Spirit, the same legates of the apostolic see presiding, adhering to the teaching of the Holy Scriptures, to the apostolic traditions, and to the unanimous teaching of other councils and of the Fathers, has thought it proper to establish and enact these present canons; hoping, with the help of the Holy Spirit, to publish later those that are wanting for the completion of the work begun.

Canon 1. If anyone says that the sacraments of the new law were not all instituted by our Lord Jesus Christ, or that there are more or less than seven, namely, baptism, confirmation, Eucharist, penance, extreme unction, order and matrimony, or that any one of these seven is not truly and intrinsically a sacrament, let him be anathema.

Canon 2. If anyone says that these sacraments of the new law do not differ from the sacraments of the old law, except that the ceremonies are different and the external rites are different, let him be anathema.

Canon 3. If anyone says that these seven sacraments are so equal to each other that one is not for any reason more excellent than the other, let him be anathema.

Canon 4. If anyone says that the sacraments of the new law are not necessary for salvation but are superfluous, and that without them or without the desire of them men obtain from God through faith alone the grace of justification, though all are not necessary for each one, let him be anathema.

Canon 5. If anyone says that these sacraments have been instituted for the nourishment of faith alone, let him be anathema.

Canon 6. If anyone says that the sacraments of the new law do not contain the grace which they signify, or that they do not confer that grace on those who place no obstacles in its way, as though they are only outward signs of grace or justice received through faith and certain marks of Christian profession, whereby among men believers are distinguished from unbelievers, let him be anathema.

Canon 7. If anyone says that grace, so far as God's part is concerned, is not imparted through the sacraments always and to all men even if they receive them rightly, but only sometimes and to some persons, let him be anathema.

Canon 8. If anyone says that by the sacraments of the new law grace is not conferred *ex opere operato*, but that faith alone in the divine promise is sufficient to obtain grace, let him be anathema.

Canon 9. If anyone says that in three sacraments, namely, baptism, confirmation and order, there is not imprinted on the soul a character, that is, a certain spiritual and indelible mark, by reason of which they cannot be repeated, let him be anathema.

Canon 10. If anyone says that all Christians have the power to administer the Word and all the sacraments, let him be anathema.

Canon 11. If anyone says that in ministers, when they effect and confer the sacraments, there is not required at least the intention of doing what the church does, let him be anathema.

Canon 12. If anyone says that a minister who is in mortal sin, though he observes all the essentials that pertain to the effecting or conferring of a sacrament, neither effects nor confers a sacrament, let him be anathema.

Canon 13. If anyone says that the received and approved rites of the Catholic Church, accustomed to be used in the administration of the sacraments, may be despised or omitted by the ministers without sin and at their pleasure, or may be changed by any pastor of the churches to other new ones, let him be anathema.

From Schroeder, Canons and Decrees, *51–53.*

83. Canons on the Eucharist (1551)

Canon 1. If anyone denies that in the sacrament of the most holy Eucharist are contained truly, really and substantially the body and blood together with the soul and divinity of our Lord Jesus Christ, and consequently the whole Christ, but says that he is in it only as in a sign, or figure or force, let him be anathema.

Canon 2. If anyone says that in the sacred and holy sacrament of the Eucharist the substance of the bread and wine remains conjointly with the body and blood of our Lord Jesus Christ, and denies that wonderful and singular change of the whole substance of the bread into the body and the whole substance of the wine into the blood, the appearances only of bread and wine remaining, which change the Catholic Church most aptly calls transubstantiation, let him be anathema.

Canon 3. If anyone denies that in the venerable sacrament of the Eucharist the whole Christ is contained under each form and under every part of each form when separated, let him be anathema.

Canon 4. If anyone says that after the consecration is completed, the body and blood of our Lord Jesus Christ are not in the admirable sacrament of the Eucharist, but are there only *in usu,* while being taken and not before or after, and that in the hosts or consecrated particles which are reserved or which remain after communion, the true body of the Lord does not remain, let him be anathema.

Canon 5. If anyone says that the principal fruit of the most holy Eucharist is the remission of sins, or that other effects do not result from it, let him be anathema.

Canon 6. If anyone says that in the holy sacrament of the Eucharist, Christ, the only begotten Son of God, is not to be adored with the worship of *latria,* also outwardly manifested, and is consequently neither to be venerated with a special festive solemnity, nor to be solemnly borne about in procession according to the laudable and universal rite and custom of holy church, or is not to be set publicly before the people to be adored and that the adorers thereof are idolaters, let him be anathema.

Canon 7. If anyone says that it is not lawful that the holy Eucharist be reserved in a sacred place, but immediately after consecration must necessarily be distributed among those present, or that it is not lawful that it be carried with honor to the sick, let him be anathema.

Canon 8. If anyone says that Christ received in the Eucharist is received spiritually only and not also sacramentally and really, let him be anathema.

Canon 9. If anyone denies that each and all of Christ's faithful of both sexes are bound, when they have reached the years of discretion, to communicate every year at least at Easter, in accordance with the precept of holy mother church, let him be anathema.

Canon 10. If anyone says that it is not lawful for the priest celebrating to communicate himself, let him be anathema.

Canon 11. If anyone says that faith alone is sufficient preparation for receiving the sacrament of the most holy Eucharist, let him be anathema. And lest so great a sacrament be received unworthily and hence unto death and condemnation, this holy council ordains and declares that sacramental confession, when a confessor can be had, must necessarily be made beforehand by those whose conscience is burdened with mortal sin, however contrite they may consider themselves. Moreover, if anyone shall presume to teach, preach or obstinately assert, or in public disputation defend the contrary, he shall be *eo ipso* excommunicated.

From Schroeder, Canons and Decrees, *79–80.*

84. Canons on Penance (1551)

Canon 1. If anyone says that in the Catholic Church penance is not truly and properly a sacrament instituted by Christ the Lord for reconciling the faithful of God as often as they fall into sin after baptism, let him be anathema.

Canon 2. If anyone, confounding the sacraments, says that baptism is itself the sacrament of penance, as though these two sacraments were not distinct, and that penance therefore is not rightly called a second plank after shipwreck, let him be anathema.

Canon 3. If anyone says that those words of the Lord Savior, "Receive ye the Holy Spirit, whose sins you shall forgive, they are forgiven them, and whose sins you shall retain, they are retained" [Matt. 16:19], are not to be understood of the power of forgiving and retaining sins in the sacrament of penance, as the Catholic Church has always understood them from the beginning, but distorts them, contrary to the institution of this sacrament, as applying to the authority of preaching the gospel, let him be anathema.

Canon 4. If anyone denies that for the full and perfect remission of sins three acts are required on the part of the penitent, consti-

tuting as it were the matter of the sacrament of penance, namely, contrition, confession and satisfaction, which are called the three parts of penance; or says that there are only two parts of penance, namely, the terrors of a smitten conscience convinced of sin and the faith received from the gospel or from absolution, by which one believes that his sins are forgiven him through Christ, let him be anathema.

Canon 5. If anyone says that the contrition which is evoked by examination, recollection and hatred of sins, whereby one recounts his years in the bitterness of his soul, by reflecting on the grievousness, the multitude, the baseness of his sins, the loss of eternal happiness and the incurring of eternal damnation, with a purpose of amendment, is not a true and beneficial sorrow, does not prepare for grace, but makes a man a hypocrite and a greater sinner; finally, that this sorrow is forced and not free and voluntary, let him be anathema.

Canon 6. If anyone denies that sacramental confession was instituted by divine law or is necessary to salvation; or says that the manner of confessing secretly to a priest alone, which the Catholic Church has always observed from the beginning and still observes, is at variance with the institution and command of Christ and is a human contrivance, let him be anathema.

Canon 7. If anyone says that in the sacrament of penance it is not required by divine law for the remission of sins to confess each and all mortal sins which are recalled after a due and diligent examination, also secret ones and those that are a violation of the two last commandments of the Decalogue, as also the circumstances that change the nature of a sin, but that this confession is useful only to instruct and console the penitent and in olden times was observed only to impose a canonical satisfaction; or says that they who strive to confess all sins wish to leave nothing to the divine mercy to pardon; or finally, that it is not lawful to confess venial sins, let him be anathema.

Canon 8. If anyone says that the confession of all sins as it is observed in the church is impossible and is a human tradition to be abolished by pious people; or that each and all the faithful of Christ of either sex are not bound thereto once a year in accordance with the constitution of the great Lateran Council, and that for this reason the faithful of Christ are to be persuaded not to confess during Lent, let him be anathema.

Canon 9. If anyone says that the sacramental absolution of the priest is not a judicial act but a mere service of pronouncing and declaring to him who confesses that the sins are forgiven, provided only he believes himself to be absolved, even though the priest absolves not in earnest but only in jest; or says that the confession of the penitent is not necessary in order that the priest may be able to absolve him, let him be anathema.

Canon 10. If anyone says that priests who are in mortal sin have not the power of binding and loosing, or that not only priests are the ministers of absolution but that to each and all of the faithful of Christ was it said: "Whatsoever you shall bind upon earth, shall be bound also in heaven; and whatsoever you shall loose upon earth, shall be loosed in heaven" [Matt. 16:19]; and "whose sins you shall forgive, they are forgiven them, and whose sins you shall retain, they are retained" [Matt. 16:19]; by virtue of which words everyone can absolve from sins, from public sins by reproof only, provided the one reproved accept correction, and from secret sins by voluntary confession, let him be anathema.

Canon 11. If anyone says that bishops have not the right to reserve cases to themselves except such as pertain to external administration, and that therefore the reservation of cases does not hinder a priest from absolving from reserved cases, let him be anathema.

Canon 12. If anyone says that God always pardons the whole penalty together with the guilt and that the satisfaction of penitents is nothing else than the faith by which they perceive that Christ has satisfied for them, let him be anathema.

Canon 13. If anyone says that satisfaction for sins, as to their temporal punishment, is in no way made to God through the merits of Christ by the punishments inflicted by him and patiently borne, or by those imposed by the priest, or even those voluntarily undertaken, as by fasts, prayers, almsgiving or other works of piety, and that therefore the best penance is merely a new life, let him be anathema.

Canon 14. If anyone says that the satisfactions by which penitents atone for their sins through Christ are not a worship of God but traditions of men, which obscure the doctrine of grace and the true worship of God and the beneficence itself of the death of Christ, let him be anathema.

Canon 15. If anyone says that the keys have been given to the church only to loose and not also to bind, and that therefore priests, when imposing penalties on those who confess, act contrary to the purpose of the keys and to the institution of Christ, and that it is a fiction that there remains often a temporal punishment to be discharged after the eternal punishment has by virtue of the keys been removed, let him be anathema.

✝

From Schroeder, Canons and Decrees, *101–4.*

85. Reform Decree on Establishing Seminaries (1563)

Since the age of youth, unless rightly trained, is inclined to follow after the pleasure of the world, and unless educated from its tender years in piety and religion before the habits of vice take possession of the whole man, will never perfectly and without the greatest and well-nigh extraordinary help of almighty God persevere in ecclesiastical discipline, the holy council decrees that all cathedral and metropolitan churches and churches greater than these shall be bound, each according to its means and the extent of its diocese, to provide for, to educate in religion, and to train in ecclesiastical discipline, a certain number of boys of their city and diocese, or, if they are not found there, of their province, in a college located near the said churches or in some other suitable place to be chosen by the bishop. Into this college shall be received such as are at least twelve years of age, are born of lawful wedlock, who know how to read and write competently, and whose character and inclination justify the hope that they will dedicate themselves forever to the ecclesiastical ministry. It wishes, however, that in the selection the sons of the poor be given preference, though it does not exclude those of the wealthy class, provided they be maintained at their own expense and manifest a zeal to serve God and the church. These youths the bishop shall divide into as many classes as he may deem proper, according to their number, age, and progress in ecclesiastical discipline, and shall, when it appears to him opportune, assign some of them to the ministry of the churches, the others he shall keep in the college to be instructed, and he shall replace by others those who have been withdrawn, so that the college may be a perpetual seminary of ministers of God. And that they may be the better trained in the aforesaid ecclesiastical discipline, they shall forthwith and always wear the tonsure and the clerical garb; they shall study grammar, singing, ecclesiastical computation and other useful arts; shall be instructed in Sacred Scripture, ecclesiastical books, the homilies of the saints, the manner of administering the sacraments, especially those things that seem adapted to the hearing of confessions, and the rites and ceremonies. The bishop shall see to it that they are present every day at the sacrifice of the mass, confess their sins at least once a month, receive the body of our Lord Jesus Christ in accordance with the directions of their confessor, and on festival days serve in the cathedral and other churches of the locality. All these and other things beneficial and needful for this purpose each bishop shall prescribe with the advice of two of the senior and more reputable canons chosen by himself as the Holy Spirit shall suggest, and they shall make it their duty by frequent visitation to see to it that they are always observed. The disobedient and incorrigible, and the disseminators of depraved morals they shall punish severely, even with expulsion if necessary; and removing all obstacles, they shall foster carefully whatever appears to contribute to the advancement and preservation of so pious and holy an institution. And since for the construction of the college, for paying salaries to instructors and servants, for the maintenance of the youths and for other expenses, certain revenues will be necessary. . . .

Furthermore, in order that the establishment of schools of this kind may be procured at less expense, the holy council decrees that bishops, archbishops, primates and other local ordinaries urge and compel, even by the reduction of their revenues, those who hold the position of instructor and others to whose position is attached the function of reading or teaching, to teach those to be educated in those schools personally, if they are competent, otherwise by competent substitutes, to be chosen by themselves and to be approved by the ordinaries. But if these in the judgment of the bishop are not qualified, they shall choose another who is competent, no appeal being permitted; and should they neglect to do this, then the bishop himself shall appoint one. The aforesaid instructors shall teach what the bishop shall judge expedient. In the future, however, those offices or dignities, which are called professorships, shall not be conferred except on doctors or masters or licentiates of Sacred Scripture or canon law and on other competent persons who can personally discharge that office; any appointment made otherwise shall be null and void, all privileges and customs whatsoever, even though immemorial, notwithstanding.

But if in any province the churches labor under such poverty that in some a college cannot be established, then the provincial synod or the metropolitan with two of the oldest suffragans shall provide for the establishment of one or more colleges, as he may deem advisable, at the metropolitan or at some other more convenient church of the province, from the revenues of two or more churches in each of which a college cannot be conveniently established, where the youths of those churches might be educated. In churches having extensive dioceses, however, the bishop may have one or more in the diocese, as he may deem expedient; which, however, shall in all things be dependent on the one erected and established in the [metropolitan] city.

Finally, if either with regard to the unions or the appraisement or assignment or incorporation of portions, or for any other reason,

any difficulty should happen to arise by reason of which the establishment or the maintenance of the seminary might be hindered or disturbed, the bishop with those designated above or the provincial synod, shall have the authority, according to the custom of the country and the character of the churches and benefices, to decide and regulate all matters which shall appear necessary and expedient for the happy advancement of the seminary, even to modify or augment, if need be, the contents hereof.

From Schroeder, Canons and Decrees, *175–79.*

86. Reform Decree on Preaching (1563)

Desiring that the office of preaching, which belongs chiefly to bishops, be exercised as often as possible for the welfare of the faithful, the holy council, for the purpose of accommodating to the use of the present time the canons published elsewhere on this subject under Paul III, of happy memory, decrees that they themselves shall personally, each in his own church, announce the Sacred Scriptures and the divine law, or, if lawfully hindered, have it done by those whom they shall appoint to the office of preaching; but in other churches by the parish priests, or, if they are hindered, by others to be appointed by the bishop in the city or in any part of the diocese as they shall judge it expedient, at the expense of those who are bound or accustomed to defray it, and this they shall do at least on all Sundays and solemn festival days, but during the season of fasts, of Lent and of the Advent of the Lord, daily, or at least on three days of the week if they shall deem it necessary; otherwise, as often as they shall judge that it can be done conveniently. The bishop shall diligently admonish the people that each one is bound to be present at his own parish church, where it can be conveniently done, to hear the word of God. But no one, whether secular or regular, shall presume to preach, even in churches of his own order, in opposition to the will of the bishop. The bishops shall also see to it that at least on Sundays and other festival days, the children in every parish be carefully taught the rudiments of the faith and obedience toward God and their parents by those whose duty it is, and who shall be compelled thereto, if need be, even by ecclesiastical censures; any privileges and customs notwithstanding. In other respects the things decreed under Paul III concerning the office of preaching shall remain in force.

✠

From Schroeder, Canons and Decrees, *195–96.*

87. Rules on Prohibited Books (1563)

Begun in 1559, the Index of Prohibited Books here is given formalized procedures by the Council.

✠

I. All books which have been condemned either by the supreme Pontiffs or by ecumenical councils before the year 1515 and are not contained in this list, shall be considered condemned in the same manner as they were formerly condemned.

II. The books of those heresiarchs, who after the aforesaid year originated or revived heresies, as well as of those who are or have been the heads or leaders of heretics, as Luther, Zwingli, Calvin, Balthasar Fried-

berg, Schwenkfeld, and others like these, whatever may be their name, title or nature of their heresy, are absolutely forbidden. The books of other heretics, however, which deal professedly with religion are absolutely condemned. Those on the other hand, which do not deal with religion and have by order of the bishops and inquisitors been examined by Catholic theologians and approved by them, are permitted. Likewise, Catholic books written by those who afterward fell into heresy, as well as by those who after their fall returned to the bosom of the church, may be permitted if they have been approved by the theological faculty of a Catholic university or by the general inquisition.

III. The translations of writers, also ecclesiastical, which have till now been edited by condemned authors, are permitted provided they contain nothing contrary to sound doctrine. Translations of the books of the Old Testament may in the judgment of the bishop be permitted to learned and pious men only, provided such translations are used only as elucidations of the Vulgate edition for the understanding of the Holy Scriptures and not as the sound text. Translations of the New Testament made by authors of the first class of this list shall be permitted to no one, since great danger and little usefulness usually results to readers from their perusal. But if with such translations as are permitted or with the Vulgate edition some annotations are circulated, these may also, after the suspected passages have been expunged by the theological faculty of some Catholic university or by the general inquisition, be permitted to those to whom the translations are permitted. Under these circumstances the entire volume of the sacred books, which is commonly called the *biblia Vatabli,* or parts of it, may be permitted to pious and learned men. From the Bibles of Isidore Clarius of Brescia, however, the preface and introduction are to be removed, and no one shall regard its text as the text of the Vulgate edition.

IV. Since it is clear from experience that if the sacred books are permitted everywhere and without discrimination in the vernacular, there will by reason of the boldness of men arise therefrom more harm than good, the matter is in this respect left to the judgment of the bishop or inquisitor, who may with the advice of the pastor or confessor permit the reading of the sacred books translated into the vernacular by Catholic authors to those who they know will derive from such reading no harm but rather an increase of faith and piety, which permission they must have in writing. Those, however, who presume to read or possess them without such permission may not receive absolution from their sins till they have handed them over to the ordinary. Book dealers who sell or in any other way supply Bibles written in the vernacular to anyone who has not this permission, shall lose the price of the books, which is to be applied by the bishop to pious purposes, and in keeping with the nature of the crime they shall be subject to other penalties which are left to the judgment of the same bishop. Regulars who have not the permission of their superiors may not read or purchase them.

V. Those books which sometimes produce the works of heretical authors, in which these add little or nothing of their own but rather collect therein the sayings of others, as lexicons, concordances, apothegms, parables, tables of contents and suchlike, are permitted if whatever needs to be eliminated in the editions is removed and corrected in accordance with the suggestions of the bishop, the inquisitor and Catholic theologians.

VI. Books which deal in the vernacular with the controversies between Catholics and heretics of our time may not be permitted indiscriminately, but the same is to be observed with regard to them what has been decreed concerning Bibles written in the vernacular. There is no reason, however, why those should be prohibited which have been written in the vernacular for the purpose of pointing out the right way to live, to contemplate, to confess, and similar purposes, if they contain sound doctrine, just as popular sermons in the vernacular are not prohibited. But if hitherto in some kingdom or province certain books have been prohibited because they contained matter the reading of which would be of no benefit to all indiscriminately, these may, if their authors are Catholic, be permitted by the bishop and inquisitor after they have been corrected.

VII. Books which professedly deal with, narrate or teach things lascivious or obscene are absolutely prohibited, since not only the matter of faith but also that of morals, which are usually easily corrupted through the reading of such books, must be taken into consideration, and those who possess them are to be severely punished by the bishops. Ancient books written by heathens may by reason of their elegance and quality of style be permitted, but may by no means be read to children.

VIII. Books whose chief contents are good but in which some things have incidentally been inserted which have reference to heresy, ungodliness, divination or superstition, may be permitted if by the authority of the general inquisition they have been purged by Catholic theologians. The same decision holds good with regard to prefaces, summaries or annotations which are added by condemned authors to books not condemned.

Hereafter, however, these shall not be printed till they have been corrected.

IX. All books and writings dealing with geomancy, hydromancy, aeromancy, pyromancy, oneiromancy, chiromancy, necromancy, or with sortilege, mixing of poisons, augury, auspices, sorcery, magic arts, are absolutely repudiated. The bishops shall diligently see to it that books, treatises, catalogs determining destiny by astrology, which in the matter of future events, consequences, or fortuitous occurrences, or of actions that depend on the human will, attempt to affirm something as certain to take place, are not read or possessed. Permitted, on the other hand, are the opinions and natural observations which have been written in the interest of navigation, agriculture or the medical art.

X. In the printing of books or other writings is to be observed what was decreed in the tenth session of the Lateran Council under Leo X. Wherefore, if in the fair city of Rome any book is to be printed, it shall first be examined by the vicar of the supreme Pontiff and by the master of the sacred palace or by the persons appointed by our most holy lord [the pope]. In other localities this approbation and examination shall pertain to the bishop or to one having a knowledge of the book or writing to be printed appointed by the bishop and to the inquisitor of the city or diocese in which the printing is done, and it shall be approved by the signature of their own hand, free of charge and without delay under the penalties and censures contained in the same decree, with the observance of this rule and condition that an authentic copy of the book to be printed, undersigned by the author's hand, remain with the examiner. Those who circulate books in manuscript form before they have been examined and approved, shall in the judgment of the

fathers delegated by the council be subject to the same penalties as the printers, and those who possess and read them shall, unless they make known the authors, be themselves regarded as the authors. The approbation of such books shall be given in writing and must appear authentically in the front of the written or printed book and the examination, approbation and other things must be done free of charge. Moreover, in all cities and dioceses the houses or places where the art of printing is carried on and the libraries offering books for sale, shall be visited often by persons appointed for this purpose by the bishop or his vicar and also by the inquisitor, so that nothing that is prohibited be printed, sold or possessed. All book-dealers and vendors of books shall have in their libraries a list of the books which they have for sale subscribed by the said persons, and without the permission of the same appointed persons they may not under penalties of confiscation of the books and other penalties to be imposed in the judgment of the bishops and inquisitors, possess or sell or in any other manner whatsoever supply other books. Vendors, readers and printers shall be punished according to the judgment of the same. If anyone brings into any city any books whatsoever he shall be bound to give notice thereof to the same delegated persons, or in case a public place is provided for wares of that kind, then the public officials of that place shall notify the aforesaid persons that books have been brought in. But let no one dare give to anyone a book to read which he himself or another has brought into the city or in any way dispose of or loan it, unless he has first exhibited the book and obtained the permission of the persons appointed, or unless it is well known that the reading of the book is permitted to all. The same shall be observed by heirs and executors of last wills, so, namely, that they exhibit the books left by those deceased, or a list of them, to the persons delegated and obtain from them permission before they use them or in any way transfer them to other persons. In each and all of such cases let a penalty be prescribed, covering either the confiscation of books or in the judgment of the bishops or inquisitors another that is in keeping with the degree of the contumacy or the character of the offense.

With reference to those books which the delegated fathers have examined and expurgated or have caused to be expurgated, or under certain conditions have permitted to be printed again, the book-dealers as well as others shall observe whatever is known to have been prescribed by them. The bishops and general inquisitors, however, in view of the authority which they have, are free to prohibit even those books which appear to be permitted by these rules, if they should deem this advisable in their kingdoms, provinces or dioceses. Moreover, the secretary of those delegated has by order of our most holy lord [the pope] to hand over in writing to the notary of the holy universal Roman Inquisition the names of the books which have been expurgated by the delegated fathers as well as the names of those to whom they committed this task.

Finally, all the faithful are commanded not to presume to read or possess any books contrary to the prescriptions of these rules or the prohibition of this list. And if anyone should read or possess books by heretics or writings by any author condemned and prohibited by reason of heresy or suspicion of false teaching, he incurs immediately the sentence of excommunication. He, on the other hand, who reads or possesses books prohibited under another name shall, besides incurring the guilt of mortal sin, be severely punished according to the judgment of the bishops.

✠

From Schroeder, Canons and Decrees, *273–78.*

The Jesuits

88. Ignatius Loyola, *Autobiography* (1553–1555)

The Reformation era, like other moments of crisis in the history of Christianity, witnessed a surge in the foundation of new religious orders. Among these, the Society of Jesus had by far the greatest impact. This new order was to combine the contemplative life with action in the world on behalf of the church's apostolic mission. Among its various ministries, it quickly became evident that education was to be the most important.

The order's founder, Ignatius Loyola (1491–1556), was a Basque aristocrat who went through a profound conversion experience and subsequently gathered about him a number of like-minded companions, dedicated to cultivation of the spiritual life, charitable work, and itinerant preaching. In 1540, Pope Paul III gave his approval to this group. What follows is an excerpt from Ignatius' autobiography (written in the third person).

✠

Up to his twenty-sixth year he was a man given over to the vanities of the world, and took a special delight in the exercise of arms, with a great and vain desire of winning glory. . . . [Wounded in the war with France in 1521] he was not able to stand upon his leg, and so had to remain in bed. He had been much given to reading worldly books of fiction and knight errantry, and feeling well enough to read he asked for some of these books to help while away the time. In that house, however, they could find none of those he was accustomed to read, and so they gave him a life of Christ and a book of the lives of the saints in Spanish. By the frequent reading of these books he conceived some affection for what he found there narrated. Pausing in his reading, he gave himself up to thinking over what he had read. At other times he dwelled on the things of the world which formerly had occupied his thoughts. . . . In reading of the life of our Lord and the lives of the saints, he paused to think and reason with himself, "Suppose that I should do what St. Francis did, what St. Dominic did." . . .

He determined, therefore, on a watch of arms throughout a whole night, without ever sitting or lying down, but standing a while and then kneeling before the altar of our Lady at Montserrat, where he had made up his mind to leave his fine attire and to clothe himself with the armor of Christ. Leaving, then, his place, he continued, as was his wont, thinking about his resolutions, and when he arrived at Montserrat [1522], after praying for a while and making an engagement with his confesssor, he made a general confession in writing which lasted three days. . . . [In 1534, after studying at university, he and six companions came to a decision as to what they were going to do.] Their plan was to go to Venice and from there to Jerusalem, where they were to spend the rest of their lives for the good of souls. If they were refused permission to remain in Jerusalem they would return to Rome, offer themselves to the vicar of Christ, asking him to make use of them wherever he thought it would be more to God's glory and the good of souls. . . .

From Jones, Counter Reformation, *38–39.*

89. An Early Jesuit Report on Rome (1538)

In 1537 the plan of the companions to go to the holy land to convert the Muslims was foiled. They found themselves instead in Rome and there they plunged into apostolic service. This report illustrates one aspect of that work.

✠

The hospitals were ignored. Nobody made any effort to find out what was happening or to organize any relief of the suffering. Piety and compassion had fled. . . . The companions took action, as far as they were able, to relieve the great need. They begged money in the streets and collected donations, both in cash and in food, from house to house. They then searched the streets to find the poor and starving and brought them back to the house. There they washed them and gave them new clothes. They gave them medicine and food and taught some catechism. . . . Sometimes there were as many as three hundred crowded into the house receiving comfort and spiritual guidance. In addition, the companions went out daily to assist the two thousand starving and shivering in the streets of Rome's poorest quarters, giving them food and money. The companions themselves owned nothing, but our Lord touched the hearts of good Romans who daily brought gifts of money and clothing and medicines for this holy work. . . .

✠

From Jones, Counter Reformation, *40.*

90. Ignatius Loyola, *Prima summa* (1539)

Gradually Ignatius seems to have clarified in his own mind what the purpose of his new order was to be. In this document, he emphasized obedience to the pope, on the assumption that the head of the universal church has a better picture of its real needs than any other individual.

✠

[This is to be] a community founded principally for the advancement of souls in Christian life and doctrine . . . for the propagation of the faith by the ministry of the word, by spiritual exercises, by works of charity, and expressly by the instruction in Christianity of children and the uneducated. . . . [T]his entire society and each one individually are soldiers of God under faithful obedience to our most holy lord Paul III and his successors and are thus under the command of the vicar of Christ and his divine power not only as having the obligation to him which is common to all clerics, but also as being bound by the bond of a vow that whatever his Holiness commands pertaining to the advancement of souls and the propagation of the faith we must immediately carry out . . . whether he sends us to the Turks or to the new world or to the Lutherans or to others.

All the companions who are in holy orders . . . shall be bound to say the office according to the rites of the church, but not in choir lest they be led away from the works of charity to which we have all dedicated ourselves . . . since as a consequence of the nature of our vocation, besides other necessary duties, we must frequently be occupied a great part of the day and even of the night in comforting the sick both in body and spirit. . . .

From Jones, Counter Reformation, *39.*

91. Ignatius Loyola, *The Spiritual Exercises* (1548)

The new Jesuit ideal of the contemplative in action, Ignatius saw, required a new spirituality. The handbook he wrote for this purpose was *The Spiritual Exercises.* It prescribed an intensive course of personal interior religious development that would ideally last for four weeks and that would be life-transforming for the serious practitioner. Only part of Ignatius' introductory observations and the "First Principle and Foundation" can be printed here. To this spiritual guidebook, Ignatius appended his famous "Rules for Thinking with the Church"—a direct assault on what he saw as the Protestant mindset.

Introductory Observations

By the term "Spiritual Exercises" is meant every method of examination of conscience, of meditation, of contemplation, of vocal and mental prayer, and of other spiritual activities that will be mentioned later. For just as taking a walk, journeying on foot, and running are bodily exercises, so we call spiritual exercises every way of preparing and disposing the soul to rid itself of all inordinate attachments, and, after their removal, of seeking and finding the will of God in the disposition of our life for the salvation of our soul. . . .

First Principle and Foundation

Man is created to praise, reverence, and serve God our Lord, and by this means to save his soul.

The other things on the face of the earth are created for man to help him in attaining the end for which he is created.

Hence, man is to make use of them in as far as they help him in the attainment of his end, and he must rid himself of them in as far as they prove a hindrance to him.

Therefore, we must make ourselves indifferent to all created things, as far as we are allowed free choice and are not under any prohibition. Consequently, as far as we are concerned, we should not prefer health to sickness, riches to poverty, honor to dishonor, a long life to a short life. The same holds for all other things.

Our one desire and choice should be what is more conducive to the end for which we are created. . . .

Rules for Thinking with the Church

The following rules should be observed to foster the true attitude of mind we ought to have in the church militant.

1. We must put aside all judgment of our own, and keep the mind ever ready and prompt to obey in all things the true spouse of Christ our Lord, our holy mother, the hierarchical church.

2. We should praise sacramental confession, the yearly reception of the most blessed Sacrament, and praise more highly monthly reception, and still more weekly Communion, provided requisite and proper dispositions are present.

3. We ought to praise the frequent hearing of mass, the singing of hymns, psalmody, and long prayers whether in church or outside; likewise, the hours arranged at fixed times for the whole Divine Office, for every kind of prayer, and for the canonical hours.

4. We must praise highly religious life, virginity, and continence; and matrimony ought not be praised as much as any of these.

5. We should praise vows of religion, obedience, poverty, chastity, and vows to perform other works of supererogation conducive to perfection. However, it must be remembered that a vow deals with matters that lead us closer to evangelical perfection. Hence, whatever tends to withdraw one from perfection may not be made the object of a vow, for example, a business career, the married state, and so forth.

6. We should show our esteem for the relics of the saints by venerating them and praying to the saints. We should praise visits to the station churches, pilgrimages, indulgences, jubilees, crusade indults, and the lighting of candles in churches.

7. We must praise the regulations of the church with regard to fast and abstinence, for example, in Lent, on ember days, vigils, Fridays, and Saturdays. We should praise works of penance, not only those that are interior but also those that are exterior.

8. We ought to praise not only the building and adornment of churches, but also images and veneration of them according to the subject they represent.

9. Finally, we must praise all the commandments of the church, and be on the alert to find reasons to defend them, and by no means in order to criticize them.

10. We should be more ready to approve and praise the orders, recommendations, and way of acting of our superiors than to find fault with them. Though some of the orders, etc., may not have been praiseworthy, yet to speak against them, either when preaching in public or in speaking before the people, would rather be the cause of murmuring and scandal than of profit. As a consequence, the people would become angry with their superiors, whether secular or spiritual. But while it does harm in the absence of our superiors to speak evil of them before the people, it may be profitable to discuss their bad conduct with those who can apply a remedy.

11. We should praise both positive theology and that of the Scholastics.

It is characteristic of the positive doctors, such as St. Augustine, St. Jerome, St. Gregory, and others, to rouse the affections so that we are moved to love and serve God our Lord in all things.

On the other hand, it is more characteristic of the Scholastic doctors, such as St. Thomas, St. Bonaventure, the Master of the Sentences [Peter Lombard], and others, to define and state clearly, according to the needs of our times, the doctrines that are necessary for eternal salvation, and that more efficaciously help to refute all errors and expose all fallacies.

Further, just because Scholastic doctors belong to more recent times, they not only have the advantage of correct understanding of Holy Scripture and of the teaching of the saints and positive doctors, but, enlightened by the grace of God, they also make use of the decisions of the councils and of the definitions and decrees of our holy mother church.

12. We must be on our guard against making comparisons between those who are still living and the saints who have gone before us, for no small error is committed if we say: "This man is wiser than St. Augustine," "He is another St. Francis or even greater," "He is equal to St. Paul in goodness and sanctity," and so on.

13. If we wish to proceed securely in all things, we must hold fast to the following principle: What seems to me white, I will believe black if the hierarchical church so defines. For I must be convinced that in Christ our Lord, the bridegroom, and in his spouse the church, only one Spirit holds sway, which governs and rules for the salvation of souls. For it is by the same Spirit and Lord who gave the Ten Commandments that our holy mother church is ruled and governed.

14. Granted that it be very true that no one can be saved without being predestined and without having faith and grace, still we must be very cautious about the way in which we speak of all these things and discuss them with others.

15. We should not make it a habit of speaking much of predestination. If somehow at times it comes to be spoken of, it must be done in such a way that the people are not led into any error. They are at times misled, so that they say: "Whether I shall be saved or lost, has already been determined, and this cannot be changed whether my actions are good or bad." So they become indolent and neglect the works that are conducive to the salvation and spiritual progress of their souls.

16. In the same way, much caution is necessary, lest by much talk about faith, and much insistence on it without any distinctions or explanations, occasion be given to the people, whether before or after they have faith informed by charity, to become slothful and lazy in good works.

17. Likewise we ought not to speak of grace at such length and with such emphasis that the poison of doing away with liberty is engendered.

Hence, as far as is possible with the help of God, one may speak of faith and grace that the divine majesty may be praised. But let it not be done in such a way, above all not in times which are as dangerous as ours, that works and free will suffer harm, or that they are considered of no value.

18. Though the zealous service of God our Lord out of pure love should be esteemed above all, we ought also to praise highly the fear of the divine majesty. For not only filial fear but also servile fear is pious and very holy. When nothing higher or more useful is attained, it is very helpful for rising from mortal sin, and once this is accomplished, one may easily advance to filial fear, which is

wholly pleasing and agreeable to God our Lord since it is inseparably associated with the love of him.

✠

From L. J. Puhl, ed., The Spiritual Exercises of St. Ignatius (Chicago: Loyola University Press, 1951), 1, 12, and 157–61.

92. Letter of Juan de Polanco to Antonio de Araoz (1 December 1551)

Like the order itself, Jesuit educational efforts proved to be fabulously successful. Jesuits acquired professorships in established universities, and they themselves founded several new universities and seminaries. More importantly, they set up and staffed colleges—approximately five hundred in the first century of the order's existence—whose rough U.S. equivalent today would be from junior high school through junior college. The inspiration for these institutions and their innovative pedagogy came from Ignatius himself. The following letter illustrates aspects of Ignatius' early educational vision. He instructed Polanco, his secretary-consultant-friend in Rome, to write it to Araoz, the Spanish provincial of the order.

✠

The peace of Christ. Seeing that God our Lord is moving his servants in your region as well as here to start a number of colleges of this society, our father has thought it good to provide counsel about the procedure and advantages which have been learned through experience regarding the colleges here (for those of the colleges there are already well known). He wants this to be fully studied, so that, as far as the matter is in our hand, nothing may be left undone for God's greater service and the aid of our neighbors.

The manner or method employed in founding a college is this. A city (like Messina and Palermo in Sicily), or a ruler (like the king of the Romans and the dukes of Ferrara and Florence), a private individual (like the prior of the Trinità in Venice and Padua), or a group of persons (as in Naples, Bologna, and elsewhere) provides an annual sum of money—some of them in perpetuity from the beginning, others not until they can test and verify the value of this work.

A suitable building is procured, two or three priests of very solid doctrine are sent, along with some of our own students, who, in addition to pursuing their own education, can aid that of other students and, through their good example, personal contact, and learning, help them in virtue and spiritual progress.

The procedure in such places is this. At the beginning three or four teachers in humane letters are appointed. One of the teachers starts off with elementary grammar, accommodating himself to beginners; another is assigned to those on an intermediate level, another for those more advanced in grammar. A different teacher is assigned to the students of the humanities who are further along in the Latin, Greek, and—if there is an inclination for it—Hebrew languages.

When the school has been advertised, all who wish are admitted free and without receipt of any money or gratuity—that is, all who know how to read and write and are beginners in [Latin] grammar. However, being young boys, they must have the approval of their parents or guardians and observe certain conditions, as follows.

They must be under obedience to their teachers regarding which subjects they study and for how long.

They must go to confession at least once a month.

Every Sunday they must attend the class on Christian doctrine given in the college, as well as the sermon when one is delivered in the church.

They must be well-behaved in their speech and in all other matters, and be orderly. Where they fail in this or in their duties, in the case of young boys for whom words do not suffice, there should be a hired extern corrector to chastise them and keep them in awe; none of our men is to lay his hand on anyone.

The names of all these pupils are registered. Care is taken not only to provide class instruction but also to have them do exercises in debating, in written composition, and in speaking Latin all the time, in such a way that they will make great progress in letters and virtues alike.

When there is a fair number of students who have acquired a grounding in humane letters, a person is appointed to inaugurate the course in the arts [i.e., philosophy]; and when there are a number of students well grounded in arts, a lecturer is appointed to teach theology—following the method of Paris, with frequent exercises. From that point on, this whole arrangement is continued. For experience shows that it is inadvisable to begin by teaching arts or theology: lacking a foundation, the students make no progress. (This plan applies to places where there is a readiness for something more than humane letters—a readiness that does not always exist. In other places it is sufficient to teach languages and humane letters.)

Beyond this, the priests in the colleges will aid in hearing confessions, preaching, and all other spiritual ministrations. In this work the young men sometimes have grace that equals or exceeds that of the priests, God our Lord being greatly served thereby.

So much for the method. Now I shall mention the advantages which experience has shown to accrue from colleges of this type for the society itself, for the extern students, and for the people or region where the college is situated (although this can in part be gathered from what has already been said).

The advantages for our own men are these:

1. First of all, those who give classes make progress themselves and learn a great deal by teaching others, acquiring greater confidence and mastery in their learning.

2. Our own scholastics who attend the lectures will benefit from the care, persistence, and diligence which the teachers devote to their office.

3. They not only advance in learning but also acquire facility in preaching and teaching catechism, get practice in the other means they will later use to help their neighbors, and grow in confidence at seeing the fruit which God our Lord allows them to see.

4. Although no one may urge the students to enter the society, particularly when they are young boys, nevertheless through good example and personal contact, as well as the Latin declamations on the virtues held on Sundays, young men are spontaneously attracted, and many laborers can be won for the vineyard of Christ our Lord.

So much for the advantages for the society itself.

For the extern students who come to take advantage of the classes the benefits are the following:

5. They are given a quite adequate education. Care is taken to ensure that everyone learns, by means of classes, debates, and compositions, so that they make great progress in learning.

6. The poor who lack the means to pay the ordinary teachers or private tutors at

home here obtain gratis an education which they could hardly procure at great expense.

7. They profit in spiritual matters through learning Christian doctrine and grasping from the sermons and regular exhortations what they need for their eternal salvation.

8. They make progress in purity of conscience—and consequently in all virtue—through the monthly confessions and the care taken to see that they are decent in their speech and virtuous in their entire lives.

9. They draw much greater merit and fruit from their studies, since they learn from the very beginning to make a practice of directing all their studies to the service of God, as they are taught to do.

For the inhabitants of the country or region where these colleges are established there are in addition the following benefits:

10. Financially, parents are relieved of the expense of having teachers to instruct their children in letters and virtue.

11. Parents fulfill their duty in conscience regarding their children's formation. Persons who would have difficulty finding even for pay teachers to whom they could entrust their children will find them in these colleges with complete security.

12. Apart from schooling, they also have in the colleges persons who can give sermons to the people and in monasteries and help people through administration of the sacraments, to quite visible good effect.

13. The inhabitants themselves and the members of their households will be drawn to spiritual concerns by the good example of their children, and will be attracted to going more often to confession and living Christian lives.

14. The inhabitants of the region will have in our men persons to inspire and aid them in undertaking good works such as hospitals, houses for reformed women, and the like, for which charity also impels our men to have a concern.

15. From among those who are at present merely students, in time some will emerge to play diverse roles—some to preach and carry on the care of souls, others to the government of the land and the administration of justice, and others to other responsible occupations. In short, since the children of today become the adults of tomorrow, their good formation in life and learning will benefit many others, with the fruit expanding more widely every day.

I could elaborate this further. But this will suffice to explain our thinking here about colleges of this kind.

May Christ, our eternal salvation, guide us all to serve him better. Amen.

From G. E. Ganss, ed., Ignatius of Loyola: The "Spiritual Exercises" and Selected Works *(New York: Paulist Press, 1991), 362–65.*

93. Letter of Ignatius Loyola to Peter Canisius (13 August 1554)

As time went on, Ignatius increasingly turned in the direction of combating Protestantism. In this letter, he frankly acknowledges the church's faults and recommends strategic weapons taken from the Protestants themselves. Above all, however, the reversal of Protestant gains would be achieved, he thought, through education.

☩

Seeing the progress which the heretics have made in a short time, spreading the poison of their evil teaching throughout so many countries and peoples . . . it would seem that our society, having been accepted by divine providence among the efficacious means to repair such great damage, should be solicitous to prepare the proper steps, such as are quickly applied and can be widely adopted, thus exerting itself to the utmost of its powers to preserve what is still sound and to restore what has fallen sick of the plague of heresy, especially in the northern nations.

The heretics have made their false theology popular and presented it in a way that is within the capacity of the common people. They preach it to the people and teach it in the schools, and scatter booklets which can be bought and understood by many, and make their influence felt by means of their writings when they cannot do so by their preaching. Their success is largely due to the negligence of those who should have shown some interest; and the bad example and the ignorance of Catholics, especially the clergy, have made such ravages in the vineyard of the Lord. Hence it would seem that our society should make use of the following means to put a stop and apply a remedy to the evils which have come upon the church through these heretics.

In the first place, the sound theology which is taught in the universities and seeks its foundation in philosophy, and therefore requires a long time to acquire is adapted only to good and alert minds. Because the weaker ones can be confused and, if they lack foundations, collapse, it would be good to make a summary of theology to deal with topics that are important but not controversial, with great brevity. There could be more detail in matters controversial, but it should be accommodated to the present needs of the people. It should solidly prove dogmas with good arguments from Scripture, tradition, the councils, and the doctors, and refute the contrary teaching. It would not require much time to teach such a theology, since it would not go very deeply into other matters. In this way theologians could be produced in a short time who could take care of the preaching and teaching in many places. The abler students could be given higher courses which include greater detail. Those who do not succeed in these higher courses should be removed from them and put in this shorter course of theology.

The principal conclusions of this theology, in the form of a short catechism, could be taught to children, as the Christian doctrine is now taught, and likewise to the common people who are not too infected or too capable of subtleties. This could also be done with the younger students in the lower classes, where they could learn it by heart. . . .

Another excellent means for helping the church in this trial would be to multiply the colleges and schools of the society in many lands, especially where a good attendance could be expected. . . .

Not only in the places where we have a residence, but even in the neighborhood, the better among our students could be sent to teach the Christian doctrine on Sundays and feast days. Even the day students, should there be suitable material among them, could be sent by the rector for the same service. Thus, besides the correct doctrine, they would be giving the example of a good life, and by removing every appearance of greed they will be able to refute the strongest argument of the heretics—the bad life and the ignorance of the Catholic clergy.

The heretics write a large number of booklets and pamphlets, by means of which they aim at taking away all authority from the Catholics, and especially from the society, and set up their false dogmas. It would seem expedient, therefore, that ours here also write answers in pamphlet form, short and well-written, so that they can be produced without delay and bought by many. In this way the harm that is being done by the pamphlets of the heretics can be remedied and sound teaching spread. These works should be modest, but lively; they should point out the evil that is abroad and uncover the evil machinations and deceits of the adversaries. A large number of these pamphlets could be gathered into one volume. Care should be taken, however, that this be done by learned men well grounded in theology, who will adapt it to the capacity of the multitude.

With these measures it would seem that we could bring great relief to the church, and in many places quickly apply a remedy to the beginnings of the evil before the poison has gone so deep that it will be very difficult to remove it from the heart. But we should use the same diligence in healing that the heretics are using in infecting the people. We will have the advantage over them in that we possess a solidly founded, and therefore an enduring, doctrine. . . .

From Van Voorst, Readings in Christianity, *211–13.*

The New World

94. Paul III, *Sublimis Deus* (1537)

The age of the Reformation, we dare not forget, was also the age of the "discovery" of the "new world." While the Spanish crown was concerned about little more than the extraction of wealth, some Catholic leaders saw in these discoveries divine compensation for the losses to Protestantism. To bring the natives into the church, of course, they had to be converted. And for this, they had to be human. Not only were they being treated inhumanely, but there was widespread doubt on the question of their essential humanity. In this bull of 1537, the church officially settled the question.

The sublime God so loved the human race that he created man in such wise that he might participate, not only in the good that other creatures enjoy, but endowed him with capacity to attain to the inaccessible and invisible supreme good and behold it face to face. . . . [The devil's] satellites have published abroad that the Indians of the West and the South, and other people of whom we have recent knowledge should be treated as dumb brutes created for our service, pretending that they are incapable of receiving the Catholic faith. . . . [But] the Indians are truly men and they are not only capable of understanding the Catholic faith but, according to our information, they desire exceedingly to receive it. Desiring to provide ample remedy for these evils, we define and declare . . . notwithstanding whatever may be said to the contrary, the said Indians and all other people who may later be discovered by Christians, are by no means to be deprived of their liberty or the possession of their property, even though they be outside the faith of Jesus. . . .

From Jones, Counter Reformation, *132.*

95. Francisco de Vitoria, *De Indis* (1532–1539)

Vitoria (1492–1546) was a Spanish Dominican who inspired a Thomist revival in Salamanca. He made important contributions in the areas of natural law, human rights, political authority, and just war theory. In this series of lectures on the "Indians," he argued against their enslavement.

✛

The Spanish were bound to use force of arms to continue their work of conversion, but I fear they adopted measures in excess of what is allowed by human and divine law. . . . Among all men there is an equal ability to found their own governments, whether they be Christian or not, which means that all men are natural masters. Therefore even if the Christian faith has been announced to the barbarians with complete and sufficient arguments and they have still refused to receive it, this does not supply a legitimate reason for making war on them. Those barbarians cannot be barred from being true owners, alike in public and private war, by reason of the sin of unbelief or any other mortal sin; nor does such sin entitle Christians to seize their goods and lands for they possess true dominion. . . . If they seem intelligent or stupid, I attribute it to their barbarous upbringing. Even among ourselves we find many peasants who differ little from brutes. . . .

✛

From Jones, Counter Reformation, *131.*

96. Bartolome de las Casas, *A Short Account of the Destruction of the Indies* (1542)

Himself a former slave owner, Las Casas (1474–1566) renounced his past, joined the Dominican Order and became the foremost champion of "Indian" rights. Having observed the Spanish treatment of the natives first hand, he gives us the following appalling report.

The Spaniards entered like wolves, tigers and lions which had been starving for many days, and since forty years they have done nothing else. . . . [Hispaniola] was the first to be destroyed and made into a desert. The Christians began by taking the women and children, to use and to abuse them, and to eat of the substance of their toil and labor, instead of contenting themselves with what the Indians gave them spontaneously, according to the means of each. Such stores are always small; because they keep no more than they ordinarily need, which they acquire with little labor; but what is enough for three households, of ten persons each, for a month, a Christian eats and destroys in one day. . . .

The Christians, with their horses and swords and lances, began to slaughter and practice strange cruelty among them. . . . They made bets as to who would slit a man in two, or cut off his head at one blow: or they opened up his bowels. They tore the babes from their mothers' breast by the feet, and dashed their heads against the rocks. Others they seized by the shoulders and threw into the rivers, laughing and joking. . . . They made a gallows just high enough for the feet to nearly touch the ground, and by thirteens, in honor and reverence of our redeemer and the twelve apostles, they put wood underneath and, with fire, they burned the Indians alive. They wrapped the bodies of others in dry straw, binding them in it and setting fire to it; and so they burned them. They cut off the hands of all they wished taken alive, made them carry them fastened on to them, and said: "Go and carry letters": that is, take the news to those who have fled. . . .

[In Cuba, Prince Hatuey] was taken and they burned him alive. . . . When he was tied to the stake, a Franciscan, a holy man, who was there, spoke as much as he could to him of the teachings of our faith, of which he had never before heard. . . . After thinking a little, Hatuey asked the monk whether the Christians went to heaven; the monk answered that those who were good went there. The prince at once said, without any more thought, that he did not wish to go there, but rather to hell so as not to be where the Spaniards were. . . .

I was induced to write this work . . . that God may not destroy my fatherland Castile for such great sins. . . . I have great hope for the emperor and king is getting to understand the wickedness and treachery that, contrary to the will of God and himself, is and has been done to these peoples; heretofore the truth has been studiously hidden from him . . . by these tyrants who, under pretext that they are serving the king, dishonor God, and rob and destroy the king. . . .

✠

From Jones, Counter Reformation, *132–33.*

Rome and Elizabeth I

97. Pius V, *Regnans in excelsis* (1570)

By 1570, we recall, the Elizabethan Settlement was firmly in place in England. The bull excommunicating and deposing Elizabeth amounted to little more than ineffectual fulminations harking back to a past which could not be recovered. Its tone of finality makes the ecumenical progress of our time all the more astonishing.

✠

He that reigns in the highest, to whom has been given all power in heaven and earth, entrusted the government of the one holy Catholic and apostolic Church (outside which there is no salvation) to one man alone on the earth, namely to Peter, the chief of the apostles, and to Peter's successor, the Roman Pontiff, in fullness of power. This one man he set up as chief over all nations and all kingdoms, to pluck up, destroy, scatter, dispose, plant and build. . . .

Resting then upon the authority of him who has willed to place us (albeit unequal to such a burden) in this supreme throne of justice, we declare the aforesaid Elizabeth a heretic and an abettor of heretics, and those that cleave to her in the aforesaid matters to have incurred the sentence of anathema, and to be cut off from the unity of Christ's body.

Moreover we declare her to be deprived of her pretended right to the aforesaid realm, and from all dominion, dignity and privilege whatsoever.

And the nobles, subjects and peoples of the said realm, and all others who have taken an oath of any kind to her we declare to be absolved forever from such oath and from all dues of dominion, fidelity and obedience, as by the authority of these presents we do so absolve them; and we deprive the said Elizabeth of her pretended right to the realm and all other things aforesaid: and we enjoin and forbid all and several the nobles, etc. . . . that they presume not to obey her and her admonitions, commands, and laws. All who disobey our command we involve in the same sentence of anathema.

✠

From H. Bettenson, ed., Documents of the Christian Church *(New York: Oxford University Press, 1963), 338–39.*

Sources

✠

Chapter 1: The Late Medieval Background

Janz, D., ed. *Three Reformation Catechisms: Catholic, Anabaptist, Lutheran.* Lewiston, N.Y.: Edwin Mellen, 1982. Copyright © 1982 Edwin Mellen Press. Used by permission.

Miller, C. H., trans. *Desiderius Erasmus: The Praise of Folly.* New Haven: Yale University Press, 1979. Copyright © 1979 Yale University Press. Used by permission.

Oberman, H. A., ed. *Forerunners of the Reformation: The Shape of Late Medieval Thought.* New York: Holt, Rinehart and Winston, 1966. Copyright © 1966 Holt, Rinehart and Winston. Used by permission.

Rabil, Albert Jr., ed. and trans. *Henricus Cornelius Agrippa: Declamation on the Nobility and Preeminence of the Female Sex.* Chicago: University of Chicago Press, 1996. Copyright © 1996 University of Chicago Press. Used by permission.

Rupp, E. G., and B. Drewery, eds. *Martin Luther.* London: Edward Arnold; New York: St. Martin's, 1970. Copyright © E. G. Rupp and B. Drewery. Used by permission of St. Martin's Press, Inc. and Edward Arnold, London.

Sherley-Price, L., trans. *Thomas à Kempis: The Imitation of Christ.* Baltimore: Penguin, 1972. Copyright © 1952 Leo-Sherley Price. Used by permission of Penguin Books Ltd.

Summers, M., trans. *The Malleus Maleficarum of Heinrich Kraemer and James Sprenger.* New York: Dover, 1971. Copyright © 1971 Dover Publications. Used by permission.

Tavard, G. H. "The Bull *Unam Sanctam* of Boniface VIII." In *Papal Primacy and the Universal Church*, edited by P. Empie and T. Murphy, 106–7. Minneapolis: Augsburg, 1974.

Wenzel, S., ed. and trans. *Fasciculus Morum: A Fourteenth Century Preacher's Handbook.* University Park, Pa.: Pennsylvania State University Press, 1989. Copyright © 1989 Pennsylvania State University Press. Used by permission.

Chapter 2: Martin Luther

Pelikan, J., and H. Lehman, eds. *Luther's Works: American Edition.* 55 vols. St. Louis: Concordia; Philadelphia: Fortress; 1955–1987.

Rupp, E. G., and B. Drewery, eds. *Martin Luther.* London: Edward Arnold; New York: St. Martin's, 1970. Copyright © E. G. Rupp and B. Drewery. Used by permission of St. Martin's Press, Inc. and Edward Arnold, London.

Tappert, T., ed., *The Book of Concord.* Philadelphia: Fortress, 1959.

Chapter 3: Zwingli and the Radical Reformation

Jackson, S. M., and C. N. Heller, eds. *Zwingli: Commentary on True and False Religion.* Durham, N.C.: Labyrinth, 1981. Reprinted from *The Latin Works of Huldreich Zwingli.* Philadelphia: Heidelberg Press, 1929. Used by permission of the American Society of Church History.

Janz, D., ed. *Three Reformation Catechisms: Catholic, Anabaptist, Lutheran.* Lewiston, N.Y.: Edwin Mellen, 1982. Copyright © 1982 Edwin Mellen Press. Used by permission.

Liechty, D., ed. *Early Anabaptist Spirituality.* New York: Paulist, 1994. Copyright © 1994 Daniel C. Leichty. Used by permission of Paulist Press, Inc.

Potter, G. R., ed. *Huldrych Zwingli.* New York: St. Martin's, 1977. Copyright © G. R. Potter. Used by permission.

Vedder, Henry C. *Balthasar Hubmaier: The Leader of the Anabaptists.* New York: AMS, 1971.

Williams, G. H., ed. *Spiritual and Anabaptist Writers.* Library of Christian Classics. Philadelphia: Westminster, 1957. Copyright © 1957 Westminster/John Knox Press and SCM Press, London. Used by permission.

Yoder, John H. *The Legacy of Michael Sattler.* Scottdale, Pa.: Herald, 1973. Copyright © 1973 Herald Press. Used by permission.

Zuck, L. H., ed. *Christianity and Revolution: Radical Christian Testimonies, 1520–1650.* Philadelphia: Temple University Press, 1975. Copyright © 1975 Lowell H. Zuck. Used by permission.

Chapter 4: John Calvin

Beaty, M., and B. Farley, eds. *Calvin's Ecclesiastical Advice.* Louisville: Westminster/John Knox, 1991. Copyright © 1991 Westminster/John Knox Press. Used by permission of Westminster John Knox Press.

Dillenberger, J., ed. *John Calvin: Selections from His Writings.* New York: Doubleday, 1971.

Manschreck, C. L., ed. *A History of Christianity.* Vol. 2, *The Church from the Reformation to the Present.* Grand Rapids: Baker Book House, 1964. Reprinted from *Concerning Heretics,* R. H. Bainton, trans., copyright © 1935 Columbia University Press, by permission of Columbia University Press.

McNeill, J. T., ed., and F. L. Battles, trans. *Calvin: Institutes of the Christian Religion.* 2 vols. Library of Christian Classics. Philadelphia: Westminster, 1960. Used by permission of Westminster John Knox Press.

Reid, J. K. S. ed. *Calvin: Theological Treatises.* Philadelphia: Westminster, 1954. Copyright © 1954 Westminster/John Knox Press and SCM Press, London. Used by permission.

Chapter 5: The Reformation in England

Bray, G., ed. *Documents of the English Reformation.* Minneapolis: Fortress, 1994.

Leith, J. H., ed., *Creeds of the Churches.* Richmond, Va.: John Knox, 1973. Copyright © 1982 John Leith. Used by permission of Westminster John Knox Press.

Chapter 6: The Counter/Catholic Reformation

Bettenson, H., ed. *Documents of the Christian Church.* New York: Oxford University Press, 1963.

Ganss, G. E., ed. *Ignatius of Loyola: The "Spiritual Exercises" and Selected Works.* New York: Paulist, 1991. Copyright © 1991 George E. Ganss, S.J. Used by permission of Paulist Press, Inc.

Jones, M., ed. *The Counter Reformation: Religion and Society in Early Modern Europe.* New York: Cambridge University Press, 1995.

Puhl, L. J., ed. *The Spiritual Exercises of St. Ignatius.* Chicago: Loyola University Press, 1951. Copyright © 1951 Loyola University Press. Used by permission.

Rupp, E. G., and B. Drewery, eds. *Martin Luther.* London: Edward Arnold; New York: St. Martin's, 1970. Copyright © E. G. Rupp and B. Drewery. Used by permission of St. Martin's Press, Inc. and Edward Arnold, London.

Schroeder, H. J., trans. *Canons and Decrees of the Council of Trent.* Rockford, Ill.: Tan, 1978. Copyright © 1978 Tan Books and Publishers, Inc. Used by permission.

Van Voorst, R. E., ed. *Readings in Christianity.* 1st ed. New York: Wadsworth, 1997. Copyright © 1997. Reprinted with permission of Wadsworth, a division of Thomson Learning: www.thomsonrights.com. Fax 800-730-2215.

Wicks, J., ed. and trans. *Cajetan Responds: A Reader in Reformation Controversy.* Washington, D.C.: Catholic University of America Press, 1978. Copyright © 1978 Catholic University of America Press. Used by permission.

Index

✠